A POSTCOLONIAL PEOPLE: SOUTH ASIANS IN BRITAIN

N. ALI
V.S. KALRA
S. SAYYID
editors

A Postcolonial People
South Asians in Britain

HURST & COMPANY, LONDON

First published in the United Kingdom by
C. Hurst & Co. (Publishers) Ltd,
41 Great Russell Street, London WC1B 3PL
www.hurstpub.co.uk

Printed in India

A catalogue data record for this volume is available from the British Library.

ISBNs
1-85065-796-3 *casebound*
1-85065-797-1 *paperback*

ACKNOWLEDGEMENTS

We would like to extend special thanks to a number of individuals whose help in so many different ways went 'above and beyond the call of duty': Sophia Ahmed, Karl Atkin, Rajinder Dudrah, Michael Dwyer, Anne Edwards, Pauline Findlay, Barnor Hesse, Jonathan Hoare, John Holt, Rupa Huq, John Hutnyk, Eesher Kalra, Nuvpreet Kalra, Shehla Khan, Ian Law, Andy Lie, Tej Purewal, Ali Rattansi, Sanjay Sharma, the Singh Twins, Alda Terracciano, Shinder Thandi, Bernard Traynor, Laura Turney, AbdoolKarim Vakil and Couze Venn.

We also thank the Centre for Research in Primary Care, University of Leeds, for hosting the workshop for the book and providing logistical assistance.

Finally, all of the editors individually acknowledge the debt they owe to their families for their often subtle but always unstinting support.

October 2005

NASREEN ALI
VIRINDER S. KALRA
S. SAYYID

CONTENTS

Acknowledgements — *page* v
The Contributors — ix

Introduction: BrAsians: Postcolonial People, Ironic Citizens — *S. Sayyid* — 1

Part I. FRAMES — 11

Narrating the Postcolonial Political and the Immigrant Imaginary — *Barnor Hesse and S. Sayyid* — 13
☐ Arrival — *Daalat Ali* — 32
The 'Asian' in Britain — *Avtar Brah* — 35
☐ Chicken Tikka Masala — *Sophia Ahmed* — 62
Politics of Blackness and Asian Identity — *Tariq Modood* — 64
☐ Curry Powder — *Apurba Kundu* — 72
The Dialectic of 'Here and There': Anthropology 'at Home' — *John Hutnyk* — 74
☐ Drugs — *Noreen Sheikh-Latif* — 91
(Im)possible Intersections: Religion, (Post-)Colonial Subjectivity and the Ideology of Multiculturalism — *Arvind Mandair* — 93
☐ Football — *Daniel Burdsey* — 108
Writing a BrAsian City: 'Race', Culture and Religion in Accounts of Postcolonial Bradford — *Seán McLoughlin* — 110

Part II. PORTRAITS — 141

Mapping the Colonial: South Asians in Britain, 1857–1947 — *Humayun Ansari* — 143
☐ Anish Kapoor — *John Holt and Laura Turney* — 157
Imperial Implosions: Postcoloniality and the Orbits of Migration — *Nasreen Ali* — 158
Demographics of BrAsian Settlement, 1951–2001 — *Ceri Peach* — 168
☐ Muslims! — *Shehla Khan* — 182

The Politics of the BrAsian Electorate *Muhammad Anwar* 188
Brown Economy: Enterprise and Employment *Shinder S. Thandi* 211
□ Newham *Dhanwant Rai* 230
Policing Diversity: Racialisation and the Criminal Justice System *Virinder S. Kalra* 234
Health Care and BrAsians: Making Sense of Policy and Practice *Karl Atkin* 244
□ Palliative Care *Gurch Randhawa and Alastair Owens* 256
Imagining the Politics of BrAsian Youth *Claire Alexander* 258
The Scandal of 'Arranged Marriages' and the Pathologisation of BrAsian Families *Fauzia Ahmad* 272
□ Queer *Shafqat Nasir* 289
A City of Surprises: Urban Multiculturalism and the 'Leicester Model' *Gurharpal Singh* 291
Capital Gains: BrAsian Suburban North-West London *Rupa Huq* 305

Part III. SIGNATURES 315

Asian Sounds *Sanjay Sharma* 317
□ Rusholme *Nida Kirmani* 327
The Singular Journey: South Asian Visual Art in Britain *John Holt and Laura Turney* 329
□ Uprisings *Paul Bagguley and Yasmin Hussain* 340
South Asian / BrAsian Performing Arts *Raminder Kaur and Alda Terracciano* 343
□ Vasco da Gama *AbdoolKarim Vakil* 358
Planet Bollywood *Rachel Dwyer* 362
□ Writings *Yasmin Hussain* 371
Metropolitan Borderlands: The Formation of BrAsian Landscapes *Noha Nasser* 374
□ Zee TV *Rajinder Dudrah* 392

Bibliography 395
Index 431

THE CONTRIBUTORS

FAUZIA AHMAD is Honorary Research Fellow, Centre for the Study of Ethnicity and Citizenship, University of Bristol.

SOPHIA AHMED is a student in the Department of Politics and International Studies, University of Leeds.

CLAIRE ALEXANDER is Senior Lecturer, Department of Sociology, London School of Economics.

DAALAT ALI is a writer and commentator on Kashmiri literature, based in Rochdale.

NASREEN ALI is Senior Research Fellow in the Centre for Primary Healthcare, University of Leeds.

HUMAYUN ANSARI is Senior Lecturer in the Department of History and Director of the Centre for Ethnic Minority Studies and Equal Opportunities, Royal Holloway, University of London.

MUHAMMAD ANWAR is Professor at the Centre for Research in Ethnic Relations, University of Warwick.

KARL ATKIN is Senior Lecturer in Ethnicity and Health, Department of Health Sciences, University of York.

PAUL BAGGULEY is Senior Lecturer in Sociology, School of Sociology and Social Policy, University of Leeds.

AVTAR BRAH is Professor in Sociology, Birkbeck College, University of London.

DANIEL BURDSEY is Lecturer in Sociology of Sport and Leisure, University of Brighton.

RAJINDER DUDRAH is Lecturer in Screen Studies, Department of Drama, University of Manchester.

RACHEL DWYER is Reader in Indian Studies and Cinema, Department of South Asia, School of Oriental and African Studies, University of London.

BARNOR HESSE is an Associate Professor of African American Studies, Political Science and Sociology, Department of African American Studies, Northwestern University, Evanston, Illinois.

JOHN HOLT is an artist and cultural activist and was a lecturer in Fine Art in the School of Fine Art, Art History and Cultural Studies, University of Leeds, and Fellow in Art and Design, Loughborough University.

RUPA HUQ is Lecturer in Sociology, Faculty of Arts and Social Sciences, Kingston University.

YASMIN HUSSAIN is Lecturer in Sociology, Department of Sociology and Social Policy, University of Leeds.

JOHN HUTNYK is Senior Lecturer, Department of Social Anthropology, Goldsmiths College, University of London.

VIRINDER S. KALRA is Senior Lecturer, Department of Sociology, University of Manchester.

SHEHLA KHAN is a PhD candidate in the Department of Government, University of Manchester.

RAMINDER KAUR is Lecturer, Department of Anthropology, University of Sussex.

NIDA KIRMANI is a PhD student in the Department of Sociology, University of Manchester.

APURBA KUNDU is Lecturer in Cybernetics in the Department of Cybernetics, University of Bradford.

ARVIND MANDAIR is Assistant Professor, Sikh Studies, Hofstra University, Hempstead, New York.

SEÁN MCLOUGHLIN is Lecturer in Islamic Studies, Department of Theology and Religious Studies, University of Leeds.

TARIQ MODOOD is Professor of Sociology, Politics and Public Policy, and Director of the Centre for the Study of Ethnicity and Citizenship, University of Bristol.

NOHA NASSER is Senior Lecturer, Birmingham School of Architecture, University of Central England.

SHAFQAT NASIR is a Lecturer in Sociology at Manchester Metropolitan University.

ALASTAIR OWENS is a Lecturer in the Department of Geography, Queen Mary, University of London.

CERI PEACH is Professor of Social Geography and a Fellow of St Catherine's College, University of Oxford.

DHANWANT RAI is Head of Corporate Research, London Borough of Newham.

GURCH RANDHAWA is Senior Lecturer in the Institute of Health, University of Luton.

S. SAYYID is University Research Fellow in the School of Sociology and Social Policy, University of Leeds.

SANJAY SHARMA is Lecturer in Sociology and Communications, School of Social Sciences and Law, Brunel University.

NOREEN SHEIKH-LATIF is a senior researcher at Lifeline and a postgraduate student, University of Manchester.

GURHARPAL SINGH is Professor of Inter-Religious Relations, Department of Theology and Religion, University of Birmingham.

SHINDER S. THANDI is Senior Lecturer in Economics, Coventry Business School, University of Coventry.

ALDA TERRACCIANO is Visiting Senior Lecturer, University of Middlesex.

LAURA TURNEY is head of the Gender and Mainstreaming Equality Team in the Scottish Executive.

ABDOOLKARIM VAKIL is Lecturer in Contemporary Portuguese History, Department of Portuguese and Brazilian Studies, King's College London.

INTRODUCTION

BRASIANS

POSTCOLONIAL PEOPLE, IRONIC CITIZENS[1]

S. Sayyid

'My illustrious friend and joy of my liver: the thing you ask of me is both difficult and useless. Although I have lived all my days in this place, I have neither counted the houses nor have inquired into the number of the inhabitants; as to what one person loads on his mules and the other stows away in the bottom of his ship it is no business of mine...' Ottoman official (Layard, 1853: 663)

Perhaps one of the most oft cited stories about the *Celestial Emporium of Benevolent Knowledge* concerns a certain French philosopher who, upon reading the entry on animals in this book, burst out laughing.[2] What motivated this outburst? In some circles the laughter is considered to have stemmed from the French character of the philosopher, while in others it is maintained that the nature of philosophy rather than that of Frenchness is responsible. The passage in question details a classification of animals according to the following schema: '(a) belonging to the Emperor, (b) embalmed, (c) tame, (d) sucking pigs, (e) sirens, (f) fabulous, (g) stray dogs, (h) included in the present classification, (i) frenzied, (j) innumerable, (k) drawn with a very fine camelhair brush, (l) et cetera, (m) having just broken the water pitcher, (n) that from a long way off look like flies...' (Foucault, 2004: i).

Perhaps the laughter was induced by the contrast between the *Encylopaedie* published in 1751 in Paris and this 'Chinese encyclopaedia'. What is striking about this taxonomy of the *Celestial Emporium* is its strangeness. For what it points to is the very incongruity of the juxtaposition between its various categories. Outside the pages of the *Celestial Emporium* where could 'animals drawn with a very fine camelhair brush' be part of a sequence that would also include 'animals that have just broken the water pitcher'? (Foucault, 2004: xviii) The character of this taxonomy can only be thought of as discrepant because it implic-

1 I would like to acknowledge the help of the following people in the writing of this chapter: Seán McLoughlin, Virinder S. Kalra, AbdoolKarim Vakil and especially Barnor Hesse and Shehla Khan.

2 See, for example, Gregory's reading of Foucault's laughter (2004: 1–5).

itly contrasts with a taxonomy based on another logical structure. This discrepancy between the *Celestial Emporium* and, let us say, *Encylopaedie* opens up the possibility of interrogating 'our' representations of knowledge. It allows us to imagine the possibility that maybe a Chinese philosopher reading the *Encylopaedie* would also burst out laughing at the attempt to systematise all diverse knowledges that entered European horizons since the voyages of 'discovery' (Venn, 2005). Or perhaps the laughter of philosophers, French or Chinese, stems from a recognition of the ultimate arbitrariness of any taxonomy, of its absurd foundations, for a taxonomy implies juxtapositions which are impossible outside a particular frame of reference.

The *Encylopaedie* only becomes comprehensible in the light of the hegemony of the classical episteme (Foucault, 1970). Similarly, it could be the Chineseness of the *Celestial Emporium* that contains the incongruity of the classifications it presents, that is, the Chineseness of the 'Chinese encyclopaedia' which confers the appearance of order rather than of randomness upon its classification scheme. The signifier of China marks out the *Celestial Emporium* as the product of a different episteme, a frame of reference that seems to be confined to the Middle Kingdom and environs. Without exercising the sovereignty of the signifier of 'China', the *Celestial Emporium* would collapse rather than become emblematic of a different way of looking at the world, an attempt to organise the knowledge of the world which does not simply replay the episteme inaugurated and consolidated by *Encylopaedie*.

What epistemological framework should be used to structure the production of knowledge of a book dedicated to the analysis of South Asian settler communities in Britain? The order of things to be found in this volume is perhaps less strange and more prosaic than that located within the *Celestial Emporium of Benevolent Knowledge*, and would thus seem to legitimate the relative paucity of epistemological considerations. The representations of South Asians in Britain have for the most part continued to rely on a conceptual vocabulary borrowed from the legacy of Indology and its allied disciplines.

Indology can be seen as a variant of orientalism: indological discourse is founded upon the opposition between normative Western practices and establishments against which South Asian ways of living appear as distortions and aberrations (Inden, 1990). These distortions and aberrations are domesticated by the use of tropes such as caste (hierarchical divisions), *izzat* (notions of honour) and *biraderi* (kinship networks). They help to identify South Asian settlers as essentially 'Indian'.

The British experience of India came to be dominated by the colonial gaze. The colonial gaze is based upon '…a distance, a space of separation, a relationship of curiosity, that made it possible to see something as "a case" a self-contained object whose "problems" could be measured, analysed and addressed by a form of knowledge that appears to stand outside the object and grasp it in its entirety' (Mitchell, 2000: 100). The ability of this colonial gaze to apprehend its objects in their entirety is only possible synchronically. Thus for the colonial gaze the temporality of the object escapes, and with it any trace of the political. What we are left with are a series of snapshots; dis-embedded, de-historicised objects frozen in time. India was knowable and governable through a cluster of disembodied 'facts'. These facts were to be processed through what Cohn calls investigative modalities, which define the '...body of information that is needed, the procedures by which appropriate knowledge is gathered, its ordering and classification, and [then] how it is transformed into usable forms such as published reports, statistical returns, histories, gazettes, legal codes and encyclopaedias'(Cohn, 1996: 5). Cohn goes on to identify six investigative modalities (historiographic, travelogue, survey, enumerative, museological, surveillance), by which 'facts' about the colonised came to be known.

It does not require too much imagination to see how these six investigative modalities have with slight reconfigurations been applied to South Asian settlers. The production of government reports, statistical surveys, legal provisions, journalistic accounts, television documentaries etc. are testimony to ways in which indological investigative modalities continue to be deployed to examine South Asian settlers in Britain. Accordingly, the contents and categorisations contained in *A Postcolonial People* would not seem to require further epistemological enquiry. This book could then have been constructed as an encyclopaedic account of South Asian setters in Britain covering themes such as arranged marriages, inter-generational conflict and the impact of Zee-TV. It would then describe these using all the usual categories of Indology. Such an endeavour would no doubt have produced an empirically rich narrative, a systemisation of the various knowledges about South Asian settlers that have accumulated over the last fifty years. The story would probably begin sometime between 1945 and 1947 at the earliest, but this would have been a mere prelude to the real story which would be presented as starting with the mass migration of South Asian communities to Britain, probably sometime in the 1960s. This process of mass migration would be the device used to represent the conjoining of two distinct spaces and temporalities, through the elaboration of the 'race-relations' paradigm or what I prefer to call the 'immigrant imaginary' (Sayyid, 2004). The immigrant imaginary is a product of the spatialisation of the ex-colonial ethnically marked settlers. It shares with Indology the squeezing out of any temporality: thus reducing the 'Indian' subject to being another example of a 'people without a History'. The immigrant imaginary with its attendant public narratives and representations is based on deploying the colonial gaze to comprehend the settlement of South Asian settlers.

Alas, while the attempt to continue with the colonial framing of ethnically marked populations has been unrelenting, it has also been largely unsuccessful in that bringing about colonial closure, either culturally, politically or epistemologically, has not been possible. The continuation of colonial framing in the context of the settlement of communities of ex-colonial populations in Britain has continually run into a series of scandals and crises. The postcolonial condition of the world order most visibly highlighted by the 'de-centring of the West' (Young, 1990; Sayyid, 2003) has disrupted the possibility of uncontested coloniality. It has meant that the attempt to impose the practices and logics of coloniality has not led to the closure enshrined in a fully formed naturalised order, but rather the constant displacement of such a possibility.[3] The continued reliance on colonial framing in the context of the postcolonial condition has been largely responsible for the inability of 'race relations' paradigms to cope with ethicised minorities' attempts to re-write the history of the nation.

The conflict between a disavowed coloniality and postcoloniality is most vividly demonstrated by the chequered trajectory of the various labels deployed to identify people from South Asia who settled in Britain in the wake of the (formal) decolonisation of British India: Black, British Asian, Asian British etc. There is a continuing debate about the most appropriate way of describing and labelling those settlers that hail from South Asia. This debate, however, is not only concentrated in academic circles dealing with issues of classification, or at the level of public policy in which overworked managers try to impose a taxonomic discipline on unruly social relations. It can also be found in kebab shops and bazaars, in streets and clubs, in homes and offices, in short in locales that bring together people who share a sense of belonging to South Asia, a sense mediated by coloniality and marked by racialised subordination, and continually represented through the currency of Indological discourse. The heart of this debate turns upon an existential question, a question that is always present in what we do, what we say, even when we are doing and saying things that seem to have no explicit obvious link to it.

Attempts to answer the question of who these 'immigrants' are have centred on the division between an ethnically unmarked majority and ethnically marked minority.[4] The privileging of national identities has cultural and legal as well as political and philosophical aspects. (An illustration of this can be seen in the rather haphazard way in which na-

3 Barnor Hesse has explored this displacement of coloniality through the category of transruption, see Hesse, 2000.

4 The concept of marking is used within linguistics to distinguish between lexemes on the basis of their range of use. Unmarked terms refer to a general category with extensive use, whereas marked terms indicate more specific usage. For example, lion and dog are unmarked whereas lioness and bitch are marked.

tional labels such as Indian, Pakistani and Bangladeshi are used in local and national state publications and media broadcasts to designate even those settlers who have British citizenship. Behind the bureaucratic convenience of such labels, lurks the confusion between ethnic and national identity, a confusion that would see ethnic homogeneity as the normal condition of membership of the national community.) More important, the division between national majority and ethic minority is over determined by a series of polarisations which play upon the constitutive split between West and Non-West.

So how should a book about South Asians settled in Britain be arranged? Under what sign could its inclusions be made intelligible and its exclusions seem not only legitimate but also necessary? Unlike either the *Celestial Emporium* or *Encylopaedie*, what signifier of distinctive destiny would marshall knowledge of South Asian settlers is not altogether clear. Through their experience, ex-colonial ethnically marked populations find themselves on the cusp of the divide between West and Non-West. Ex-colonial settlers have to be understood within the context of the postcolonial condition. The postcolonial here refers to a conceptual not just a chronological category. Perhaps the story of ex-colonial ethnically marked populations can best be told in the pages of a postcolonial encyclopaedia. However, the idea of systematising and totalising all knowledge as part of a postcolonial project of accumulation of knowledge runs into a number of difficulties. First, there is an obvious problem as postcolonial marks something beyond colonialism but not something intrinsic in itself, in other words, the 'post' in the postcolonial reminds us that we have not arrived at something that can have its own name; thus a postcolonial encyclopaedia would still be parasitic. It would deconstruct the colonial without replacing it. Second, given the idea of an encyclopaedia itself and its Enlightenment rationality, would a postcolonial encyclopaedia still be postcolonial except in a descriptive/temporal sense? Perhaps a postcolonial encyclopaedia would be no more impossible than the Chinese encyclopaedia.

If such an encyclopaedia were possible then the entry on South Asian settlers would appear under the label 'BrAsian'. We use the term throughout this volume to designate members of settler communities which articulate a significant part of their identity in terms of South Asian heritage. The choice of this term was not only a stylistic device aimed at avoiding circumlocutions like 'people of South Asian heritage', but, more important, a recognition of the need for a category that points one in a direction away from established accounts of national identities and ethnicised minorities. The idea of BrAsian builds upon previous discussions that respond to the inadequacies of the various descriptions (Kaur and Kalra, 1996). As has been pointed out, 'Asian' as the most common way in which BrAsians are addressed does not translate very well outside the context of the British Isles. In the United States and Australia, for example, Asian refers to people of East Asian or South East Asian heritage. (In the United States, South Asians labour under the name of East Indians, another misnomer to account for American Indians.)[5] Partly in order to specify what Asians we are referring to, one could see the merit in terms which foreground the British context of this group of Asians, so that British Asian or Asian British or Asian Britons become equivalent to South Asian communities settled in Britain. Such usage would seem to have a great deal of merit to it as it accords with popular and academic usage in the British context and to some extent the South Asian context as well.

Unfortunately the difficulty of implementing such a straightforward solution arises from the contested nature of the term British. British refers both to a civic constitutional identity and to a term heavily implicated in the racialised narratives of the *'herrenvolk'* of the British Empire. Attempts to re-define Britishness away from whiteness have run into resistance from the usual suspects of xenophobic columnist-provocateurs and right-wing elements.[6] Further, they have also prompted the recognition that such a transformation would entail a major debate about the nature of British identity in relation to its imperial past and its post-colonial future—a debate that most practical politicians would seem to want to avoid. As a consequence there is an embarrassing phenomenon of ethnic self-abnegation in which prominent public figures of the ex-colonial ethnic minority in their attempt to lay claim to the inheritance of an unreconstructed British identity may find themselves declaring, 'when we had the British Empire…' without any consideration of the elisions and disavowals that this particular narration of Britishness entails, either for them or for others of the ethically marked and subordinated residents of Britain. There are of course many who continue to hope and work towards a definition of Britain and British that would be open to the ethnically marked, a vision of a cosmopolitan Britannia or world island. Such a transformation of the idea of Britishness cannot be accomplished without the dis-articulation of coloniality in its constitution. This is not simply a gesture that recalls the horrors of Empire, a gesture which can be met by a counter-gesture challenging the invocation of any polity with

5 The underlying difficulty is of course that the geography of the world for the most part was mapped as part of the process of European expansion, and as such reflects not only European interests and concerns but more significantly means that the rest of the world was often represented as a residual category to Europe. Often the contemporary terms like Asian, African and of course American have no pre-European analogue. See Hall, 1994. There is nothing specifically European about this, after all India continues to be known via an Islamicate designation which ultimately follows ancient Persian usage.

6 See, for example, the furore created by the suggestion in the Parekh report that British be used to designate a community of communities.

a pure history. Rather it entails the recognition of the need to replace the colonial *telos* with a vision in which the distinction between West and Non-West is no longer privileged: a vision that articulation of British and Asian makes difficult since its constituent elements are clearly over-determined by the West and Non-West opposition.

Thus the use of British as prefix or suffix establishes a superficial relationship between Asian and British. The identity of British or Asian is not radically transformed by being conjoined—thus allowing for the possibility of disaggregating the British from the Asian (or as right-wing circles in Britain would express it, re-patriating Asians to their home-lands). Such an arrangement maintains the distinction and distance of the West and Non-West. This split produces cultural representations which describe South Asian settlers as 'frozen' in time, or belonging to a culture regarded as static, patriarchal and authoritarian, in contrast to British/Western culture, with its gleaming (post-)modernity, its dynamism and gender egalitarianism.

The category of BrAsian has four main features. First, it refuses the easy decomposition of the British and Asian dyad into its Western and Non-Western constituents. BrAsian is not merely a conflation of the British and the Asian, it is not a fusion but is a confusion of the possibility of both terms.

Second, BrAsian occupies an intermediate terrain on the cusp between West and Non-West. The physical location of BrAsian settlers is not sufficient to mark them out as being incontestably part of a Western trajectory, nor does their heritage determine their non-Western character. BrAsian signifies the impossibility of a hyphenated identity. In the context of the postcolonial, ethnically marked identities cannot be mere superficial additions to the national identity which remains basically the same. BrAsian demonstrates that transformations occur across the national majority/ethnic minority divide, and disrupts that balance of power in which the national majority holds all the cards, since the boundaries that constitute that national majority are themselves subject to the process of social and cultural transformations.

Third, the signifier of BrAsian needs to be conceptualised in the Derridean sense of being 'under erasure' (Derrida, 1976). A concept can be said to be 'under erasure' when it has to be crossed out since it is clearly inadequate; however, the crossing has to remain visible, it cannot be snow-paked out, since there is no adequate replacement (Slater, 2004: 10). BrAsian is not the correct answer to the question of British Asian subjectivities, but nor is there a better answer we can turn to.[7] The line that crosses out and puts the category of BrAsian under erasure can be

7 I would like to thank Seán McLoughlin and Virinder S. Kalra for their insights in the discussion of the nature of BrAsian identity.

described as the postcolonial line: crossing out and cancelling the colonial, without the crossing being able to erase the concept. It is the postcoloniality of South Asian settlers that transforms them into BrAsians, and distinguishes them (along with other ethnically marked ex-colonial settlers) from preceding groups of settlers who might serve as a comparator (the Huguenots, East European Jews). By placing BrAsian under erasure we accept that BrAsian is not a fully formed name that marshalls all the various forms of experiences of South Asian settlers.

Fourth, BrAsianness is defined by what can be described as a sense of ironic citizenship.[8] That is, BrAsians experience persistent and deep-seated skepticism about the dominant mythology of Britishness. They have recurring doubts about their inclusion within the conversation of the nation as interlocutors and peers. Their sense of irony arises from a recognition (often tacit rather than explicit) of the distance between the narratives available to them and the entrenched sense of Britishness. The legal status that most BrAsians are entitled to is too often undermined by extra-legal conventions, e.g. institutionalised racism. Racism acts not only as a barrier in the fields of law and order, education, employment but also at a more diffuse level in which BrAsians' relationship to the dominant story of these isles continues to see them and their presence as something supplemental to the nature of what it means to be British. The BrAsian experience of racially induced segregation and subordination raises doubts about the inclusive claims made about membership of British society. BrAsians (like other ex-colonial ethnically marked people) are often reminded that to be in Britain but not a part of Britain is not the same as being British. This sense of ironic citizenship is manifested by the ease with which BrAsians fail the 'cricket tests' of xenophobic politicians (Marquese, 1994: 137–41). Hence, the ironic citizenship that is made available to BrAsians is represented within xenophobic discourse as dual loyalty and 'failure to integrate'. Consequently, the BrAsian recognition of the role of contingency in the construction of their way of life is belied by accounts which continue to see them and their communities as essentialist fragments of the Non-West.

BrAsian is the signifier around which selections of knowledge (benevolent or otherwise) that make up *A Postcolonial People* are organised. The volume is arranged in three main sections. The first part, Frames, is mainly concerned with investigating epistemological and theoretical debates by which the BrAsian experience has been approached. The second part, Portraits, is an attempt to present a comprehensive survey of aspects of BrAsian life. A special effort has been made to bring together dimensions of BrAsian life-worlds that are often kept apart due to disciplinary

8 This use of irony is similar to and inspired by Richard Rorty, but it is not identical to his use. See Rorty, 1989: 73.

considerations. This section is partly a response to one of the common complaints against critiques of Indology, namely that such a Saidian-inspired, scorched-earth critique leaves nothing but epistemology, dissolving all substantive themes into epistemological questions which are increasingly removed from the concerns of people and their lives. The third part of the book, Signatures, covers the way in which BrAsians have signed themselves on the landscape of these islands, in particular it explores the way in which cultural representations by BrAsians have contributed to the construction of BrAsian identity as almost a distinct 'way of life' with its internal divisions, conflicts and fragments but also with its commonalities and unities.

Each of the main sections contains a number of essays, along with which there are a number of 'boxes', smaller notes that appear throughout the volume at regular intervals, disrupting and deflecting the possibility of a stabilised narrative. The articles are not meant to carry encyclopaedic information that echoes the usual stereotypes populating the narratives of ethnically marked communities. The interrelationship between boxes and chapters is purely arbitrary, an interruption of the epistemic coherence by the juxtaposition of topics of very different scale and substance. It destabilises the possibility of BrAsian emerging as an unproblematic category, the mere object of ethnographic field-work or empirical surveys, or an improbable entry in an impossible encyclopaedia.

An aspect of the 'de-centring of the West' is weakening and increasing contestation of the relationship of power/knowledge which established and legitimated Western hegemony as political, cultural, economic and epistemological enterprise. The relationship between power/knowledge became more explicit in the wake of the British government joining the United States in its global crusade against terrorism and rogue regimes. One understanding of this 'war on terror' is to see it as an attempt to re-centre the West through military coercion which can no longer be legitimated through other means (Sayyid, 2003; Reus-Smit, 2004). The so called 'war on terror' has so far tended to be mainly directed at the political mobilisations under the banner of Islam. *A Postcolonial People* has been put together in the context of this global postcolonial war, in which the separation between colonial as space of violence and metropole as space of peace has been threatened and the distinction between 'race relations' and international relations become increasingly blurred. It is in this context that intelligence agencies have suddenly discovered the merits of diversity as they aim to recruit members from key ethnic minorities, thus replaying an aspect of the colonial drama as native informants are increasingly turned into police informers.[9]

9 See, 'CIA outrages UK academics by planting spies in classroom', *Times Higher Education Supplement*, 3 June 2005.

In this set of circumstances it is hard not to sympathise with the Ottoman official (cited above) who when confronted with the interrogative Western imperative refuses to oblige. There is a certain irony that A.H. Layard's citation of the response was possibly interpreted as another illustration of the 'oriental repose', reflecting the absence of the will to truth, and perhaps an element of comedy in the petty-minded Ottoman bureaucrat's lackadaisical reluctance to harness the accumulation of knowledge for the exercise of power. In the wake of the bombing in London (7 July 2005), and the renewed quest for native informants and police informers, the Ottoman official's response seems a far more prudent gesture than a simple capitulation to the logic of the colonial.

There is a popular *hadith* which states that one should follow the road to knowledge even if it takes one as far as China. The quest for knowledge of how to encapsulate the BrAsian experience began with a Chinese encyclopaedia and the laughter of a philosopher trying to make sense of the strange ways of organising knowledge in strange lands. Alas, the strange land of course is not China, or at least not the China of the Chinese, for the *Celestial Emporium of Benevolent Knowledge* is not an encyclopaedia, nor is it really Chinese. Rather it is an invention forged at the edge of the West (Almond, 2004) by the brilliant imagination of a blind *porteño* librarian. In 'The Analytical Language of John Wilkins', Jorge Borges mentions in passing the perhaps apocryphal Chinese encyclopaedia. In the space of a few lines he evokes a China that recalls the Western imagining of China. Thus for Foucault it is this Western representation of 'China' which comes to connote 'China' as the radical Other (Gregory, 2004: 3). This could suggest that the laughter of Foucault as he pored over the pages of the *Celestial Emporium of Benevolent Knowledge* arose from beholding a distorted reflection in the mirror. Or it could be that the laugher recognised that the dream of otherness may not be the same as what the Other dreams.

When Foucault stopped laughing he went on to say: '...leave it to our bureaucrats and our police to see that our papers are in order. At least spare us their morality when we write' (Foucault, 1974: 17). This suggests perhaps that postcolonial interventions only refuse the colonial rather than invoke another order of being. Consequently, without the possibility of a radical rupture towards a new order of things, the postcolonial condition condemns us to continue to play with concepts and categories that are played within and against the colonial lineage, while awaiting the possibility of a new language game that has yet to begin. *A Postcolonial People* is made possible by articulating the unnecessary but unavoidable category of BrAsian, a category whose relevance and persistence is inscribed in the idealisation of its obsolescence; in other words, this volume is custom-built to be out of order.

Part I. FRAMES

N. Ali, V.S. Kalra and S. Sayyid

The following chapters are mainly concerned with investigating the epistemological and theoretical debates through which the BrAsian experience has been articulated. Central to the argument of the book is the description of BrAsian as a postcolonial people. Postcoloniality is deployed here as a term that is not merely empirical or descriptive, but also conceptual.

The first chapter, by Barnor Hesse and S. Sayyid, provides an analytical narrative of the postcolonial context of the BrAsian settlement and sets out to reframe the way in which the 'normal' science of 'race relations' accounts for racially marked ex-colonial settlers in Britian. Hesse and Sayyid politicise the notion of postcoloniality, extending its significance beyond the field of literary and cultural studies, where it has tended to reside, to the arena of political and social enquiry. The political aspect of the postcolonial is not, however, limited to a change of scope, that is, the nature of the postcolonial is not political simply because it focuses on issues traditionally associated with politics, but rather, as Hesse and Sayyid argue, it arises from its capacity to question the construction of social relations as being already given. This focus on the political aspect of the postcolonial condition provides the context for the difficult emergence of a BrAsian subjectivity.

The next two chapters, by Avtar Brah and Tariq Modood respectively, focus directly on the politics that surround the articulation of a distinct BrAsian subject position. Avtar Brah's chapter outlines the historical trajectory that oversaw the transition from Asian, as a signifier of immigrants, to BrAsian, as a signifier of settlers. Brah shows how over a period of almost fifty years the figure of the 'Asian' has been contested between ethnically marked populations hailing from South Asia and the discursive practices of an ethnically unmarked national imagination. Tariq Modood's chapter examines the way in which the usage of 'black' as a means of identifying all of Britain's ethnically marked ex-colonial populations obscured the very different ways in which populations with Caribbean and those with South Asian heritage adapted to and were accommodated by Britain. Modood's intervention highlights how the politics of ascription, in the context of ethicised communities, have often had more to do with orientalist fantasies of various élite discourses rather than the concerns and actualities of the communities themselves.

The following three chapters explore the conceptual assumptions behind some of the dominant representations of South Asians and BrAsians. John Hutnyk alerts us to the difficulty of applying a particular kind of anthropological gaze derived from the colonial experience to postcolonial phenomena. He does this through a reading of absence within anthropological accounts of left-leaning political organisations that empowered BrAsians. This empowerment demonstrates the limits of various models of Western supremacist discourse, whose function was to discipline ethnically marked ex-colonial populations. According to Hutnyk, the absence of analysis of the radical leftist tradition within the BrAsian communities is one of the ways in which depoliticisation of BrAsians is represented and regulated. Thus Hutnyk argues that a positivist anthropology focusing on essentialist categories (however skilfully re-described) is bound to produce an account in which the BrAsian experience constantly reacts to an essence based on alterity as a cultural rather than a political category. Arvind Mandair picks up on the essential otherness of South Asians as it is expressed in the seriousness of their religious affiliations. Mandair's chapter recounts how South Asians (subsequently BrAsians) become the place of religion. He notes the decisive influence of Hegel in the formation of Indology and its attempt to appropriate and contain South Asians and examines the implications of Derrida's arguments for the untranslatability of the concept of religion for the way in which BrAsianness is regulated and represented. The final chapter in this part, by Seán McLoughlin, examines these themes of representation and regulation in the specific case of Bradford. The centrality of Bradford in Britain's ethnoscapes means that its representations in academic, journalistic and literary discourses provides a generalised commentary on the dialectical relationship between some members of Britain's ethnically marked populations and the representation of the British nation as ethnically unmarked. Bradford's status as a metaphor for BrAsian at its most radically Other transforms McLoughlin's historiography of Bradford into a conceptual history of BrAsianness.

This part outlines some of the processes that helped to form a distinct BrAsian identity. The relationship between the presence of ethnically marked ex-colonial people in Britain and the postcolonial condition provided the context for this formation. The two parts following this one continue the story of BrAsians by mapping out the complex forms of their settlement of Britain.

NARRATING THE POSTCOLONIAL POLITICAL AND THE IMMIGRANT IMAGINARY

Barnor Hesse and S. Sayyid

'Imperialism did not end, did not suddenly become "past", once decolonisation had set in motion the dismantling of the classical empires. A legacy of connections still binds countries like Algeria and India to France and Britain respectively. A vast new population of Muslims, Africans and West Indians from former colonial territories now resides in metropolitan Europe; even Italy, Germany and Scandinavia today must deal with these dislocations, which are to a large degree the result of imperialism and decolonisation as well as expanding European population.' (Said, 1993: 282)

'If the law is the apparatus that binds and seals the universality of the political body of the nation, then the "immigrant", produced by the law as margin and threat to that symbolic whole, is precisely a generative site for the critique of that universality.' (Lowe, 1996: 9–10)

Britain in the 1960s: A man arrives at Heathrow airport, stands in line before passport control. He has no family with him, he does not speak the language and he has no more than five pounds in his pocket. His clothes, bearing and face mark him out as a foreigner, from India or Pakistan, who has come to work in Britain. Possibly he will find a job in the textile mills up North, a tyre factory in the Midlands, or maybe at London Transport. As he stands in the queue his thoughts wander back to family and friends, perhaps he is thinking of the day when he will have earned enough to return. Maybe he is preoccupied with the strange sights that greet him, surrounded by images and sounds that confound him. It would not be surprising if he is overcome by a mixture of excitement and anxiety, realising he stands in a country he has previously known only through travellers' tales and myths. Could it be that what he feels is not that different from the emotions that must have been felt by another group of voyagers from another, much earlier time and different place?

OVER 500 YEARS EARLIER

In May 1498 the Portuguese Vasco da Gama arrived off the coast of what is now called Kerala bearing letters for Prester John, who was thought to be the monarch of a realm described as the 'extreme Orient beyond Persia and Armenia'. Da Gama's encounter with unfamiliar Indians was mediated by a knowledge of the familiar, the vocabulary of which he had to resort to in order to describe what he saw. However, he was not able to transform South Asia so that it conformed to his descriptive scheme; da Gama's arrival was still pre-colonial. In contrast, the subsequent colonial project sought to recast South Asia in terms of the Western imagination—constructing 'South Asia' as we know it—and was part of a re-ordering of the world in European terms. Or as one writer puts it, in reference to the conception of Asia as a *continent*: 'The term, it is recognised, is essentially Western. There is no equivalent word in any Asian language nor such a concept in the domain of geographical knowledge' (Chaudhuri, 1991: 23). In this way we can understand the emergence of a *South* Asia, a geographical expression and a cultural formation initiated as part of the imperial process by which Europe sutured the globe, and so established its distinctive identity in relation to rest of the world. The mapping of South Asia coincided with the formation of the West as a global enterprise, the latter signalled by the appropriation of the Americas, which, underwritten by imperial processes emanating from the peninsula on the western edge of the Asian continent, elaborated a gradual shift from the idea of Christendom to the idea of Europe, and introduced into the Americas various administrative categories of 'non-Europeanness' (e.g. 'Indian' for native Americans, 'Negro' for Africans) and proto-anthropological discourses of 'race' to govern and conceptualise human diversity (Wolf, 1982; Todorov, 1984; Rabasa, 1993).

Initially the presence of South Asia in Europe was contained in and spread through exotic commodities, fabulous legends and the embellished first hand experiences of a few hardy travellers. The entry of South Asia into the European imagination therefore was not an event like the appropriation of the Western hemisphere, in which an unknown landmass and its inhabitants were consumed by Europe. Many of the traits considered to be specifically South Asian were constituted by networks of trade, pioneered by the Portuguese. Early modern India, therefore, can be seen in terms of the ways in which control of the Indian Ocean passed from Islamicate and Chinese ships to Portuguese, Dutch and British fleets. The spices brought by the Portuguese from the Americas helped to define a global cuisine, which is now known perhaps too un-problematically as Indian. The voyages of Vasco da Gama in effect inaugurate the beginning of the process by which South Asia becomes a looming presence on European horizons. Thus Portuguese voyages to *Al-Hind* coincide with the major transformation of European identity, in particular, the way in which racialised discourses emerged from the imperial establishment of 'Europeanness' and the colonial creation and rule of 'non-Europeanness' (Scammell, 1990; Wink, 1997).

EMPIRE/NATION

The expansive migration and settlement of South Asians in Britain cannot be accounted for outside the context of the relationships established between Europe and South Asia in general and between post-Timurid India and the British Isles in particular. Indeed, Asian settlement is a postcolonial suffix to the colonial relationship between Britain and its Indian empire. This is one of the reasons why there has always been something distinctly colonial about modern Britishness racially exceeding the conventional parameters of its history and the official memory of its national institution. So when in 1997 the Union Jack was being lowered in a televised ceremony to publicise Hong Kong's official return to China, the irony that it was only a hundred years ago that the British Empire was celebrating Queen Victoria's Diamond Jubilee seemed lost. The zenith of the British Empire came in the wake of the First World War, when it comprised 14 million sq km of the earth's land surface (133 million sq km, including Antarctica)[1] and ruled over approximately 400 million people (of which 322 million were to be found in its Indian dominions). The irony might be underlined by remembering the period between Pakistan and India's independence in 1947 and the official decolonisation of Hong Kong, as fifty years of Britain resuming, with a postcolonial indifference, political and cultural developments in which its national and local meanings continued to be deeply marked by the combined and uneven effects of colonial, racial and multicultural formations. Of course the post-Second World War period is not usually remembered or conceived in this way, centring as it does on the upheavals and dislocations internal to the discontinuities that periodise the well-being and idealisations of Western democratic culture (principally Europe and the United States). In Britain it is conventional to speak of the post-war condition of labour shortages as the catalyst for migration from the colonies, without any consideration of the impact of coloniality, as a political and social culture, on Britain's 'nation-Empire', as if nation and empire belonged to incommensurable temporalities, polities and spaces. Were we to re-employ the usual sociological narrative implied here, endorsing the nation-empire separation, symptomatic of analyses that divorce national race-relations from global international relations, we would fail to see the British continuities of race, empire and nationalism across the twentieth century as a whole.

Here we want to point to three conjunctural dimensions around which our alternative postcolonial/coloniality narrative might be contrasted to the ubiquitous post-war/race-relations narrative. First, there was in the last half of the twentieth century, Britain's redeployment within its cities

1 This based on Taagapera (1978), but excluding the self-governing white dominions of Canada, Australia, South Africa and New Zealand.

and institutions of a liberal-colonial racism arising from the unanticipated, rapid unravelling of the British Empire, in which the colonial regulation of international relations became subsumed into the regulation of immigration and race relations within a liberal discourse that formally denounced the idea of racial superiority. Second, there were the creolising, hybridising effects of the social and cultural movements of migrations from South Asia, the Caribbean and West Africa which entrenched and transformed the ethnic-urban meanings of localities in major British cities, entangling idioms of Britishness in new forms of representation and contestation, greatly unsettling local white investments in the nation as a community racially unified in the imagination. Third, presiding over the shock waves of these developments were the indifferently postcolonial regimes of British institutions, whose implications in the post-war national commitment to the welfare state, full employment, peace and prosperity had also to contend with social challenges to housing, policing and education, posed by unrelenting, unsettling questions of racism and multiculturalism, flowing from imperial histories that greatly exceeded the narrow preoccupations of race-relations (Hesse, 2000). While the exact chronology of these shifts in British identity was far more confused and contradictory than is sketched here, its main contours are fairly clear, despite the attempt of revisionist historians to seek in the complexities and hesitancies associated with real historical phenomena the negation of the phenomena themselves (e.g. David Carradine, Niall Ferguson).

Continuing to invoke the term 'post-war' to describe the context and temporality of these events, reiterates a descriptor that is not only exhausted but also increasingly anachronistic. The end of the cold war ushered in the official demise of the so-called post-war period, displacing the bi-polar world characterised by the Soviet and US nuclear-armed empires, which were always the continuation of consequences of the Second World War by other means. Since then the question of the world order has been a frequent topic of debate, yet it continues to be underpinned by a Western imperium, both residual and renewable, with its hegemonic assumptions that there is no alternative to its basis of a world order. The passing of the cold war must now be understood as an interregnum, since European and American cultures of coloniality have clearly remained intact, albeit reframed, reformed and reformulated with regard to refugees and asylum seekers, Third World debt, anti-immigration, rogue states, global poverty, racial profiling, racist attacks, institutional racism, multiculturalism and the 'war on terror'. Therefore what we refer to as the postcolonial is not to be understood empirically as simply referring to the conventional etchings or endings of empire as a formal regime or set of institutions, but rather conceptually as a way of narrating the deregulated presences of past economic, political and cultural colonialities transformed within the postcolonial present to naturalise and depoliticise the world order (e.g. the world economic and political hegemony of the United States and European Union; Third world poverty). In other words, the postcolonial describes the limitations and incompleteness of anterior decolonisation, and indicates renewed circumstances in which the challenge to resist and overcome the residuum and excess of coloniality continues to disturb, question and unsettle Western practices of normalising, disavowing and depoliticising the contemporary colonial architecture of the world order.

COLONIALITY

What we call European coloniality should not be confused with the formal existence of empires and colonies, as in references to colonialism, nor should its persistence be treated as something exempt from the American experience. For us the idea of coloniality points to a governmental cultural form or social regulatory process, assembled in formal and informal practices of 'racial rule' (Goldberg, 2002). Despite the liberal humanist commitments of the European Union and the United States, coloniality is routinely sustained in their deliberations, which enshrine the hegemonic authority of the West over the *non*-West, the moral high ground of Europeanness over *non*-Europeanness, and the global value of white populations over *non*-white populations. Such a Western spectacle (Hesse, 1999) overflows and exceeds the previous formal institutionalisation of Western empires (e.g. colonialism). In contemporary political, social, economic, legal and intellectual practices, the reflexes of European coloniality have become so normalised as to be complicit even with the apparent counter claims of Western liberal-democratic discourses. Despite any putative humanitarian gloss, coloniality expresses the languages, practices and relations that gave meaning to the kinds of distinctions, nuances, representations and interactions that culminated in the racially hierarchical and segregated formations of European empires across the world, including the United States. Coloniality, detached from the institutions of empire is particularly expressed, marked and initiated through the continuing associations of 'race', racism and multiculturalism with Western forms of governance and culturally occidentalist dominated representations (Venn, 2000). It can be read as symptomatic of Western regulatory formations, processes, knowledges and identities because it has congealed historically from the social transformation of colonised cultural differences into administered, inferiorised 'Otherness' (e.g. 'savages', 'primitive', 'underdeveloped', 'minorities'). We cannot overestimate the historic transformation of the relation between coloniality and modernity because the Eurocentric (including the Americas) lineage of colonised 'Otherness' continues to be appropriated, exploited, interrogated, exoticised, infantilised and pathologised under the rubric of international relations and race relations. Within these terms, an official postcoloniality subsists fraudulently, continuing to underwrite liberal-democratic administrations of racially polarised, gendered, sexualised 'non-European-Otherness'. This, it must be understood, is not something that only occurs between the 'West' and the 'non-West', but also between 'Europeanness' ('whiteness') and 'non-Europeanness' ('non-whiteness') within the very contours and criteria defining and explaining the West to itself.

Our colonial reference to whiteness in parentheses should perhaps also be made explicit at this point. As Edward Said pointed out, the colonial relation meant the rule of the white man, it was a way of being in the world and appropriating that world. The 'white man' was a hegemonic disposition, a dominating cadre of comportments that made possible a specific authoritarian colonial cultural style: 'Being a White Man was therefore an idea and a reality. It involved a reasoned position towards both the white and the non-white worlds. It meant—in the colonies—speaking in a certain way, behaving according to a code of regulations, and even feeling certain things and not others. It meant specific judgements, evaluations, gestures' (Said, 1978: 227). In addition it meant embodying the administrative cultivation of 'race', in which policies implementing a governing form of racism, were indispensable attributes of the colonial authority, ascribed to the disposition and the orientation of the 'white man'. As far as the lineage and legacy of coloniality is concerned, the modern, global, colonial way of being the 'white man' involved,

> ...the culturally sanctioned habit of deploying large generalisations by which reality is divided into various collectives: languages, races, types, colours, mentalities, each category being not so much a neutral designation as an evaluative interpretation. Underlying these categories is the rigidly binomial opposition of 'ours' and 'theirs', with the former always encroaching upon the latter (even to the point of making 'theirs' exclusively a function of 'ours'). (Said, 1978: 227)

This of course raises the question, to what extent and how does this symbolics of whiteness remain relevant in relation to the non-West and the West's designated non-white populations? In the move from the oscillations between the authoritarian and paternal imperialisms of formally recognised empires, to the humanitarian imperialism of the postcolonial era, the symbolics of whiteness appears to have folded into an assumingly benign liberal-democratic universal culture.

Heuristically the failure to understand the contemporary meaning of coloniality has generated a great deal of uncertainty if not confusion about the meaning of the postcolonial in political terms. As a cultural intervention or intellectual practice, postcolonialism has been mainly associated with the field of literary and cultural studies, where it has referred to a genre of writing which reflected on the complex and often contradictory ways in which European empires shaped and continued to influence societies which, though no longer subject to direct imperial control, were haunted by the spectral resonances of empire, whether in the field of law, economy, polity or social institutions. When the postcolonial has been used to address political issues, for example the 'right' or the 'good', it has done so largely by being refracted through a cultural prism, seeing culture broadly as practices of representation defining what Charles Taylor has called in the context of multiculturalism, a 'politics of recognition' (Taylor, 1993). Thus the postcolonial analytic has tended to focus on politics as practices of cultural representation. Consequently, the political aspect of the postcolonial has often been found at points at which culture (as ethnic representations or ways of life) and politics (the domain of the state or the rule of law) converge, or, to be more precise, at the point at which cultural questions consume political questions (e.g. nationalism, so-called fundamentalism). While useful within the realms of cultural studies, this has left unattended transnational political questions of power and coloniality, which can only be summarised under the theme of *interrupted decolonisation*, as a persisting and relevant idea in the contemporary age. In this sense the postcolonial becomes an idiom for reflecting on the historical logics of decolonisation and mobilising its contemporary logics—if by decolonisation we understand both the removal and elimination of the forms of coloniality described above.

At least three contemporary logics of decolonisation that arise within the political prism of postcoloniality can be identified. The first can be described as *decolonising the representations of the decolonised*. Here coloniality is not understood so much in terms of material exploitation or political subordination, though these are conditions of its existence, but as an unaccountable organised structure of authoritative knowledge exerted over the formerly colonised and their descendents. The sense of coloniality used depicts forms of power/knowledge that describe Western projects of mastering and regulating the 'non-European' world and communities comprising people of colour in terms of Eurocentric knowledges, representations and administrations. Decolonising the representations of the decolonised takes the form of a politics of interrogation (not recognition), where the objective is to expose, challenge, remove and eliminate hegemonic 'white'/'Western' claims of the right to theorise and legitimate 'non-Western'/'non-white' experiences of postcoloniality.[2]

The second logic can be described as *decolonising representative decolonisation*. Here coloniality is understood in terms of authorising and

2 The main catalyst for this kind of approach is the work of Edward Said, particularly his book *Orientalism*, though we can probably add to this Valintine Mdimbe's *Invention of Africa*, Johanas Fabian's *Time and the Other* and Ronald Inden's *Imagining India*.

allocating global resources, power, or what Anibal Quijano has referred to as the 'coloniality of power', which refers to the continued ways in which modern categories of citizenship, democracy and national identity are shaped by the unequal power differentials between 'European'/'white' and 'non-European'/'non-white' assemblages and comportments. Despite the eradication of juridical and political institutions of colonialism, colonial practices and discourses continue to proliferate across time and space on a global level, particularly under auspices of global capitalism. For us the logic of decolonisation here takes the political form of challenging and replacing the limited and inadequate previous processes of decolonisation in the political, juridical and economic arenas, particularly under the rubric of globalisation (e.g. candidates for decolonisation here range from the IMF, the World Trade Organisation and the United Nations to NATO). It also extends to striving for political and economic forms of cosmopolitan democracy, within and beyond Western nation-states, regulated globally by a transformation of unfair terms of trade imposed by the West to the detriment of the non-West.

The third logic can be described as *decolonising the representatives of decolonisation.* Here coloniality is understood in terms of what Homi Bhabha (1994) has described as liberal-colonial doubleness, in which coloniality extends as much to the liberal as to the colonial part of the institutions and discourses conjoined in this way. It questions the idea that the Western liberal institutions involved in inaugurating and administering the formal decolonising process are no longer involved in sustaining coloniality. Rather than accepting a radical discontinuity between metropole and colony, in terms of civilisation and barbarism, it understands, as Stokely Carmichael and Charles V. Hamilton (1967) argued in the late 1960s, that something like institutional racism is very much associated with respected Western institutions and that it points to the persistence of coloniality. Here the logic of decolonisation takes the form of exorcising coloniality from the liberal-democratic culture of Western nations themselves. The political in postcolonialism, or the *political postcolonial* should now be thought of as a series of reflections, conceptions, interventions, practices in the arena and analysis of decolonisation, ranged against the terms of resumed and renewed coloniality, mobilised for its continual eradication. The prospect of decolonisation becomes something akin to what Jamaica's national poet Louise Bennet once ironically referred to as 'colonisation in reverse', in describing the migrations from the former colonies to the former imperial metropole. We should note, however, that it is not the exchange of the hegemonic and subaltern positions within the colonial hierarchy that is being signified by 'colonisation in reverse' but rather the critical reversal of the colonial relationship itself, its reversion and revision, not merely the swapping of positions within that relationship.

IMMIGRANTS

If we now return to considering the arrival of the ex-colonial ethnically marked 'immigrant' in the British metropole it should be seen immediately how postcoloniality confused the spatial and racial distinction between centre and periphery, nation and empire, citizen and native, and thus signalled the unsettling and unpredictable effects of an exceedingly provisional decolonisation of all the political, social and cultural manifestations made possible by the imperial enterprise. The ex-colonial 'immigrants' were pejoratively portrayed as bringing the Empire home, underlining the disavowed reality of the 'nation-empire', and in some quarters deeply resented for closing the gap that colonialism had opened up between liberal-democracy and its racial Other. The administrative machinery of what Couze Venn calls 'imperial governmentality' (in our terms *racialised governmentality* [Hesse and Sayyid, forthcoming]) began to assert itself in relation to the management of the presence of the ex-colonial 'immigrant' (Venn, 2000). Because the history of ex-colonial immigration to Britain is most often told in terms of the post-war labour shortage, which was to be filled by semi-skilled and unskilled labour from the Caribbean, South Asia and West Africa, we can easily lose sight of its deeply re-inscribed colonial dynamics. In these accounts, the movement of people is reduced to the working of an implacable economic logic, which transcends any particular embodiments, and works in a universal space, the invisible hand of the market, outside of historical processes or cultural formations. Invariably this sets in train a series of nationalised explanations (push-pull, chain migration) designed to account for the transfer of people from the edge of a contracting empire, the official moment of postcoloniality, to the war torn, battered and bombed heartlands of the officially designated post-war Britain. These host-community/immigrant-community accounts provide an overwhelmingly inadequate way of narrating the migratory and settlement experiences of ethnically marked postcolonial subjects across Britain; nevertheless they sustain the fictions in British public culture of a termination between the imperial past and the nationalist present, as well as of a structural and political separation between a racially unmarked indigenous British society and racially marked migrants who become carriers of cultures for British consumption or proscription.

What these official and media accounts cannot do is place these migrations within the history of postcoloniality. The absence of any analysis of the postcolonial condemns the stories of 'immigrants' to replay the colonial drama inscribed in various scenes of the 'immigrant' imaginary (Sayyid, 2004). Formed by the intersection of discourses organised around the figure of 'immigrant' as signifier of ex-coloniality, the 'immigrant' imaginary constitutes 'immigrants' as ontologically distinct, to be celebrated as exotica or to be dismissed as being unworthy of specific representation. It projects a future in which the 'immigrant' minority will be indistinguishable from the national (i.e. ethnically unmarked) majority, but consecrates a present that permanently defers such a possibility. It tends to reduce social, political, cultural and economic changes within an 'immigrant' minority to generational conflict and succession. Generations emerge as the dominant analytical trope, used to mark out transformations, which see the immigrant process as the key component in changing the lives of ethnically marked populations. Routine-ised narratives, which cite the movement from first to second to third generation, are represented as containing self-evident explanations. Often portrayed with the certainty of biological processes, the generational movements of immigrants are depicted as analogous to a life cycle in which tadpoles eventually turn into frogs. While there is an argument to be made that age cohorts may in some contexts have sociological and political significance, it does not follow that the only transformations having significant impact on the 'immigrant' community result from their socialisation into the 'host' society. Here we have the dominant representation of the migratory experience always associating it with the importation of inscrutable cultures and bizarre practices from another time and distant lands, in which generational movement, from immigrant to citizen, seen as absorption into the British way of life, requires movement from Urdu and Hindi to Cockney and Brummie. Absorption, meaning *being assimilated rather than assimilating*, is seen as the only engine of transformation, where continued movement from one generation to another, particularly in terms of success or failure, becomes a significant anthropological if not biological predicator of future social behaviour.

On the face of it perhaps there is nothing new here. The 'immigrant' imaginary resembles in its emphasis the strategies and policies that were used to reconcile post-national minorities to the national majority during the early modern period of Europe's successive waves of state formation and consolidation. Post-national ethnically marked populations arose as a result of being left out (for a variety of contingent historical reasons) of the process by which the Westphalian template of peoples, territories and government was institutionalised. The construction of national belongings often left some communities outside the process even when they were located within the boundaries of the nascent state-nation projects. Post-national communities tended to be either those ethnically marked populations that were unable to transform their ethnicity into a nationality (i.e. they were unable to build the bridge from cultural, linguistic ethnic community to political community armed with all technologies and powers of a state). For example, Bretons or Welsh or Sicilians could have easily become national majorities in their own state-nations. The second type of post-national group that failed to be accommodated in the initial process of state sponsored projects of centralisation and nation-building were populations that can be loosely termed dispersed or nomadic (i.e. groups that were considered to be too territorially scattered and *not* having a specific dwelling—in today's terminology, diasporas). The most important examples were the Roma people and the Jews. Post-national communities were constructed as minorities by the process of boundary drawing that saw the hegemonic group as a national majority. The minority status of ethnically marked populations was not simply a symptom of their demographic size, but reflected more closely an (im)balance of forces and resources between ethnically marked and unmarked populations. Historically the European domestication of post-national ethnic minorities has been protracted, often violent and authoritarian. Where domestication was successful it enabled the national majority to more or less absorb its ethnic minorities and produce a more or less unified national majority in which traces of the former ethnic minorities did not resonate significantly either politically, socially or economically. This did not mean, however, that all the ethnicised minorities dissolved but rather that they became accepted as a legitimate, de-ethnicised part of the national majority. Through such a process the French and the English were created from a number of different ethnicities. Post-national ethicised minorities became part of the national majority, through the expansion of the process of nation-building. It was the establishment of national languages with national standards (rules of grammar, dictionaries), compulsory or wide-spread schooling, conscription, expanded administrative machinery, dislocations and relocations of national economies, which induced and coerced the domestication and eventual absorption of European ethnic minorities.

Unsurprisingly then the 'immigrant' imaginary articulates the arrival of ethnically marked ex-colonial people as another instance of the post-national minority thesis, hence postcolonial people become available if not ready to be domesticated and assimilated into the national fold by using the same techniques and practices that made nation-states out of diverse ethnic, cultural, linguistic, economic groupings. The problem of course is that such a thesis cannot identify or countenance immigrants and their descendants as belonging to ethnic minority formations that are decidedly postcolonial, since the thesis cannot concede the idea that ex-colonial immigrant formations are not signifiers of the incomplete process of nation-building but are rather signifiers of the incomplete social, political and racial developments surrounding decolonisation. The failure of British politics to come to terms with these postcolonial conditions since the latter half of the twentieth century has led to mainstream and extremist discourses attributing many social problems to the presence of the ex-colonial ethnically marked populations. We place in this context the recurrent claim made by most mainstream politicians, even by virtue of certain turns of phrase, that racialised exclusions and violations directed against people of colour is the product of their presence, or to put it in the vernacular, they were attacked or discriminated against *because* they are Asian. As absurd as it is common, this is one of the reasons always suggested for strict immigration control, that the presence of the racially Othered is the cause of racism. The index of racism is linked not with its routine rationalities and practices established within the lineaments of British imperial culture at home and abroad, but rather with the (ascribed) refusal of these postcolonial people to cross over into a national hearth of belongingness and absorption, thereby almost obliging the national ethnically unmarked majority to racially exclude, deride and violate the ethnically marked minorities.

What we can see from the postcolonial reframing of the cycle of 'race relations' in Britain are the limits and shallowness of many policy interventions around racism. It allows us to break with the primacy of the domestic in determining the proper responses to racism and its persistence, and clearly locates the decolonising impact of the ethnically marked. It has to be remembered that ethnic marking, the process of designating ethnic minorities and national majorities, is not a simple reflection of underlying realities, rather it is the product of a particular construction which has been foundational to the articulation of British identity. Attempts to re-articulate a British identity in the wake of ex-colonial settlement, loss of geopolitical prominence and the unravelling of the United Kingdom continue to founder upon the insistence that a serious consideration of the postcolonial be excluded from this. Consequently the presence of ex-colonial 'immigrants' becomes a symptom of the failure of British identity to reconstitute itself following the loss of empire, the ravages of the hot war, the end of the cold war and the return of the depoliticised colonial world order. If the 'immigrant' imaginary helps to prevent the incomplete decolonisation of the British Empire from becoming the effective postcolonisation (recolonisation?) of Britain, it is because it also represents the postcolonial condition as something that happens to other people in other places. This may become clearer if we turn our attention to what might be described as the postcolonial understanding and response to racism.

POSTCOLONIAL RACISM

Reviewing or re-reading the migratory postcolonial experience is now crucial to understanding and contesting the British incidence and impact of racism. In recent years, for all the welcome liberal discussion about 'race' in the social sciences and humanities, the tendency has been to collapse race into a sign of ethnicity or difference rather than to invoke an interrogation of racism. The idea of 'race' has generally been detached from the idea of racism, though bizarrely in some instances it has to be acknowledged that discussions of race have often masqueraded for discussions of racism. It should be acknowledged that since the late 1990s the entry of a nationally invoked 'institutional racism' into the political lexicon of the public sphere momentarily suggested that some things were about to change even though British public culture had enormous difficulty both understanding and accepting it. Nevertheless the advent of institutional racism as an object of redress for public policy proved to be a false dawn. Racism is still not something that is seen to merit national government discussion like privatisation, education, global warming or the National Health Service; there is as yet, no war against racism. Despite the long traditions of black, BrAsian and generally anti-racist struggles across its major cities, British public culture continues to have great difficulty accepting that racism is as British as liberalism and as institutional as nationalism. Where both liberalism and nationalism have British histories and institutional force, it would seem British public culture has felt racism is a different kind of phenomena, that it is more recent perhaps, of less sure footing and certainly not a formative part of the British experience. Although Britain has a small but honourable tradition of political activists, community workers, journalists and academics striving to expose and explain the impact of racism across social life, the effect on British public culture has always been negligible. Atlantic slavery, British colonialism or Western imperialism were instrumental in shaping what contemporary Britain inherits and understands as nationalism and liberalism. Yet in the fields of knowledge regularly and conventionally produced in and disseminated through the public culture, racism is somehow exempted from these historical and social formations.

Perhaps part of the answer lies further afield. Any acknowledgement of racism in the public domain appears to be understood less as having the social morphology of liberalism and nationalism, and more as having the psychological attributes of irrationality, hatred, superstition and prejudice. The mainstream attitude had been to associate these presumed psychological associations with the impact of post-1945 immigration and the contested emergence of race-relations in the context of scare resources or competition for resources. Between the late 1950s and the early 1970s this media view easily prevailed, with little or no sustained exposure for the concerns of black and BrAsian communities in the local and national media. For a brief moment in the late 1970s and mid 1980s a more public and direct anti-racist network of ideas, movements and campaigns managed to place racism, rather than prejudice, on various local public and national agendas. The riots in Brixton, Southall and Toxteth in 1981 and Tottenham and Handsworth in 1985 introduced middle England to the *local idea* of racism, the problem of policing and the robust presence of black and BrAsian communities. More than this, in cities like London, Birmingham and Liverpool the concept of a *locally invoked* institutional racism was added to the exigencies of urban anti-racist lexicons, though not the national concerns of a parliamentary vocabulary. Despite some gestures to social change and some useful equal opportunity developments introduced in local government, the voluntary sector and the police, by the beginning of the 1990s racism was no longer an issue that could be raised publicly, even in the watered down version of prejudice. Although the so-called Rushdie Affair, symbolised by television pictures of a staged book burning in Bradford and a gathering of mass prayers in Hyde Park, heralded the media's discovery of large Muslim communities in Britain, this tended to promote a media and political obsession with understanding cultural diversity rather than racism. British public culture stood outside and hovered above the fray that had not entered it (Hesse, 2000, 2004b).

It was not that the problems of racist attacks, racist policing, racism in employment, education, immigration and health had diminished. During the greater part of the 1990s they simply continued to be relegated to what the imagined British community chose not to imagine about itself. The racist murder of Stephen Lawrence, one of many at the beginning of the 1990s, managed to change what the nation could talk about in relation to racism, but only after a long public campaign had been undertaken and a change of government allowed an official inquiry to be set up. The report produced by the Macpherson inquiry declared for the first time nationally that institutional racism was a problem in Britain. But the imagined community still had one problem; apart from arriving at an understanding of institutional racism, it had to understand where it came from, how it got here. The concept of institutional racism had entered a public domain that had no specification of a history or cultural formation in which it could be located (Hesse, 2004b). This gave rise to a Macpherson definition of institutional racism in terms of unwittingness, unintended consequences and organisational failures in policy, all of which could continue to be explained in the time-honoured, more comfortable terms of prejudice, immigration and race-relations established since 1945.

Nevertheless, some things did change. The accelerated globalisation of the 1990s, the end of the cold war and the end of apartheid effectively brought to a close the developments and discourses that had traditionally defined the post-war period *as a period*. Britain had become a significant, if at times reluctant, player in the neo-liberal economic and federal expansion of the European Union. The 1992 removal of internal immigration barriers across the Union compromised the vernaculars of British national identity with European cosmopolitanism, while the increasing prominence in social life of asylum seekers and refugees began the expansion and redefinition of the British template of nationalist and racist mobilisation. At the same time Britain became a captive audience to a socially mainstreamed passion for all things culturally diverse. Through sports, music, cinema, the fashion industry and business, especially the food industry, the cultivated lure of a multicultural Britain revolutionised the images of advertising, broadcasting and entertainment. Since the ethnic look and ethnic looking came in somewhere in the last third of the 1990s, neither has ever looked back. At the same time, there were still influentially hysterical elements in the popular press and restrained versions in the political discourse of Government, which continued to resent and traduce the ethnically or racially marked foreigner in our midst.

At times overwhelming the ethnic love and hate fest was the emergence of a global Muslim subjectivity, which by the beginning of the twenty-first century was officially indicted if not proscribed by the rise of the 'war on terror', which intentionally or not chose the reflex of following the contours of a colonial undertaking. East continued to be East and West, West: Afghanistan, Iraq, Iran and North Korea (the 'axis of evil') now all resemble colonial problems to be resolved through 'Empire' (Hardt and Negri, 2001) or the 'Western conglomerate state' (Shaw, 2000), both inside and outside the West. Hence the British position of Asian communities, as postcolonial people, particularly those marked by Muslim affiliations, intimacies or resemblances, are not so easily separated from the racial profiling emanating from policing strategies associated with the 'war on terror'. Such a postcolonial presence cannot be explained outside the rupturing of the membrane, which separated metropole from periphery, or the space of law and peace from the space of violence and chaos. The intrusion of the periphery into metropole (which is, as we noted, constitutive of the postcolonial condition) can no longer be contained within the interior of the metropolitan nation-states. 'Race-relations' which have for far too long been conceived as matters of domestic policy are being subverted by the increasing difficulty of sustaining the act of spacing that divides it from international relations; the myth of the national majority historically and politically distinct from developments surrounding the ethnically marked and colonially overdetermined minority should now be laid to rest. Indeed what amounts to a subversion of the colonial idea of 'race relations' draws attention to the genealogical formation of contemporary racism in the context of a world polarised and policed as the 'West' over the 'non-West', 'Europe' over 'non-Europe', 'white' over 'non-white' that is often surrounded by official silence.

PARADOXICAL RACISM

It is necessary to recall that racism as a critical concept first emerges in the 1930s to describe the experiences of people of Jewish heritage living under the racial laws imposed by the newly elected Nazi government (Fredrickson, 2001). However, the Nuremberg Laws, the Nazi political programme and the associated legal and extra-legal practices had a strong family resemblance to what was going on throughout the rest of the world as colonialism, in which European settlers or administrations regulated the conduct of what were deemed to be 'non-European' peoples. The colonial frame here refers not only to the empires of the British, French and Dutch etc., but also to the 'inner' empires, in which European settlers confronted indigenous peoples of the Americas and Australasia, as well as the Africans who were enslaved and the Indians who were pressed into indentured servitude. Given the homology between racial practices in Nazi Germany and normalised practices in the rest of the world subject to European coloniality, it is worth asking what circumstances motivated the invention and formulation of racism as a concept describing German imperial practices across Europe, especially when these practices resembled those carried out by European authorities in the colonised territories? Each one of the racialised techniques of social exclusion, segregation, demonisation, marginalisation and violence was already operating under the rule of coloniality. Concentration camps, discriminatory legal codes, repression through native collusions, clandestine or semi-official systems of violations, none of these were new to European political culture in the colonies (Du Bois, 1947; Cesaire, 1955). If anything, the innovations of the Nazis lay in the efficiencies achieved in their excesses, the industrialisation and bureaucratic systematisation of the killing process (Bauman, 1989). Indeed in the decade after the Holocaust, both the French in Algeria and the British in Kenya (Anderson, 2005) continued and escalated their range of brutal, vicious colonial practices in their efforts to sustain colonial rule against indigenous anti-colonial movements. In many ways what was radical about fascism was not its precise meaning, but its dislocation of the Europe/Empire divide: fascism was colonialism re-applied to Europe (Cesaire, 1955; Du Bois, 1947; Mazower, 1999). All of this begs the historical question as to why these resemblances were not sufficient to motivate usage of European colonialism as a concept describing Nazi governmental practices? Or conversely, why was it that the newly formulated concept of racism was not systematically and generally applied to European colonial practices in India and Africa? The answers are conceptual, ideological and political. Broadly, concepts induce reflection on marked relations between different aspects of reality, which pass unnoticed and undistinguished from the flow of everyday experiences or freely available empirical descriptions, unless brought into concentrated focus as an abstracted, condensed idea. To conceptualise some things in particular is often not to conceptualise other things in particular, it defines an ideological orientation. The 1930s concept of racism, accredited and taken up by the European powers and the United States after the Second World War, despite the opprobrium it placed on the biologisation of the 'race' idea, was only a partial discrediting of its politicisation. In politically denying European colonial resemblances in German dreams of imperium, the indictment of racism was detached from any indictment of European coloniality. It thereby preserved the latter's routine governmental forms for the continuities of colonial relations in both international relations and race-relations, where administratively 'race' became normalised and depoliticised.

Perversely this undoubtedly Eurocentric concept of racism (Hesse, 2004a, 2004b) emerged to account for the misapplication of coloniality in the heartlands of Europe and to peoples of European physiognomy and comportment (i.e. assimilated European Jewish populations), in effect conceptualising it as a pathological as opposed to a normalised coloniality (which was always reserved for the natives). Although the circulation of something as indictable as racism has in the second half of the twentieth century provided many social moments and political struggles with a significant basis for analysis and mobilisation, the hegemonic inflections of the concept suggested that racism was an exceptionalist form of an extreme ideology beyond the pale of even colonial Western culture (Hesse, 2004a). The circulation of the concept of racism as ideology marked the disavowal of the violence of normalised Western colonialism and the reinforcement of the ascribed moral and political distinction between Europe and non-Europe, the West and the rest, white and non-white, centre and periphery. The ideology of racism, symbolised in the political experiments and fantasies of the Nazis, became in the Western imaginary the template for the racial 'state of exception'. The idea of the state of exception describes those circumstances under which the juridical order is suspended and emergency powers or martial law, or governmental powers unbound by existing law, are exercised (Agamben, 2005). By analogy racism, in being articulated with the inscription of fascism, was defined as extremist politics. Unlike anything with the democratic credentials of Western culture or the British way of life, it was designated as the constituent of a state of exception. This conceptualisation of racism as exceptionalist ideology had global ramifications. It privileged the understanding of racism as an issue of national domestic policy. In other words, the critique of racism addresses the problematic of the regulation of ethnically marked 'minorities'. The operating theatre of racism became the nation-space, hence the speed with which issues of immigration become racialised, problematised and contested. The conceptual containing of racism within the nation-state-space meant that those subject to racism have always had limited options, since they could not outflank the racial order by evoking transnational/diasporic alliances; the sovereign primacy of the Western plutocratic nation state prevents such challenges to the global racial order. In addition it occludes the indictment of any intrinsic colonial relationship between racism and democracy or liberal and colonial state assemblages. These designs which continue to underpin Western polities have been constructed as the basis of the world order and have become normalised as the property of international relations, even where they are sometimes exposed as structures of the colonial hierarchy that orders the planet. The split between coloniality (international governance) and racism (nationalist ideologies) is not necessarily the product of different meanings but rather the different spaces in which they are deployed, such that the split is another means by which the spacing between West and the Non-West (and its analogies in 'European'/'non-European', 'white'/'non-white') becomes constitutive of the Western representation and domination of the world through international relations and race-relations. Of course one of the most prominent ways in which this constitutive split is represented is through the undecidable figure of the BrAsian, the racialised ex-colonial 'immigrant' who stands betwixt and between citizen and foreigner, a colonial past and a national present, West and 'non-West', one of us or one of them.

The establishment of 'immigrant' communities in Britain has occurred in the context of an unsettling, ambivalent and interrupted postcolonial transformation of the West. The colonial continuity of race-relocated regimes and formations has obliged BrAsians like other 'immigrants' to bridge the divide between West and the 'non-West'. The pioneer BrAsians were often people whose formative years passed in the crucible of the anti-colonial struggle. They were often the first South Asians for a hundred years to witness a South Asia in which British rule had receded from the horizon. They arrived in Britain during a period of global turmoil, itself the product of anti-colonial movements in the Third World and the civil rights movement in the United States. They arrived in a Britain that had won a world war at the cost of losing its empire and its place in the world. Their arrival coincided with, and to some extent contributed to, what has been described as the 'de-centring of the West' (Young, 1990; Sayyid, 2003a). In circumstances in which the capacity of the Western enterprise to project itself as the destiny of humanity is weakened, being BrAsian does not necessitate conformity to the disciplinary matrix of the 'immigrant' imaginary.

Cleary we have come a long way since the narrative of post-war migration to Britain, race-relations and the multicultural society were quickly ushered in to aid and abet not only the 'forgetting of empire' (Hall, 2000a) but the disavowal of its incomplete decolonisation, perpetuated in the postcolonial condition. If the break with the post-war paradigm is to be complete, and the postcolonial paradigm to emerge, we will need to re-think some of the claims made for the political formation of the post-war period, particularly where the presence of postcolonial people point to a very different account. The post-war paradigm was in part held together by the Western eulogising of liberal democracy and its defeat of fascism, together with the symbolic discrediting of racism sutured to fascism and nationalism, excluding the credibility of any suggestions of racism's organic link with the articulation of liberalism and coloniality evident in the European empires. In nations like Britain and throughout the West the need for new forms of postcolonial governance is urgent; such a need is unlikely to be met as long as the dream of re-establishing the certainties of coloniality remains the policy option of choice in both international relations and race-relations. Alas, it is difficult to see how there can be colonial solutions to postcolonial problems.

ARRIVAL

Daalat Ali

I was born in Kotli, which was a sub-district of Mirpur. Although there is no record of my date of birth, I know I was born at the end of the First World War, a year or so after my father returned from an Ottoman prisoner-of-war camp. I did not go to school because there were no schools to go to, so I was a farm hand. When I had grown up I used to go to *Angrazi Alaqa* (British India) to work on the construction of railways or canals. The money I raised by labouring was used to pay for land tax and to buy grain and other necessities. Unlike some of my friends I did not fight in the Second World War. When the British were driven out, Kashmir was invaded by India and Pakistan. There was no work, and times were bad. People were leaving for wherever they could go. I wanted to go to England, but I had no money. So I sold all my cattle, leased out my farm, and persuaded my mother to sell the little jewellery she had. My wife even sold her jewellery. It all came to 3,000 rupees. I was still 3,000 rupees short. It looked like I would not be able to go, but I was really determined, so I left in the middle of the night. I did not tell anyone. I walked 17 miles to Mirpur and got a bus from there to Jhelum. From Jhelum I caught a train to Karachi, where a few men from my village worked. I took a job in Karachi because I did not want to spend the money for the England trip. I started looking for an 'agent', someone who would lend me the rest of the money, get me a Pakistani passport and help me get to England. This was not that easy as the police were cracking down on the trade in passports. After three months I found an agent. He was called Babu Mohammed Latif. He was from Mirpur and his mother was from our village. He agreed to send me on, half money up front and half later. The passport was still a problem. So Babu Mohammed helped get a passport that would specifically allow me to travel to holy places in the Middle East, but could only be used to travel to other countries if it was stamped by a Pakistani embassy. I took a ship to Iraq, eventually arriving in Baghdad. I got the Pakistani embassy there to stamp my passport allowing me to travel to *Walayat*.

I was helped by some of Babu Mohammed's contacts to catch a flight to London. On the aeroplane I wore my best suit, I had a five pound note in my pocket and a paper with addresses given to me in Karachi by Babu Mohammed. The aeroplane landed in London

Airport. At passport control there was only one woman sitting in a shed-like room. She stamped my passport without comment and I collected my little raggedy bag, and came out of the airport. I wanted to get to London, so I started showing the paper with the address on it and the five-pound note to anybody and everybody, hoping they would help me. A police officer saw me doing that so he took me to a bus stop. I got on the bus and gave the driver the full 5 pounds, he took the fare and gave me change. The bus took me to Kings Cross. The driver came out and handed me over to a porter. The porter took me to a ticket office, took my money, bought my ticket and gave me the right change. He then made me sit down on a platform. It was very cold, I was hungry, and most of all I was very scared. I wished I had stayed home. The train pulled up, and I got in. The porter came and said something, which I could not understand. The next train came. I tried getting on it, but again the porter prevented me. I thought that I had been arrested. I wanted to run, but did not get a chance. Finally the right train came. The porter took me into the train and went round until he found a person in uniform (a naval officer). They made me sit near the window. Now I was convinced that I had definitely been arrested and they were taking me to jail. Eventually, the train pulled into Bradford and the naval officer helped get a taxi and took me to Arcadia Street, where Babu's brother opened the door. I ran towards him shouting 'hide me, hide me, they have arrested me.' He laughed. I brushed both aside and ran into the house and went upstairs from where I saw the officer get in the taxi and drive away.

A few days later I was taken to a house in Dane Street in Rochdale. I was ecstatic to see so many of my countrymen of whom some were relatives. There were sixteen of us crammed into a four-bedroom house. The kitchen was in the cellar. We also washed clothes there as well as bathe. Not only us but other friends, who had no bath tubs in their house, used to come to Dane Street for baths. The house had very little furniture and no carpets. It was really hard staying warm. Whenever we went out we would bring anything that could be used as firewood to heat up the house. Most of our time was spent playing cards, talking about back home. I remember, if we heard someone had got a letter from home, we used to go and hear it, or at least ask about the weather, crops, who has died, whose child was born. Once one of us had a letter from home and it mentioned it is 1st Ramadan today. The letter took fifteen days to arrive. We did not know it was Ramadan. We started fasting. Everybody who was employed paid BC (basic consumption) kitty. The unemployed were not charged rent or BC; they were free. Instead the unemployed cooked for those who were working. So everybody paid or cooked, except Babu Sahib who did neither. He also had his own bedroom, while the rest of us had to share. This was because Babu Sahib was the only one amongst who could speak, read and write English. He would write everybody's letters, filled in forms etc. He was reaping the benefits of education. Babu Sahib was treated like a *pir*.

We used to look from the top window of the house to see which mill chimney was giving out the most smoke, because that would be the busiest mill and most likely to have vacancies. So we would head towards it in the hope of finding work. As none of us could speak English, as soon as we got close to the Mill's gates we would push each other to be in the front. So the one in the front would have to find out if there was work. Sometimes, somebody from the mill would see us coming and they would wave their arms like an umpire signals a dead ball, which meant there were no jobs.

Based on conversations with Fazal Ali and Choudhary Mohammed Hussain.

THE 'ASIAN' IN BRITAIN[1]

Avtar Brah

The presence of Asian and other black people in Britain has added a new dimension to discussions about 'culture', 'politics' and 'identity'. This chapter is an attempt to identify how, and in what ways, the various debates acquired saliency during the different phases of black settlement in Britain after the Second World War with particular emphasis on the period between the 1950s to the 1980s. It examines how the figure of 'the Asian' was constructed in different discourses, policies and practices; and how these constructions were appropriated or contested by the political agency of Asian subjects. *Inter alia*, this chapter is also concerned with mapping the general parameters of inter- and intra-generational continuity and change.

THE CONCEPTS OF CULTURE AND IDENTITY

Discussions about culture must be understood within the context of the power relations among different groups. Accordingly, analyses of South Asian culture formations in Britain must be informed by an understanding of the colonial history (cf. Dutt, 1901; Palme Dutt, 1940; Mukherjee, 1974 [1955]; Jenks, 1963; Gopal, 1963; Hutchins, 1967; Greenberger, 1969; Kiernan, 1969; Morris *et al.* 1969; Bagchi, 1973; Patnaik, 1975; Nazir, 1981; Hall, 2001), as well as the power hierarchies that currently characterise the British social formation.

Identity, as we know, is simultaneously subjective and social, and is constituted in and through culture. Indeed, culture and identity are inextricably linked concepts. The sections that follow are concerned with identifying how, and in what ways: a notion of 'Asian culture and identity' became a major subject of political and cultural debate in Britain; this debate panned out over the different phases of post-war South Asian settlement; South Asian groups appropriated or resisted the meaning of these representations; and the everyday life of Asian people articulated with these discourses. The chapter is divided into three parts, dealing with: the experience of arrival and finding one's bearings during the 1950s and early 1960s; the settlement phase of the 1960s and the early

1 This a revised and updated version of 'Constructions of the Asian' first published in Avtar Brah, *Cartographies of Diaspora*, London: Routledge, 1996.

1970s; and the period of the 1970s and the first two years of the 1980s, when young Asians born in Britain started to make their presence felt. The chapter concludes with a brief commentary on the major shifts in the debate over the last decade and a half.

COMING TO 'VILAYAT' (1950s–EARLY 1960s)

Britain experienced severe labour shortages during the post-war period of economic expansion. At the same time, having been systematically exploited during the colonial period, Britain's ex-colonies faced a future of poverty. They had a large labour force, but insufficient means to make this labour productive (Sivanandan, 1976). Migration of labour from the ex-colonies to the metropolis during the 1950s was thus largely a direct result of the history of colonialism and imperialism of the previous centuries. If once the colonies had been a source of cheap raw materials, now they became a source of cheap labour.

The South Asians who came during the 1950s were part of this broader movement of labour migrations in Europe. Almost all the jobs available to them were those that the white workers did not want. In the main these were unskilled jobs involving unsociable hours of work, poor working conditions and low wages. Hence Asian workers came to occupy some of the lowest rungs of the British employment hierarchy. Additionally, as ex-colonial subjects, they belonged to a group whose country was once ruled by Britain. From the beginning, therefore, the encounter between Asians and the white population was circumscribed by colonial precedents. As Zubaida points out:

> These cognitive structures (beliefs, stereotype and 'common-sense' knowledge) in terms of which people in Britain experience coloured [*sic*] minorities must be profoundly imbued with accumulations of colonial experience. The beliefs and stereotypes acquired and disseminated by generations of working-class soldiers and middle-class administrators in the colonies are available to our contemporaries. Many of these cognitions are derogatory, some are patronising, a few are favourable, but there is one theme underlying all of them: the inferiority and servility of 'native' populations. In this respect, immigrant communities from the ex-colonies are not entirely new to the British people. At times when the economic and political conditions are conducive to increased tensions between the communities, the more negative elements of these cognitions are aroused and modified. (Zubaida, 1970: 4)

Partly by virtue of the location of their jobs and partly because they needed cheap housing, the 'immigrants' tended to settle in the rundown parts of working-class areas. Housing shortages, inadequate social services, high levels of unemployment and poor educational facilities were common features of these areas long before the arrival of the 'immigrants'. However, in the minds of the local residents these problems gradually became associated with the presence of 'immigrants'. The 'immigrant', rather than the social institutions and social policies responsible for the problems of what later came to be described as 'inner-city' areas, became the object of their resentment. This resentment was reflected in the negative constructions of the 'immigrant'. As was the case during the British Raj, it was Asian cultural practices which first came under attack. According to the stereotype, the Asian was an undesirable who 'smelled of curry', was 'dirty', wore 'funny clothes', lived 'packed like sardines in a room', practised 'strange religions', and so forth (Brah, 1979).

As the number of Asian and other black children in schools increased, many white parents began to demand that the local schools restrict their intake. In response, a number of local authorities began to introduce quotas for the proportion of black pupils permitted to enrol in a particular school. The excess numbers were 'bussed' to schools outside these areas. For example, in October 1963 white parents in Southall lobbied Sir Edward Boyle, then Minister of Education, during his visit to a local school. Following this meeting, and within the same year, the Southall Education Committee adopted a policy of dispersal, although it did not become the policy of the Department of Education and Science until June 1965 (Ealing International Friendship Council, 1968; Department of Education and Science, 1965).

At the same time the Government came under pressure to restrict black immigration. In Parliament Cyril Osborne, Conservative MP for Louth, initiated the campaign as early as 1952. In the period 1952–7 his campaign was conducted largely in the House of Commons and the press and, although for a variety of reasons it met with little success, there are indications that 'many members of the cabinet shared popular concern about coloured immigration and were not in principle opposed to the introduction of controls' (Layton-Henry, 1980: 54; see also Moore, 1975; Sivanandan, 1976). Black resistance against racial harassment in Nottingham and Notting Hill in 1958 served to bring the issue of 'race' to the forefront. Simultaneously pressure began to mount from the local authorities to restrict black immigration. After 1955 Cyril Osborne was joined in his campaign by fellow parliament members Norman Pannel (Kirkdale) and Martin Lindsey (Solihull): the campaign attracted white support at the grassroots level, and local disaffection and resentment was further fed through active anti-black campaigning by the fascist fringe (Moore, 1975). The Government capitulated by introducing the Commonwealth Immigration Act of 1962. Thus, even during this phase of economic expansion, Asians and other blacks felt less than welcome in their new country of residence.

The liberal opinion of the time (and this included sections of academic, professional and political opinion) also saw the question of 'race relations' primarily in terms of cultural differences. It was likely to subscribe, either implicitly or explicitly, to the general preoccupation of the period with notions such as the 'assimilation of coloured minorities'. The problem tended to be couched primarily in terms of 'helping the immigrant to adjust to the host society', despite the fact that sections of the 'host society' were acting in rather an un-host-like fashion towards the new arrivals. To those who subscribed to the assimilation model, the Asian represented the epitome of the outsider, 'the alien' whose culture constituted an antithesis of the 'British way of life'. The assimilationist was likely to predict that future generations of Asians would abandon what the assimilationist deemed to be their 'archaic cultures' in favour of a 'Western lifestyle'.

During the early phase of migration there was an under-representation of women among the Asian population, as the majority of Asian men had come initially without female relatives. They came primarily with the idea of accumulating sufficient savings and then returning home. They were prepared to work long, arduous shifts in order to make up for very low basic wages. Many lived in all-male households. Their busy working schedules left little time for any meaningful participation in the social or political life of the locality in which they lived. In view of the antipathy shown towards them by many of the white residents, it is doubtful if such participation would in any case have been feasible.

A majority of the migrants at this stage had rural origins, and belonged mainly to the peasant proprietor class. Their new role as industrial workers demanded many adjustments and adaptations. For instance, their working schedules were now governed by the clock, which marked the beginning and the end of a particular shift, rather than by the seasons. Overnight a villager from the subcontinent arriving at Heathrow would be faced with the requirements of an urban, industrial society. The innumerable adjustments which this migrant had to make in day-to-day life often went unnoticed by the media or the white population, who were likely to characterise such a person as 'culturally encapsulated'—as if 'culture' was something entirely separate from lived experience. In general the migrants faced up to their new circumstances with stoicism and a pragmatic attitude. Sikh men, for instance, found that it was easier to find jobs if they took their turbans off, and many did so. Since there was no formal banning of the turban, the Sikhs did not as yet perceive this covert discrimination as an attack on their religious practices. When the direct challenge came in 1959, and a Sikh was banned from wearing a turban at work, the issue became a political one and the Sikhs launched several campaigns in order to retain the right to wear turbans at their places of work (Beetham, 1970).

In these early stages, questions of cultural identity as a political issue did not loom large in the minds of the Asians. The early migrants were quite secure in their sense of themselves, rooted as it was in the social milieu from which they originated. Social norms derived from this milieu were the main reference point. But as their children began to attend local schools, the parents became attuned to the possible influence of '*gore lok*' (whites) on their children.

In the main, Asian parents were initially quite favourably disposed towards Western education. During colonialism acquisition of a Western education had represented an important means of social mobility. In the contemporary world Western countries continue to play a dominant role in the international social and economic order. Consequently, Western education remains a coveted possession in the 'Third World'. It is not surprising, therefore, that the early Asian immigrants, including those with middle-class backgrounds, held the British education system in great esteem. Educational qualifications acquired in Britain, they assumed, would enable their offspring to get better jobs than those which they had themselves. At this stage most parents were unfamiliar with the history of the educational disadvantage suffered by the white working classes in the localities where they themselves had now come to settle. The correlation between class and educational inequality was not fully established in their minds. Their disquiet was centred primarily on issues such as the strongly Christian ethos of school assemblies. Some parents were disconcerted by the requirements of the compulsory school uniform which stipulated that girls must wear skirts. Such parents were likely to regard the wearing of skirts as not in keeping with the norms of 'modesty', but, as yet, they rarely translated this discontent into public protest. Nevertheless, a collective concern about the potential undermining of Asian lifestyles under the influence of the British educational system was by now beginning to take shape.

By the early 1960s the anti-immigration campaigns, 'bussing' of Asian children to schools outside the areas in which they lived, discrimination in housing and employment and the experience of being subjected to racial abuse came to constitute significant facets of the day-to day social experience of Asians in Britain. Issues of cultural identity now began to assume importance, and strategies designed to foster positive cultural identities amongst the young came to be seriously considered.

A HOME AWAY FROM HOME (1960s–EARLY 1970s)

When the 'assimilation' model was shown to be generally unacceptable to large sections of the black communities, while at the same time evidence of racial discrimination against them kept mounting (see, for instance, Daniel, 1968), liberal rhetoric adopted a new terminology. In a frequently quoted speech delivered in 1966 Roy Jenkins, the then Home Secretary, argued against the notion of 'assimilation' but in favour of 'integration'. He said that the latter would be viewed, not as a 'flattening process of assimilation but as equal opportunity, accompanied by cultural diversity, in an atmosphere of mutual trust' (Jenkins, 1966: 4).

On the face of it this statement seems reasonable and fair, but its underlying assumptions warrant examination. First, this view of integration seems to imply that equality of opportunity for the different segments of British society was already in existence at the time when the migrants first began to arrive, and hence the difficulties facing the newcomers could be overcome quite straightforwardly by the introduction of a social policy that would place the migrant on the same footing as the native. Yet, as is well-known, material wealth, power and privilege are differentially distributed among different sections of British society. Second, to speak of 'cultural diversity' in an 'atmosphere of mutual trust', without reference to the socio-economic and political factors which sustain social inequality and give rise to intolerance, is to explain away racism merely in terms of human failing. It is perhaps not surprising, therefore, that while this definition of integration came to be accepted as conventional wisdom by many bodies, welfare agencies and individuals active in the 'race relations' field, racism has continued to grow.

The liberal sentiment paved the way for the emergence of the so-called 'race relations industry' which included the Community Relations Commission (later reconstituted to form the Commission for Racial Equality), the Race Relations Board, locally-based community relations councils, the Institute of Race Relations (which underwent radical change in its structure and political orientation in 1972), the Runnymede Trust, the Research Unit on Ethnic Relations sponsored by the Social Science Research Council and community relations sections of churches and other organisations. The work of these organisations, which contributed to the effort that led to the enactment of anti-discrimination legislation, should be set against the simultaneous entrenchment of racism in stricter immigration controls. The race relations legislation of the 1960s proved to be so ineffective that it had to be replaced by the 1976 Race Relations Act. The 1968 Immigration Act, on the other hand, was far more successful in meeting its primary objective of reducing black immigration. It removed the right of entry of British passport holders unless they had a 'substantial connection' with Britain—i.e. unless at least one parent or grandparent of the applicant was born in Britain. In other words, the overwhelming majority of black people—who, it might be argued, have had quite a substantial connection with Britain through the Empire—were now excluded because they could not claim to have grandparents who were born there. The 1971 Immigration Act was even more restrictive. A non-patrial Commonwealth citizen could no longer enter Britain (other than as a temporary visitor) unless she or he had a work permit for a specific job with a specific employer. Initially the person would be admitted for a year and permission might be renewed at the discretion of the Home Secretary. Dependants would be admitted for the duration of the work permit only. The Act also extended the power of deportation (Moore, 1975).

Extensive anti-immigration lobbying preceded the Immigration Acts. A highly distorted but pervasive mythology about the presence of black people in this country came into currency: blacks were here to sponge off the state; were running down inner-city areas; were receiving priority in housing and other services; their presence was making Britain overcrowded and, unless controlled, their numbers would increase beyond an acceptable proportion (which was never defined); their children were holding British pupils back in their studies and so on.

Each one of the above claims has, of course, been contradicted by evidence gathered by some of the most respected data-collecting bodies, but their collective influence has proved difficult to dislodge from the popular imagination. The media's treatment of 'race' issues remained at worst biased and at best ambivalent (cf. Hartman and Husband, 1974; Husband, 1975). Asian cultural specificities were often represented as wanting against certain unspecified Western standards which, implicitly if not always explicitly, were held up as being superior. Politicians such as Enoch Powell, being fully aware of the potency of cultural symbolism, made speeches which consistently used metaphors that evoked images of the Asians as the archetypal 'alien'. The practice of 'Paki bashing' (an epithet naming the violence perpetrated against South Asians in this period) reached its peak during the late 1960s. The education system and the welfare system were likely to characterise almost any difficulty facing Asians as the result of 'cultural problems'. In other words, during the 1960s the focus shifted away from 'the problems facing the immigrant' and instead Asians and other black people came to be seen as themselves constituting a 'problem'.

It is against this background that the initial intent to 'return' began to recede as a priority and the Asians started to make emotional and financial investments in a long-term stay in Britain. The 1950s for them had been a period of finding their bearings in a new country. The 1960s was the decade during which a large number of families were reunited. Asian businesses sprang up to meet their special needs in terms of food products, clothing, entertainment etc. Lifecycle rituals and religious festivals could now be celebrated with greater pomp and ceremony. Older patterns of family life were modified to adjust to the exigencies of the new situation. Neo-local residence, for instance, became fairly typical, partly because not all members of the extended family lived in Britain, but equally because the houses were often too small to accommodate any but the immediate family: similarly, women, who might hitherto have been unfamiliar with wage-labour, now started to take up employment on a substantial scale. This became a necessity due, in large part, to the increasing expense of buying and furnishing houses, meeting the continually rising cost of living and maintaining the essential obligations towards the extended family. In time these changes were to initiate important restructuring of the sphere of gender relations.

The 1960s witnessed the first industrial disputes involving a predominantly Asian workforce. When they first arrived the Asian migrants tended to be unfamiliar with their basic labour rights. They worked under extremely unfavourable conditions, but for the most part were unaware that they might try to improve these through the trade union system. As knowledge about the system grew, trade union branches were formed in a number of factories which relied almost entirely on immigrant labour. In 1963, for instance, the Indian Workers Association helped launch a campaign to unionise Asian workers at Woolfe's rubber factory in Southall. An overwhelming majority of the membership of the Indian Workers Association at this stage consisted of manual workers employed in nearby factories. According to Marsh (1967), village-kin and friendship networks were made full use of in an effort to convince Asian workers of the need to join the unions. Meetings would be held in people's homes and Asian holy books would sometimes be brought in to solemnise and underscore the commitment to workers' unity on the shop floor. It is interesting to note the ways in which these cultural resources were mobilised in order to address their new circumstances as industrial workers. Unity as an ethnic group and ties of communal loyalty were as important in this context as the bonds of labour.

Having become organised, these workers went on strike, first in 1964 and again in 1965. These earliest strikes highlighted not only the nature of the conflict between white management and black workers, but also the ambivalent attitude of the unions towards black membership. The complexity of the intersections between 'race' and class was amply demonstrated by these events, as it was in the disputes which later followed in other parts of the country (see, for instance, Marsh, 1967 and Moore, 1975). Asians were now beginning to react against their subordinate position as workers from the ex-colonies. Their activism drew on the political cultures of both their country of origin and Britain. A number of community activists of this period, many of whom were university graduates, were later to leave their factory jobs and set up in businesses or take up employment in some aspect of the expanding 'race relations industry'.

As we have already seen, by now the notion of 'cultural diversity' had caught the imagination of the liberal segments of British opinion. Community Relations Councils were formed in areas of high 'immigrant' concentrations in order to 'promote friendship and harmony' between blacks and whites. Middle-class whites predominantly ran these organisations: among other activities, they organised 'cultural evenings' to which everyone in the community would be invited. But the type of Asian who could socialise with ease in these situations was typically one who could speak English. A number of these English-speaking Asians would be co-opted as members of the executive committees of these councils. Many of them later became spokespersons for their respective communities and were often referred to as the 'leaders' of these communities.

In contrast, contact between the Asians in manual occupations and the white population was generally limited to the workplace. In so far as Asians were likely to be employed in unskilled jobs which white workers did not now need or wish to do, they would occupy a very low position in the occupational hierarchy. As ex-colonial subjects, Asian workers would be regarded as inferior even by unskilled white workers. There were few opportunities for these groups to engage in meaningful cultural exchange, although workplace cultures did provide an arena where friendly or antagonistic relations could be played out. Many Asians did not speak English, but racism was often a bigger barrier than language. This is not to deny, however, that individual Asians and whites might form strong and binding attachments. Indeed, in an earlier piece of work I gave examples of such individuals and households who seemed able to communicate happily, either through non-verbal signs, forms of creolised English or through children (Brah, 1979).

Asians, on their part, did not necessarily use Western criteria to measure their own status. They might be industrial workers in this country but many came from comparatively well-off, land-owning peasant families. The social hierarchies according to which they were most likely to rank themselves were the ones internal to Asian cultural formations, although, of course, the processes leading to the restructuring of these hierarchies were already under way. The prohibition against certain castes eating together, for example, could not be maintained in British workplace canteens. This is not to suggest that caste became irrelevant in Britain. Indeed, as communal life became more established, caste associations proliferated with the effect that caste became re-inscribed in the British context. But the point is that caste in Britain is not an exact replica of caste in India; rather, British-based configurations of caste have their own specific features. In any case, even in India caste is a highly differentiated heterogeneous, variable and contested institution.

The emergence of the 'East African Asian'

The mid 1960s witnessed the augmentation of South Asian populations in Britain by new arrivals from East Africa. Although South Asian traders and administrators were to be found in East Africa long before the advent of the British in that region, South Asian migrations to the area in significantly large numbers resulted largely from the policies of the colonial government in pre-partition India (Ghai and Ghai, 1970). As part of this policy Indians were recruited during the late nineteenth century as 'indentured labour' in order to build the East African railways. The practice of indenturing labour (a system of contract labour which constituted a form of semi-slavery), predominantly using Indian and Chinese workers, was adopted in much of the British Empire, and carried on for a number of years after its formal abolition in 1916 (Tinker, 1977). In East Africa illegal indenture persisted until 1922. When it ended most Indians returned to India, but some of the labourers stayed on after their contracts expired and took to petty trades because the colonial government would not permit them to buy land. Subsequently, as new opportunities began to open up, 'voluntary' migration from India was set in train. The primary thrust of the colonial policy was to restrict the activities of the Africans to the agricultural economy and those of the Indians to petty trade and commerce, at the same time maintaining both groups subordinate to the white settlers with large plantations or dairy farms and to the metropolis bourgeoisie. The substance of this policy is encapsulated in the following comment from Captain Lugard:

> Being unaffected by the climate, much cheaper than Europeans, and in closer touch with the daily lives of the natives than it is possible for a white man [*sic*] to be, they [the Asians] would form an admirable connecting link (under the close supervision of British officers), their status being nearly on par with the natives, while their interests are entirely dependent on the Europeans. As they would establish themselves permanently, with their families, in the country, they would have a personal interest in it. (Quoted in Mamdani, 1976: 71)

This policy was crucial to the processes of class formation in East Africa. With their activities confined largely to retail trade and middle-level clerical and administrative posts in the civil service, South Asians came to constitute the middle layer of the 'colonial sandwich', occupying a position below the white colonist but above black Africans. The South Asian commercial bourgeoisie consisted of a mere handful of families and it remained subordinate to metropolitan capital. A substantial number of South Asians were employed in enterprises owned by other South Asians, with whom their relationship was mediated through caste and kinship ties. Since the South Asians (and, up till Independence, also the Africans) were excluded from structures of governance, they had no political base in the colonial state and little political clout to deploy in situations of crisis. Political power remained in the hands of the British until its transfer at Independence to the Africans.

To be the middle layer in the colonial sandwich meant that a substantial number of Asian households led a lifestyle that was comparatively more affluent than that of the overwhelming majority of Africans, and substantially less affluent that that of the Europeans. This is not to suggest, however, that the 'middle layer' was a uniform configuration. Indeed, there was considerable differentiation of income and wealth amongst South Asian groups and, given the absence of socialised welfare, it was not uncommon for many Asian households to be living in conditions of considerable hardship and poverty. That is, a significant proportion of the Asians were quite poor and small sections were wealthy. But since even the richest families had been wealthy for only one or two generations, social distinctions arising from sharply distinctive lifestyles and institutionalised forms of social distance had not yet congealed in rigid forms. Religious, linguistic, regional and caste differences, although retaining their importance in matters of marriage, did not form barriers to social mixing. For example, at the time of the Hindu festival Diwali Sikhs and Muslims alike would take part in the non-religious aspects of the celebrations, such as the firework displays. Similarly the sports tournaments organised by the mosques or the *gurdwaras*, as part of the events to celebrate Eid and the Gurpurbs respectively, would include participants from the various Asian communities.

Despite the partition of India in 1947, which resulted in the creation of Pakistan, most Asians continued to refer to themselves as 'Indian', save perhaps in times of severe political conflict as when India and Pakistan were engaged in war during 1965. A collective identity was maintained vis-à-vis the European on the one hand and the African on the other. A number of communal differences and divisions amongst Asians were normally (though not entirely) submerged in this shared identity and, over a period of time, the lifestyles and attitudes of the diverse Asian groups settled in Africa developed common features. Of course there was a sense in which 'cultural difference' continued to be constructed in terms of the regional differentiations prevailing in South Asia: Punjabi, Gujarati and so on, but East African-based axes of differentiation would cut across such 'difference'. In sports, for example, several identities would simultaneously come into play: one was a Kenyan-Punjabi hockey player, or a Ugandan-Gujarati cricket player and so on. Religion was constructed less as a signifier of 'culture' than one of 'belief'. The construction of this distinction marked an inter-subjective space for non-antagonistic identification among different South Asian groups.

Vocabulary drawn from Swahili became an integral component of the South Asian languages spoken in East Africa. Popular culture was another major site for cultural syncretism. Radio, cinema and (from the 1960s onwards) television exercised immense influence in this respect. Many Asian teenagers in Africa idolised Western pop-singers as much as the playback singers or the film stars of Indian movies. The East African musical form 'Hi Life' was another interconnecting strand of cultural fusions. This cultural creolisation was crucial to the constitution of East African Asian identity. However, it was not without its contradictions, for such creolisation was also one of the crucial sites for the mediation of the social hierarchy vis-à-vis Africans and Europeans.

The state institutions, together with the education system, were also critical as primary vehicles of 'Western' influence. It is worth noting that the education system remained segregated until independence from colonial rule. The medium of instruction was mainly English, and both the 'O' and 'A' level examination papers were set and marked in Britain. There was very little about Africa itself in these curricula, although Africa stalked every nook and cranny of the mind. The power and authority of 'the European' seemed distant and aloof to both Asians and Africans. As Captain Lugard had hoped, colonialism did succeed in carving a context in which, 'much cheaper than the Europeans, and in closer touch with the daily lives of the natives', the Asians did indeed 'form an admirable connecting link' (Mamdani, 1976). This closer contact meant that the social relationship between Asians and Africans was simultaneously more intimate and passionate in its affect and affection as much as in its antagonistic ramifications. It was not surprising, therefore, that when post-Independence East Africa witnessed intense struggles and shifts in alliances between different segments of the local populations, these conflicts emerged in the idiom of either 'tribalism'—i.e. conflict between different African ethnic groups—or antagonism against the 'wamayindi' (Asians). However, the political management of these conflicts differed in Kenya, Tanganyika and Uganda.

East African Asians in Britain differ from those from the South Asian subcontinent in several respects. First, they are mainly, though not exclusively, of urban background. Second, in contrast to the subcontinental migrants amongst whom the Punjabis constituted the largest single linguistic group, the East Africans were predominantly Gujaratis. Third, as a group, they had comprised the largest component of the emerging middle classes of East Africa. However, while they might be described as being middle class, they were culturally marked different from the longer-established middle classes of the South Asian subcontinent. In the main, Asians from East Africa are the descendants of immigrants to East Africa who had rural backgrounds, and most of them continued to maintain relatively close links with their kin in the subcontinent. Thus Asian cultures constituted in East Africa were characterised by traces of this rural influence, evident especially in lifecycle rituals, in regional dialects and in cuisine. But, above all, these new cultures were *East African Asian*, constituted in the capillaries and sinews of the economic and social-life world of Asians in East Africa.

When Kenya, Uganda and Tanganyika achieved independence in the early 1960s South Asians living there were offered the choice of British citizenship, which evidently included the right to enter and settle in Britain. When this news reached Britain a strong anti-immigration lobby grew around the issues of the right of entry for South Asians from East Africa, resulting in the introduction of the Immigration Act of 1968. So effective was the anti-immigration lobby that the Bill passed through the House of Commons and the House of Lords and received Royal Assent in *two days*. The 1968 Act institutionalised racial discrimination in law by removing the right of entry of British passport holders to Britain unless they had at least one parent or grandparent born here. At a stroke thousands of Asians in East Africa became stateless, and families were torn apart. In 1972 Idi Amin, the then President of Uganda, expelled all Asians from Uganda irrespective of whether or not they were Ugandan citizens. The Amin edict resulted in a new dispersal of South Asians to various parts of the globe, but most notably to Britain, Canada and South Asia.

Apart from the tragedy of being uprooted, Ugandan Asians were faced with racism as soon as they set foot in Britain. According to government policy they were to avoid settling in areas of 'high' Asian concentration. In order to disperse them, Britain was divided into 'red' and 'green' zones. The 'red' zones were those where the size of Asian populations was deemed to be already 'too high' and hence they were designated as out of bounds for Ugandan Asian refugees. The 'green' zones, on the other hand, were defined as places where the Asian population was non-existent or so low that a slight rise in their numbers would be 'tolerated'. Thus many Asian families found themselves flung to remote parts of Britain, without communal channels of support. In Uganda they were used to a life of daily contact with relatives, neighbours and friends—visiting them in the home; chatting on the streets; congregating in parks and public spaces and in temples, mosques and churches. A large part of daily activity was conducted outdoors. The comparatively regimented life of an advanced capitalist society, with its individualistic ethos of privacy, together with the cold and grey of the proverbial British weather, did not make for a welcoming scenario. At first the refugee response was to withdraw into themselves. The early experience of isolation led to depression and despondency, particularly amongst the older members of households: but the spirit was not broken, and communal networks were soon revived through letters, telephone calls and visits to fellow Ugandans living in other parts of Britain. Once these links were established, the refugees deployed their own initiative and, in defiance of government policy, moved to 'red' zones, which offered greater security and a sense of familiarity and belonging.

The expulsion from Uganda did not make a major impact on the material circumstances of the very rich Ugandan refugees. There is no doubt they had suffered massive losses in their business activities, but their investments were not confined to Uganda, so the likes of the Madhvanis and the Mehtas simply moved their operations elsewhere. Similarly, the more prosperous sections of the petty bourgeoisie also had some savings transferred abroad. They too were able to establish themselves relatively quickly. But the majority of the refugees—the small shopkeepers with all their capital tied up in Uganda, the salaried professionals and the workers—had lost everything and had to start from scratch. Every member of the family of working age had to find employment. Although some women had helped run family enterprises in Uganda, and others had held professionals jobs in fields such as medicine and teaching, the great majority were unused to paid work outside the home. But now most women who could find a job took one. Living in rented accommodation, and paying high rents for property of poor quality, the refugees gave high priority to buying their own houses. People worked long hours and saved every penny in order to obtain a mortgage on a house.

With the exception of Asians from Uganda who came to Britain as refugees, a majority of the Asians from Africa were able to transfer their savings and other movable assets to Britain when they left Africa. Those who possessed the necessary entrepreneurial skills and capital set up in business; others sought employment in the professional fields; but a great majority became employed in the factories as semi-skilled or unskilled workers. For this sector of the Asians from Africa, migration involved considerable downward social mobility. Like other labour migrants, they found themselves engaged in low-status, poorly paid jobs. Racial discrimination on the shop floor was fairly common, taking the form of limited opportunities for in-service training and promotion, different rates for the same job, the nature of the tasks allocated to them in the production process and verbal racial abuse. Coming as they did from a comparatively privileged position in Africa, the processes of proletarianisation brought the status contradictions between their previous and current social positions into sharp relief. Their discontent was marked by some of the best-known industrial disputes involving Asians, such as Mansfield Hosiery, Imperial Typewriters and Grunwicks. Kinship and other communal networks were mobilised in order to provide both moral and financial help. Financial assistance became critical because, in some cases, the local unions refused to make the strikes official and thereby deprived the workers of strike pay.

By the early 1970s Asians from the subcontinent too had come to accept that their stay in this country was unlikely to be temporary. Once a family had been reunited, and financial investment made in a house or a business, the 'myth of return' would become largely accepted as such, and attention was directed much more towards life in Britain. The thrift and economy of the earlier years tended to be replaced by the same consumerism that was prevalent in Britain at large.

Asian parents were becoming increasingly aware that the ethnocentric nature of the educational curriculum and racialised practices in schools and other educational institutions could seriously undermine their children's intellectual aspirations and sense of belonging. The issue of cultural identity now became crucial. Many parents began to make a conscious effort, albeit an unsystematic one, to teach their children about their background and history. Temples, mosques and *gurdwaras* began to offer classes in religious instruction and mother-tongue teaching. The notion of self-help, which gained currency in the 1970s, was born of the efforts made by the black communities across the country to provide the type of information, advice, support and education to the members of their communities which the official agencies were either unable or unwilling to provide. These initiatives ranged across the social, medical, educational and welfare fields. With the continuing erosion of even the veneer of liberalism which had previously accompanied public discussion of 'race relations', Asians were compelled to acknowledge that in order to safeguard their interests they would need to organise against forces which could potentially undermine their group identity. If they were being construed and treated as a 'problem', it was incumbent upon them to challenge this conception. The form in which the new mood was articulated varied according to whether you were a 'community leader' accompanying a deputation to the Home Office, an unskilled worker in a factory or a young person who had just left school. But in all cases there was an emerging rejection and defiance of the processes of subordination. The onset of the 1970s thus heralded a new stage in Asian reaction and response to life in Britain.

HERE TO STAY (MID 1970s–EARLY 1980s)

During the 1970s Britain witnessed a deepening of the economic recession on the one hand and racial conflict on the other. As we have already seen, racial antipathy was not absent even during the period of the economic boom, but the recession helped to create a fertile ground for the rejuvenation of fascist organisations which openly admit to having racist policies. These groups capitalise on the frustrated energies and hopes of the white working class, especially those of the youth. In their recruitment campaigns they consistently made scapegoats of the 'immigrants' or the 'Jews' for the state of the economic crisis. In the style of Enoch Powell and others of his persuasion, these right-wing organisations raised the spectre of the supposed threat to the British way of life posed by 'immigrants with alien cultures' (Nugent and King, 1979; Taylor, 1979; Troyna, 1982).

The 'anti-immigration' and 'alien culture' theme found reverberations in a pre-election speech of Margaret Thatcher. During a television interview in January 1978 she pledged that, if elected, her party would 'finally see an end to immigration'. She plumbed the depths of fear of a defensive identity when she suggested that the British way of life needed special protection, for 'this country might be swamped by people with a different culture'. It is worth noting that these comments were made at a time when, due to the enforcement of the 1971 Immigration Act, primary immigration had virtually ceased. The argument therefore was not about numbers. The speech was calculated to act as a vote-catching device. It is a commentary on the centrality of 'race' in British politics that such a subject should prove an effective means of soliciting votes. It is a device regularly deployed by politicians. When the 'mainstream' politicians resort to using language which has the ring of that of the extreme right-wing groups, the rhetoric and the political position of the latter acquires increasing credibility and respectability.

When elected, the Government kept its promise to do everything in its power to reduce immigration further. However, the only immigrants who could enter after the enforcement of the 1971 Act (apart from the small proportion who still qualified for a visa on the grounds that their skills were in very short supply), were the dependants or fiancés of those already settled here, and special categories of British passport holders such as those in Hong Kong. The state dealt with the case of the latter by excluding their entry through the 1981 British Nationality Act, and changes were introduced in the immigration rules which were designed to end the arrival of the apparently small number of people who entered as fiancés. The new Immigration Rules came into effect in 1980 and were mainly directed at South Asians. Their imposition was justified on the grounds that the 'arranged marriage system' supposedly constituted a 'never-ending flow of primary immigration'. The allegation, never substantiated, was that there was a widespread abuse of this cultural practice by Asians. This piece of legislation openly discriminates against groups who subscribe to 'arranged marriage'; in particular it targets young Asian women. It has come under attack from various sources as being both sexist and racist. For instance, David Steele, the leader of the Liberal Party, told Parliament:

> I can understand the air of embarrassment that always surrounds the Minister of State and the Home Secretary when we debate this subject. The reason for that embarrassment is that, while the Minister of State may say that the rules are not racialist in intent, they are certainly racialist in effect. Moreover, some Conservative Back Benchers intend them to be racialist in intent as well.... May we be told how many people will be prevented from coming into this country as a result of these miserable regulations? ... The best estimates that I have been able to get have been between 2,000 and 3,000. We are going through all this paraphernalia of introducing rules which I believe are thoroughly repugnant, and of causing an uncertain degree of suffering to families of those already settled here in respect of their elderly people, their fiancés, their husbands and their children. (Hansard, House of Commons, 1979–80, vol. 980, columns 1032–4)

It is worth noting the way in which the proponents of the rules selected a cultural issue, namely arranged marriage, and exploited it to their own advantage, with the result that Asian women resident in Britain came to be denied the right to settle in Britain with a partner from abroad. The example illustrates how a cultural practice may become racialised and serve as a means of social control. It is also important to note that this legislation is only concerned with heterosexual relationships; the immigration law does not recognise gay and lesbian relations, thereby exercising *de facto* discrimination.

How did Asians experience the decade of the 1970s and the dawn of the 1980s? They witnessed a further entrenchment of institutionalised racism, particularly in the form of immigration laws and the British Nationality Act. Reports of harassment at the hands of the immigration service were widespread. There were cases of Asian women arriving in Britain being subjected to 'virginity tests', and of Asian children undergoing x-ray examinations in order to establish their age. Asian marriages involving a fiancé from the subcontinent were likely to be subjected to acutely embarrassing forms of surveillance for the first year. The police and the immigration service in search of alleged illegal entrants and over-stayers raided a number of factories and other workplaces with an Asian workforce. Despite widespread criticism of these raids, which led to a review of these procedures by the Home Secretary in 1980, the practice continues. People suspected of immigration offences were required to prove their innocence, reversing the normal principles which underlie other criminal investigations. In addition, magistrates were empowered to issue 'open' warrants to the police without the names of specific individuals on them (State Research, 1981).

A number of well-publicised deportation cases (e.g. that of Nasira Begum, who served a deportation order when she divorced her husband who held British citizenship) and other types of immigration cases (e.g. that of Anwar Ditta, a British-born Asian woman who was refused permission to bring her children from Pakistan to live with her in Britain until a massive campaign was mounted and a current affairs television programme, using the technique of 'DNA fingerprinting', demonstrated that the children were indeed hers and her spouse's, and not some distant kin that they were trying to pass off as their own for the purpose of 'illegal' entry into Britain) have further highlighted the many and different ways in which the immigration laws operate against Asians settled in Britain.

Discrimination in employment continued. As the recession deepened, Asians' jobs were among the most vulnerable, and the unemployment rates in areas of high Asian concentration rose quite dramatically. Racist attacks remained on the increase, and this period witnessed the murder on the streets of several Asians, including Gurdip Singh Chaggar and

Altab Ali. According to a report in the *New Statesman* (24 July 1981), a Home Office minister announced in Parliament that during 1980 in the Metropolitan Police District alone there had been 2,426 violent attacks on Asians compared with 2,075 in 1979 and 1,865 in 1977.

It was pointed out earlier that during the early phase of settlement both middle-class and working-class Asian parents showed considerable enthusiasm for the British education system and wanted their children to succeed at school. Educational opinion at that time tended to favour the notion that bilingualism hindered the progress of Asian children, and that one of the primary educational priorities must be to 'integrate' children. Some Asian parents were influenced by this view and tried to use English with their children. Middle-class parents who, in any case, were the group that was best able to speak English adopted this practice most eagerly. By using English at home these parents wished also to differentiate themselves from their counterparts from the villages. However, the political scene of the late 1960s and the 1970s soon brought home to these parents that, even if their children were fluent in English and held good educational qualifications, their life-chances in Britain would, most likely, still be shaped by their position as children of black colonial immigrants. Asian communities, together with other black communities, had to confront the possible effects of racism in education on attainment levels, self-image and the identity of black children. There were two main responses to this situation. First, politically active parents, community activists and some of the 'leaders' formed part of the lobby which was seeking to effect changes in educational and other social policies. Second, the communities undertook to promote initiatives of their own, such as the provision of supplementary education involving the teaching of Asian languages and religious instruction, and the setting up of welfare centres offering advice on a wide variety of topics. This type of provision owes its existence to the combined efforts of religious, political and other community organisations as well as to the hard work of committed individuals. Of course, to the extent that a part of this provision is organised on a religious and communal basis, it tends to perpetuate certain types of cleavage among Asian groups. Nonetheless, this self-help has been a cornerstone of Asian people's sense of self-determination and independence.

'Second-generation' or BrAsian?

The 1970s also witnessed the emergence of the first generation of young Asians with a formal education acquired mainly, if not entirely, in British schools. The media, professional and political opinion and popular imagination all tend to construct Asian youth predominantly as the object of 'culture clash'. It is argued that a young Asian growing up in Britain is exposed to *two cultures*, one at home and the other at school, and as a result, the young person experiences stress and identity conflicts. This argument is problematic on several counts. First, to posit a notion of two cultures is to suggest that there is only one 'British' and one 'Asian' culture. Yet, as we have already noted, there are some significant differences in the upper-, middle- and working-class cultures of Britain, with each further differentiated according to region and gender. Similarly, 'Asian cultures' are differentiated according to class, caste, region, religion and gender. Therefore, theoretically at least, there would seem to be as many possibilities of intra-ethnic as of inter-ethnic 'clashes of culture'. To think in terms of a simple bipolar cleavage, then, is quite untenable.

Second, the emphasis on 'culture clash' disavows the possibility of cultural interaction and fusion. There is no *a priori* reason to suppose that cultural encounters will invariably entail conflict. Conflict may or may not ensue and, instead, cultural symbiosis, improvisation and innovation may emerge as a far more probable scenario. Indeed, even conflict cannot be seen as an absence of these dynamic processes of cultural synthesis and transformation. Moreover conflict is often a sign of the power relations underpinning cultural hierarchies rather than of 'cultural clash' *per se*.

Third, there seems to be an implicit assumption in much of this debate that cultural transmigration is one-way traffic. Hence, the centuries of cultural contact and mutual influence between 'Asian' and 'British' cultural forms during the pre-colonial and colonial period, as well as since political independence, is rarely acknowledged. Indeed, India's earlier cultural and commercial links with 'Europe' extend back to the Greek and Roman times when the Western hemisphere was not yet known as 'Europe' and Greece and Rome freely acknowledged their indebtedness to the East and to Africa (Hiro, 1971). Hence, indirectly Britain has carried the imprint of Asia, Africa, and the Middle East for at least two millennia. In comparison, British colonial rule over India lasted just over a century and a half, until 1947. The point is that inter-cultural travel across the globe is an ancient phenomenon, and Britain is constituted out of these multifarious influences. The more recent, post-war, cultural interactions and reconfigurations within Britain have their own historically specific features, but the influence remains irreducibly multidirectional.

Fourth, the caricature invoked by terms such as 'between two cultures', 'culture clash', and 'identity conflict', which portrays young Asians as disoriented, confused and atomised individuals, is not supported by the evidence. There are many and varied influences that impact differently upon different young Asians, which makes for very heterogeneous and variable outcomes. This is not to deny that *some* young Asians do indeed experience conflicts, and that *some* aspects of this dissonance could well be associated with specific cultural practices. The problem arises when this explanation becomes a central paradigm for addressing young Asian people's experiences. Moreover while emotional and psychic distress warrants sympathetic attention, the supposed 'cultural conflict' cannot be assumed to be the sole underlying contributory factor. The question of 'identity conflict' is a very complex one which cannot be reduced to any single determinant. Racism, gender, class, the specific trajectory of an individual biography, for instance, are no less relevant to understanding processes of identity formation. In any case there is no single 'identity' that each and every young Asian avows (Brah, 1978, 1979).

Another variation on the theme of 'cultural clash' comes into play when uncertainties of lifecycle transitions are explained primarily by attributing them to the effects of 'inter-generational' conflict. The argument is presented along the lines that young Asians growing up in Britain internalise 'Western' values which are at variance with the 'traditional' world view of their parents; and in the process of emulating 'Western' forms of behaviour, youth comes into conflict with the parental generation. Undoubtedly the *potential* for conflict may well be there, especially when the early years of parents and their children are separated not only in time but also by country, so that the two age groups are exposed to differing cultural and political influences during their formative years. For instance, it has already been shown that the process of migration has involved a major change in social position and this change has been experienced in different ways by the two generations. Nevertheless, inter-generational *difference* should not be conflated with *conflict*. The emergence of conflict cannot be predicted in advance, not least because generational relationship might easily have been negotiated and managed in such a way as to favour understanding and shared perspectives. The parental age group may not always be as inflexible as is sometimes assumed. The great majority of post-war Asian immigrants were themselves quite young and impressionable when they first migrated to this country. They too have been subjected to new influences. That is to say they are not always oblivious to the cross-pressures which bear upon their children.

In my own study (Brah, 1979) the great majority of Asian parents interviewed expressed sympathy towards the predicament of young Asians growing up in Britain, although certain areas of experience of the young people were sometimes outside the range of experience of their parents. Equally, the young Asians seemed to understand, if not always agree with, the constraints which were binding upon the parents. There was considerable overlap in the attitudes, norms and values of the two age groups. Indeed, the incidence of 'conflict' was no higher than amongst white young people (attending the same schools as the Asians) and their parents. There were many similarities between Asians and whites as to the type of issue that was likely to produce agreement or disagreement among members of a household. There can be a variety of intersecting factors which may help generate solidarity rather than conflict between age groups. These include: the subtle cultural meanings we learn to associate from childhood with particular relationships, events, forms of behaviour and social perspectives; the psychic investments in emotionally charged bonds with family and relations; the security derived from a sense of belonging to a community and the shared experience by both parents and children of their structural position in society.

At this point it may be helpful to make a distinction between 'age group' and 'generation'. Age group is a category that delineates a vertical relationship between subjects at a specific stage of a lifecycle (e.g. adolescents and their middle-aged parents), whereas 'generation' is a unit of analysis articulating a horizontal relationship between cohorts. As a conceptual category, 'generation' is indexed and calibrated in relation to large units of historical time (Manneheim, 1952; Eisenstadt, 1971). The discourses examined above operate mainly at the level of age group. However, when the attention is shifted to generation it would seem that while the value systems of Asian age groups may retain some similarities, there may simultaneously emerge some significant new cultural forms that, *inter alia*, mark generational change.

During the late 1970s the political activism of Asian young people hit the news headlines as they adopted a highly visible and militant stance against racist oppression. They took to the streets to express their anger at racial attacks and murders. Several youth groups and 'youth movements' were formed during the aftermath of these public demonstrations. The media represented this activism as a new form of youth militancy singularly different from the political behaviour of their more 'docile' parents. But this representation erases the history of militant struggles of the 1950s, 1960s and early 1970s noted earlier. It misreads the criticism levelled by some youth groups at 'community leaders' as a form of protest at 'parental values'.

In addition the reports focused almost entirely on young men. These male groups came to be constructed as 'youth groups' *par excellence.* Yet some of these groups, such as the Bradford Black, consisting of young people of both Asian and Afro-Caribbean descent, included women. Most important, a 'Young Girls Support Group' formed in 1978 by young Asian community workers based in Southall, West London, was transformed into the feminist group 'Southall Black Sisters' in 1979, and it played a central role in the events considered below. Significantly, young women organised on the basis of their position as women rather than as 'youth', even though the membership of the groups was often almost entirely young. These women's groups addressed patriarchal issues simultaneously with those of class and racism, and in the process found themselves interrogating the gender politics of the male-dominated youth movements and 'Left groups', as much as the ethnocentrism and 'race' politics of white feminist groups. Indeed, these women's groups emerged and operated at the sharp edge of the highly charged politics of the period.

A large-scale police operation on 23 April 1979 involved the arrest of nearly 700 (predominantly Asian) men and women of all age groups, of whom 344 were charged and tried in court. This took place in the heart of one of the oldest established Asian communities, Southall. The arrests were made when the people of Southall began to gather in order to demonstrate against the overtly racist National Front, which was holding a pre-election rally at the local town hall. The National Front had virtually no support in Southall and they had not fielded a local candidate there since 1970. So their decision to hold a rally there was seen as a calculated act of provocation. Nearly five thousand people had marched to Ealing Town Hall on the previous day to prevail upon the local Council not to let its premises in Southall be used by a fascist group to hold a political rally, but the Council had decided that the meeting should go ahead. So community organisations in Southall drew up plans to hold a peaceful protest, and these plans had been agreed with the local police. But on the day people trying to get to the site of the planned demonstration, together with those who were simply trying to return home from work or after collecting young children from school, found themselves trapped between police cordons. As a pamphlet produced by the Campaign against Racism and Fascism/Southall Rights notes:

> 2,756 police, including Special Patrol Group units, with horses, dogs, vans, riot shields and a helicopter were sent in ... the evidence of hundreds of eye witnesses shows that ... police vans were driven straight at crowds of people, and when they scattered and ran, officers charged at them, hitting out at random.... A *Daily Telegraph* reporter saw 'several dozen crying, screaming coloured [*sic*] demonstrators ... dragged bodily along Park View Road to the police station.... Nearly every demonstrator we saw had blood flowing from some sort of injury; some were doubled up in pain. Women and men were crying' ... (Campaign against Racism and Fascism/Southall Rights, 1981: 2)

A white teacher, Blair Peach, was killed. Later eleven eyewitnesses gave evidence under oath that they had seen Blair Peach hit by one, or in some cases two, police officers attached to the Special Patrol Group. The jury turned a verdict of 'death by misadventure' and the Director of Public Prosecutions decided that there was insufficient evidence to prosecute any police officer. This announcement generated much public controversy and led to the setting up of separate enquiries by three public agencies: the Commission for Racial Equality, the National Council for Civil Liberties and the Runnymede Trust. The depth of concern may be gauged from the following quote from the supplementary report of the

NCCL Committee of Enquiry, chaired by Michael Dummett, Professor of Logic at the University of Oxford. Adding to its earlier criticism of the extent of force used by the police in Southall, the Enquiry declared:

> We deplore the fact that no police officer has been brought to account for Blair Peach's death.... We deplore the fact that neither the Commissioner of Police nor the Home Secretary, as Police Authority, has publicly recognised the failings in the police operation.... We are astonished by the failure of both Sir David McNee and William Whitelaw to explain publicly the reasons offered for the presence of unauthorised weapons in SPG lockers.... We regard the inquest into Blair Peach's death as deficient in conduct and procedure. The evident bias of the coroner, Dr John Burton, combined with his confused and inaccurate direction to the jury, made a fair hearing of the issues impossible. (NCCL, 1980: 50–1)

Clarence Baker, a member of the local band 'Misty in Roots', formed by a group of young Southallians of Afro-Caribbean descent, was wounded and lay unconscious in hospital for some time. He had suffered injury when the police raided the building occupied by the community organisation 'Peoples Unite Education and Creative Arts Centre', of which the musicians' co-op to which 'Misty' belonged was a part. Their music equipment was totally destroyed. On the day of the demonstration these premises had been converted into a makeshift centre for emergency legal advice and medical treatment. Lawyers and medical staff (black and white, men and women) who were there to provide assistance claimed that they had been roughly handled by the police and forced out of the building amid a barrage of sexist and racist abuse. The events of the day generated a massive political campaign. They represented a watershed in the creation of new youth politics.

In July 1981 Southall witnessed one of the first of a series of 'riots' (or 'uprisings', as these events have been called by the black communities) which swept across the country that year. Asian youth reacted when skinheads arrived in Southall in buses decked with National Front banners and stickers. A group of skinheads attacked an Asian woman in her shop and the news of the incident spread quickly through the various informal communication networks operating among Asians in the area. Large numbers of young Asians came out on the streets and besieged the public house where the skinheads were attending a rock concert. During the pitched battles that followed, between Asian youths and the police, and between Asians and the skinheads, the pub was set ablaze by petrol bombs. The anger triggered off that day was yet another reaction against the growing number of violent attacks on Asians and the alleged lack of police protection against these attacks.

During the same month in Bradford twelve young Asian men were arrested and charged with conspiracy; all were community activists and some had been actively involved in the campaigns which grew around immigration cases such as those of Anwar Ditta and Nasira Begum referred to above. For two days after the arrests in July 1981 the young men were not allowed to see their solicitors. They were all held in custody for varying periods, and the majority did not receive bail until 22 October. All of the defendants pleaded not guilty. Their case is seen by many as a deliberate attempt by the police to weaken black resistance against racism, and support groups for the local defence committee have been formed all over Britain. This necessarily brief overview of the realities of Asian life in contemporary Britain does not include the less dramatic episodes, most of which never hit the headlines.

The emergence of the youth groups marks the coming of age of a new form of Asian political and cultural agency. It is not that these groups are more 'progressive' than the parental age group, as they tend to be described in some public discussions. Rather having grown up in Britain they articulate a *home-grown British political discourse*. They lay claim to the localities in which they live as their 'home'. And however much they may be constructed as 'outsiders', they contest these psychological and geographical spaces from the position of 'insiders'. Even when they describe themselves as 'Asian', this is not a reaching back to some 'primordial Asian' identity. What they are speaking of is a modality of 'British Asianness'. These home-grown BrAsian identities inaugurate a fundamental *generational* change.

1990s–THE NEW MILLENIUM

This chapter has focused on the period from the 1950s to the end of the 1980s. However, it concludes with a general commentary on the subsequent decade of the 1990s and the onset of the twenty-first century. This period has been hugely eventful with wars, genocides, traffic in people and political resurrections all over the world as its mainstay. The reconfiguration of the global balance of power following the demise of the Cold War, the attack on the Twin Towers in New York and the two Gulf Wars, have all combined to create a global crisis. As is increasingly acknowledged even by the sceptics, the contemporary world is being reinvented through a postmodern form of imperialism. The figure of the 'Asian' has been impacted upon by these global changes in a particularly acute way. The publication of Salman Rushdie's *Satanic Verses* and its distressed reception by many Muslims, and the subsequent *fatwah* of 1989 by the Ayatollah Khomeini of Iran, issuing a death sentence on Rushdie, converted a relatively local British event into a global incident of major proportions. For years the 'Rushdie Affair', as it came to be known, sharply divided public opinion (Appaiah, 2003; Asad, 1993a; Sayyid, 1997). There emerged a simplistic and dangerous binary through which opponents of the book became represented as deluded, backward and uncivilised in contrast to the supposedly enlightened liberal supporters of Rushdie. This binary, reminiscent of colonial discourses, became a prime site for mobilising anti-Muslim opinion in Britain and abroad. The figure of the Asian was now fractured in a new way across religious lines creating a postcolonial positionality of Muslim/non-Muslim. One significant outcome of the wide circulation of this binary was that among Muslims it became the basis of a new consciousness of a pan-national Muslim political identity. Alongside this, the 1984 attack by the Indian army on Harmandir Sahib, the Sikh temple in Amritsar, to flush out militants seeking to establish a separate Sikh state, fuelled Sikh militancy not only in India but also in the diasporas. Concurrently the rise of the extremist Hindu Right nationalist movement seeking to establish Hindu hegemony led to major incidents such as the demolition of Babri Masjid in India by 'Hindutva' activists (Appaiah, 2003; Bhatt, 1997, 2001). In Britain supporters of Hindutva sent funds and bricks for the building of a temple at the site where the Babri Masjid had stood. Such events resulted in some internal dissention among Asian communities in Britain, but there were also examples of a show of solidarity as was evident in the opposition to the Iraq wars. The 9/11 attacks of 2001 in New York have further aggravated the political situation. There is now the powerful chameleon-like discourse of the 'terrorist' that can pounce on and instantly criminalise a wide variety of 'suspects'. Among these the young South Asian—or Middle Eastern—looking young men, especially Muslims, are assumed to be the prime suspects. This has created a 'state of siege' climate amongst some South Asian Muslim communities. In contrast to the 1970s and 1980s image of young Asians, especially those with higher education qualifications, as being supposedly more 'Westernised' and by implication somehow less 'traditional', the educated young people of today are likely to be viewed as posing more of a threat. This is partly due to the élite educational and class backgrounds of political figures such as Osama Bin Laden and the young men who are supposed to have masterminded the attack on the Twin Towers.

There have been significant levels of social class differentiation among South Asian groups over the decades. There is now a fairly well established small bourgeoisie and a professional/entrepreneurial middle class. This has significant consequences in terms of the power dynamics of Asian social life. The consumption patterns, for instance, are beginning to be clearly differentiated across class. These social groups are able to procure élite educational facilities for their children, thus improving the children's future material life trajectories. As a category, the majority of Asians are, however, still working class. This is especially the case where Pakistanis and Bangladeshi groups are concerned. In areas such as Blackburn, the site of 'riots' in 2001, both Asians and whites are predominantly from one of the lowest socio-economic groups. The 'Blackburn riots' could be seen partly as a clash of white and Asian working-class masculinities, the animosity nurtured by years spent on low income in poor housing estates. The 'them' and 'us' division was fuelled by circulating racist discourses, including gendered discourses which pathologised the lives of Muslim women. Indeed the figure of the 'veiled woman' is a significant icon that is mobilised both locally, as in places such as Blackburn, and globally in the White House by the president of the United States and his colleagues when they claim to have gone to war in order to free the veiled women. Unveiling the Eastern woman is, of course, a longstanding fantasy of orientalist discourses, but rarely have we seen her made into an overt centrepiece of trans-national politics. The image of the veiled woman is seen as the epitome of Eastern backwardness and unreason. The longstanding episode of the 'headscarf affair' is now being replayed as the wearing of headscarves in schools has been made officially illegal (Brah, 2002, 2004; Puwar and Raghuram, 2003).

Orientalism is a key dynamic within current regimes of imperialism. For instance, on a visit to the British forces in Basra in Iraq in early January, Tony Blair, the British Prime Minister, described the soldiers as 'the new pioneers of soldiering' who were there to deal with the threat of 'rogue states and the virus of Islamic extremism' which could reduce the 'world system to chaos' (*Guardian*, 5 Jan 2004). Writing in the same newspaper, Eric Hobsbawm discusses the dangers of this new imperialism with the United States at its helm. The British Empire, he says, was probably the only one that was global in so far as it operated across the planet. But it saw its purpose as that of championing British interests. The new empire on the other hand sees itself as having a universal purpose and as Hobsbawm argued 'Few things are more dangerous than empires pursuing their own interest in the belief that they are doing humanity ur'(*Guardian*, 14 June 2003). The future of South Asia and its diasporas is inextricably linked with these imperial ambitions.

At the beginning of this chapter it was noted that identity is not a singular but rather a multifaceted and context-specific construct. In the case of Asians, religion, caste and language, for example, are important features of group identity. The complex interplay of these factors marks intra-Asian relations in Britain. These relations are not a straightforward replay of social relations in the subcontinent, rather they are mediated via cultural, political and economic dimensions as these are forged in Britain. The cultural sphere is crucial in affirming or contesting these identities. For instance, sports tournaments with a focus on some specifically South Asian game such as *kabadi* may help underwrite a BrAsian Punjabi male identity when Punjabi teams from Birmingham, Coventry and London play against each other. Similarly, the religious ritual dance performed during 'Navratri' as worship of the goddess Durga is an arena for the play of gender and caste-inflected Hindu-Gujarati identities. Caste inequalities may be reinforced, since Navratri congregations meet under the aegis of various caste-based organisations, but these same organisations could well be used by the lower castes as a ground from which to contest these very hierarchies. The ritual fast during Ramadan, the observances during Muharam, or the celebration of Eid, may underscore a Muslim identity at the same time as highlighting the intra-Muslim differentiations such as Sunni and Shia.

In the same way the performance of *mushaira* (Urdu poetry readings) all over Britain inscribes a BrAsian institution against the echoes of a complex South Asian history from the Timurid (Mughal) period onwards. Similarly, the tradition of 'revolutionary' poetry recitation, which is marked in Britain at events held to commemorate the political activism of, say, Shahid Bhagat Singh—who was hanged by the British for his part in anti-colonial insurrection—is an instance of the BrAsian form of political culture. Old and new forms of Asian music, dance and theatre groups, drawing upon classical as well as contemporary traditions, are beginning to mushroom all over Britain. Literature produced by Asians living in Britain—in English as well as in various South Asian languages—is fast becoming an established feature of Britain's literary production. These art forms simultaneously interpret, translate and interrogate the subtleties and intricacies of South Asian life-worlds in and outside Britain, drawing out their global interconnections as well as what is distinctive about each. BrAsian identities are in flux and whatever form these political and cultural identities take they are interwoven into the British social and cultural fabric.

CHICKEN TIKKA MASALA

Sophia Ahmed

Supermarkets claim to sell more than 18 tonnes of it each week. Over 23 million portions of it are sold through South Asian restaurants each year. So acclaimed has it become that the Newport chef Iftikar Haris felt a musical was the best way to sing its praises. The phenomenon is of course chicken tikka masala.

The latter part of the twentieth century witnessed the emergence of chicken tikka masala as the newly acclaimed national dish of Britain, representing a time of multiculturalism. The former Foreign Secretary Robin Cook described it as a 'true British national dish'. Although chicken tikka masala as we know it today was created for the palates of the British, its origins are situated in Mesopotamian history. The earliest known recipe for cooked meat enriched with spices engulfed in a pool of sauce can be found on cuneiform tablets near Babylon dating back to 1700 BCE, and is attributed to the Black-Headed people (sag-gi-ga, i.e Sumerians).

Fast-forward a few thousand years and the dormant recipe is revived and transformed to create what we today call chicken tikka masala. Legend tells us it was created when a diner demanded some form of gravy with his tandoori chicken. An astonished chef responded by simply adding a can of Campbell's soup and a few spices. Although in the latter part of the twentieth century many restaurateurs have claimed it was they who invented the dish, no compelling evidence has been found to substantiate these claims.

Different South Asian restaurants throughout the country cook the masala in different ways according to their South Asian geographical origin. The only certainty about the dish is that it commonly includes chicken, yogurt, spices and tomatoes. Everything beyond this is left to the chef's discretion.

Chicken tikka masala can be seen as a metaphor for the BrAsian experience. Had it not been for colonisation and migration South Asian foods such as tandoori chicken would not have arrived on Britain's shores. Similarly, had it not been for the British experience there would have been no gravy (masala) with our chicken today. In other words chicken tikka masala, which existed neither in South Asia nor in Britain, occupies a distinct 'third space' between the purities of South Asian and British cuisine. It exists only because of the fusion of these cultural experiences and as a consequence is now eaten both in Britain and throughout South Asia.

Recipe

Ingredients

Part 1

1 lb boneless chicken breast
¼ cup plain/natural yogurt
2 t. grated/minced ginger
2 crushed cloves of garlic
¼ t. white pepper
¼ t. cumin powder
¼ t. chilli powder
¼ t. turmeric
2 T. lemon juice
2 T. vegetable oil
Salt to one's taste
Melted butter (for basting)

Part 2

1 onion
1 T. tomato paste
2 tomatoes
3 t. crushed ginger
3 t. garlic cloves
3 whole green chillies
1 t. red chilli powder
4 T. butter/cooking oil
1 cup of cream
Salt to one's taste

Method

• Chop the chicken breast into roughly 2 inch cubes then place to one side.
• Mix together all of the ingredients from part one of the recipe, excluding the chicken, in a large bowl.
• Add the chopped chicken and stir.
• Marinate the mixture overnight in a refrigerator.
• Preheat an oven to 360° F.
• Place chicken in an ovenproof dish and bake for 8–10 minutes, basting with melted butter twice.
• Drain the excess marinade and continue to bake for a further 3–5 minutes.
• While the chicken is being cooked prepare part two of the recipe.
• Heat butter/oil in a heavy non-stick pan and add ginger and garlic. Once these have become golden brown add the chopped onions, tomato puree, chopped tomatoes, green chillies, red chilli powder and salt. Cook on a very low heat until the mixture becomes pureed. Add one cup of water and simmer until the butter/oil comes to the surface.
• Add the cooked chicken to the mixture and continue to cook on a low heat.
• Add the cream (yogurt can be used instead of cream for a low fat alternative) and simmer for a few minutes.

POLITICS OF BLACKNESS AND ASIAN IDENTITY[1]

Tariq Modood

Most people who have been active in British race-relations debates over the last decade or so, whether at political, academic or administrative levels, have participated in, or acquiesced to, the idea that an, perhaps the, important social fact about non-white people in Britain is their common participation in a political 'blackness'. The single most important and common manifestation of this idea has been the use of the term 'black' to describe people of African, Caribbean and South Asian origins in Britain. Sociologists have been both at the forefront of this development and amongst the slowest to abandon it. Yasmin Ali, following the lead of Stuart Hall (1992a: 252), has described the fortunes of the concept of 'black' in the following way:

> At the beginning of the 1980s 'communities originating in some of the countries of the old empire' would have been expressed unselfconsciously as 'black communities'. At the end of the decade 'black' is a much more contentious label than it was previously. 'Black' in its British usage was intended to convey a sense of a necessary common interest and solidarity between communities from the old empire (or the New Commonwealth); it was a usage predicated on the politics of anti-racism. As such 'black' 'became "hegemonic" over other ethnic/racial identities' in the late seventies and early eighties. The moment was not to last. From within marginalised communities and from without there was, in the 1980s, a steady assault upon this fragile hegemony. (Ali, 1991: 195)

As one of the people cited as responsible for contributing to the defeat of this hegemony (Ali, 1991: 207), I would like to return to this topic to consider an aspect of why it was so vulnerable to criticism. It is important to be clear, of course, that what has been defeated is not the concept of 'black' but its hegemony, and even then, as far as terminology is concerned, the effect of the change in political writing and academic research is negligible. Hence, while the Commission for Racial Equality in December 1988 ceased to recommend that 'black' as an ethnic monitoring category encompassed Asians (Commission for Racial Equality, 1988), British academic writing on race has continued with the older

1 This is a version of a paper that was first published as 'Political Blackness and British Asians', *Sociology*, 28, 4 (November 1994), pp. 859–68.

terminology. I therefore understand the loss of the hegemony of 'black' to mean a pushing back from the mainstream public discourse to its original location, left-wing politics and race sociology, where, of course, it still flourishes.

Because my primary concern is with current affairs reportage, together with the speeches and documents produced by political parties, trades unions, big employers, central and local government officials and professionals and so on (this is what I mean by 'mainstream public discourse'), I would date the hey-day of the concept of 'black' differently from Ali. For her the high-point was the late 1970s and early 1980s (Ali, 1991: 201) and others would confine it yet again to the earlier of these two periods when the concept of 'black', devised by New Left radicals to mark a transcendence of ethnicity and origins in favour of a new colour-solidarity and political formation, is said to have been taken up by Afro-Caribbean and Asian communities who found that their separate struggles were actually bringing them together; a moment that was soon to be lost when the concept was appropriated by the set of race professionals that emerged in the responses of local and central government to the riots of 1981 (Sivanandan, 1985; Gilroy, 1987: 25). Yet it was the incorporation of these anti-racist pressures into the British polity that led to the ascendancy of the inclusive concept of 'black' within the mainstream (Banton, 1987; Anthias and Yuval-Davis, 1992: 159). For with the enactment of the 1976 Race Relations Act, and particularly with local government racial equality initiatives after the 1981 riots, a tranche of radical activists were brought into work with the state, with 'the system' (Dhondy, 1987). It was their anti-racist rhetoric, often contradictorily mixed up with the very different 'black is beautiful' rhetoric of ethnic pride, which came together with the more social scientific and administrative language of statistics and policy recommendations, which too favoured a white-black tidiness, to create the favoured consensus which was around the term 'black' in the early to mid 1980s, first within the specialist lobby and then more widely.

Hence, the important mainstream hegemony came to be established just as the original left-wing, extra-state radicalism and the consequent Afro-Caribbean-Asian solidarities that arose from community self-defence from skinheads or police harassment, were giving way to struggles within the Labour Party and the (local) state in which Afro-Caribbeans and Asians lobbied for ethnic or sub-ethnic interests (usually the distribution of jobs, social grants and control of state-aided community centres and projects) which belied the increasing and uncritical use of the rhetoric of political colour-unity. The contrast, then, between radicals, like Sivanandan, Hall, Gilroy and Ali, dating the hegemonic period as the late 1970s and early 1980s, and my dating it as early to late 1980s, primarily arises from the difference in our respective interests in radicalism and mainstream discourse. For those whose starting-point was extra-state agitation as a way of amplifying and connecting with histories of class struggle and global anti-imperialism, the transformation of their 'black' movements into 'the race relations industry' and competing ethnic lobbies could not help but be seen as, to use Sivanandan's phrase, a 'degradation'. For those like me, whose community relations work perspective was, in the period of the 'degradation', increasingly obliged to adopt a 'black' discourse perspective which (as the radicals note) was inconsistent with the emerging ethnic realities, the problem was not about the decline of the concept of 'black', but how such a concept was ever foisted upon the various ethnic minorities.

Given, then, that the origins of 'black' lie in the egalitarian desire of grouping those people together who suffer similar forms of discrimination and marginality, so that their condition can be highlighted and remedial action taken, including ethnic mobilisation, law and policy, how can I argue that 'black' is harmful to Asians? I offer some reasons below, most of which depend upon the fact that the term 'black' is not neutral amongst non-white ethnic groups. It has a historical and current meaning such that it is powerfully evocative of people of sub-Saharan African origins, and all other groups, if evoked at all, are secondary. It is not an empty term that can be picked up and given a meaning such that any group other than those of African origins can be the core group (just as masculine vocabulary, even when intended to be gender-neutral, as in legal and academic language, cannot but put the image of the male gender in the reader's mind). Some of the effects for Asians, in extending an Afro-based term to describe them, are as follows (for a related viewpoint, see Hazareesingh, 1986).

TOO NARROW A CONCEPTION OF RACIAL DISCRIMINATION

A focus on 'colour' as the basis of uniting and mobilising those who suffer from racial discrimination falsely equates racial discrimination with colour-discrimination. While there is good evidence that in the case of face-to-face discrimination, for example in the context of seeking accommodation or employment, colour is a decisive factor (Brown and Gay, 1985; Centre For Research Into Ethnic Relations, 1990; Foyster *et al.*, 1990), this is really only the ground floor of racism rather than the whole building. It is generally recognised that class is a factor which contributes to racial discrimination and to racial disadvantage. Inferior treatment on the basis of colour can create a subordinate class which, by virtue of its socio-economic location, could continue to suffer comparative disadvantage even were colour prejudice to wane. Thus, for instance, employers who prefer a public school, Oxbridge background will disadvantage the majority of society, which may have a disproportionately greater impact on racial minorities, and this fact is acknowledged in the British legal concept of indirect racial discrimination. While proponents of the concept of 'black' recognise how class is interrelated with race, they overlook how cultural differences can also disadvantage and be the basis of discrimination, e.g. in employment on the grounds of one's dress, dietary habits, or desire to take leave from work on one's holy days rather than those prescribed by the custom and practice of the majority community. An emphasis on discrimination against 'black' people systematically obscures the cultural antipathy to Asians (and, no doubt, others), how Asian cultures and religions have been racialised, and the elements of discrimination that Asians (and others) suffer. If colour (or colour and class) were the sole basis of racism in British society, it would be impossible to explain the finding, of all the white attitude surveys over more than a decade, that self-assigned racial prejudice against Asians is higher, sometimes much higher, than against black people (e.g. Brown, 1984: 290; Jowell *et al.*, 1986: 150 and 164; *Today*, 14 March 1990; Amin and Richardson, 1992: 19–21). Moreover, explanations to do with length of settlement and mutual familiarisation belie the fact that the difference in the prejudice against the two groups may be growing (Young, 1992: 181).

The emphasis on colour-discrimination and colour-identity denies what otherwise would be obvious: the hostility of the majority is likely to be particularly forceful against non-white individuals who are members of a community (and not just free-floating or assimilated individuals) that is sufficiently numerous to reproduce itself as a community and has a distinctive and cohesive value system that can be perceived as an alternative to and a possible challenge to the norm; this phenomenon is currently growing in Britain and disproportionately impacts upon Asians. It is what explains some of the contradictions in contemporary racism, such as the observation that white working-class youth culture is incorporating, indeed, emulating, young black men and women, while hardening against groups like South Asians and Vietnamese (Cohen, 1988: 83; Boulton and Smith, 1992; Back, 1993). A glance at the newspapers will quickly reveal that as many race relations battles turn on issues of culture and minority rights as on colour discrimination and socio-economic deprivation. 'Black' obscures this and prevents Asians from fully articulating and mobilising against the nature of their oppression.

'BLACK' OBSCURES ASIAN NEEDS AND DISTORTS ANALYSIS

Because 'black' is powerfully evocative of people of African origins, its usage inevitably gives prominence to Afro-Caribbeans. I have elsewhere given examples of how this marginalisation of Asians is widespread in research and political literature (Modood, 1988a: 399–400). Where there is marginalisation, it naturally follows that the distinctive concerns of the Asian communities will be marginalised. It is notable, for example, that despite the high levels of attacks on Asians and their property from the 1960s onwards, attempts to get the police and policy makers to address this basic issue of security had, till very recently, been less effective than the attempts to get them to focus on the equality of treatment of offenders by the criminal justice system, an issue up to now of far less importance to Asians. Immigration rules, transmission of parental culture to children, minority religious observance in schools, support for large families and self-employment are a number of issues that are of greater importance to Asians than to others, but because Asians have not been in a position to push them to the top of the agenda, these have received relatively less attention in the race equality movement than Asians have felt they deserved.

Asians (and for that matter any other group) need a richer and more rounded public identity than one focused on politics can allow. People of African origins can use the concept of 'black' with a historical depth and a cultural texture through freighting it with an African diasporic ethnic pride, as famously captured in the 'black is beautiful' slogan, or in the newer idea of 'black Atlantic' (Gilroy, 1993b). For Asians 'black' can be no more than 'a political colour', a reference to a limited aspect of their being, which inevitably requires them to give greater prominence to an aspect of their political being than is important to them or than they consider sensible; and it gives a leadership role to those Asians who, whatever their standing in, or commitment to, the various Asian communities, can identify with and internalise the politics of anti-colour discrimination. This is too gross a strait-jacket for Asian community concerns and qualities which Asians may wish to promote.

Even if there is a descriptive, sociological concept of 'black' based upon statistically inferred colour discrimination (and I have already suggested that the concept of racial discrimination is more complex than colour discrimination), this concept is of a negative condition, of how *others* treat oneself, not the basis of a positive identity likely to foster pride in one's origins and establish a secure psychological platform for active participation in British society. For while mobilisation to secure rights requires a dynamic of group pride, 'black' serves to obscure Asian identities and smother the basis of ethnic pride.

The crux of the issue here rests on a distinction between the values, aspirations and community structures of an oppressed group (its mode of being) and the social structures and ideological forms which oppress that group (its mode of oppression). A cardinal error of 1980s anti-racism was to substitute mobilisation around opposition to a mode of oppression (racism), for the freedom to be what one is and aspires to be, for one's mode of being. By understanding minorities such as Asians *primarily in terms of racism and anti-racism*, anti-racists in effect create group identities exclusively from the point of view of the dominant whites and fail to recognise that those whom white people treat as no more than the raw material of racist categorisation have, indeed, a mode of being of their own which defies such reduction (Modood, 1990a). Many anti-racists' interest in Asians is not in Asians but in the condition of victim; Asians who experience racial discrimination are reduced to discriminated beings ('blacks') who happen to be Asians, and who should publicly proclaim their mode of oppression as their primary identity, while confining the symbolic power of their mode of being to secondary occasions. But this is too superficial a view of oppression and of ethnic mobilisation against racial subordination. We need a concept of race that enables us to understand that any oppressed group feels its oppression most according to those dimensions of its being which *it* (not the oppressor) values most; moreover it will resist its oppression from those dimensions of its being from which it derives its greatest collective psychological strength. We see this very clearly with working-class Asian (and other) Muslims. Despite being the most racially disadvantaged group in Britain, measured in terms of unemployment, over-representation in manual work, educational qualifications, poor housing, attacks on person and property and so on (Jones, 1993), they have borne this marginal and oppressive condition with stoicism and kinship self-help, but exploded on an issue of religious honour, when it was perceived that *The Satanic Verses* not only limited one's material opportunities but attacked the very core of one's being (Modood, 1990b, 1992b). It is most revealing that the Muslim protesters neither looked for nor were offered any 'black' solidarity and that one of the leaders of 'black' politics, Paul Boateng MP, dismissed Muslim anger as having nothing to do with 'the black discourse' (Kramer, 1991: 75).

It has been argued that as all identities are situational, individuals are capable of identities of several sorts, and that Asians can be found who have a strong Asian identity and a sense of political blackness, even if not fully acknowledged by themselves (Drury, 1990). Drury offers as evidence that 92 per cent of a sample of about a hundred teenage Sikh girls in the early 1980s rejected the term 'black' as a self-description, but a significant number thought there were commonalities of experience between all non-white people. Yet this surely confirms that a sense of being 'black' is for most Asians a forced identity, on the periphery of their conception of themselves and not a source of pride or even of self-defence. The general point is not peculiar to Muslims or Asians. Materialistic theories of anti-racism typically underestimate the defence of group dignity and the positive role of ethnic pride. The 'black is beautiful' campaign in the long term reached far more American blacks than the civil rights campaign and, indeed, provided a personal and collective psychological dynamic which fed into the latter, and which enabled blacks to take advantage of the socio-economic opportunities created by the politics.

NEW IDENTITIES

The hegemony of 'black' over other ethnic/racial identities was doomed. If one single remark combines and epitomises these criticisms it is Yasmin Alibhai's contention that when most Asians hear the word 'black', they are unlikely to think of themselves, so many fail to apply for jobs where advertisements specifically welcome black people (*Woman's Hour*, BBC Radio 4, 17 November 1988). Therefore, it is not surprising that in 1988 some Asians decided that an anti-racism which was so out of touch with or defiant of basic Asian community concerns had to be challenged. The year began with the National Association of Asian Probation Staff boycotting the Home Office staff ethnic monitoring exercise because it classified Asians as a sub-division of Black, and was followed by an on-going debate in the minority press, especially in *New Life*, *Asian Herald* and the Afro-Caribbean *Voice*, with occasional overspills into the national media (Modood, 1988b; Roy, 1988; Uppal, 1988; Kogbara, 1988; *Heart of the Matter*, BBC TV, 10 July 1988) and academic journals (Modood, 1988a).

This critique bore fruit when in December of that year the Commission for Racial Equality (CRE) decided to cease to recommend that people of Asian origin be classified as Black and in the following month the Office of Population Censuses and Surveys (OPCS) announced that they were proceeding to the next stage in the ethnic question trials for the 1991 Census with the same categories as the CRE. It is perhaps an open question as to the significance of these administrative decisions: were they just petty terminological changes or did they mark an important milestone in the philosophy of race relations? The CRE, which was disinclined to read too much into them, was told by a *New Statesman and Society* editorial that it 'should be publicising its decision with confidence instead of weakly whispering out an important decision, almost hoping nobody will notice' (23 December 1988). Phillip Nanton has argued that 'these attempts to capture an acceptable ethnic categorisation suggest that a fundamental change has taken place in the definition of ethnicity, for ethnic categories can no longer be regarded as "given" but are open to interest group pressure and negotiation' (Nanton, 1989: 556).

One response of theorists such as Hall and Ali to the end-of-the-hegemony-of-'black' has been to shift attention from organised politics and social structures to cultural identities and their manufacture and communication, from 'a struggle over the relations of representation to a politics of representation itself' (Hall, 1992a: 253). With this goes a celebration of 'new ethnicities' and cultural hybridity, and a critique of 'ethnic absolutism'—the idea that ethnic identities are simply 'given', are static and ahistorical and do not (or should not) change under new circumstances or by sharing social space with other heritages and influences. The emphasis on the historical nature of ethnicity (as opposed to conformity to an atemporal essence or an imagined golden age), on hybridity without loss of integrity or self-respect, on cultural openness and multi-textured identities, rather than on the coercive simplicities of 'black' absolutism, is to be welcomed, and may allow Asians to develop a more authentic repertoire of self-images than 'black' allowed. Yet this new turn is not without its dangers. If 'new' simply comes to describe the *avant-garde*, then it is clear that most British Asians will once again suffer marginalisation. A rejection of theories of primordial ethnic absolutism should not prevent us from accurately describing where most Asians are, regardless of whether it seems sufficiently 'new' or progressive. We must not pit 'new' and 'old' ethnicities against each other: we must avoid the élitism of cultural vanguardism that devalues and despises where the ordinary majority of any group or social formation is at—an élitism so thoughtlessly exemplified in Salman Rushdie's *The Satanic Verses*, to the loss of us all, new and old. And yet in the loss of hegemony there may be wisdom (Modood, 2005).

CURRY POWDER

Apurba Kundu

Curry powder and curry as a South Asian dish are unknown on the subcontinent. Indeed, the origin of the word 'curry' is not easy to trace. Curry is variously understood to be from: the Tamil '*kari*', translated as spiced sauce or, more simply, gravy; the Hindi '*karai*', a special cooking vessel; or even the Old English 'cury', a term for cooking derived from the French 'cuire', to cook, boil, grill (Davidson, 1999; Grove and Grove, 2000; Panjabi, 2000; Wickramasinghe *et al.*, 2002). Indian 'curry' powder is common in both British kitchens and BrAsian restaurants ubiquitous on British streets. Conventional wisdom appears to accept Sharwood's, founded by James Allan Sharwood in 1889, as the oldest firm importing and marketing blends of Indian spices as curry powder to London's public (http://www.sharwoods.com/, accessed 10 December 2002) and the Veeraswamy, established in London's Regent Street in the late 1920s, as the oldest surviving South Asian restaurant (see http://www.veeraswamy.com/; and Grove and Grove, 2000). However, since South Asians started to arrive in Britain centuries before—as *ayahs* and servants, seamen and soldiers, entrepreneurs and professionals—it is not surprising that some historians have traced the commercial creation of curry powder to 1780, the first appearance of curry on a menu to 1773—in the Coffee House in Norris Street, Haymarket, London—and the first eating place dedicated to Indian cuisine—the Hindostanee Coffee House at 34 George Street, Portman Square, also in London—to 1809 (Grove and Grove, 2000).

However, there are other competing claims. The tale of one such competitor, known only as Abdul, is told by the former Ambassador and Indian Army officer Mirza Rashid Ali Baig. As a 'dressing boy' to Baig's father, Mirza Abbas Ali Baig, C.S.I., K.C.I.E., Abdul travelled with the family to London in 1910, when Baig senior arrived to take up his appointment within the newly formed Secretary of State's Council of India (Baig, 1967: 10). The young Baig remembers how Abdul, also an 'excellent cook', used his father's influence at the India Office to win the catering contract for a rest and recuperation camp set up for Indian soldiers taken from the French frontlines in the Great War (1967: 11). In addition to this profitable contract he was soon importing spices from India and marketing '*Abdullah's Curry Powder*' which was in great demand amongst those who had served in India and had developed a taste for Indian food. He also started *the first, and for many years the only*, Indian restaurant in London, to which Indian students flocked (1967: 11). The young Baig recalls how, far from resenting his former servant's good fortune, 'Father used to say with pride… [that] Abdul was earning very much more than he had ever done'(1967: 11).

Abdul was far from finished. Along with his wife, 'an excellent business woman', he invested in property and went on to found the import-export firm of Messrs A. Abdullah & Sons, Manufacturers, Importers and Exporters of Helmet Court, Wormwood Street, London. Years later, when Saudi Arabia broke off diplomatic relations with Britain over the Suez Canal episode, Abdul was 'appointed their Agent in London and the embassy building and property placed in his charge… [subsequently] he was invited to Saudi Arabia and received and honoured by no less a person than King Saud himself' (1967: 11–12). Throughout Abdul remained close to the family he used to serve, happy to host their members whenever they visited London. 'It gave us, and him, great pleasure when our two sons… went to England and over whom he kept an avuncular eye', writes Ambassador Baig (1967: 12). Abdul's rise from dressing boy and cook to restaurateur, entrepreneur and Royal Agent is, as Baig succinctly concludes, 'A romantic tale by any standard' (1967: 12).

THE DIALECTIC OF 'HERE AND THERE'

ANTHROPOLOGY 'AT HOME'[1]

John Hutnyk

Ethnographers in Britain seem to have by and large ignored left political activity among South Asian settlers on these islands. However, the lustrous career of South Asian communists active in Britain is not to be romanticised and, of course, the number of communist champions is far fewer than those not involved in class politics. Nevertheless, the groundwork for many of the kinds of political positions taken for granted today were forged in adversity and struggle under scarlet flags. Thus given the conditions into which most South Asian youth are born in multi-racist Britain, and given the heritage to which they can, if they wish, lay claim, it should be no surprise that comprehension of the struggle is 'imbibed as if with mothers milk', as one informant described it to me. Why then has scholarship singularly failed to register this?

ANTHROPOLOGY 'AT HOME'

'... labour in the white skin cannot be free if in the black it is branded.' (Marx, 1867: 301)

In a short story collected in *Where the Dance Is* Ambalavaner Sivanandan tells the tale of a meeting of a Marxist study group in a pub in Hampstead, probably sometime in the 1970s. In this engaging (semi-autobiographical?) story a Sri Lankan PhD student at the London School of Economics, going by the name of Bala, is invited to a meeting by Clarence, an acquaintance from home now resident in the 'mother country'. Bala is uncertain as to just what is required of him:

> I was not sure how to play my role: as a red insurrectionary or as black militant. (Sivanandan, 2000: 48)

The four white comrades bought him drinks for both affectations, but when the discussion turned to the issue of immigration into Britain it was Clarence, the 'senior immigrant', who won the most approval, and a kiss from one of the women, for a position that should readily be recognised

1 Thanks to Tia Chowdhoury, Sivanandan, Tariq Mehmood, Bobby Sayyid and Virinder S. Kalra for comments that have helped get this project started, as it should continue.

even amidst the smoke and fug of the mid-afternoon local boozer. As the story tells it, Clarence 'mumbled and spluttered incoherently about the responsibility of the mother country to its children and ended up declaring, "we are here because you were there"', something Bala had heard before. The meeting broke up, with the next Saturday scheduled for a discussion of Marx's *Eighteenth Brumaire*.

The story continues with various intricacies: the woman who kisses Clarence cooks a curry for Bala, Bala gets to know something of Clarence's life in Britain, and so on, but the main point in retelling this scene is neither appreciation of Sivanandan's accomplished literary talents, nor to rehash some scenario in mockery of the curry-cooking, patronising, white, left woman Tessa, but to register the movement that Sivanandan always tries to effect: the complication and extension of thought beyond platitudes and slogans, achieved always also from an activist's perspective. The formula 'we are here because you were there' may in fact have the ring of truth, and it makes an excellent chant, and must needs be said. But saying it for approval, saying it into the ether, saying it without consequence deserves critical attention too. Sivanandan questions the motives and context of sloganeering even in the very heart of a Marxist cell meeting discussion of immigration in the days when Compendium bookshop was still a fixture and visits to Cuba were the norm. Sivanandan shows us exactly where romantic attachments and the deceits of too easy acceptance only allow platitudes when more is required. As to what happens at the end of the tale, without giving the story away—its called 'The Man Who Loved the Dialectic'—a nuanced Marxism makes more sense of the predicament of contemporary life than that afforded in any other conception.

What then for writing about BrAsians that would do more than rehearse either the trite axioms of identity politics or the romantic attachments of essentialist stereotype? On two sides there is a seductive danger and all too easy exoticist trap—playing the ethnic card and falling for ethnicist stereotypes have been the preserve of many who would write, with good intentions, the history of South Asians in Britain. On the one hand those who have appropriated the role of documenting Asian identities in the metropole, on the other metropolitan identities playing up to expectations. For convenience sake this essay identifies this double trap in the congealed positions of anthropologists writing on BrAsians, and in their identitarian informants, using the critical position of a BrAsian communist history (the subject matter that stems from Sivanandan's fictional study group) as the counterfoil that disrupts this duality.

The procedure of taking category and classification in advance of observation and discussion has reified and fixed a conservative set of stereotypes. To assume that caste, kinship, arranged marriages and religious tradition are the main keys to comprehension of the social and political experience of South Asians in Britain is a common delusion, born from the work of anthropologists bent on finding rural and village subjects conveniently replicated in metropolitan settings. This is a conservative anthropology in the extreme, owing more allegiance to old categories found 'over there' than politics and experience of people with agency 'over here'. Not to say, of course, that caste, kin and religion are or were unimportant, but, as we will see, equally worthy of attention could be workplace and neighbourhood organisations, trades unionism, political activism, socialist and communist party affiliation, rallies and other such associations. It can be argued that the organisational history of South Asians in Britain has been particularly obscured by a blinding culturalism attuned only to the exotic. The worst consequence of this exoticism is to reduce the 'migrant' worker to a timeless and rural pre-political unconsciousness—an imperialist oversight that replicates ethnicist fantasy and depoliticises by means of reified culture.

Ethnographic approaches to BrAsians have been culturalist and conservative in exactly this way (as we will see, Werbner, 1990a; Gillespie, 1995; K. Hall, 2002). In the postcolonial framework, we should agree at the beginning that it is important to avoid the stupid generalisations of voyeuristic social science. To extrapolate from one or two cases of some behaviour or other and then ascribe that behaviour to a cultural, national or ethnic group as a whole would be an error. The imaginary god-like observations that declare 'Muslims are X' or 'Sikhs do Y' is as unacceptable as the old anthropological attributionism of 'Nuer think…' 'Nuer say…'. Certainly there can be no final assertion that BrAsians are or are not more or less politically engaged than anyone else—though like everyone else, some BrAsians are and some are not… these arabesques are farcical. In the discussion of a diasporic Asian presence in Britain the designation must be 'not postcolonial, not not postcolonial'. (Similarly, the critical position in this paper might be 'not communist, not not communist'.)

This is not just a methodological concern of relevance to anthropological categories; it has current political purchase. In the discussion, for example, of participation by Muslim groups in the anti-war coalition, or as 'targets of security forces' at home, in the context of the 'war on terror', a host of cascading racist substitutions appear, sliding rapidly from the shock image of fundamentalist suicide bombers to a spurious link with asylum seekers, generalised to all Muslims, then further extended to Asians and to non-white people in general. This often unexamined cascade inevitably draws sustenance from the general, more influential and wider social and culturalist limits of understanding of Asians, Islam, Hinduism and politics disseminated in Britain through the artefacts of white academia. Monographs of BrAsian experience in Britain are few, but telling. In numerous university course offerings, as well as in the popular media, all South Asians are characterised in a double strategy, either as demons or as exotica, and neither stereotype comes close to an appreciation of the diversity of those under anthropological examination. This double strategy makes Asians either, and both, a people of curious culture—Bhangra, spicy food, Bollywood—and a people of fanaticism—Islam, Hindutva, religious extremism. Sometimes both at the same time—militant spiritualism, spicy sweetmeats—the pathologies of categorisation reveal more of the West than is seen in other domains. This 'exotica-fanatica' two-step is found in academic texts explicitly to the exclusion of the large sections of the history, and present, of South Asians in Britain. The culturalist discourse actively ignores organised political activity, at best offering asides to collaborationist or merely community level action. This is as true of the historical period of the anti-colonial movement, and the Mahatma, as it is of the present where the local Asian Labour Party glamour candidate might be fore-grounded. There is no discussion of, for example, the leading contribution to the Communist Party of Great Britain of the likes of Saklatvala, Palme Dutt or Krishna Menon, and it is very rare to see mention of similarly motivated activists in any of the major anthropological studies of South Asians in Britain today. In part the effort of this essay is to suggest a way to reconstruct this absent history by way of the field of biography (Callaghan, 1993; Wadsworth, 1998), the historical survey work of Visram (2002) and the living memory of so many Uncles, Aunties and the others involved in organisations like the Indian Workers Association, The Pakistani Workers Association, the journal *Lalkar* and so forth (see Sharma *et al.*, 1996 for a beginning attempt to acknowledge the recent history of the IWA; Brah, 1998 for a collection of more contemporary documents).

It is worth remembering from the start, in these days of ahistorical and culturalist appreciation of South Asian ethnicity in Britain, that there could be no ethnic trip, for academics or for cultural entrepreneurs alike, without the initial project of colonialism and its co-constituent consequence of labour exploitation. The British Raj and its global extractive orientation over several hundred years, and the brute fact that consequent migration into Britain from the colonies was not philanthropy cannot be underestimated. Conventionally, ritual mention of imperial history is made in most scholarly studies—if not quite chanting 'we are here because you were there'—but the drawing of inferences and implications does not necessarily inform general understandings in a political way. More often that not a political context is registered then diplomatically relegated, as culturalist commentary seeks out more flamboyant and exuberant themes than that so-called ethnic peoples were brought to Britain with one purpose in mind—white industry wanted to work them hard (in a way that war weary organised white workers would not accept). Immigration shaped by imperialism and the exploitative requirements of manufacturing is the inescapable condition that frames British Asian settlement.

Of course it should not be thought that South Asian 'migrant' labourers had no agency in migration, or that the pull factor of labour shortage on the part of British industry was not complicated by diverse negotiations and structuring factors such as those called 'chain migration' and *biraderi* processes—as indeed named in anthropologist Werbner's *The Migration Process*. Of course South Asians were not mere passive subjects of exploitation, but the study of these processes stresses the cultural in an ethnicist way, ignoring any analysis of contextualising circumstances. *The Migration Process* foregrounds an ethnographic gaze blinded in its micro exoticism to the wider realities that perhaps only politicised groups could tackle. It is a matter of record that anthropologists preferred to study kinship and culture while activists stressed struggle and exploitation. Ignoring left political activity with a vengeance, Werbner herself starts out by noting that the literature on South Asians in Britain is not clear on 'how people have organised themselves to resist being passive victims' and notes that 'forms of cultural resistance vary from community to community' (Werbner, 1990a: 6). However, her interest is primarily in symbolic and culturalist categories and she fails to mention either the Indian or the Pakistani Workers Association, or any level of class or political association (beyond reference to anthropological notions of the 'big man' [Werbner, 1990a: 310]) and prefers to quote anthropologists like Gluckman and Mauss (much) rather than engage with Marx or Marxist influences (never).

It is not as if Werbner is unaware of the politics of BrAsian organisation in Britain, its just that anthropologists have somehow been inclined to ignore this aspect as part of a rush to rustic and ethnic caricature. It is interesting that the use of anthropology to study people within the West aimed to break a division of labour between sociology and anthropology in which the former discipline had focused upon 'advanced societies' and anthropology had monopoly over 'the Rest of the World'. But by deploying anthropology to examine South Asians in Britain without acknowledgement of political articulation and organisation, a refashioned othering 'at home' marks the BrAsian presence out as a scandalous interruption of the 'Rest' within the West. This BrAsian interruption then opens up the possibility of constant refrains about the fundamental illegitimacy of settlement as a threat to the coherence of the nation—exactly one of the key areas of BrAsian organisational work. Sadly, this was not of interest to anthropology, as old school exoticism was imported whole from the colonial theatre. Sasha Josephides faults the two early anthropological studies of the pre-1970s Indian Workers Association, identified in her 1991 essay (the reference is to Desai, 1963 and John, 1969), with a methodological individualism derived from Frederick Bailey's

Stratagems and Spoils (1969), Mayer's 'action sets' (1966) and models of social organisation approaches made popular by Fredrik Barth (1966). In offering an alternative to these approaches (Josephides, 1991: 253), the possibility of a more adequate comprehension of the story of the IWA was promised. Unfortunately this beginning was not developed and the culturalist-ethnicist hegemony prevailed in anthropological work 'at home'. Gerd Bauman is one of the few (tenured) anthropologists writing in the 1990s to mention the IWA at all—in his study of Southall entitled *Contesting Culture* (1996)—yet even here the focus is on fairly old school anthropological notions of community and negotiation. There does seem to be an injunction against taking any contemporary tone in analysis of the BrAsian contribution to Britain.

Asian workers 'at home' have been organised, culturally and politically, and have provided a critique of anthropological categorisation themselves by focusing on political and organisational issues. It is salutary to find that the communist or Marxist inspired authors and activists that should be discussed here were able to provide a critique of Eurocentric models of social science writing long before such critiques—under the guise of reflexive anxiety and postmodern doubt—became common rhetoric within the social sciences as taught in white institutions. The need to challenge slavish mimicry of received versions of positivist and quantitative sociology, or exoticist and primitivist anthropology, has been nurtured amongst militant organisations much more than can be said of the credentialist teaching factories we call universities. A watchful vigilance against the pitfalls of complicity in surveillance knowledge production and the seductions of token-incorporation should not mean non-participation in those still dominant institutions—only that such participation is best thought of, and practised, first as critical and oppositional. In contradistinction to a culture of liberal alibi, the non-token stance is not to enact left posturing within the colleges, but to institute pathways and openings for further critical gains that refuse to replicate voyeuristic scholarship—collaborative critical production projects, cross-sectoral alliances, campaign-based resourcing and knowledge production is far more useful than merely interpreting the world according to hitherto existing structures. How to avoid voyeuristic replication of the anthro-gaze? Place South Asians in the subject, not the object, position in your research. How does the world look if seen from the position of British South Asians, and what can we learn from that? Not how does the white world look when invaded by exotic-fanatic, other worldly, inscrutable ethnics. Is it possible to re-orient (or dis-Orient) minds away from the demographic ethnographic and voyeuristic position and rethink the history of the metropolis as made by outsiders with an investment in coming inside without forgetting the co-constitutive origins of here and there, not just 'there'.

The unsung heroes of the Workers Movement and the communist tradition in Britain are many; more than the deployment of numerous sociologists and oral historians could possibly document in present circumstances. There are of course several high profile and well known names to be acknowledged—including Saklatvala, Palme Dutt and Sivanandan himself—but the naming of names of course should not be offered without due recognition that without considerable support from anonymous comrades, tireless mill and factory worker-organisers, fellow travellers and family there could be no communist movement at all.[2]

Not every South Asian migrant to Britain joined the communist party or some other left group, but the history of such struggles is known amongst the South Asian communities today and is 'imbibed as if with mothers milk' ('Informant A', interview with author). How could anthropologists miss it? Largely because they have focused their gaze upon relatively unformed sectors of the population—quite often school children—and read off culture from small survey samples. This can be seen for example in Mary Gillespie's ethnographic study of school kids watching television in Southall (Hutnyk, 1996) and can be found again in Kathleen Hall's study of Sikhs in Leeds—*Lives in Translation: Sikh Youth as British Citizens*—neither work managing to mention organised left activity, or organised anti-racism even as they discuss liberal stances on that theme.[3] Much like Gillespie, Hall deploys the terminology of 'second generation' and 'caught between two cultures' on the first pages

2 This is possibly the most convenient place to admit I have a personal investment here. The argument that it was as stokers on British Merchant Navy ships that Pakistanis, specifically Mirpuris, first initiated chain migration to Britain (Saifullah Khan, 1977; Ballard, 1987: 24; Kalra, 2000a: 63) is interesting to me particularly as my grandfather Thomas Moat Tate was himself a stoker in that same navy during the second imperialist war and often told stories of the camaraderie, and racism, among those below decks. Not wanting to buy into the argument that (Azad) Kashmiri migration begins with the stokers leaving their ships to work in munitions factories (the overall significance of which Kalra disputes as a mythic foundation for the 'chain migration' thesis), I nonetheless hope to support this critique by publishing my grandfather's memoirs one day (imperialist history resides in most closets, none can deny it).

3 Written with a wider brief, yet in no significant way does the anthropological approach of K. Hall advance on that of Gillespie, published eight years earlier. The school setting, the camaraderie via knowing transgression, the selective interviews and the realist ethnographic convention remains pretty much the same. Hall seems slightly more alert to issues of power, and is unduly obsessed with turbans, but there is not much to distinguish her study from the many other anthropological reports on the children of diaspora in that it does little to address the redistributive justice so much needed and so often articulated by those Asian organisations that the likes of Gillespie and Hall choose to ignore. At least Hall can recognise some 'campaign' activity in her (brief) discussion of the efforts to get Punjabi language classes on to the curriculum at her school. But we have to ask just what it is that makes anthropologists so keen to generalise on culture from the basis of a handful of interviews with school-aged teenagers—why pick on the kids? Clearly authority plays its part.

of her study of Sikhs in Britain. By 'second generation' might we hear a kind of insistence that the people under investigation (all of them) are forever named as arrivees from elsewhere? Though approving of Homi Bhabha's notion of third space and seeing hybridity as the place where migrant people (?) live their lives through acts of cultural translation, Hall also, briefly, approves Kaur and Kalra's notion of Transl-asia (K. Hall, 2002: 5, 142; Kaur and Kalra, 1996), but perhaps misses the ironic and critical dimension to that intervention. Clearly for Kaur and Kalra Transl-asia does not equal third space hybridity, but also explicitly underlines the political and debated context of varied responses to these translated discussions and their context in multi-racist Britain.[4] In studies like this, the characterisation of people who 'arrived' in Britain some thirty years before publication as either school children or 'second generation' is not merely empirical in its consequences—as a study of Sikhs, or even Sikh youth, it leaves much aside. Perhaps because the fieldwork was conducted so long before publication (it is, she says, a study marked by Thatcherism), the attached afterword mention of racial violence in Oldham and Bradford in the summer of 2001 (K. Hall, 2002: 204) adds little to counter the impression in the main text that white anthropologists working on South Asians 'at home' see them primarily as visitors 'over here'. Certainly only a few historical studies of organised left Asians are available (and it is because Hall, Werbner, Gillespie are not interested in the left that these are most often biographies of great leaders written by academic fellow travellers without ethnographic skills, though the survey of Visram is of impressive scope [Visram, 2002]). In most cases, however, any notion of Asian left organisation is excluded or actively avoided (fear of restless natives perhaps?). It is particularly astonishing that Hall manages an entire book on Sikhs in Britain without mention of the IWA—and though it would not be enough to simply correct the record with the history of great names of that organisation, studies that are no longer beholden to uncritical tropes of anthropology would actually be a start. It might be a chance to move beyond the pathologies of myopic interpretation and comprehension; the point would be to change the ways ethnography represents.

There are a few BrAsian writers who escape the apparent anthropological agreement to avoid examination of everyday political associations. As already mentioned, there were and are vast differences among South Asians in terms of participation in organised political groupings, just as there is in the population in general. Kalra shows that there has been considerable union and other organisation of South Asian labour from

4 Kalra's essay in TCS (2000b) on non-translation makes this political aspect even more pertinent. All the same, Hall's appreciation of the work of the Transl-asia group is welcome.

the earliest days of settlement in Britain (Kalra, 2000a: 122). Although participation by black workers in the workplace union organisations was substantial, 'their incorporation into the wider union movement was not' (Kalra, 2000a: 117). It is certainly the case that the majority of workers only come in contact with their unions when some issue particular to their own employment necessitates representation, but this too reflects the general case. What accounts for the disarticulation of BrAsian unionisation in particular with the wider union movement in general if not racism? This is yet another parallel that obscures history and fails to normalise understandings in an exotico-fanatic vein. At any rate workplace union participation is not to be ignored as it is in the ethnographic literature.

The exposure of the anthropological and sociological construction of South Asian migrant workers' malleability, acquiescence and compliance, of their putting up 'with unattractive work if it is temporary and they have an alternative life to return to' (Kalra, 2000a: 20) is well taken. What this construction does is deflect scholarly attention away from the varied ways in which BrAsian agency and political engagement—in the workplace, in terms of class, race and indeed culture—does manifest itself and is not convincingly rejected with an anthropological *laissez-faire* view where 'black workers are assumed to lack the cultural and political resources with which to adapt to the customs of the industrial workforce' (Kalra, 2000a: 20).

This is reinforced by Kalra's analysis of the 'myth of return' thesis (2000a: 19) which has it that South Asian workers in Britain retained an ever less likely ideology of wanting to return to their countries of origin. Proponents of this line of explanation saw migrants as having limited political engagement because they saw themselves as resident in a 'host' country (Kalra, 2000a: 19; Anwar, 1979). Kalra finds examples in Rose (1969) and again repeated twenty years later in Werbner (1990a: 7). The inference that should be drawn, however, is not that migrants were politically conservative. The monolithic 'myth of return', like its later counterpart the 'second generation' problem, insists that a migrant is a migrant is a migrant—and by implication really belongs elsewhere, overseas, over there in their proper home. Revealingly, as Kalra's usage demonstrates, the terminology of ethnicist scholarship insists on migration, not settlement. An anthropology predestined to insist on this myth is not far from the more explicit racism of the 'Paki go home' politics of the National Front and BNP.

Who then were the South Asians who not only did not 'go home' but who stayed 'here' because the British were 'there' and who refused to fall into the trap of ignoring the co-constitution of here and there as a factor in the political, cultural and economic circumstances of contemporary Britain? These were the people who organised politically as South

Asians and as communists in trades unions, in anti-racist groups and in party formations. There is much work that could be done by a reconfigured anthropology on these matters. It is only an indicative survey, a kind of initial listing or a first register of issues for examination that will be attempted here—the names mentioned are not exhaustive and offer only a kind of red interlude and reminder. As already mentioned, the list of the great and the good as found in published biography are never the full story. I would argue for a wider range of studies that would pay different kinds of attention to political organisation, and would do so in a variety of ways. There will be opportunity later to set out the research programme for a wider appreciation.

SKETCHES

Shapurji Saklatvala was first elected to the British parliament in 1922, standing as member of the Labour Party though never secretive about being a communist. Though he was a nephew of the Tata business empire, he married Sally Marsh in Oldham, after being sent to England in 1905 and became a friend of Sylvia Pankhurst. By 1907 he was a member of the Marxist group the Social Democratic Foundation—a forerunner of the Communist Party of Great Britain, the CPGB (Wadsworth, 1998: 23–4)—and sought a position in representative politics in Battersea. The Labour Party of course had reservations about endorsing someone associated with the Communist Party, but sanctioned his candidature on condition that he accept the Labour whip and constitution—'the first and only time the Labour Part endorsed a Communist Party member for a parliamentary seat' (Wadsworth, 1998: 42). In 1924 the Labour Party had taken a decision to expel communists from their party and Saklatvala then won his seat running as a communist. He was imprisoned in 1926 for sedition, at the time of the general strike. As the Labour Party excluded him, the Tories chanted 'send him back to India' as well as 'send him back to Moscow'. Saklatvala indeed departed for a successful tour of India, greeted by wellwishers wherever he spoke as a fighter against the imperialist power. Interestingly he was criticised by the founder of the Indian Communist Party, M.N. Roy, for hanging about with Gandhi during the visit. Saklatvala's support, though, was never uncritical: indeed, he questioned the Mahatma's promotion of *khaddar* in terms that stressed the importance of egalitarian workers' organisation, at one public meeting stressing that the jute workers in Dundee had to realise the urgent need 'of making the Bengal jute workers as well as the Bengal jute growers, a part and parcel of the British Jute Workers' Federation, demanding a six hour day and £5 a week minimum wages, whether the factory be in Dundee or Calcutta' (Wadsworth, 1998: 55). This position of proletarian internationalism clearly goes an organisational step further than Gandhi's photo opportunity with Oldham's mill workers in the 1930s. Amusingly, in a letter to Gandhi, Saklatvala made the point that it seemed contradictory to encourage people in spinning, so as to make more clothes, at the same time as giving the example of wearing less and less himself. Saklatvala's visits to India were curtailed when the Government revoked his passport, with the Secretary of State for India, William Wedgwood Benn (father of Tony Benn), confirming the ban in 1929 in what has come to be known as 'ghastly imperialist mode' (Wadsworth, 1998: 68–70). Saklatvala's call for the CPGB to organise at the ports among Asian seamen was ignored in much the same way as the white left today has failed to take up the cause of asylum seekers and refugees. Yet his influence upon rank and file cadre was immense. Visram reports that Bengali workers celebrated Saklatvala Day in 1937 and British communists fought in the Saklatvala Battalion in The Spanish Civil War (Visram, 2002: 319). When Saklatvala died, George Padmore paid him tribute, along with Nehru and Palme Dutt.

Rajani Palme Dutt, first cousin of the Swedish Prime Minister Olaf Palme, via his mother Anne, was born in 1896 at Cambridge. Rajani and his bother Clemens were both involved in left-wing politics at university, with Rajani being expelled from Oxford in 1917 for refusing conscription into the army—though he did eventually take out a first class degree. He unsuccessfully ran in Birmingham as a communist for the parliament in 1945 and in 1950. Palme Dutt started the CPGB's theoretical journal 'Labour Monthly' in 1921, editing it for more than fifty years, with two years—1936–8—as editor of 'The Daily Worker' and more than forty years on the Central Committee. He died in 1974.

As it was for Palme Dutt and Saklatvala in the 1920s, it remains important today to make the connection between anti-colonialism and the struggle for emancipation 'at home'. Imperialism overseas is co-constituted with inequalities in the domestic sphere. The one bound up with the other, neither resolvable alone. Palme Dutt opposed the First World War as 'an imperialist abomination' (Callaghan, 1993: 14), and this at a time when an anti-war voice would have had even less support than today. Palme Dutt led the way, though many did not realise how much it was in their interests to follow.

Along with Saklatvala, Palme Dutt insisted that the leadership of Lenin was important because the old Bolshevik had made imperialism a key focus of revolutionary struggle. The Comintern was the vehicle of an organised anti-colonialism. It is important not to forget how much this meant for people in India, Malaya, Indonesia, China and other subjugated colonies, and also how it resonated with the diverse British working class, and how such alliance and interest in internationalism continues today (albeit usually depoliticised under studies of cultural diasporas).

Udham Singh: When arrested for shooting dead former Amritsar

Governor Michael O'Dwyer in 1940 Udham Singh gave his name as Mohamad Singh Azad, signifying a Muslim-Sikh alliance for freedom (Visram, 2002: 272)—his name was recently celebrated in song by Asian Dub Foundation on their album R.A.F.I. (1998, see Hutnyk, 2000) though it is unusual to hear the name mentioned in British anthropology or sociology (but see Clark, 1975; Kalra, 2000b).

These, however, are the old names, and there are many that remain unacknowledged, and it is the task of historians and commentators to write these stories without reaching out to exoticist categories. The tale of the Southall Indian Workers Association, for example, is not only its relation to Indian based political groupings but also its relations to the British communist tradition and issues of separate or joint organisation. Should black organisations organise separately from the white left given the historical propensity of that left—mostly in its Trotskyite variants—to see black organisations as areas for recruitment and for 'parachuting in' to do publicity for their own campaigns? What are the requisite organisational forms that can fight the co-constituted violence of imperialism there and racism here, based as it is on the modern fantasy of the nation state as sole arbiter of population and border control for the purposes of capitalist production?[5] Alongside such questions, there might be room for research investigation of the issues raised by Tariq Mehmood in his forthcoming novel that would require interrogation of police actions tracking BrAsian activists in Bradford and other Northern towns. The relation of BrAsian organisations and various associated activisms to the reformist populism of the Labour Party, including its 'Black Sections', deserves continued attention, as does the activity of various anti-deportation campaigns, asylum-seeker support, immigration group work in general and community self-defence organisation (see *Dis-Orienting Rhythms* for some discussion of this last theme in particular, Sharma *et al.*, 1996).

Would ethnographic and documentary history not find fitting subjects in the formation of the Black People's Alliance and responses to Enoch Powell's 'rivers of blood' speech? The participation of BrAsian activists in the Vietnam Solidarity Campaign and other anti-imperialism struggles as well as campaigns against apartheid in South Africa remain to be written. In struggles like these people were 'not fighting for culture', in Sivanandan's phrase, and not likely to sell out to the management of racism inaugurated in the wake of the Scarman Report—which was at least engaged with to some degree by the early Birmingham Cultural Studies School (in anticipation of this management, see Hall *et al.*, 1978). It is a matter of record, however, that cultural studies in general has abandoned

5 On the primary role of the nation state here, see Angela Mitropoulos who argues that the 'refugee problem … [is] … the greatest challenge to the principle role of the nation state: the "right" of nation states (whether as one nation or "united" nations) to allocate, regulate and control bodies for the purposes of capitalist production' (Mitropoulos, 2001).

this more political terrain, and the morphing of anthropology with that discipline is part of the problem. Scholarship becomes popular in inverse proportion to its irritant charge and the establishment of anthropology at home and a cross-disciplinary take up of a bland ethnicist ethnography is symptomatic. It cannot just be left to magazines like *Lalkar*, newspaper of the IWA (GB), and *Spark*, of the Youth Wing of the Socialist Labour Party, to make the agitational moves.

Sivanandan himself offers a sketch of part of this missing history in his essay 'From Resistance to Rebellion', but doing history always takes second place to activist engagement. Siva was a member of the Black Unity and Freedom Party. As editor—of *Race and Class*—organiser-director—of the IRR—campaigning public speaker and accomplished novelist he spent many years advising and involved with anti-racist and working-class struggles—the special issue (of *Race and Class*) full of tributes to his work attests to this. It was probably not an unusual occurrence, then, when Sivanandan abandoned his prepared speech to launch an attack on a fellow panellist at a conference marking the fiftieth anniversary of the 6th Pan African Congress meeting in Manchester, the indication to many in the audience that political struggle remained more important than either personality or the polite protocols of scholarly decorum. It was to the palpable relief of activists in the audience that Siva railed against hapless anthropological-cum-exoticist assumptions in treatment of the history of pan-Africanism as a culturalist curio rather than a *political* legacy.

Like Saklatvala, Sivanandan's politics were never specific to BrAsian interests, but without departing from those interests he also took up the interests of the entirety of humanity and so entered into debates on themes as diverse as technological change and the 'silicon age' in the capitalist production process; the 'hokum' of New Times thinking in the reinvention of the British Labour Party (as 'Thatcherism in drag'); on South Africa; teaching; and globalisation, as well as self-defence work; racism; Sri Lanka and imperialism.

The issues are important and resonate today. The themes need to be contextualised not in terms of ethnic organisation as such, but related to the narrative of changes to labour force/class composition and imperialist restructuring after so called globalisation (sweatshops, off-shore labour, mill closures, service sector and the class struggle). Unexhausted and inexhaustible histories remain to be documented and to inspire. Tales for that scene round the kitchen table, tales for the summer afternoon. The work to be done builds communities of resistance with memories. The simple and undeniably normal fact that South Asians of all stripes have been involved in active left activity in Britain was and remains a key to the politics of this country. Whether it be the current conjuncture and the mobilisation against the war on Iraq and the anti-terror persecutions of the paranoid Blair government, or the anti-racist movements of the 1970s and the 1990s, in struggles around workplace conditions and exploitation of cheap labour (Grunwick, Hillingdon), or other examples, South Asians can be counted. In each of these cases and more, without romanticising, BrAsian engagement in politics in Britain has as often as not taken a simultaneously anti-racist and anti-colonialist cross-sectoral orientation reaching back even to core participation in the Communist Party of Great Britain of Palme Dutt, and in the Comintern by Dutt and M.N. Roy, and even in the beginnings of anti-colonialism in general, and working-class politics in particular, Menon, Saklatvala and so many others.

Faced with racist and class confrontation every day, situated in contexts of prejudicial attack and the struggles, and contradictions, of class mobility, there is a diverse range of political awareness to be tapped among the BrAsian community that seems less readily accessible for white youth unless they retain a specifically 'working-class' formation. Even then this can often take reactionary form in any community. The trouble with the available documentation on BrAsian experience in Britain is that those making such documentation have not been interested in political and organised responses to racism so much as a kind of liberal celebration of their own anti-racist credentials—it must be mentioned—which then transmutes and transforms Asian agency to the machineries of anthropological categorisation.

The studies available of contemporary British Asians—Werbner *et al.*—hardly ever mention the communist contribution to the history of struggles against racism, or other modes of oppression in capitalist Britain, in the terms articulated by those involved in such struggles. Baumann sometimes does, Gillespie and Hall not at all. Admittedly, the available biographical histories of the communist left may sometimes be more alert, but they are always couched in the context of great names. The text of Visram's *Asians in Britain* is an exception, but it stops far too early. Reconstructed ethnographers need now be deployed.

LOOKING FORWARD: 'A HOMELESS ANTHROPOLOGY'

The question to ask might be not what are these Asian settlers doing, but, knowing something of the struggles for which they devoted their lives, can this knowledge, vouchsafed to scholars, commentators, critics, be transmuted into learning and motivation, or must it add merely to the edification of inmates of the administered bland academia-industrial-infotainment complex? There is an imperative that is more important than prestige and sales, and that is not to become apologists by imitation, capitulating to the paradigms and perspectives of imperialist social science like loyal coolies or the comprador class of old.

Against a surveillance knowledge production on Asians, there is already a critique built into working-class history and twisting it towards identity politics or ethnicist ends does a disservice. That this ethnicist anthropology is taught for all intents and purposes in unchanged (Malinowskian) form to the increasing numbers of black students entering the universities is as ironic as it is perverse. To note the limited number of black graduates that continue into the teaching profession at research level is to recognise a grand disparity and suggests provocative questions: for example, would it be possible to imagine a black British anthropology?[6] It would not be a surprise to find the only condition for such an anthropology to thrive would be if it reproduced the platitudes and certitudes of an imperial anthropology of the Rest, now with 'coloured' practitioners, alongside the usual 'at home' exoticism of minority and 'second generation' migrant surveillance.

The cultivation of what Sivanandan once called 'a class of collaborators' who would be useful in 'the political control of a rebellious "second generation"' (Sivanandan, 1982: 101) is not obviously countered by simple celebration of the commitment and contribution of South Asian comrades in Britain. Obviously there are interests vested in such a 'class' on the part of anthropologists and on the part of 'identity politicians', and the promotion of such positions cannot remain innocently unremarked. It is, however, the case that if these narratives are not set out as either role models or nostalgia, they might possibly serve to indicate the diversity and complexity of BrAsian experience in Britain, as elsewhere. The story might also show how the reductive type-casting so beloved of 'identity politics', as with collaboration and even complicity with the

6 A test to gauge the elimination of racism from British anthropology might be to ask this hypothetical and fantasy question: What if, in just one department anywhere in the system, or a newly formed department, exactly no Anglo-Saxon, white, anthropologists were involved in any way with the teaching of the discipline, yet all the tasks of teaching anthropology were performed by fully accredited and qualified British anthropologists, i.e., by black or Asian British anthropologists? Can such a scenario be imagined and would this department still be considered to teach 'British' social anthropology? Would it be considered a British department? People will dismiss this as impossible, impracticable and unworkable—they might say there is not the staff, no new departments are planned, it would be a ghetto, it would cause 'imbalances', separatism etc. But the abstract absurdity of even suggesting a black anthropology department indicates that white supremacy prevails as normalcy, as a never challenged standard and essential core. Race is the criteria for ensuring a 'proper' representation among the teaching staff—which is to say, race is used as criteria for exclusion of at least one possibility—an all black, all British department—and at best a tolerant tokenistic mix might be approved. Why would it be so unimaginable to appoint ten black Britons to one anthropology department in Britain? For those who think critically about knowledge and politics, the impossibility of a black anthropology means only that the entire system, disciplinary forms and protocols, appointments, teaching programmes and curricula must be done away with—anything less maintains an unexamined white supremacy that will never relinquish its presumptuous right to rule.

avowed enemy racist stereotyping, does not match how things are for those who look closely and with eyes open.

Sivanandan was among the first to recognise that the personalised politics of identity was dangerous in that this identity politics can sometimes morph into an apolitical 'postcolonialism' in the metropolitan centres and remain wilfully ignorant of politics on the other side of the international division of labour. Gayatri Spivak (1999) also usefully targets the ways in which arrivee settlers cloak themselves in the comforts of an accommodationist migrancy or multiculturalism, making the 'postcolonial' a problematic category. Who benefits here? What is served by an erudition that remains in the comfort in the élite salon? As Brennen points out, a radicalism of belief survives, though those radicals of the activist left are more often found 'hibernating in academia' (Brennan, 1999: 26) and especially in anthropology and in cultural studies: that place which Gargi Bhattacharyya calls one of the 'most well-meaning sections of higher education' (Bhattacharyya, 1998: 56). From here, there is no guarantee that the deployment of fieldworkers to document the activities of the masses of South Asians involved in political work would necessarily mean this work was immune from the publishing industry and corresponding tenure system that thrives on making product, not politics. Kalra refers to 'a bludgeoning of literature about Muslims in Britain' that has emerged in academia since 1990 (Kalra, 2000a: 196). This onslaught gained sales, if not spectacular impetus, in the post September 11 book market as publishers fell over themselves to supply shelves with any back title that mentioned Islam or Afghanistan. The quality of this work is of course mixed; the purpose for which it is now read is often different to that with which it was written. In this context the problem with anthropological approaches to cultural groups in Britain is much the same as the problem of white left approaches—a homogenising project of knowing that ignores agency and ignores wider geo-political implications. Here the Black and White Unite and Fight slogan is important so long as it is not merely a slogan that substitutes for critical analysis—as Sivanandan had pointed out with the 'over here over there' couplet. To market publications that are readily open to be read as 'ethnic' or 'identity' documentary reportage is little different from the exoticist-fanatisist routines of the tabloid press.

The production of knowledge of BrAsian popular culture in Britain should no longer be driven by antiquated anthropological concerns that recycle metaphors of caste, tribe and village to account for South Asian settlers in a so-called 'advanced' capitalist society. The old mission of an anthropology at home is now forever obsolete. Those who maintain its ghost are orientalism's latter-day profiteers, the comprador class and its calculating employers, working in the teaching factory, replicating their own system themselves. In contradistinction to this, it might be plausible to write the story of BrAsian political engagement in Britain in a different way. To collect moments of BrAsian popular culture in Britain in a more radical register—one that did not minimise agency in favour of categories (from Gluckman, Bailey *et al.*)—to hold together the multiple locations of diaspora without imposing an origin-ist or anthro-exoticist privilege to geographical South Asia itself. Along the way to link up a politics that made more than historical niceties out of a history of struggle. The 'subcontinent' is involved, but it is not by any means always the key geographical or political, or even cultural, co-ordinate to be considered. Communist histories may be co-constituted in multiple ways—the project to realise these histories remains to be done. This text schematises such a project, which continues yet to begin.

DRUGS

Noreen Sheikh-Latif

Evidence surrounding the deprivation, discrimination and economic disadvantage of black and minority ethnic (BME) people is overwhelming (SEU, 1998), with BME groups featuring disproportionately in figures of unemployment (e.g. CRE, 1995), poverty (e.g. Jones, 1996) and the criminal justice arena (e.g. Home Office, 1998), thus positioning young people from BME groups at risk of problematic drug use (Patel and Wibberley, 2002). However, both general population surveys (Leitner *et al.*, 1993; Ramsey and Spiller, 1997) and school-based surveys (Parker *et al.*, 1995) suggest respondents from BME communities, in particular BrAsians, are less likely than their white counterparts to use illicit substances, which has subsequently been interpreted as drug use occurs less frequently amongst BME communities.

Despite this, over the last fifteen years a growing body of local evidence indicates that drug use amongst BME communities does exist and is increasing. Indeed, the inclusion of heroin and crack cocaine in the repertoires of some black and minority drug users has been documented since 1993. Studies since the early 1990s have also revealed: young BrAsian women using drugs (Gilman, 1993); drug service providers and carers becoming increasingly worried about younger BrAsians using heroin, steroids and cannabis (Gooden, 1999); new cases presenting for treatment in the Regional Drug Misuse Database for Anglia and Oxford 1997/8 being mostly BrAsian (Sheikh *et al.*, 2001); and in Manchester a senior community development worker stating 'five or ten years ago I used to say it [drug use] was a white man's problem.... Asians are not involved. [I was] absolutely wrong.' (Patel *et al.*, 1998: 14).

In Tower Hamlets Carey (2000) reported heroin as the drug of choice amongst Bangladeshi youths in the borough, and one drug agency stated that 'five years ago Bengalis would have accounted for approximately 10 per cent of the client base, now they are over 40 per cent and this is expected to rise,' and that Bengali clients were 'considerably younger' than others (Patel *et al.*, 2001: 16).

Young BrAsian men, in particular Pakistani and Bengali, are also seen to be at particular risk of becoming involved in dealing, with local knowledge suggesting they have close links to cheap sources of heroin (Sheikh *et al.*, 2002). Furthermore, many 14–15 year olds have been found to be involved in drug distribution as 'runners'. In areas characterised by poverty the financial incentives are very appealing, not only to the dealers, but also to their families, who may ignore the issues surrounding drug use because of the advantages of the extra income. Such cases can result in denial—by drug users and their families—that drug use is occurring in their homes (Sheikh *et al.*, 2001; Sheikh *et al.*, 2002).

Such a situation leads to a certain racialisation of drugs, with specific drugs associated with specific ethnic groups: black African-Caribbean communities with crack and cannabis; and BrAsians with the supply of heroin. These suggested correlations have led to conflict with the police, for example, 'stop and search' powers resulting in a significant number of young black people being stopped by the police because of their colour (Murji, 1994).

Patel (1997) also points out that although there has been a steady increase in research into substance use by black and minority ethnic communities, there has nevertheless been a shortage of sophisticated analysis. This has often lead to replicated studies with little result or impact on service delivery. This is reflected in the comments of communities, and young people in particular, who feel that little action has been taken despite recurrent 'research' about their own and their peers' drug use (Sheikh *et al.*, 2001).

(IM)POSSIBLE INTERSECTIONS

RELIGION, (POST-)COLONIAL SUBJECTIVITY AND THE IDEOLOGY OF MULTICULTURALISM

Arvind Mandair

A certain repetition of the colonial event seems to haunt the very manner in which BrAsians have attempted to engage the political present. This repetition can be visualised in terms of an aporia: on the one hand the possibility of refiguring their subjectivity, and on the other the impossibility of avoiding objectification of their subjective experience. It is the seemingly inevitable and reductive nature of this—the reduction of experience to subject-object, Self-Other relations, indeed the automatic process of othering—that constitutes this repetition of the colonial event. This chapter explores the possibility of forging connections between the design of a past imperialism with its repetition in the lives of postcolonial peoples today. Specifically the aim is to trace the circuit of repetition to the nexus of ideas feeding the main site where the subjectivity of diasporic South Asians is formed, namely the site where religious tradition is retrieved and reproduced, projected and introjected. Based on the assumption that subjectivity is founded on the ability to respond, response-ability as both the condition for response and the obligation to respond, this chapter will pursue an oblique and often impossible engagement between several discourses not usually thought to be connected: (i) the theorisation of religion and 'world religions' in relation to the specialist discipline of Indology; (ii) the secular anti-imperialist criticism inspired by Edward Said, particularly as it impinges on modern South Asian studies; (iii) the study of the relationship between the religious reform movements and the formation of the colonial subject in nineteenth-century South Asia; (iv) the discourse of multiculturalism in Britain today and its relationship to postcolonial engagement through the politicisation of religious traditions; and (v) underpinning all of the above, the continuing ideological influence of G.W.F. Hegel, a philosopher whose presence was thought to have been safely exorcised by postcolonial writers.

Far from being accidental the juxtaposition of these seemingly disparate themes points to their mutual imbrication in colonial and contemporary South Asian experience. More important, it focuses attention on religion as the principal driving force behind the circuit of repetition. Despite the predictions of secular modernity, recent years have witnessed a resounding global 'return of religion' from the periphery to the centre of debates on the future of democracy, multiculturalism and globalisation. The redefining of politics in South Asia in terms of pan-continental religious traditions is a good example of this return. Less obvious, but in perfect consonance with this development, is the effort expended by South Asian immigrants and settlers in Britain to reproduce their religious traditions in a manner that does not necessarily conform to the ideological demands of contemporary multiculturalism.

The latter scenario is highlighted by Talal Asad in his perceptive article 'Multiculturalism and British Identity in the Wake of the Rushdie Affair'. In his polemic response to the hysteria of British liberal intellectual élites over the political mobilisation by British Muslims to get *The Satanic Verses* banned, Asad identifies the insidious tactics of institutionalised and interventionist power respectively at work in the liberal/conservative and radical left notions of multiculturalism. For Asad the real dilemma for BrAsian immigrants in Britain was how to defend, develop and elaborate the collective historical difference exemplified by their religious traditions, but under the proviso that the politicisation of religious traditions has no place within the cultural hegemony that has defined British identity over the last century. Although Asad is perfectly correct in emphasising the reproduction of religious tradition as a site of postcolonial contestation, an impression given, however unintentionally, is that 'religion' and religious tradition is conceptualised as something that both is universally translatable and has strictly defined boundaries. While evidence suggests this is indeed the case (in addition to the seemingly straightforward case of Islam and British Muslims, one has only to cite the revival or return of religious nationalisms—Hindu, Sikh, Muslim—in India and the diaspora, or the seeming transparency of the relationship between religion and identity in the enunciations 'I am Hindu', 'I am Muslim', 'I am Sikh', to show how empirically unassailable this position is), there is a problem in simply assuming the same is true of South Asian traditions. Recent thinking about the *question* of religion, as opposed to assuming ready-made definitions of it, suggests there is a much stronger, and often invisible, connection between religion, enunciation and subjectivity than is normally recognised. Questioning this link may help to expose the insidious bond between the empirical and the imperial—indeed the constant return of the imperial as the empirical.

IMPERIALISM AND THE GLOBALATINISATION OF RELIGION

The enunciation of subjectivity by South Asians in terms of strictly defined religious traditions is now increasingly recognised as mimicking a colonial gesture that was effected through the institution of the Anglo-vernacular mission schools during the nineteenth century. The avowed aim of this gesture was to give back to Indians, as a gift, their original religion(s) and their mother tongues, both of which were perceived to have been lost during their fall from a Golden Age, a fall caused by the mixing of races and religions, with the resultant long history of despotism and foreign domination that continued until the redeeming advent of British rule. Recent research on colonial and pre-colonial India conducted in the form of detailed micro-studies has convincingly shown that the mimicry of the native élites in fact entailed a process of cultural and psychological transformation during their encounter with European imperialism. In brief, the central mechanisms of these transformations included: (i) the imposition of English as the official language of India (King, 1994); (ii) the establishment and proliferation in mid-nineteenth-century North India of a vast network of Anglo-vernacular mission schools (Oberoi, 1994; Dalmia, 1996); (iii) as a result of the previous two, the emergence of boundaried vernacular languages (Urdu, Hindi, Punjabi) corresponding to and organised under strictly religious identities (Muslim, Hindu, Sikh), a religio-linguistic situation that had not existed before and which laid the epistemological foundations for the indigenous élites to enter into discursive relations ('dialogue') with European-style thinking; (iv) the introduction of print-capitalism which brought about the switch in cultural codes from a predominantly oral culture to print culture (Oberoi, 1994); (v) the influence, direct and indirect, of a factor that continues to be underestimated and to which more attention shall be devoted shortly, namely, intellectual developments in early-nineteenth-century Europe and the birth of autonomous disciplines such as Indology, the science of religions, philosophy of religion. A major conclusion of these microstudies, which has been endorsed elsewhere (Balagangadhara, 1994; Derrida, 1998; King, 1999), is that Indian languages do not possess a word for 'religion' as signifying something like a uniform and centralised faith community. Moreover, prior to colonialism what came to be classified as 'proper' Indic religions and languages possessed fluid boundaries with the result that most Indians participated in multiple religious and linguistic identities. In other words the distinct entities known as Hindu-ism or Sikh-ism, which philosophers and phenomenologists have long posited as the natural Other of Western religions and Western thinking, are in fact recent formations.[1]

Although it is not immediately obvious, developments such as these are dependent on a reorientation of thinking about the translatability of

1 The presence of Islam in India is normally cited as the main cause for the subsequent development of Hindu identity. However, it should be noted that Islam did not precipitate the same kind of religious identity (or indeed the formation Hinduism) that the encounter with European thinking gave rise to. The latter can be distinguished by the prevalence of ontotheology (see later in this chapter).

the term 'religion', indeed the history of the translation of this term, or, stated differently, the intrinsic link between religion and translatability as interchangeable concepts. If translatability here implies much more than semantic exchange, referring also to the creation of an economy of colonial desire and the consequent transactions between coloniser and colonised, the question arises as to whether the work of translation as the site of this encounter is as innocent or transparent as continues to be presumed. How did the representation of Indic cultures in terms of religion come to be regarded as natural?

The connection between religion and the principle of translatability has rarely been questioned, especially in the context of Indic traditions. One could even say that the genesis and continuity of Western scholarship's relation to the Other via disciplines such as anthropology, Indology, philosophy of religion, has been based in no small degree on the seemingly incontrovertible fact that non-Western cultures have provided, and continue to provide, reciprocal terms for concepts such as 'God', 'religion', 'faith', 'nation' from their indigenous linguistic and conceptual resources. But *what if* that which South Asians have continued to reciprocate since the colonial event as God/faith/religion has been and continues to be no more and no less than a *response* to the colonial *demand for* religion, and even before that, a demand for correct representation, a demand for identity? To paraphrase Derrida, what if *religio*—and along with it God, faith, theology—remained untranslatable? (Derrida, 1998: 30). What if 'religion is the response. Is it not there, perhaps, that the beginning of a response must be sought? No response, indeed, without a principle of responsibility: one must respond to the other, before the other and for oneself. And no responsibility without a *given word*, a sworn faith without a pledge, without an oath, without some *sacrament* or *ius iurandis*. Before even envisaging the semantic history of testimony, of oaths, of the given word…, we must formally take note of the fact that we are already speaking Latin. This point is made in order to recall that the world today speaks Latin (most often via Anglo-American) when it authorises itself in the *name of religion*' (Derrida, 1998: 36–7).

But what if *religio* remained untranslatable? Derrida's question invokes more than just a deconstruction of the history of colonial translation of South Asian culture under the category 'religion', or idea of history as a reawakening of South Asian culture. Rather the question focuses on the undecidability or incommensurability that exists even before any encounter between coloniser and colonised is overtaken by the demand for representation, the well known mutual conferral of recognition between Self and Other, or by what has long been misrecognised as 'dialogue': the *sponsio* by the coloniser—we promise to save you if you confess the truth about yourself. Who are you? What is your true religion?—and the *re-sponsio* by the colonised—'I am Hindu/Sikh/Muslim etc.' The invocation of untranslatability reveals the context of the colonised not as a ready-made subject, agent or self, but as a subjecti*vity* in the process of being figured out between the *sponsio* and the *re-sponsio*; that is, through the native's ability to inform or answer to a demand for religion. From this viewpoint the notion of untranslatability exposes the degree to which secular postcolonial theorising continues to gravitate around one version or another of the politics of recognition intrinsic to Hegel's master-slave dialectic *even as it contests this very model.*

A good example of this disavowal can be seen in the work of a diverse group of scholars who have appropriated and applied Edward Said's secular anti-imperialist critique to the orientalist imagining of India.[2] At the risk of oversimplifying, a more or less consistent narrative emerges from this group, one which pinpoints the figure of Hegel and specifically Hegel's lecture courses on the Philosophy of History (LPH) as ur-texts in the colonial and neo-colonial constructions of India. The genius of the LPH texts was that while perpetuating the myth of a 'religion obsessed' India, or the idea of a mysticism/transcendental wisdom that is unique to India, they kept India politically and intellectually consigned to this ('un-free') representation and, therefore, outside history. This narrative expresses the hope that once the overtly imperialising tendency of the LPH is dismantled, it may be possible to stem the mechanism that enables the reproduction of orientalism and orientalist constructions of India within academic institutions today. Any movement beyond orientalism must constitute, following Said, a secular anti-imperialist critique, one that would guard against the 'return of religion' or any form of repressed religiosity (Hart, 2000: 152). Though rarely acknowledged, versions of this narrative have since the mid 1980s influenced more than just the discourses that utilise South Asia as an archival resource. They also, inadvertently, provide support for an unspoken political and intellectual alliance between liberal-conservative and radical left views on the ideological limits of multidisciplinarity in the humanities and social sciences and multiculturalism in mainstream politics. Although this narrative has revealed the outer contours of this ideological alliance, its conceptual matrix remains remarkably resistant to exposure because of a dogma that underpins the ideology of multidisciplinarity and multiculturalism. The dogma consists in the idea that critical thinking—or the proper standpoint of the intellectual and activist—is only possible through a historicist overcoming of religion or the religious. While this point is merely implicit in the LPH texts, it is explicitly worked out in Hegel's lesser known *Lectures on the Philosophy of Religion* (LPR), specifically in the transition from the 1824 to the 1827 lectures. In this lecture course Hegel

2 See, for example, Ronald Inden, Tejaswini Niranjana, Gayatri Spivak etc.

can be found attempting to theorise an intellectual relationship between history and religion in the context of an ever-increasing influx of knowledge of non-Western cultures into Europe, but also, significantly as far as this chapter is concerned, in the context of a discussion about the proper place of India, Indology and Indian 'religions' within the emerging discourse of the *Wissenschaft*.

THE UNBEARABLE PROXIMITY OF THE ORIENT: HEGEL, INDOLOGY AND THE SCIENCE OF RELIGIONS

As the indologist Wilhelm Halbfass reminds us, one of the most poignant contributions to the intellectual association between India and Europe was Hegel's reading of, and engagement with, the emerging discipline of Indology (Halbfass, 1988: 84–99). In ways that are not altogether obvious the influence of Hegel's ideas brought about an important though overlooked reversal in the nature of Indology.[3] This reversal has influenced seemingly unrelated events such as, on the one hand the nature of enunciation by native nineteenth-century North Indian élites which gave rise to the kind of constructs we know today as Hindu-*ism* and Sikh-*ism*, and on the other hand the ideology of modern multiculturalism and multidisciplinarity and the terms by which BrAsians have negotiated religious identity and difference. Hegel's role in effecting this reversal is an important example of the continuity between the operation of imperialist discourses in the past with their effects in the present.

3 To quickly illustrate this reversal, the early phase of indological research (pre-1840s), which had its beginnings in the work of William Jones, Charles Wilkins and H.T. Colebrook, posited *Advaita Vedanta* as the central philosophy and theology of Hinduism (Halbfass, 1988; King, 1999). According to this particular representation, which continued to be propagated throughout the nineteenth century by 'indophiles' such as Schelling, Schopenhauer and Max Muller, Hinduism could in essence be considered a philosophy but not a true religion as the term was understood in the West. The nearest thing to 'genuine religion' in India was the mélange of cults and sects based on the worship of chthonic deities. If Hindus had had a true religion it could only have existed in the remote and ancient past, a Golden Age from which the originally Aryan race of Hindus had fallen into their present state through centuries of domination and racial mixing (Dalmia, 1996: 176–210). However, after the 1860s the work of a new generation of indologists—amongst them H.H. Wilson, Albrect Weber, Freidrich Lorinser, Ernest Trumpp, Monier Williams and George Grierson—began to 'discover' what soon came to be regarded as the 'only real religion of the Hindus' or 'monotheistic' *Vaishnava bhakti* (Sharma, 1986; Dalmia, 1996). Not surprisingly this view received intellectual support from orthodox Hindu scholars and publicists, which led during the last two decades of the nineteenth century to the integration of the mélange of *sampradayas* (sects) under the all encompassing political leadership of the *Vaishnava sampradaya* (Dalmia, 1996: 396). As a result *Vaishnava bhakti*, often solely identified with Hindu sectarianism or religious nationalism, has constantly vied for political representation, resulting in the late 1990s in the transformation of the previously secular Indian state into an overtly self-conscious Hindu state (Pandey, 1989; Jaffrelot, 1996; Singh, 2000).

To illustrate this consider the case of what is today called Hinduism. Contrary to conventional wisdom the ideological framework underpinning the two most important articulations of modern Hinduism, namely the monistic *Advaita Vedanta* (or philosophical Hinduism) and monotheistic *Vaishnava bhakti* (devotional or religious Hinduism), have been drawn largely from Western experience. These two articulations of modern Hindu identity should be perceived as the outcome of two very different and competing responses from Hindu colonial élites to the translatability and appropriation of the term 'religion'. For over two centuries the dominant articulation has been a representation of Hinduism centred on *Advaita Vedanta* as the underlying principle of indigenous Indian civilisation, one that encompasses both the idea of religion in general and the diversity of religious sects and cults of which *Vaishnavism* is but one. The influence of this articulation is due to its propagation by a long line of well known Indian reformists, politicians and academics, notably Ram Mohan Roy, Vivekananda, Aurobindo Ghosh, Mohandas Gandhi, Jawaharlal Nehru and Sarvepali Radhakrishnan. In contrast, *Vaishnava bhakti*, the other main articulation of modern Hindu identity, had until quite recently remained politically repressed despite its vast public support base. Previously seen as little more than the driving force behind sectarian nationalism in India, *Vaishnava bhakti* has now come to be recognised as a legitimate expression of the shift from secularism to religion within mainstream Indian politics (Van der Veer, 1994). An analysis of this phenomenon is beyond the scope of this chapter. However, it is safe to assume that what seems to have been consistently overlooked by conventional narratives of modern Hinduism is that the very distinction between these two movements—*Advaita Vedanta* as the central philosophy of Hindu civilisation and therefore inclusive of all religious diversity versus *Vaishnava bhakti* as the 'only real religion of India'—could only have come about after a far reaching reversal in the nature and orientation of the indological enterprise (Sharma, 1986).

What brought about this change in the nature and orientation of Indology? At the risk of being too summarical this reversal occurs at the intersection of a whole series of intellectual debates that were occurring simultaneously during the early nineteenth century including the theorisation of religion, aesthetics and the history of philosophy. Much of this activity which was centred particularly in Germany during the 1790s around two parallel movements. First, what Bernard Reardon describes as the 'intellectual rekindling of Christianity both Protestant and Catholic without parallel since high middle ages' (Perkins, 2000: 357). Second, the growth of national consciousness motivated in particular by a need felt by leading European intellectuals to respond to a proliferating knowledge of oriental religions and cultures particularly as this was presented through its most effective vehicle, the new discipline of Indology (Bernal, 1987; Perkins, 2000). Yet despite its common concern for rethinking Christianity, responses to the 'Oriental Enlightenment' were motivated by opposing desires. On the one hand, exemplified by the responses of Schelling and Schopenhauer, a desire to present a cultural difference or foreignness that is already at the heart of Christian European traditions, a difference that precedes anxieties relating to perceptions of native and foreign, inside and outside.[4] On the other hand, exemplified by the dominant tradition of modern Western philosophy and illustrated most powerfully by Hegel, the desire to see oriental knowledge systematically ordered and controlled. The most effective way to achieve this was to suture any gaps present in the growing databank of knowledge about oriental cultures, thereby keeping the possibility of any harmful influence at a safe distance. The problem was achieving this intellectually and in a way that removed the threat of oriental religions and at the same time the threat of those like Schelling who colluded with such ideas.

Perhaps the best example of this process in Hegel's *oeuvre* can be found in Part II of his posthumously published *Lectures on the Philosophy of Religion* (LPR) which present his most sustained encounter with South Asian religious thought. From a postcolonial point of view, starting with Part II provides an important insight into present dilemmas and a 'natural' point of departure. A close reading of Hegel's key moves in this lecture course reveals three main concerns. First, the 'need' to establish a firm theoretical standard for thinking about religion in general. Second, to use this standard as the basis for bringing the growing diversity of oriental religions into some kind of manageable order. Third, to order them in a way that counters the influence of indophiles such as Schelling in whose philosophy the prevailing definition of God/religion brought the origins of oriental and occidental civilisations unbearably close, such that the dominant vantage point of Euro-Christian identity based on its exclusionary claims to history, reason and metaphysics, not to mention the colonial enterprise itself, would be threatened. To even suggest that true metaphysical thinking could be coeval with the type of thinking possessed by Orientals would render the very source of Western thinking to be impure.[5]

The clearest articulation of Hegel's concern can be seen in the transition from the 1824 to 1827 lecture course and most noticeably in the long discussions about the proper constitution of the first two stages of the dialectic: the stage of primal unity associated with religions of nature

4 It is now increasingly recognised that this kind of response, which has since been caricatured as indomania or as a perversion of Christian thinking, anticipates important aspects of the post-structuralist movement which opens up new avenues of contact between Western and Eastern traditions. (See, for example, Graham Parkes, 1987; 1991.)

5 For a more detailed argument see Mandair, *Religion, Language and Subjectivity: translating cultures between East and West*, Manchester University Press (forthcoming).

exemplified by oriental religions, and the stage of artistic religion exemplified by Graeco-Roman religions (Hegel, 1987: 144–8). For Hegel the need to rationally account for a qualitative difference between these two stages was crucial both in order to justify a cultural boundary between India and Europe, and for any systematic classification of the religions of other nations or races. The entire argument in this section revolves around the problem of beginning. More specifically the problem of identifying the nature of this beginning which is also the 'original condition of mankind' (Hegel, 1987: 147). The dilemma for Hegel was how to classify Indic culture *as* religion and yet keep it outside of history which properly speaking belonged to the West. There were two obstacles here. First, there was an abundance of seemingly compelling evidence relating to the antiquity of Sanskrit as the source of Indo-Aryan languages and race. This evidence, which was backed by the philological authority of Sir William Jones and the philosophical arguments of Schlegel and Schelling amongst others, tended to suggest that Orient and Occident shared the same origin, given which there could be no moral justification either for the colonisation of India or for placing Indian religions outside the pale of history. Secondly—and what in fact stemmed from the purely metaphysical/conceptual definition of religion, which, being grounded on the notion of *pure* movement or the *aufhebung* as the principle not only of historical motion and therefore historic*ism*, but also of the very first impulse whereby spirit definitively extricates itself from nature, the negation of negation, this *pure* movement being at the same time the very definition of religion as such—this moment of emergence must account for history and religion simultaneously: the co-origination of history and religion.

Hegel's resolution to this problem was to implement a move originally formulated in his 1812 *Science of Logic* in which the ontological proof for God's existence, with its implicit assumption of the identity of being and thinking, is made the central criterion for thinking about religion as such and the phenomenal appearance of determinate religions during the course of human history. This allowed Hegel to think *philosophically* about religion in general and *historically* (which means *phenomenologically*) about other religions and thus to classify them based on the degree to which a particular culture was capable of thinking God's existence, its remove from the ontological proof as the ultimate standard for measuring the progress of religion(s) in world history. History could *begin* only when a culture became capable of thinking properly about God.

What emerges in the transition to the 1827 lectures is not simply an improved system for describing other religions and therefore a precursor to the phenomenological method, but a specific device which prefigures the very possibility of phenomenology, namely an ontotheological schema—indeed Hegel's own reworking of ontotheology—which ensures the production of stereotypical versions of Hinduism. With the ontological proof providing the law for thinking about religion—God cannot *not* be thought, therefore God cannot be nothing or thought as nothing—schematisation consists in a prior operation of marking out a visual time chart upon which any culture encountered by the ontological proof is automatically compared and fixed in its proper place. This time chart is of course the history or phenomenology of religions whose primary axis is drawn automatically by the Hegelian narrative itself.

As Gayatri Spivak suggests in her readings of Hegel on the *Srimadbhagavadgita*, 'Hegel places all of history and reality on a diagram. By reading off the diagram the law of motion of history is made visible as the Hegelian morphology is fleshed out' (Spivak, 1999: 39). Spivak rightly suggests that what we have in Hegel's narrative is not an epistemo*logy* i.e. an account of how individual subjects produce religion, but an epistemo*graphy*, a graduated diagram of how knowledge comes into being. Whereas in the West the proof of God's existence provides the ontological law for thinking about God's existence as an exclusion of the nihil, oriental religions by comparison, i.e. by automatically reading off the epistemograph, have not sufficiently evolved to this stage of thinking. As is well known, the LPH marks out a similar time chart as the path of world-historical progress, where the spirit of each nation (*Volksgeist*) embodies the world spirit in a given epoch. But whereas in the LPH the work of ontotheology forms the subtext of Hegel's narrative, the LPR is a more rounded statement in which ontotheology is history and history is ontotheology. Accordingly each epoch on the graduated diagram correlates spatially to a bounded localised configuration. Each configuration is designated as a quasi-cartographical realm. Thus the spatial boundaries of a nation/culture corresponds to its spirituality-cum-historicity. By this logic cultures mired in an existence that remains bound to a particular area can only have a limited life-span on the time-chart of world history. They can only exist today as static, frozen objects, i.e. as phenomena to be known and studied by conceptually more advanced cultures. They become raw material, empirical data that can be fully understood and retrieved by those who possess the proper conceptual tools.

Although it is often overlooked, the ontotheological nature of the Hegelian epistemograph mediated through the two new disciplines of the philosophy of religion and the history of religions, whose essential form Hegel had outlined in the LPR, exerted a theoretical and practical influence with important consequences for the colonial and ongoing postcolonial encounters between India and Europe. For our purposes brief mention will only be made of the two most relevant ones: (a) the reconstitution of Indology in relation the historicised *Religionswissenschaft* programme; (b) related to this, the enunciation and retrieval of 'religious tradition' by the indigenous colonial élites.

The reconstitution of Indology

The second phase of indological research after the 1860s focused mainly on the translation and exegesis of North Indian *bhakti* or devotional texts and traditions by a new generation of indologists trained at institutions such as Tübingen, Göttingen and Berlin where Hegel's ideas continued to set the tone for thinking about religion long after his death. In contradistinction to the previous phase dominated by British indologists, which had found philosophy but no true religion in Hinduism, this 'post-Hegelian' generation of indologists were now able to identify *bhakti* as the 'only true religion of the Hindus' (Sharma, 1986: 83; Dalmia, 1996: 396–9). This important shift in perception was made possible by a new framework for thinking about religions that was both ontotheological (allowing indologists access to Hindu thinking about God's existence) and phenomenological (allowing them to introduce classificatory distinctions, i.e. the correct degree of historical spacing between different phenomena). As a result, at a time when European intellectuals could be accused of being indophiles and thereby perceived as potential threats to the Christian substratum of European civilisation, indologists, many of whom were also active missionaries, could remain committed to a Euro-Christian standpoint, and yet claim scientific status for their work.[6] Consequently, for the first time in Western intellectual history, terms such as monism, monotheism and pantheism became standardised world-historical categories for classifying non-Western cultures. They became formulaic concepts imposing a logic of the stereotype into the activity of thinking about religion (and religions) and its relationship to the concept of culture.

Although the new distinction between pantheism and monotheism overtakes earlier traditions of distinguishing between heathens and Christians, a more important issue arises here than a merely improved procedure for classification. Given that this world-historical categorisation (mono- versus pan-theism) is part of the colonial procedure for managing the multiplicity of new religions that were flooding the knowledge market—one that finds its most comprehensive expression in Hegel's various Berlin lecture courses and will only be refined in Husserl's version of phenomenology—is there not a transparent slippage between the concepts of religion and culture? That is to say, isn't the *mono*- versus *pan*-theism distinction, as it comes to be understood after Hegel, effectively also the basic measure of what counts *most* as culture in the multicultural frame despite its supposedly secular-humanist formulation. If these world-historical categories are simply part and parcel of the evolution of metaphysical thinking, the historico-comparative (or phenom-

6 Many indologists, it should also be remembered, also doubled as Christian missionaries.

enological) enterprise becomes visible as an apparatus that has continued to protect Western secular-humanism either from a cross-fertilisation of ideas or a radical questioning of its ground, both of these possibilities being caricatured as the approach of 'Eastern' nihilism.

In his important work *Capital Times* Eric Alliez points to precisely this problem. Alliez qualifies the notion that historico-comparative phenomenology as a tool for encountering non-Western cultures is a purely modern development reflecting the separation between religion and secularism. Instead, for Alliez, phenomenology must be regarded as a continuation of the tradition of distancing non-Christian otherness inaugurated by St Augustine's treatment of time and consciousness in Book IX of the *Confessions*. As a result the modern sense of phenomenological positioning, as elaborated in the tradition of comparativism that runs from Augustine through Hegel and Husserl to Eliade and Ricoeur, 'in its most dynamic effects must be considered the ultimate process of covering over the Christian conception of the world' (Alliez, 1996: 134). If Alliez is right then the positioning of cultural multiplicity can be conceptually traced to the manner in which Augustinian theology has distanced and installed its non-Christian interlocutors.

Colonial subjectivity and the comparative imaginary

Though rarely acknowledged, the ontotheological schema exerts an influence on the formation of colonial and postcolonial subjectivity. One reason for this is the prevailing dogma in the social sciences about the nature of communication between coloniser and colonised. This dogma dictates that knowledge simply 'diffused' from coloniser to the native élites who then 'internalised' new knowledges (the ontotheological or historico-comparative schema being one example) which duly facilitated a 'dialogue' or fluent exchange of ideas between coloniser and colonised. Clearly this model of dialogue as fluent exchange between two equal ('free') minds is part of a social science ideology of historicism grounded in a hermeneutics of trust and goodwill. It is a hermeneutic that serves the purpose of (re)writing social history and thus requires a subject-object or historico-comparative horizon to be already in place. If a subject or agent of history is not immediately recognisable as such, as in the case of colonised Indians, historicist description can provide agency for the natives. A more realistic model would suggest that the work of internalising the ontotheological schema is itself a subjective technology involving a process of *co-figuration* between the cultures of the colonised (Self) and coloniser (Other).[7]

As a subjective technology the mechanism of co-figuration is automatically comparative, that is, the subject is concretised through an

7 The term 'co-figuration' is borrowed from Naoki Sakai.

availability of terms for comparison (history, religion etc.) in which the familiar and the foreign are rendered representable. But the relation to the Self cannot be determined unless the relation to the Other has beforehand been determined as an interlocutor, a witness who confirms the concretisation of one's own self. Properly speaking, then, prior to any 'politics of recognition' the Self that is capable of responding to the figure of the West as its Other, has to be figured out. Consequently, the ontotheological schema is also practical in that it fashions the shape of desire of those influenced by it. One is seduced into reading one's self-positioning in history as an autonomy, a standpoint from which one perceives oneself to be *equal* to others and at the same time *free* to assert the distinctness of one's culture. But this equality, freedom and the perceived cultural difference is an illusion bought at the cost of conceding reality, authority, freedom to the phantasmal figure of the West. In effect this concession amounts to no more than the self-imposed task of 'confirming and policing the West's own boundaries in the very act of invoking, on behalf of its interlocutors, the promise of global translation of *religio*' (Derrida, 1998: 29–30). Seen from this comparative standpoint, autonomy and cultural difference are intrinsically connected to the logic of the reserve, the museum, or the zoo.

BEYOND RECOGNITION: MULTICULTURALISM(S) AND RELIGIOUS TRADITIONS

Reasons for linking the situation of South Asian settlers in multicultural Britain to the seemingly outdated writings of Hegel should now be clearer. What alarmed occidentalists like Hegel in the early nineteenth century continues to surface in the writings of advocates of contemporary Anglo-American multiculturalism whose ranks include on the one hand liberal intellectuals such as Charles Taylor (who has helped to solidify the view that 'recognition' is central to multiculturalism) and on the other intellectuals of the radical left such as Homi Bhabha. Both share a certain blind spot in regard to the formation of BrAsian postcolonial subjectivity in Britain. South Asian settlers are intimately bound up with the *religious* history of colonisation which includes the translation of indigenous categories and traditions under the rubric of 'religion'. It is this blindness toward religion that Talal Asad exposes in 'Multiculturalism and British Identity'. Recalling Asad's argument, neither the liberalist invocations of the equal dignity of distinct ethno-cultural forms, nor the post-modern fissuring of national identity hybridisation, fusion and creolisations, really threaten the authority of British or Western identity. Both alternatives are in fact 'comfortably accommodated by urban consumer capitalism and by the liberal celebration of British cultural diversity' (Asad, 1993b: 266). Moreover the authority of British/Western identity lies in the ability to impose the religion/secularism divide on others yet to transcend this very distinction, or to reserve the ability to translate between religion and secularism infinitely at will—which is precisely what Hegel was theorising. Asad locates the perceived danger to British identity in the politicisation of religious traditions by BrAsians or in their ability to access liberal law for the purpose of instituting their own deeply held religious traditions. Based on the foregoing argument, however, to go a stage further than simply counter-posing religious tradition to multiculturalism is both possible and necessary. After all, the enunciation by BrAsians of their cultural traditions as specifically *religious* has been the standard political (neo-colonial) response and the standard entry point into the politics of recognition. That is, by asserting the *distinctness* of their religious traditions Sikhs, Muslims, Hindus have automatically conferred recognition and legitimacy on the West (British Identity) as their Other, and in so doing have consistently been accommodated within the multicultural frame. For neo-colonials the inability to question the translatability of *religio* appears to have compromised their cultural politics to retrievals of tradition as repetitions of the same.

But what if *religio* were to remain untranslatable? What if BrAsian settlers were to exercise a definite undecidability in the process of translating received traditions according to a mechanism which automatically inserted them into a global circulation as proper representatives of the many particular and therefore ethnic 'religions'? What if the ideological relay responsible for this automatic translation were to be circumvented? What if they were able to avoid entering into the politics of recognition by dissipating the desire for recognition from the Other, or the need for the Other to legitimate oneself? What if BrAsians were to stop talking about the Other?

The potential of this relatively simple gesture should not be underestimated. Far from paralysing postcolonial BrAsians within a traditionless post-modern limbo, undecidability is positively empowering. Going beyond mere access to liberal enlightenment thought, undecidability can enable postcolonials to retrieve traditions other than identity. It allows a redefining and repetition of tradition(s) but not according to an origin, not as 'religion' but as religion-without-religion that is beyond the overdetermined distinction between church and state, or between religion and secularism. Nevertheless, a useful indicator might be to suggest that this differential repetition of traditions enables the opening of modes of perception, epistemologies, possibilities for thinking and especially different modes of forming and transforming subjectivity that have been repressed under the sign of the nation. Yet this is far from being an exercise in nostalgia, a return to an imagined pre-colonial scenario. The release of differential subjectivities is incommensurate with the production of social and individual desire for installation in an historico-comparative imaginary. It refuses any entry into the arena of 'dialogical' responsivity based on Self-Other rivalry that is intrinsic to the historico-comparative imaginary. Also it does not respond to the seduction of permanence offered by the secular religion or religious secularism of the nation-state. Rather it creatively cultivates impermanence as the ground of social relations.

For occidentalists and multiculturalists alike such possibilities will no doubt evoke deep rooted fears of the return of 'Eastern' nihilisms; the fear of losing control of the devices that have so far prevented the anarchistic scenario of multiple cultures routinely infecting one another with their differences, or more important, from infecting the 'Sources of the Self' (to use the title of Charles Taylor's influential book outlining the moral basis of Western identity). The real threat to authority is that these alternative modes of retrieving tradition are perfectly viable and equally justifiable means of ushering in the promise of modernity as the advent of the new. They contest Western hegemony over the task of thinking about the futures of man and democracy. However, before 'we' fall prey to fears of being contaminated by the varieties of Eastern nihilisms now on the market, it needs to be remembered that such fears are no more than the projection of a particular cultural imaginary. To paraphrase Eric Alliez, perhaps 'we' ought not to look to the East as the source of a contamination which the West has always feared. Perhaps Western Europe is where that very pestilineal disease germinates. Perhaps the trick of this history, which is still our own, was in its wanting the university authorities to perceive the prodrome of a black plague about to ravage Europe (Alliez, 1996: 238).

FOOTBALL

Daniel Burdsey

The early twenty-first century has witnessed a number of significant breakthroughs by BrAsians in a variety of popular cultural and media fields, from pop music to soap opera, yet arguably one of the most unique has been in the sphere of professional football. This occurred during the 2004–5 season when Zesh Rehman of Premier League club Fulham FC became the first BrAsian to play regularly in the highest division of the domestic game. Born in 1983 in Birmingham to Pakistani parents, and having already played for England at youth level, Rehman's achievements represent the current pinnacle of the increasingly significant role that football plays in the lives of many young BrAsians. However, whilst BrAsian participation in professional football can be traced back to the end of the nineteenth century, when Anglo-Indian brothers Jack and Eddie Cother played for Watford, just over a century later, and for a variety of reasons, BrAsian representation at élite level— in terms of both players and spectators—still remains minimal.

This state of affairs, together with wider processes of racial discrimination and exclusion, and inveterate (post)colonial discourses that have sought to emasculate the South Asian body and construct participation in contact sports as anathema—often articulated within stereotype-invoking 'jokes' about corner shops and corner kicks or patronising, uninformed media coverage—have conspired to conceal the fact that a burgeoning BrAsian football culture has existed since the early 1960s. At this time the 'chain migration' of (at this stage, predominantly) men from parts of South Asia to Britain meant that playing football together became a practical and sociable leisure activity. In the coming years this recreational participation became more formalised and a number of competitive amateur teams were established. Due to patterns of geographical settlement many of these emerged from particular ethno-religious groups, often with specific local referents to South Asia, and today football clubs continue to represent important aspects of political identity, tradition and community for some members of the South Asian diaspora. From the foundation of clubs, such as Guru Nanak FC (in Gravesend) and Coventry Sporting FC, by pioneering Punjabi migrants in the 1960s to those established by more recent settlers, football has become an increasingly popular and socially significant facet of the cultural landscape for young BrAsians.

As a result of overt racial abuse in amateur football—which remains frequent and often severe—together with the more covert cultures of exclusion that permeate the game's structures, many BrAsian clubs have been forced to compete in all-Asian leagues. Whilst this continues to pose a number of problems with regard to the transition of players into the professional game, an important cultural corollary has been the establishment of BrAsian football federations and tournaments. For example, the Khalsa Football Federation and Bangladesh Football Association (UK) provide organisational and representative functions for their member teams, whilst the UK Asian Football Championships provide an annual forum for the cream of BrAsian talent. Furthermore, in recent years, a number of hugely progressive and comparatively successful clubs, such as London APSA and Sporting Bengal United (both based in east London) have taken BrAsian football cultures and structures to a new level. As well as rapidly progressing up the amateur football pyramid, these clubs have been proactive in establishing formal connections with professional clubs, contributing to wider projects of community engagement and development, and even forging football-centred links between communities in the subcontinent and the diaspora.

Whilst football is traditionally associated with BrAsian men, young women are also making significant strides within the game, subverting not only ethnic and cultural, but also gender stereotypes in the process. This development was reflected in Gurinder Chadha's 2002 movie *Bend It Like Beckham*, in which Jess, a young Sikh girl of Kenyan Asian parentage, eventually fulfils her dream of becoming a professional footballer in the United States. Such a marketing opportunity was quickly seized upon by FIFA, the game's global governing body, which subsequently selected Parminder Nagra, the actress who played Jess, to be their Football Personality of the Year. Perhaps more significantly, it was a young woman who became the first BrAsian to represent England at football when Aman Dosanj, a goalkeeper, was selected to play at under-16 level. Furthermore, in 2001, when Britain became the first non-Islamic nation to send a team to the (third) Muslim Women's Games, futsal—a small-sided, indoor variation of football—was one of the two sports in which they competed.

WRITING A BrASIAN CITY

'RACE', CULTURE AND RELIGION IN ACCOUNTS OF POSTCOLONIAL BRADFORD

Seán McLoughlin

'But then Asians happened.... Not that a huge horde of them swamped the place overnight. Took decades. Little by little, house by house, the Asians moved in and the whites moved out. The trouble with Asians, especially pakis, is they're different. Different clothes, different language, food, skin, and, of course, we got a different God. That's why the whites move out.... After that, the only ones who'll move in are more pakis because whites don't want to know, not once the place has become polluted. And on and on it goes until you get these little enclaves, some would say ghettoes, sprawling up all over town. And then when the young punks start kicking up a fuss for whatever reason, in comes some smart ****** who tells the world that a place like Bradford suffers from self segregation. No ****ing shit Einstein. The whole world is segregated in a million different ways so why should Bradford be any different?' (Alam, 2002: 300–1)

The organic 'Asianisation' of geographical, social, economic and political spaces within postcolonial Britain has been described and analysed most often in terms of a shifting but dominant discourse of ethnic, 'racial', cultural and religious difference. This chapter explores a case study of how Asianised Britain has been 'written' in this way, with reference to just one city, Bradford, in West Yorkshire. Whether for its *mela* (fair), said to be 'Europe's biggest Asian event', or for the burning of Salman Rushdie's novel, *The Satanic Verses* (1988), the story of 'Brad-istan', as it is sometimes dubbed locally, has been consistently documented, perhaps more than any other centre of the South Asian diaspora worldwide. Over a period of forty or more years the iconic status of Bradford has been very publicly inscribed: 'a miniature Lahore' (*Bradford Telegraph and Argus*, 9 July 1964); a 'Black Coronation Street' (*Sunday Mirror*, 4 June 1978); and 'the Mecca of the North' with Ayatollahs of its own (Ruthven, 1991: 82). The argument here is that, beyond the headlines, a body of writing about Bradford now exists that is worthy of a new sort of reflection.

Considered individually, works some will have read many years ago, and perhaps forgotten, provide only 'snapshots' of a 'BrAsian' city from particular viewpoints at particular moments in time. However, considered together, such 'snapshots' can also begin to map, in broad outline, the emergence and changing shape of 'Brad-istan'. The intention here is to present a historical retrospective of sorts, based upon a close reading of a small selection of the many writings about the city, dwelling on the detail of these accounts and allowing them to speak more on their own terms, and of their own contexts, than would normally be the case. Moreover, it will become apparent that many of the authors that have written about Bradford, as well as pioneering the study of 'BrAsian' cities in the diaspora per se, have made definitive contributions to their own academic disciplines or genres of literature.

This chapter, then, first re-examines the pioneering work of two anthropologists, Badr Dahya (1974) and Verity Saifullah Khan (1977). Taken together their writing represents some of the earliest accounts of the social, economic and political functions of Pakistani 'ethnicity' as migrants settled in Britain during the 1960s and early 1970s. The second snapshot revisits Tariq Mehmood's political novel, *Hand on the Sun* (1983), which is a unique account of resistance to the realities of racism in the 1970s. Set against actual events in Bradford, it provides much of the context for the emergence of a militant and politically 'black' Asian Youth Movement in 1978. Snapshot three focuses on Bradford Council's trailblazing, but ill-fated, experiment in multicultural policy-making during the early 1980s. The main interest here is the insightful assessment of these new policies advanced by travel writer Dervla Murphy (1987). A monograph by Philip Lewis (1994/2002), interfaith adviser and scholar of religious studies, provides the fourth and final snapshot. Set against the impact of local-global events such as the Rushdie affair, recent 'race riots' and 9/11, more than a decade after its first publication *Islamic Britain* remains one of the pre-eminent studies of the contemporary valency of religious identity amongst South Asian Muslim diasporas.

As the narrative unfolds here, section by section, account by account, the particular significance of each of these snapshots is further contextualised, culminating in an extended analysis of the sum of their parts by way of conclusion. However, one of the overall arguments, worth anticipating here, is that unless we have a better understanding of social and historical change in 'BrAsian' cities like Bradford, we can not properly evaluate the reality of their contemporary dilemmas. While Bradford has, for example, often been represented, and presented itself, as an icon of 'the multicultural society', former chief of the Commission for Racial Equality, Herman Ouseley, has identified the city as representing, 'a unique challenge to race relations' (Ouseley, 2001: 1). The publication of *Community Pride Not Prejudice: Making Diversity Work in Bradford* is an overdue admission of the failure of 'multicultural' policies in the city. However, set against the political context of a revived government emphasis on 'integration' under the banner of 'community cohesion' and 'citizenship', Ouseley's report, read alone, is in danger of decontextualising the emergence of Bradford as a particular sort of postcolonial, trans-national, 'BrAsian' city that has been in the making for at least half a century now.

Finally, Bradford may well be seen by some as a 'microcosm' of BrAsian (Asianised) postcolonial Britain. However, the effects of globalisation and cultural pluralism have been writ especially large in the city. Uniquely (trans)local dynamics are at work, dynamics which increasingly make 'Brad-istan' look like the (often quoted) exception rather than the rule. The following factors begin to explain its particularity. First, the *size* of the BrAsian heritage population of Bradford has made its presence especially visible; in 2001 there were 85,465 people of Pakistani, Indian and Bangladeshi heritage living in a city of 467,665 people.[1] Second, the Census also suggests that the overall *dominance and concentration of a single minority 'ethnic' group* in the inner city—that is, the Pakistanis—is especially marked. Bradford is home to Britain's highest proportion of Pakistanis (67,994) relative to overall population (15 per cent), and other groupings—such as Indians (12,504) and Bangladeshis (4,967)—are relatively small.[2] Third, the *ethnic category 'Pakistani' is reinforced by religion* with the vast majority of Pakistanis being Muslim. In 2001 there were 75,188 Muslims living in Bradford compared to just 4,748 Sikhs and 4,457 Hindus.

Fourth, since the 1970s Bradford has been a city beset by *economic problems*, in particular the almost terminal decline of its, once world famous, woollen-textiles industry. Nearby Leeds, as well as Manchester and others, have all managed to regenerate in the post-industrial age to a greater or lesser extent. However, for smaller former mill towns in the north of England like Oldham, Burnley and Bradford, this has proven more difficult.[3] Fifth, against this context, Pakistani Muslim ethnicity is also reinforced by a shared position in terms of social class. While there are plenty of examples of BrAsian Muslims in Bradford having achieved 'success', both in their own terms and those of wider society, many have not yet accumulated the *social and cultural capital* necessary for upward mobility in a knowledge-based economy. There are many 'structural-cultural' reasons for this including the failure of the education system to tackle 'underachievement' and the continuing consequences of the con-

1 For all 2001 Census statistics on Bradford cited here see: www.statistics.gov.uk/census2001/profiles/00cx.asp

2 Projections for the Pakistani population of Bradford in 2011 are 102,350 or 21 per cent of the district's numbers with the figures for 2021 being 132,950 or 26 per cent (*Bradford Population Forecasts Information Bulletin*, 2000: 2).

3 Attempts have been made to re-package Bradford as the home of art, culture and tourism. In the 1980s the 'institutional completeness' of South Asian communities in the city was commodified in the 'Flavours of Asia' tourist campaign. More recently Bradford bid unsuccessfully to become European Capital of Culture 2008.

text of migration. For example, the majority of Pakistanis that migrated to Bradford post-war were actually unskilled and illiterate farmers, most especially from Mirpur district in Pakistani administered 'Azad' (Free) Kashmir. Sixth and finally, the size, concentration and predominance of the now largely 'working-class', Pakistani and Kashmiri heritage, Muslim population in Bradford has seen this constituency able to exert levels of political pressure, and achieve *levels of political mobilisation*, rarely seen amongst Asians elsewhere in Britain. It is selected versions of this story of a 'BrAsian' city that we turn to now, beginning with anthropological accounts of the earliest period of settlement.

URBAN ETHNICITY: ANTHROPOLOGY AT HOME AND PAKISTANIS IN BRITAIN DURING THE 1960s AND 1970s

'Many of the earlier sociological studies of ethnic minorities and "race" relations in Britain stressed objective conditions of the host society and discussed the response of various cultures in terms of the ways, and degrees to which, they "assimilated" or "integrated". The significance of the actor's perception of his [*sic*] situation, his orientation and resources were underplayed. More recent anthropological work incorporating studies of the home society … have attempted to balance that perspective without disclaiming its significance.' (Saifullah Khan, 1977: 58–9)

One way in which anthropology managed to extend its traditional object of study in a postcolonial world was to 'write' non-European immigration to the post-war West. In Britain studies of 'West Indian' settlement were conducted from the late 1940s into the 1950s and 1960s. However, as Benson (1996) has observed, overall anthropologists have tended to produce many more studies of 'Asian' as opposed to 'African-Caribbean' migrants. Her explanation is that, ultimately, anthropologists much preferred to study what they supposed to be the 'strong' cultural systems of South Asia, based on institutions and practices such as caste, kinship and religion. While this may be true, the definitive early collection of anthropological writing about 'ethnic minorities' in contemporary Britain, *Between Two Cultures* (Watson, 1977), included chapters on migrants from a variety of countries, including China and Greek Cyprus as well as Pakistan and India. Moreover, as the editor of the collection, James Watson, and the quotation above make clear, a critique of the prevalent assumption that assimilation might be a priority for minorities was at the heart of this new anthropological project.

Watson's theoretical inspiration in this respect was Abner Cohen's conceptualisation of 'ethnicity'. In a key edited volume, developing his own work on custom and politics in urban Africa, Cohen (1974) argues that ethnicity can be best seen as a manifestation of informal interest groups in a formal political system where there is competition for scarce resources. In contexts of dynamic social change such as those involving migration, groups often adapt to their new context by situationally 're-organising' traditional customs, or 're-inventing' new ones under traditional symbols. So 'ethnicity' represents not a conservative reproduction of culture, but rather an enhancement of 'cultural distinctiveness' which can be 'manipulated' to express political and economic interests. Unfortunately the sophistication of this theorising is not always reflected in *Between Two Cultures* and, like *Urban Ethnicity* itself, the volume sometimes overstates the unhindered agency of ordinary people. However, today the collection is remembered most for its title, which was thought to essentialise the relationship between 'cultures' and 'roots', tending to assume that people are unable to improvise multiple and more hybrid 'routes' in new directions.

In his contribution to *Urban Ethnicity* Badr Dahya (1974) examines the single male Pakistani presence in industrial Bradford and the various ways in which ethnicity was at work during the 1960s and early 1970s. Emphasising why the 'definition of the situation' was different for Pakistanis compared to the white working class, Dahya dissented from the generally accepted view of sociologists Rex and Moore (1967) that migrant housing patterns were determined primarily by racial discrimination. However, while this remains an important contribution, as suggested above, Dahya underestimated the extent to which Pakistani 'choices' were already made within the limits of deeply structured constraints.

While Dahya illuminated traditionally 'male' spheres of activity, it is only in the work of another anthropologist, Verity Saifullah Khan, that the experiences of Pakistani women and children, reunited with their husbands and fathers in Britain, begins to receive attention. Having conducted research in both Bradford and the villages of Mirpur during 1972 and 1973, she contributed the chapter on 'Pakistanis' to *Between Two Cultures* (1977). Saifullah Khan's is perhaps a more nuanced account of Pakistani 'ethnicity' than Dahya's, clearly showing it to be a socially constructed and contextual process, capable of producing social 'stress' as well as 'support'. However, she refers to very few contemporary events, a characteristic which effectively de-politicises the experiences of Mirpuris in 1970s Bradford.[4] Therefore, for all the nuance in her account, she was criticised for failing to question all but the most common-sense racism or challenge the ways in which colonialism continues to shape contemporary Britain (Centre for Contemporary Cultural Studies [CCCS], 1982).

Both Badr Dahya and Verity Saifullah Khan were pioneers in the study of the 'BrAsian' city. They played a pivotal role in establishing

4 For example, there is no explicit discussion of the Yorkshire Campaign to Stop Immigration or the National Front.

the main tropes of the 'urban ethnicity' genre: 'chain migration', 'fusion and fission', 'institutional completeness', 'community leadership' and so on.[5] While their work continues to be cited nationally and internationally, back in the 1970s the authorities would seem to have thought anthropologists' observations about insider accounts of 'encapsulation' unimportant or, more likely, unpalatable.[6] Indeed, in the context of a dominant discourse about 'integration' and 'segregation', a retrospective on the work of Dahya and Saifullah Khan highlights the relative lack of research on social actors' perceptions of ethnic clustering today.[7]

Custom and politics in urban Britain

By 1964 there were already 12,000 Pakistanis in Bradford: 5,400 originating from Mirpur; 3,000 from Chhachh in Campbellpore District on the Punjab/North West Frontier Province border; 1,800 from Punjab itself; and 1,500 from East Pakistan (now Bangladesh). As Dahya explains, the origins of this presence can be traced back to the economic success of some thirty or so former Mirpuri and Chhachhi *lascars* (seamen) in 1944–5 (1974: 84). It was they who first provided the draw to other seamen who had jumped ship and then, after 1950, to kinsmen who were sponsored to travel from the subcontinent. Eventually the Pakistanis sealed their predominance in Bradford with the rush to 'beat the ban' imposed by the Commonwealth Immigration Act of 1962. The Act reinforced the process of highly selective 'chain migration' with established migrants seizing the opportunity to obtain employment vouchers for their kin.

Perhaps surprisingly Dahya has little to say about the working lives of Pakistanis in Bradford.[8] His focus instead is on early settlement patterns, businesses and community politics. For example, Dahya explains that when the pioneers of Pakistani labour migration first came to the city, they lodged in houses owned by Poles in an area already marginal to local people and containing the 'ethnic' institutions of these earlier migrants: a Roman Catholic Church, a social club and a delicatessen.[9] In these early days single male migrants from the subcontinent boarded

5 This work continued in the 1970s, 1980s and 1990s with anthropologists such as Anwar, Ballard, Bhachu, Shaw and Werbner.

6 Dahya was recently quoted in *The Observer* (15 July 2001) and reference to Saifullah Khan can be found on the websites of UNESCO and the British Foreign and Commonwealth Office amongst others.

7 One important exception is the work of my colleague at the University of Leeds, Deborah Phillips (2003).

8 A glimpse of this is presented by Rajput, 'a leading Karachi journalist', in *Bradford Telegraph and Argus*, 8–9 July 1964.

9 Even in the 1960s it was argued that one of the reasons 'race' had not become a political issue in Bradford was 'the long history of invasion by outsiders' (*New Society*, 19 November 1964).

together in Bradford, but with the violent partition of India in 1947, and the arrival of a new wave of immigrants, workers began to organise themselves along lines of region, religion and denomination. 'Fusion' gave way to 'fission' and segmentation so that, as immigrants bought their own houses, distinct patterns of settlement amongst Gujaratis, Sikhs, Pathans, Chhachhis, Punjabis, Shi'as, Bangladeshis and Mirpuris all became discernable within the 'inner ring' of the city. Dahya argues that residing within the inner-city of Bradford was a 'rational choice' for the Pakistanis because housing was cheap and freely available; it was close to work, shops and transport links. Moreover, given that, at this stage, the majority of immigrants were transients committed to remitting a significant portion of their wages back home, they

> ...*voluntarily segregated* themselves because they realized their economic goals were more likely to be achieved through conformity to group norms, by means of mutual aid and under austere living conditions than through dispersal into the wider society. (Dahya, 1974: 112 [my emphasis])

One of the tropes of the literature on diasporas worldwide, is the description of the range of 'ethnic' services available to immigrants as 'communities' become established. Dahya, for example, documents the phenomenal expansion and diversification of Pakistani enterprise in Bradford between the late 1950s and early 1970s:

> In 1959 the only Pakistani-owned economic concerns were 2 grocery/butchery businesses and 3 cafés. By 1966 the number of Pakistani concerns had grown to 133, which included 51 grocers/butchers and 16 cafés. In 1970 there were over 260 immigrant-owned and -operated businesses, all of which were located in the areas of immigrant settlement. The number of food businesses has risen to over 180, which includes 11 wholesale premises, 1 canning factory, 112 grocery and butchery businesses, 25 cafés, 15 private clubs and 2 confectioners and bakers. (Dahya, 1974: 91)

However, moving beyond mere description of this 'institutional completeness', Dahya offers an analysis of the way in which early Pakistani businesses became a vehicle for 'ethnicity'. Apart from catering for everyday needs they emphasised a sense of 'Pakistani-ness' in a number of ways: by displaying Urdu signage, posters depicting the Holy Places at Mecca and pictures of Pakistan's national poet-philosopher Muhammad Iqbal; by disseminating information about Islamic festivals; and by selling Pakistani newspapers. Dahya maintains that these 'extra economic functions' (1974: 94) helped to reinforce the idea of a distinctive group-belonging amongst Pakistanis, both for themselves and for others, resulting in the relative encapsulation of migrants. However, crucially Dahya tends to present 'ethnicity' as a simple reproduction of culture, rather than in terms of Cohen's (1974) more sophisticated theorising.

During the 1960s and 1970s most Pakistanis seemed to judge that their interests in Bradford were best served by the relative self-sufficiency of the communities they had built. In this regard Dahya does describe how this evolving 'ecological' base could become transformed into a 'political' base, especially at election time or as emergent leaders gradually began to make the case for limited public recognition. Pivotal in this respect was a religious institution, the local 'Mosque Committee', which was made up of both religious functionaries and influential Pakistani entrepreneurs. No doubt with their own vested religious and business interests in reinforcing 'ethnicity' amongst Pakistanis, the committee sought 'to mobilise public opinion … and influence … political behaviour' (Dahya, 1974: 93). For example, representatives spoke out against a 'policy of dispersal' from the slums of Bradford and lobbied the local education authority with regard to female dress and physical education in schools. During the 1971 elections the committee also exhorted Pakistanis to vote against a Bangladeshi who contested the Manningham ward.[10] At the time, Bangladesh (formerly East Pakistan) had recently been at war with (West) Pakistan and the 'effectiveness' of this campaign, at least from a (West) Pakistani point of view, was underlined when a Conservative was returned in the context of an anti-Tory swing in the rest of Britain. In this context, then, religion, in the institutionalised form of the 'Mosque Committee', did not transcend, but rather became a resource for, Pakistani ethnicity, although Dahya does not draw out the significance of these events, or the role of 'community leaders' thus.

A tale of two pinds: Mirpuris in Bradford

In her contribution to *Between Two Cultures* Saifullah Khan underlines the heterogeneity of the Pakistani population of Britain and is one of the first authors to focus on the particular experiences of Mirpuris in Bradford. At the time she estimated that of around 30,000 Pakistanis 60 to 70 per cent came from Mirpur in 'Azad' Kashmir (1977: 57). She examines how some of the main institutions of village life in 'Azad' Kashmir were being variously 'strengthened, modified and altered' in Bradford (1977: 76). In this respect she comes much closer than Dahya to an understanding of ethnicity as a vehicle for situational 'innovation' to advance interests under the banner of 'tradition' (Cohen, 1974). For example, she identifies the continuing strength of village-kin networks in Bradford and reports a continuing preference for solidarity with *biraderi* (patrilineal descent group) members. But she also notes that given the contingencies of the new setting, 'many families have incorporated neighbours from the same region of origin into their social network' (1977: 77).

10 As early as 1963 three Pakistani candidates stood as 'independents' at the local elections in Bradford (Singh, 1994: 17).

Like Dahya, Saifullah Khan presents Bradford's Mirpuris as a relatively 'segregated' minority. However, in an extremely detailed explanation of this clustering, she is more careful than Dahya to maintain a judicious balance between the different structural and cultural forces which together, even by the early 1970s, had left 'the individual arrival with an ever-decreasing series of limited options' (1977: 73). There is reference to several structural factors constraining Mirpuris in Bradford, including enforced segregation and 'differential treatment' at work (1977: 72), a pathological white prejudice against 'dark skinned colonials', the more blatant examples of 'permissiveness' in wider society and 'insecurity due to immigration controls' (1977: 73). However, Saifullah Khan also acknowledges that, against this context, the Mirpuris of Bradford had already established their own strategy for survival which maintained 'an independence from the host society', and that they increasingly exerted a 'pressure to conform' to such an extent that, even relatively early, 'the skills required for communication and participation [in wider society] could not be acquired so easily' (1977: 80). It is precisely this sort of detailed contextualisation that is so often missing from contemporary accounts of 'segregation' in Bradford.

While Dahya was able to speak of lower than average unemployment and strong competition for labour during the 1960s, in the 1970s Bradford was a city of low incomes with Pakistanis, in particular, dependent on 'declining industries' (1977: 75–6). With an increase in prejudice and stereotyping too, Saifullah Khan argues that, 'Returning home or organising resistance to such pressures in Britain are not easy options' (1977: 73). Of course Dahya (1974) identified an emerging political 'leadership' amongst immigrants in Bradford, however Saifullah Khan (1977) maintains that despite this there was still a general lack of Pakistani 'grass-roots' organisations in the city. For example, unlike Sikh women who could go to the 'temple', there was no tradition of Pakistani women attending the local mosque and there were no community centres (1977: 81).[11] Indeed, Saifullah Khan makes some very insightful observations about the nature of the relationships between the Pakistani 'community', 'ethnic' leaderships and the perceptions of the state and wider society:[12]

> The leaders known to British authorities are frequently of the urban middle class whose values and life-style differ markedly from the majority of their countrymen. Many villagers have no contact with or knowledge of these individuals and their organisations nor of the bodies such as the local Community Relations Councils.... The English are generally unaware of the internal differentiation of

11 According to Singh (1994: 13) Bradford's first Sikh *gurdwara* was established in 1964 and a Hindu Cultural Society was established in 1968; the latter took charge of a *mandir* on Leeds Road in 1974.

12 These debates were taken up in earnest only a decade or more later. See Werbner and Anwar (1991).

the Pakistani population and through their unquestioned use and reification of the notions regarding 'the Pakistani community' and 'Pakistani leaders' they presuppose a cohesion which rarely exists. (Saifullah Khan, 1977: 74)[13]

Saifullah Khan suggests that, in the 1970s at least, for most Mirpuris in Bradford their priority was not formal political organising against racism or unemployment but simple day-to-day survival. This usually meant maintaining 'an unobtrusive life-style, aimed at minimal disruption of the host [*sic*] society' (1977: 74). Indeed, life in Britain was still 'perceived as an extension of life back home and both must be seen as one system of socio-economic relations' (1977: 58). However, while Saifullah Khan is clear that the second generation of British-Mirpuris are likely to maintain 'a distinctive identity and life-style' (1977: 87), and 'remain encapsulated enough to accept arranged marriages' (1977: 86), she acknowledges that, for them, there is a 'difference of orientation ... resulting from time of birth, background and subsequent experience' (1977: 85). In short, Bradford will be their main reference point and not Mirpur. 'Mono-lingual' and 'mono-cultural' schools, where minority languages and cultures are 'not acknowledged or recognised' (1977: 83), at once expose BrAsians in Bradford to levels and forms of acculturation and institutional racism that differed markedly from the experiences of their parents. Without giving much of a feel for the energy and anger of this generation, Saifullah Khan does at least hint at the moment of 'pan-Asian' identity in Bradford that we must consider next:

These younger people will not accept the prejudices internal to the Pakistani population and between Asians of different regional or religious origin. Nor will they ignore the external definitions, myths and stereotypes circulating in the majority society. (Saifullah Khan, 1977: 74)

THE 'EMPIRE' WRITES 'BLACK': 'RACE', A SUBALTERN NOVEL AND ASIAN YOUTH IN THE 1970s – 1980s

In the 1960s and 1970s, Hiro (1991) argues, Asians were generally seen as a 'soft touch' by so-called 'Paki bashers'. However, by the end of the 1970s, in response to racist murders and an increase in profile for the National Front (NF) and British National Party (BNP), Asian Youth Movements (AYMs) emerged around the country in Birmingham, Bradford, London, Manchester and Sheffield. With an anti-fascist analysis that began by identifying the roots of racism in colonialism, the AYMs' focus was very much on a secular and politically 'black' identification coupled with working-class solidarity born of common experiences of life in Britain. However, as Kalra *et al.* (1996) argue, while there were

13 Community Relations Councils, established after the 1966 Race Relations Act, often acted as early advocates for minority ethnic organisations. See Singh (2002).

always attempts at co-ordination between AYMs, a formal sense of national organisation was missing until things came to a head in Bradford during 1981. The so-called 'Bradford 12', led by a splinter group of the local AYM, were arrested having been found in possession of a crate of petrol bombs. The '12' maintained they had been prompted in their actions by the widely broadcast threat of National Front skinheads marching through Bradford and attacking Asian areas. Eventually, in 1982, a Crown Court accepted their plea of 'self-defence is no offence'. Soon after these events one of the acquitted, Tariq Mehmood, wrote a semi-autobiographical novel, *Hand on the Sun*, which describes the politicisation of a group of Asian youth in 1970s Bradford.[14] At a time, today, when religiously defined identity politics would seem to have overtaken the 'black' and 'Asian' project, the novel provides a reminder of other histories and other forms of solidarity.

Somewhat overlooked, and now out of print, *Hand on the Sun* was significant enough to find a top ranking publisher in Penguin during the early 1980s. Indeed it represents one of the earliest accounts to emerge out of the experience of childhood immigration from the rural Indian subcontinent and a subsequent adolescence and schooling in urban Britain. Perhaps it is for this reason that *Hand on the Sun* has been read as a 'set text' for literature examinations in English schools and colleges. Many of the 'diasporic' themes dealt with in later, more explicitly hybridising, 'Asian Cool' novels are present, including a sense of loss, the negotiation of identity, issues of gender and generation, conflict and social change. However, although, like Hanif Kureishi, Mehmood speaks from the margins of any putative 'Asian community', he is more the Gramscian 'organic intellectual' than the cosmopolitan Londoner and is positioned very differently in both literary and epistemological terms. Interestingly, when Kureishi visited an 'Asian' bar during his brief visit to Bradford during the 1980s, he reports that he was introduced to a local 'political star', one of the 'Bradford 12'. While Kureishi greeted the man 'enthusiastically', when it was confirmed that the former was the author of *My Beautiful Laundrette*, Kureishi was attacked as 'a fascist, a reactionary' (1986: 156).

Where *Hand on the Sun* receives a mention today, for example on some of the more scholarly pages of the internet, it is rightly located in terms of 'postcolonial', 'world' and 'third-world' literatures. As the title of this section suggests, Mehmood writes '*black*' from an 'empire' now relocated inside postcolonial Britain. At a time when few 'Asian' interventions in the debate about the politics of 'race', culture and nation

14 Mehmood's new novel, *While There is Light* (2003), revisits the experiences of the 'Bradford 12'. See www.tandana.org/AYM.html for an online archive of images which tell the story of the AYMs.

were being made—and more than a decade before they emerged in cultural studies (for example, Sharma *et al.*, 1996)—Mehmood's narrative establishes clear relationships between the lives of his characters and the social, economic and political structures of capitalism and colonialism. While *Hand on the Sun* is often polemical, it is sufficiently well crafted to give agency and voice to the complex dilemmas and contradictions of 'real people'. In this respect Mehmood achieves what so little of 1970s and 1980s sociology of 'race' and ethnicity was able to. The final political analysis of the activists in the book is unlikely to have been representative of most Asian youth at the time. Nevertheless, many of the experiences described in the novel undoubtedly were.

'Here to stay, here to fight'

'To hold a people down forever is like putting a hand on the sun.' (graffiti, El Salvador)

Mehmood's is a generation, often born in South Asia, for whom the discrepancies between the image and reality of life in 'Wallait' (Britain) were particularly stark. Having listened to the tales of the returnee migrants, when he arrived as a child in Bradford, the main character of *Hand on the Sun*, Jalib, is shocked that the streets are home to beggars rather than 'paved with gold' (1983: 19–20). There are wistful diasporic moments of reflection, too, on the village childhood spent swimming, smoking and talking, all this to be exchanged for 'a system which told him that he was a wog and that he must assimilate into a new way of life and forget his backward ways' (1983: 24). At school in Bradford children are segregated into 'girls', 'boys' and 'blacks' (1983: 9). There is racial abuse and graffiti; staff are totally indifferent to the culture and history of the 'black' and Asian children. However, there are also small acts of resistance. One teacher who is disliked, Mr Ramsey, becomes Mr 'Rami' ('bastard' in Punjabi) (1983: 11). While the power of the *goras* (whites) was writ large for Jalib when he entered Britain, and an immigration officer spoke to him in his own language (1983: 24), all 'fear and wonder' disappears when he hits a white kid at junior school, and the latter bleeds red blood the same as his own (1983: 25). At high school Jalib gets into a fight with Jim, the 'cock of the school', and individual impotence turns to communal empowerment as the 'black' and Asian youth secure victory with a combination of knives and chilli powder. Mehmood uses all these incidents to prefigure later conflicts in the novel and establish the principle that 'self defence is no offence'.

In many unobtrusive ways Mehmood's account subtly values and affirms the integrity of South Asian cultural practices including male friends holding hands in public (1983: 26), something ridiculed by the *goras* (whites). However, Mehmood is not uncritical of power relations and social divisions within 'communities'. Indeed, while the 'issues' rarely feel 'forced', most of the individual stories, of both major and minor characters, tend to perform a didactic function. Shaheen, the heroine, is just as politicised as Jalib by racial attacks on her community and is frustrated by the attitudes of those that restrict her to domestic chores or present her with an unwelcome marriage proposal (1983: 70). *Hand on the Sun* also documents the many hidden costs of the migration process for the first generation. Mehmood tells of mothers who rarely go out and compares their existence in Bradford to the laughing, joking and singing songs in praise of Allah that takes place in the villages of Pakistan (1983: 56–9). Husbands are distanced from their wives and fathers rarely see their children. Work in the mills has made them joyless and brutalised; they have 'melted into the machines' (1983: 54).

Seeing their parents so crushed begins to anger Jalib and his friends as they themselves find only 'shit jobs' available when they leave school. However, there is frustration too at the first generation's seeming resignation when illegal immigrants are kicked out of Britain, or when one third of the workforce at a local mill is threatened with redundancy: 'It is as Allah would have it' (1983: 77).[15] At this stage in the novel Jalib's political education really begins. In the mill a radical, Hussain, tries to organise the men and compares union officials in Bradford to corrupt government employees back home in Pakistan. Echoing events in 1970s Britain, he tells Jalib and the others about racist murders in Southall and argues for the need to fight back against imperialism with capitalism in crisis (1983: 62). However, no doubt reflecting the political journey of many radicals, perhaps even Mehmood himself, when Hussain is challenged he eventually accepts that organisations such as the International Socialists and Socialist Workers' Party 'had achieved nothing' for 'black' people; too often they have glossed the realities of racism with empty slogans about unity (1983: 93). With the feeling that what is happening in London will most likely soon find its way to Bradford, Jalib commits himself to countering skinhead attacks on 'his people' by any means necessary.

To illustrate the continuities of colonial and postcolonial contexts, and that the generations need not be divided over politics, Mehmood continues the education of Jalib and his friends in an encounter with Dalair Singh, a veteran freedom fighter from the days of the Raj (1983:

15 The Indian Workers' Association was one of the more politicised organisations among the first generation (Kalra *et al.*, 1996). Together with the Kashmir Welfare Association and the 'white left' it organised against racist groups in Bradford during the 1960s and 1970s. It also took a leading role in the campaign against the 'bussing' of Asian children (1964–80) and protested against discrimination in the promotions policy of West Yorkshire Passenger Transport Executive. It was closely associated with the *gurdwaras* (Singh, 2002).

86). He lived through the Second World War and recounts stories of guerrilla raids against the British. In contrast to many of their parents, Dalair's advice to the youth is 'never give up'. He tells them of things that official histories do not remember, citing the example of Udham Singh who bided his time and travelled to England to assassinate General O'Dwyer, the British officer responsible for the massacre of Indians in Amritsar in 1919 (1983: 88). Mehmood is also very careful to remind us that Singh symbolically signed his name 'Ram Mohammed Singh', suggesting an easily forgotten heritage of political unity amongst Hindus, Muslims and Sikhs in the wake of Partition. Accordingly, the novel depicts friendships across religious, ethnic and racial boundaries as a matter of routine, making a deliberate intervention against the pervasiveness of communalism.

The climax of *A Hand on the Sun* draws very closely on the real events surrounding the so-called 'Battle of Bradford' in 1976.[16] The National Front, having organised a large 'anti-immigration' march through the city, were eventually chased out of town by an angry crowd of West Indian and Asian youth. Mehmood begins his account when an Ad Hoc Committee Against Racism and Fascism is formed, but in a passage describing a public meeting it becomes clear that the youth, and Mehmood himself, disdain the usual 'community' leaders as *chamchas* (lackeys) who beg the police not to allow the NF to come to Bradford. Echoing an attitude central to the AYMs, Jalib and his friends protest, 'Let them come—we must smash them!' (1983: 113). On the day of the NF march an 'anti-fascist' counter-demonstration supported by a temporary alliance of the mosques, *gurdwaras* and *mandirs*, the trades unions and left-wing organisations rallies in the city centre. However, foreshadowing more recent events in Bradford, a youth suddenly grabs a microphone at the rally, shouting, 'The fascists are marching on Lumb Lane. What are we all doing here? If you want to defend your community, go to Lumb Lane!' (1983: 121). Jalib and the other youths break through the ranks of stewards and police heading for Manningham Middle School where the NF have been moved under police escort. A 'pitched battle' ensues with mounted police charging the youths, while the NF and their Union Jacks—'the symbol of the enemy'—are 'shepherded away' to waiting coaches under a 'hail of missiles' (1983: 119).

For the young Asians in the novel the 'Battle of Bradford' represents a 'victory' that they feel moved to consolidate; the activists all agree on the need for a dedicated AYM (actually formed 1978), an organisation that is independent, secular and cuts across their different communities and political affiliations. The possibility of an Afro-Asian organisation is

16 A brief description and analysis of these events is given by Ballard in 'Up Against the Front', *New Society*, 6 May 1976, pp. 285–6.

considered but, reflecting on religious communalism evident even on the march, it is felt that 'our own house is in such a mess we'd better start by sorting it out' (1983: 128). As time passes and the novel draws to a close there are reports from Southall of the AYM there securing government funds to open its own centre and similar offers eventually emerge in Bradford. At a party celebrating the victory of a campaign against the deportation of one of the workers at Hussain's mill, two uninvited guests, the chief Community Relations Officer and someone from the Commission for Racial Equality, are busy buying drinks for the AYM's leaders. They offer grants and the chance to meet Prince Charles on his forthcoming visit to Bradford. Some are against such co-operation with the system but others think it will bring the influence that comes of respectability. Fittingly, it is Mehmood himself who has the last say. At once he echoes the analysis of the Centre for Contemporary Cultural Studies (CCCS, 1982) that public recognition can be a form of state incorporation and control, and anticipates the dissipation of the AYM by the late 1980s as many members took up jobs within the emerging 'race' relations industry:

> Only years later did these young Asians understand that, even if the state was pouring huge amounts of money into the emerging movement, it was a small price to pay to buy off the militancy of a people's struggle. (Mehmood, 1983: 156)

It is to the limits and possibilities of this public recognition of BrAsians in 1980s Bradford that we shift our attention now.

TURNING POINT? MULTICULTURAL POLICY-MAKING AND TRAVELOGUE IN THE 1980s

> 'My attitude is that we must become part of the community. At present we are looking from the outside. We are being discussed and governed by whites although they know little of our problems.' (Mahamid [*sic*] Ajeeb, Chair of Bradford Community Relations Council, *Sunday Mirror*, 4 June 1978)[17]

In the late 1970s Bradford and other city councils in Britain came under pressure from the newly formed Commission for Racial Equality to demonstrate how they were seeking to comply with Section 71 of the Race Relations Act (1976). They were charged with both eliminating unlawful discrimination and promoting good race relations. However, the expansion of multiculturalism and anti-racism in Britain hinted at by Mehmood, which eventually saw central government finance high profile grants for the inner-cities, was only really catalysed by the widespread uprisings of disaffected youth from Brixton to Toxteth during the early

17 Ajeeb was to become the first Asian Lord Mayor of Bradford in the 1980s. See Kureishi (1986) and Lewis (1994).

1980s. Of course in Bradford the case of the 'Bradford 12' had been a very close call and, based on a mapping of demographic and economic trends in the district, the council became one of the first in the country to develop a fully-fledged 'race-relations' policy.[18] This was announced in 1981 with the publication of *Turning Point: A Review of Race Relations in Bradford.*

Turning Point is a bold, urgent but still somewhat belated attempt to confront the challenges facing Bradford at the beginning of a new decade. In the knowledge that the inner-city would eventually become more or less 'Asianised',[19] it marks a moment of transition in the balance of power between 'ethnic' majority and minorities. In a postcolonial moment, perhaps with echoes of Indian independence in 1947, BrAsians are finally recognised, more or less on their own terms, and promised a degree of respect, representation and self-determination. On the defensive after two decades of largely ignoring this presence, half expecting 'them' to 'fit in' and half wondering whether 'they' would even stay, *Turning Point*'s starting point is that, compared to Bradford's many white European migrants, those from the 'New Commonwealth' are challenging 'many of the more simplistic ideals of "integration" or "assimilation"' (*Turning Point*, 1981: 5).[20]

However, despite being home to the third largest 'immigrant community' in Britain during 1981, the report revealingly admits that 'as a counter to the claim often made of Bradford having good race relations ... rather ... it has no race relations at all' (1981: 7). *Turning Point* forecasts that in the coming decade, due to industrial decline and an expanding Asian population, any previous 'slack' in the system is likely to be replaced with growing levels of competition for jobs and housing. Therefore, it is the report's worried conclusion that, without intervention to tackle racial prejudice and afford all cultures 'parity of esteem', a second generation of young Asians, with greater skills and higher expectations than their parents, could form 'an economic sub class, structurally disadvantaged, and increasingly difficult to accommodate' (1981: 15). The time for 'benign neglect' ('the Asians will help themselves') is past (1981: 44).

In the early to mid 1980s Bradford's leading role, nationally and internationally, in the development of 'multicultural' policy drew a wide range of authors to the city, including Hanif Kureishi and Dervla Mur-

18 *Sunday Mirror*, 4 June 1978, describes Bradford as 'one of the country's liveliest and most progressive authorities'.

19 Today, South Asian heritage children are projected to make up 40 per cent of the city's school population by 2011 (Bradford Metropolitan District Council, 2000: 2)

20 *Turning Point* tends to present the assimilation and integration of white Europeans as 'natural' and uncontested. However, during 1852 and 1862, for example, there were anti-Catholic riots in Bradford, a 10 per cent Irish city at the time.

phy. In 1986 Kureishi contributed a piece entitled simply 'Bradford' to a special issue of travel writing for Granta, Penguin's paperback magazine of new writing. One of the things that interests Kureishi about Bradford is the so-called Honeyford affair, a detailed and 'generally accurate' (Halstead, 1988: 81) account of which is provided by Dervla Murphy (1987). When Honeyford, the headmaster of a predominantly BrAsian school in Bradford, made various ethnocentric asides in his public criticisms of council policy, a multi-ethnic alliance mobilised to have him removed from his post. Murphy, who spent much longer in the city than Kureishi, taking a flat in inner-city Manningham for several months, has also written about her travels to India, Nepal, Tibet, Pakistan and many other countries. Nevertheless, for both Kureishi, the cosmopolitan Londoner and Karachi-ite, and for Murphy, a white, bourgeois, middle-aged, Irish woman, postcolonial Bradford proved just as much an encounter with 'difference' as these other, more far-flung destinations. Moreover they discovered that the white working classes of Thatcherite Britain, just as much as the Mirpuris of Manningham, inhabited worlds far away from their own.

Kureishi and Murphy both begin by rehearsing a familiar trope, the 'institutional completeness' of Asian Bradford. Kureishi stays in a working-class Pakistani area with an Islamic Library, Asian video shops and the Ambala Sweet House. Somewhat predictably, he remarks, 'If I ignored the dark Victorian buildings around me, I could imagine that everyone was back in their village in Pakistan' (1986: 152). However, it soon becomes clear that things have changed radically since Dahya and Saifullah Khan were writing in the 1970s. The focus then was on Pakistani 'insider' accounts and the transformation of discrete neighbourhoods. Into the 1980s, for 'ethnic' majorities and minorities alike, the 'Asianisation' of Bradford starts to become a far more public and civic, as opposed to simply 'communal', matter. Moreover, as the controversy surrounding Honeyford illustrates, local events were also becoming national affairs. Murphy's detailed descriptions and analyses are often especially reflective in this respect, situating 1980s Bradford in the context of much wider debates about social change and 'race' relations, liberal universalism and cultural relativism.

Travels of a different sort: racists, anti-racists and a liberal travel-writer

'These policies seem at first glance humane and responsible.... But there was a fatal flaw in the Council's thinking—its emphasis was on the effects of racism rather than its causes.... Its attempt to take the bull of British racialism by the horns merely set that bull loose in the china-shop of local race relations.' (Murphy, 1987: 94)

As her account unfolds it becomes clear that Murphy is extremely critical of the implementation of *Turning Point* in Bradford, suggesting the local council has been 'brave but foolish' (1987: 94). 'Moderate' 'race-relations' workers she speaks to maintain that it moved 'too far too fast, having apparently been unaware (inexplicably!) of the virulence of local racialism' (1987: 95). Murphy is surprised at the ignorance of racism in the city because in pubs, out shopping, waiting for buses or on the street, her ears are filled with hate speech about 'their filthy habits', 'their drug pushing', 'their wife beating' and 'their Paki religion' [*sic*]. It is amongst the city's white 'have-nots', then, that Murphy most meets 'resentment of Bradford's take-over', the feeling that 'there's no one left to stand up for us, all they care about is them Pakis [*sic*]—making life easier for them' (1987: 73). In developing a 'race' policy Bradford Council had failed to take account of how altered relations of power and access to scarce resources in the city would impact on 'relations' with disenfranchised whites. Murphy reflects:

> I was soon to become familiar with these half-truths, suspicions, exaggerations and distortions: symptoms of fear, ignorance and angry frustration. If something has gone dreadfully wrong with the management of your own society, it's comforting to feel that 'They' are really to blame. (Murphy, 1987: 6)

While Murphy was resident in Manningham the so-called Honeyford affair of 1984–5 came to a head. In a series of articles in the *Times Educational Supplement*, *Yorkshire Post* and *Salisbury Review* (a New Right journal committed to repatriation), Ray Honeyford, the recently-appointed head teacher of a predominantly 'Muslim' school, Drummond Middle, argued that the Council's 'anti-racist-cum-multi-cultural' initiatives were prioritising cultural identity over social integration. While in hindsight this reflects the tone of much current debate in the 2000s, it was his stereotyping of 'black' and Asian parents and their cultural practices that 'inflamed racial prejudice' (1987: 104). Honeyford was responding to the issue of BrAsian parents taking children on extended holidays to the subcontinent during term-time. However, his criticisms strayed from purely educational matters:

> He referred to the Mirpuris' motherland as a country which is corrupt at every level, which cannot cope with democracy and which since 1977 has been ruled by a military tyrant who, in the opinion of at least half his countrymen, had his predecessor judicially murdered. He dwelt on the Pakistani ill-treatment not only of criminals but of those who dare to question Islamic orthodoxy as interpreted by a despot. Also, he condemned Pakistan as 'the heroin capital of the world' and alleged this 'fact' is now reflected in the drug problems of English cities with Asian populations. (Murphy, 1987: 111)

Translations of Honeyford's work proved enough for more than half of the Drummond parents to sign a letter calling for his dismissal. A pro-Honeyford faction also emerged which presented the 'Honeyford Out!' campaign as 'an alliance of reactionary Muslims and rabid Lefties' (1987: 109). Certainly, Murphy maintains that most parents were 'not remotely interested in debates about multi-cultural and or anti-racist education' (1987: 115). Nevertheless, presaging the Rushdie affair, what was undoubtedly key was that Honeyford had insulted Islam, Pakistan and the local Asian community. Eventually, in December 1985, Honeyford was forced to retire on an enhanced pension, but not before 10,000 Bradfordians had signed a petition backing him, and Conservative Prime Minister Margaret Thatcher had invited him to 10 Downing Street for consultations.

The Honeyford affair was the culmination of a series of controversies played out in Bradford as the Council sought to turn the theory of *Turning Point* into reality. For example, having decided that it would consult with the 'credible representatives' of ethnic minorities (1981: 49), in 1982 the Council agreed to various 'concessions' put forward by the newly formed Bradford Council for Mosques (BCM), a latter day incarnation of the 'Mosque Committee' (Dahya, 1974). At Drummond these included: the serving of *halal* meat; separate-sex physical education and swimming lessons; the adoption of a multi-faith syllabus for religious education (1987: 116–17). However, in the wake of this decision in early 1983, pressure from Animal Rights activists, rumoured to have NF support, forced a full Council debate on the commitment to serve *halal* meat (1987: 109). With one of their hard won concessions under threat, BCM was successful in having up to 10,000 children boycott their lessons on the day of the debate and demonstrate outside Bradford Town Hall. In any event, the Council voted to retain *halal* meat in Bradford schools but, as Murphy argues, this and other conflicts over the redistribution of power and resources, 'had left a lot of diffuse hatred in the atmosphere' (1987: 109).

Murphy's argument is that Bradford Council's new policies hardened opinion amongst whites and so made 'life more difficult for Browns and Blacks' (1987: 87).[21] Indeed, she seems to approve or advocate a response to racism which does not move beyond the largely 'internalised' survival strategies of the 1960s and 1970s described by Saifullah Khan, where minorities 'keep in the shadows, keep their heads down' (1987: 70) or adopt 'a heads-below-the-parapet choice' (1987: 129). Murphy acknowledges that compared to the 'flaccid non-racialism' of the 'ineffectual' 'race' relations industry and the 'two-faced' trades unions, vigorous anti-racism suggested a means of 'blacks' and Asians securing racial

21 One discomforting aspect of Murphy's account is that she appears fascinated with 'race' as a physical characteristic, so much so that she insists on calling 'Asians' 'Browns'.

justice 'through tough positive action' (1987: 89–90). However, she is particularly critical of the 'Race Awareness Training' which saw 'truculent zealots' facilitate 'unlearning and dismantling racism' amongst resentful Council staff. For Murphy, it is naïve to think that such an aggressive approach, so often identified with the 'Far Left', can be the only way to cultivate 'race awareness' in Britain. Finally, perhaps in the same way that Gilroy (1992) is 'anti' the anti-racism which reproduces an ethnic absolutism of its own, she remarks:

> Yet in Britain now it seems that whites (anti-racists no less than racists) are so 'Race Aware' that they relate to ethnic minorities almost as though they belonged to a different species who deserve better or worse treatment (depending on which camp you are in) because 'they're not like us'. (Murphy, 1987: 101–2)

Murphy raises questions too about *Turning Point*'s notion of 'parity of esteem' for all cultures and describes friends' 'howls of protest about racist interference' when she personally involves herself in the 'domestic dramas' of young BrAsian women (1987: 26). Not alone amongst feminist and liberal universalists then or now, she wonders where the limits of 'cultural self-determination' might be.[22] However, in a position on arranged marriages, which foreshadowed that of Keighley MP, Ann Cryer, in the 2000s, Murphy goes so far as to suggest that 'there is a strong case to be made for legal interference in their [British-Mirpuri] domestic affairs' (1987: 24). Nevertheless, she acknowledges that 'this will mean confronting the wrath of British Muslim males' (1987: 24), one of the constituencies that Murphy does not venture to talk to.[23]

Despite her unrestrained liberal frankness, Murphy is sympathetic to the way in which, for rural to urban international migrants especially, a 'disconcerting' pluralistic environment such as modern Britain 'has the potential for strengthening rather than eroding hard line attitudes' (1987: 27). For Murphy, Islam has had a positive impact on 'citizenship' in Manningham—in the mid 1980s the area is 'safe' and 'lacks its fair share of crime, by British standards, because as yet its Muslims are an uncommonly law-abiding lot' (1987:29). However, after she meets up with a group of chauvinistic young 'Mirpuri drop-outs' over a 'strong brew' in a 'Sikh pub', she does not feel that the increasingly acculturated and 'jobless young Muslims' will remain 'tamed' by Islamic traditions and authorities for that much longer: 'my forecast is Big Trouble Ahead' (1987: 29).

22 See Saghal and Yuval-Davis' (1992) critique of state-sponsored multiculturalism as lending legitimacy to the patriarchy of religious leaders.

23 Kureishi does talk to the President of BCM who wants single sex, not Islamic or racially segregated, schools: 'No, no, no! No apartheid!' (1986: 160).

TRANS-NATIONAL TRADITIONS: 'ISLAMIC BRITAIN' AND RELIGIOUS STUDIES TO THE PRESENT

'Muslim communities from South Asia have largely dictated public perceptions about Islam in Britain. In this regard no city has featured so centrally and consistently in shaping such attitudes as Bradford.' (Lewis, 1994: 24)

In 1994 Lewis published *Islamic Britain* which is the product of the most sustained period of engagement with the city of Bradford of all the work considered in this chapter. It reflects the author's ten years experience as Advisor to the Bishop of Bradford on inter-faith issues and six years research in Pakistan. As the title of Lewis' monograph suggests, his account writes religion back into the account of 'Brad-istan', underlining its current salience as perhaps the most significant marker of identity amongst BrAsians today. Lewis argues that both the *halal* meat and Honeyford affairs signalled that many Muslims in Bradford, and certainly 'community leaders', wanted specific public recognition for their religious identifications (1994: 4). However, during the 1980s discussions of 'Islam' and 'Muslims' in Britain were often subsumed under the categories of ethnicity, 'race' or culture. All that began to change of course when on 14 January 1989 members of the Bradford Council for Mosques burned a copy of Salman Rushdie's novel *The Satanic Verses* (1988).

Although he does not explicitly acknowledge it himself, Lewis can be seen as writing in the tradition of religious studies associated with the Community Religions Project (CRP) at the University of Leeds. As Knott (1986; 1992) suggests, during the mid to late 1980s religious studies was only just beginning to respond to the more longstanding interest of the social sciences in migration and ethnicity. Compared to sociologists, anthropologists had shown more concern with the 'cultural stuff' of 'migrant religion'; however, as Knott argues, 'with a few notable exceptions, they … failed to provide plausible accounts of the role and significance of religions in the lives of the groups they … described' (1992: 4–5). In terms of setting a religious studies agenda, Knott firstly submits that, in the social scientific literature on religion and ethnicity, religion is too often seen 'as the passive instrument of ethnic identity' (1992: 12). While there is little doubt that religion can operate in this way, she cites the Rushdie affair, reasoning: 'there are times when religion plays a more active role in the definition of an ethnic group's identity and behaviour than many of these accounts suggest' (1992: 12). Secondly, Knott (1986) argues that religious studies scholars should investigate the empirical dynamics of what happens to the 'content' of religion under conditions of contemporary migration: 'How does a religion and the religiousness of its people change in an *alien* milieu? How are they different from their parent traditions in the homeland?' (Knott, 1986: 8).

Reflecting on Knott's work now, it is fair to say that the empirical project of mapping transformations of religion has been more significantly advanced than the theoretical project of exploring the relationship between religion, ethnicity and identity (McLoughlin, 2005). The CRP has published a number of monographs documenting various dimensions of the religions of South Asian and other minority ethnic communities.[24] However, despite the detailed ethnography produced, an interest in conceptualising the particular salience of religion—the specific 'work' it seems to do—has not been taken up with the same vigour in the literature. It is against this context that *Islamic Britain* must be understood.

Reading the book it is easy to be drawn towards accounts of community politics and public recognition, Lewis' major contribution here being the documentation of BCM's leadership during the Rushdie affair and after. However, while this remains important, it is not Lewis' only, or perhaps even his main, concern. As a historian much more than a theorist of religion or ethnicity, Lewis' key focus is a mapping of the various Islamic 'traditions' re-located in Britain. Thus his study includes an assessment of Islam's institutionalisation in Bradford and the authority of its scholars (*'ulama*), as well as problems of transmission and the need for 'intellectual and imaginative resources ... to engage with the religious, intellectual and cultural traditions of the West' (Lewis, 1994: 208).

Scholars of other disciplines do not always appreciate the significance of such issues, not least for Muslims themselves. For this reason religious studies has an important role to play in taking such matters seriously and engaging other disciplines in producing more sophisticated accounts of religion. However, for this to be at all possible, religious studies scholars must return to, and develop, Knott's more theoretical agenda. Indeed, given the current prominence of religion in Britain's public life, there is now a special need for scholars to be better able to identify the relative 'agency' and 'explanatory power' of 'religion', 'tradition' and their cognates, within the intricate webs of culture and structure that comprise any given context. Lewis' (2002) updated commentary on BrAsian Muslims in Bradford after the 'northern' riots and 9/11 can perhaps be seen as just one example of why this might be necessary.

Movements, mosques and mobilisation: from the institutionalisation of Islam to the Rushdie affair

While Lewis follows Dahya (1974) and Saifullah Khan (1977) in documenting the role of 'ethnic' businesses and community organisations in sustaining distinctive 'cultural worlds' in Bradford, he leads the way in exploring the role of religious institutions in this process. Certainly

24 The CRP monograph series includes accounts of Christians, Buddhists, Hindus, Muslims and Sikhs in Britain.

earlier ethnographers had relatively little to say in this respect, partly because they were working within the paradigm of social anthropology criticised by Knott (1986; 1992). However, it is also fair to say that the institutionalisation of Islam in Bradford accelerated only with the reuniting of families, a process which continued into the 1980s amongst Mirpuris and Bengalis. Indeed, Lewis concurs with Barton (1986), arguing that the first single male migrants almost entirely lapsed in their practice of religion. It was only with the arrival of wives and children from the late 1960s onwards, that the need for mosques and religious teachers to reproduce Islam for a new generation was obviated.[25] While the first mosque in the city was established in Howard Street during 1959, as 'fusion' gave way to 'fission' (Dahya, 1974), different ethnic and sectarian groupings founded their own separate institutions. For example, the small, but still very influential, Gujarati Muslim community reunited quickly and its two mosques were both established by 1962 (Lewis, 1994: 58). In contrast, while the first mosque of the majority Mirpuris was founded as early as 1966, the relatively late reuniting of their families meant that fourteen out of eighteen centres were not opened until the 1980s (1994: 60).

As noted above, BCM was formed in 1981, against the context of Bradford Council's experiment in 'multiculturalism' and in order to provide a platform for issues of common concern to Muslims regardless of ethnic or sectarian differences.[26] A 'credible' channel of communication with the authorities, BCM also played a significant role in mobilising Muslims in defence of this hard won recognition during the *halal* meat and Honeyford affairs. However, as Lewis' account demonstrates, it was the Rushdie affair that gave BCM a national and international profile. The organisation was first informed of the content of *The Satanic Verses*, said blasphemously to defame the Prophet of Islam and his family, by a network of co-religionists in India via an organisation of largely Gujarati Deobandi scholars based in Blackburn. Lewis suggests that 'it is hard to exaggerate the veneration of the Prophet which informs Islamic piety and practice in South Asia in all traditions, but especially amongst the Barelwis' (1994: 154).[27] Indeed, while outrage at Rushdie's novel united the various Islamic movements in Britain temporarily, the book burn-

25 In 1991 there were thirty mosques and nine supplementary schools in Bradford, all 'located within a radius of 1½ miles from the city centre, within seven inner city wards' (Lewis, 1994: 62). In 2004 there were around fifty mosques.

26 Similar organisations were established by Sikhs and Hindus in 1984, but, given the size of their constituencies, they have not had the same impact as BCM (Singh, 2002).

27 Lewis makes a distinction between those Islamic movements which seek to 'defend' (the Barelwis), 'reform' (the Deobandis), or 'reject' (Ahl-i Hadis, Jama'at-i Islami) the traditional paradigm of South Asian Islam, exemplified by Sufi *pirs* (mystical guides, saints) and their shrines (1994: 28).

ing of 14 January 1989 was no spontaneous reaction. Instead, against the general context of a backlash against 'multiculturalism' in Bradford since the Honeyford affair, it can perhaps best be seen as a desperate attempt by BCM to 'draw attention to their continued anguish and anger when confronted by [the] incomprehension of politicians and media alike' (1994: 156).[28]

The book-burning put Bradford centre stage amongst Britain's Muslims. However, Lewis considers that BCM quickly lost control of the debate as Muslims were portrayed by liberals and conservatives alike as 'Nazis': 'For the national media Bradford had become the epicentre of the shock waves convulsing the Muslim communities across Britain' (1994: 158). In Bradford itself Muslims retained only a few allies including the Anglican Bishop. The Community Relations Council, despite a history of long collaboration with BCM, decided to adopt 'no position on the book' (1994: 160). Things took a graver turn when, on 14 February 1989, Ayatollah Khomeini of Iran intervened in the affair with a *fatwa* (legal opinion) calling for the death of Rushdie for blasphemy (1994: 158). Disastrously, argues Lewis, two members of BCM were alleged to have supported the Iranian cleric. However, the Bradford-based Muslim Parliament activist, Mohammed Siddique, challenges this, suggesting that, 'The *fatwa*, remarkably, elevated Muslims from the position of hopeless despair to a position of strength and power' (Siddique, 1993: 72). Empowering fables of a united global Muslim *umma* (community) notwithstanding, Lewis reports that BCM soon realised that local investments in Bradford were at stake as the world's press descended on the city. The organisation quickly made a public statement disassociating itself from Khomeini, insisting that Muslims should stay within the law of the land (1994: 159).

While it is always likely that 'minority' groups will have to rely on a range of political strategies from violence to reform, Lewis argues that the BCM learned important lessons from the events of the Rushdie affair. He contrasts the shift from 'book-burning to vigil' (1994: 163), maintaining that the latter form of protest began to earn BCM a more sympathetic hearing, as did its involvement with a national lobby, the UK Action Committee on Islamic Affairs (UKACIA), which did not approve of the book-burning.[29] However, as we shall see, the experiences of the Rushdie affair did not put an end to violent conflicts in the city although the events do seem to have marked the height of the BCM's powers. The solidarity achieved in response to *The Satanic Verses* tended to obscure

28 BCM wrote to the Prime Minister, Rushdie's publishers, MPs, local Councillors and even the United Nations, all to no avail. As Muslims, no protection under Britain's legislation on 'race' relations or blasphemy was open to them.

29 Interestingly, UKACIA paved the way for a new national umbrella organisation, the Muslim Council of Britain (inaugurated 1997). However, BCM has not, as yet, affiliated.

divisions within the organisation. For example, during the first Gulf War of 1990–1, Lewis notes that Sufi-oriented Barelwi members of the BCM showed themselves ready to unilaterally criticise the British government and their 'anti-Sufi' allies in Saudi Arabia but not the regime in Iraq where some of Islam's holiest Sufi shrines are located (1994: 166–8). In this context some 'Muslim' councillors, who between 1981 and 1992 had increased from just three to eleven in number, publicly distanced themselves from BCM. Perhaps recalling Saifullah Khan's (1977) remarks about leadership cited earlier, one local candidate for the Tories suggested at the time:

> The views, actions and emotional statement by any individual or Muslim organisation does not do justice to the city's 60,000 Muslims since no individual nor organisation has ever been given the mandate by … the Muslims of Bradford to act as their representative or spokesman. (Lewis, 1994: 168)

The worst of times

In the 1990s and 2000s Bradford has continued to be a focus for national and international attention, mainly because of 'riots' involving youth of Pakistani (and especially Kashmiri) heritage. In a new 'Postscript' to a second edition of *Islamic Britain* Lewis provides a brief summary of the most recent report on 'what's wrong' in the city (Ouseley, 2001). He suggests that the findings largely confirm those of the earlier 1996 Bradford Commission report published after the first disorders in 1995. In many ways both reports also realise the fears expressed in *Turning Point* (1981), although neither Ouseley nor Lewis mention this fact:

> There was evidence of rising mistrust and polarisation of Muslim and non-Muslim communities, a rapid increase in the numbers of disaffected Muslim youth, the emergence of exclusionary clan politics, the failure of traditional imams to connect with the world of British Muslim youth and the cumulative impact of such issues on educational underachievement. The city was judged to be 'in the grip of fear' unable to talk honestly and openly of problems within and between communities: fear of being racist; fear of confronting a gang culture and the illegal drugs trade. (Lewis, 2002: 216)

Lewis reports that in such 'official' accounts, 'There has been a recognition that ethnicity is a key factor' (2002: 216). Indeed, he reflects that 'community consolidation and separation … is more not less marked' in Bradford than a decade ago (2002: 220). In Ouseley's (2001) terms, what were once 'comfort zones' (as described by anthropologists in the 1970s) have now become 'closed zones'. However, significantly there is no suggestion here that ethnicity might be theorised, as it was by Cohen (1974) and Watson (1977), in terms of the reorganisation of cultural distinctiveness to advance minority economic and political interests. Ethnicity is not seen as a *situationally functional* strategy of 'survival'. Rather, like Ouseley and others (for example, Macey, 1999), Lewis is mainly interested in the way in which in the 1990s 'ethnicity' has become (situationally) *dysfunctional*, perhaps for BrAsian Muslims themselves, but especially for the city of Bradford as a whole.

One continuity between 1970s anthropology and 1990s public policy, however, is that all argue, in effect, that structural explanations which invoke 'deprivation' and 'racism' tell only part of the story of 'Bradistan'. For Lewis and Ouseley such paradigms have encouraged a 'political correctness', perpetuated by both local government and community leaders, that has inhibited the development of open debate and critical dialogue about tensions and conflicts of the city (see especially Mahony, 2001). Against this context there is a renewed interest in the significance of cultural (and religious) traditions in reproducing patterns of 'self-segregation' in inner-city Bradford, something which increasingly sets Muslims apart from many Hindus and Sikhs. Lewis, for example, argues that for 'significant sections of traditional Muslims from South Asian backgrounds cultural and religious norms do render socialising in conformity with British norms problematic' (2002: 217). The 'norms' that Lewis mentions in this respect include *izzat* (family honour) and (transcontinental) cousin marriages. He also describes how an 'ethnic' media can reinforce encapsulation and the sheer size of the Pakistani Muslim constituency in Bradford supports the maintenance of 'separate' sports leagues and 'parallel' professional and business sectors (2002: 217).

While this language of 'conformity' and 'norms' may appear somewhat loaded, it does underline the persistence of religious and ethnic 'boundaries' in Bradford. Lewis' intervention also represents a novel, if not very self-conscious, revisiting of difficult structural-cultural questions about how, in particular social contexts, cultural and religious 'traditions' can become *resources* for the reproduction of a 'self contained social world' (2002: 217). In particular he argues that, 'The difficulties for a majoritarian religious tradition [such as Islam] to develop the social and intellectual skills to live comfortably as a religious minority are exacerbated in a social context of relative encapsulation' (2002: 18). Committed anti-essentialists might protest that no tradition, even one with the history of political power associated with Islam, is necessarily or inherently 'majoritarian'. However, what Lewis is apparently inviting us to reconsider here, although he does not articulate it explicitly, is the idea that Islam (or Hinduism, Buddhism, Sikhism or Christianity) might be more than some sort of 'empty' signifier, capable of legitimating an endless variation of interpretations and strategies. Contrary to the thrust of most contemporary social science, does not Islam actually comprise a complex of symbols, discourses and practices, in Bourdieu's (1992) terms, a *habitus*, a repertoire of dispositions, that has some sort of real and structuring 'content' and 'agency' in the world?

In this regard Lewis' emphasis on social context is certainly important. However, a discussion of another of Bourdieu's notions, the idea of 'cultural capital' (Bourdieu and Passeron, 1977), is also essential here. The particular 'cultural capital' of any individual or community structures the extent to which the 'resources' of any given 'tradition' can be (i) 'accessed' and/or (ii) 'reproduced' and 'practised' in a given context. Any discussion of the explanatory power of religious traditions needs to take more account of the dialectical relationship between 'culture' and 'structure' as enmeshed formations, something suggested by Cohen (1974), Werbner and Anwar (1991) and others. Lewis, for example, considers that while some Muslim movements, notably Jama'at-i Islami heritage 'moderate Islamists', are creatively re-making tradition through 'engagement' with wider society, others have followed strategies more suggestive of 'isolation' or 'resistance' (2002: 219). What is crucial to draw out here, however, is that the new, articulate and 'engaged' British-born Muslim leadership, which proved effective interlocutors with the state and wider society in the immediate aftermath of 9/11, is increasingly composed of an élite of young educated professionals with a great deal personally invested in Britain. Indeed, for all its 'engagement', Lewis himself maintains that to date such a leadership has been perceived as 'neither able nor interested in connecting with Muslim street culture' (2002: 216) at the grassroots level.

By contrast, Lewis sees 'sections of the traditional political and religious leadership', usually associated with Barelwi and Deobandi mosques in Bradford, as 'isolationists' who have failed 'to connect with the world of British Muslim youth' (2002: 220). By continuing to appoint *imams* from South Asia rather than British-born and English-speaking graduates with a knowledge of British custom and practice, elders have contributed to the creation of an 'intellectual vacuum' (2002: 223) with the 'unfocused resentment' of some young Muslims producing the 'worrying growth of an assertive Muslim identity' (2002: 218). In Bradford this is manifest in a macho culture, which 'can impact negatively on women and minorities deemed to be outsiders living within "their" territory' (2002: 218). Against the context of gangs, drugs, prison and especially educational underachievement, 'Islam becomes a cultural resource' for the sort of defiance and rebellion signalled by real and imagined affiliation to 'rejectionist' anti-Western utopianists such as Hizb al-Tahrir. Lewis' 'dispiriting picture of traditional religious leadership' (2002: 224) finds many echoes in the accounts of BrAsian Muslims in Bradford. Nevertheless, even after thirty to forty years of settlement, neither the ongoing predicament of diaspora for many first generation migrants, nor the importance of continuity of religious and cultural 'norms' to their sense of self, can be ignored. Against the context of changing structural circumstances there is thus a need to understand the limits and possibilities of their repertoire of adaptation strategies, past and present, as suggested by their individual and collective 'cultural capitals'. As Phillips (2003) argues, 'preference'—whether for 'isolation' from, 'engagement' with, or 'rejection' of, wider British society—is always a 'bounded' choice.

THE EMERGENCE OF A 'BRASIAN' CITY: A CONCLUDING ANALYSIS

'The whole world is segregated in a million different ways so why should Bradford be any different?' (Alam, 2002: 300–1)

As stated at the outset, this chapter contends that by considering together various 'snapshots' of 'BrAsian' Bradford, from the 1960s through to the 2000s, it should be possible to glimpse something of how the city has come to be the way it is. Indeed, to Lewis it would appear that the 'self-contained world' (Lewis, 2002: 217) of Bradford's Muslims today must be understood as the product of the long-term interactions with wider society outlined here. Similarly, part of the problem with Ouseley's (2001) account is that he does not sufficiently contextualise the structural constraints within which Pakistani Muslims have been able to make culturally and religiously constructed choices over a period of more than forty years in the city. This concluding section, then, summarises and elaborates some of the main themes introduced above, in the hope that such a discussion might encourage more deeply contextualised accounts of 'Brad-istan'—and other such postcolonial translocalities—in the future.

The ethnographies of Dahya (1974) and Saifullah Khan (1977) illustrate that the evolution of various 'self-sufficient' Asian 'communities' in Bradford is best seen as an organic response to the ongoing uncertainties and risks of living as a 'minority' of largely rural origins in an urban setting characterised by racism, immigration controls and a permissive majority culture. The often-cited absence of racial and ethnic conflict in 1960s and early-1970s Bradford was due mainly to the cautious adaptation strategies of the first generation. Moreover, even by the early 1970s, the social reproduction of such 'communities' had established real momentum, exerting a 'pressure to conform' which made it difficult for many new arrivals to acquire 'the skills necessary for communication and participation' in wider society (Saifullah Khan, 1977: 80). This dynamic encapsulation of 'Pakistanis' also served the vested interests of 'community' business and religious élites (Dahya, 1974), who actively manipulated 'traditional' cultural symbols to their own particular political and economic ends. Indeed, at least a decade before the expansion of state multiculturalism in the 1980s these same élites were authenticating fictions of ethnic unity in transactions with government and wider society (Saifullah Khan, 1977).

While more acculturated than their parents, Bradford-born and educated generations of BrAsians have also periodically adopted more confrontational political strategies than the first generation. For example, the initial militancy of the AYM during the late 1970s was born of a lack of recognition and the experience of institutional/popular racism. However, significant mobilisation was catalysed mainly by the physical threat posed by racist organisations to the safe 'Asianised' spaces of Bradford such as Manningham. Indeed, the 1976 'Battle of Bradford', described by Mehmood (1983), has one important characteristic in common with the later events of the Honeyford and Rushdie affairs, as well as mobilisations in the name of the Muslim *umma* and the riots of 1995 and 2001 (Murphy, 1987; Lewis, 1994/2002). To a greater or lesser extent, each and every mobilisation can be seen as a reaction to actual or perceived attacks on the 'sacredness' of *apna* (our) 'community', variously identified, both territorial and imagined.

Of course it was only against the context of economic decline and urban unrest in Britain that the local state finally introduced a race-relations policy in 1981. However, as Murphy (1987) suggests, this probably came too late for Bradford and, ultimately, the politicians were unable to control the powerful forces that their decision-making had unleashed. This was true both in terms of the vehemence of hitherto suppressed 'BrAsian' claims and a white backlash against the redistribution of power and resources. The local state subsequently retreated into tokenism, and eventually institutional racism by the early 1990s (Samad, 1997). This destroyed any possibility of a multicultural policy based on cross-cutting 'critical' dialogue (Mahony, 2001), entrenching instead an essentialised 'difference' multiculturalism. Indeed, more than a decade before Ouseley (2001), Halstead (1988) spoke of political acquiescence with *de facto* separatism in the city.

The valency of a 'pan-Asian' political project did not survive the 1980s. By the end of the decade social divisions between Pakistani and Bangladeshi heritage Muslims on the one hand, and Hindus/Sikhs of Indian and especially African-Asian heritage on the other, were becoming more marked, most especially in terms of class, education and upward mobility. The *laissez-faire* approach of British governments to global economic restructuring left large numbers of unskilled migrant workers from peasant families in 'Azad' Kashmir with little prospect of working again and, despite a reliance on state benefits, this has reinforced a perceived sense of, and need for, self-sufficiency and encapsulation.

Against this context BrAsian Muslims in Bradford today represent an economic underclass. 'They' also remain racially and ethnically marked as 'Pakistanis', 'Bangladeshis' and so on, but amongst the British-born there is a deep ambivalence about 'back home'. Therefore, the salience of Islam as a diasporic badge of religious, but also of ethnic and class, pride, something reinforced by one geo-political crisis after another since 1989 (Werbner, 2002), is not difficult to comprehend. While the state, concerned commentators (Murphy, 1987; Lewis, 1994/2002), and many *babas* see Islam as a way of 'taming' the youth and instilling in them the values of good citizenship, there is evidence that Islam too is a vehicle for genuine working-class anger and protest. However, one negative by-product of this can be the aggressive 'masculinity' confronted by Mehmood's (1983) character, Shaheen, and criticised more recently by Macey (1999).

Something else is striking about the contemporary situation. For all the history of political mobilisation amongst BrAsians in Bradford, in *their* moments of protest, the current working-class youth of Pakistani and Kashmiri Muslim heritage do not obviously have a political project around which to organise. Indeed, perhaps quite unremarkably, just as 'pan-Asian' identity politics deconstructed (but never displaced) 'Pakistani' identity politics in the late 1970s, and just as 'Muslim' identity politics deconstructed 'Asian' identity politics in the 1980s, so the 1995 and 2001 'riots' can be seen as deconstructing the seeming hegemony of a 'Muslim' identity politics in contemporary Britain.[30] In the wake of the Rushdie affair Modood rightly suggested that 'the new strength among Muslim youth in not tolerating racial harassment, owes no less to Islamic re-assertion than to metropolitan anti-racism' (Modood, 1992a: 272). However, in the decade or so since Rushdie, Muslim identity politics has often become the preserve of the upwardly mobile and educated middle classes, focused as much (if not more) on relations with the British state and wider society than on social uplift amongst the Muslim grassroots.

Despite the increasing evidence of its particular dynamics, four decades after Badr Dahya first began his fieldwork amongst single Pakistani male migrants, there is no sign of a waning in contributions to the literature produced about Bradford. However, rather than the 'insider' critique of a prevailing 'assimilationism' which typified 1970s anthropology, much of the contemporary literature too often fails to challenge the 'outsider' emphasis of the nation-state on 'citizenship' and 'community cohesion', a discourse which has (re)emerged in the context of New Labour's communitarianism and new moral panics about immigration and trans-national terrorism. One of the few authors publicly intervening in this debate, interestingly, is a relatively new BrAsian novelist, perhaps the only one of any note to have emerged in Bradford since Tariq

30 By 'identity politics' I mean the sort of political recognition, respect and equality that has been sought by groups that 'identify' themselves in terms of 'ways of life' that are somehow 'different' from the dominant culture. See Parekh, 2000.

Mehmood. Mohammed Yunas Alam, British-born of Pakistani heritage, has recently published two novels (1998; 2002) which illuminate that, beyond the dominant discourse of ethnicity, 'race', culture and religion, 'Brad-istan' today continues to be a city of highly differentiated, pluralised and competing interests.[31]

Kilo (2002), for example, is the account of how Khalil Khan, the son of an inner-city shop-keeper, is attracted to the much discussed but little researched career of drug-dealing after his hard-working father is broken (and ultimately dies) as a result of the intimidation of a multi-ethnic gang of protection racketeers. As Khalil, whose nickname is 'Kilo', in turn, seeks independence, revenge and peace with himself, the novel touches upon a wide range of complex issues: everyday acculturation and segregation; gangsters, drug smuggling and street violence; families, marriage and Pakistan; good cops and bad cops; religiosity, transgression, hypocrisy and morality; racism and the 'fantasy world' of community relations. Indeed, anyone writing about Bradford in the future would do well to ponder the following retort from Kilo to a local policeman who accuses him of 'killing your *own people* [my emphasis added]'. Here, there appears to be a defiant challenge to all that would too easily ascribe an ethnicised, racialised, culturalist or religious identification in contexts where none necessarily exist:

> Me killing people? My people? ... Had someone just made me non-elected leader of Asian and black people without having the decency to have asked first? I had no people. I didn't claim to be a politician, nor did I push myself as one of those selfish bastards who claimed to lead the community. (Alam, 2002: 118)

31 Thanks to Philip Lewis for alerting me to Alam's work.

Part II. PORTRAITS

N. Ali, V.S. Kalra and S. Sayyid

Part II of this volume attempts to present a comprehensive survey of various aspects of BrAsian life. Our contention that the BrAsian presence has radically altered the shape of Britishness is illustrated in this section by a series of empirical portraits that cover the formation of the diaspora; the geographies and political economy of settlement; and its impact on social institutions.

The first two chapters look at, respectively, the historical formation of the BrAsian diaspora and the salience of the migration process. Humayun Ansari's chapter follows the historical journey of the South Asian presence in Britain between the beginning and end of the Raj (1857–1947). It examines the South Asian settlers in Britain prior to the formation of BrAsian identity and traces the early presence of princes, *ayahs*, *lascars* and students, a sizeable group of people who are absent in conventional historical narratives. Nasreen Ali contextualises post-Second World War migration from South Asia to Britain by placing it within the relationship established between Europe and India from the fifteenth century onwards. Ali identifies and differentiates pre-colonial, colonial and post-colonial linkages thus placing BrAsian settlement within an appropriate historical perspective. The narrative presented in Ali's chapter provides much of the background for the subsequent chapters in the book since it deals with the crucial role that migration plays in BrAsian settlement.

The inclusion of a question on ethnicity in the Census of 1991 has meant that a range of quantitative indicators is now available for those interested in Britain's racialised minorities. Ceri Peach, utilising the Censuses of 1991, 2001 and other data sources, provides a demographic picture of BrAsian settlement. These statistical frames are filled in by the next four chapters, which examine the relationship between public institutions and practices and BrAsian communities. Political voting patterns are the subject of Mohammed Anwar's chapter. By providing a quantitative and historical assessment of BrAsian voting patterns, Anwar illuminates the level of political participation and voter preference. Shinder Thandi's chapter focuses on the economic story of BrAsians. By contrasting the perception of BrAsian business success with the reality of unemployment rates and typologies of entrepreneurial engagement,

Thandi makes a significant contribution to the literature on the economic activities of minority groups. Virinder S. Kalra looks at the question of policing and BrAsians. Historically BrAsians have been constructed as the victims of crime rather than its perpetrators, but in either case have received poor services from the police. The changing contours of this relationship are explored in the aftermath of the 2001 civil disturbances in Oldham, Burnley and Bradford. Karl Atkin provides an overview of the way in which ideas of multiculturalism, anti-racism and institutional racism have been central at various times in promoting change in the Health Service. Unfortunately, none of these approaches has managed to alter the fundamental inability of the institutions of the NHS to provide an adequate service to BrAsians. These chapters interrogate the extent to which public institutions have been able to provide services targeted to the specific needs of a BrAsian citizenry.

The next two chapters, by Claire Alexander and Fauzia Ahmad respectively, examine the way in which BrAsian youths and families are problematised within the terms of the sociological imagination of racialised others. Specifically, Alexander traces the various ways in which BrAsian young people have been represented and demonised by public and academic discourse. Fauzia Ahmad takes up the issue of poor service delivery through a case study of marriage. Ahmad looks at the way in which the legal profession, allied with social workers has managed to pathologise the institution of 'arranged marriage'. The variety of practices that take place under the term are thereby reduced to a function of patriarchy, which needs to be opposed by state structures. Ahmad argues that a more nuanced approach, which can distinguish between various kinds of marriages, is required.

Lastly, Gurharpal Singh and Rupa Huq present case studies of Leicester and North West London. Singh makes a cogent argument about the way in which Leicester has come to be represented as a 'model' multicultural city, a status which, however, often belies the political contradictions that are ever present. Huq takes us on a tour of Southall and Wembley, two suburbs of London, which have a national iconic status in BrAsian geographies. As early centres of settlement they are different from the rest of the country (and London) in that they are suburbs rather than inner cities, giving them an ambiguous status in relation to the city.

Each of the chapters in this part add to the mosaic of understanding BrAsian life. The authors' viewpoints vary according to their disciplinary background, but each highlight the tensions besetting the concept of Britishness as it confronts its particularity through the presence of BrAsians. The ruptures created by this interaction have occasionally been violent, but even in their less jarring manifestations are never without some form of social cost. It is perhaps in the creative medium that the fissures of BrAsia find their most positive aspect, as Part III will highlight.

MAPPING THE COLONIAL

SOUTH ASIANS IN BRITAIN, 1857–1947

Humayun Ansari

The pattern of South Asians arriving in Britain in the decades between 1857 and 1947 did not take the shape of a uniformly rising curve. The periods of most intense activity coincided with the consolidation of Britain's reputation as a leading imperial and industrialised nation in the late nineteenth century, and the First World War when meeting the demands of the war effort acted as a catalyst in stimulating migration. In contrast, the economic stagnation and very high levels of unemployment that characterised the inter-war period acted as a brake inhibiting any particularly large numbers of new arrivals. Therefore, South Asian movement to Britain was marked by peaks and troughs as well as many disjunctures brought about by the combination of material and ideological circumstances experienced by socio-economically, religiously and culturally differentiated individuals and groups of migrants and the societies from which they came.

While a South Asian presence in Britain can be traced as far back as the beginning of the seventeenth century, it was during the course of the nineteenth century that migration, leading to the evolution of 'settler' communities of any significant size, took place. At that time the first relatively permanent South Asian populations (mainly Muslim), amounting to no more than a few hundred in total, were established in Cardiff, Liverpool and the East End of London. Over time these communities of 'sojourners' grew with people of South Asian origin being born in Britain. But it was not until the end of the First World War that South Asians started to form a significant part of the 'visible' migrant population. This shift was primarily the result of the evolving relationship between Britain and its colonies, a relationship that had given rise to conditions that precipitated the earlier migratory flows from the latter to the former. Caught in the web of relationships between the metropolis and the colony, and the demands and needs of imperial trade and industry, these South Asians were less able than before to determine how they lived and where they worked. Consequently, whenever a demand for cheap labour appeared in any part of the British Empire, South Asian labourers were exported to work on terms that offered the possibility of a relatively better future than the hardship and bare subsistence at home. Hence many, eventually, found their way to Britain.

By the end of the nineteenth century South Asians were attracted to Britain by its growing reputation as the land of opportunity. One major factor, for instance, was that for a comparable job, the wages were considerably higher. Estimates state that in 1895 the *per capita* income in Britain was £36.94 compared with £2.65 in India (Brown, 1994: 110). For South Asian seamen arriving in Britain this, combined with the brutal treatment they suffered on ships, made desertion highly compelling.

Furthermore, once the British had established their dominance over India, in particular after crushing the Rebellion of 1857, the perception had grown among Indian élites that it was the superiority of the British educational system that had enabled the British to acquire the mental capacity and the material capabilities to achieve such immense power. Since many of the élites were now convinced that colonial rule was here to stay, it appeared that the best way of achieving their social and economic aspirations in the new dispensation would be through participation in the running of the colonial system, for which Western education probably offered the most convincing and suitable credentials. Consequently, from the mid nineteenth century a steady trickle of Indian students began to arrive in Britain. From a mere four in 1845 their numbers steadily grew to 207 in the 1890s, and by 1910 there were around 700. Scottish universities were particularly popular, perhaps because of the disproportionately large number of Scots who taught in India. These institutions gained a high reputation in engineering and medicine. At the turn of the twentieth century the Edinburgh Indian Students Association alone boasted a membership of 200. Some of these students eventually settled in Britain making significant contributions in their local communities.

A variety of others came in search of opportunities—for example, teachers of Asian languages such as Professor Syed Abdullah who taught Hindustani at University College, London in 1869. There were merchants and traders, many of whom were involved in peddling and many of whom had initially arrived as employees of British Indian firms, but with a flair for enterprise some established their own businesses. In addition, there were street hawkers and musicians; itinerant surgeons, ear and eye doctors; a petitioner class, mainly comprising small scale farmers from the Punjab who came to make their land claims; and, higher up the social scale, Indian *nawabs* (for example, Nawab Nazim of Bengal), with their retinue in tow. Then there remained the maritime workers and domestic servants who for long had formed part of a transient population that connected Britain with its empire—thousands of South Asian seamen, or *lascars*, who were employed on ships plying between India and Britain, and hundreds of mainly female domestic servants, or *ayahs*, who travelled with their employers on extended visits to Britain.

Occasionally during the late nineteenth century an individual South Asian acquired fame or notoriety. The most famous example was Munshi Abdul Karim, who arrived soon after Queen Victoria's Golden Jubilee in 1887 and quickly rose from waiting at her table to teaching her rudimentary Hindustani, eventually becoming her 'Indian Secretary' in 1894. Given the growing negative perceptions of Indians that had developed in the second half of the nineteenth century, the Queen's courtiers and government officials, especially those connected with Indian affairs, began to resent the 'social and official position accorded him in Court Circulars and on all occasions by the Queen' (Visram, 2002: 46). They accused him of spying and after Victoria's death sent him ignominiously packing to India where he died in obscurity.

UP TO 1914

As South Asians became familiar with the British social and cultural environment, they established centres where they engaged in intellectual and political exchanges among themselves and discussed practical matters of concern in relation to wider British society. They also set up a range of religious organisations. As their memberships increased in number and in confidence, all these organisations, associations and societies gradually grew in influence, serving a range of moral and welfare functions. The Edinburgh Indian Association was created in 1883 and the Indian Gymkhana in 1916. The Religious Society of Zoroastrians was established in 1861, and the Anjuman-i-Islam in 1886, which was a precursor to the Central Islamic Society (1910), and the Woking Mission (1912). Sikhs likewise established the Khalsa Jatha in 1908, followed quickly by the founding of the first *gurdwara* in 1911.

From this cross-section of South Asian institutions one can discern the presence, by the early twentieth century, of a significant population from diverse backgrounds scattered individually and in groups of various sizes around Britain. Some had been settled for several generations, others more recently, and yet others could still be described as broadly 'transient'. Although there was certainly a South Asian presence, whether, by 1914, a clearly identifiable self-conscious 'Asian' entity existed in Britain remains questionable.

The experiences of South Asians in Britain during this period also need to be understood in relation to the wider developments taking place in British society. By the mid nineteenth century British society had become deeply conscious of race and class. However, in respect of race, new meanings had gained popularity. The 'ethnocentric' racism of the earlier periods, in which South Asians had been viewed as inferior in terms of their civilisation, and, as heathens deserving of Victorian paternalism, in need of being rescued, gave way to notions of racial supremacy underpinned by Social Darwinist biological determinism. The British now thought of themselves as a race destined to govern and subdue. After the 1857 Rebellion, or so-called Indian Mutiny, South Asians were increasingly perceived by many in Britain as naturally, 'obsequious, deceitful, licentious and avaricious' with 'no right whatever' (Kincaid, 1973).

Hence these notions shaped interaction between the 'respectable classes' in Britain and the *ayahs* and *lascars*, who in the mid nineteenth century continued to arrive at an estimated annual rate of 10–12,000. The number of *lascars* employed on merchant ships registered in Britain increased rapidly in the next few decades and by 1891 had risen to over 24,000 and by 1914 to over 51,000 (Hughes, 1855; Ommer and Panting, 1980). Consequently the numbers of those settling in the East End of London and Glasgow grew too. Having arrived in Britain some were mistreated and instances of cruelty were not unknown. Indeed, many fled their employers and, unable to find an alternative, slid into criminal activity or resorted to begging, living in conditions of extreme poverty and overcrowding (Mayhew, 1873). *Lascars*, who had deserted to escape cruel treatment, could end up being looked after by missionaries, who regarded them as a 'moral challenge'. Because of their dire circumstances they were considered 'vulnerable' and were provided with accommodation and recreational facilities in institutions such as 'The Strangers' Home for Asiatics' established in 1857 and later 'The Ayahs' Home' set up in 1897. At the same time, given their situation, *lascars* and *ayahs* presented promising opportunities for conversion, and converts such as Reverent E.B. Bose in London and Aziz Ahmad in Glasgow were assigned to proselytize among *lascars* at the turn of the century.

On the whole, therefore, large numbers of South Asians in late-Victorian Britain survived on the margins. However, the more resilient and resourceful fended for themselves, going about the streets selling religious tracts, as hawkers of Indian jewellery, playing drums and even sitting as 'models' for artists. Some continued in domestic service or worked as casual labourers. But they also survived because of the generosity of, at one end of the scale, wealthy Indian benefactors such the Maharaja Duleep Singh, and at the other end, the white working classes among whom they lived. While colour prejudice certainly dogged the lives of the South Asian poor, evidence also suggests that their indigenous counterparts seemed, on the whole, to be fairly racially tolerant. They mingled with ease—in public houses, theatres and music and dance halls. Here 'colour or country [was] considered no obstacle.... Everybody free and easy—*lascars*, blacks, jack tars, coal heavers, dustmen, women of colour, old and young, and a sprinkling of remnants of once fine girls ... all jigging together.' (Visram, 1986). Despite the widespread opposition to cohabitation and miscegenation, there were always some Englishwomen who willingly consorted with and married South Asians without any feeling of shame or degradation (London City Mission Magazine, 1857). Many former *lascars*, supported by their wives, ran lodging houses and cafés for their compatriots.

The children of South Asian settlers, unencumbered by the state's policy of preventing settlement through repatriation, were better placed to move up the social ladder since they were less prone to impediments of language and religion. While still taunted and abused, gradually they merged during this period into the local, English and Christian, community. Among them was Frederick Mahomed (1818–88), son of Sake Dean Mahomed (1759–1851) a notable early nineteenth-century settler. Author of *The Travels of Dean Mahomet*, the first book written and published by an Indian in English (Fisher, 1996), he became known as the innovative and accomplished 'Shampooing Surgeon' of King George IV, and also set up a fencing academy and gymnasium. Conscious of his South Asian background, he 'took pride in some elements of his Indian Islamic heritage'. Later on his own son, Frederick Akbar Mahomed (1849–84), through his work on hypertension, made a major contribution to medical science (Swales, 1996). Another notable, Albert J. Mahomet was 'possibly the first British-born Indian photographer'. His reminiscences *From Street Arab to Pastor*, first published in 1894, gave an interesting account of the life of the poor in the East End of London (Shephard, n.d.). As Mukherjee (1944) has illustrated, with the case of the Bonnerjee family, although many prosperous and educated South Asians became immersed in 'British' values and culture, participating actively in the social life of their white counterparts, they also expressed hybridity in their ceremonies and rituals, in their cuisine and in other aspects of their social existence. This process of acculturation equipped their subsequent generations to pursue successful professional careers enabling them to live in considerable comfort. By 1914 the number of South Asians entering self-employment had increased (Visram, 2002). Others were students who, on obtaining their qualifications, decided to settle permanently in Britain, making careers as physicians, surgeons, lawyers, journalists, engineers, teachers and in a wide range of other professions.

During the later decades of the nineteenth century, while most members of South Asia's élite continued to view their futures in terms of being junior partners within the British imperial enterprise (Mancherjee Bhownagree, Tory MP for Bethnal Green from 1895 to 1906 is a case in point), the Indian nationalist movement was gathering momentum. As a consequence, some educated Indians sought to influence political opinion in Britain in favour of self-rule. The East Indian Association, established in 1866, had started campaigning for the promotion of Indian interests nineteen years before the founding of the Indian National Congress in 1885. A number of South Asians, convinced of the damage that imperial rule had wreaked in India, felt that their country's voice needed to be heard at the highest level at the heart of the Empire—in the British Parliament—if they were to harbour any hopes of having their aspirations met. Men such as Dadabhai Naoroji (1825–1917), who was eventually elected to Parliament in 1892, despite racist jibes from the likes of the incumbent Prime Minister Lord Salisbury, presented powerful critiques of colonial rule and lobbied for economic and political reform in India (Ralph, 1997).

However, Naoroji represented by no means the only political strand that existed among South Asians in Britain. By the early twentieth century the politics of pan-Islamism and Muslim modernism formed the twin pillars on which Muslims from Western-educated classes of Indian society—administrators, merchants and professionals—built strategies to pursue their individual interests as well as those of their community. Syed Ameer Ali (1849–1928), from a distinguished Muslim family, like many South Asian Muslims of his class, suspected Hindu hegemony in India at Muslim expense. Having retired from his position as Judge of the Calcutta High Court in 1904, he settled in England with his English wife. There he chose to advance specifically Muslim interests, pursuing separatist political ambitions through organisations such as the London branch of the All India Muslim League (established in India in 1906), which he founded in 1908. Through substantial lobbying of Parliament, he, together with other prominent South Asian Muslim pressure groups, helped to shape and modify British policy on Indian issues. He was appointed to the Privy Council—despite King Edward VII's opposition to this 'clever' but potentially 'very dangerous' 'native'—'in the hope that such a prize would stop him "rocking the boat" of imperial rule'. This ploy failed to stop his criticism of British policy. Undeterred by the British government's lack of response on pan-Islamic concerns, he set up the Red Crescent Society in 1912, through which funds could be gathered and provisions sent to help the Turks in Tripolitania, and after the First World War he continued 'to stir up against the British Government in connection with their Turkish policy sentiments of hostility and hatred among his co-religionists...' (Forward, 1995).

As attacks against the Ottomans increased, many younger generation Muslims—Rafiuddin, Syed Mahmud and Mushir Husain Kidwai among them—influenced by Bolshevik ideas, began to favour an anti-British, pan-Islamic struggle with the aim of achieving the freedom of the Muslim world from Western dominance, not entirely or necessarily by constitutional means. As a consequence, a range of political societies emerged with the broad aim of stemming the decline of the Muslim worldwide brotherhood, or *umma.* They published pamphlets and articles disseminating information about Muslim issues, and involving members of the British establishment to positively influence both public perceptions and official policy. However, the British establishment was never confident enough to allow these Indian Muslims to play any significant role in policy making.

Beyond the leading figures, whose approach, on the whole, was loyal, moderate and constitutional, there emerged a group of students altogether more radical in their political ideology, who were prepared to use revolutionary methods in their fight to rid India of alien rule. At the turn of the century India House, established in London in 1905 by Krishnawarma, acknowledged as 'the architect of the revolutionary movement in England' (Datta, 1978), became the centre of activity for this more extreme strand of nationalist opinion. Convinced that the constitutional path to Home Rule was ineffective, and impatient with the slow progress towards independence, activists, such as Savarker and Cama, advocated force and violence as part of their strategy to overthrow British rule. The most dramatic moment in this anti-colonial agitation came in London in 1909, when Sir William Curzon Wyllie, a civil servant notorious for keeping a close eye on Indian students' political activities and movements, was assassinated by Madan Lal Dhingra, who saw the killing as 'an act of patriotism and justice' and the laying down of his life for the cause of his motherland as a matter of great pride and honour (Visram, 2002).

THE FIRST WORLD WAR

Although the more radical wing of the nationalist movement attempted to make capital in the turbulent political climate of the First World War, nationalist South Asian opinion had broadly supported the war effort. Indeed, the First World War proved to be a turning point in Indian-British relations, with important knock-on effects for South Asians living in Britain. With a large proportion of the British male population joining the armed forces, the needs of industry compelled employers to meet labour requirements by drawing on resources in other parts of the Empire. *Lascars*, who by 1914 formed nearly 17.5 per cent of the maritime workers in the British merchant fleet, thus had their contracts extended and many, lured by the possibility of higher wages and better terms and conditions 'jumped ship' and obtained European articles. On-shore industries around London, Liverpool, Sheffield and Glasgow, struggling to meet their labour demands, attempted to entice *lascars* with offers of higher remuneration while turning a blind eye to their desertion. Firms, such as John Walker and Tate sugar refiners, and Lever Brothers at Port Sunlight in Cheshire, ignored government warnings against 'harbouring' absconders and recruited them until more white workers became available. Other South Asians, artisans and mechanics from Bombay and the Punjab, found jobs in industry including in munitions factories. Many of these South Asian workers had been living in Britain for some time and had decided against returning to India. While there was pressure from some quarters to repatriate them, the government could find little justification for doing so. Thus by the end of the war a reservoir of South Asian labour had developed in Britain, which was further supplemented by seamen and soldiers discharged as the war ended.

The First World War also brought about a radical change in personal relations between, and mutual perceptions of, South Asians and the British. In Britain young men of South Asian descent successfully joined the armed forces—some, despite the War Office's reluctance (influenced by racial assumptions) to award them commissions, achieved officer rank in the army and the air force. Indra Lal Roy, a nineteen-year-old ace pilot, who was killed in 1918 in a dogfight over France, was perhaps the most prominent of these volunteers (Visram, 2002). Indian soldiers fought gallantly against their enemies, and acquitted themselves bravely on the battlefield, 'springing like cats and surmounting obstacles with unexampled agility' (from a German soldier's letter quoted in Mason, 1986: 413). As the war progressed, it was increasingly acknowledged—often through the award of top honours such as the Victoria Cross—that South Asians could fight in battle as well as their white counterparts, and so they came to command much respect right across Britain. The British public appreciated their sacrifices (3,427 *lascars* lost their lives and 7,700 Indian soldiers died on the Western Front [Visram, 2002]) for King and country, and the authorities were compelled to take interest in their welfare. Having suffered heavy casualties, over 14,500 Indian soldiers were brought to England where they were treated in makeshift hospitals in Brighton, Netley and other south-coast towns. Some of the survivors subsequently made Britain their home. Others returned from India to settle in Britain after the war.

Politically too, it was considered necessary for the Indian wounded to be to be looked after as well as their white counterparts and with due regard to their cultural sensitivities. Indian students in Britain, working in hospitals alongside the British as physicians, assistant surgeons, dressers, nurse orderlies, storekeepers and clerks, made it difficult for white British people to maintain social distance or retain stereotypes of racial and cultural inferiority and incivility. Other Indians, some from the Strangers' Home for the Asiatic sailors, were recruited as cooks, ward sweepers, water carriers, washer men and tailors, and through physical proximity and practical interactions, all helped to undermine the kind of aloofness that had reflected paternalism and dominance in relations between the British and Indians in the past.

That said, many of the old attitudes of racial superiority and bigotry, especially among the upper classes, persisted and were detected by some of the wounded soldiers in the differential treatment they received at the hands of English doctors. Great efforts were made to prevent South Asian soldiers from mixing socially with the general public lest it should narrow the social distance on which the mystique and prestige of the Empire had partly been created. In particular the authorities were greatly concerned to minimise interaction between white women and South Asians, whether students, *lascars* or soldiers. These men were presumed to imbue dubious morality and to possess 'crude ideas ... about European women; they cannot understand the freedom with which the sexes mingle' (Visram, 1989). Hence during this period the authorities became obsessed with guarding the 'honour' of white women and, in their effort to avoid 'scandals', prohibited even the most innocent of liaisons. Instructions accordingly went out that nurses were to work only in a supervisory capacity; Indian soldiers were to be confined to hospitals; those seen talking to women would be severely punished. Women, white and Indian, were only allowed to visit the wounded if they were armed with proper credentials.

The entry of the Ottoman Caliphate into the war on the German side created a dilemma for South Asian Muslims in Britain. Loyalty to Britain was demanded, but it was emotionally impossible for them to oppose the Ottoman Caliphate, the most important symbol of the worldwide Muslim community. Many could not avoid being concerned about the hostility directed at the Ottoman Empire, which was being expressed both in official circles and in the press, and they responded by articulating their views with much feeling, taking many risks and expending considerable energy and personal resources in defence of the Ottoman Empire's integrity. Through a web of pressure groups and organisations, and with the help of prominent establishment men, they tried to influence government policy. Public meetings were organised; resolutions were passed; debates were conducted through letters to *The Times*; petitions were sent to the Prime Minister; and regular bulletins were issued providing a counterpoint to what they perceived to be anti-Turkish propaganda. Very often these individuals found it hard to arrive at a comfortable balance between their sympathy for the Ottoman Caliphate and their loyalty to Britain, and, given the apparent ambivalence of their position, many were kept under close surveillance.

1918–47

The period between the two world wars saw a downturn in the migration of South Asians to Britain. The need for cheap labour, that had created a substantial acceleration in migration during the First World War, quickly dried up after the economic boom fizzled out, and as a result the flow during the 1920s and the early 1930s slowed to a trickle. With the economy stagnating, and unemployment in shipping particularly high, the government and employers introduced numerous policies and practices that excluded 'aliens' from job opportunities, and so discouraged further migration.

However, during the late 1930s and the Second World War migration from India picked up again. Although the inter-war period was undoubtedly one of mass employment and continuous economic gloom, the picture was in fact much more complex. While older export industries continued to experience decline, new industries such as car manufacturing, chemicals, electrical and consumer goods began to grow in regions such as the Midlands, creating substantial job opportunities and raising the living standards of the majority of the population. Prosperous regions—southern England and the Midlands—contrasted with those suffering decay—the north of England, Wales and Scotland. South Asians were encouraged to migrate from those parts of Britain where structural employment, particularly among the unskilled—seamen, coal miners and dock and harbour labourers—had already reached a very high level (Constantine, 1980). Externally, the pressure to leave places in India such as the Punjab was generated by the devastating impact of the Depression on agriculture. Migration within the Empire offered one outlet for economic survival to those plagued by debt. Furthermore, after the First World War unemployment increased rapidly in those regions of the subcontinent from which recruitment into the Indian armed forces had been disproportionately high. So Britain presented an opportunity for the demobilised soldiers too. Moreover, as the economy in Britain began to recover in the late 1930s, a growing number of *lascars*, still often working on iniquitous contracts and in appalling conditions, began to 'jump ship' and escaped inland in an attempt to move into less arduous and better paid work in trade and industry. Even though many were repatriated, it was estimated that two-thirds succeeded in settling in Britain (Banton, 1955). Supported financially and materially by existing networks and institutions—lodging houses, cafés, religious centres—many lived communally in cheap and overcrowded accommodation in close proximity of the city docks, some eking out a meagre existence as petty hawkers selling Indian perfumes and herbal medicines, others labouring on a casual basis in the catering and rag trades.

During this period, while many instances can be found of South Asians being helped by indigenous people among whom they lived and worked, prejudice and racism remained widespread, finding expression in both individual and institutional interactions. Since South Asians in Britain at this time were overwhelmingly male, inter-racial marriages were not uncommon. But with 'scientific racism' and eugenicist theories taking a firm grip on the popular mind, this intermingling was severely frowned upon and described as a 'serious social evil', which, it was claimed, would lead to 'moral decline' and thus needed to be eradicated (Visram,

2002). Men and women involved in such partnerships were stigmatised and denigrated. Indian peddlers similarly felt the brunt of racial prejudice. They were frequently accused of employing sharp practices in their dealings, of undercutting British textiles and of duping housewives into believing that they had something special to offer. Suffering social and economic exclusion, they set up bodies such as the Indian Workers Association and the Indian Seamen's Welfare League, through which they attempted to resist discrimination. These kinds of organisations facilitated the protection of their interests, at the same time catering for their cultural and welfare needs (Adams, 1987).

One of the groups that remained largely unaffected by the steep downturn in the global economy was that of the students from élite South Asian backgrounds. From the early nineteenth century a key object of British policy in India had been the promotion of Western education, especially among the upper strata so that its members would be equipped to become the interpreters of the 'Raj' to ordinary or less privileged Indian people. These élites, encouraged by prospects of lucrative jobs, power and social status within the established order, became convinced of the superiority of Western education and indeed, aspired to it, pursuing its acquisition with great enthusiasm. By the 1920s the scions of such families were travelling to Britain in substantially increased numbers and could be found not only at such traditionally prestigious institutions such as Oxford and Cambridge but also at universities in London, Birmingham, Manchester, Liverpool, Sheffield, Leeds and Bristol. By 1927 there were around 1,700 Indian students at British institutions (Singh, 1963). Many of the students who came to study medicine and engineering, once qualified, secured jobs and decided, like others before them, to settle more or less permanently in Britain.

During the inter-war period a greater number of South Asian enterprises were established, covering a range of goods and services. They supplied Indian cloth, perfumes, herbs, pickles and spices both to South Asians and to white customers with Indian connections (Choudhury, 1993). With a demand for Indian cuisine, restaurants such as Shafi's and Veeraswamy's in London were set up, which, at least initially, relied on Sylheti galley chefs who had 'jumped ship'. Their success attracted others to the catering trade. By 1946 the number of Indian, mainly Sylheti owned, restaurants in London had risen to twenty, with some of them functioning as 'clearing houses', meeting a variety of migrant needs including accommodation, the provision of advice and guidance on jobs and other opportunities and acting as general contact points and networking hubs (Adams, 1987).

Indian professionals, in particular medical doctors, began to make substantial contributions during this period. By 1945 their number had risen to an estimated one thousand or so. Other than medicine, South

Asian professionals, considering their relatively small presence in Britain, were involved in a surprisingly diverse range of occupations. Among academics, Ratnasuriya lectured in Sinhalese at the London School of Oriental Studies and Radhakrishnan was a professor at Oxford. Barristers and solicitors included M.A. Jinnah, who lived with his sister Fatima and daughter Dina in Hampstead, and Krishna Menon, who became politically active, represented St Pancras as a local Labour councillor, set up the India League and became India's first High Commissioner in London in 1947. He edited the Pelican series 'Penguin Books' (founded in 1935) while also producing many pamphlets on social and political themes. Among writers Mulk Raj Anand became an active member of the group of 'progressive writers' in London and produced some of their most acclaimed literary work. Noteworthy among those who made religion their vocation was Pastor Kamal Chunchie (1886–1953), a Muslim convert to Christianity. He played cricket for Essex, became vice-president of the League of Coloured Peoples (LCP) and a member of the Royal Empire Society. While carrying out missionary work in London, he condemned racism and urged acceptance of 'black' peoples as equals (Visram, 2002).

Middle-class South Asians, committed to creating a 'home' in an environment shaped by British norms and values, often tended to discard aspects of their culture and instead to adopt Western mores—Indian dress, language, cuisine, even religion, saris and vegetarian food were abandoned by most Hindus living in Britain during this period. Sikhs shaved off their beards. Muslims danced the waltz. In general, the majority strove to integrate, all in an effort to avoid being perceived as the 'Other' and thus being excluded from British society. In contrast to 'working-class' South Asians, many of whom clustered in specific geographical areas, 'the professional groups did not form separate geographical or social units and many became anglicised, practicing in white communities' (Allen, 1971). All the same, they were able to carry on expressing multiple identities through various professional, social and religious organisations—the Indian Social Club, the Zoroastrian Association, Jamiat-ul-Muslimin (Muslim Association)—whose existence reflected the gradual formation of at least an embryonic Asian community during these decades.

The outbreak of the Second World War greatly affected the South Asian presence in Britain. As the war had approached, migrants from middling rural backgrounds had begun to enter into petty trading and other entrepreneurial activities, in particular peddling. During the late 1930s scores of South Asians had gravitated to the Midlands and the north of England, encouraged by the many stories circulating among migrants regarding the economic successes of earlier 'pioneers', particularly in the 'door business'. Having saved up enough money, they set up stalls in markets and then moved on to drapery shops and wholesaling (Maan, 1992). South Asian peddling, denounced as a 'growing evil' by the police, was perhaps one of the few occupations through which South Asians, especially the unskilled, could earn a reasonable wage with dignity at this time (Visram, 2002).

Furthermore, the war gave a fillip to the growth industries of the 1920s and 1930s, many of which were converted to the manufacture of essential wartime products, which had knock-on effects where Indians lived and worked. With demand for war matérial rocketing, migrants from India, particularly those finding it hard to obtain work, were directed by the authorities to factories in cities such as Bradford, Leeds, Birmingham and Coventry. The prospects for relatively well paid skilled and unskilled work—for example, as blacksmiths, porters and sweepers in aircraft factories—offered opportunities to, among others, the small numbers of South Asian seamen stranded without employment because of the war (Adams, 1987; Banton, 1955). For instance, it was some of these ex-seamen who first settled in Bradford in 1941; by 1944–5 there was a nucleus of thirty or so South Asians, all former seamen, lodging in the city (Dahya, 1974). Perhaps more markedly, the South Asian population of Birmingham—mainly peddlers— in 1938 estimated to be about one hundred Sikhs and Muslims, had increased to one thousand by 1945 (Wood, 1960; Desai, 1963). Among the arrivals there in early 1940 were merchant seamen who were instructed to go to Birmingham by the Ministry of Labour to work in factories producing military matérial.

Looking back over the period from 1857 to 1947, it is clear that while the South Asian population grew to significant proportions, it lacked homogeneity. Nevertheless, and despite the fact that the numbers were relatively small, compared with the mass migration that began after the Second World War, the movement of South Asians that had occurred during that period clearly formed the basis of later migratory processes. Just as 'push' and 'pull' factors operated from the 1950s onwards, so a similar combination of factors played a crucial part in drawing South Asian migrants to Britain over the preceding century. South Asian settlers comprised people from different religious, linguistic, ethnic and socio-economic backgrounds, including those who were born in Britain as products of inter-racial unions. The picture that emerges of their lives, experiences, reactions and responses is a complex one. Throughout this period South Asians experienced much racial hostility and social exclusion, which they resisted in myriad ways. On the whole the development of a wide range of socio-cultural, welfare and occupational organisations suggests they continued to retain a sense of South Asian identity and community solidarity—indeed, the cultural impact of their efforts has endured and this is reflected in the architecture and cuisine of the period (see Nasser, this volume). A significant number became involved in the struggle for colonial freedom and social justice and during the inter-war years, as the freedom movement intensified, they took increasingly politically active and radical stands. Of particular significance was the work these 'pioneering' settlers conducted in forging the primary links in the chain that would connect these earlier setters with their later counter-parts, while at the same time laying the foundation of the kaleidoscopic BrAsian community.

ANISH KAPOOR

John Holt and Laura Turney

Kapoor is described as one of the most internationally influential sculptors of his generation. He was born in Bombay but has lived and worked in London since the early 1970s where he was educated at Chelsea School of Art. His work has been exhibited all over the world and is held in a number of public and private collections. Kapoor's creativity is concerned with an engagement with deep-rooted metaphysical polarities. These polarities are manifest in his work, for example, absence/presence—to be/not to be—the intangible/the tangible.

Kapoor's sculptures reveal a fascination with light and darkness as he confronts us with notions of space/not space. Pier Luigi Tazzi writes that Kapoor achieves this effect (a manifestation of 'the void') through:

> ... his knowledgable use of materials—the pigments and their dispersability, stone and its hardness, surfaces that are reflective and others opaque, chasms and protrusions—with the 'spiritual' import of his own research and the illusions of sight and the mind. Kapoor's work is always metonymic, never metaphorical, even when it draws from the vast repertoire of universal symbolism. (Bhabha and Tazzi, 1998: 104)

Kapoor is an enormously inventive and versatile artist whose works not only take over the physical space of the gallery but psychological space as well, as his work is transformed by the physical, psychological (and for some spiritual) experiences of the viewer. Drawing on Greek mythology, *Marsyas* is Kapoor's most recent work. Composed of three steel rings joined by a single span of red PVC membrane, *Marsyas* occupied the whole length of the Tate Modern's Turbine Hall.

IMPERIAL IMPLOSIONS

POSTCOLONIALITY AND THE ORBITS OF MIGRATION

Nasreen Ali

Migration is the movement from one locality to another distinct locality for settlement. It is a common phenomenon within human history and the world can be mapped in terms of crystallisations of previous waves of migration. The expansion of the British Empire saw administrators, soldiers, traders and settlers from the British Isles spread like a thin veneer over much of its imperial possessions. Conversely the collapse of the Empire (1947–60s) saw many of them return to the British Isles. The end of the Empire also signalled the migration to Britain of a significant number of colonial and ex-colonial subjects of the Crown who were racially marked within the architecture of the Empire in contrast to the white populations of, for example, Australia or Canada. Their arrival from the English-speaking Caribbean and parts of South Asia illustrated that the 'Empire' was coming 'home'—a sense of what this meant was captured in the slogan: 'we are here, because you were there'—which set the stage for an intense and compulsory engagement with the postcolonial, an engagement explored in other chapters of this book.

This chapter aims to describe and account for the wave of migration into Britain that has crystallised to produce the BrAsian phenomenon. This wave's immediate antecedent was the immigration that, following the end of the Second World War, brought millions of people to the devastated industrial core of Europe. But having peaked in the years 1962–75 migration from South Asia tailed off as racialised immigration controls were put in place by successive Conservative and Labour governments. However, this postcolonial movement is better put into perspective by considering the *longue durée* of migration to Britain from South Asia that began at least 400 years ago (Ansari, this volume; Visram, 2002).

THE PRE-COLONIAL PHASE: 1608–1757

The first ships of the East India Company arrived in India at Surat in 1608. The Company, incorporated eight years earlier by a group of English merchants, had managed to obtain a monopoly of all trade between England and the East Indies. The first settlers to arrive in England were those associated with the East India Company: *lascars* (South Asian sailors), who staffed many of the Company ships, and *ayahs* and domestic servants brought back by Company officers. By the eighteenth century the growing prominence of the East India Company in India's affairs meant that many emissaries and petitioners found themselves travelling to Britain seeking redress against the Company. During this period the South Asians to be found in Britain, aside from those *lascars* and domestic servants who ended up settling, were generally transient visitors.

Conventionally the end of Aurengzeb's reign in 1707 is seen as the moment that signalled the fragmentation of the Mughal Empire which in turn opened the possibility of the exercise of European rule in South Asia. Until then the Mughals' power and wealth had ensured the relationship between India and England continued outside the colonial frame.

THE PROTO-COLONIAL PHASE: 1757–1857

Generally the exercise of British power over India is considered to begin with the consolidation of the British conquest of Bengal following the battle of Plassey on 23 June 1757 and with its gradual incorporation of large parts of post-Mughal India culminating with the formal replacement of the Mughal dynasty and the crowning of Victoria as Empress of India in 1857. During this period Europeans continued to play the part of Mughal gentlemen and on occasion curiosity would still inform the Indo-European exchanges rather than assumptions of racial and cultural superiority (Dalrymple, 2002). However, so-called 'tolerance' and 'inter-cultural dialogue' were increasingly underpinned by relations of power which tended to subvert the possibility of dialogic encounters between Britain and South Asia. Consequently the period is marked by the increasing incorporation of the latter into the colonial frame at political, social, economic and cultural levels. During this period Britain began to host students from South Asia seeking qualifications, client princes on official visits, political activists working for decolonisation and entrepreneurs engaged in business between the two regions.

THE COLONIAL PHASE: 1857–1947

The suppression of the 1857 rebellion against British rule ('Indian Mutiny') and the consequent establishment of direct Crown rule marks not only a tightening of the regulatory and disciplinary techniques by which the British Empire started to exercise its power, but also the clearest articulation of the racialised colonialism that re-configured South Asia and its people as secondary elements in binaries indicative of the concept of 'the West and the Rest'. Consequently the extensive contacts between Britain and India were increasingly mediated through the structures and mentalities of empire and race. Despite this, the number of South Asians settled in Britain increased, forming a community which, though numerically small, was multi-ethnic, multi-class and multi-religious (see Ansari, this volume). This community began to establish itself with its own places of worship (e.g. the first mosques were established in Woking and Liverpool in 1889), its own shops and other facilities and even involvement in British politics (e.g. Dadabhai Naoroji who in 1892 became the first South Asian elected to the House of Commons).

THE POSTCOLONIAL PHASE: 1947–

The formal ending of the British Empire in India in 1947 did not mean the severing of links between Britain and South Asia, and in the period that followed relations between the two are most clearly marked by the wave of mass migration from parts of the latter to the industrial urban landscapes of the former. As a consequence, the conurbations of London, the West Midlands, Yorkshire and Lancashire became the homes to substantial numbers of settlers that laid the foundations for the formation of the BrAsian 'nation'. However, the incomplete nature of decolonisation in South Asia, marked by the persistence of the culture of 'brown sahibs', was mirrored in Britain, where South Asian settlers and other ethnically marked migrants were increasingly confronted with the racial logic of colonialism as they attempted to make a home. From a few thousand in the 1950s, the population of South Asian settlers grew to over 400,000 in 1971 (Ballard, 1994b: 7), accounting for about 0.85 per cent of the total population of Britain. Since 1971 the South Asian population (with the exception of the Bengalis) has expanded mainly through natural increase rather than further immigrations (see Peach, this volume).

Although, at first glance, the number of South Asians in Britain would appear large, overall the total population of South Asia found outside its immediate environs is estimated at less than 1%, compared to perhaps 3% of Chinese, 50% of Europeans and 54% of Africans (Peach, 1994: 38), suggesting South Asians make reluctant migrants compared to other regional populations. However, migration to Britain from South Asia has been from five primary sources: the Punjab, Gujarat, Azad Kashmir,[1] Sylhet and East Africa, the latter, whose circumstances of migration were rather different, accounting for a fifth of BrAsians. Relatively the Punjab (Pakistani and Indian) Gujarat and Sylhet are prosperous areas and Azad Kashmir poor (though remittances have transformed the living standards of some of the areas), while East Africa was home to mainly urbanised South Asians who originally mostly came from either Gujarat or the Punjab. Although other very large areas of South Asia are notably absent from the ranks of the migrants, e.g. Uttar Pradesh and West Bengal, the

[1] Azad Kashmir means 'Free Kashmir', that is, the part of Kashmir controlled by Pakistan. The status of the territory of Kashmir is currently disputed.

five regions that constitute the main sources do not exhaust the profile of South Asian migrants to Britain, all of whom have become part of BrAsia. Nevertheless, accounting for the mass migration of South Asians to Britain requires not only a theoretical understanding of why some people migrate and others do not, whatever their profession and place of origin, but also an explanation of what in particular were the dynamics in each of these five regions that produced the incentive to do so.

SOUTH ASIAN MIGRATION: A VERY PECULIAR PRACTICE

The earliest systematic approaches to the study of migration derive from the nineteenth-century geographer Ravenstein, who suggested that migration can be attributed to socio-economic imbalances between regions. Certain factors 'push' people away from the area of origin and others 'pull' them to the area of destination. 'Push factors' include demographic growth, low living standards, lack of economic opportunities and political repression, while 'pull factors' include demand for labour, availability of land, good economic opportunities (Ravenstien, 1885).

The post-war migration of South Asians to Britain is often explained in terms of structural factors in which the interplay between push and pull produces the movement of large groups of workers (Light and Bhachu, 1993). Accordingly, major reconstruction following the Second World War produced a demand for labour that 'pulled' South Asians to Britain and conditions in the various successor states to the British Raj was what 'pushed' some South Asians out. Indeed, the campaign of the Minstry of Labour in Britain to recruit workers from British colonies and ex-colonies provides a concrete illustration of the way in which pull factors directly encouraged South Asian migration.

Although push-pull theories are useful in demonstrating how structural factors could create the conditions under which migration might occur—principally, the difference between regions of high labour demand and regions of high labour supply—they are less able to provide the level of analysis that accounts for the mechanism and specificity of actual migratory movements that are clearly more complex. It is rarely the poorest people from the least-developed countries that move to the richest countries. More often the migrants are of intermediate social status and from areas undergoing economic and social change. Similarly migration is rarely from densely-populated to under-populated areas. In fact countries of immigration are among the worlds most densely populated. Furthermore the push-pull model treats state intervention as merely disruptive of the 'normal' functioning of the market, whereas the state invariably plays a major role in shaping and controlling population movements. Therefore the notion that migrants make free choices in order to 'maximise their well-being' and as such produce 'an equilibrium in the market place' is far from historically correct (Castles and Miller, 1993: 20–1). Perhaps more important, the push-pull model does not explain the localised nature of migration. Why does a certain group of migrants from a particular town in one country move to a particular town in another? To answer such questions, analysts of South Asian migration have focused on more agent-centred approaches, mainly those grouped under the rubric of 'chain migration'.

The process of chain migration may begin with the success of a single immigrant, news of whom reaches home and encourages friends and relatives to join him/her. This is the first stage of chain migration. The second stage starts when early migrants become sufficiently established to call their spouses, children and in many cases spouses-to-be to join them. This leads to both the reuniting and establishment of families, which in turn leads to the recreation of home culture. Traditional ceremonies and social occasions become more numerous and the customs and values of the place of origin become more strongly rooted with greater emphasis being placed on education and religion. Once community life becomes well established, and news of this reaches the area of origin, it has the effect of enticing the older, younger and the less enterprising. Thus the chain is completed and a full community life is the result. 'Chain migration' can be defined as the movement in which prospective migrants learn of opportunities, have transportation provided and initial accommodation and employment arranged through primary social relationships with previous immigrants (Anwar, 1979; Shaw, 1988; Ballard, 1994b).

Most recent explanations of South Asian mass migration to Britain employ a combination of push-pull (structural) and 'chain migration' (agent-centred) approaches (Kalra, 2000a). Since traditions of international migration usually arise from the existence of prior connections between the countries involved, for example connections based on colonisation, political influence, trade, investment or cultural ties, migrations can be understood best by using, it is suggested, the conceptual framework of 'migration systems' (Fawcett and Arnold, 1987: 456–7). A migration system refers to a set of places linked together by flows and counter-flows of people, information, goods and services and ideas. These links can be categorised as state-to-state relations and comparisons, mass culture connections and family and social networks. Hence migration systems account for institutional factors such as the political economy of the world market, inter-state relationships and the laws, structures and practices established by the states of the sending and receiving countries. Also considered are the beliefs and informal networks and practices developed by the migrants themselves to cope with migration and settlement. These informal networks include psychological adaptations, personal relationships, family and household patterns, friendship and community ties and mutual help in economic and social matters.

Combining push-pull theories, which provide the structural contexts enabling migration, with network theories, to account for the shape of South Asian migration to Britain, would appear the most efficacious approach. However, although such a unified explanation would have the advantages of economy and elegance, it would still have a number of limitations, not least because the relationship between structures and networks remains under-explored. Specifically, what is the relationship between structures and agents? Accounts which privilege structural (in this case 'push-pull') factors will suggest the actions of the agent are determined by structure in which case the agent is merely a product of the structure. Conversely, approaches that privilege agency tend to minimise the outcome of structures or see structures as nothing more than the regularities produced by individuals freely choosing to act in a specific manner. Furthermore the 'Solomanic' concept of 'relative autonomy of the agent' is no solution to the determinism of structural accounts and the contingency of agent-centred approaches for it has little explanatory value: if the relative autonomy is produced by the structure it is not relative autonomy, and if it is independent of structures and based on the capacity of agents, it is still clear that the autonomy is not relative. This is not only a matter of mere theoretical niceties since the answer to the question of why so many South Asians who 'chose' to live outside the region chose to live in Britain turns upon this tension. For although Britain is home to perhaps 15 per cent of all South Asians outside South Asia—probably the world's largest South Asian population after India, Pakistan, Bangladesh, Sri Lanka and Nepal[2]—given the apparent general reluctance of South Asians to migrate, it is difficult to account for the very concentrated nature of migration from a few key regions—Kashmir, Punjab, Bengal and Gujarat—and even if it is argued that the first three, having been divided during partition, produced the phenomenon of 'twice migrants', this does not explain why only certain places within these regions, for example, Sylhet in Bengal and Mirpur in Kashmir, furnish the bulk of migrants.

At moments of dislocation the terrain of the 'undecideable' expands, which allows agents to exercise autonomy. In other words, the autonomy of agents is determined by contexts in which structures are open and no longer able to govern agent's 'choices': thus moments of decision arise in circumstances where structural influences are weak (Laclau, 1990). In these moments agents can act in ways that lay the foundations for subsequent actions; agents can at these moments reformulate weakened structures. The period of postcolonial migration from South Asia to Britain was ushered in when a postcolonial interruption of the Empire pro-

2 Figures are based on Peach, 1994:38, while the actual numbers maybe out of date the order of magnitude is indicative of the significance of BrAsia.

vided the dislocation through which mass 'coloured' migration to Britain became possible despite the logic of racism and colonialism that had sought to insulate Britain from its racially marked subjects. Prior to this initial colonial constructions had provided the impetus for the formation of embodied practices that are the basis of network explanations. Colonial contact and appropriation into particular relationships can be seen as the beginning of the process by which South Asians began to be incorporated into the international system of labour divisions based on their mobility. The postcolonial confusion between centre and periphery and its racial underpinning is evident in the way immigration legislation began with a notion of empire wide citizenship (determined by a meeting of the Prime Ministers of the 'white' dominions in 1946) and was formalised so that Australians and Canadians could claim right of abode in Britain (a right denied to the indigenous peoples of these settler states). With the independence of Pakistan and India, citizens of these countries also become commonwealth citizens with right of abode in Britain, a right that successive legislation from the 1961 Immigration Act sought to restrict by creating multiple tiers of citizenship which limited 'immigrants of colour' from entering and settling in Britain. The 1971 Immigration Act replaced all existing immigration laws and became the basis of present immigration control. This act defined the 'true citizens' as 'patrials' and others as non-patrials. Patrials included: citizens of Britain and the colonies born, adopted, registered or 'naturalised' in Britain, or those who had a parent or grandparent who had obtained citizenship by those means; British citizens who had been settled in Britain for five years; Commonwealth citizens born or adopted to British citizens born in Britain; or the Commonwealth wives of men who were patrials. In essence this meant that individuals of British descent, who were likely to be white, were free from control, could enter, settle and take employment thus enjoying full citizenship. All others were non-patrial and subject to the above conditions. Immigration legislation since 1971 has concentrated on further restricting the entry of migrants. However, with primary migration over, this has primarily concentrated on two functions. First, the restriction of family reunification and second, on more recent refugee migration to Britain.

Postcolonial migration from South Asia was made possible by the erosion of the binaries that defined the colonial world order, specifically by the way in which subaltern subjects of colonialism were able to make use of colonial connections to transcend their position. The crisis of the British Empire caused by, among other things, the cost of the War and the rising price of holding on to restive colonial populations, forced a situation in which Britain not only had to abandon piecemeal its possessions, but in doing so also had to try to re-articulate its sense of what it meant to be British (Hesse and Sayyid, this volume). This dislocation of the structures of colonialism opened the path for the colonial subject to cross the centre-periphery divide. Consequently most of the South Asian settlers who came to Britain during the peak period of mass migration (1962–72) had either experienced the end of empire as children or been involved, vicariously or directly, in the nationalist mobilisations against British rule. Thus those who participated in nationalist struggles had a significant influence over the settlement and formation of South Asian communities in Britain, e.g. Kashmiri nationalists (Ali, 2002).

Chain migration or network approaches are correct to point out the embedded practices and institutions through which the process of migration can occur, however, there is a need to emphasise how the practice of migration from South Asia to Britain was institutionalised in the context of the postcolonial situation, which saw the translation and reworking of colonial links and practices to postcolonial ends. For example, the process of migration practices that came to be sedimented as a result of colonial contact and the construction of South Asia along colonial lines also meant the construction of its population along the lines of those who were deployed and considered capable of migration and those who were not—Lord Roberts' (1885–93) articulation of the discourse of 'martial races', for instance, which transformed the basis of recruitment from territorial to ethnic (caste) background based on the idea that some ethnicities had an inherent military prowess while others did not. Muslim and Sikh Punjabis were considered 'martial races' and assigned to protect the Empire at home and away. (The concept of 'martial races' tended to exclude or minimise the military contribution of communities that either had been politicised through over 100 years of dealing with British imperialism or were majority communities—i.e. Hindus—such that, in the case of a nationalist uprising, the Army of India might not support the nationalist position.) By the First World War Sikhs constituted a third of the armed forces and the Punjab provided three-fifths of army recruits (Tatla, 1999). Opportunities abroad made them aware of foreign economies and the obvious potential for individual and family development therein. Colonial links also provided considerable opportunities for tradesmen and craftsmen in other British colonies and in the early twentieth century a significant number of Punjabi Sikh craftsmen (Ramgarhia Sikhs) migrated to East Africa as indentured labour primarily to build the Kenya-Uganda railway.

Similarly the Azad Kashmiris have a long established relationship with the British armed forces. In Azad Kashmir's mainly agrarian economy poor quality land and little industrialisation had led to a surplus male labour force in the area. Consequently, many Mirpuris joined British steamships operating from Bombay as stokers and by the end of the nineteenth century a high proportion of engine-room and stoke-hold *sirhangs* were from Mirpur (see Ballard, 1990). As the British coal-powered merchant fleet expanded, more and more men were recruited. Then during the First and Second World Wars many joined the Allied armies and navies, in particular, again, from the Mirpur district. As with their Punjabi contemporaries the armed services provided the opportunity to travel overseas and gain knowledge of the advantages in foreign lands. In the nineteenth century many Kashmiris also migrated to East Africa, the Indian Ocean Islands and the Caribbean.

TRADING PLACES

The experience of South Asian settlers has been dominated by the 'immigrant imaginary' (Sayyid, 2004), an imaginary that sought to restore the disruptive effects of postcoloniality by re-inserting South Asians into the colonial framework despite their relocation and unravelling of the colonial world order. The binaries of rural/urban, tradition/modern, religious/secular and centre/periphery continue to haunt the way in which the relationship between South Asian migration and settlement is represented.

For most South Asians migration meant a switch from rural to urban lifestyle as most migrants were from peasant farming communities. For example, many Punjabis were encouraged by the British to settle in the 'canal colonies' in western Punjab, which had been developed for the Muslim and Sikh peasantry during colonial rule. There was already a long tradition of Punjabi migration, but the partition of the Punjab in 1947 created pressure on the land resources. Thus the main impetus for migration from the Punjab in the 1950s was the dislocation, and the associated shortage of work, caused by partition.

The main migration of Azad Kashmiris from Mirpur Town and Mirpur District began in the late 1950s and early 1960s as migrants followed the routes of pioneers to look for work. Upheavals caused by partition were exacerbated with the related problem of the Kashmir issue. The constant threat of war between India and Pakistan has, since 1947, resulted in further displacements of large numbers of Mirpuris and continues to do so albeit on a much smaller scale as Kashmiri refugees seek asylum in Britain. Important impetus for the large-scale movement was provided by the construction of the Mangla Dam through which large numbers of Azad Kashmiris were displaced, having huge implications for the people of Mirpur district, and Mirpur Town itself. The initial stages of construction involved the relocation of approximately 200 villages and the old town of Mirpur, which comprised approximately 13,000 inhabitants. By completion in 1967 about 100,000 people had been relocated (Ballard, 1990). Some Kashmiris were relocated in other parts of Pakistan and some individuals no doubt were drawn by the economic possibilities in Britain. Many Kashmiris settled in Britain see themselves as political migrants driven from their home by economic and political marginalisation and the ambiguous status of the Azad Kashmir Government and Kashmir (Ali, 2002). As a consequence many Azad Kashmiri migrants hold Pakistani passports and have been conflated with Punjabi migrants.

In East Africa (mainly Uganda, Kenya and Tanzania) mostly Gujarati South Asians arrived to work predominantly in the banking and financial sectors and to service the wholesale and distributive trade in Africa. The Africanisation policy after independence meant that banks and businesses were nationalised and South Asian roles made redundant unless they were willing to continue under strict African regulation. Although many South Asians held British passports and opted to migrate to Britain during the 1970s, the majority were expelled or fled from the nationalist regimes in Kenya from 1965 and Uganda from 1969—culminating in Amin's expulsions in 1972.

Generally South Asians have moved from a space described as traditional to one described as modern. With the exception of 'East African Asians', and in contrast to South Asian migration to Canada and the United States, most South Asian migrants to Britain were from 'traditional' societies and thus the process of migration was also presented as a form of time travel in which the migrant moves not only across space but also from the past into the present. Thus the division between tradition and modern becomes focused on South Asian settlers as reminders of simpler times, implicitly denying the historicity of the South Asian experience and the historical transformations that made South Asian migration possible. Hence even those from the educated élites, those with royal links, and those working for the Indian Civil Service had to bridge the divide between the centre and periphery.

Migration literature based on the American experience has built in certain assumptions about the way migrant identities would be transformed once migrants began to settle in their host societies. Popular and academic accounts of South Asian migration have tended to decontexualise the South Asian migratory experience. In other words, the process of migration becomes an 'economic' activity in which people from the Third World move to the First World in search of a better life. While such accounts may point to the structural factors such as the need for labour to carry out the post-war recovery, they rarely point to the weakening of the colonial world order except metaphorically. Such points of view disavow the postcolonial, and neglect what is perhaps the most remarkable aspect of South Asian (and Caribbean) migration to Britain: an almost poetic inversion of the imperial enterprise that continues to haunt the ethnoscapes of Britain and relocates the theatre of the postcolonial in the heart of the ex-empire.

DEMOGRAPHICS OF BrASIAN SETTLEMENT, 1951–2001

Ceri Peach

In the 2001 Census there were over two million people of South Asian ethnic origin living in Britain. Of this total Indians form one million, Pakistanis 750,000 and Bangladeshis 280,000. While most census data are available in terms of national ethnicity, these larger national aggregations are composed of religious, linguistic, regional and caste or quasi-caste groups, which the census is only now beginning to touch. The 2001 Census contained for the first time a question on religion. Pakistanis and Bangladeshis are almost exclusively Muslim and together with Indian Muslims accounted for about 70 per cent of the 1.6 million Muslims in Britain in 2001. While Islam is multi-ethnic, Indians are multi-religious. About half of the Indian ethnic population is Hindu, a quarter is Sikh and a fifth is Muslim. Nearly all of the Sikhs and Hindus are of South Asian origin, but not all come directly from India. About 30 per cent of Britain's ethnic Indians come from, or are descended from East African Asians expelled during the Africanisation campaigns of the 1960s and 1970s (Robinson, 1986, 1996). Smaller numbers of Indians come from diasporic communities in Guyana, Trinidad, Singapore and Fiji.

Although there has long been a South Asian presence in Britain (see Ansari, this volume) large-scale immigration and subsequent natural

Table 1. GROWTH OF THE SOUTH ASIAN POPULATION OF BRITAIN, 1951–2001

	Indian	*Pakistani*	*Bangladeshi*	*Total South Asian*
1951	31,000	10,000	2,000	43,000
1961	81,000	25,000	6,000	112,000
1971	375,000	119,000	22,000	516,000
1981	676,000	296,000	65,000	1,037,000
1991	840,000	477,000	163,000	1,480,000
2001	1,051,831	746,612	282,808	2,081,251

Source: 1951–91 figures from Peach, 1996: 9, table 5 (detailed description of data is given in the notes to this table). 2001 figures from Census, April 2001, http://www.statistics.gov.uk/STATBASE/Expodata/Spreadsheets/D6589.xls

growth has been a feature of the post-Second World War period (see Ali, this volume). Table 1 illustrates the growth of the South Asian population from less than 50,000 in 1951 to over 2 million in 2001. From 1951 to 1981 the figures are based on birthplace and are best treated as estimates. However, in 1991 and 2001 the figures are based on self-identified ethnicity. About half of the South Asian ethnic populations are now British-born so that natural increase has replaced immigration as the main source of ethnic population growth.

Table 2 illustrates the main periods of primary immigration. It can be seen that the most dramatic rise came in the period 1955 to 1974. In the case of the Indian ethnic population, the flow was increased by the expulsion of the Indian minority population from former British colonies in East Africa (Uganda, Kenya, Tanzania and Malawi). About 30 per cent of the born-abroad Indian population of Britain in the 1991 Census originated from East Africa. There were also small numbers who originated from other twice-migrant Indian societies in Trinidad, Guyana, Fiji and Singapore. The migration flow from Bangladesh peaked in the 1980s, much later than from either India or Pakistan which peaked in the 1960s and 1970s. Furthermore data are complicated because Bangladesh was East Pakistan until 1971 and migrants were counted as Pakistanis. However, while the bulk of the Indian and Pakistani immigrant population arrived at the time of British post-war economic expansion, Bangladeshis peaked at a time of rising unemployment (Peach, 1990).

All three national ethnic groups, which originated from the subcontinent, came from remarkably limited regional origins: the Punjab, Gujarat and the Sylhet district of Bangladesh. The Indian population is largely northern from the Punjab and Gujarat. The Pakistani population also comes largely from the Punjab, Azad Kashmir and the Campbellpore District (Ballard, 1994a). The Bangladeshi population originates overwhelmingly from Sylhet Province in the north-east of the country (Eade *et al.*, 1996). The regions of origin of all three groups were strongly affected by the large-scale population movements that took place at the time of Partition in 1947. This is not the only reason of course. In the

Table 2. COMMONWEALTH-BORN POPULATION OF BRITAIN, 1989–91, BY YEAR OF ENTRY ('000)

	Pre '55	*'55–64*	*'65–74*	*'75–79*	*'80–84*	*'85–88*	*No reply*	*Total*
Caribbean	17	131	52	–	–	–	11	211
India	54	75	134	52	29	25	19	388
Bangladesh	–	11	15	14	23	16	–	79
Pakistan	–	34	68	40	33	24	11	210

Source: *Labour Force Survey 1990 and 1991*, London: HMSO, 1992, p. 38, table 6.39.

case of the Mirpuri population from Azad Kashmir, the displacement of population through the construction of the Mangla Dam was a major factor. Ballard makes the point that many of the migrants were from peasant farming families. That is to say they were people who owned land rather than tenants. This gave such migrants the sense of psychological and financial independence, which proved crucial to their success as settlers (Ballard, 1994a). There were also links with Britain dating back to imperial days. The British Army policing the North West Frontier region recruited bearers from the Campbellpore District. The East India Company recruited cooks and stokers for its ships from Sylhet.

SOCIO-ECONOMIC STATUS

Since settlement in Britain the socio-economic trajectories of the three national ethnic groups has diverged significantly. Figure 1 shows male employment of the Indian, Pakistani and Bangladeshi populations compared with other populations in 2001. The columns are arrayed in decreasing order of percentage in the white-collar classes (the bottom three categories on the columns).

While of all the groups concerned Indians have the highest proportion of professional men, the Pakistanis and the Bangladeshis have the lowest. This polarisation of the three groups is due partly to differential success after arrival, but more to differences in their socio-economic starting points, capital and social capital on arrival. Both the Pakistani and the Bangladeshi populations came largely from peasant farming backgrounds. While there were significant peasant elements in the migration from the Indian Punjab, they were from a richer irrigated area rather than the poorer rain-fed areas of Pakistan (Ballard, 1990). The Indian population, in any case, contained a significant proportion of academic and medical élites. In the case of the East African Indians there were additional benefits. The East African Indian population had been middlemen in Kenya, Uganda, Tanzania and Malawi. They were the civil servants, the lawyers, doctors, accountants, bankers and entrepreneurs. They were English-speaking and thoroughly conversant with civil service procedures. In some cases of anticipatory migration they were able to bring capital assets with them.

The economic performance of Indian, Pakistani and Bangladeshi women are significantly different. The 2001 figures indicate that only 29% of Pakistani women of working age were in the formal labour market and even fewer (25%) Bangladeshi women. This contrasts with 57% for Indian women and 60% of the total female population. These figures for Pakistanis and Bangladeshis did, however, represent a growth over the 1991 figures. Pakistani and Bangladeshi women also participate in home-working, particularly in the rag trade in Tower Hamlets.

Academic qualifications disaggregated by gender are not yet available. However, taking men and women together, Bangladeshis and Pakistanis have the lowest level of qualification of all ethnic minority populations (Figure 2). 50% of Bangladeshis and 45% of Pakistanis lack any academic, vocational or professional qualifications.

Pakistani and Bangladeshi women also married much earlier, on aver-

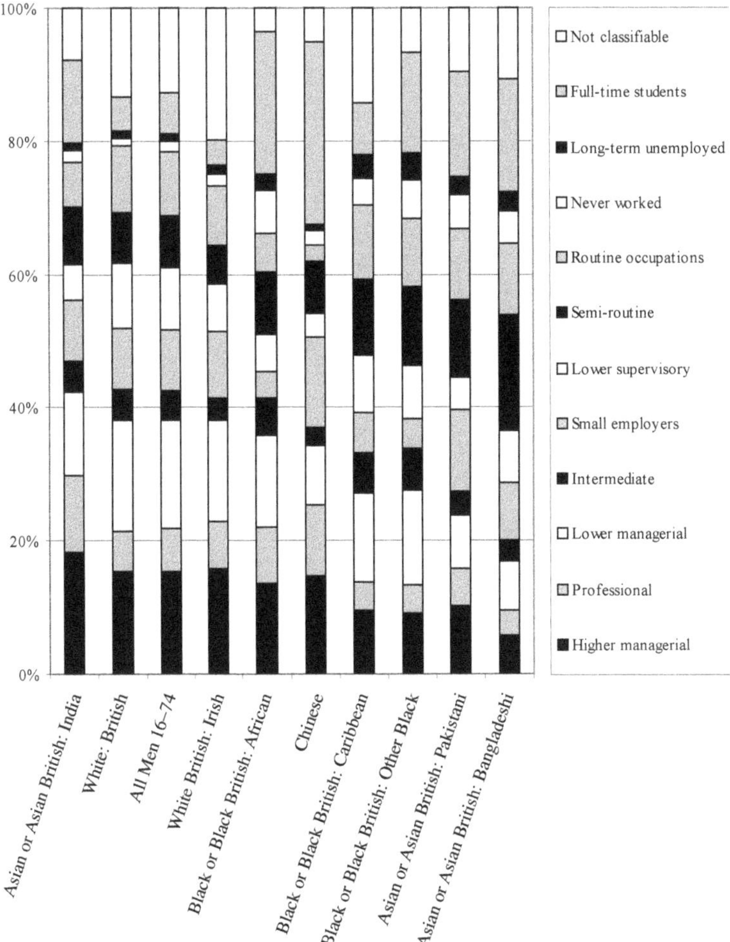

Figure 1. MALE EMPLOYMENT BY ETHNICITY, ENGLAND AND WALES, 2001

Source: Census 2001, table S112 Sex and NS-SeC by ethnic group.

age, than Indian women, began childbearing sooner, and had larger average family sizes. 36% of Pakistani women, 40% of Bangladeshi women, but only 14% of Indian women and 12% of all women were engaged full time in looking after their homes and families (Table S108 sex and age and economic activity by ethnic group, 2001 Census). Compared with Indian households, therefore, there are fewer breadwinners and larger numbers of dependants. However, as children grow up and enter the work force the situation of household incomes may improve.

UNEMPLOYMENT AND SELF EMPLOYMENT

The average unemployment level for White British men in England and Wales at the time of the 2001 Census was 5.3%. The figure for Indians was marginally higher at 6.2%. However, the Pakistani and Bangladeshi levels of unemployment were nearly three times higher than average at 13.8 and 15.9% respectively. The self-employment rate for Indians and Pakistanis (17.4 and 17.1% respectively) was higher than that for the White British (14.2%), but the Bangladeshi rate was lower at 11.1%.

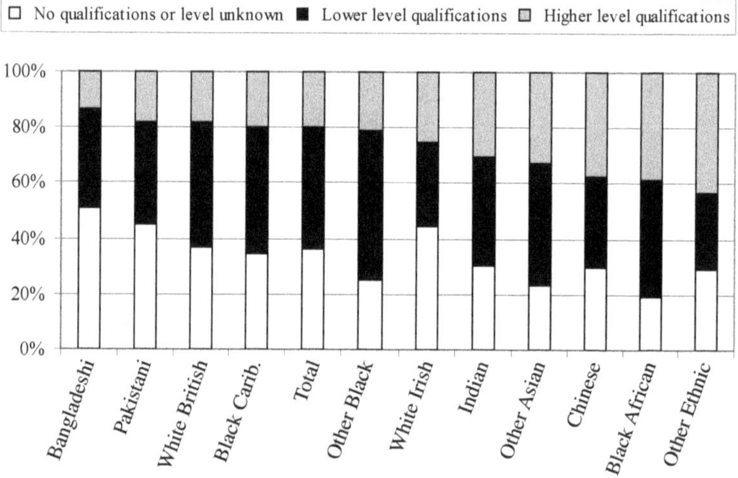

Figure 2. QUALIFICATIONS BY ETHNICITY, ENGLAND AND WALES, 2001

Note: The term ‘no qualifications’ describes people without any academic, vocational or professional qualifications. The term ‘lower level’ qualifications, is used to describe qualifications equivalent to levels 1–3 of the National Key Learning targets (i.e. GCSEs, ‘O’ levels, ‘A’ levels, NVQ levels 1–3). The term ‘higher level’ refers to qualifications of levels 4 and above (i.e. first degrees, higher degrees, NVQ levels 4 and 5, HND, HNC and certain professional qualifications).

Source: Table T13 Theme Table on ethnicity. http://www.statistics.gov.uk/STATBASE/Expodata/Spreadsheets/D6833.xls

The degree of self-employment is roughly the same as it was in the 1991 Census, but the Indian figure has now overtaken the Pakistani figure.

DEMOGRAPHIC AND FAMILY STRUCTURE

All three BrAsian groups had a younger age structure than the White population and in the case of the Pakistani and Bangladeshi population the contrast is striking. Table 3 shows that 22% of the Indian population, 35% of the Pakistani population and 38% of the Bangladeshi population were under sixteen. This compares with 19% for the White population. While 16% of the White population was 65 and over, the percentages for the Indians, Pakistanis and Bangladeshis were 6, 4 and 3 respectively. The proportion of BrAsians of working age was correspondingly about 8 to 11 percentage points higher than for the White population.

Marriage and families were almost universal among South Asian groups and single parenting was rare. Taking families with dependent

Table 3. BRITISH POPULATION: BY ETHNIC GROUP AND AGE, 2001–2 (%)[1]

	Under 16	*16–34*	*35–64*	*65 and over*
White	19	25	40	16
Mixed	55	27	16	2
Asian or Asian British				
▪ Indian	22	33	38	6
▪ Pakistani	35	36	25	4
▪ Bangladeshi	38	38	20	3
▪ Other Asian	22	36	38	4
Black or Black British				
▪ Black Caribbean	25	25	42	9
▪ Black African	33	35	30	2
▪ Other Black[2]	35	34	26	–
Chinese	18	40	38	5
Other	20	37	39	4
All ethnic groups[3]	20	26	39	15

Notes
[1] Population living in private households 2001–2. See source Appendix, Part 1: Classification of ethnic groups and Part 4: Local LFS.
[2] Sample size was too small for a reliable estimate of the 65 and over age group.
[3] Includes those who did not state their ethnic group.

Source: Annual Local Area Labour Force Survey, Office for National Statistics, http://www.statistics.gov.uk/STATBASE/Expodata/Spreadsheets/D6300.xls

children, 91% of Indians, 89% of Bangladeshis and 85% of Pakistani families were of couples, whereas this was true of 77% of the White population and only 46% of Caribbean families. (These estimates for 2002 from the Labour Force Survey have not been adjusted to take account of the 2001 Census results). Traditional extended family structures were also significant for South Asian groups. Table 4 shows that 7% of Indian households were multi-family units and for the combined Pakistani and Bangladeshi population the equivalent percentage was 10.

Table 4. ETHNIC GROUP OF HEAD OF HOUSEHOLD[1]: BY TYPE OF HOUSEHOLD, BRITAIN, SPRING 1999

	White	*Black*	*Indian*	*Pak./ Bangla.*	*Other groups*[2]	*All*[3]
One person	29	30	14	7	25	28
Two or more unrelated	3	6	–	–	8	3
One family households: couple: no children[4]	29	10	18	9	13	28
One family households: couple: dependent children[4, 5]	23	12	42	56	33	24
One family households: couple: non-dependent children[4]	7	3	8	7	–	7
One family households: lone parent: dependent children[4, 5]	6	24	5	8	13	7
One family households: lone parent: non-dependent children only[4]	3	5	4	–	–	3
Multi-family households	–	–	7	10	–	1
All households (=100%) (millions)[6]	22.2	0.4	0.3	0.2	0.2	23.7
Total one couple family household	65	58	73	80	59	66
Total one couple family with children	36	48	55	71	46	38

Notes

[1] Percentages of heads of household in each ethnic group living in each household type.
[2] Includes those of mixed origin.
[3] Includes ethnic group not stated.
[4] Other individuals who were not family members may also be included.
[5] May also include non-dependent children.
[6] Includes same sex couples.

Source: Social Trends 30, http://www.statistics.gov.uk/STATBASE/expodata/files/7739050591.csv, Spring 1999.

HOUSING

The Indian population has a notably high degree of home ownership, nearly 80%. For Sikhs the percentage was even higher than for the Indian average, at 85%; for Hindus it was 76%. The White British average is 72% and the Pakistani very close at 71%. Bangladeshis, however, have a much lower proportion, 38%, 10 points lower than the Caribbean population. Nearly half of the Bangladeshi population live in council or other social housing. This is the second highest degree of dependence on social housing after the African population (Figure 3). The type of housing occupied by the three groups differs appreciably. The Indian population has a significant concentration in outer-city suburban detached and semi-detached housing. The Pakistanis have concentrations in inner-city Victorian terraces and the Bangladeshis in inner-city council flats.

GEOGRAPHICAL DISTRIBUTION

All of the ethnic minority groups show a high concentration in England rather than Scotland, Wales or Northern Ireland (Table 5). England contains 98% of Indians, 97% of Bangladeshis and 95% of British Pa-

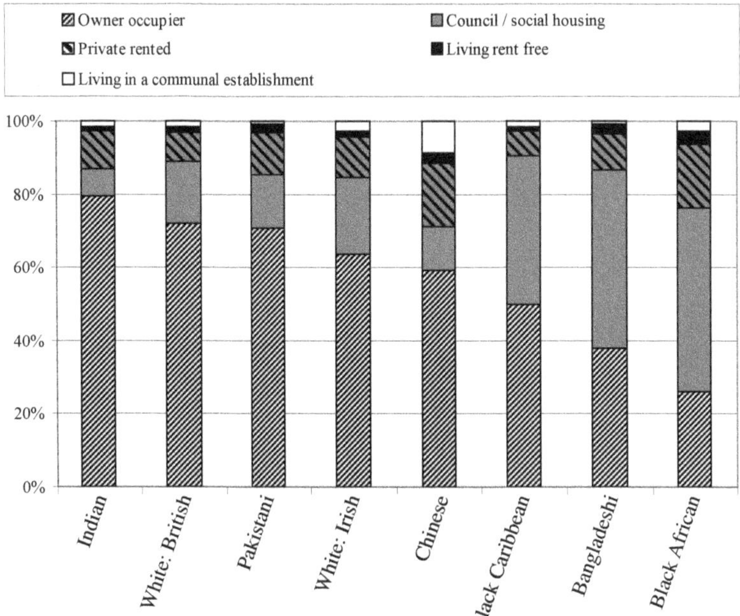

Figure 3. TENURE BY ETHNICITY, ENGLAND AND WALES, 2001

Source: 2001 Census.

Table 5. PERCENTAGE REGIONAL DISTRIBUTION OF ETHNIC POPULATIONS IN BRITAIN 2001

	North-East	*North-West*	*Yorks and the Humber*	*East Midlands*	*West Midlands*	*East*	*London*	*South-East*	*South-West*	*Scotland*	*N. Ireland*	*UK Base = 100%*
White	4.53	11.74	8.57	7.20	8.63	9.46	9.42	14.05	8.89	9.16	3.09	54,153,898
Indian	0.96	6.86	4.89	11.61	8.63	4.84	41.48	8.47	1.56	1.43	0.15	1,053,411
Pakistani	1.88	15.65	19.58	3.72	20.68	5.19	19.10	7.83	0.90	4.25	0.09	747,285
Bangla-deshi	2.18	9.19	4.36	2.45	11.09	6.54	54.37	5.43	1.70	0.70	0.09	283,063
Black Caribbean	0.16	3.61	3.77	4.72	14.54	4.63	60.71	4.85	2.19	0.31	0.05	565,876
Black African	0.54	3.28	1.98	1.89	2.47	3.50	78.09	5.07	1.27	1.05	0.10	485,277
Black Other	0.44	5.43	3.41	3.72	10.01	5.43	61.84	5.00	2.40	1.16	0.40	97,585
Chinese	2.44	10.87	4.99	5.22	6.51	8.24	32.42	13.37	5.14	6.59	1.68	247,403
Other	1.83	5.78	4.11	3.19	6.11	6.31	49.01	12.69	4.03	4.15	0.56	230,615

Source: Annual Labour Force Survey, 2002.

kistanis. In regional terms, the Pakistani population has a much more northerly and West Midland distribution than the Indian or Bangladeshi populations. The 1950s and 1960s Pakistani immigrants were particularly strongly drawn to the declining mill towns of the North West and the West Riding of Yorkshire. Nearly 20% of the Pakistani population lives in the Yorkshire and Humberside region, compared to 5% of the Indian and 4% of the Bangladeshi populations. For the North West the respective figures are 16, 7 and 9%; for the West Midlands the figures are 21, 9 and 11%. The Indian and Bangladeshi populations, on the other hand, show notable concentrations in London (42% and 54% respectively) compared to only 19% of the Pakistanis. The Indian concentration in the East Midlands (12%) notably in Leicester is exceptional among the South Asians and owes much to the concentration of East African Asians there after their expulsion from East Africa.

All of the migrant groups show a high concentration in the metropolitan counties, the largest urban areas of the country. Table 6 shows that while 27% of the White population of Britain was living in metropolitan counties in 2001, the corresponding figure for the Indian population was 65%, Pakistanis 68% and Bangladeshis 78%.

SEGREGATION LEVELS

By the time of the 1991 Census significant differences in the degrees of residential concentration of BrAsians was already evident. The segregation of the Bangladeshis was particularly striking at a number of different levels. In the first place, nearly a quarter (23%) of the total Bangladeshi population was concentrated in the single London Borough of Tower Hamlets. In 2001 this percentage was the same despite the fact that the national total itself had increased by 74% during the intervening period.

Secondly, at the intra–urban level in 1991, the Bangladeshi population was the most segregated of all minority ethnic populations in Britain. Using the Index of Dissimilarity (ID), that measures the percentage of a group—which would have to shift its area of residence in order to replicate that of the population as a whole—the average un-weighted index, at ward level, for urban areas in which there are 1,000 or more Bangladeshis, was 68. Against the White population the ID was 73. This is a high level characteristic of African-Americans in the US (though there are differences between the two situations).

The Pakistani levels of segregation were lower than for the Bangladeshis and the Indian levels lower than for the Pakistanis. For Pakistanis, the average ID was 55. This is 13 points lower than for the Bangladeshis; against Whites the Pakistani ID was 61 or 12 points lower than the comparable figure for the Bangladeshis. There were, nevertheless, high values (in the 1970s) in relation to British Whites in some cities.

Table 6. POPULATION RESIDENT IN METROPOLITAN COUNTIES OF BRITAIN BY SELECTED ETHNIC GROUP, 1991 AND 2001

		Greater London		*Greater Manchester*	*West Midlands*	*West Yorkshire*	*Other metropolitan counties*	*Ethnic group total*	*% living in metropolitan counties*
		'000	%	*'000*	*'000*	*'000*	*'000*	*'000*	
White	2001	5,103	9	2,261	2,043	1,843	3,570	54,154	27
	1991	5,289	10	2,350	2,176	1,848	3,679	51,811	30
Black Caribbean	2001	344	61	16	76	14	8	566	81
	1991	287	58	17	72	15	8	493	81
African/ Black African	2001	379	78	10	10	4	9	485	85
	1991	161	77	5	4	2	5	208	85
Indian	2001	437	42	36	157	42	15	1,053	65
	1991	347	41	30	141	35	10	840	67
Pakistani	2001	143	19	75	138	122	30	747	68
	1991	88	18	49	88	81	18	477	68
Bangladeshi	2001	154	54	20	29	8	8	283	78
	1991	86	53	11	18	6	5	163	77
Chinese	2001	80	32	12	11	6	15	247	50
	1991	57	36	8	6	4	11	157	55
UK total	2001	7,172	12	2,482	2,556	2,079	3,704	58,789	31
	1991	6,680	12	2,499	2,552	2,014	3,761	54,889	32

Sources: Office of Population Census Survey (OPCS) 1993, volume 2, table 6; and 2001 Census.

Birmingham had an ID of 74, Oldham 76, Sheffield 71 and Wolverhampton 70. In turn, the Indian segregation levels averaged over twenty cities, was 16 points lower than the Pakistani. The un-weighted ID against the White population was 46 compared with 61 for the Pakistanis and 73 for the Bangladeshis.

The high levels of segregation for the Bangladeshis and to a lesser extent for the Pakistanis were true not only of their comparisons with the White population and the population as a whole but for comparisons with other ethnic minorities. Bangladeshis were slightly more segregated from the Indians than they were from the Caribbeans and the Africans. Pakistanis were less segregated from Indians than they were from Bangladeshis. Indeed, while Pakistani IDs were exceptionally low for Bangladeshis, Bangladeshi IDs were not exceptional for Pakistanis. Pakistani IDs with other groups were generally in the 40s and lower than they were with the White population as a whole or with the Irish. This indicates that at ward level, at least, Pakistanis tend to live in areas of greater ethnic diversity than the Bangladeshis. Bangladeshi segregation levels with other groups were generally in the 50s and with the White population as a whole and with the Irish, in the 60s.

Another measure of segregation is the P* index of isolation. The principle of P* is that segregation is asymmetric: a 10% minority is more exposed to a 90% majority than vice versa. A way of conceptualising the measure is to say that P* measures the probability of a minority group member bumping into another member of the group in the street where he or she lives. The normative expectation under conditions of no segregation would be that the P* of each group with each other group would be a reflection of their percentages of the total population. If we concentrate our attention on the group interaction with itself, the 'expected' figure is the percentage that the group forms of the total population. For example, if we examine the intersection of the White in its row with White in its column and so on (the leading diagonal of Table 7) we would 'expect' a value of 79.9 (the White percentage of London's 1991 population). In fact the figure is 83.5. This means that the White population is slightly more isolated than expected, but not much. The final column of Table 7 indicates the degree of excess of observed isolation compared with the expected for each group. Bangladeshis are massively more isolated (18.5 times) than expected; Indians are 11.7 times more isolated and Pakistanis 5.5 times more isolated than expected. BrAsians appear to have the highest degree of encapsulation of any ethnic group in London in 1991. To put this in perspective, the Caribbean population of London was only slightly smaller than the Indian population and a lot less socio-economically secure, but its P* measure of isolation was only 2.7 times greater than random while the Indian population was 11.7 times more isolated than randomly expected. Pakistanis are, however, 11 times more exposed

Table 7. LONDON 1991 P* WITH COMPARISON OF P* VALUE DIVIDED BY GROUP'S LONDON PERCENTAGE

	White	*Carib-bean*	*African*	*Other Black*	*Indian*	*Pakistani*	*Bangla-deshi*	*Chinese*	*Asian other*	*Other other*	*N*	*% London population*	*P*/ London % of ethnic group*
White	**83.5**	3.6	2.0	1.1	4.0	1.0	0.9	0.8	1.5	1.7	5,303,748	79.9	1.0
Caribbean	66.5	**11.6**	5.1	2.6	5.6	1.8	1.5	1.0	1.9	2.4	289,712	4.4	2.7
African	66.2	9.2	**7.5**	2.4	5.3	1.7	1.9	1.3	2.1	2.4	161,660	2.4	3.1
Other Black	69.4	9.3	4.9	**3.2**	4.9	1.6	1.5	1.0	1.9	2.3	80,368	1.2	2.6
Indian	60.7	4.7	2.5	1.1	**20.5**	3.6	1.2	0.8	2.7	2.1	345,901	5.2	3.9
Pakistani	59.9	6.1	3.2	1.5	14.2	**7.2**	2.2	0.9	2.8	2.1	87,452	1.3	5.5
Bangladeshi	54.4	5.0	3.6	1.4	4.8	2.2	**23.7**	1.1	1.8	2.0	85,298	1.3	18.5
Chinese	74.2	5.1	3.7	1.4	5.2	1.3	1.7	**2.7**	2.4	2.2	55,499	0.8	3.2
Asian other	70.9	5.0	3.0	1.3	8.5	2.2	1.4	1.2	**4.3**	2.4	111,701	1.7	1.4
Other	73.7	5.7	3.3	1.5	6.0	1.5	1.4	1.0	2.2	**3.6**	120,118	1.8	2.0

Source: Peach, 1996.

Small-scale data are not yet available for the 2001 census, so that it is not possible to analyse whether segregation levels have increased or decreased in the inter-censal period.

to Indians than random while Indians are only three times more exposed to Pakistanis than expected.

The South Asian population in Britain has shown a dramatic increase from less than 100,000 in 1951 to over 2 million in 2001. During that time sharp economic differences between BrAsians have become accentuated. The Indians tend to be professionals and suburban. The Pakistanis and Bangladeshis have a much more blue-collar profile and tend to live mainly in inner cities. Their educational levels tend to be low and their unemployment rates tend to be high. Bangladeshi and Pakistani women tend to have relatively low participation rates in the formal economy.

The picture that emerges is one of economic integration but social segregation. In other words, BrAsians are part of the political economy of Britain, but they seem to constitute distinct civil societies within that political-economic frame. This is most acute in the case of the Bangladeshis and Pakistanis where social encapsulation is manifested within high levels of residential segregation. The groups are residentially separate also from each other. It is important to note that this trajectory is the opposite of what would be predicted from the American model of assimilation. In the American model, economic success and sub-urbanisation are accompanied by residential diffusion and intermarriage. In Britain what seems to be happening is that economic success is decoupled from social assimilation and sub-urbanisation is decoupled from residential diffusion. This provides the context for the emergence of a distinct BrAsian identity.

MUSLIMS!

Shehla Khan

On Valentine's Day 1989 Imam Khomeini issued a *fatwa* against Salman Rushdie, author of the *Satanic Verses.* Khomeini's invocation of the friend/enemy polarity (Schmitt, 1996) signified the radical politicisation of the conflict surrounding the *Satanic Verses* and its imbrication within the Islamic revolution's discursive articulation of Muslim subjectivity. One of the constitutive elements of this discursive field inhered in the rejection of *gharbzadegi* (Al Ahmad, 1997) or Westoxification as a pre-requisite for the emergence of a Muslim subject position. This antithetical linkage underscored one of the ways in which the architects of the Islamic revolution politicised the notion of Muslim identity, relating it to the modalities of inclusion within a specific political community (Sayyid, 2003). Thus, to be a Muslim meant to resist inclusion within a world that was not constructed around the signifier of Islam, more specifically a world that 'Europe' had conjured in its own image. Al Ahmad's thesis of *gharbzadegi* had been directed primarily at the incidence of formal and informal colonisation in the Muslim world, and remained confined to the territorial boundaries of the state. In contrast, Khomeini, by deterritorialising Muslim subjectivity, implicitly deterritorialised the concept of *gharbzadegi*, extending its relevance beyond the borders of individual Muslim states. It was not only this double-edged deterritorialisation, which came to the fore in the issuing of the *fatwa*. More significantly, the *fatwa* also evoked the possibility of Muslim subjectivity as an agent of reterritorialisation, and thus of a radical inversion of the process by which 'Europe' had routinely sought to impose its imperium across the globe.

It is significant that the crisis triggered by the publication of the book, including Khomeini's subsequent intervention, mark a critical moment in the articulation of Muslim subjectivity in Britain. In many ways the sets of issues surrounding the emergence of Muslims as subjects during the ferment of the Islamic revolution, notably inclusion and *gharbzadegi*, deterritorialisation and reterritorialisation, have also become pertinent in the processes marking the mobilisation of Muslims in Britain. Taken in their totality these issues point to the anomalies associated with articulating a Muslim subject position within the confines of Britain's liberal polity. This articulation as it extends across an increasing number of sites—for example law, media, government, education—poses a mounting challenge to the unacknowledged writ of the liberal state and its assimilationist structures (Modood, 2005). Specifically it points to the ways in which the universalism of the Enlightenment, and its construction of 'Europe' as the repository of Reason and ultimately of Imperium, continue to be inflected within the inclusionary logic of liberalism as it seeks to incorporate the 'Other'. The assertion of Muslim identity produces a series of seismic tremors, which unsettle the norms and practices devised by the liberal state to promote depoliticisation and conformity amongst its 'alien' minorities. Furthermore, given the dichotomised construction of 'European' and 'Non-European' identity, the articulation of Muslim subjectivity implicitly invokes the deconstruction of 'European' subjectivity. It is the combination of these twin processes, which endows the emergence of a Muslim subject position with a transformative potential.

The articulation of identity in an Islamicate rather than in an ethno-national register marks the advent of a new kind of politics in Britain, which exceeds those envisaged by the state's economy of 'race relations'. By articulating a trans-ethnic subject position that cannot be contained within ascriptions of Britain's ethnoscapes, it anticipates a splintering of the taxonomy deployed by the state to organise and discipline its ethnically marked populations. This has particular significance for the idea of BrAsian, since over two-thirds of the Muslims in Britain are located in BrAsian communities. However, their increasing identification with a Muslim subject position hollows out BrAsianness, which becomes a residual category that is largely associated with Indocentric motifs, for example Bollywood, Bhangra and *bindis*.

The challenge posed to the existing topography of 'race relations' is also apparent in facets of Muslim mobilisation, and encompasses two interrelated processes. On the one hand, the activist stance reflects the projection of a specifically Muslim presence upon the public arena, rather than one that is delimited by ascribed ethnicised markers. On the other hand, the mobilisation of Muslims as Muslims reflects a parallel process of politicisation in which an equivalential logic is established between a particularistic demand, and a more diffuse one in which such demands are exceeded. This double-edged mobilisation is manifest in the demand for Muslim grant maintained schools, which has gained a currency that transcends particular interest. Thus over 50 per cent of Muslims endorsing state funding were not committed to sending their children there (Modood, 2005: 199). Instead the issue of state funding became a metaphor for Muslim-British state relations in which the state came face to face with a new form of political solidarity. In the demand for schools, as well as their extensive participation in the anti-war demonstration of 2003, Muslims featured as Muslims rather than as BrAsians. The far-reaching consequences of politicisation are also evident in the increasing tentativeness of Muslim political party allegiance. The defection of a large percentage of the Muslim electorate from Labour party support, and the victory of Respect in the seat of Hackney in the 2005 election are illustrative of this trend.

Above all, the fluid and expansionary aspect of Muslim identity formation becomes evident in the emergence of the global as its frame of reference. Khomeini's intervention implicitly evoked the possibility of restoring the logic of caliphal authority in a post-Westphalian world, of projecting Muslim subjectivity beyond the boundaries of the nation state and on to an inchoate transnational political formation. It drew the Muslims of Britain into the currents of the global Muslim resurgence, which occurs at, but exceeds the level of the state.

In the years since the *fatwa* the mobilisation of Muslims in Britain has proceeded apace; it is evident, for example, in their willingness to make common cause with beleaguered Muslim populations across the globe, for example in Palestine, Iraq, Afghanistan, Chechnya and Kashmir. However, the process of Muslim assertion, in Britain as elsewhere, has encountered resistance at multiple, interrelated levels. In the context of the British state, it is manifest in recastings of loyalty tests issued by politicians and media men as Muslims come to be viewed through a double lens in which Bradford becomes home to a mountain pass in the Tora Bora, an Apache-ravaged alley in the Gaza Strip, or a *medressa* in Peshawar. In the global context, it is manifest in the creation of new forms of governmentality via the so-called 'war on terror' in which military force, ideological initiatives and penal and surveillance systems coalesce to stem the rise of a Muslim political subjectivity insofar as it aims to challenge an iniquitous world order.

In turn, the transnationalised governmentality of the 'war on terror' has become inflected within the discursive vocabulary of racism. This is seen most vividly in attempts to outsource the definition of terrorism to the Other, who exists outside the pale of the liberal state. It finds its most polarised expression in the phrase 'home-grown terrorists', which has become common currency since the attacks in London in July 2005, and which replays the opposition between metropolitan home and violent periphery.

The logic of racialised governmentality in turn paves the way for the raft of legal-institutional initiatives advanced by the liberal state in the guise of counter-'terrorism' measures, for example shoot-to-kill policies, increased surveillance, the revocation of British citizenship and deportation. Arguably these measures represent in extreme form the ongoing liberal quest to re-suture Muslim identity to the British state via domestication and pacification or above all by disciplining a form of identification whose affiliations have come to exceed territorial boundaries. However, in resembling measures adopted by the colonial state to discipline 'native' populations in the periphery, their cumulative effect is, paradoxically, to blur distinctions between 'home' and 'away', between the colonial past and the postcolonial present. This melding provides an ironic contrast to the liberal celebration of the 'borderless worlds' of contemporary globalisation, of time-space compression, of converging lifestyles and ideologies.

The complex formation of Muslim as a political category illustrates how at the conceptual level, it serves to undermine biologically determined notions of race in which racial identity is construed as a matter of destiny. As such it constitutes a refutation of the putative dichotomy of 'race' and religion, which occurs with some regularity in Islamophobic interventions via the assertion that demonising or ridiculing persons on the grounds of race is unacceptable since racial affiliation is involuntary. Religious affiliation, meanwhile, is voluntary, and therefore undeserving of a comparable restraint. However, this view ignores the way in which 'race' functions as an entire civilisational discourse or, as Hesse notes, the nexus of 'meanings and significations of social existence' within a hierarchised dichotomy (Hesse, 2005: n44). 'Cultural racialisation' denotes a mobile and expansionary notion of race, which also subsumes for example, language, history and religion. Racism, therefore, invokes the spectrum of cultural reproduction as an affirmation of its constitutive split between 'Europe' and a subordinate 'Non-Europe' (Hesse, 2005).

An understanding of racism's incremental tendencies reveals how conflictual moments between Muslims and the liberal establishment are often depoliticised and essentialised. The burning of the *Satanic Verses*, for example, was caricatured as a clash between freedom and fundamentalism/fascism. In being denounced as fanatical, fascistic and grotesque, Muslims became the living exemplars of the cultural racialisation attending the representation of 'Islam' within the book. Echoes of this logic have been discernible in the recourse to race-centric accounts in the aftermath of the London attacks. These accounts serve to insulate the liberal state through the dismissal of a structural-political dimension which could situate the attacks within the context of the global 'war on terror'. Instead, the debate over causes and consequences has featured attempts to direct critical enquiry towards questions of multiculturalism, integration and assimilation. These attempts, which have met with considerable success, hinge upon the pathologisation of Muslims, ascribing blame and prescribing remedies via the iteration of familiar orientalist/indological tropes, for instance the role of 'hate preachers', the cultural schizophrenia engulfing Muslim youth, the need for an Islamicate Luther (despite the non-existence of a Muslim pope) and the general Muslim antipathy to 'our freedoms' and 'our way of life'. The consequences of pathologising Muslims are twofold: on the one hand, this serves to present Muslim 'dysfunction' as endogenous, as the symptom of the community's self-ghettoisation from the state's liberal ethos; on the other hand, it allows for the state's racist policies to pass unchallenged, thus maintaining the frontier between white, liberal Britain and its marked ethnic minority.

Significantly, the only ethnically marked individual given leave to cross the frontier is the ethnic informer, who has internalised the racist and orientalist readings of Islam that colour the dominant discourse. The authority of the ethnic informer, typified by figures such as Rushdie or Hanif Kureishi, derives from the ostensible claim to access both worlds; however, as the 'insider' echoing the hegemonic constructions of the 'outsider', such an individual reinforces the allied processes of pathologisation and of depoliticisation by providing an 'authentic' note of endorsement to prevailing relations of power. The informer's role is not to deny the struggle for hegemony; it is rather to parochialise the political by relocating hegemonic struggles away from the frontier and into the interior of the ethnically marked subordinate group. As such the informant absolves the dominant culture of its excesses, which are reconfigured as the internecine feuds and rivalries typifying the 'otherness' and specificity of the 'outsider'. This is demonstrated, for example, in the attempted displacement of Islamophobia upon the myriad divisions that allegedly exist, for instance, between Sufis and Islamists, between members of different clans or *biraderis*, between individuals of different generations.

The struggle to articulate a Muslim subject position occurs across a plurality of sites around the globe. It becomes the common denominator linking seemingly disparate events such as the publication of a book and the pursuit of the 'war on terror'. This is not a struggle which can be conceptualised as the aggregate of various local conflicts. Rather, in being organised around the signifier Islam, these heterogeneous conflicts are co-constitutive: they draw upon, intersect and sustain one another as they cut across discursive, institutional and territorial boundaries. As such they coalesce to pose a momentous challenge to the legacy of Enlightenment reason and the diverse ways in which it has contributed to the entrenchment of colonial as well as neo-colonial forms of rule both at the level of the individual nation-state and within the global order at large.

THE POLITICS OF THE BRASIAN ELECTORATE

Muhammad Anwar

Most BrAsians have a right to vote and to stand for elections both as British citizens and as Commonwealth citizens. Their concentration in some inner-city areas of Britain has implications for their participation in the British political process and their concentration in particular conurbations means that, at least in statistical terms, BrAsians are in a position to influence the political process in those areas. The integration of BrAsians into the British political process is of fundamental importance because political involvement, power and influence can highlight issues both through the ballot box and through politicians, party officials and committees and these channels are fundamental to influencing political decisions, which affect all aspects of BrAsian life. This chapter examines BrAsian participation in the British electoral process since 1974, by using empirical data from the studies undertaken at the 1997 and 2001 General Elections. The registration and turn out levels of BrAsians as well as their voting patterns are analysed. In addition the responses of the political parties to the participation of South Asian settlers and their representation in politics are presented. In this context the issue of entryism is also discussed.

ELECTORAL IMPORTANCE OF THE BRASIAN VOTE

The 1991 Census showed there were 78 parliamentary constituencies with more than a 15% ethnic minority population (23 with over 30%), of which the majority were BrAsian. In 1981 there were 58 constituencies with more than 15% of the total population living in households with the head born in the New Commonwealth and Pakistan (NCWP). It is estimated that in 2002 there are now more than 80 parliamentary constituencies with a 10% BrAsian population. Topping the 1991 list was Birmingham Small Heath constituency with a BrAsian population of almost 40%, followed by Ealing Southall with a similar percentage (see Table 1).

There are also now several hundred local election wards with a BrAsian population of 10% or more. Of these, Northcote ward in the London Borough of Ealing recorded, in 1991, the highest percentage of BrA-

Table 1. TWELVE TOP PARLIAMENTARY CONSTITUENCIES IN TERMS OF SOUTH ASIAN POPULATION (1991) % OF TOTAL POPULATION

Parliamentary constituency	*Total pop.*	*Ethnic minority pop.*	*Ethnic min. pop. (%)*	*Black (%)*	*South Asian (%)*
Birmingham Ladywood	80,008	44,503	55.6	17.3	34.6
Birmingham Small Heath	81,280	44,689	55.0	11.7	39.6
Newham North East	81,896	43,747	53.4	12.2	35.2
Ealing, Southall	97,280	49,829	51.2	6.9	39.0
Birmingham Sparkbrook	75,492	36,975	49.0	7.9	36.8
Newham North West	60,457	28,856	47.7	19.3	23.6
Bethnal Green and Stepney	80,394	34,479	42.9	5.5	34.4
Brent North	81,002	34,371	42.4	8.6	25.3
Leicester East	85,472	32,461	38.0	2.3	33.5
Ilford South	77,681	28,625	36.8	6.7	25.8
Bradford West	97,058	35,450	36.5	2.3	31.9
Leicester South	95,504	30,884	32.3	3.1	26.1

Note: Birmingham Small Heath and Birmingham Sparkbrook have now been merged into one constituency.

Source: 1991 Census.

sians as part of the overall population (79%), followed by Brookhouse in Blackburn (75%) and Spinney Hill in Leicester (71%) (see Table 2).

However, it must be stressed here that it is not only the number of BrAsians in certain areas which makes those people electorally important, but also whether they actively take part in the political process. In other words, are they on the electoral register, do they come out to vote, and how do they compare with non-Asians in terms of such participation? However, before we deal with these questions, let us analyse the views of BrAsians and non-Asians about ethnic minorities' participation in politics.

ATTITUDES ABOUT PARTICIPATION IN POLITICS

The initiatives taken by the political parties to encourage BrAsians and other ethnic minorities are important. However, the attitudes of ordinary electors and candidates on this subject are equally important. In this context, we asked respondents in our 1998 survey whether ethnic minorities should be encouraged to participate in the political process and an overwhelming majority of BrAsians and non-Asians felt that they should (Anwar, 1998b). See Table 3 for details.

Table 2. LOCAL ELECTION WARDS WITH MORE THAN 50% SOUTH ASIAN POPULATION, 1991

District ward	*Population*	*Ethnic minority pop.*	*Ethnic min. pop. (%)*	*Black (%)*	*South Asian (%)*
Ealing, Northcote	11,177	10,083	90.21	5.93	78.76
Leicester, Spinney Hill	10,035	8,281	82.52	4.95	70.67
Ealing, Glebe	12,858	10,424	81.07	7.56	68.55
Blackburn, Brookhouse	8,121	6,339	78.06	0.58	74.66
Leicester, Crown Hills	9,585	7,261	75.75	2.96	69.42
Newham, Kensington	7,902	5,910	74.79	9.43	56.82
Bradford University	18,898	13,970	73.92	2.80	66.67
Newham, Monega	8,060	5,910	73.33	14.70	53.68
Tower Hamlets, Spitalfields	8,861	6,448	72.77	4.15	65.17
Newham, Upton	10,209	7,325	71.75	16.64	50.71
Leicester, Latimer	7,952	5,630	70.80	1.66	67.14
Newham, St Stephens	7,412	5,162	69.64	11.58	51.52
Leicester, Rushey Mead	11,479	7,498	65.32	1.67	61.15
Birmingham, Sparkhill	26,251	16,353	62.29	6.51	51.56
Luton, Biscot	11,662	7,044	60.40	5.39	52.18
Leicester, Charnwood	9,290	5,538	59.61	4.00	50.66

Source: 1991 Census.

Table 3. SHOULD ETHNIC MINORITIES BE ENCOURAGED TO PARTICIPATE IN THE POLITICAL PROCESS? 1998 (%)

	Yes	*No*
White	97	3
Black	96	4
Asian	98	2
Other	96	4

Source: Anwar, 1998b.

These findings were consistent with the author's previous research in 1979, 1983 and 1990 (Anwar, 1994). In the 1998 survey of electors, we asked the respondents what form this active participation should take: 1) getting involved in the present political parties; 2) having their own political party; and 3) any other method. An overwhelming majority of the respondents supported the first method. Among ethnic groups 92% of Whites, 86% of Blacks and 94% of BrAsians supported this method. We

Table 4. ETHNIC MINORITY PARTICIPATION IN POLITICS
CANDIDATES' VIEWS IN 1979 SURVEY (%)

Candidates' views	*Total (542)*	*Con (219)*	*Lab (107)*	*Lib (216)*
Yes, should be encouraged	89	83	98	92
No, should not	3	6	–	2
Unsure	8	11	2	6

Source: Anwar, 1980.

also asked about the reasons for encouraging ethnic minorities to take an active role in British politics. The majority of the respondents—Whites, BrAsians and other ethnic minorities—felt that it was good for integration and for providing equal opportunities for ethnic minorities.

It is interesting to mention here that in the 1979 survey, 71% of BrAsian electors compared with 58% of Whites, felt that ethnic minority participation in elections should be encouraged. However, 32% of White respondents at that time were opposed to their participation as were 6% of BrAsians (Anwar, 1980). Therefore, the attitudes of both BrAsians and Whites after twenty years have shown a very significant positive change. The 1979 study also included a survey of candidates, which showed that candidates of all three main political parties were generally in favour of encouraging ethnic minorities to participate in politics. Only 6% of Conservative candidates and 2% of Liberal candidates thought they should not be encouraged to participate. See Table 4 for details.

The survey of candidates at the 1997 General Election showed that for the same question 95% of the respondents said 'yes', ethnic minorities should be encouraged. As shown in Table 5, the only major difference between the responses of the candidates of the three main political parties was the comparatively greater percentage of Conservative Party candidates who said 'no'. Like the electors, the vast majority of candidates agreed that participation should take the form of 'getting involved in the present political parties'. Altogether, almost 95% of candidates in the survey supported this method and there were no significant differences between the three main political parties. The results from the survey of candidates at the 2001 General Election are similar.

Table 5. SHOULD ETHNIC MINORITIES BE ENCOURAGED TO TAKE A MORE ACTIVE ROLE IN THE BRITISH POLITICAL SYSTEM? (%)

	Con	*Lab*	*Lib Dem*
Yes	88.7	99.0	95.2
No	8.0	–	2.4
Unanswered	3.3	1.0	2.4

Source: Anwar, 1998b.

ELECTORAL PARTICIPATION

The settlement of BrAsians has been largely an urban phenomenon and focused on a number of regions (see Peach, this volume; Ali, this volume). It is in this context that we now examine the participation of BrAsians in British politics, for which registration is a fundamental prerequisite.

Registration

In the early period of South Asian mass migration and settlement very few Asians were registered (Deakin, 1965). A sample survey in 1974 of 227 BrAsians and Afro-Caribbeans and 175 Whites showed that, despite improvements, ethnic minorities were still five times more likely not to have registered to vote than Whites (Anwar and Kohler, 1975). It was found that only 6% of Whites, compared with 27% of Asians and 37% of Afro-Caribbeans, were not registered. However, further research in two areas, Birmingham and Bradford, where fieldwork had been undertaken in 1974, showed a great increase in the registration levels of Asians. In Birmingham it was found that 5% of Asians and 13% of Afro-Caribbeans were not on the electoral register, compared with 4% of Whites, and in Bradford 9% of Asians were not registered, as against 5% of Whites (Anwar, 1979). It appeared that this change had occurred because of the efforts of the then Community Relations Commission (CRC), the two local authorities, local community relations councils, political parties and also some ethnic minority community groups. The ethnic minority press had also played an important role.

In 1979 a survey in twenty-four parliamentary constituencies showed that 23% of BrAsians and 7% of Whites were not registered (Anwar, 1980). Another survey in 1981 showed that in inner London BrAsians had double the non-registration rate of Whites (27% and 12% respectively) (Todd and Butcher, 1982). And in 1983 a survey showed that 21% of BrAsians, but also 19% of Whites from the same areas were not registered (Anwar, 1984). The fieldwork for this survey was undertaken in inner-city wards, where registration levels are generally low, and there were wide area variations due to the policies of the local electoral registration officers (EROs) and the efforts of others concerned. Another national study of registration still showed that gaps existed with 15% of BrAsians, 24% of Blacks and only 6% of Whites not registered (Smith, 1993). More recent research in five local authority areas, undertaken in 1998, found that registration for BrAsians and Whites was fairly similar, but non-registration among Black respondents was still very high (26%) (see Table 6).

However, even within the BrAsian category there were differences in the level of non-registration: Indian, 24%; Pakistani, 17%; and Bangladeshi, 13%. It is interesting to compare these figures with the findings

Table 6. REGISTRATION—FOUR ETHNIC GROUPS 1998 (%)

	Registered	*Not registered*
White	82	18
Black	74	26
BrAsian	81	19
Other	54	46
Total non-White	73	27

Source: Anwar, 1998b.

from the question of whether they were registered. In the same 1998 survey nine out of ten respondents *claimed* that they were registered to vote (Anwar, 1998b). Saggar (2000) also found that in 1997 96.9% of Indians, 90.2% of Pakistanis and 91.3% of Bangladeshis *claimed* they were registered to vote. It must be pointed out that there are always area variations in terms of registration levels, which are sometimes linked to the policies and practices of the registration offices and sometimes because of the interest taken by BrAsian organisations and political parties in persuading and helping people to register. It is expected that with the new rolling register, introduced from February 2001, the registration levels will improve: it is now updated each month and people can register to vote in the weeks before the election, though not once the election has been called. As a result there was an increase of 1.3% in the number of those registered to vote between the 1997 and 2001 General Elections (The Electoral Commission, 2001). However, a study by MORI on behalf of the Electoral Commission showed that 15% of non-voters were not registered. Some would argue that if individuals could register to vote on the day of the election, as happens in the United States, the turn out could increase by at least 10% and possibly 15% (Lijphart, 2001).

Reasons given for non-registration among BrAsians include language difficulty, alienation, concern about anonymity and confidentiality, fear of harassment, fear of officialdom, administrative inefficiency and doubts about residence status.

Voter turn-out

If BrAsians are on the electoral register, do they come out to vote? Monitoring of various local and General Elections in the last twenty-eight years has shown that, on average, the BrAsian turn-out is generally higher than that of non-Asians from the same areas. For example, at the October 1974 General Election, a survey in Bradford and Rochdale showed that the turn-out among BrAsians was 57.7%, compared with 54.6% for non-Asians (Anwar, 1980). At the 1979 General Election BrAsian turn-out rates, in eighteen of the nineteen constituencies monitored, were higher than non-Asian: on average, 65% for BrAsians and 61% for non-Asians. In 1983 once again we found that the BrAsian turn-out was higher than that of non-Asians: overall 81% for BrAsians and 60% for non-Asians (Anwar, 1984). A survey at the 1987 General Election and another in 1991, before the 1992 General Election, also showed that there was a greater likelihood of BrAsians turning out to vote (*Asian Times*, 11 June 1989; Amin and Richardson, 1992). A similar pattern—a higher turn-out of BrAsians—was discovered in various surveys undertaken at local elections (Le Lohe 1975, 1984; Anwar, 1986, 1994). The trend was confirmed at the 1997 General Election. A survey in six parliamentary constituencies across the country showed that the BrAsian turn-out was higher than non-Asians, with area variations as shown in Table 7.

Another study at the 1997 General Election, based on the British Election Survey, also confirmed that BrAsian turn-out levels were higher than those of non-Asians (Saggar, 2000). It showed that 82.4% of Indians, 75.6% of Pakistanis and 73.9% of Bangladeshis compared with 68.7% of Black Caribbean, 64.4% of Black Africans and 78.7% of Whites claimed to have voted. It should be pointed out that the author's calculations are based on marked registers and not the recall method. Therefore, like the *claim* about registration, which is normally higher than the *actual* situation, the same could apply to turn-out. Our survey of five areas, which asked respondents to state whether they would vote in the 1998 local elections, found that 64% of BrAsians were likely to vote compared with 52% of Blacks and 55% of Whites (Anwar, 1998b). The survey also found that BrAsian respondents were also the most likely to have voted at the 1997 General Election.

At the 2001 General Election we undertook another survey of turn-out by using marked registers in four parliamentary constituencies. The results are presented in Table 8. Once again the results show that on the

Table 7. BRASIAN VS NON-ASIAN TURN-OUT, 1997 GENERAL ELECTION (%)

Parliamentary constituency	*BrAsian turn-out*	*Non-Asian turn-out*
Bradford West	63.1	51.5
Birmingham Edgbaston	61.6	58.2
Birmingham Ladywood	67.5	55.9
Birmingham Sparkbrook and Small Heath	60.2	52.2
Rochdale	64.4	42.4
Walthamstow	60.0	63.0

Source: Anwar, 1998b.

Table 8. BRASIAN VS NON-BRASIAN TURN-OUT, 2001 GENERAL ELECTION (%)

Parliamentary constituency	*BrAsian turn-out*	*Non-BrAsian turn-out*
Ilford South	52.6	47.4
Walthamstow	56.6	53.3
Birmingham Perry Barr	53.5	33.5
Birmingham Sparkbrook and Small Heath	56.5	44.5

whole the BrAsian turn-out was higher than non-BrAsian. A study by MORI for the Electoral Commission confirmed this trend. It showed that over 85% of BrAsians compared with 80% of Whites claimed they had voted in the 2001 General Election on 7 June (Electoral Commission, 2002). If higher levels of registration plus higher levels of turn-out are seen in relation to mobilisation and participation, then BrAsians are capable of being more reliable voters and, consequently, in a better position to influence the outcome of elections in their areas of settlement.

Voting patterns

This section deals with the voting patterns of BrAsians and other ethnic groups, including Whites, in General Elections since 1974 to see what changes have taken place over time. Analysis also includes expressed voting intentions before some General Elections. However, we start with the 1972 parliamentary by-election in Rochdale—an interesting case study of BrAsian participation— where the part played by Pakistanis appears to have been a decisive factor in the election result (Anwar, 1973), a victory for Cyril Smith of the Liberal Party. In 1974 both the Labour and Liberal parties worked hard to gain Pakistani support in Rochdale (Anwar, 1975). At the February and October General Elections of that year, in Rochdale over 50% of the BrAsians voted Liberal and over 40% Labour. However, in Bradford West over 70% of BrAsians voted Labour and only 2% Liberal (Anwar and Kohler, 1975). These differences were clearly linked to very special local situations. A survey in six parliamentary constituencies showed that there was strong support among ethnic minorities for the Labour Party (Anwar and Kohler, 1975). For example, 49% of BrAsians compared with 41% of Whites claimed to have voted for the Labour Party at the February 1974 General Election and 61% of BrAsians compared with 45% of Whites were inclined to support the Labour Party at the October 1974 General Election.

At the 1979 General Election an exit poll in twenty-four parliamentary constituencies revealed that 86% of BrAsians, 90% of Afro-Caribbeans and 50% of Whites voted for the Labour Party (Anwar, 1980).

However, in some constituencies like Rochdale, up to 50% of BrAsians voted for the Liberal Party candidate, while in some other constituencies over 15% of BrAsians voted for the Conservative Party. At the 1983 General Election a national exit poll showed that the majority of ethnic minorities had voted Labour (57%) but 24% and 16% had voted Conservative and Alliance respectively (Anwar, 1986). However, it appeared that while the solid support for Labour among Afro-Caribbean voters remained, BrAsians were slowly moving towards other parties as well. For example, the highest ethnic minority vote (93%) for the Labour Party was recorded in Bristol East, with a mainly Afro-Caribbean population; for the Conservatives the highest was in Croydon North East (27%) and for the Alliance in Rochdale (54%), the last two with a predominantly BrAsian electorate. This trend continued. At the 1987 General Election 66.8% of BrAsians intended to vote for the Labour Party, 22.7% for the Conservative Party and 10% for the Alliance (*Asian Times*, May 1987). An exit poll confirmed this pattern, showing that 61% of BrAsians had voted for Labour, compared with 20% for Conservatives and 17% for the Alliance. Once again there were area variations. Decrease in Labour Party support among BrAsians was also shown in a survey carried out by National Opinion Polls (NOP) before the 1992 General Election. It showed that 55% of BrAsians intended to vote for the Labour Party and, while 18% of respondents were still undecided, the others were likely to vote for the Conservatives and Liberal Democrats.

Overall, surveys between 1974 and 1992 showed that the vast majority of ethnic minorities voted for the Labour Party. However, over time the growth of a significant minority, particularly of BrAsians, that voted for the Conservative Party and for the Liberal Democrats, could be noted (Anwar, 1994). This trend was confirmed at the 1997 General Election.

Table 9. VOTING PATTERNS BY ETHNIC GROUP, 1997 GENERAL ELECTION SURVEY (%)

	Lab	*Con*	*Lib Dem*	*Other*
White	61	27	7	5
Black Caribbean	94	2	4	–
Black African	96	1	3	–
Black other	88	2	4	6
Indian	72	18	4	4
Pakistani	55	39	1	4
Bangladeshi	83	13	1	3
Other	67	24	3	4

Source: Anwar, 1998b.

On polling day the author undertook a survey in five parliamentary constituencies—Birmingham Edgbaston, Birmingham Ladywood, Birmingham Sparkbrook and Small Heath, Bradford West and Walthamstow—to identify how ethnic minorities and Whites from the same areas had voted (Anwar, 1998b). Voters were asked, in a totally voluntary and confidential process, to record again their votes on 'duplicate' ballot papers which they then placed in a box.[1]

It appears from our analysis that the majority of ethnic minorities voted for the Labour Party candidates (60% of BrAsian, 92% of Black), but a significant minority also voted for the Conservative Party candidates and a yet smaller proportion for the Liberal Democrat candidates. However, there were area variations and different trends for different ethnic groups. For example, in Bradford West our survey suggested that the majority of Pakistanis (61%) voted for the Conservative candidate (Mohammad Riaz) compared with 35% for the Labour Party candidate (Marsha Singh). For the Indians the pattern was just the opposite: 74% voted for the Labour Party candidate and 23% for the Conservative candidate. Overall, out of the total sample of 3,232 voters (more than two-thirds of whom were categorised as ethnic minorities), 65% voted for the Labour Party, 27% for the Conservative Party, 4% for Liberal Democrats and 4% for other parties (Anwar, 1998b). See Table 9 for details.

Another survey at the time of the 1997 General Election showed similar voting patterns for ethnic minorities (Saggar, 2000). This study showed solid support for Labour amongst Afro-Caribbeans (93.5%); similar support for the Conservatives among Indians (17.5%) to that recorded by our survey; less support for the Conservatives among Pakistanis (7.1%); and more support for the Liberal Democrats among Bangladeshis (10.3%). These differences can be explained thus: our survey was in five parliamentary constituencies, with a larger sample of ethnic minorities, while the Saggar survey was part of a wider study of the 1997 General Election, and had a smaller sample of ethnic minorities. For example, there were only eighty-five Pakistanis and thirty-nine Bangladeshis in the Saggar sample while in our survey, in the constituency of Bradford West alone, there were 704 Pakistanis in the sample.

A survey by the author on polling day at the 2001 General Election (in five constituencies with a sample of 2,837 voters) showed that overall 62.3% had voted for the Labour Party, 13.2% for the Conservative Party, 12% for the Liberal Democrats and 12.5% for smaller parties and independent candidates. Voting patterns of various ethnic groups are presented in Table 10.

1 It should be noted—because of the possible implications for the results of the survey—that all five constituencies except Edgbaston, which had a Conservative Party MP, were held by the Labour Party. However, our main interest here was to compare the political behaviour of ethnic minorities and Whites from the same geographical areas.

Table 10. VOTING PATTERNS BY ETHNIC GROUP, 2001 GENERAL ELECTION SURVEY (%)

	Lab	*Con*	*Lib Dem*	*Other*
White	50.6	16.3	24.6	7.5
Black Caribbean	86.3	3.1	7.1	3.5
Black African	91.6	1.7	4.2	2.5
Black other	78.0	7.3	4.9	7.8
Indian	62.9	27.0	4.9	5.2
Pakistani	60.0	7.0	5.0	28.0
Bangladeshi	59.9	14.0	7.6	19.5
Chinese	57.9	36.8	5.3	-
Other	68.8	9.1	11.1	11.0
Total	62.3	13.2	12.0	12.5

This table again confirms the downward trend of BrAsian support for the Labour Party and the continuing solid support for the same party among Blacks. However, due to the Iraq war a significant number of British Asian Muslims voted against the Labour Party in the 2003 local elections and 2004 local and European elections, and consequently many Labour Party candidates were defeated in inner-city areas where the party had previously had safe seats. As a result the Labour Party lost control of local councils in many important areas such as Birmingham, Leeds and Leicester. The Liberal Democrats have benefited from this shift. Generally the Labour Party activists claim that this is a temporary phenomenon and that the vast majority of these BrAsians would in due course come back to support the Labour Party.

One reason why the majority of BrAsians and ethnic minorities still vote Labour is the perception that it is more sympathetic to ethnic minorities and 'supports the working class'. A similar perception affects the pattern of voting in the United States, where the Democratic Party has always received the majority of the black votes (Cavanagh, 1984). Nevertheless, it appears from our research evidence that in Britain a variety of important factors are involved in attracting electoral support from BrAsians: the policies of the political parties; the organisation and mobilisation of BrAsians at local and national levels; the candidates' personal contact and familiarity with BrAsian communities; and the presence of BrAsian candidates. In this context it is relevant to discuss the policies and initiatives taken by the parties to attract BrAsian support.

POLITICAL PARTIES' RESPONSES

The participation of BrAsians in the political process is also affected by the policies and initiatives taken by the political parties. These include special arrangements to attract BrAsian support, manifesto commitments at elections and the number of BrAsian candidates and elected BrAsian MPs and councillors. It is also clear now that initiatives to attract the electoral support of BrAsian and other ethnic minority communities can be taken by parties and their leaders without the fear of losing white voters. Hence the number of set-ups arranged to do just that.

The Conservative Party set up an Ethnic Minority Unit in the Conservative Central Office's Department of Community Affairs in 1976. Its objective was to make party members aware of the growing importance of BrAsians and other ethnic minority electors, to influence party policy, to improve the image of the party among BrAsians and other ethnic minorities, and, as a result, to seek their support. The Unit helped form an Anglo-Asian Conservative Society through which it recruited BrAsians directly into the party. It had about thirty local branches. The formation of the Anglo-West Indian Conservative Society followed with the same objective. However, more recently these societies have been replaced by a national organisation, the One Nation Forum. Nevertheless, some Anglo-Asian and Anglo-West Indian Societies continue their activities at the local level. Members of these societies and the One Nation Forum get involved in election campaigns as Conservative Party workers, and some come forward as party candidates in local, parliamentary and European elections. Leaders themselves have also made direct overtures towards BrAsians. For example, in a February 1997 speech Michael Howard, the then Home Secretary, voiced his appreciation of the role of BrAsians in making Britain prosperous and stated that since Asian values were closer to the philosophy of his party, BrAsians were natural Conservative Party supporters. And William Hague, the Conservative Party leader, speaking as chief guest at a dinner for Asian millionaires at the Café Royale, expressed the hope that one day an Asian would be Conservative Party leader, adding, 'though you'll forgive me for saying not quite yet. As far as I am concerned, I see Asians as no less British than the Scots, the English, the Welsh and the Northern Irish' (*Daily Telegraph*, 22 April 1999). He also announced the creation of a 'Cultural Unit' at the Conservative Central Office to attract more BrAsians. Mr Hague said he wanted more British blacks and BrAsians playing a full part in 'the mainstream of our national life. Not just in business, the professions, sports, the arts or in the media but also in politics.' Similar sentiments were expressed by another Conservative Party leader, Iain Duncan-Smith (at the time a Deputy Chairman of the Party, Shailesh Vara, was BrAsian). Clearly the party is making an effort to attract support from BrAsians.

The BrAsian vote is also clearly valuable to the Labour Party. The Labour Party Race and Action Group (LPRAG) was set up in 1975 as a pressure group to educate and advise the party on relevant issues. There was also a long campaign to set up Black Sections in the Labour Party (Shukra, 1990; Jeffers, 1991) and although this issue was defeated at several Labour Party annual conferences in the 1980s, the Labour Party NEC finally set up a Black and Asian Advisory Committee, followed by a Black Socialist Society, similar to the party's women's and local government committees. The Society's primary objective is to obtain and maintain ethnic minorities' support for the party and an officer is also appointed at the party's national headquarters to deal with ethnic minorities. In September 1995, following pressure from Pakistani and Kashmiri Labour supporters, including Labour councillors, the party agreed a policy on the Kashmir issue (Labour Party Debates, September 1995)[2] and in the following month the party leader, Tony Blair, met the then Pakistani Prime Minister, Benazir Bhutto, during her brief stopover *en route* to the United States (he was the only leading British politician to do so and received appreciation from Bhutto for the party's approved policy regarding Kashmir). With his wife, Blair also visited the Regent's Park Mosque in London in February 1997 when the Muslim community celebrated *Eid ul fitr*, a move some saw as an initiative to garner Muslim support ahead of the 1997 General Election. Between the 1997 and 2001 General Elections Tony Blair, now the Prime Minister, was again seen to attend several events organised by various BrAsian groups.

The Liberal Party, for their part, used to have a Community Relations Panel in the 1970s, which included ethnic minority members. It met regularly to discuss relevant issues and formulated not only policies to attract ethnic minority members, but also election campaign strategies specially directed towards them. The Liberal Democrats are following a similar arrangement. In June 1991 the 'Asian Liberal Democrats' was formed to attract BrAsian support. One BrAsian was also a member of the Liberal Democrats National Executive. The leader of the Liberal Democrats has also held important meetings with Asian businessmen and others to attract both financial and electoral support. More recently an Asian, Lord Dholakia, became the President of the Liberal Democrats.

The Scottish National Party (SNP) is also trying in various ways to secure BrAsians' support. The organisation 'Asians for Scottish Independence' has been formed. BrAsian candidates were put forward at the 1997 and 2001 General Elections and some have also contested the Scottish Parliament elections.

2 Following their success, Pakistanis and Kashmiris campaigned for the approval of a similar policy at the Conservative Party Annual Conference, which, unlike the Labour Party's, is advisory and not policy-making.

BRASIAN REPRESENTATION

One way to examine the response of the political parties to the participation of BrAsians is to examine the number of BrAsian candidates put forward in General Elections in the last thirty years, although of course MPs from the Indian subcontinent were elected to the House of Commons even before the Second World War. The first, Dadabhai Naoroji, was elected in 1882 as a Liberal, with a majority of five, at Finsbury Central. The second, Sir Mancherjee Bhownagree was twice elected as a Conservative for Bethnal Green North East in 1895 and 1900. The third, Shapurji Saklatvala was also twice elected, for Battersea North as a Labour candidate in 1922 and as a Communist in 1924. All three were Parsees. In the House of Lords there was one member from the Indian subcontinent, Lord Sinha of Rajpur (1863–1928). At a local level, in 1934, Chunilal Katial, a medical doctor, was elected as a Labour councillor in Finsbury, North London, and in 1938 he became the first BrAsian Mayor in Britain. Krishna Menon, a teacher, was also elected in 1934 as a Labour councillor for St Pancras ward in London and in 1936, another doctor, Jainti Saggar, was elected as a Labour councillor in Dundee and served for eighteen years. And these were not the only Asians elected by their mainly white electorate. Similarly, Asian women took an active role in politics, for example, participating in many suffragette organisations at the beginning of the century: Sophia Duleep Singh, who lived in London, being just one example.

After the Second World War the first Asian candidate selected by a major political party was Sardar K.S.N. Ahluwala, who contested Willesden West for the Liberal Party in 1950. At the February 1974 election the Labour Party put forward an Asian from Glasgow to contest East Fife, and the Liberal Party selected an Asian for Coventry South East. There were no Asian candidates selected by the main political parties at the October 1974 General Election, but at the 1979 General Election three of the five ethnic minority candidates put forward by the main political parties were Asians (seven others stood for the minor parties): two Conservative and one Liberal. This was the first time since 1945 that the Conservative Party had selected ethnic minority candidates. In the event, all the BrAsians—and other ethnic minority candidates—lost, because they had contested seats where there was no chance of winning, irrespective of the party. At the 1983 General Election, two-thirds of the eighteen ethnic minority candidates who stood for the major political parties were BrAsians. However, as in 1979, none contested a winnable or safe seat. Nevertheless, the main parties continued to attract BrAsian electoral support, and selected eighteen BrAsian candidates at the 1987 General Election (a total of twenty-seven ethnic minority candidates were selected that year). Only one, Keith Vaz (Leicester East), was returned—for the

Labour Party. Another Asian Labour Party candidate, Mohammad Aslam (Nottingham East), lost by only 456 votes, because Labour Party support was divided over his selection. Three Afro-Caribbean Labour MPs were also returned in this election: Paul Boateng (Brent South), Diane Abbott (Hackney North and Stoke Newington) and Bernie Grant (Tottenham). The three London MPs were all elected in safe Labour seats. However, Keith Vaz won his seat with a swing of over 9% from the Conservative candidate. Aside from this, the general performance of BrAsian candidates was like that of other party candidates in the same regions, proving that BrAsians and other ethnic minority candidates were certainly not vote-losers and, in some cases, improved the party position by attracting more votes.

One clear indication of white voters' acceptance of BrAsian candidates came in the November 1991 parliamentary by-election for Langbaurgh, an area in which only 0.7% of the voters were from ethnic minorities. With a swing of 3.6%, Dr Ashok Kumar (Labour) took this seat from the Conservative Party, increasing the number of BrAsian MPs to two. At the 1992 General Election, sixteen of the twenty-three ethnic minority candidates selected by the main political parties were BrAsian: four Labour, six Conservatives and six Liberal Democrats. In one constituency, Ealing Southall, two BrAsian candidates stood against each other, one for the Labour Party, the other for the Liberal Democrats, Piara Khabra (Labour) being the eventual winner. Of Labour's sitting MPs, although Dr Kumar lost his seat—by a small margin to the Conservative candidate—Keith Vaz managed to gain re-election. At the same time, Nirj Deva (Brentford and Isleworth) became the first BrAsian in recent times to win for the Conservative Party. Of the twenty-two constituencies contested by ethnic minorities as a whole, six had ethnic minority populations of less than the national average of 5.5%. Political parties were obviously now prepared to put forward BrAsian and other ethnic minority candidates in predominantly white areas. Table 11 shows the details of the BrAsian candidates' constituencies and their respective parties, ethnic minority population in 1991, and the political parties' majorities at the 1987 and 1992 General Elections.

At the 1997 General Election, of the forty ethnic minority candidates representing main political parties, twenty-six were BrAsians (eight Labour, eight Conservative and ten Liberal Democrat). Five BrAsians, all Labour, were elected as were four blacks. Although Nirj Deva was defeated, the two other BrAsian sitting MPs—Vaz and Piara Khabra—improved their vote significantly, as shown in Table 12.

M. Sarwar won Glasgow Govan, a Labour Party held seat, and the first seat in Scotland to be won by a BrAsian. He was also the first Pakistani and the first Muslim to enter the House of Commons. M. Singh (Bradford West) was the other new BrAsian MP.

Table 11. BRASIAN CANDIDATES REPRESENTING MAIN POLITICAL PARTIES, 1992 GENERAL ELECTION (%)

Party	*Candidate*	*Constituency*	*Ethnic minority populations 1991*	*Majority at 1987*	*Majority at 1992*
Lab	Claude Moraes	Harrow West	22.5	Con 25.0	Con 32.7
Lab	Piara Khabra	Ealing Southall	51.2	Lab 15.3	Lab 13.9
Lab	Ashok Kumar*	Langbaurgh	0.7	Con 3.3	Con 2.4
Lab	Keith Vaz	Leicester East	38.0	Lab 3.7	Lab 22.8
Con	Abul Q Chaudhary	Birmingham Small Heath	55.0	Lab 35.2	Lab 39.2
Con	Nirj J Deva	Brentford and Isleworth	18.4	Con 14.5	Con 3.9
Con	Mohammed Kamisa	Birmingham Sparkbrook	49.0	Lab 45.2	Lab 40.2
Con	Mohammad Riaz	Bradford North	20.7	Lab 3.3	Lab 15.7
Con	Mohammad Rizvi	Edinburgh Leith	n.a.	Lab 26.5	Lab 12.4
Con	Andrew Popat	Bradford South	8.0	Lab 0.6	Lab 9.3
Lib Dem	Mohammad A Ali	Liverpool Riverside	12.5	Lab 59.4	Lab 64.4
Lib Dem	Zerbanoo Gifford	Hertsmere	4.6	Con 32.8	Con 33.1
Lib Dem	Pash Nandhra	Ealing Southall	51.2	Lab 15.3	Lab 13.9
Lib Dem	Vinod Sharma	Halesowen and Stourbridge	3.6	Con 22.3	Con 15.0
Lib Dem	Marcello Verma	Cynon Valley	0.7	Lab 56.7	Lab 56.2
Lib Dem	Peter Veruna	Cardiff South and Penarth	6.4	Lab 10.2	Lab 21.9

*In the 1991 by-election Dr Kumar's (Lab) majority was 3.8%.

Source: 1987 and 1992 General Election results; 1991 Census of Population, produced by NEMDA, January 1994.

Table 12. PERFORMANCE OF BRASIAN SITTING MPs AT THE 1997 GENERAL ELECTION

MP	*Constituency*	*Party*	*Majority in 1992*	*Majority in 1997*
Nirj Deva	Brentford and Isleworth	Con	1,675	Lost
Keith Vaz	Leicester East	Lab	11,316	18,422
Piara Khabra	Ealing Southall	Lab	5,031	21,423

Source: Adapted from Anwar, 1998b.

Dr Ashok Kumar's (Lab) performance in Middlesborough South and Cleveland at the 1997 General Election, where he turned a 1,401 Conservative Party majority at the 1992 General Election into a Labour Party majority of 10,607, together with the evidence presented in Table 12 shows not only that BrAsians are now accepted as 'party candidates', but that even in opposing 'safe' seats that have full party support, and even in areas with very few BrAsians and other ethnic minorities, they can win.

In 2001 the number of BrAsian candidates put forward by the three main political parties had increased to thirty-nine (twelve represented the Labour Party), seven of whom were elected (see Table 13). All were in safe Labour seats. Of the twelve BrAsian Conservative candidates, none were elected. Although Shailesh Vara in Northampton South was considered to have had a good chance, he lost by 885 votes to the sitting Labour MP. None of the fifteen BrAsian candidates put forward by the Liberal Democrats stood any chance of winning. Despite the advances, the number of BrAsian MPs still does not reflect the presence of the BrAsian population in Britain nor even the electoral support that the Labour Party, in particular, received from BrAsians at the 2001 General Election. It is also worth noting that so far no BrAsian woman has been elected to the House of Commons.

Overall the electoral performance of BrAsian candidates was generally in line with the regional vote share for the relevant political parties. Nevertheless, some BrAsian candidates did increase their share of the vote while others saw theirs fall by small percentages. This was due either to local factors, including controversial selections, or the intervention of independent candidates, several of them BrAsian. Although such independent candidates, and BrAsian representatives of minority parties, generally performed poorly, suggesting that outside the main political parties BrAsian candidates have little chance of winning, they can clearly influence the voters. For example, in Birmingham Small Heath and Sparkbrook the People's Justice Party (PJP) received 4,770 votes. This was 13.02% of the total vote cast, almost equal to that received by the Liberal Democrat candidate (13.2%). This party (PJP) already had five local councillors in Birmingham and was supported mainly by Brit-

Table 13. BRASIAN CANDIDATES IN THE 2001 GENERAL ELECTION

Party	*No. of ethnic minority candidates*	*No. of BrAsian-origin candidates*
Con	16	12
Lab	18	12
Lib Dem	25	15
Total	59	39

ish Pakistanis. The importance of the concentration of a large number of Pakistanis in this constituency and their support for the PJP is clearly reflected in the result.

On the whole, the representation of BrAsians in the House of Commons did not change dramatically between 1997 and 2001 and still does not reflect their numbers in the population. Thirty BrAsian MPs would be a more accurate representation. In the House of Lords the number of BrAsian members has increased to fifteen, two of whom are women. However, as in the House of Commons, the total number reflects neither the diversity nor the number of BrAsians in society. Of British MEPs in the European Parliament four are BrAsian (two Labour and two Conservative), one of whom is a woman. There is no representation of BrAsians in the Scottish Parliament or in the Welsh Assembly.

At the local council level, it appears that slow progress is being made over time. In the London borough elections in 1974, only twelve BrAsian and other ethnic minority councillors were elected, while outside London in the 1973 local elections only six BrAsians and other ethnic minority councillors were elected, of whom one was Liberal and the rest Labour. However, in the London borough elections of 1986, of the 142 ethnic minority councillors, sixty-eight were BrAsian and in 1994 the number increased to 139. Outside London similar progress was made. For example, in 1982 Birmingham had five BrAsian councillors out of 117, but in 1992 the number increased to fourteen and in 2002 to eighteen. Other areas with a significant number of BrAsian councillors are Bradford, Leicester and Luton. In 2005 the number of BrAsian county councillors was thirty.

Three points are worth making regarding local elections and BrAsian representation. One, nationally the number of BrAsian councillors changes every year with local elections taking place in different areas. Two, the number of BrAsian councillors is estimated to be over 350 nationally (out of almost 21,000 local councillors), including Scotland, and over 80% of them belong to the Labour Party. Three, the number of BrAsian women councillors is less than 5% nationally and in some areas non-existent. Once again, if we compare the number of BrAsian councillors with the total BrAsian population, the number is very small. It is clear that all political parties and BrAsian communities need to do more to achieve fair representation.

ENTRYISM OR RACISM

In 1990, as part of a wider study, we interviewed party agents (Anwar, 1994). Like the party candidates, the party representatives did not want BrAsians and other ethnic minorities to have separate parties, but wanted them to join the existing political structures. Both the Labour Party and Conservative Party representatives said theirs was the best party to represent BrAsians' interests, and claimed they had the support of most of the BrAsians in their areas. However, Labour Party representatives were in a better position than other parties to give examples of BrAsian members and BrAsian elected councillors and candidates. They were also better placed to provide examples of their regular contacts with BrAsians. One respondent suggested the fear of rejection and/or discrimination as a possible problem limiting the involvement of BrAsians and other ethnic minorities. More recently, several examples had been reported of many BrAsians, particularly young BrAsians, who felt they had been banned from becoming members of the Labour Party or that problems had been created for BrAsians standing as candidates. For example, in the 1990s some BrAsian Labour Party activists had tried to increase the membership by recruiting more BrAsians, but some constituency parties had been suspended and inquiries had been set up to delay the selection process. Areas in which this happened include Small Heath and Sparkbrook in Birmingham, Bradford West, Nottingham East and Manchester Gorton. All these constituencies have a significant BrAsian presence.

During that period several sensational headlines appeared in the press fronting stories that suggested BrAsians were trying to take over parliamentary constituency parties. Examples include: 'Muslims "bought" anti-Kaufman votes'—referring to Gerald Kaufman's parliamentary seat of Manchester Gorton (*The Times*, 4 October 1994); 'Entryism or racism: Labour turns down one in four Asians for party membership amid fears of a local take-over' (*Independent on Sunday*, 25 September 1994); 'Labour alarm at Asian take-over' (also in the *Independent on Sunday*); 'Asians seize on safest route to Westminster' (*The Times*, 30 September 1994); an editorial, 'Labour's Asians, deselection, democracy and the New Labour Party' (also in *The Times*); and so on. The Manchester Gorton selection of the parliamentary constituency, in which a BrAsian, a Muslim and an ex-Labour councillor from Brent had challenged the sitting MP, in fact ended up with an inquiry by the Labour Party's NEC, and the Labour Party being taken to the High Court by three BrAsians who accused the party of blocking the membership applications of 600 BrAsians in the constituency. There was also a BBC television programme on this selection, which concluded that without the intervention of the Labour Party and the Labour Party NEC, there had been an equal chance of the BrAsian candidate, Mr Shahzad, winning the selection. There were several other examples of local wards and parliamentary constituencies where BrAsians felt they were not being treated equally by the political parties, and some had even accused the parties of racial discrimination. In particular many young BrAsians had expressed such views. In this context a complaint against the Labour Party was also made to the Commission for Racial Equality (CRE) in which some BrAsian members in Birmingham accused the party of possibly exercising discrimination in the membership and selection process. It was reported that as a result some discussions took place in 1996 between the legal director of the CRE and Labour Party officials. Younger BrAsians are also in the forefront of the campaign to increase the representation of BrAsians at both national and local levels. A new group, the Association for Active Asians in Labour (AAAL), was formed in March 1995 to fight racial harassment and racial discrimination within the Labour Party.

In October 1994 211 BrAsians resigned from the Conservative Party, alleging they had encountered racism there (*Muslim News*, 28 October 1994). The Conservative Party had also been accused of barring BrAsians from the Hayes and Harlington Conservative Association (*The News*, 2 November 1995), and the sitting MP, Terry Dicks, highlighted this problem by saying that the association's treatment of BrAsian people, who represent a stronghold of 10,000, was unfair. It appeared that due to overt racism a former party branch chair, Lynda Reed, was forced to resign after twenty years. She said, 'When I recommended a good local Conservative who happened to be Asian for the 1994 Council elections I was told it was out of the question and me and my Asian friends would not be welcome' (*The News*, 2 November 1995). The Conservative Party chairman had been urged by Nirj Deva, the only Conservative Asian MP in Britain at the time, to investigate the allegation. The Conservative Party was also accused of 'blatant racism in their selection of candidates' (*The Times*, 27 September 1995).

In November 1993 the Tower Hamlets Liberal Democrats were accused of distributing a leaflet, as part of their campaign in the area, which was condemned by the Liberal Democrat leader as racist (*Daily Telegraph*, 11 November 1993). Following an inquiry relating to this and another leaflet, it was recommended that three local Liberal Democrats be suspended from the party. There was also a feud about playing a 'race card' between the local Labour Party and the Liberal Democrats in Tower Hamlets (Anwar, 1994).

It is clear from various reported stories of racial harassment and racial discrimination within the political parties, and from the author's interviews with BrAsian activists in all three major political parties, that there are still some obstacles, such as procedures, practices and less favourable treatment of BrAsians and other ethnic minorities, to achieving equality of opportunity within the various parties. Also, when 'race' is seen as an electoral advantage, it is used by political parties without due consideration to race relations. At the 1992 General Election all three major political parties included statements concerning migration and race relations in their party manifestos. They used different terminology and put different emphasis on various issues in this context. Although it was generally assumed that in 1992 'immigration' would not become an election issue, it was made so by the Conservative Party towards the end of the election campaign when they felt they were behind in opinion polls. It appears this move won them some white votes, which perhaps made some difference in the outcome of a close election contest. The facts of immigration did not justify the rhetoric of the then Home Secretary and others in his party. The issue also revived the debate about the numbers and presence of ethnic minorities in Britain. It is worth adding here that, before the 1992 election, the debate was renewed by the speeches of Conservative MP Winston Churchill, who made non-white immigration an issue. At the 1997 and 2001 General Elections the 'immigration card' and 'race card' were used mainly by the National Front (NF) and the British National Party (BNP) candidates. In the local elections in May 2002 three BNP councillors were elected in Burnley and a fourth one was elected in a by-election in Darwin in November 2002. This ward is in the constituency (Blackburn) of Mr Jack Straw, the Foreign Secretary at the time. In 2004 the number of BNP councillors nationally had increased to sixteen.

Overall it appears that all three main political parties have failed to integrate BrAsians sufficiently in their structures. If parties do not radically improve involvement and representation of BrAsians it is possible that BrAsian voters will switch off from the electoral political process.

However, through their organisations the BrAsian leaders might find ways of promoting participation of their communities in the institutions of British society, including political participation. There are several hundred BrAsian organisations throughout the country. These include religious, social, welfare, educational, political and professional organisations at local, regional and national levels. The role of BrAsian leaders and BrAsian organisations is very important in the political process and their activities in terms of pressure groups and political participation are ongoing. However, their presence is more noticeable at election times when they often organise their members and mobilise support for political parties.

Some events have also made BrAsians more determined to mobilise. For example, the 'Rushdie affair' has made Muslims in Britain more politicised and, as a consequence, they have been mobilised by community leaders on other issues as well. Many Muslims have realised that they are not being treated equally as a religious community and as a result some young Muslims have recently become more ardent supporters of the genuine demands of the Muslims in Britain. Some in particular point to the tiny representation of Muslims in the House of Commons and the House of Lords. This is seen as deliberate by some and as anti-Muslim policy by others.

It is clear that the concentration of BrAsians in some areas of Britain has maximised their statistical significance in the political process. The evidence presented in this chapter shows that the participation of BrAsians in the electoral process has increased over time—as in previous elections, BrAsian turn-out increased at the 1997 and 2001 General Elections—but that their representation has made slow progress. The voting patterns of BrAsians show that a majority of BrAsians still vote for the Labour Party, but a significant minority are also voting for the Conservative Party and Liberal Democrats. No doubt there are area variations in terms of Labour Party support among BrAsians. Overall the Conservative Party and Liberal Democrats have not done enough to increase their share of the vote among BrAsians and need to do more to attract them, in particular, by taking positive action to provide representation for BrAsians. At the same time the Labour Party has not done enough to increase the number of BrAsian people in the decision-making process to reflect our multi-ethnic society. No doubt at the local level there are several BrAsians who have become Mayors or Lord Mayors, council leaders and a few Chairmen and Deputy Chairmen of committees, or more recently, members of local authority cabinets, but at the national level no elected or appointed BrAsian member currently holds any ministerial or other senior position. Having said that, one BrAsian, Keith Vaz, served as the Minister for Europe for a short period before the 2001 General Election.

The number of BrAsian candidates for the main political parties increased from 26 in 1997 to 39 in 2001. However, the number of elected BrAsian candidates at national level is still only 7 out of 659 members of the House of Commons. This does not reflect the number of BrAsians in the population, nor does it reflect the results of our 1997 survey of electors and candidates that showed that over 98% of ethnic minority as well as 91% of White electors, agreed that there should be more elected representatives from ethnic minorities both at national and local levels. In the same survey 90% of candidates also agreed with this. Our survey at the 2001 General Election shows similar results. In this context, it is worth mentioning that the overall performance of BrAsian candidates has been in line with the regional party share of the vote. BrAsian candidates, therefore, are accepted as party candidates and if they are given safe or winnable seats to contest they can win, even in areas with very few BrAsians and other ethnic minorities. There is also overwhelming support, both among electors and main political party candidates, for encouraging ethnic minorities to participate in the existing political parties rather than having their own ethnically based political parties. At the same time, there seems to be more willingness among BrAsians to get involved in the main political parties. However, there seem to be some problems in terms of opportunities for BrAsians and other ethnic minorities in this context. Therefore, it is the responsibility of the political parties to increase the number of BrAsians in the decision-making process. The candidate selection process is the crucial gateway into the House of Commons. But while the positive action taken by the main political parties such as 'training', 'zipping' or the Additional Member System (AMS) for the Scottish Parliament, and the Welsh and London Assemblies has focused on promoting women, no such action by the political parties has been taken so far regarding BrAsians and other ethnic minorities. Despite this, it appears that overall BrAsians are likely to have an increasing influence in British elections and politics.

BROWN ECONOMY

ENTERPRISE AND EMPLOYMENT

Shinder S. Thandi

In March 2003 *Eastern Eye* produced their seventh annual list of Britain's richest Asians, entitling it 'Success' to reinforce the point about the increased visibility of BrAsians in the business field and to dispel the stereotype of the over-worked, struggling Asian corner-shop owner. By focusing on the top 200 wealthiest business families, the publication itself tries to create the myth of success of Asian business across the board, when in effect there is great polarisation and unevenness in business success rates across different BrAsian communities and when an overwhelming majority of businesses, numerically at least, still remain small and family run. A similar hype could be manufactured about BrAsian labour market experience: BrAsians have benefited greatly from upward social mobility and their labour market experience is now almost comparable to the majority community. Such representations, well-meaning and important for building a positive image, are useful for understanding the contribution of BrAsians to the British economy, both in terms of participation and in generating employment and entrepreneurial activity, especially at the local level. However, there is a danger that they may camouflage serious structural difficulties faced by BrAsian labour in Britain. There is a need to address the paradox of apparent success and growing differentiation. Are BrAsian entrepreneurs really not glorified corner-shop owners or has there been real and considerable achievement and breakout both in terms of scale and diversity in sectors?

The main purpose of this chapter is to provide an evaluation of the BrAsian labour market experience, especially of BrAsian's participation both as employees and as employers. This will enable us to build their socio-economic profile and assess their labour market achievement. The main focus of the first part is to examine the different types of economic activities that BrAsians are engaged in and their labour market experiences and outcomes. The second part discusses factors in the rise of BrAsian business, their main characteristics, the different sectors of involvement and the constraints on future growth. The chapter combines empirical material with theoretical debates to enable the reader to make an assessment of the contribution of BrAsians to the British economy.

However, there are other important reasons for evaluating the labour market achievement of BrAsians, especially given the contemporary British context. Issues pertaining to social exclusion and community cohesion have assumed increased importance in British political discourses and have posed important challenges for public policy. First, there is the growing recognition that if certain ethnic groups appear to be significantly disadvantaged in the British labour market, this leads to a higher incidence of unemployment and a widening earnings gap. These in turn have negative effects on economic opportunities and social mobility, contributing to even greater levels of social exclusion. Second, achievement of some ethnic groups may be disappointing especially when considering their experiences of employment to education returns. For instance, many BrAsian groups may have benefited from higher levels of education, but show poorer rates of return as indicated by low productivity and under-utilisation at both individual and economic levels. Third, for some groups, discriminatory behaviour by employers in particular sectors may act as a deterrent for further entry into those sectors and may lead to excess entry into others. This acts as a distortion and results in lower earnings across the board for all. Fourth, significant differentials in labour market achievements can have an impact on wider relations between different ethnic groups. Poor achievement among some groups in the labour market may lead to cultural and ethnic stereotypes within and beyond the workplace. So, for instance, a relatively poor performance among some young Pakistani and Bangladeshis may generate negative stereotypes of Pakistanis and Bangladeshis in general. This will have the effect of suppressing both the aspirations of these young people and others' expectations of their potential. This can perpetuate the cycle of disadvantage and discouragement and lead to even further social exclusion, alienation and diminished trust. As recent studies on the race riots in some northern English towns have illustrated, this may act as an important factor in increased incidence of civil disorder. The apparent social and economic causes of civil disorder and limited social cohesion may well be rooted in persistent failures to deal with ethnic minorities' labour market differentials especially in employment. Collectively these reasons pose a strong challenge for public policy-makers.

BrASIANS IN THE LABOUR MARKET: PARTICIPATION, EXPERIENCE AND ACHIEVEMENT

De-industrialisation, rise of knowledge-based economy and BrAsian labour

BrAsian employment prospects, along with those of other ethnic groups, have been profoundly affected by changing patterns in the British labour market. Employment growth has been very uneven over the last ten years—the business services sector has seen the largest growth in jobs (29 per cent growth since 1991) followed by distribution and transport and non-market services. Also 'new jobs' have been created in design, finance and leisure services where skill requirements are both higher and different than those in manufacturing. The manufacturing sector, on the other hand, has continued to shed employment (over a third of a million jobs between 1991–9), as has the primary sector. Especially in the manufacturing sector the decline in jobs has come in areas such as the north-west West Midlands and London where a majority of the BrAsian communities have traditionally been located. Thus changing labour market demand and skill requirements have led to an acute mismatch between these and the characteristics and location of BrAsian labour. Another important change in labour market conditions, which has had a disproportionate impact on BrAsian labour, has been the change in work patterns. While there has been a decline in full-time shift work in the male dominated manufacturing sector in favour of part-time and flexible work, there has also been an increase in new growth sectors where female and part-time jobs predominate. The emergence of a 'knowledge-based economy' and employment growth in ICT related services has particularly disadvantaged Asian male labour.

Assessing BrAsian labour market experience: how well do BrAsians achieve?

Traditionally labour economists have used a number of indicators to assess labour market achievement. Below we consider five main indicators to assess BrAsian labour market achievement using data obtained from recent Labour Force Surveys.

1. *Economic activity rates*

According to the June 2002 Labour Force Survey, at the end of 2001 there were 3.1 million members of ethnic minority groups in Britain over the age of sixteen. Of these, 1.7 million were in employment. BrAsian workers numbered 841,000, split 63% male and 37% female.

As Table 1 shows, the overall economic activity rates are lower for BrAsians than for whites and this is especially more pronounced for women. According to the table, Asian or Asian British women only had activity rates of 48% compared with white women at 74%. It is in fact the lowest among all ethnic minority groups. There also appears to be a significant gap between Indian and Pakistani and Bangladeshi women both in terms of activity rates and income. Data provided by Labour Force Surveys and Youth Community Service also shows that a significant proportion of certain ethnic minorities are not in employment, training

Table 1. ECONOMIC ACTIVITY BY ETHNIC GROUP, BRITAIN, WINTER 2001/2

Categories	*In employment ('000)*	*ILO unemployed ('000)*	*Total economically active ('000)*	*All aged 16 and over ('000)*	*Economic activity rate (%)*	*Employment rate 16–59/64 (%)*	*ILO unemployment rate for all 16+ (%)*
All							
White	26,637	1,309	27,947	44,159	79	76	4.7
All ethnic minority groups	1,679	200	1,879	3,103	65	58	10.6
Mixed	127	20	147	220	70	60	13.5
Asian or Asian British	841	93	934	1,603	63	56	10.0
Black or Black British	484	66	551	872	69	61	12.0
Chinese	83	*	88	143	63	60	*
Other ethnic groups	144	16	160	265	64	58	9.9
Men							
White	14,609	814	15,423	21,614	85	80	5
All ethnic minority groups	976	129	1,105	1,564	75	66	12
Mixed	67	13	79	104	79	66	16
Asian or Asian British	533	62	595	826	77	69	10
Black or Black British	247	42	389	427	74	63	14
Chinese	45	*	47	68	72	69	*
Other ethnic groups	84	10	94	140	69	62	11
Women							
White	12,029	495	12,523	22,545	74	71	4
All ethnic minority groups	703	71	774	1,539	54	49	9
Mixed	60	0	67	116	61	55	*
Asian or Asian British	308	31	339	777	48	43	9
Black or Black British	237	25	262	445	64	58	9
Chinese	38	*	40	76	55	51	*
Other ethnic groups	60	*	66	125	57	52	*

* sample size too small for a reliable estimate.

Source: Labour Market Trends, June 2002, NSO.

or education. For instance, for age group 16–18 year-olds amongst BrAsians, the highest percentage not in education, training or employment is the Bangladeshi group (approx. 17%), followed by Pakistani (approx. 13%) and then Indian (approx. 3%). Available research shows that risks of non-participation increase if parents are poor or unemployed or they belong to certain minorities. In other words, younger groups entering the labour market already start from a disadvantaged position.

2. *Occupational attainment*

This indicator enables us to look at the extent of success in upward mobility in the labour market. Looking across all ethnic minorities, data shows there has been some overall improvement in occupational attainment, usually measured in terms of number in professional/managerial employment. Indian men, for instance, appear to have similar attainment to whites but Pakistanis and Bangladeshis lag behind markedly. Although no precise data is available to confirm this, rough calculations indicate that it is 28% for Indians, 17% for Bangladeshis and 15% for Pakistanis. Similar differences emerge for women, although their overall percentages (in terms of attainment) are lower.

Figure 1 illustrates the basic occupational structure among BrAsian labour. It indicates that around 35% are in the managerial and profes-

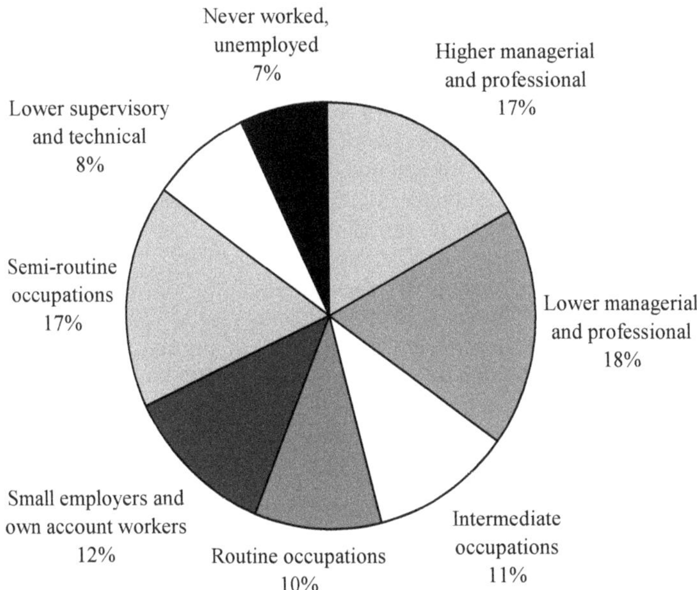

Figure 1. OCCUPATIONS OF ASIAN LABOUR FORCE

sional categories (both high and low) and if we exclude those who are self-employed (12%), the majority of the remainder are in routine or semi-routine jobs or unemployed.

3. *Unemployment rates*
Data indicates that unemployment rates for Asians or Asian British stand at 10%, which is just over double the rate for whites at 4.7%. These rates have persisted over a long period of time, indicating there is a pattern of unemployment risk associated with certain ethnic minorities. Disaggregated data shows considerable variation in unemployment rates among BrAsian communities with Pakistanis and Bangladeshis experiencing the worst rates. More worrying, available time series data shows that unemployment rates for some British born second-generation ethnic minority groups have worsened compared with unemployment rates of first generation migrants in the 1970s. For example, for Pakistanis unemployment rates are twice those of whites of the same age group. So although the second-generation may appear to have closed the gap in terms of occupational attainment, this is far from the case with respect to unemployment.

4. *Earning differentials*
If we consider those in work, data shows there is a marked difference in earnings levels of ethnic minorities and their white counterparts. In fact almost all ethnic minority men (less so for Indian men) earn less than white men. But there is a significant variation in earning power between ethnic groups. Figures show that in terms of earnings Bangladeshi men are the most disadvantaged and Indian men the least. Furthermore Labour Force Survey data reveals that whilst just over 25% of white households had incomes at or below the national average, the comparable figures are 80% of Pakistani and Bangladeshi households and 40% of Indian households. These confirm the results of other findings that BrAsian labour tends to be concentrated in low paying occupations. Given these low household incomes, certain BrAsian communities will also suffer the long-term effect of labour market disadvantage—the 'double jeopardy' effect of lower private pension coverage (due to low contribution) and a shift to pension provision towards the private sector (due to withdrawal of state pension). In such circumstances this will only increase BrAsian communities' dependence on means-tested benefits in later life.

5. *Rates of self-employment*
Although there are popular perceptions about high levels of self-employment among BrAsians, figures show that of all ethnic minorities, the Chinese, in fact, had the highest self-employed rate at 24%, followed by the BrAsian groups at 14%. But the BrAsian rate is higher than both the whites and the average rate among all ethnic minority groups. However,

again there are significant differences in rates of self-employment among BrAsians. The 1998–2000 figures show that Pakistanis had the highest rate at around 25%, Indians next at around 14% and 8% for Bangladeshis. If anything the figures show that the trend for the latter two is one of decline, although there are no apparent reasons why this should happen.

To summarise, it appears that in certain areas—occupational attainment, earning power and unemployment rates—there are clear signs of low achievement in the labour market. The evidence also shows that there are significant differences between different BrAsian groups.

While the above indicators are useful in measuring overall labour market achievement, there are still other dimensions of labour market experience that they do not adequately capture. Two other factors are also important influences on labour market achievement. The first of these is geographical location. Figures show an overwhelming majority of the BrAsian population is concentrated in larger urban areas of Greater London, West Midlands, Greater Manchester and West Yorkshire. Employment rates do vary according to location and among different BrAsian groups. They are the highest in Greater London and lowest in Greater Manchester. There are also major differences at sub-regional and at local authority levels. Evidence indicates that Pakistanis and Bangladeshis are the most disadvantaged (Peach, this volume). The second factor relates to the fact that BrAsians tend to be over-represented in some sectors and under-represented in others. All BrAsian men, as with all ethnic minorities, are under-represented in primary-related sectors but over-represented in others. Indian men, for instance, are over-represented in engineering, textiles and clothing, distribution, transport and communication and public health and education sectors and Indian women are over-represented in engineering, textiles, clothing and distribution; Pakistani men are over-represented in textiles and clothing (10% employment for this group compared with 1% for all men), distribution and transport and communication and the same applies for Pakistani women; Bangladeshi men are over-represented in textiles and clothing (9% for this group) and distribution (60%). If we look at the industry level the variations increase even further. For instance, 52% of Bangladeshi male employees and self-employees are in the restaurant industry (compared with 1% for white men) and a third of them are cooks or waiters; looking at Pakistani male employees and self-employees, 12% are taxi drivers or chauffeurs compared with the national average of 1%; looking at Indian men, 5% are medical practitioners, almost ten times the national average. Unfortunately no comparable figures are available for Asian females. This data reinforces the point made earlier that most BrAsians tend to be disproportionately concentrated in declining sectors; sectors with large labour turnover since they are most at risk from forces of international competition and lowly paid.

BrAsians and the labour market

Evidence presented above clearly demonstrates low levels of labour market achievement among BrAsians in Britain. However, a more detailed look at the structural characteristics of the labour markets in which ethnic minorities operate will provide a better understanding of BrAsian labour market disadvantage. This entails looking at both the demand and supply forces and how they operate to disadvantage BrAsian groups. The factors suggest the prevalence of significant imperfections in the labour market, which results in discrimination against BrAsians. They also suggest BrAsian labour operates in highly segmented markets; markets that may be secondary or informal and where mainstream legislation on wage and working conditions may have little relevance.

There are a number of factors operating on the demand side of the labour market that limit the demand for BrAsian labour. Since most BrAsian communities are located in inner city districts, where there is a low level of business activity, labour demand remains low. Furthermore whatever business activity does exist, it tends to be of a small size, limiting both job opportunities and low career progression. For example, around 70 per cent of the Bangladeshi working population is in the catering industry, where most workers are not able to progress above the cook or waiter status. Another important factor, also highlighted above, is the radical change in the industrial landscape of Britain. De-industrialisation and re-structuring towards a post-industrial economy has meant a change in demand from low to high skilled labour. If BrAsian communities happen to be over-represented in the declining industries, as is the case with the high concentration of male Pakistani labour in the textile industry in Oldham (Kalra, 2000a), then the impact of re-structuring will have a disproportionate effect on this community. The spatial mismatch— concentration in geographical areas where jobs are declining rather than being created—can have serious social and political consequences too. Evidence also suggests that ethnic minority small businesses are mainly concentrated in areas of ethnic minority settlement (see discussion on ethnic enclaves in the second section). But ethnic minority businesses, many of which depend on family labour, expand slowly and thus only produce a nominal increase in demand for labour. Furthermore, very rarely do these businesses employ labour across ethnic lines. For example, an Indian owned business would only employ Indian labour, a *halal* butcher unlikely to hire a Sikh, and Hindu or Christian or Sikh associations unlikely to hire people of other religious denominations. These cultural and religious barriers are a reality in business practices and have the overall effect of reducing labour demand and also employment across ethnic lines. Nor do these businesses expand very much given their limited capital and problems with getting start-up finance. As they tend to be clustered in a small space and in a small range of sectors, they are often engaged in cut-throat competition and in such a context expansion is hardly a priority—survival and sufficient profitability to sustain security in family income remain primary objectives. In any case, evidence suggests there is a higher failure rate among such businesses.

Government statistics show that around 56 per cent of ethnic minorities live in the forty-four most deprived local authorities in the country (Social Exclusion Unit, 2000). These are areas that suffer from multiple deprivation, especially from poor levels of public infrastructure—education, transport and social services. This leads to a cycle of economic deprivation, low business development and low employment generation. Successive governments have attempted to tackle this problem, but no tangible results are permanently visible. Surveys also continue to show that, despite financially bigger and newer initiatives, BrAsian businesses make little use of professional advice and information services or business links, but instead rely heavily on community networks.

The private sector does not have a good track record either when it comes to recruitment from areas of BrAsian settlement. Many companies simply do not use local agencies for recruitment and evidence from company recruitment practices suggests that BrAsian job applicants are disproportionately likely to fail to get jobs they have applied for even when class, education and location is accounted for. This can only be explained by direct or indirect forms of racism or lack of cultural awareness. Some writers have argued there may be a form of 'unwitting discrimination' built into recruitment systems: for example, major companies not recruiting from new universities—the source of most BrAsian graduates; or companies expressing a preference for experience over qualification, which BrAsian groups may lack.

On the supply side of the labour market there are also a number of important factors that continue to inhibit both the quality and quantity of labour. Evidence shows that different BrAsian communities have different endowments of human capital—level of education, skills, language fluency and so on. Research reveals that differences in labour market outcomes are linked to educational qualifications. Among BrAsians educational qualifications (measured by five GCSEs at A*–C grades) do vary, with the Indian group at around 60% and Bangladeshi/Pakistanis at around 28%. Studies also show that although BrAsians have disproportionately higher rates of participation in higher education compared with whites, a vast majority of them are concentrated in the 'new' post-1992 universities. For instance, in some of the new universities in the Midlands region BrAsian students may comprise up to 40% of the total population and on some courses, especially computer science, business studies and finance, BrAsian students may account for up to 80% of the total course enrolment. If the major employers only visit 'traditional' universities or they discriminate against 'new university' graduates, this acts as a disadvantage for BrAsian students.

There is also the issue of attainment of non-academic employability skills among some BrAsians despite the fact that overall they tend to experience longer periods in post-school education. Analysis of skills attainment shows marked differences across different BrAsian groups. Figures show that individuals from Bangladeshi (24%) and Pakistani (19%) backgrounds are considerably more likely to hold no qualifications at all. Only Indians do slightly better at 10% compared with whites at 12%. Figures also show that only 28% of Bangladeshis and 39% of Pakistanis are qualified to NVQ level 3 or above, or its equivalent, compared with more than 50% of whites. These low levels of skill attainment among some groups act as significant barriers to entering and remaining within the workplace. The situation appears to be even worse for post-school sixteen-year-olds as they are more likely to be unemployed and not on the many government financed training programmes. Research indicates that there is a divergence in performance, especially between Indians in one group and Pakistanis and Bangladeshis in another, but also within each particular BrAsian group. Whilst quite a large number do well in the workplace, there is a significant minority of youth from BrAsian backgrounds who simply fall out of the system. They become discouraged, demoralised and alienated, affecting their chances of employability even further.

Some have suggested that differences in the class profile of different BrAsian groups have an important bearing on labour market achievement. It may well be that Indians are more successful in managerial and professional jobs because of their relatively wealthier socio-economic background, including homeland occupations, compared with other BrAsian groups. However, this is a rather simplistic explanation given the very complex interplay between the many processes at work and the different types of labour markets in which these groups participate.

BrAsians and social capital: the colour of money

Although it has been suggested that cultural and religious factors may be at work in inhibiting both the quantity and quality of labour supplied and labour market experience, measuring the influence of such factors is extremely difficult. According to the very limited research examining economic activity rates by different religious groups (Brown, 2000), Muslim men and women were the least likely to be in paid work, while Hindus were the most likely. Looking at employment profiles and income differentials, Sikhs and Pakistani and Bangladeshi Muslims show particular under-representation in professional employment, whereas Hindus and Indian Muslims dominate. In terms of earnings, Muslim men and women are over-represented in the lowest income band, with almost a quarter earning less than £115 per week compared with only a tenth of Hindus and Sikhs. While this may be an interesting way to connect religion and differences in labour market outcomes, it becomes impossible to demonstrate any causality between them.

Social capital metrics attempts to measure the connectedness of individuals to their local communities. Measures of social capital are usually divided into two types: bridging and bonding. 'Bridging social capital' consists of formal and informal networks that link the members of a given social group with the wider society, whereas 'bonding social capital' connects members of the social group with each other (Putnam, 2000). Therefore, bridging social capital would be far more important in understanding labour market experiences and outcomes. Thus an isolated community, which lacks bridging social capital, is not likely to benefit from employment opportunities. According to this view, geographically concentrated communities such as Pakistanis and Bangladeshis may develop high levels of bonding social capital but lack bridging social capital. The former provides the basis for a successful local economy (as reflected in the rise of Pakistani owned businesses) and contributes to group economic success via that route. Bonding capital is thus partly compensating for the lack of bridging social capital. The corollary of this should be that ethnic minorities who are considered to be less exclusionary would be able to acquire bridging capital, but the example of Britain's Caribbean population demonstrates this is not the case.

Economists have offered a variation of the above argument to explain labour market experiences by using the concept of 'human capital externalities'. Basically, the argument states that people are influenced not only by their own individual human capital (acquired through their own education and work experience) but also by that of their co-ethnic associates. In other words, the stock of human capital should be seen as a collective resource (a form of public good) for the ethnic community as a whole. Evidence from research on educational attainment among BrAsian groups does indicate that processes such as peer-group pressure or demonstration effects are at work. Thus we would expect to find the smallest disadvantage for those groups who have a high collective stock of human capital, and higher disadvantage for those with lower collective levels of human capital. Superficial and anecdotal evidence may suggest that this is a reasonable explanation for different outcomes among BrAsian groups, but this view requires further investigation.

There are a number of other factors that may also act as a barrier to labour market participation. For example, for females poor access to childcare (due to location, socio-economic status and affordability) may be an important factor. For others, a poor state of health may be an important barrier—evidence shows that, compared with whites, BrAsians tend to

Table 2. COMPARISON OF GROSS AND NET DIFFERENTIALS IN LABOUR MARKET ACHIEVEMENT BETWEEN ETHNIC MINORITIES AND THEIR WHITE COUNTERPARTS IN BRITAIN

	Metric	*Gross: men*	*Gross: women*	*Variables taken into account*	*Net: men*	*Net: women*
Black	Unemployment	2.59	2.56	Education, training, experience, marital and parental status, region	2.51	2.38
	Occupational attainment	0.56	0.68	Same as above	0.36	0.57
	Earnings	Carib.: £115(-) African: £116(-)	n/a	Age, migration, education, economic environment, family structure	Carib.: £81(-) African: £132(-)	Born in Britain: statistically insignificant
Indian	Unemployment	1.50	1.38	Education, training, experience, marital and parental status, region	1.64	1.44
	Occupational attainment	1.10	2.00	Same as above	0.61	0.48
	Earnings	£5(-)	n/a	Age, migration, education, economic environment, family structure	£23(-)	Born in Britain: statistically insignificant
Pakistani/ Bangladeshi	Unemployment	2.67	1.18	Education, training, experience, marital and parental status, region	2.85	2.71
	Occupational attainment	0.71	1.00	Same as above	0.56	0.48
	Earnings	£150(-)	n/a	Age, migration, education, economic environment, family structure	£129(-)	Born in Britain: statistically insignificant

Notes: (i) the figures for unemployment and occupational attainment should be read as the likelihood ethnic minorities have of being, respectively, unemployed or working in the professional class as compared to their white counterparts. One would indicate that they were equally as likely; (ii) the figures for earning power are the amount of disadvantage (-) or advantage (+) ethnic minorities experience relative to their white counterparts; (iii) all figures for unemployment are based on Carmichael and Woods (2000); all figures for male earnings are based on Berthoud (2000); (iv) in the case of female earnings, figures for gross and net were taken from two different sources and therefore cannot be compared, and hence are not included.

Source: Performance and Innovation Unit, Ethnic Minorities and the Labour market: Interim Analytical Report (2002), Tables 4.11 and 4.12, pp. 109–10.

suffer disproportionately from certain kinds of ailments, for example, diabetes and coronary heart disease (see Atkin, this volume). Poor public infrastructure of inner city areas—poor housing, poor transportation and lack of mobility—can also act as an important supply-side barrier.

Taking into account all the observable and quantifiable variables, on both the demand and supply side of the labour market, a reasonable assessment of the extent of disadvantage experienced by BrAsian communities compared with their white counterparts can be made. These variables can also explain the significant differences that persist in labour market outcomes among BrAsian communities themselves. However, the explanatory variables do not account for the disadvantages completely and even after allowing for them, significant differences still persist. These net differences in employment, occupational attainment and earnings, between BrAsians and whites, can thus only be explained by unobserved or unquantifiable variables. Table 2 shows that there is a significant difference between the gross and net values in labour market achievement, especially for Pakistanis and Bangladeshis. For example, looking at earning power, figures show that Pakistani and Bangladeshi male workers earn £129 less than their white counterparts even after allowing for the possible observable explanatory variables. The net differences—sometimes referred to as ethnic penalties—illustrate a persisting disadvantage for ethnic minorities as a whole even after key observable variables have been taken into account (Carmichael and Woods, 2000; Berthoud, 2000). An important explanation for this remains the existence of racial discrimination in the labour market towards ethnic minority communities. Indeed, wide-ranging evidence suggests that although the more overt forms of racism that existed in the 1950s and 1960s may have become less visible, various complex and institutionalised forms of racism still remain. Much of the evidence on the existence of racial discrimination is qualitative, gathered from the personal experiences of the minorities, employment tribunal decisions and public opinion polls. This indicates that racial harassment and discrimination takes many different forms and has a negative influence on both the ability and motive to participate fully in the labour market. Thus this still remains an important explanation for the persistence of disadvantage for BrAsians in the labour market despite the fact that anti-discrimination policies have been operating for over thirty years.

BrASIAN BUSINESS ENTERPRISE: RHETORIC OR REALITY?

Profile of BrAsian business: its significance in British economy

Earlier it was mentioned that BrAsians have high levels of self-employment compared with whites. Indeed, there has emerged a strong, diversified and vibrant BrAsian business sector, which has even led to the creation of specialist business directories of ethnic minority firms in major cities and in the emergence of annual Asian rich lists compiled by leading Asian newspapers *Eastern Eye* and *Asian Express*.

As the period of BrAsian settlement has increased and the communities have grown and matured, the numbers of BrAsian businesses have also grown, and especially rapidly in the last twenty years. Despite the fact that ethnic minorities only comprise about 6.4% of the British population, ethnic minority businesses comprise about 10% of the total business start-ups. One estimate puts the annual income of ethnic minority businesses at £10 billion per year (Nat West, 2000), indicating their significance for the British economy. As nearly half the ethnic minority population is concentrated in the Greater London area, it is not surprising that ethnic minority businesses should be concentrated there too. According to one estimate (LSFU, 1999) there were 62,000 ethnic minority businesses in London, representing 19% of all businesses. The same source estimates that ethnic minority entrepreneurs own over 50% of new start-ups and around 7% of all small businesses. BrAsian owned enterprises account for the majority of these ethnic minority businesses, thriving in all areas of BrAsian settlement, with many now becoming national labels. There is now substantial literature exploring their emergence, the sectors in which they operate, the major constraints they face and the various national and local government initiatives providing them with support and networking opportunities (Barrett *et al.*, 1996).

Explaining BrAsian enterprise

Why is there a higher propensity for self-employment among BrAsian communities, and among ethnic minorities in general? Are ethnic minority communities more entrepreneurial than white? Are some ethnic minority communities more entrepreneurial than others? What motivates the BrAsian community towards self-employment? There have been several mainstream theories of entrepreneurship, each emphasising an important single factor of motivation (Aldrich and Waldinger, 1990). Factors identified range from the profit motive, risk-taking under uncertainty, greater access to information or knowledge that can be exploited, and the desire to innovate and create new products. Although these are all sound economic and psychological reasons for motivating business entry, they only emphasise the positive. There may be circumstances in which individuals or families have, or feel they have, no option other than self-employment, for example, having encountered personal experiences of racism or having perceived obstacles to upward social mobility or career advancement. Mainstream theories of entrepreneurship clearly fail to acknowledge these negative or reactive reasons for business entry and are therefore of limited value here. But an explanation based on a wholly negative experience would have equally limited value since that on its own may not be a sufficient condition for business entry.

Early research on ethnic enterprise emphasised the combined role of negative experiences, including exploitation encountered in the labour market and the resulting social cohesiveness. Ivan Light (1994), for example, argued that the greater the hardships and frustrations experienced by immigrants, the greater was their propensity to seek self-employment and develop stronger economic and social bonds within their own ethnic community. Nascent informal business networks or social capital—essential for developing the exchange of market information, sources of credit, a loyal consumer base and a steady supply of co-ethnic labour—strengthened the capacity and sources of competitiveness over time and enabled ethic businesses to compete successfully in the market.

Another explanation, that continues to be popular, characterised ethnic enterprises as the 'middleman minority'. Bonacich, for instance, observed that many of the ethnic groups active in business were historically trading peoples of minority status. The group's cultural characteristics and traditions and their greater tendency to be sojourning abroad gave them the 'reactive social solidarity' that helped to support, perpetuate and reproduce its economic success. The 'middleman minority' concept was applied quite widely to explain the business success of different immigrant groups across the globe. However, following the Weberian tradition, it was essentially a 'culturalist' argument, which focused on the group's system of beliefs, attitudes and patterns of behaviour to explain their business success. Its major weakness lay in its inability to explain the business success of those groups who had no historical tradition of entrepreneurship. The argument was also tautological in nature: members of certain ethnic groups were entrepreneurial because they were by nature entrepreneurial. Some of the early research in Britain on BrAsian entrepreneurship, for instance by Werbner (1990b), suffered from this same limitation.

Further research into ethnic enterprise offered other explanations of why and how ethnic communities organise themselves economically and socially. Michael Piore's work, *Birds of Passage*, was extremely influential in developing new theoretical understandings of how ethnic minorities are incorporated into the local labour market and why ethnic enterprise emerges. According to his approach, ethnic minorities, along with other disadvantaged native workers, encounter a segmented, two-tiered labour market: the primary and the secondary. In the primary market job selection is based largely on skill and educational qualifications and there are clear and established labour contracts that specify pay scales, performance criteria and formal channels for career advancement. The secondary segment, in contrast, uses selection criteria that emphasise employment or immigration status and ethnicity, rarely uses formal labour contracts, generally pays poorly, and offers virtually no opportunities for career advancement. In this perspective ethnic minority communities would typically be found in the secondary segment where their lack of marketability in the primary labour market and their willingness to work for low wages made them attractive to employers. Given the difficulties of crossing over into the primary labour market, ethnic minority communities would largely remain confined to the secondary segment with its long-term implications for socio-economic mobility. Indeed, the preceding section of this paper has shown how such may be the case for some BrAsian communities, especially in the textile, hosiery and catering sectors. Portes (1995) extended this theory by arguing that under certain circumstances migrant groups will create their own 'ethnic enclave' in which their economic and social activities dominate. These ethnic enclaves have several distinctive features: geographical concentration (often in inner-city areas); interdependent networks of social and business relationships, or embeddedness; and an informal and localised labour market. This enclave functions almost as a substitute, self-sufficient unit that keeps ethnic minority communities protected from the vagaries of the wider economy and society (Aldrich *et al.*, 1981). The positive dimensions of this enclave include a path towards upward mobility: employment in ethnic businesses provides a good training ground for developing, and an environment that inculcates and nurtures, entrepreneurial qualities. One could argue that business success in ethnic neighbourhoods is not simply the aggregate sum of the attributes of individual businessmen, but is a tangible outcome of social capital created in such communities. This supports the argument discussed above regarding how bonding social capital and powerful demonstration effects or peer influences can lead to positive outcomes for some BrAsian communities.

Most of the explanations given above argued that immigrant business success was due either to qualities inherent in the ethnic group itself or to a reaction to the harsh external socio-economic environment. These explanations began to be questioned when they were used to try to explain differences in rates of business participation among different ethnic groups (Rafique, 1992; Metcalf *et al.*; 1996). Waldinger (1990 and 1995) proposed a more inter-active model, that overcomes the either/or deficiency of the earlier ones, in which ethnic entrepreneurship results from a wide range of factors such as market conditions and ethnic social networks that generate, encourage and impact upon such activity.

The complexity of BrAsian entrepreneurship is best captured in a synthesised inter-active model adapted from Waldinger and reproduced in Figure 2. In this model the opportunity structure facing prospective entrepreneurs is determined both by the prevailing market conditions and by the ability of BrAsian groups to access or own businesses. Some of these opportunities may be very apparent, for example, supplying the daily needs of the local ethnic population. Thus one would expect to see BrAsian groups owning grocery stores selling ethnic foods and vegetables, newspapers and other culture-specific goods from their country of origin. Most of these businesses would be expected to have low start up costs. Over time, there would also develop BrAsian owned businesses

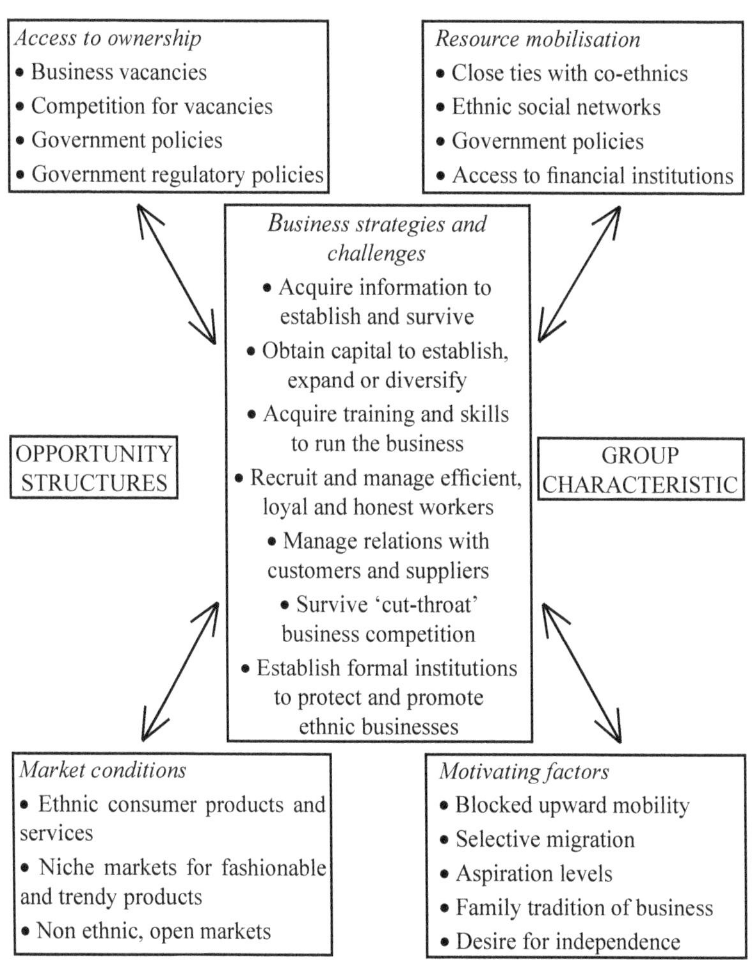

Figure 2. INTERACTIVE MODEL OF BRASIAN ENTREPRENEURSHIP

Source: Adapted from Waldinger *et al.* (1990).

providing a range of specialist services in fields such as travel, law, tax and accountancy and property. However, over time these businesses need to grow and achieve economies of scale. Typically some of the more profitable businesses will exploit the possibilities of setting up a supply chain link with businesses in their homeland, with a view to serving a larger market and moving up the value chain. Among BrAsian businesses, food retailing and female ethnic clothing serve as classic examples. In the former case companies such as East End Foods, Natco, Tilda and Patak all started on a small scale and expanded and diversified into importing, packaging and distribution and also into domestic manufacture. In the latter case, a number of boutiques catering for female fashionable clothing (supplying bespoke, designer or customised *salwaar kameez* suits or *lenghas*), and located in prime sites in major areas of BrAsian settlement, have developed trans-national production and distribution chains (Bhachu, 2004). Although the opportunity structures are very important, the inter-active approach also emphasises that BrAsian groups are both predisposed to create economic opportunities for themselves and able to draw upon a variety of ethnic forms of social capital. Some important factors here are the high savings rates and frugal living among BrAsian groups, use of family labour and getting financial help from friends and family. Formal and informal channels, often taking the form of business and traders' associations, may develop, facilitating the exchange of market information and lobbying for mainstream and local resources.

Despite the lengthy existence of BrAsian enterprise, there is still a severe lack of data on self-employment or economic activities that ethnic groups are engaged in. Hence the assessment of their overall contribution to the economy is difficult to measure. One major problem is associated with the procedures used by surveying agencies. The data collection agencies try to slot individuals into one job per individual, but a common feature in some BrAsian communities is the participation of individuals in both the formal (the main occupation) and the informal part-time economy—taxi-driving, helping in family grocery store, other part-time work and, for females, home working, providing child-care facilities, cleaning and laundry services, sewing etc. None of these informal activities are captured in national statistics yet they are important sources for household income and may even be beneficial in training for future entrepreneurial activities. Statistics therefore tend to underestimate the contribution of BrAsians to the economy.

It would be wrong to suggest that the BrAsian entrepreneurship and enterprise narrative is a one-dimensional success story. No doubt there are many rags to riches stories, especially associated with pioneering migrants. But it would be simplistic to assume that the major players in BrAsian business today fall mainly into that category. Certainly, quite a few of them are truly trans-national entrepreneurs, but many have thrived because of their extensive associations with, or because of assistance from, other business friends and families. Also, the vast majority of BrAsian businesses are small, family owned and suffer from not only the same constraints as any other small businesses, but the additional ones arising from operating in deprived areas with the limited clientele base they cater for. Many continue to survive through long working hours, generating profits that are just enough to provide economic security for the family (Basu and Goswami, 1999; Jones *et al.*, 1994). In many cases priority attached to economic freedom and independence overshadows the need for material gain. For some, then, life on the margins is better than subjecting oneself to the humiliation and drudgery associated with working in lowly paid, dead-end jobs. This is the aspect of BrAsian business life that becomes marginalised in the continuing hype of BrAsian business success and which public policy needs to acknowledge.

The overall position of BrAsians in the labour market has undoubtedly improved over the past forty years, as shown in the data on labour market achievement. Some groups aside, BrAsians are not the most recent migrants to Britain and therefore would not be expected to be found in 3-D jobs that immigrants tend to take around the world. However, success is not universal across BrAsian groups and, as demonstrated in this chapter, they experience significant differences in labour market achievement. While many of the relatively poor outcomes can be explained by economic, social and demographic factors operating on both sides of the labour market, there is still a large residual that remains unexplained. This points to the operation of both direct and indirect forms of covert discriminatory practices in the labour market. Despite many years of anti-discrimination legislation and specifically earmarked support for ethnic minorities, many BrAsian communities remain disadvantaged.

Although BrAsian business success fits in neatly with the larger narrative on cultural, gastronomic and musical 'Asian Cool', that success is, numerically at least, confined to a very small segment of the total BrAsian business sector and even more marginally relative to the total BrAsian population. There is a growing polarisation between the small group of trans-national entrepreneurs, which all political parties want to appropriate for their own political agendas, and the vast majority of BrAsian businesses that engage in the daily struggle of survival. For many of them the concepts of expansion, growth or breakout, which have become the mantras of business support agencies, don't have much relevance, as they continue to provide vital services in localised communities knowing full well that the odds are stacked against them.

NEWHAM

Dhanwant Rai

The London Borough of Newham, located in East London has the most ethnically diverse non-white population in England and Wales (Census 2001), with a fairly equal spread of different ethnic minority communities. The population of ethnic minority communities has increased significantly, from a total of 43% in 1991 to 61% in 2001, an increase of 18% in ten years. This trend is expected to continue. BrAsians comprise nearly a third of the total population in Newham, up 6% in the ten years from 1991 to 2001. The largest change has been among the Bangladeshi community, which has more than doubled. The Indian population on the other hand has decreased by 0.9%. Table 1

Table 1. NEWHAM POPULATION BY ETHNIC GROUP: 1991 CENSUS COMPARED WITH 2001 (%)

	1991 Census	*2001 Census*
White	57.4	39.4
White British	-	33.8
White Irish	-	1.3
Other White	-	4.3
White and Black Caribbean	-	1.2
White and Black African	-	0.7
White and Asian	-	0.7
Other Mixed	-	0.8
Indian	13.0	12.1
Pakistani	5.9	8.5
Bangladeshi	3.8	8.8
Other Asian	3.0	3.1
Black Caribbean	7.2	7.4
Black African	5.7	13.1
Other Black	1.6	1.1
Chinese	0.8	1.0
Other	1.4	2.1

Source: Office for National Statistics, 2001 Census (KS06) and 1991 Census (LBS06).

compares the distribution of ethnic minority groups between the 1991 and 2001 censuses. Although the 2001 Census categories are somewhat different from those of 1991, and hence exact comparisons are not possible, variations affecting BrAsian communities are marginal.

From the mid nineteenth century Newham experienced a rapid growth of industry: the docks and riverside industries in the south and railway lines in the north (which had declined by the 1970s). Over the years this attracted workers from various backgrounds, for example, Irish, German, Scottish, Lithuanian, African, Indian, Chinese, Jewish and Italian. African seamen settled with their families in the south of the borough, and by the 1930s Newham had the largest African population in London. The migration of other communities followed and by the 1960s and the 1970s Indians and Pakistanis followed by Bangladeshis in the 1980s had begun to settle in high proportions. Newham has been a cosmopolitan area for over a hundred years, with different communities settling over different time periods.

The settlement patterns of BrAsians in Newham reflect the general patterns of migration of BrAsians into Britain, with generally Indians migrating first followed by Pakistanis and Bangladeshis. This is reflected in the proportions of each born in their country of origin (Indians 39%, Pakistanis 46% and Bangladeshis 53%). Bangladeshis also have a much younger age profile: 40% aged under 16 years compared with 34% Pakistanis and 26% Indians (Newham average is 25%).

With 25% of the total population being Muslims, Newham has the second largest Muslim population in a borough in England and Wales

The economic context

The closure of the docks and the decline of industry associated with the railways, which were historically the main sources of the jobs in the area, led to major unemployment in the borough with around half the jobs disappearing between the mid 1970s and the mid 1980s. Much local employment had been based on unskilled tasks, the availability of which was limited elsewhere. Only in recent years have new firms and new types of employment been established in Newham, mainly in the retail and service sectors.

Newham is ranked the eleventh most deprived borough in the country and the fourth most deprived in London (The English Indices of Deprivation, 2004). Poverty, unemployment, poor housing and poor health are among some of the challenges faced by the local population, and some ethnic groups face more hardship than others. However there are some interesting statistics regarding BrAsians in Newham which are likely to be reflective of the national pattern. A high proportion of Indians live in owner occupied housing (71%) compared with 55% Pakistanis and 38% Bangladeshis (Newham average is 45%). Pakistani and Bangladeshi people in particular experience high rates of labour market disadvantage compared with other groups and employment rates are lower among these two. Lower educational qualifications and lower levels of skills combined with discrimination in the labour market are likely to account for these variances.

Despite experiencing relatively high rates of disadvantages (particularly Pakistani and Bangladeshi groups), Asian people in Newham have made a significant contribution to the local economy through the small retail sector. Newham is known for its vibrant Asian retail street, Green Street, dubbed as one of the best shopping streets for BrAsian goods in Europe. Aside from its excellent Asian restaurants, a few of which have received acclaimed reviews in magazines and papers, it houses some of the best clothes and specialist fashion accessory shops and is also the base for some of the best Asian clothes fashion designers in Britain. Green Street attracts a large number of mainly Asian customers from both outside and within Newham, who all make a positive contribution to the local economy.

The political context

BrAsians in Newham have taken an active part in local politics for many years. About a quarter (16 out of 60) of all elected members are now Asian. All of these are from the Labour party which is the predominant party in the borough (59 out of 60 members). One of the contestants at the Mayoral elections was a BrAsian, indicating an active BrAsian engagement in local issues and in the political management of the borough. However, there has been a number of successive BrAsian ceremonial Mayors from the elected Members.

Newham is interestingly juxtaposed in terms of 'race relations'. While a relatively high proportion of Asians tend to say that different communities in Newham get on well together, (Newham Annual Residents Survey, 2004/5), Metropolitan Police records in the borough show one of the highest rates of racial incidents in the country. The majority of Asians are residentially polarised in the north-east of the borough, whereas high proportions of the white population live in the south-west and south and a high proportion of the black population live in the west. Community activity addressing issues of racial harassment appear to have lessened since the mid 1990s, perhaps reflective of the pattern across the country. The council has adopted an all inclusive approach, addressing ‘race’, gender, disability, religion and sexual orientation inequalities under the equalities policy context, while at the same time adopting the notion of (celebrating) diversity, which appears to be the trend across the country. This current thinking of amalgamating two conceptually different approaches is perhaps resulting in limited active intervention to address inequalities and discrimination.

Newham is fast improving through large scale physical and social regeneration programmes. These initiatives are likely to improve employment opportunities and related benefits for local people. It remains to be seen how the Pakistani and Bangladeshi groups in particular benefit from regeneration activities to move them out of their highly disadvantaged positions compared with other groups in Newham.

POLICING DIVERSITY

RACIALISATION AND THE CRIMINAL JUSTICE SYSTEM

Virinder S. Kalra

'The police are not an intrusion into that society, but a threat, a foreign force, an army of occupation—the thick end of the authoritarian wedge.... It was once held that the British police were governed more by popular morality than the letter of the law. There is no criticism of them they would brook, no aspect of society they do not pronounce on...' (Sivanandan, 1982: 49–50)

This observation came after the policing of the 1980s civil disturbances and clashes with police in inner areas of England, from Brixton to Blackburn. Those events were racialised in terms of a rampant black (mainly African-Caribbean) male youth out of control and ready to undermine all that was cherished in British societies. In contrast the presence of BrAsians in these events (especially in Birmingham and London) has all but been erased by selective recording and the differential operation of racist stereotypes. The image of BrAsians as passive and law abiding fulfils one of the central fantasies of colonial control—of the docile Orientals, and the configuration of racialisation in British society (see Alexander, 1996) with African and African-Caribbean heritage people (especially males) being seen as the greatest threat to law and order. In this chapter, the relationship of BrAsian young people with the key state institutions of the criminal justice system, and the police in particular, is put under scrutiny. Systematic racialisation of BrAsian young people has been a routine aspect of policing these communities since their arrival in Britain. This process has often been subsumed within the more urgent discourse of dealing with the extraordinary levels of racism against African/African-Caribbean peoples, although the recent exposé of police racism in the North West of England highlighted how 'Pakis' were the prime target.

Racialisation is a central mechanism operating within the Police Force, which mediates experiences of the criminal justice system in specific ways and hence the police play a key role in shaping that mediation. The process of differential ethnic marking of groups in the criminal justice system is primarily through the mechanism of policing, but there are both continuities and changes in the way this process has developed over recent years. The way in which the criminal justice system operates differentially towards racialised groups with varying effects is not a new feature of the implementation of law and order in Britain. Indeed, the police and courts' response to the civic disturbances that marked a number of England's Northern towns in the middle of 2001 is evidence as much of a continuing differential marking of populations, as of any new shift. However, a novel if not entirely new feature of that marking process concerns the shift of target from African-Caribbean to BrAsian Muslim males. The situation prior to the 1990s could be described as an over-zealous application of the law and police activity in relation to African-Caribbeans, as demonstrated by statistics on stop and search, arrests and prison population. By contrast, BrAsians were marked by an under-zealous application of the law, demonstrated by low levels of arrest for racial intimidation and attacks perpetrated against them. This crude set of distinctions serves to illustrate that diverse outcomes have long been a reality for different racialised groups in Britain when engaging with the criminal justice system. What the Northern riots achieved was to balance the equation, with an over-zealous application of sentences to both the BrAsian young men accused of rioting and the white young men involved. However, before considering these events and their outcomes in detail, a background check on the workings of the criminal justice system is in order.

RACIALISATION IN THE OPERATION OF THE CRIMINAL JUSTICE SYSTEM

A mass of quantitative evidence shows increasing discrimination in the workings of the criminal justice system since the 1970s. Both academic and policy literature points to many discrepancies at all stages of the workings of the various aspects of the law.[1] Indeed, an analysis of the workings of the police, judiciary and prison service shows a consistent pattern of differential treatment. Following the Criminal Justice Act, 1991, the Home Office has been obliged to collect information that can help to tackle discrimination in the performance of the criminal justice system and perhaps the most comprehensive collation of statistics in this regard was published in the document *Statistics on Race and the Criminal Justice System 2000* (Home Office, 2000). A summary of some of the main findings of this document illustrate the extent to which the criminal justice system works differentially in terms of both ethnicity and gender, and impacts on the way that BrAsians are treated and perceived by the criminal justice system. Perhaps the best starting point is the outcome of this process, the prison population.

Table 1 shows that about 3% of the male prison population and 1%

1 Usefully summarised with a large and comprehensive bibliography in Bowling and Phillips, 2002.

of the female population can be categorised as BrAsian. However, while for male Indians and Bangladeshis the prison population in percentage terms is slightly greater than their population as a whole, for Pakistanis it is almost three times as much (from the 2001 Census and see Peach, this volume). This is not the case for females. However, this is much less than the over-representation of African and African-Caribbean males and females in the prison population (when compared to the general population of England and Wales, British nationals aged 15–64). Black males constituted 12% of the prison population and black females a shocking 19%. The data is complicated by the troubling fact that the Home Office uses the same ethnic category for foreign nationals and British minority ethnic groups, rendering British born people in the same ethnic category as foreign nationals. Since a large proportion of those categorised as 'ethnic' are actually foreign nationals, 4,490 (30%) males and 680 (5%) females at the end of January 2002, this tends to inflate the proportion of prisoners from minority ethnic groups as compared with the general population. However, we should also note, in the context of the distinction between British and foreign 'ethnics', that a considerable number of settlers of BrAsian origin (i.e. those with rights to stay in Britain) have not taken up nationality.

Table 1. PRISON POPULATION BY ETHNICITY, NATIONALITY AND GENDER, 1999

	All males	*British males*	*All females*	*British females*
White	81.5	85.7	75.3	84.8
Black	12.0	10.2	19.0	11.9
African	2.0	1.1	2.7	0.8
Caribbean	7.1	6.3	9.9	5.7
Other	2.8	2.8	6.4	5.4
Asian	3.1	2.3	1.1	0.7
Bangladeshi	0.3	0.1	0.1	0.1
Indian	1.1	0.8	0.4	0.3
Pakistani	1.7	1.3	0.5	0.3
Other	3.4	1.8	4.5	2.4
Chinese	0.1	–	0.2	–
Other Asian	1.4	1.0	0.5	0.4
Other	1.9	0.8	3.8	2.0
Not known	–	–	0.1	0.1

Source: Home Office, 2000.

From 1994 to 1999 the ethnic proportion of the prison population has remained quite stable despite increases in the overall population of prisoners. The only notable rise has been in BrAsian groups, mainly an increase in Pakistani males (Home Office, 2000). This apparent racialisation of Pakistani males raises the important question of whether BrAsian Muslims are a new target for police harassment.

The Home Office also considers religious difference in its monitoring of prison populations. In the year 2000 Christian denominations accounted for the majority of the prison population (57%) while 7% were of the Islamic faith. Table 6.6 of the report *The Prison Population in 2000* (Elkins and Olagundoye, 2001) gives a detailed breakdown of the prison population by ethnic group and religion, covering a large range of faiths, from Buddhists through to those with no religion. According to the 2001 Census Muslims represent 2.7% of the national population, revealing a stark over representation in prisons where Muslims account for 7% of the population. This is in contrast to the Sikh prison population which is proportionate to its national population (0.7%) and the Hindu population which is under-represented. However, these religious populations do not map directly on to ethnic groups—especially in the case of Muslims, where the majority are from the black ethnic group (Elkins and Olagundoye, 2001). Indeed, Arab Muslims make up a much smaller percentage of the prison population than their general numbers. The increasing criminalisation of Pakistani males as evidenced by the prison population does, however, have resonance with the previous association of black males with mugging.

The association of black Caribbean young people with crime was used as a political tool to mobilise against immigration in the 1970s (Hall *et al.*, 1978; Solomos, 1989). In the most recent analysis of the statistics Bowling and Phillips conclude, using self-reporting studies by offenders, that the volume of offending echoes 'the official view of 30 years ago that the African-Caribbean crime rate is much the same as that of the "white" population and that the rate for BrAsians is much lower' (Bowling and Phillips, 2002: 106). The perpetuation of the official view on African-Caribbean offending is an example of institutional racism in the workings of the criminal justice system. Quite possibly Pakistani males are a new target for this process of criminalisation. An examination of stop and search operations might reveal whether this is the case.

More than any other form of police activity, stop and search, or SUS as it was then known, was cited as one of the key factors behind the alienation of black youth in the build up to the 1981 and subsequent civil disturbances (Keith, 1993). Under the *Police and Criminal Evidence Act, 1984* (PACE), police officers have the power to stop and search any person either suspected of having carried out a crime or acting in a suspicious manner. This factor obviously allows for the subjective experience of officers to play a large role in determining whom they consider suspicious. When the perception of officers is that black people are more likely to commit crime, the conditions for a cycle of harassment are created (Bowling and Phillips, 2002). Anecdotal evidence gathered by the BBC for the documentary *The Secret Policeman* (2004) in areas such as the North West certainly illustrates how police officers' prejudices inform their decisions for stop and search. Filmed secretly by a BBC journalist, the officers were explicit in their targeting of 'Pakis', seeing this as a fairly entertaining part of their role.

This anecdotal evidence is confirmed by the general figures on stop and search from Home Office research which once again illustrate a pattern of differential treatment. Of all stops carried out in 1999/2000 4% involved BrAsian suspects, 8% black suspects, and 1% other non-white. More stark are figures for searches and arrest rates. Black people are five times more likely to be searched than white people, while the figures for BrAsians vary widely by force. While the general reason for deploying SUS related to stolen property, for BrAsian and black people the most cited reason was 'drugs'. Notably, however, the proportion of those arrested from a stop and search were 13% for white people, 17% for black and 14% for BrAsians with a further 17% of other ethnic groups also facing arrest. These national figures, taken on regional inflections, depended on the population of racialised minority in each part of the country.

RIOTS AND CRIMINALISATION

With regard to policing, the weight of statistical evidence provides a particular understanding of racialised groups, especially young people from these groups. In simple terms, black young people are seen as pathologically criminal, while BrAsian Muslims are overly involved in fraud and drugs. The diversification of statistical analysis therefore allows for the development of nuanced stereotypes. But the central conundrum remains. If heavy handed policing was partly to blame for the 1981 riots, what role did it play in the 2001 disturbances, when the evidence given above still shows much lower rates of criminalisation for BrAsian Muslims than black groups? There is an element of conjecture in this, as at the time of the 1981 riots there were no statistics available on stop and search by ethnicity as there are now. Indeed, it is perhaps the concentration of a certain type of policing in certain areas, as brilliantly described by Michael Keith for the Metropolitan Police in the book *Race, Riots and Policing* (1993), that leads to unrest, rather than broad levels of discrimination.

While the statistical data only weakly indicates an emerging pattern of criminalisation of BrAsian Muslim youth, recent ethnographic work (Alexander, 2000), and the few voices heard in the reports into the disturbances (four in total, from Oldham, Burnley, by Ted Cantle and Lord Denham), offer a different picture. Here BrAsian Muslim young people are alienated both from the police and from 'community leadership'. Segregation and poor employment opportunities, rather than racism in housing and education, have led to a resentment that has found no other avenue of expression (Kundnani, 2001a). Although these reports suggest the social conditions that create resentment are largely similar to those of black Caribbean/African youth of the 1970s and early 1980s, the criminalisation suffered by this group still far outweighs that of BrAsians. This might explain why interactions with the police were not highlighted in respect of the more recent disturbances, while Lord Scarman's 1981 report recognised a clear link between the impact of policing and civil disorder. For Scarman the riots were 'essentially an outburst of anger and resentment by young black people against the police' (Scarman, 1981: 15). No such clear connection has been made in any of the reports following the disturbances in 2001. Indeed, in the Burnley report the police authority had a major role in its editing, and in Oldham the police were only subject to minor criticism, and were in the large exonerated for any role they may have had in perpetuating the conditions that led to the riot.

The Burnley task force was set up after the June disturbances and was chaired by Lord Tony Clarke and consisted of a wide range of representatives, primarily local, from the voluntary as well as statutory sector. Differential treatment by the police is invoked only in claims of them *favouring* the BrAsian population. For instance: 'There is a perception in the town that the police and the council fall over themselves to protect them [the Asians]' (Burnley Task Force, 2001: 63). Another quotation argues that all people should be treated the same regardless of race. No mention is made in any of the submissions of the possible criminalisation of certain sections of the BrAsian population.[2] A similar story appears in the Oldham Independent Review led by David Ritchie, a career bureaucrat. Only one chapter of the final report related to policing, but the central philosophy underpinning the approach is highlighted in its opening paragraph: 'The police do not create the environment in which they work, but need to influence it, reflect it and respond to its problems' (Oldham Independent Review Panel, 41: 2001). This populist view, of the police as an agent that is somehow above society and not susceptible to its norms, is generally contradicted by most of the policies on policing that have emerged from the Home Office in recent times (Bowling and Phillips, 2002). Of most significance, perhaps, is the fact that the report

2 Interestingly, the subsequent trials of young BrAsian men in Preston for the Burnley disturbances revealed a complete lack of ability by the Burnley police to handle the situation. This was glossed over by the inquiry as the police were one of the main commissioning bodies.

does not mention as an important factor the alienation of BrAsian young people by the police force. This is despite the overwhelmingly negative attitudes towards the police revealed in the views of the Oldham BrAsian community—old and young—summarised in Appendix 7 of the report. While the report attempts to tackle the source of this distrust, it does so within an overall thesis that highlights segregation as the main cause of social unrest. While the role of the local authority in providing housing and education is identified as contributing to segregation, the role of the police in creating and maintaining it is dismissed. Instead, while the focus has been on deprived social conditions, the police are viewed as outside agents, acting as referees imposing regulation on communities of which they themselves were not a part. Missing from the picture is a clearer appreciation of the police's role as active agents in the creation of the conditions that led to the rioting rather than as the passive recipients and controllers of social disorder created due to deprivation and social poverty. However, the racialisation of BrAsians, and BrAsian Muslims in particular, has progressed to such an extent that they are now viewed as the new pariahs. The furore that erupted following the BBC documentary *The Secret Policeman* largely failed to address the underlying issues that promote racialisation as a method of policing. Indeed, one racist officer in the programme remarked that policing is impossible without some element of discrimination.

The relationship between the police and BrAsian Muslim and white young males is often assumed to be structurally similar. However, both groups maintain the police discriminate against them. This suggests the police are caught between these two groups, rather than having a particular institutional position in relation to the BrAsian Muslim youth, which consequently places the riots firmly in the context of debates about maintaining social order. A number of commentators have played on this argument suggesting the bottom line was the problem of thuggery (see Kundnani, 2001b for a critique of this). The natural response to this should be an extension of police powers to tackle the issue of youth criminality. But the reality of the disorders in Oldham and Bradford indicate these were not about conflict between BrAsian and white youth, but between BrAsian communities and the police (the Burnley case was an exception in that a white mob essentially attacked the BrAsian community and targeted hostility towards asylum seekers).

A consideration of the disturbances in terms of those arrested and police injured, as shown in Table 2, clearly indicates that the main conflict, especially in Bradford, was between the police and BrAsian young people. Overall 395 people were arrested during the riots, the majority of whom were BrAsian young men. Sentencing varied from between three to five years for serious offences, though concern has been expressed regarding the length of sentences handed down to those with first

Table 2. POLICING IN THE AREAS OF DISTURBANCE

	Bradford Easter	*Bradford July*	*Burnley*	*Oldham*
Numbers involved	100	400–500	400	500
Injuries – police	–	326	83	2
Injuries – general public	20	14	28	3
Cost of damage	£117,000	£7.5–10m.	£0.5m.	£1.4m.

Source: Denham Report, 2001.

time offences.[3] This alone is evidence of differential treatment, but when compared to the sentences given to the white young people arrested, there is much more cause for concern. Only twelve white people were arrested following the Oldham riots and they were given sentences of nine months each. One of these is an active member of the far right, neo-fascist, British National Party, who was instrumental in inciting the rioting. The distinction in terms of sentencing between the BrAsian and white youth rested on the judge ordering the jury to disallow the charge of riot due to lack of evidence. This was also the case for incitement to racial hatred, despite CCTV footage showing racist chanting. The conflation of white and BrAsian youth as disenfranchised yobs fails when encountering the criminal justice system, which is well able both to distinguish and to discriminate between minority racialised and racist youth.

POLICING THE CRISES: RACIALISING BRASIAN YOUTH

'... more complex story of the striking deterioration in police–black relations, especially between the police ... and section of black youth.' (Hall, 1978: 52)

Written in the 1970s, the seminal volume *Policing the Crises* (Stuart Hall *et al.*, 1978) indicated how the nexus of media coverage, police manipulation and racist institutions created and propagated a close linkage between mugging and African-Caribbean youth. At its most general level this is an example of what Keith (1993) calls Police lore—the routines and customs that the police apply when dealing with people—that marks certain groups for special treatment—in this case negative. This has an impact on how that group—and other groups involved in the same process—perceives itself in relation to the police. This lore is not static. As argued in this chapter, BrAsian Muslim youth are increasingly considered new targets for the operation of police lore. Changes in atti-

3 Indeed, the House of Lords overturned some of the sentences given to the 'rioters' (30 January 2003) but did not accept the principle of mitigating circumstances which many had argued were of importance.

tudes and changes in policy can result in different outcomes for different groups, and changes in police lore can either ease tensions or produce new pariahs. This relationship with the police in turn creates a whole set of negative relations with the criminal justice system that leads to the disproportionate presence of blacks and Muslims in Britain's prisons. Writing in the 1970s, Hall *et al.* (1978) drew a clear link between the police as representatives of the state and black youth as targets for repression justifying racist language and serving class antagonism.

In the 1980s urban unrest was also linked to the role of the police and their treatment of minority racialised groups. The civil disturbances of 1981 were followed by the Scarman Report, which as previously indicated, explicitly focused on role of police and their relations with black youth. Subsequently a whole range of government programmes were enacted to deal with what were perceived as the 'problems of the inner cities'. This was a euphemism for trying to deal with the 'problem' of black (African-Caribbean) young people, who were perceived as alienated. Throughout the 1980s a range of measures were put in place aimed at quelling discontent, which to some extent succeeded in creating a lower-middle-class, predominantly public-sector-located black (African-Caribbean) strata. Nonetheless, there was an understanding that the police had an ongoing and explicit leading role in creating the conditions for the alienation of African-Caribbean youth. Indeed, the Macpherson report into the death of Stephen Lawrence was, in some respects, the product of the culmination of years of resistance to the misunderstanding of African-Caribbean youth and, to some extent, an exposure of the depth of racism within the British police force.

The urban unrest of 2001 came two years after the Macpherson report and the rioting took place in those areas that had been the recipients of numerous regeneration initiatives. Certainly many more reports have been produced about these disturbances than those of the 1980s, but still some of the key questions about the relationship between the police and BrAsian Muslim young men appear beyond the serious questioning of public policy. Following the 1980s unrest Stuart Hall declared his difficulties with speaking at yet another conference following yet more urban unrest—which he considered part of a recurring cycle in which a problem is followed by a conference followed by research—'the research reinforces what we already know, but in elegant and scholarly language. Then nothing happens. There is another problem.... Everyone expresses surprise ... and calls another conference' (Hall, 1987: 45). In the 1990s there was a change in this pattern, as the focus shifted northwards and the population rioting began to become increasingly BrAsian Muslim there have been fewer and fewer conferences. Indeed, academia and the research community have found it almost impossible to take this round of urban unrest with the same commitment as that of the 1980s.[4] The possible explanations for this are myriad, but conjecturally, the emergence of BrAsians as a target for police activity coincides with a resurgent nationalism in English society that has little tolerance for those who fall outside the narrow confines of a post-religious liberal individualism. BrAsian Muslims in both the local and global context are therefore somehow not able to be integrated and therefore not subject to the processes of civil society response that Stuart Hall outlines. Rather it is state intervention and police control that are seen as the only possibilities for tempering the difference that these communities represent. However, there is a difference between these attempts at control and the earlier ones. While in the 1970s the targeting was limited to Britain's urban areas, in the post-9/11 climate there is a trans-national dimension that cannot be contained within the relationship between the nation-state and its citizens. It may be argued that this is the reason why the civil society opposition to the treatment of those BrAsians imprisoned for rioting in 2001 has been mute. Indeed, this also allows for a level of repression of BrAsian and specifically BrAsian Muslim communities by the police (using measures such as the anti-terrorism legislation) which has hitherto not been witnessed since the era of extra-judicial killings in the north of Ireland.

4 Indeed, the editors of this book found no journal willing to take the papers from a workshop organised into the causes of the urban unrest of 2001.

HEALTH CARE AND BrASIANS

MAKING SENSE OF POLICY AND PRACTICE

Karl Atkin

At the beginning of the 1990s government policy acknowledged the importance of providing accessible and appropriate health and social care to minority ethnic populations living in Britain (Department of Health, 1990). Since then there has been considerable activity aimed at reducing health inequalities and establishing equitable public services (Mason, 2000). However, what this has actually meant for South Asian populations is less clear. The disadvantages experienced by South Asian people and the process of racist service delivery are now reasonably well understood (Atkin, 2003). Nonetheless, the translation of this understanding into improved health outcomes and better service support has been slow (Mir and Nocon, 2002).

This chapter, using a combination of theoretical and empirical debates, will make sense of this tension and explore its implications for the present understanding of health care and South Asian populations and in doing so will unravel the discursive practices that have contributed to our understanding thus far. This is important for orientating future debates and ensuring we learn from previous mistakes. Policy discussions, by presenting inadequately contextualised accounts, can, for example, perpetuate disadvantage and discrimination by encouraging ill-advised service developments (see Ahmad, 2000). There is also a more general need to provide those working in public services and local communities with a critical understanding that will enable them to tackle, rather than be overwhelmed by, the problems of providing accessible and appropriate health care in an ethnically diverse society (Anionwu and Atkin, 2001).

We begin our analysis by briefly reviewing the changing explanations, over the past fifty or more years, of ethnic, racial and cultural differences in Britain. If nothing else, this acts as a reminder that understanding occurs within a historical context, subject to shifting definitions and solutions. The chapter then offers a broader theoretical introduction to institutional racism, the current framework used to explain the failings of public institutions to respond to the needs of minority ethnic populations. The chapter concludes by arguing that future work must further sensitise our understanding of institutional racism, first by critically evaluating what we mean by 'ethnicity', and second by linking our awareness and understanding of discriminatory outcomes to a transformation of public policy and practice.

DIFFERENCE AND DIVERSITY: AN HISTORICAL ACCOUNT

Mass immigration from the Commonwealth began in the late 1940s and early 1950s in response to the needs of the British economy. Post-war reconstruction led to labour shortages in key industries which was beginning to jeopardise economic growth. However, little consideration was given to how welfare provision should respond to these changes in the make-up of the British population (Cashmore and Troyna, 1990). There was perhaps a vague understanding that 'these people' would return home, once their work was done (Mason, 2000): otherwise, if 'immigrants' and their families did settle, they would become assimilated into British society, adopt British values and thereby lose their identity as distinct ethnic groups (Solomos, 1992). This crude understanding informed social policy for nearly twenty years and explains why public services, including health and social care agencies, did little to respond to the needs of an emerging diverse society (Ohri, 1988). If ever ethnic difference did emerge as an issue for welfare provision it was either ignored or assumed to be a temporary phenomenon, as 'immigrants' adjusted and accommodated themselves to the British way of life (Cashmore and Troyna, 1990). Furthermore familiar racist discourse still operated and informed debates. Immigrants were suspected of being inferior to the general populations and hence were encouraged to fill unskilled or semi-skilled jobs (Mason, 2000). There were also debates about the threat that minority ethnic populations bore to the 'well-being' of the general population, with the British Medical Association, for instance, regularly calling for health checks before 'immigrants' were allowed to enter the country (Ahmad, 1993). Nonetheless, *assimilation* represented the convenient policy solution, which meant public services did not have to address the issues raised by the influx of immigrants with cultural and religious values different to those of the general population (see Rex and Moore, 1967).

Throughout the 1970s mainstream policy and practice still failed to engage with the consequences of a multi-ethnic society, although there was a gradual realisation that public services were failing the needs of minority ethnic populations (see Rex and Tomlinson, 1979). However, there was no coherent policy framework in which to make sense of these problems and the more theoretical explanations of disadvantage and discrimination had little impact on policy and practice responses (Mason, 1986). This slowly began to change with the rise of multi-culturalism—which reached the height of its influence during the early to mid 1980s—and the emergence of its anti-thesis, anti-racism (Atkin, 1996). Debates, in which these two opposing positions engaged, dominated the policy and practice agenda well into the 1990s and, as we shall see, their influence is still evident today.

Multi-culturalism and anti-racism

According to multi-cultural approaches, diversity in language, religion and cultural norms hindered effective communication between the majority and distinct minority communities. Promoting awareness of each other's culture was seen as helping overcome linguistic and cultural barriers and preventing misunderstandings. This, it was argued, would result in more sensitive and responsive service provision (see Atkin, 1996 for a review of these debates). However, the relationship between ethnically distinct minorities and the majority 'white' society was seen exclusively in terms of cultural practices, in which 'white' culture became the 'norm' (Gilroy, 1987). This approach to 'difference' diverts attention from the wider power relationships within society and in particular fails to recognise that the dominant 'white' culture and the 'distinct' minority culture do not meet on equal terms (Pearson, 1986). The situation of South Asian people cannot be understood solely in terms of cultural artefacts; the political, social and economic position of minority populations is equally important (Ahmad, 1989). This was the starting point of anti-racism, which emphasised the importance of structural disadvantage in understanding the experience of minority ethnic populations (Ahmad, 1993).

Anti-racism associates the policies and practices of an essentially racist society with inaccessible and inappropriate welfare provision (Roys, 1988); focusing on cultural practices distracts from this. Hence, for example, anti-racist strategies explicitly dismiss cultural descriptions as a surrogate form of racism (Pearson, 1986). At the same time, however, anti-racism could be criticised for emphasising structural influences at the expense of individual agency (Atkin, 1996). Minority ethnic populations are more than the product of the racisms they experience, so by dismissing ideas such as 'cultural difference' and 'identity' anti-racist approaches made it difficult to explore how South Asian people made sense of their own lives (Atkin, 1996).

Anti-racist strategies, with their emphasis on structural disadvantage, had a huge influence on our understanding of institutional racism (Mason, 2000). However, during the 1990s awareness of the importance of cultural values in understanding the experience of minority ethnic populations increased (see Kelleher and Hillier, 1996). This suggested the conceptualisation of 'culture' by multi-cultural approaches was the problem, rather than the concept of 'culture' *per se*, particularly since multi-cultural approaches tended to strip culture of its broader socio-economic context (Ahmad, 2000). Difference is not a problem in itself and perceptions of culture need not be identified as 'inferior' or deviant. Furthermore, the notion of 'otherness' does not address the extent to which the taken-for-granted norms of the general population are equally socially constructed. It is not that South Asian people are culturally different: rather we are all different culturally (Ballard, 1989).

The tensions in both multi-culturalism and anti-racist strategies explain the present theoretical concern with explaining cultural difference and diversity within the broader context of the political, social and economic disadvantages faced by minority ethnic populations (see Parekh, 2000 for a rethinking of multi-culturalism within this context). Policy and practice, however, has not completely adopted such an approach. Ideas of assimilation—in which the difficulties of providing equitable provision could be solved if minority ethnic people were more like the general population—and multiculturalism—in which cultural differences become misunderstood and used against minority ethnic groups—can still be found in present day debates.

THE RISE OF INSTITUTIONAL RACISM

'Institutional racism' is now offered as the official explanation for the failure of British public services to respond to the needs of an ethnically diverse society (see Macpherson, 1999). This became embodied in law with the introduction in April 2001 of amendments to the 1976 Race Relations' act, which made statutory agencies responsible for identifying and tackling institutional racism within their organisation. However, the idea of institutional racism is not new and was first introduced over twenty years ago (Glasgow, 1980). Since then it has gradually emerged as an extremely helpful and productive idea in making sense of health inequalities as well as inappropriate and inaccessible service provision (Law, 1996). Institutional racism, at its most straightforward, occurs when the policies of an institution lead to discriminatory outcomes for minority ethnic populations irrespective of the motives of individual employees of that institution (Mason, 2000). It is often called camouflaged racism, because it is not immediately obvious, but is embedded in the taken-for-granted assumptions informing organisation practices (Atkin, 2003).

Institutional racism thus refers to the uncritical application of policies and procedures that ignore the needs of an ethnically diverse society. It combines two specific discursive practices, which explain the type of response health and social care agencies make to the needs of South Asian populations. First, potential difference in need, between South Asian people and the general population, is disregarded and 'one service' is assumed to 'fit' all. Second, when difference is recognised, it is recognised in such a way as to misrepresent the needs of South Asian populations, thereby encouraging inappropriate policy and practice responses (Ahmad, 1993). Myths and stereotypes emerge to deny South Asian people access to appropriate health care.

Constructing need: ignoring difference and diversity

Fundamental to our understanding of institutional racism is the idea that the same service for all equates with an equal service for all. Hence public services, by assuming they treat everyone the same, obscure their failures to meet the needs of minority ethnic people. Policies, procedures and practices are seen as equally appropriate for all (Atkin, 1996). In effect, this means public services become organised according to a 'white norm', in which service users are assumed to have Western attitudes, priorities, expectations and values; and act according to Western ways (Butt and Mirza, 1996). Such an approach legitimates non-recognition of the care needs of minority ethnic communities and specifically disregards the dietary, linguistic and cultural needs of South Asian populations.

The inability of the National Health Service (NHS) to provide adequate support for those whose first language is not English is a more obvious example of this (Robinson, 2001). The lack of interpreters, the use of family members, the inability of individuals to engage with what is being said and practitioners' lack of training in the use of interpreters, creates barriers to effective communication and often leaves an individual without important information about their health; important for understanding, coping and caring as well as for deciding what course of action to take (see Atkin, 2003 for a review of these problems). Poor language support thus denies South Asian people the opportunity to exercise choice over their lives; choices the general population take for granted (Walker and Ahmad, 1994).

Furthermore the failure to recognise diversity can have more subtle consequences. The social model of disability, despite its valuable and important role in asserting the rights of disabled people, has been criticised for its Eurocentric assumptions (Stuart, 1996). For example, independence and autonomy—central to the disability movement—represent social and cultural constructs, which may not have the same meaning among different ethnic groups (see Modood *et al.*, 1997). In Britain a young Asian person's sense of independence is informed by how they interpret their ethnic and religious culture within the broader British culture to which they are also exposed (Ahmad *et al.*, 2002). Hence establishing autonomy and independence, which is as important to Asian young people living in Britain as it is to their 'white' counterparts, can assume different connotations (Hussain *et al.*, 2002). Developing and sustaining an identity separate from their parents and exercising some control over their own lives, for example, is not always equated with leaving home as it often is for their 'white' counterparts. Asian disabled young people have to balance the need to exercise control over their lives with a sense of mutuality, interdependence and an ability to reciprocate.

Misrepresenting the health care needs of South Asian populations

Ignoring diversity and difference is only one element contributing to institutional racism. Occurring simultaneously and equally important is the *misrepresentation* of the health care needs of South Asian people. Here there is an ill-founded concern with the 'Other'. When the differences of South Asian populations are recognised by health and social care agencies, it is often to their disadvantage. Sometimes this is the consequence of ill-informed views about the cause of problems presented by South Asian populations; at other times it is the use of inappropriate myths and stereotypes, which although purporting to explain the behaviour and beliefs of South Asian populations, do little more than falsify their experience.

To begin with, health and social services often identify cultural practices as the cause of South Asian health and social 'problems' (Walker and Ahmad, 1994). Consequently, South Asian communities are held responsible for their problems and are frequently characterised as in some way to blame for their needs because of their so-called deviant, unsatisfactory and pathological lifestyles (Ahmad, 2000). There is a history of defining health problems faced by South Asian populations in terms of cultural deficits, for which the main solution offered would be a shift towards a 'Western' lifestyle; past examples include discussions on maternity and child health (see Rocherson, 1988) and diet and rickets (see Ahmad, 1993). The views of front-line practitioners working in health and social services further reflect this concern with 'the pathological Other' (see Ahmad, 1993). Practitioners working in local authorities often list South Asian people as 'high risk' clients, 'uncooperative' and 'difficult to work with'. Similarly, evidence suggests that racism within the NHS affects minority ethnic people because of common stereotypes portraying them as 'calling out doctors unnecessarily' and 'being trivial complainers' and 'time wasters' (Atkin, 1996).

The process by which impairment and more generally 'poor birth outcome', becomes attributed to consanguineous marriages offers a more complex example of how the health care needs of South Asian populations become misrepresented (Ahmad *et al.*, 2000). Health professionals often relate congenital conditions among Pakistani families to consanguineous marriages. They therefore consider congenital conditions to be self-inflicted and located in the presumed cultural and biological pathologies of these communities (Darr, 1997; Atkin *et al*., 1998). The relationship between consanguineous marriage and the incidence of impairment and poor health is of course complex (Ahmad *et al*., 2000). In some cases, marrying a first cousin can increase a family's risk of giving birth to a disabled or chronically ill child, especially if there is a history of certain conditions in the extended family (Modell and Darr, 2002). However, first cousin marriage is not the only cause of disability or chronic illness in Pakistani or Bangladeshi families, and there is good evidence to suggest its influence has been over-emphasised (see Ahmad *et al*., 2000 for a review of the evidence). Such an approach not only carries with it an implicit (and misleading) criticism of Asian cultural practices, thereby creating mistrust between health professionals and their patients (Ahmad, 1993), it also misrepresents the origins of ill health and therefore leads to misguided policy approaches (Atkin *et al*., 1998). The preoccupation with blaming consanguineous marriage for causing impairment means other important potential causes—such as poverty, poor maternal health, inappropriate housing or inadequate service support—are rarely mentioned. Low socio-economic status, for example, seems far more likely than ethnic origin or cultural difference to be responsible for ill-health among South Asian populations (Nazroo, 1997). We also know that poor ante-natal and post-natal care are just as likely to explain impairment and ill health in South Asian families as cultural practices (Mir and Tovey, 2003).

An over-emphasis on the consequences of first-cousin marriages, at the expense of other more relevant explanations, illustrates the elaborate nature of institutional racism. However, misrepresentation of South Asian beliefs and values has another dimension. As part of this preoccupation with culture, minority ethnic groups also have to contend with inappropriate generalisations of cultural practices and the use of simplistic explanations to explain their behaviour (Law, 1996). Such explanations tend to present static and one-dimensional views of cultural norms and values, which are devoid of context and allow no room for individual interpretation (Atkin, 2003). A useful example, illustrating the dangers of such approaches, emerges from an exploration of provision of pre-natal diagnosis. Myths, often derived from simplistic accounts of Islamic beliefs, explain why pre-natal diagnosis is sometimes withheld from Muslim families (Anionwu and Atkin, 2001). Termination is assumed unacceptable to such families because it is incompatible with Islamic values. However, the empirical reality is far more complex than this. Like in other sections of the British population (see Green and Statham, 1996), termination is acceptable to some Muslim families but not to others (Atkin *et al*., 1998). There is no one Islamic interpretation of the acceptability of termination and a family's decision-making process is informed by its own values and beliefs, the views of other family members, the role of health care professionals and whether they already have a child with a condition (Atkin *et al*., 1998). The imposition of ill-informed views about Islam, therefore, deny South Asian people choice over their own lives.

Another more general myth, that contributes further to our failure to recognise the support needs of South Asian families, is the convenient idea that 'they' virtuously 'look after their own'. Since the 1980s this idea has been used as an excuse by health and social care agencies for not planning or providing services for disabled or chronically ill individuals or their families (Pearson, 1986; Connelly, 1988; Cameron *et al*., 1989; Atkin and Rollings, 1996; Walker and Ahmad, 1994; Bhakta *et al*., 2000). The assumption that Asian people live in self-supporting extended family networks is simplistic for several reasons (Ahmad 1996 provides a detailed account of these reasons). Household structures, for example, are changing, as are the expectations that inform family obligations (Modood *et al*., 1997). However, this is not the real issue. The assumption that extended Asian families have the necessary material, emotional and social resources to cope with chronic illness or disability, with limited professional support, is at best misguided and at worst a denial of their support needs (Atkin and Rollings, 1996).

BEYOND INSTITUTIONAL RACISM

Institutional racism enables us to make sense of the discrimination and disadvantages faced by South Asian populations as they try and gain access to appropriate health care. However, providing responsive and equitable service provision for South Asian populations requires us to further 'sensitise' our conception of institutional racism. By doing so we can outline the possible concerns of future debates. Two distinct principles—one broadly theoretical, the other more practical—emerge as relevant. The first is concerned with how we make sense of terms such as ethnicity, difference and diversity. The second is more concerned with how we can translate evidence about the process of disadvantage into improved outcomes for South Asian populations.

Making sense of ethnic differences

Ethnicity is a notoriously difficult concept to define as many of the chapters in this book illustrate. Previous understandings that classify people according to their country of origin seem no longer sustainable, particularly since nearly 40 per cent of what we regard as minority ethnic populations are born in Britain (Modood *et al*., 1997). Consequently, young people are beginning to redefine their identity by adopting such terms as

British Muslim or British Asian or even British-Indian. Young people are also increasingly using religious affiliations, such as Muslim or Hindu or Sikh, to describe who they are (see Ahmad *et al.*, 2002 for a discussion of these broad issues). This perhaps reflects fundamental differences in how young people and parents make sense of their identities and the variations in their broader engagement with British society (Hall, 1990), although this is not to say that young people are wholly rejecting their parents' identifications. Indeed, there is considerable continuity in values between the different generations (Atkin *et al.*, 2002).

The emergence of these debates also highlights diversity both between and within South Asian populations. At the beginning of the 1990s it was possible for policy to present South Asian populations as a discrete group. We now recognise differences in both socio-economic positions and cultural values among Indian, Pakistani and Bangladeshi populations (Nazroo, 1997). As part of this we are also beginning to understand the importance of religion in making sense of the lives of South Asian populations (Modood *et al.*, 1997). But religion too is not a simple marker of cultural difference. The socio-economic position of Indian Muslims, for example, reveals they have more in common with Pakistani Muslims than other Indian populations (Chamba *et al.*, 1999). Regional identification is also important in explaining ethnic differences, even when people share the same country of origin (see Mir and Tovey, 2003).

However, as we attempt to tackle disadvantages and discrimination, the multi-faceted nature in which 'ethnicity' has come to be understood has both pros and cons. Conceptual confusion can occur and 'ethnicity' can be used to obscure more fundamental differences among populations. Consequently, policy and practice can sometimes misunderstand what makes South Asian populations 'different' and fail to take into account the multifarious markers of diversity and identity. At the same time, however, the loose definition of the term 'ethnicity' provides us with flexibility, and the complex and shifting nature of ethnicity provides a useful framework in which to explore diversity and differences between and among populations. Ethnicity is not a neutral term and has come to embody language, religion, culture, nationality and a shared heritage (Ahmad *et al.*, 2002). Furthermore, ethnicity has increasingly been seen as a political symbol, defining not just exclusion by a powerful majority, but also a source of pride and belonging (Ahmad *et al.*, 2002); in other words, a mobilising resource that enables South Asian populations to celebrate their difference and make legitimate demands as British citizens (Husband, 1996). By understanding this, policy and practice can begin to reflect the diversity of the populations it serves.

However, making sense of diversity and explaining difference is only part of the process of tackling discriminatory outcomes. We need to recognise that South Asian populations may not be all that different from the general population. Patients with end stage cancer, for example, articulate many similar concerns, worries and needs irrespective of ethnicity (Chattoo and Ahmad, 2003). This is further reflected in their service needs.

Not every problem or difficulty a person encounters as they attempt to gain access to appropriate service delivery can be attributed to his or her ethnic, cultural or religious background. The challenge for future policy and practice is to know when ethnicity makes a difference and mediates a person's relationship with service support and when it does not. There is increasing evidence that socio-economic status, age and gender are as important as ethnicity in making sense of a person's health and social care needs. Policy and practice needs to recognise this and understand how ethnicity relates to other aspects of an individual's identity. Otherwise it will once more offer solutions on the basis of misguided and mistaken premises. South Asian women, for example, sometimes struggle to convince doctors that their child is seriously ill and find themselves being dismissed as 'neurotic' or 'overprotective' (Atkin *et al.*, 1998). Lack of language support and assumptions about the passivity of South Asian women contribute to such views. Nonetheless, their treatment is not wholly a consequence of their ethnic background, and can sometimes be explained by doctors' more general sexist attitudes (Green and Murton, 1996).

Using evidence to improve policy and practice

In addition to the theoretical concerns outlined above, the idea of institutional racism needs to accommodate more practical issues. Offering an analysis of the problems facing South Asian populations is one thing; doing something about it is another. Accounts of institutional racism tend to focus on the unfair structuring of opportunities (Law, 1996). The critical emphasis of the literature is perhaps understandable and has successfully highlighted the negative consequences of racism, marginalisation and unequal treatment (see Ahmad, 2000). However, two related problems occur. First, by constantly focusing on disadvantage, policy and practice discourse is in danger of adopting a 'victim orientated' viewpoint that undervalues the significance of struggle and empowerment (Jeyasingham, 1992). Despite a sometimes hostile environment, community action on haemoglobin disorders offers an example of positive achievement (see Anionwu and Atkin, 2001 for a broader discussion of these issues). For example, many of the advances in service delivery have not occurred as a consequence of 'needs assessment' undertaken by statutory agencies, but have been informed by the activities of national and local voluntary organisations, such as the UK Thalassaemia Society (Anionwu and Atkin, 2001). Thus the discrimination experienced by South Asian populations is not inevitable and there are often opportunities for change (Walker and Ahmad, 1994).

Second, by constantly highlighting the negative consequences of service provision, we do little to advance thinking and practice (Levick, 1992) and are in danger of leaving a 'waste ground' devoid of meaning (see Bauman, 1992). A good deal of evidence outlining the process and outcomes of institutional racism has been accumulated. However, policy and practice has been less successful in translating the ensuing insights into improvements in service delivery. There is a need to understand, for example, more about what constitutes good practice and how such practice can be sustained and replicated in other localities (Atkin, 2003). Future research, outlining the difficulties facing South Asian populations is perhaps unhelpful. Research, policy and practice needs to refocus its attention on understanding how services can best meet the needs of South Asian populations by exploring more about how services are delivered and suggesting ways they can be improved. Apart from defining problems, the growing evidence base must also lead to solutions. Without such a commitment to change, service initiatives are not only in danger of wasting valuable public resources, but are also in jeopardy of becoming little more than token gestures, leading to increasing disillusionment and estrangement among South Asian populations (see Mir and Nocon, 2002).

By looking at the problems surrounding the provision of health and social care for South Asian populations in Britain within the historical perspective, the previous theoretical positions and their influence on current thinking becomes evident. So does the fact that our understanding of discrimination and disadvantage requires constant reconciliation, not only with how we chose to frame the issue, but also with the changing empirical circumstances in which South Asian people find themselves.

Insights informed by 'institutional racism' explain how the health care needs of South Asian people are either ignored or, if they are recognised, are seen as a problem subject to various stereotypes and myths. Understanding this offers an initial starting point for developing accessible and appropriate public services. However, there is also a need to recognise the complexity associated with ideas such as ethnicity, difference and diversity. This means acknowledging differences between and within different 'ethnic' populations as well as accepting that ethnicity is not always the only explanation for disadvantage and discrimination. Diversity and difference, therefore, need to be understood within a broader context in which socio-economic status, age and gender can sometimes be as equally important as ethnicity in making sense of a person's health and social care needs.

Finally, awareness of institutional racism needs to be grounded in a commitment to improving outcomes for South Asian populations. Focusing on the needs of South Asian populations is not the same as responding to those needs. Using the available evidence to make improvements in service delivery is a far from straightforward process and in the past, policy and practice has seemed overwhelmed by the difficulties of responding to the needs of South Asian people. Policy and practice needs to shift its focus and ensure the present evidence base is used more effectively to improve outcomes for South Asian populations. This is the future challenge for public services, as they attempt to meet the needs of all British citizens.

PALLIATIVE CARE

Gurch Randhawa and Alastair Owens

Although the BrAsian population as a whole is relatively young compared to other population groups in Britain, its members are inevitably aging. As a consequence an increasing number of BrAsians are now encountering palliative care services either as patients or as carers. Palliative care is the total care both of patients with life threatening diseases and of their families. It has been argued that palliative care services for ethnic minority populations are not only often culturally insensitive but institutionally racist. Attempts to meet the needs of BrAsian patients have led to the oversimplification of cultural differences and an over-reliance on stereotypes of the BrAsian community and its practices. Culture and ethnicity are frequently reduced to religious beliefs and customs often described in fact-file booklets used by health care professionals to understand their ethnic communities, effectively legitimating discrimination rather than eliminating it. Indeed, the fact-files are an example of the way in which practices institutionalise and fix people's ethnic identities.

While palliative care is increasingly embracing the needs of patients with a range of life-limiting conditions, cancer remains the key focus of most services. The belief that BrAsians do not get cancer and therefore rarely need palliative care services is an inaccurate perception that has been forcefully challenged in recent years. Detailed research by epidemiologists suggests that cancer prevalence across a range of different sites does vary among Britain's minority ethnic populations. While overall BrAsians appear to have lower rates of cancer than the rest of the population, this alters according to the type of cancer and, significantly, by age. A recent study carried out in Leicester, for example, concluded that 'although older South Asians had much lower rates of cancer than the rest of the population, younger South Asians were at increased risk compared with non-South Asians' (Smith *et al.*, 2003: 70). Other recent research has shown that cancer mortality among BrAsian migrants increased with duration of residence in England and Wales (Harding, 2003). Indeed, 'over the last ten years cancer rates have increased among South Asians while they have been falling among the rest of the population' (Smith *et al.*, 2003: 72).

These shifts, and the resulting potential increase in demands for services, clearly need to be acknowledged and anticipated in the fields of preventative medicine and health promotion. In line with other studies, our research suggested that awareness and understanding of cancer, its causes and the services available for its treatment and palliation were low among the BrAsian populations in Luton (Randhawa and Owens, 2004). The individuals that we spoke to were keen to learn more. They highlighted a need for promotional literature to be available in a variety of South Asian languages and indicated a desire for information to be disseminated through a range of media (such as video, radio and the internet) and through community networks and institutions. Addressing awareness problems and access difficulties has been a key area of service development over the past few years and includes initiatives such as the appointment of a Macmillan Ethnic Minority Liaison Officer to work with cancer patients, community palliative care nursing staff and others in Bradford (Jack *et al.*, 2001).

These experiences and observations suggest there is a need to think more carefully and critically about training for and working with people from different ethnic backgrounds. In part this is a matter of understanding that service providers (as well as users) also have a complex ethnic and cultural identity in order to move beyond a binary understanding of difference: the white professional 'Self' caring for the foreign Asian 'Other'. It also involves a greater recognition of the emotional demands of palliative care, for both service providers and users, which exert particular pressures on nursing practice. The most significant challenge in the provision of palliative care to BrAsian people therefore is to develop a more reflexive understanding of cultural difference that empowers nursing staff to work more effectively in the complex arenas of service provision at the end of a patient's life (Owens and Randhawa, 2004). Given the discipline of palliative care's commitment to innovative forms of patient-centred 'total care', there is surely scope for building these new approaches.

IMAGINING THE POLITICS OF BRASIAN YOUTH

Claire Alexander

One of the distinctive features of BrAsian communities is its markedly younger age profile by comparison with other ethnic majority and minority groups (Peach, this volume). It is perhaps surprising, therefore, that comparatively little is known about Asian young people themselves. Although the post-war period has seen a proliferation of academic and popular interest in black British/African-Caribbean youth and youth culture, BrAsian youth have remained largely invisible and ignored. This is partly because of the still prevalent assumptions around the all-powerful, controlling influence of 'Asian culture', in which BrAsian young people are seen as simply reproducing the static traditions of their parents and their 'community', and partly because, until recently, BrAsian youth were viewed as not constituting a 'problem' group and consequently, as being rather dull. Where it appeared at all, the issue of 'youth' was framed within the notion of cultural conflict and crisis—as young people caught 'between two cultures'. As Dick Hebdige has argued, 'In our society, youth is present only when its presence is a problem' (in Giroux, 1996: 3).

Although there has been an ongoing fascination with the issue of arranged marriages amongst Britain's Asian communities, and the occasional flurry of political and tabloid media moral panics over the cultural by-products of 'forced' marriage, runaway girls and 'bounty hunters' (CCCS, 1982; Samad and Eade, 2002), it is only in the last fifteen years, in the wake of the 'Satanic Verses' affair (1989) and the Gulf War demonstrations (1990–1), that BrAsian youth have become the focus of public and academic concern. With the Bradford 'riots' of 1995, the disturbances across the North of England in the summer of 2001 and the growth of so-called 'fundamentalism' amongst Muslim youth BrAsian young people—and notably young men—have rapidly become a new 'folk devil'. Fears around 'Asian gangs', rising crime rates, violence and drug use on the one hand, and of religio-ethnic militancy, conflict and social alienation on the other, have served to re-energise long-established notions of generational conflict and identity crisis. At the same time the past few years have seen the explosion of BrAsian youth cultural forms into the mainstream, in music, literature and cinema. This points to the creation of new, hybrid youth identities which challenge and subvert the notion of what it means to be 'second generation' BrAsian.

This chapter will trace the contours of the construction of BrAsian youth identities in the sociological imagination. Taking as its starting point the early concerns about 'between two cultures' identity crisis, the chapter will explore the contemporary pathologisation of Asian youth identities through the stereotypes of 'fundamentalism' and 'the Asian gang'. It will also explore the more 'hidden' history of BrAsian youth resistance and struggles against racism. The chapter will consider the roles of gender, religion and the fragmentation of the term 'black' within the construction of youth identities. Finally, it will touch on the current debates around 'new ethnicities' and the creation of innovative and hybrid youth identities and cultures.

FRAMING BRASIAN YOUTH: THE 'BETWEEN TWO CULTURES' DEBATE

The dominant paradigm for understanding BrAsian youth identities remains the 'between two cultures' analysis, which became popular as a form of academic and common-sense/media construction of ethnic minority youth identities throughout the 1970s (CCCS, 1982), particularly when faced with growing unrest amongst black communities during this period. Rooted in the assimilationist assumptions of the 1960s, BrAsian youth were seen as torn between the repressive traditional regimes of their parents and the more permissive freedoms of wider British society. This inevitably led, the argument continues, to 'culture clash' between Asian parents and children, and to 'identity conflict' in trying to reconcile two opposing, and ultimately irreconcilable, worldviews. The titles of works during this period reflect these foundational assumptions—*The Second Generation... Punjabi or English?* (Thompson, 1974); *The Half-Way Generation* (Taylor, 1976); *Culture Conflict and Young Asians* (Ballard, 1976); *In Search of Identity* (Meadows, 1976).[1] An early publication of the Community Relations Commission (later to become the Commission for Racial Equality), tellingly titled *Between Two Cultures: a study of relationships between generations in the Asian community in Britain* (1970), clearly outlined the premises of this approach:

> The children of British-Asian parents born or brought up in Britain are a generation caught between two cultures. They live in a culture of their parents at home, and are taught a different one at school, the neighbourhood and at work.... Parents cannot fully understand their children, children rarely fully understand their parents. (cited in CCCS, 1982: 122)

The notion of being 'caught' between cultures captures the problem-

1 These texts are all cited in CCCS, 1982.

oriented core of this approach, focusing on inter-generational crisis and conflict. The conflict model was underscored by an anthropological understanding of 'culture' and 'cultural identity' as an unchanging essence possessed by discrete and homogeneous 'communities' or 'ethnic groups' (Benson, 1996). This approach is reflected in Watson's (1977) edited collection, also called *Between Two Cultures*, in which each chapter focuses on a distinct ethnic minority group and traces processes of cultural change and adaptation to British society. The two chapters on Asian communities, 'The Sikhs' and 'The Pakistanis', lay strong emphasis on intergenerational difference and latent conflict. Verity Saifullah Khan thus writes of 'The Pakistanis':[2]

> The divergent culture and orientation of British Asians and their parents ... produce tensions that arise from a mutual inability to appreciate the priorities and preoccupations of the other. (Watson, 1977: 86)

Similarly, Roger and Catherine Ballard write of 'The Sikhs':

> The most important change in the character of Sikh settlement in the 1970s has been the emergence of a second generation.... These young people have been exposed to socialisation in two very different cultures, at home and at school. The crucial questions are, firstly, how successfully are they managing to resolve the contradictions between these two cultures and, secondly, whether and in what form are they sustaining their Punjabi ethnicity? (Watson, 1977: 43)

Although the authors in both cases claim to challenge the notion of identity conflict, stressing the ability of BrAsian young people to move 'between' cultures, negotiating the demands of each, the overarching picture is of two distinct and opposed sets of values—tradition versus modernity, community versus the individual, duty versus freedom, family versus school—that inevitably lead to 'particular stress' and 'contradictions'. In a later collection, *Minority Families in Britain: support and stress*, Catherine Ballard thus writes of 'the strange half-British, half-Asian behaviour' of Asian young people (Ballard, 1979: 110).

The sticking point for the 'between two cultures' advocates is, perhaps unsurprisingly, the issue of arranged marriage[3] and, by extension, the 'problem' of the BrAsian family in relation to young women (see Ahmad, this volume). Indeed, it is significant that in the otherwise generic category that marks out debates around 'Asian youth' identities, the only source of distinction is that of gender. The notion of identity crisis is sharpened in relation to BrAsian young women because of the assumed

2 It is significant that a nationality-based label 'Pakistani', rather than the more recent religion-based identifier 'Muslim', is used here.

3 Cf. Ballard and Ballard (1977), 'It is at this point that the conflict between loyalty to the family and personal independence is *finally brought into the open*' (1977: 48, my emphasis).

cultural traditions that at once devalue women and place them as the repository of family honour. Young women thus find themselves facing direct, and incommensurable, conflict between their home and school life. Saifullah Khan asserts:

> However *orthodox* a girl's home life, she is influenced by other ideas at school: mixing with friends who discuss boyfriends, the cinema and fashions. She is also *taught to question and develop her individuality*. (Saifullah Khan, 1977: 85, my emphasis)

Ultimately, it is argued, after a 'period of rebellion', most young people return to their parental culture and 'the strength of fundamental Asian values and institutions' (Saifullah Khan, 1977: 86). While Khan attributes this to the strength of early socialisation and family ties, Ballard and Ballard also (and uniquely, for this perspective) point to the role of racism in the formation of youth identities. They argue that identity crisis is precipitated by not only the challenge to parental norms, but also a rejection by wider British society. They thus point to the emergence of a 'reactive ethnicity' (Ballard, 1979: 126), which stresses cultural difference and 'renewed pride in their separate cultural identity', and which 'encapsulates Asians in their own communities' (ibid.: 127) as a form of 'ultimate security'.

The 'between two cultures' thesis has been subject to a sustained critique by emergent, mainly black, scholars, who have seen the argument as perpetuating a 'blame the victim' approach to ethnic minority communities. Errol Lawrence, for example, argues that 'ethnicity studies' view minority cultures as static and as inherently problematic, leading to a pathologised account of Asian cultures and BrAsian youth identities (CCCS, 1982). This has laid the blame for black disadvantage on cultural practices and choices rather than on wider structures of racism and discrimination. Avtar Brah (1996) has also argued that the notion of 'culture clash' is problematic for a number of reasons. First, it assumes that there is only one 'British' and one 'Asian' culture and it ignores differences of class, region, gender, religion etc. Second, the focus on conflict denies the possibility of cultural interaction and fusion, and ignores the power relations that structure cultural hierarchies and conflict. Third, the debate asserts that cultural change is a one-way process, ignoring the mutuality of 'Asian' and 'British' interaction since pre-colonial times. It could also be argued that it assumes an assimilative trajectory, in which Asian cultures are expected to move towards, and be dissolved within, dominant British culture. Fourth, the notion of 'identity conflict' portrays young BrAsians as disoriented, confused and atomised individuals, which is not supported by the evidence. It also reduces the complex formations of identity to one dominant factor—ethnicity—ignoring other influences and identities. Fifth, it conflates generational difference with conflict, and ignores any possibility of commonality or mutual understanding across generations. Lastly, and echoing Lawrence, it misreads as 'cultural conflict' and 'reactive ethnicity' the political activities of BrAsian young people against racist oppression and discrimination.

As mentioned above, the 'between two cultures' approach was at its most influential in the 1970s and early 1980s, although it still retains some power in framing the understanding of contemporary youth identities. It is important, and significant, that this period also saw the emergence of youth to the forefront of active, and angry, resistance to racism amongst Britain's African-Caribbean and BrAsian communities. While the 'between two cultures' theorists saw this as an expression of culture conflict and crisis, others have argued for the growth of an inclusive 'black British'[4] political sensibility that demanded inclusion within, rather than withdrawal from, the mainstream of British life and culture. While this period has been predominantly represented by images of African-Caribbean youth protest, culminating in the 'riots' of 1980/81 in Brixton and elsewhere (Solomos, 1993), BrAsian young people also played a defining role in challenging racial discrimination. It is to this alternative, 'hidden' account of BrAsian youth identities that this chapter now turns.

RESISTING THE IMAGE: THE 'HIDDEN HISTORY' OF BRASIAN YOUTH

A number of authors have argued that the mid 1970s in Britain saw the emergence of black youth at the forefront of struggles against racism (Brah, 1996; CCCS, 1982; Sivanandan, 1986). While distinctive in its mobilisation of a section of young people who largely had been born and/or brought up in Britain—the second generation—it is important to see these activities within the context of the longer struggles of their communities. Sivanandan thus writes:

> By the middle of the 1970s, the youth had begun to emerge into the vanguard of black struggle. And they brought to it not only the traditions of their elders but an experience of their own, which was implacable of racism and impervious to the blandishments of the state. (Sivanandan, 1986: 140)

Issues of racial attacks, police discrimination and youth unemployment were central to the public and often angry confrontations between black young people and the police, moving Britain's black communities into the media spotlight. For BrAsian youth, the growth of fascism and the level of racist attacks in their communities, and the blatant racism of the police formed the main issues for protest. These concerns were galva-

4 'Black' throughout this section is used as an inclusive political category covering African, African-Caribbean and Asian communities.

nised in the aftermath of the racist murder of eighteen-year-old Gurdip Singh Chaggar in Southall in June 1976.

One immediate consequence of Chaggar's murder was the birth of the Southall Youth Movement, which signalled the move away from the traditions of protest of the community elders in favour of a more proactive stance. Sivanandan describes the shift:

> A meeting was held and the elders went about it in the time-honoured way, passing resolutions, making statements. The youth took over—marched to the police station, demanding redress, stoning a police van en route. The police arrested two of them. They sat down before the police station and refused to move—until their fellows were released. They were released. The following day the Southall Youth Movement (SYM) was born. (Sivanandan, 1986: 142)

The role of SYM in both symbolising and mobilising BrAsian resistance was given further credibility in the Southall 'riots' of 1979 and 1981 (Bains, 1988). As Avtar Brah has argued (this volume and 1996; see also Sivanandan 1986), in the wake of the SYM, a number of other BrAsian youth groups were born, usually locally based and formed in response to racist attacks and murders, and the failures of the police to protect BrAsian communities. Youth organisations and defence committees, such as the Asian Youth Movement, were formed in London, Bradford, Leicester and Manchester, often in association with local African-Caribbean groups, such as People's Unite in Southall and Bradford Blacks (Sivanandan, 1986; Brah, 1996). Although these organisations have been criticised for their almost exclusively masculine membership, and masculinist/misogynist focus (Bains, 1988), both Brah (1996) and Sivanandan (1986) argue that these groups formed the foundation for later more broadly inclusive black anti-racist political organisations, publications and activities. Brah has argued further that the proliferation of BrAsian youth organisations, such as SYM and Southall Black Sisters,[5] across Britain 'marks the coming of age of a new form of Asian political agency' (Brah, 1996: 47) articulating a '*home grown political discourse*' (ibid., emphasis in original) that points to a distinctive second generation political consciousness (cf. Westwood, 1991).

It is not accidental that as BrAsian youth became more active and more visible in the anti-racist struggle they also became a target of state and media control. Well known cases such as the 'Bradford Twelve' and the 'Newham Eight' (Westwood, 1991) are discussed in greater detail by Avtar Brah in (this volume). However, it is important to underscore how discourses of BrAsian youth criminality and crisis are closely interwoven with discussions of BrAsian youth identities, cultures and politics.

5 Brah notes that Southall Black Sisters, established in 1978, grew out of this period of activism and was almost entirely composed of Asian young women (cf. Southall Black Sisters, 1990; Patel, 1997).

The two approaches outlined above—generational/cultural crisis and anti-racist resistance—form the broad parameters of contemporary formulations of BrAsian youth identities. However, there have also been significant transformations in the ways in which BrAsian youth identities have been conceptualised, most notably around the fragmentation of the category 'black' and the move away from anti-racist organisation towards cultural politics and the so-called 'politics of difference'. These shifts centre upon a reclamation and reworking of the notion of 'culture' and 'ethnicity' that was at the heart of the 'between two cultures' thesis, though in two distinct and opposed ways. The first centres on the idea of cultural difference, which stresses processes of continuity and change in forming increasingly fragmented and specific religio-cultural identities. This notion of cultural difference also lies at the heart of the ongoing pathologisation of BrAsian youth identities, as reflected in popular moral panics around 'Asian gangs' and 'fundamentalism'. The second approach focuses on 'new ethnicities' and places BrAsian youth identities as part of an ongoing and ambiguous struggle over representation, particularly through new, hybrid, forms of cultural production. The following two sections will explore the contours of these debates and their implications for understanding BrAsian youth identities.

CULTURAL DIFFERENCE AND CULTURAL IDENTITY: CONTINUITY AND CHANGE

In 'Old and New Identities, Old and New Ethnicities' Stuart Hall points to the salience of an inclusive black identity in anti-racist struggle in Britain throughout the 1970s and 1980s, 'The black I am talking about is a historical category, a political category, a cultural category' (Hall, 2000b: 149). The mobilisation of this 'black' identity was particularly important in challenging the static and culturally over-determined understandings of 'ethnicity', which perpetuated pathologies of ethnic and cultural difference as a primary cause of racism and racial disadvantage. However, from the mid 1980s onwards this political category was fractured by the re-emergence of notions of 'culture', which laid the emphasis on differences between 'black' (now redefined as African/African-Caribbean) and 'Asian' communities and concerns. This was particularly focused on the silencing of Asian experience, traditions and identities, and the negation of what Tariq Modood has termed the Asian 'mode of being' (Modood, 1992b: 55). These divergent sensibilities were highlighted in the aftermath of the 'Satanic Verses' affair in 1989 and the demonstrations against the Gulf War in 1990/1 (in which again Asian/Muslim young men featured prominently).

The 1990s witnessed the rebirth of 'ethnicity' as the central paradigm for understanding BrAsian identities, with the emphasis placed again on the assertion of cultural—and increasingly, religious—difference. The category 'Asian' has itself been replaced with a proliferation of narrowly defined religious, national and regional identifications—what Sivanandan has characterised as 'cultural enclaves and feuding nationalisms' (Sivanandan, 2000: 423). As a consequence Asian youth have been re-absorbed into the conceptual confines of cultural identity and 'community', and become largely invisible in academic, political and media discourse—except where they appear, traditionally, as a problem.

The little work on Asian young people that has appeared in recent years (Anwar, 1998a; Modood, Beishon and Virdee, 1994; Modood *et al.*, 1997) bears the traces of the earlier 'between two cultures' approach, though with some significant differences. On the one hand the work attempts to trace generational change through traditional 'cultural' markers, such as mother tongue proficiency, marriage practices, clothes and religious affiliation.[6] On the other the work lays emphasis on processes of cultural change as inevitable and positive rather than as a necessary source of intergenerational conflict and identity crisis. The stress is thus on what Anwar terms 'continuity and change' and the growth of 'a new culture which is a synthesis of the "old" and the "new"' (Anwar, 1998a: 192).[7] Modood *et al.* (1997) argue further that even where BrAsian young people do not adhere to the cultural practices of their parents, they retain a strong 'associational' identity—often in response to racial rejection.[8] Thus they note, 'In discussing their ethnic identity some young Asians explicitly affirmed what they took to be the family-centred and religion-centred values of their community' (Modood *et al.*, 1997: 337).

The second significant change is the stress on diversity within the category 'Asian', and in particular the difference between Muslim (Pakistani and Bangladeshi) and non-Muslim (Indian and East African Asian) communities. Although this can be seen to perpetuate the essentialising religio-cultural identities criticised by Sivanandan and others (Housee and Sharma, 1999; Sharma, Hutnyk and Sharma, 1996), this work points to variation within the category 'Asian', and notably the emergence of an Islamic identity (tied to the growth of Islamophobia in Britain and globally). Muslim young people are thus seen as having a stronger 'behavioural identity' (Modood *et al.*, 1997) than their Hindu and Sikh counterparts, in each of the areas mentioned above. Anwar likewise argues, 'young Muslims seemed to be more "conservative" in their outlook

6 Modood *et al.* define 'seven elements of South Asian identities', comprising: clothing, religion, language, marriage, description, self-identity and schooling (Modood *et al.*, 1997: 338).

7 Although he also cannot resist noting 'the approach of young Asians seems to be continuity and change, sometimes leading to *tensions between generations*' (Anwar, 1998a: 192, my emphasis).

8 The echoes here of Ballard and Ballard's notion of 'reactive ethnicity' are tangible.

and had a higher conformity to religio-cultural norms than did Hindu and Sikh young people' (Anwar, 1998a: 192).[9] This research also reveals significant discrepancies in the life experiences of Muslims vis-à-vis non-Muslim young people, in the areas of education and employment.[10]

Both Anwar and Modood point to the importance of different class, migration and settlement patterns in explaining variations between BrAsian groups, but the overwhelming explanation has remained one of 'culture' and 'cultural difference'. Anwar, for example, states that most policy makers traced the different experiences of Asian youth in education and the job market to 'cultural and language difficulties' (Anwar, 1998a: 191). Issues of structural disadvantage, racism and racial discrimination then get translated into cultural stereotypes and pathologies about 'backward' Asian (particularly Muslim) cultures. This can be clearly seen in the reports on the 'riots' in Oldham, Bradford, Leeds and elsewhere in the summer of 2001,[11] which placed the emphasis on cultural difference and Asian 'self-segregation' as primary causes of the disturbances (Amin, 2002; Kundnani, 2001a).

Coverage of the 2001 'riots' in the media also constructs a clear common-sense linkage between BrAsian cultural pathologies and criminality—an image that is particularly focused on the images of BrAsian young men. The 'riots' were thus seen to be as much about drugs, violence and 'gangs' as they were about poverty and racism. This coverage reflects wider transformations in the representation of BrAsian youth, most notably in the period after the 'Satanic Verses' affair. First, it points to the increasing visibility of BrAsian youth in the public imagination, and to the re-gendering of concern away from the 'plight' of BrAsian young women towards the 'problem' of BrAsian young men. Second, it marks the move of BrAsians from 'victim' to 'aggressor' status. Third, these 'problems' are seen as rooted in a dysfunctional BrAsian culture, so that racism and racial disadvantage appear instead as a cultural preference or cultural disadvantage. This is most clearly seen in the debates around the emergence of a 'Muslim underclass' in Britain (Modood, 1992b). Fourth, it highlights the ongoing process of criminalisation of BrAsian youth identities, so that young men now primarily appear in one of two guises—'the gang' or 'the fundamentalist'.

9 Anwar (1998a) notes that Muslim young people were more likely to pray, support single-sex religious schools and more likely to socialise within their own ethnic group. Muslim young women were more likely to wear Asian clothes for the majority of the time.

10 Pakistanis and Bangladeshis aged sixteen to twenty-four were nearly twice as likely to have no qualifications than white, Indian and African-Asian groups. Rates of unemployment amongst Pakistani and Bangladeshi men are nearly three times that of the white population and over twice that of Indian men (Modood *et al.*, 1997).

11 Cf. 'Building Cohesive Communities' (The Cantle Report), Home Office, 2001 and H. Ouseley, *Community Pride not Prejudice*, 2001.

CULTURAL DIFFERENCE AND CULTURAL PATHOLOGY: THE NEW ASIAN 'FOLK DEVILS'

In the wake of the 'Satanic Verses' affair and the Gulf War demonstrations, through the Bradford 'riots' of 1995, to the disturbances of 2001 and the aftermath of the 9/11 attacks, it is perhaps inevitable that Britain's Muslim communities have moved into the spotlight of popular, political and academic concern. The same can be said of Muslim young people—notably Pakistani and Bangladeshi young men—who were at the highly visible forefront of these events. This has generated two distinct and seemingly opposed trajectories for BrAsian youth identities, 'the Asian gang' and 'the fundamentalist'.[12] Modood thus writes of the growth of 'political alienation, sometimes expressed in terms of a political Muslim identity' and of 'a possible trend of criminalisation among young Pakistanis and Bangladeshis' (Modood, 1997: 147).

There has been very little substantive scholarly work done on contemporary Asian youth identities, so such characterisations remain primarily at the level of speculation rather than fact. Indeed, my own work on *The Asian Gang* (Alexander, 2000) suggests that such constructions of BrAsian youth reflect more a series of common-sense assumptions about the nature of ethnic, gendered and generational dysfunction than any discernible empirical reality. The idea of 'the gang', then, fuses ideas about problem/alien/black cultures, failing masculinities and identity crisis in a form of 'triple oppression' which places BrAsian young men at the margins of society and as a threat to it. 'The Asian gang' is seen as an inevitable response to low self-esteem, alienation from both their own communities and wider society and an inability to achieve legitimate success through education and employment—a reach for imagined strength actualised in violence and criminality.

Interestingly, the alternative route for Asian young men—into a 'fundamentalist' Islamic identity—is similarly posited as a response to low self-esteem, racial rejection and identity conflict. It has been argued that Islam thus functions as a defensive psychological barricade behind which young Muslims (usually men) can lay claim to a fictional strength founded in the *umma* (Gardner and Shakur, 1994; Jacobson, 1997; Macey, 1999).[13] Like 'the gang', this militant religious identity is

12 It is worth noting that the idea of 'the Asian gang' in recent years is usually implicitly Muslim, though it does occasionally include Sikh groups. Similarly, 'fundamentalism' usually refers to Islamic identities, though there is some evidence of a growth of strong religio-cultural identities amongst Sikh and Hindu young people (Bhatt, 1997). In neither case are non-Muslim identities regarded as generating the same degree of threat or concern.

13 'Their new allegiances are a reaction to, and a defence against, their experience of racial exclusionism.... Islam provides both a positive identity, in which solidarity can be found, together with an escape from the oppressive tedium of being constantly identified in negative terms' (Gardner and Shakur, 1994: 193).

often seen as founded on a rejection of the parental culture in favour of a global, culture-free alternative.[14] Also like 'the gang', 'fundamentalist' identities become inseparable from notions of violence, crime and a threat to wider British society (Macey, 2002)—particularly in the aftermath of the 9/11 attacks.

These two folk devils can thus be seen as two sides of the same culturalist coin: both arise from the apparent failures of the parental culture, giving rise to feelings of inadequacy and alienation and fuelled by rejection from mainstream society. It is worth re-emphasising the highly gendered nature of these concerns: both 'the gang' and 'the fundamentalist' are visioned as male, and are defined through increasingly similar forms of hyper-masculine behaviour, notably violence. Chetan Bhatt (1997) has thus noted that the 1990s saw growing alliances between youth 'gangs' and more traditionalist religion-based organisations, particularly in the exercise of territorial control and the policing of BrAsian women's sexuality. This is linked in turn back to the wider representation of Asian/Muslim cultures as inherently patriarchal and misogynist. Thus young women appear only as the victims of culturally rooted masculine control and oppression (Macey, 1999), an image which belies the ongoing struggle by BrAsian young women for their own space (Southall Black Sisters, 1990; Drury, 1996; Puwar and Raghuram, 2003).

As with the 'between two cultures' approach outlined earlier, these updated versions of BrAsian youth identities centre on a very particular version of 'ethnicity' and 'cultural identity'. This sees BrAsian cultures as discrete and internally homogeneous 'ethnic bubbles', which have clearly defined boundaries and membership, core values and traditions, and which are, crucially, perceived as different from (and in the case of Muslim groups, opposed to) wider British society. BrAsian young people are then seen as either trapped within these ethnic bubbles and perpetuating problematic cultural identities, or as facing identity loss and crisis when they move outside these boundaries. Even within the more progressive and optimistic interpretations, which stress processes of continuity and change, this version of culture ignores both the ongoing experience of racism and disadvantage that structures the lives of BrAsian young people, and the more complex and multiple forms of youth identities and cultures. However, there is an alternative version of 'culture' which stresses power and complexity in its formation of identities and forms of cultural production—the 'new ethnicities' debate.

14 'The Asian Gang' is often linked to the globalisation of African-American hip-hop culture (cf. Macey, 1999). Bhatt has also noted the way in which religious identity forms the basis for 'gang' identification, although he notes the fluidity of these groupings (Bhatt, 1997: 269).

CONTESTING CULTURE: RE-IMAGINING ASIAN YOUTH IDENTITIES

Unlike the version of cultural difference outlined above, which places the emphasis on ethnicity as the primary source of identity creation, and insists on a coherent and bounded sense of self and community, 'new ethnicities' are defined through processes of fragmentation, change and contestation. Rather than a celebration of 'the mode of being', 'new ethnicities' are an assertion of the shifting, partial and contingent constructions of identity—on 'becoming'. This views ethnicity as only one axis of identity, which intersects with, and is inseparable from, other factors such as gender, class, sexuality, religion, locality, age and so on. While 'culture' remains at the centre of analysis, the 'new ethnicities' approach sees it not as a birthright or possession—something to be measured through language, dress, religion, marriage, food etc.—but as part of a socially, historically and politically located struggle over meaning and identity. Hall writes:

> Cultural identity, in this second sense, is a matter of 'becoming' as well as of 'being'.... Cultural identities come from somewhere, have histories. But like everything which is historical they undergo constant transformation ... subject to the continuous 'play' of history, culture and power. (Hall, 1992a: 225)

Rather than a unitary and stable whole, then, identity becomes something that is always in process, multiple and complex. The focus is not on bounded cultures or communities, but on networks, border zones and boundary crossings, where individual and collective identities are challenged and transformed. Central to this creation are the structures of power and inequality that intersect and constrain subordinated identities, but do not wholly determine the forms of their imagination or their resistance. Identities become open ended, unpredictable and often ambiguous in the ways they appear and are lived through.

The focus for the so-called 'politics of difference' has been primarily on new forms of cultural production, in cinema, literature, photography, fashion and particularly in music. This work has been concerned with exploring the hybrid and subversive forms of cultural 'cut-and-mix', which challenge dominant paradigms of ethnic minority identities (Gillespie, 1995). Perhaps unsurprisingly, these interests have been mainly concerned with emergent youth cultural styles and expressions, particularly those of the 'Black Atlantic' diaspora (Gilroy, 1993a). The engagement with contemporary forms of BrAsian youth cultural expression has been rather more tentative, seen as hidden within the confines of 'the community' and largely impenetrable to 'outsiders' (Baumann, 1996). Nevertheless, the successes of BrAsian youth cultural expression from the 1990s—from the musical interventions of artists from Apache Indian to the contemporary global achievements of Talvin Singh, Nitin Sawhney and Asian Dub Foundation, and the emergence of BrAsian cinema from *My Beautiful Laundrette* and *Bhaji on the Beach* to *East is East* and *Bend It Like Beckham*—point to the engagement of a new BrAsian sensibility with the British cultural mainstream. More broadly, youth cultural forms, from Bhangra to *Bollywood Dreams*, highlight the syncretic and globalised nature of BrAsian identities and their role in challenging racism and racial stereotypes (see Dwyer, Sharma, this volume).

The celebration of 'the new Asian cool', and its commodification of BrAsian 'new ethnicities', has, however, been subject to severe criticism for its neglect of structures of power and continuing racial inequalities. Thus Sharma, Hutnyk and Sharma (1996) argue that such an approach valorises ideas of 'the hybrid' and 'the marginal' as positive in and of itself, and ignores the relationships of dominance, exploitation and violence that constrain identity formation. Furthermore they critique the sociological interest in BrAsian cultures, and especially youth cultures, as part of a process of knowledge production inextricably linked to forms of social control and criminalisation. *Dis-Orienting Rhythms* (1996) aims to explore both these continued structures of control, and the more fractured, temporary and ambivalent spaces from which a 'cultural politics' may be articulated, recognising the unfinished and untidy nature of these encounters.[15]

My own work on *The Asian Gang* (2000) similarly explores the cross-cutting processes of freedom and constraint in the construction of Asian youth identities, though at an empirical level. Focusing on a small number of Bengali young men in London, the study examines the changing stereotypes of BrAsian youth and the ways in which these representations impact on the lives and identifications of young men themselves. The notion of the 'gang', as argued above, carries with it dominant ideas about culture, gender and generational crisis that has everyday implications for the lives of the young men, whether at school or in their leisure activities, or in their encounters with the police, teachers, youth workers and the local media. However, these structures and stereotypes do not wholly determine the choices and experiences of the young men, and the study also explores the complex and shifting forms of identity creation, particularly in their intersection with notions of community, masculinity, family and friendship. As with the *Dis-Orienting Rhythms* collection, *The Asian Gang* stresses the multiple and often contradictory stances that make up the category 'Asian youth', and the ways in which identities are used to lever open spaces for self-creation and contestation. 'Asian youth' identities are then formed in the encounter between

15 Bhatt (1997) also argues that supposedly essentialist/'pure' forms of Asian youth identification, such as those articulated around religion, also need to be placed within this framework of hybridity and new cultural politics.

(individual and collective) agency and historical and social process—a state of 'becoming' rather than 'being'.

It is perhaps worth reflecting that although BrAsian communities have been established for over forty years in Britain, the notion of 'the second generation' remains intact in the popular and sociological imagination. It carries with it ingrained ideas of an originary/parental culture and of a 'next' generation trapped between this ancestral homeland and the 'host' country—between old and new worlds, and the threat of belonging nowhere. The spectre of 'the between' continues to haunt accounts of Asian youth identities, even into the twenty-first century, providing a convenient explanation for everything from marriage partners and consumption patterns to religious practices, and from educational under-achievement and unemployment to crime and violence. Although there has been a shift in sociological accounts of Asian youth, away from generic accounts of intergenerational conflict and crisis, towards assertions of diversity and continuity, the primary focus has remained on ideas of 'ethnicity' and 'culture' as constituting the core, defining feature of ethnic minority identities.

At the same time, however, the idea of 'the second generation' has been taken up by Asian young people themselves and used to generate new cultural practices and new identities. Building on a history of anti-racist struggle and resistance, these 'new ethnicities' are challenging the ongoing structures of racism and racial disadvantage, and redefining what being 'Asian', 'British' or 'BrAsian' might mean. These identities recognise the fragmented and multiple ways of 'being' and 'becoming', with ethnicity/culture constituting only one amorphous element in intersection with cross-cutting axes of gender, class, religion, sexuality, age, location and so on. 'The second generation' is then being constantly imagined and re-imagined—from moment to moment, person to group, and from one 'second generation' to 'the next (second) generation'. It is perhaps here that its conceptual power, as a way of both marking and challenging difference, lies.

THE SCANDAL OF 'ARRANGED MARRIAGES' AND THE PATHOLOGISATION OF BrASIAN FAMILIES

Fauzia Ahmad

'For Zahida Sohrab, arranging the marriage of her sixteen-year-old daughter seemed perfectly normal. Like many Muslim women, she believed she was merely following tradition, but yesterday she admitted she had been wrong to force her child into the loveless union. Speaking after a judge annulled the marriage, Mrs Sohrab said: "I am really, really happy. I thank God that it's over. I can't explain how happy I am because it was our own mistake. It was nothing to do with my daughter."' (Starrs, Robertson and Holme, *Herald*, 24 April 2002)

Aneeka Sohrab was a sixteen-year-old student of Pakistani origin living in Glasgow, studying for her Scottish Highers when her mother, Zahida Sohrab, coerced her into marrying another Pakistani student, Raja Sulman Khan, then aged nineteen. Aneeka's story came to prominence in the spring of 2002 after she was granted an annulment on the grounds that the marriage was conducted under duress. This tragic tale of a marriage turned sour and of Asian parental pressure to conform was one of a number of cases that received wide press attention following a much publicised campaign by social and community activists and the British government in reaction to an increase in 'forced marriages'.

Reading this somewhat sensationalised, dramatic account of a practice that is representative of a tiny minority of the marriages conducted amongst BrAsian families in Britain, one might interpret this as an attempt to promote a discourse of pathology and stereotypes. However, a closer examination of the story reveals other aspects of the events and elicits questions about the ways in which BrAsian families and the practices surrounding their marriages are represented both in the populist press and within academic texts. In this particular case two key issues were significantly under-played by the media. One, Aneeka reconciled with her parents and sought their support very soon after the marriage. The parents, upon realising the severity of their mistake, were prepared to remove their daughter from what they realised was an unsuitable union that was causing her distress, regardless of the consequences to their public 'honour' (concepts of which will be briefly touched upon later). Two, the mother—identified along with the mother of the groom as one of the main instigators of the marriage—took the opportunity both to explain publicly her reasons for forcing her daughter into the marriage and to accept responsibility, again publicly, and renounce her own actions, including emotionally blackmailing her daughter into agreeing to the marriage. Consequently, the reductionist accounts so often presented in the media, of over-bearing, unsympathetic and unrelenting parents in such cases, were momentarily disrupted.

Nonetheless, in his summing up the judge, Lord McEwan, though obviously sympathetic to the situation in which both bride and groom found themselves, interpreted events in terms of a 'culture clash', where:

> 'It may be that in the multi-cultural society in which we now live such situations will continue to arise where ancient Eastern established cultural and religious ethics clash with the spirit of twenty-first-century children of a new generation and Western ideas, language and what these days passes for culture. There is inevitable tension, and clashes will happen.' (Quoted in *The Times Online*, 24 April 2002)

Both his comments and his language—note '*ancient* Eastern cultural and religious ethics'—reflect a general sense of confusion around definitions of 'arranged' versus 'forced' marriages that permeate public debates, betraying a certain hegemonic assumed superiority that prioritises 'Western' concepts of modernity over others. The Asian practice of 'arranged' marriages has always been viewed with a certain fascination in the West, even though historically the custom also had currency within European royal and aristocratic families. Yet despite Britain's colonial relationship with the Indian subcontinent, numerous anthropological accounts and, more recently, statements issued by senior politicians that attempt to draw distinctions between 'forced' and 'arranged' marriages (the former considered 'incompatible with British values' and the latter deemed 'acceptable' and even reflective of Britain's cultural diversity), the confusion exemplified by Lord McEwan's remarks, tempered with some imperialist disapproval, persists in both public and academic arenas.

'Arranged marriages' are among the main practices used to define the distinctiveness of the BrAsian in relation to other communities found in Britain. Indeed, 'arranged marriages' symbolise BrAsians and thus continue to be commonly abstracted as a metaphor for BrAsian life-styles. This chapter aims therefore to explore the ways in which the trope of 'arranged marriages' circulates as a sign of BrAsian 'otherness' and as a site for intervention and domestication of that otherness.

THICK DESCRIPTIONS

Early ethnographic monographs on South Asian families in the subcontinent and on South Asian settlers from the 1950s onwards typically concentrated on documenting kinship systems and household structures, specifically '*biraderis*' and '*khandans*', 'extended' and joint family systems and patrilineal descent, and on the inter-relationships and reproductions of social formations such as the 'giving and taking' of gifts, concepts of '*izzat*' (honour) and '*sharam*' (shame), gender relations, arranged marriages and purdah (C. Ballard, 1978; R. Ballard, 1982; Brah, 1978, 1993; Jeffrey, 1976; Saifullah Khan, 1977; Shaw, 1994, 2000; Werbner 1988; Wilson, 1978). 'Insularity' was a defining feature of migrant families then (and some would add still is) as the 'myth of return' seemed at first a possibility. However, this prospect appeared increasingly distant as families began to settle, grow and adapt to life in Britain (Saifullah Khan, 1977; Shaw, 1994, 2000; Ballard, 1994a; Brah, 1996; Anwar, 1998a) and as a consequence certain cultural practices were modified. Within this diasporic context migrant women, far from confirming stereotypes of secluded and 'passive Asian women', played key roles in contributing towards household economies, the reconstruction of cultural traditions, labour movements and emerging political dialogues (Wilson, 1978; Saifullah Khan, 1977; Bhachu, 1988, 1991, 1996; Werbner, 1988; Brah and Shaw, 1992; Brah, 1993, 1996).

All the while, the study of BrAsians has been dominated by a handful of themes ('inter-generational conflict', cultural conflict and negotiations and 'arranged marriages'), themes that have remained remarkably persistent, constituting the grammar by which BrAsian experiences are mediated and disseminated throughout society.

'ARRANGED' MARRIAGES / 'LOVE' MARRIAGES

What do 'arranged marriages' signify in a contemporary BrAsian context? 'Arranged marriages'—where, in the most general sense, parents, with their children's consent, take a lead role in choosing their spouses—are often presented as diametrically opposed to 'love marriages'. Of course, in cultures that value chastity, marriage is often viewed as the appropriate institution or avenue for the regulation and expression of sexuality for both sexes, but particularly so for women, and studies on the practice have almost exclusively focused on women as the objects of the 'process', situating other senior women and men as instigators and as their social controllers (for examples, see Brah on teenagers in West London, 1978; Basit on Pakistani and Bangladeshi schoolgirls in East England, 1996, 1997; Bhachu on Sikh women, 1991; Bhopal on South Asian women in East London, 1997, 1998, 1999, 2000; Bradby on young Punjabi women in Glasgow, 1999; and Shaw on Pakistanis in Oxford, 2000). However, the ambiguity around the term 'arranged marriage' (Bauman, 1996) attests not only to the complexity, variety and significance of definitions and practices that actually constitute 'arranged marriages', but also to the different meanings different groups of people and individuals attach to the term—meanings that are obviously subject to religious, sectarian, caste, cultural, class, educational and generational influences. Since 'love marriages'—an equally subjective term—are often presented as the polarised opposite of 'arranged marriages', the underlying assumption is that the choice of one or the other is in some way reflective of cultural or religious conformity and conservatism and also symbolic of the degree of integration into, and influence of, Western lifestyles.

Academic literature also describes arranged marriages as being circumscribed by rules determining matches based on religious, caste or regional affiliations. Hindu and Sikh marriages have been characteristically identified as exogamous, with members forbidden to marry within the kin group, but seeking unions with partners sharing similar, or higher caste backgrounds. Whilst their marriages are regarded as sacramental, Muslim marriages are contractual and are traditionally typified (though not exclusively so) as endogamous, within kinship groups (see Anwar, 1998a; C. Ballard, 1978; R. Ballard, 1982; Brah, 1978; Jeffrey, 1976; Saifullah Khan, 1977; Shaw, 1994, 2000; Stopes-Roe and Cochrane, 1990; Werbner, 1988; Wilson, 1978). Stopes-Roe and Cochrane (1990) additionally distinguish between four types of arranged marriage: 'traditional', in which parents and significant other family members would play an active part in selecting and contracting marriages, with limited, if any, consultation with the individuals concerned. Here emphasis would be placed on the union being conceptualised as a marriage between two families; 'modified traditional', in which the individual concerned would have the final say in agreeing to a union, but only with one of a selection of potential partners offered by the parents; 'co-operative traditional', in which, depending on circumstances, either the individual or the parent(s) would make the selection, but the final decision would be a joint one for which parental approval would be essential; and finally 'independent', which would most likely appropriate Western lines of courtship and marriage, but with emphasis placed on seeking parental approval. Stopes-Roe and Cochrane add that the key difference between this and Western models is that parental approval would be an expectation rather than a hope.

Shaw (2000) in her study of Pakistani Muslims in Oxford noted a process of social change in the practices and expectations that many of her respondents had when considering the marriage prospects of their children. When once the ideal was to satisfy obligations to family in Pakistan by seeking partners there, many parents and young people now acknowledged that differences in education and outlook, between those born and raised in Britain and those in Pakistan, meant that kinship marriages were not always reliable indicators of compatibility or marital success. However, the importance of securing matches with members of appropriate castes within Britain was still stressed. According to Shaw's predictions (supported by other research, e.g. C. Ballard, 1978; Brah, 1978; Stopes-Roe and Cochrane, 1990; Basit, 1996, 1997), the availability of suitable caste members and an extended definition of *biraderi*, coupled with a greater desire to find partners within Britain, would eventually lead to a decrease in the number of trans-national marriages with kinfolk. This is a prediction at odds with those made by a recent Foreign and Commonwealth report on community perceptions of 'forced marriages' (Samad and Eade, 2002).

Many studies, particularly the earlier ones, reported that their respondents viewed arranged marriages as more stable than 'love' marriages, and pointed to the significantly lower rates of divorce within Asian communities and the supportive role played by the extended family should problems arise. However, arranged marriages were often portrayed within an idealised European perspective as an ancient and rigid duty-bound system that suppressed individual freedoms and subjugated women, and as already noted were, and still are, sometimes confused with 'forced' marriages.

From as early as the late 1970s concerns were raised about the unduly negative focus Asian families and the practice of arranged marriages received both in the press and from government quarters, some of whom talked of 'discouraging the arranged marriage system in the hope that (Asian) parents would *respect* the rights of their children' (C. Ballard, 1978, my emphasis). Catherine Ballard also drew attention to how both populist and academic literature on arranged marriages tended to adopt a simplistic problem focus, highlighting mostly negative outcomes and attitudes, or stressing inter-generational and inter-cultural conflicts (ibid.). Not much has changed since. The 'clash of cultures' thesis that still underpins many melodramatic accounts, especially from the media, is supplemented by additional fears, voiced by Home Minister David Blunkett and Member of Parliament for Keighley, West Yorkshire, Ann Cryer, that BrAsians will continue to select partners from the subcontinent and thus be responsible for 'importing poverty' (*Evening Standard*, 2001). This concern is publicly and politically couched within the racialised discourse of the emancipation of women from forced marriages, the women being either recipients of spouses from overseas or the overseas subjects themselves. An additional criticism of academic treatments of arranged marriages noted how emphasis was placed on seeking the views of adolescents whose experiences and expectations of marriage were likely to be limited (C. Ballard, 1978). This point was echoed by Ahmad (2001) who also noted how young Asian informants were often expected to assume the role of 'cultural expert'. Challenges to authority and growing independence and individuality—natural manifestations of adolescence—tended to be viewed primarily as 'cultural rebellion' against Asian 'traditional' values, especially in the case of Asian girls and the question of marriage.

Recent studies on BrAsian women reveal a great diversity of attitudes towards marriage choices and document the increasing significance education, qualifications and/or professional employment hold when considering marriage and securing a suitable husband (Basit, 1996, 1997; Ahmad, 2001; Dale, Shaheen, Fieldhouse and Kalra, 2002a, 2002b; Ahmad, Modood and Lissenburgh, 2003). These support earlier findings from Bhachu's (1991) work in which she described how younger Sikh women's entry into the labour market was not 'dominated by patriarchy', as Bhopal (1997) would suggest (see below), but instead marked a dramatic shift in women's roles within the domestic sphere where women exercised considerable control over their lives both inside and outside the private domain. This was most significantly noted in relation to their consumption patterns particularly in the elaboration of dowries, which we shall discuss later.

HOW ARE SOUTH ASIAN FAMILIES PATHOLOGISED?

While earlier, anthropological accounts were discourses developed from the point of view of the 'outsider looking in' and were descriptive in nature, many contemporary academic accounts of BrAsian families and marriage practices acknowledge the developing processes of continuity and change, of adaptation and innovation, and the modification and renegotiation of cultural values that are mediated via ethnic or religious frameworks, and hence are careful to avoid perpetuating stereotypes based on simplistic and reductive binaries between 'modern' and 'traditional' values. Nevertheless, some accounts of arranged marriages still adopt an uncritical and assumed universalistic understanding of the expression that situates arranged marriages as immutable, static institutions fixed by both temporal and spatial boundaries. When conceptualised in this way, arranged marriages and Asian cultures are inclined to be presented in a wholly negative light. For example, Talbani and Hasanali, based on their work with Canadian schoolgirls, and with only limited reference to the wider issues of gender inequality in Canada, present an uncritical and generalised reference to the 'inertia of South Asian culture' (Talbani and Hasanali, 2000: 623), which they assert encourages the (*de facto*) subordination and subjugation of women through arranged marriages:

> The arranged marriage plays a central role in maintaining the subordinate role of women in society. Female subordination is expressed, validated and perpetuated through rites and symbols related to marriage. (Talbani and Hasanali, 2000: 626)

This view of homogeneous South Asian cultures and families necessarily excludes possibilities of diversity across religious and cultural expressions, and alternative positionalities that may allow for definitions that are fluid and fluctuating, subject to change and open to negotiation within and without immediate social groups. It also negates prospects for individual agency.

Similarly, other research on BrAsian women serves to invoke emotional responses of pity by reproducing stereotypes of Asian women as passive victims of (again) a homogenised South Asian culture that is inevitably oppressive towards them (cf. Wade and Souter, 1992; Bhopal, 1997, 1998, 1999, 2000). Although some differences in the meanings of 'arranged marriage' may be explored in such texts, these are often not contextualised sufficiently to account for religious, cultural or class locations, but are rather situated within a racist discourse of patriarchy, which, from its outset, assumes 'the family' to be a repressive and constraining structure. Like Talbani and Hasanali's analysis above, individual 'agency' within the framework of the 'Asian family' in these contexts appears to be limited and can only be achieved through active promotion of, and mobilisation around, clearly perceived Western discourses.

The forced marriage controversy (mentioned earlier) is another key example of how BrAsian families are publicly stigmatised and problematised. Despite public pronouncements by politicians acknowledging that 'forced' marriages are relatively rare, and that the vast majority of 'arranged marriages' are between freely consenting adults making them, therefore, 'compatible with British social values', the continued emphasis by both the media and politicians on the minority occurrence acts to negatively and disproportionately highlight and problematise 'arranged' marriages and thus BrAsian families. Little context is offered in order to help deviate from the inevitably damaging confusion that arises. For instance, there is still a dearth of quality research exploring in detail why some marriages result in varying elements of force, even less detailing the after-effects on both parents and children in such situations. However, crude hypotheses and conclusions about the 'over-bearing' and '*izzat*-obsessed' nature of BrAsian families abound.

Indeed, other facets of the arranged marriage process, such as defining concepts like '*izzat*' and '*sharam*' and the practice of dowry giving, can also be interpreted in ways that contribute to the pathologised discourse of Asian cultures as fixed and homogeneous. However, before discussing these further some consideration must be given to the ways in which certain theoretical structures are operationalised, effectively resulting in the reproduction of racist and stereotyped assumptions about 'the Other'.

Limits of patriarchy theory

Both Lazreg (1988) and Mohanty (1988) draw our attention to the broad influence of Western ideologies that not only construct fixed representations of the non-Western world, but also wield authority over 'Third World' women who themselves utilise these ideological tools when writing about their own communities. The resulting perpetuation of myths and stereotypes is observable when, for example, such approaches negatively problematise South Asian families and women. 'Patriarchy theory' is a good example of a 'grand' and over-arching Western feminist concept that is often discussed in relation to non-Western families. However, Ann Phoenix discusses the pathologisation of black families when gender theories based on white middle-class norms are applied without taking into account other structural issues such as race and class (Phoenix, 1997). Similarly, when discussing BrAsian families and arranged marriages, the application of theories that are culture-specific raises important questions that have significant implications for the ways in which data can be interpreted.

For example, as noted above, in recent years a number of new research publications have documented the processes of rapid social change amongst younger, British born and educated South Asian women, who are taking advantage of educational opportunities in their search for upward social mobility (Basit, 1996, 1997; Ahmad, 2001; Dale, Shaheen, Fieldhouse and Kalra, 2002a, 2002b; Ahmad, Modood and Lissenburgh, 2003). Brah's earlier work on South Asian Muslim women in the labour market also documented these emergent themes and like Bhachu (discussed above), acknowledged the influence patriarchal relations had on women's lives and their relationships with men in their families and communities, both local and wider (Brah, 1996). However, she was careful to avoid imposing patriarchy theory *per se* uncritically upon the Asian families she studied, in order to allow for fluidity and variation within male/female relationships.

We can contrast this approach with other recent publications on BrAsian families, women and attitudes and practices in relation to arranged marriages, that also document similar social changes as a result of higher education and professional occupational status, but have been less cautious and uncritical in adopting interpretive frameworks such as Walby's theories of patriarchy (cf. Bhopal, 1997, 1998, 1999). These inevitably tend to produce pathologised discourses of BrAsian families that imply that *all* South Asian family structures and gender relationships are inherently oppressive, placing particular emphasis on 'arranged marriages' in which Asian women are mere 'objects' or 'victims' rather than active subjects. Despite the wealth of research emphasising difference, diversity and complexity between and within social groups, their identities and their individuals, such interpretive structures also encourage rather than challenge the perpetuation of stereotyped, polarised and simplified dichotomies between 'traditional (Asian) women' and 'modern (Westernised) women'. One particular study on Asian women in Britain that advocates patriarchy theory as an appropriate analytical tool to examine South Asian family structures and practices, not only promotes such extreme dichotomies but further characterises 'traditional women' as those possessing few or no qualifications and 'therefore' likely to have arranged marriages with dowries, contrasting them with 'single, independent women' (or 'deviant' women), typified as highly educated and 'therefore' likely to have unanimously rejected dowries and arranged marriages (Bhopal, 1999: 129–32). This analytical framework also suggests that in order to achieve 'success' (which remains undefined), South Asian women have little option but to 'turn their backs on their religion and culture' and that individual 'agency' can only be exercised once the subject has consciously dissented from the familial and cultural group (Bhopal, 1997, 1998). Here it seems the only way to achieve a separate, individual identity is to 'assimilate' into British society. It concludes:

> It is through marriage that women are able to achieve respect and status in south Asian communities. Single women are stigmatized and regarded as having failed the community.… South Asian women's identity is achieved through the men in their communities. (Bhopal, 1999: 133)

In addition, the notion that 'arranged marriages' are representative of a male dominated South Asian identity becomes further re-emphasised and essentialised so that within this analytical framework, a rejection of an 'arranged marriage' is interpreted as a rejection of identity (Bhopal, 1997). Clearly this form of analysis presents us with a number of conceptual problems. As highlighted by the above example, the adoption of patriarchy theory as an interpretive framework for understanding Asian families and cultural practices effectively essentialises arranged marriages both as fixed in practice and experience, and as a representative feature of Asian women's identities that, incidentally, were not their own but belonged to their respective families and communities. Apart from masking the diversity of experiences and differences within South Asian communities and their practices and beliefs around marriage, and failing to situate the above work within a wider social context (for example, by referring to social class differences and racism, or even accounting adequately for the apparently contradictory evidence from other studies), sweeping and simplistic generalisations and stereotypes are made. For instance, the 'modern/traditional' binaries that this theoretical perspective invites bear little resemblance to the various forms of agency exhibited by South Asian women in numerous other research studies (e.g. Bhachu, 1991, 1996; Brah, 1993, 1996; Brah and Shaw, 1992; Shaw,

1994, 2000; Jhutti, 1998; Bradby, 1999; Dwyer, 1999; Ahmad, 2001; Ahmad, Modood and Lissenburgh, 2003; Ramji, 2003) and serves instead, to further promote a set of static stereotypes that contribute to a general problematisation of South Asian women, their families, cultures and their identities.

Social realities such as a general rise in marrying ages among educated Asian women (itself a national statistic for the population as a whole) and difficulties in securing a suitable marriage partner—which could be attributed to wider difficulties and/or a product of limited leisure time due to expectations to work longer hours—are interpreted either as a 'rejection of arranged marriages' or as a failure on the part of the woman (Bhopal, 1997, 1998). Alternative conceptualisations of marriage practices that remain sympathetic to cultural and religious sensibilities are similarly not accounted for. Nor is the prospect that younger Asian men, or even parents, are also experiencing and expressing social change and differences in expectations with regards to marriage.

In the broader context of South Asian and BrAsian relationships and cultural practices, 'tradition' and 'traditional' are commonly associated with oppressive patriarchal relations of power. However, certain contradictions exist both in the definitions of the terms 'tradition' and 'traditional' as understood by respondents in some studies and within the sociological and anthropological literature. For instance, 'traditional' can in some carefully defined contexts mean 'un-Westernised', 'backward' or 'un-educated', but it can also signify a historical link with cultural practices that have positive connotations. This may be better illustrated by reference to certain aspects of a 'traditional' marriage, many of which, such as the *mehndi* (henna) night, the clothes and jewellery etc., are greeted with enthusiasm. 'Traditional' can also refer to modes of behaviour such as displaying respect towards elders. Consider also its usage when describing a 'traditional English pub' or 'traditional family values'. However, 'Westernised' or 'modern' may be interpreted by researchers and respondents alike as inter-changeable terms that represent the alternative to being 'traditional'. Clearly to equate only Western cultures with being 'modern' is patronising to say the least, yet few studies adequately define these terms, which is ironic given their wide employment. Both Hall (2000a) and Sayyid (1997) offer interesting contemporary discussions on the ways in which these binaries are easily and uncritically reproduced.

While accepting the persistence of genuine gender inequalities within some Asian familial practices is necessary, equally important is the need to adequately address and contextualise the racialised nature of gender relationships and the capitalist structures that underpin them, highlighting not only where complexities and ambivalences lie, but also where resistance to inequities exist, and the forms these inequities take. Without such an understanding, any analysis that relies solely on highlighting gender inequalities within racialised families is in danger of re-enforcing not only stereotypes, but also the racialised inequalities that act to mask diversity within groups and areas of mutual struggle. These points are well made by Parmar (1982) in relation to Amrit Wilson's early work, the acclaimed *Finding A Voice*, and more recently by Puwar (2003).

Patriarchy theory then, when applied uncritically to explore BrAsian marital practices, has a number of significant limitations. Specifically, and in the context of the current discussion, these can include the promotion of extreme binaries, a homogenising of culture and failure to account for diversity not just within South Asian ethnic groups but also within individual families, and the privileging and promotion of a hegemonic, colonialist-inspired discourse of Western cultural superiority. Such theoretical inadequacies can produce pathologised analyses of BrAsian families that are seriously flawed, essentialised and reductive. These in turn only serve to detract from key empirical findings (such as the educational success of younger BrAsian women), which unfortunately become secondary to the analytical framework. Of further concern are the ways in which such Western structural theories, when operationalised to describe non-Western societies, can act not only to pathologise certain social groups but also to silence forms of agency and difference that do not conform. The resulting racialised discourses can suggest that to be 'educated' and South Asian is to be 'Westernised', 'modern' and secular while to be 'traditional' and accept an arranged marriage and partake in dowry production and consumption is to be 'un-educated' and 'backward'. The choices and opportunities to exist within or outside these boundaries become necessarily constrained and negatively problematised. These pathologies are not restricted to everyday stereotypes employed by the media as part of its on-going orientalist discourse, but are normalised and deeply ingrained misconceptions that extend into the academic working environment.

Izzat and sharam

The related and oft recurring themes of *izzat* (honour) and its antonym *sharam* (shame) are also considered deterministic elements of South Asian cultures (and of Mediterranean and Middle Eastern societies too), but the extent to which these concepts are developed is limited. Many authors have typically defined *izzat* as a facet of male honour while female relations are situated as the subordinates who are its 'carriers' or representatives. For example:

> A woman can have '*izzat*' but it is not her own—it is her husband's or her father's. Her '*izzat*' is a reflection of the male pride of the family as a whole. (Wilson, 1978: 5)

Implicit within such fixed definitions is an underlying assumption, in keeping with anthropological accounts, of *izzat* as a strategically manipulated outcome of actions and alliances. The extent to which cultural norms of *izzat* and purdah are reproduced from the subcontinent to Britain vary according to factors such as kinship group, particular family practices, degrees of education and socialisation with the host community and the concentration of clan group members or townsfolk from the country of origin. However, this is rarely acknowledged in the literature. Scant attention has been given to expanding concepts like *izzat* and *sharam* to encompass female-centred narratives of personal honour or shame (or indeed male-personalised renderings), or to offer alternative accounts that might suggest shifting boundaries and dynamic conceptualisations. One of the few to do this is Bradby (1999) who, in discussing younger Muslim women and their marriage choices in Glasgow, suggests that female honour may alternatively be mediated through a positive assertion of religion, or through professional employment. This is in stark contrast to Wilson (1978) and others (e.g. Bhopal, 1997, 1999), who present more immutable, essentialised views of *izzat*. By failing to fully account for definitions of *izzat* and *sharam* as dynamic and evolving processes that are both gender and context specific, the majority of the academic literature inadvertently reproduces a regulative and deterministic discourse that contributes to pathological and stereotyped representations of Asian families.

Dowries—oppression or expression?

'Dowry' is subject to differing interpretations dependent on religion, caste and social location, amongst others (see Menski, 1998 for some discussion of its varying forms). For instance, Muslim marriages are contractually dependent upon the payment of a dower (*mahr*) from the bridegroom to the bride, but South Asian Muslims also engage in the broader cultural practice, shared with Hindus and Sikhs, of 'dowry giving' from the bride's parents to the bride upon her wedding of items which will also include a number of gifts to the bridegrooms family. The extent to which these are 'demands' from the bridegroom's family or are voluntary gifts is subject to much variation.

Changing patterns in, and perceptions of, dowry production and consumption across BrAsian groups and the noted rise in marrying ages, particularly amongst women, are both features that are reflective of continuity and change within contemporary British contexts. Dowry giving, dowry elaboration and dowry abuse are areas that have recently received attention within the academic literature though, as already noted, the theoretical frameworks employed to interpret them are as important as the empirical data itself. Dowry abuse, the issues around which are particular and detailed and will not be dealt with here, should be acknowledged as another significant aspect of female oppression that is particular to Asian families but remains specific in its context and scope. It is also one that retains powerful and disturbing images and insights that the media are often quick to sensationalise. Interested readers should consult the many detailed and contextualised accounts in Menski (1998).

However, representations of dowry within the broader academic literature are still worth exploring, particularly to compare two very differing analyses of the ways in which the concept of dowry production in BrAsian marriages relates to issues of identity formation, agency and control, and to representations of BrAsian women and families.

Bhachu's (1991, 1996) work from the early 1990s, later supported by Jhutti's work with Sikh women in Britain (1998), documented the relationship between BrAsian Sikh women's economic participation and independence and the construction and elaboration of their dowries or *daj*. While recognising the hierarchical nature of Asian family structures and the asymmetrical relationship between dowry givers and dowry takers, both presented an analysis of social change and cultural renegotiation that was reflective of women's changing roles in the domestic sphere and the public realm as more Sikh women became more economically active. Instead of remaining passive in the process of dowry exchange, their greater financial autonomy meant that they exercised a high degree of control over the content of their dowries, with the often full expectation of maintaining control over the contents once they were married. Although the content was subject to local and personal variations in taste and spending power, it essentially reproduced the main constituents of the 'traditional' *daj* (clothes, gold, household items and affinal gifts). Thus the women became active participants in the cultural elaboration of their dowries, which illustrated how 'cultural baggage' is re-modelled and re-appropriated in order to fit-in with local, postcolonial environments and localised identities. By adopting a postcolonial view of identity construction, Bhachu explored consumption patterns and elaborations of dowries as a means to challenge stereotypes of Asian women as 'passive victims'. In contrast, Bhopal's analysis of patriarchy served to reproduce stereotypes of dowries as fixed processes that situated Asian women within a structure of 'degradation and despair'. Despite a broad variety of definitions, and respondents offering assorted reasons for the giving of dowry—with the majority stating that dowries were gifts given to daughters by parents—Bhopal maintains that women are 'objects of social control in the family' and that marriage practices such as dowry exemplify and act to sustain her subordinate position:

> Dowry property is not women's wealth, but wealth that goes with women. Women are the vehicles by which it is transmitted, rather than its owners. Dowry

functions to disinherit women and promote their economic dependence upon men. (Bhopal, 1997: 87)

Bhopal's extension of patriarchy theory to the processes of dowry giving and taking once again demonstrate how dominant, hegemonic discourses are used to construct pathologised accounts of arranged marriages and Asian families. When discussing dowry giving, the desire to pander to an interpretive framework of patriarchy renders other forms of self-realisation, expression and agency, such as those described by Bhachu (1991, 1996) and Jhutti (1998), absent.

The patriarchal analysis cited above consistently fails to account for diversity in practices of dowry giving even across religious groups, preferring instead to reiterate and accept as given a simplified, overly generalised and stereotyped discourse of women's subordination, 'religious and social inferiority', subservience to both family and husband, subjugation and passivity, citing a lack of education as the cause of women choosing to engage and renegotiate with cultural practices and processes (Bhopal, 1997). Given these assertions, it is a wonder that any woman would wish to marry into an Asian family. And yet this vision of BrAsian cultures and family life stands in isolation not only from other studies but from social realities such as the huge globalised flow of commercial goods and cultural artefacts, proof of which can be found in the expanse of boutiques and wedding emporiums found in many high streets in densely populated Asian areas, not to mention the rapid rise in BrAsian glamour magazines (such as *Asian Woman* and *Asian Bride*) that cater for young, dynamic, educated and professional Asian women, with a heavy emphasis on BrAsian fashion, wedding features and relationships with a strong 'BrAsian' theme. While the readership of such magazines may well be influenced by Western attitudes—none of the other studies referred to suggest otherwise—they are active participants in the reconstruction, re-appropriation and re-negotiation of cultural formations.

SOCIAL CHANGE AND MARRIAGE

Changing forms of matrimonial practice may appear to be somewhat at odds with more 'traditional' methods of partner selection—notions of *khandan*, *biraderi* or caste may still persist, but to what extent are these seen as significant by BrAsians searching for their own partners?

Of those discussed so far, the vast majority of the studies that examined attitudes towards marriage noted a wide diversity of opinions and changing practices and accepted norms within and across religious, caste, class and ethnic groups, though Muslims were generally reported to be the most 'traditional' or socially conservative. Some survey evidence suggests slight increases in the numbers of marriages with partners outside cultural and religious groups, although at the moment men are more likely to 'marry out' (Modood *et al.*, 1997). Nevertheless, anecdotal evidence also shows that women are displaying similar patterns, although caution must be exercised to avoid assuming that such marriages represent active dissent from cultural and religious backgrounds.

Another interesting feature to emerge from some studies on BrAsian women, and on Muslim young women in particular, was the reported role parents played in encouraging their daughters' education, if only partly to increase their chances of success in the 'marriage market' (Basit, 1996, 1997; Dale *et al.*, 2002a and 2002b; Ahmad, Modood and Lissenburgh, 2003). Ahmad (2001) further identified the role fathers in particular played in encouraging their daughters' higher education. This is in stark contrast to research that characterises Muslim fathers and families as exercising extreme patriarchal restraints on the education and careers of their daughters (cf. Wade and Souter, 1992; Khanum, 1995).

There is even some evidence to suggest that within Westernised and contemporary contexts attitudes towards sexual relationships are also changing—more so amongst Hindu and Sikh communities than for Muslim—although across all three faiths pre-marital sex is generally frowned upon (Hennink, Diamond and Cooper, 1999). It was also found that those less likely to engage in sexual relationships were those who identified strongly with their religion and that these tended to be Muslim and Sikh young women, many of who expected their marriages to be arranged. Drury (1991) found similar attitudes among the young Sikh women she interviewed, some of who had secret relationships but still expected their marriages to be arranged and were conscious of the need to maintain their parents' *izzat*. Similarly, the significance of marriage, how a partner is sought, when it occurs and to whom are all subject to much variation according to differences in religion, sect or caste, culture, education and social class.

From Auntie Gee's to cyber love to speed dating

While many pioneer settlers either arrived married or returned to their country of origin to marry before bringing their spouses to Britain, BrAsians face a different set of issues when looking for a partner. The rise of matrimonial agencies catering for the needs of BrAsians is a relatively new phenomenon that warrants further scrutiny, not least because of their growing acceptance as an appropriate means of finding a spouse in the absence of more extended family networks. The sheer variety of options, ranging from parental led adverts suggesting a more 'traditional' approach that invites family and parental participation, to matrimonial parties (again hugely different in style from familial based ones) to 'singles nights' and internet dating, is vast, and demand suggests a growing need for 'outside' assistance in securing a matrimonial partner. Some of these are general and are open to South Asians from all faiths, while others, such as the huge numbers of Muslim matrimonial websites and agencies, are religion specific. All represent significant, contemporary responses to trans-national migrations and changing cultural landscapes. The following two examples are illustrative of the variety that suggests the marriage industry is indeed 'big business'.

Sunni Muslim family seeks suitable match for their British born daughter. BSc Hons medical professional, age 32 years, height 5′ 4″, very attractive, slim, sophisticated, articulate, appreciates both East/West values. We are seeking a British national, graduate professional doctor, dentist, pharmacist, optician, lawyer or chartered accountant. Age up to 37 years. (Typical example of an ad from the British-based Urdu newspaper, *Daily Jang*)

Asian Dating Service for Muslims, Hindus, Sikhs, and all other faiths and lifestyles. Friendship, fun, marriage.... Full access to the Asian Introduction Agency's database. Your own detailed profile online, with a photo if you like. No monthly or annual membership. You're a member for as long as you need us! The freedom to write as many secure e-mails as you like. Flexible service; your details can be amended at any time. Meet single Asian men and women from all over UK. London, Birmingham, Bradford, Manchester. (support@asians4asians.com, http://www.asians4asians.com/html/contact_us.html)

The first of these examples betrays a number of other persistent features that are briefly worth noting, such as the emphasis placed on physical attributes and the importance of attracting a 'good' *rishta* (match) such as a doctor, dentist, lawyer etc. Note also the preference for a British national and the weight attached to an appreciation of 'East/West values'. It may also be significant that the majority of ads in the paper and on many matrimonial websites are from women.

'Asian speed dating' is the newest phenomenon to dominate the current BrAsian scene with separate evenings catering for Hindu, Sikh and Muslim groups. These have so far proved to be immensely popular (with much media interest), although it is too early to assess their long-term success in terms of securing future marriages. Originally based on an idea developed by US Jewish groups to facilitate marriages within the religion, a 'speed dating' evening usually consists of between 20–30 three minute meetings with prospective partners, following which participants indicate preferences on a form which is then returned to the organisers at the end of the evening, while a copy is retained for the participant. Matches are secured on the basis of 'mutual liking' after which e-mail details are exchanged for couples to continue correspondence if they wish (http://www.asianspeedd8.com).

The rapid increase in alternative forms of marital introductions from within the BrAsian community and the BrAsian Muslim community alone suggests that dynamic re-negotiations of Asian and Islamic concepts around methods of partner selection and marriage are taking place, especially in light of educational and economic success. For Muslims these remain within the bounds of religious acceptability, which for many takes precedence over culture.

Ethnographic material on BrAsian families, though no doubt rich in detail, is primarily based on families from peasant or rural backgrounds, and often overlooks families from semi-rural or urban backgrounds, with distinctly different attitudes, expectations and obligations towards the family. This can result in the production of deterministic accounts where the researcher actively highlights key features and structures that s/he deems significant. The interest in arranged marriages, religion, *izzat*, purdah or veiling for Muslim women are examples where over-arching reductionist frameworks are used to impute meaning to the lives of those studied and to limit the scope of discourse on BrAsian families. Furthermore, by focusing fieldwork in areas of high Asian concentration, the search for structure that underpins much ethnographic work sometimes inadvertently 'tribalises' and essentialises Asian families in a way that limits their participation to 'objects' of social research (Ahmad, 2003). This influences not only the media and wider public opinion, but also Asian men and women working within academia who may reproduce such discursive formations. Social classes, histories, specific regional and family dynamics etc. can all play roles in the ways South Asian practices may, or equally may not, impact on the lives of women. To ignore these in discussions of religion and gender produces reductive categories.

With divorce rates for BrAsian couples also on the increase, more attention needs to be paid to research that looks at the breakdown of marital relations within Asian families and whether culturally and religiously sensitive mediation services are available and are utilised. Similarly, research on the divorce experiences of BrAsians from Hindu, Sikh and Muslim backgrounds, and the ways in which cultural and religious considerations are accommodated for, if at all, within the current judicial system is urgently needed (Shah-Kazemi, 2001).

Given a whole host of reasons—including the wide ranging descriptions attributed to 'arranged marriages' within both cultural and religious perspectives, the new dimensions of the ways in which marriages are conceptualised and contracted, the changing formations and negotiations within BrAsian family structures and the shifting boundaries of continuity, change, acceptability and unacceptability—it may well be appropriate to adopt newer terminologies such as 'assisted marriage' (cf. Ahmad, 2001) and fresher approaches to researching and writing about Asian families in general. Indeed, such may be overdue.

QUEER

Shafqat Nasir

Despite critiques of binarism and the knowledge of the ways in which we use identity strategically, in naming and claiming social constructions, we still invest in a sense of self. The mathematical additive formula (Black + South Asian + Woman + Gay…) is not only unwieldy but returns us to a sense that the sum equals the person, leading to closure. Neither binarism nor addition addresses the complexities of our experience of ourselves or others. The search for a term that describes oneself in relation to others, one that allows us to feel a sense of belonging, can involve both an implicit and an explicit rejection of identities. This is the case when that identity is chosen or imposed, because both are part of the force-field of attraction and repulsion, preference and denial.

The mental images and connotation that accompany 'South Asian Diaspora' are somewhat different to 'Paki'. While the first can be seen as a positive affirmation—the sound of the sitar sampled into an 'ethnic' remix of 'golden brown', colourful spices, sumptuous silk, sensual, oriental and exotic—the second is a disharmonious jarring of dirt, grease and the smell of stale take-away curries. Clearly, class-based notions of culture, reflecting different profiles of migration are at play, but so too is sexuality and its articulation through 'race' (and vice-versa). The incompatibility of 'Paki' with 'sexy' means that being the first precludes the possibility of having a sexual identity, particularly when that sexual identity also exists in an environment of highly charged alterity.

The Gay Village in Manchester is often talked of as a safe space, and although in my twenty years in the city I had seen racism here, I was taken aback when the taunt 'you kissed a Paki in the club' came hurtling in my direction. Three white women, slightly drunk, leaning on each other, one looking embarrassed, saying 'get lost', laughing. At the time, I was walking towards the taxi rank. I didn't, as Nike suggest, 'Stand up and speak out about racism', but having had a drink I felt safe enough to say sarcastically 'that's nice!'

The woman who had been actively taunting the other turned around and, saying 'Are you talking to me?', punched me in the face. She then turned away laughing and resumed her position in the group. I was stunned. As they walked away, I had a knee-jerk reaction, followed them and managed to hit my assailant lightly on the back. As she and her friends turned, I realised I should be scared. I stepped back and called, 'Police'. As the group moved towards me, an older white woman in the passing crowd stepped in front of me and calmly said 'leave her alone', to which the woman who had punched me replied, 'she's not getting away with that.'

I turned to the crowd and asked if anyone had seen her hit me. People turned away. I even asked the taxi drivers, mostly Pakistani, in Punjabi, whether they would back me up, but they made it clear they didn't want to get involved. The police arrived and went straight to the group of three women, who had changed their demeanour, hands stuffed into pockets, aggression tamed and all smiles for the police. It seemed like everyone had been here before. When the police came over they didn't ask me what happened, but said the women claimed I had been calling them 'dirty lesbians'. Amazed that it hadn't occurred to them, I exclaimed, 'I'm a fucking lesbian.' The police's only response was a caution about my language. I explained the series of events, but to be honest I don't think they were listening. At one point one of the women said, 'if you don't like it here you shouldn't come', following which the police told them to be quiet, and several people in the crowd became angry—with me, because they assumed the three white women were *bona fide* lesbians and that the 'Paki' had indeed upset them in 'their space'. When I asked the police what they were going to do they said I could either spend the night in a cell with the three women or let it go. I asked for their names and numbers, at which point they turned accusatory, saying they had me 'starting it' recorded on camera. Leave and forget it was their only advice.

It seems that even in these days of diaspora, hybridity and fluid identity there remains amongst the public and in police discourse a fixed notion of 'race' and place, both geographical and ethereal. On the 'gaydar' of the internet terms like 'No GAMs'—no Gay Asian Males—circulate. There are of course sites like *Asian Babes* which transform their Barbie dolls by replacing Shalwar Kameez with tight short skirts, but debasing 'ethnic identity' is often a necessary ingredient in producing a sexually 'tasty dish'.

Public spaces are in part constructed by public policy and policing hate crime is a term most members of metropolitan police forces are aware of, but the simplistic orientation to reducing such crimes to a single factor often makes nonsense of victims' attempts to name and define criminal behaviour. Indeed they can lead to a questioning of who the victim is, and perhaps even a questioning of the discourse of victimhood itself. Policing identity is both a wider and more intimate issue.

A CITY OF SURPRISES[1]

URBAN MULTICULTURALISM AND THE 'LEICESTER MODEL'

Gurharpal Singh

The understanding of multiculturalism as a public policy in Britain has been greatly influenced and shaped by the lived experience of ethnic minorities in the large cities. Beginning with the first pioneering studies in the 1960s (Rex and Moore 1967), the urban disturbances of the 1980s (Beynon and Solomos 1987) and the more recent riots in northern industrial towns in the summer of 2001, the urban landscapes where ethnic minorities have settled have always provided a testing ground for the effectiveness of public polices; and the dramatic manifestation of breakdown, as evident in recent riots, often call into question wider ideals of multiculturalism. The disturbances of 2001 were no exception. In retrospect they will probably mark a turning point for the Labour government that came to power in 1997 as 'New Labour' with its agenda of a 'Cool Britannia' in which cultural diversity was to be celebrated. In a brief period of four years, against the background of the pressures generated by asylum seekers, the hostility to the report by the *Commission on the Future of Multi-Ethnic Britain* (2000), the urban riots and the fallout from September 11th, Labour policy has performed something of a *volte-face*. Increasingly the language of a 'cohesive nation' and 'community cohesion' has superseded the rhetoric of 'Cool Britannia' with its promise of a 'community of communities'.

This policy reversal can be seen most clearly in the official analyses and recommendations for dealing with the 2001 disturbances in the northern industrial towns (*Building Cohesive Communities*, 2001; *Community Cohesion*, 2001; *Community Pride*, 2001). Eloquently captured in the dramatic phrase 'parallel lives'—of whites and non-whites where riots broke out—the new approach concentrates on the need to build community cohesion alongside the pursuit of racial and ethnic equality. Cultural pluralism and diversity, it is argued, has to be tied more firmly to a clearer definition—and obligations—of citizenship and the

[1] This chapter first appeared as 'Multiculturalism in Contemporary Britain: Reflections on the "Leicester Model" ', *International Journal on Multicultural Societies*, 5, 1 (2003), pp. 40–54.

need to develop a shared conception of nationhood. A *laissez-faire* approach to multiculturalism, it is conjectured, can be a prescription for *de facto* apartheid (*Community Cohesion*, 2001: 9–12). This new emphasis in policy is envisioned as being realised in practice through a set of promotional policies, national legislation and targeted local policies. The broad array of urban regeneration programmes and local authorities are seen as the best agents for promoting community cohesion while recognising the need to value diversity. In the future local authorities are likely to be required to develop community cohesion strategies that, among other things, prioritise the need to promote inter-cultural contact (Local Government Association, 2002).

The emphasis on community cohesion as the explanatory cause of recent riots can perhaps be explained by an understanding of the disassociational nature of community relations in the northern industrial towns, a disassociation fostered, it is claimed, by the policies of local authorities which failed to arrest separate development. In contrast the apparent 'success' of local authorities like Southall and Leicester in avoiding such riots, it is suggested, can be attributed to a range of policies and institutional practices that have, over time, checked the development of community dissonance, at least enough to avoid any cause for concern (*Community Cohesion*, 2001: 15). These assertions, as we shall see, remain to be critically evaluated. Nonetheless, the official recognition of its achievements has led Leicester City Council (LCC) to begin the process of evolving a new community cohesion strategy that it is hoped 'will put Leicester at the forefront of national initiatives on this sensitive issue and will be suitable for dissemination to other authorities' (Leicester City Council, 2002).

This chapter explores how this state of affairs has come about and to what extent the rhetoric about Leicester reflects developments in the locality, by focusing on: (1) a brief background to the development of Leicester as a multicultural city; (2) a review of the explanations offered for Leicester's 'success'; (3) a reflection on the contemporary challenges of managing diversity; and (4), the extent to which the Leicester experience throws a meaningful light on community cohesion and the contemporary debate on multiculturalism in Britain.

LEICESTER AND ETHNIC DIVERSITY

The city of Leicester, once described by a local historian as 'wholly uninteresting', and by J.B. Priestly as 'lacking in character', today portrays itself as a model of civic multiculturalism, a place of 'many surprises'. This transformation of a provincial East Midlands market city into a vibrant multicultural locality is a process that began after the Second World War and only reached its climax in the 1990s (Martin and Singh, 2002).

ETHNIC GROUP COMPOSITION OF LEICESTER AND BRITAIN, 1991

	Leicester		*Britain*	
	%	*Population*	*%*	*Population ('000)*
White	71.5	193,502	94.5	51,873.8
Black Caribbean	1.5	4,112	0.9	500.0
Black African	0.3	745	0.4	212.4
Black other	0.6	1,756	0.3	178.4
Indian	22.3	60,279	1.5	840.3
Pakistani	1.0	2,644	0.9	476.6
Bangladeshi	0.4	1,053	0.3	162.8
Chinese	0.3	770	0.3	156.9
Asian other	1.0	2,570	0.4	197.5
Other	1.1	3,044	0.5	290.2
Total	100.0	270,493	100.0	54,888.8

Source: Vertovec, 1994.

According to the 2001 Census Leicester's ethnic minority population is over 35 per cent; some projections suggest that by 2011 it will exceed 50 per cent. Furthermore, 45 per cent of the pupils in primary and secondary school are from ethnic minorities.[2] Ethnic minorities are increasingly attracted to Leicester from other locations in Britain and the European Union. Leicester is synonymous with a thriving BrAsian business sector with a rich cultural life that increasingly plays host to a wide variety of festivals such as *Diwali*. As lead articles in the *International Herald Tribune* (10 February 2001), the *New York Times* (8 February 2001) and the *Guardian* (1 January 2001) have pointed out, Leicester is popularly seen as, and officially views itself as, a prosperous East Midlands city that has developed a relatively successful approach to managing ethnic diversity and promoting tolerance.

However, this image contrasts remarkably with the picture of the city in the 1970s as the 'most racist' place in Britain where the white provincial equipoise was shattered by the arrival of East African and Ugandan Asians in the late 1960s and the early 1970s (Marett, 1988). More than 20,000 Ugandan Asians settled in Leicester after 1972 despite determined efforts by the political leadership of the LCC to discourage this influx. By 1981 the ethnic minority population of the city had increased to 59,709, an almost three-fold rise in a decade. By 1991 it had increased

2 Estimates based on interviews with LCC officials, *Guardian*, 1 January 2001.

by an additional 17,264 to 76,973. Gujarati East Africans constitute the largest segment of this population, representing about a fifth of the city's total population. In addition to East African Asians and the migration of New Commonwealth immigrants from India, Pakistan and the Caribbean, since the Second World War Leicester has also been the magnet for European migrants from Poland (3,000), Ukraine (3,000), Serbia (500) and Lithuania (Winstone, 1996). Therefore, Leicester's ethnic diversity is not merely bi-polar (whites vs. non-whites): there is considerable diversity *within* these two categories.

The sudden change in the city's demography in the 1970s set off a wave of local racism through which the neo-Nazi National Front established a significant foothold. Bitter conflicts in the workplace and on the streets ensued. In scenes reminiscent of the riots in the northern industrial towns in recent years, an anti-racist movement emerged led by local activists to counter not only the activities of overt racists but also, and perhaps more significant, institutionalised racism within the Labour movement (Marett, 1988: chapters 1 and 3). Young activists within the Labour Party seized the opportunity to outmanoeuvre 'Old Labour' and construct a new political programme around a civic vision of multicultural Leicester. In so doing they were responding as much to local needs as to national developments such as the Race Relations Act (1976) which placed special duty on local authorities to promote racial equality. The multicultural turn in Leicester's politics strengthened Labour's position, ushering in a one-party dominance; it also created new challenges for how the vision was to be implemented, sustained and redefined in the light of continuing pressures from both within and without.

EXPLAINING LEICESTER'S 'SUCCESS'

Given the political capital invested in the advocacy of Leicester's relative 'success' in managing ethnic diversity, it is surprising that these claims have so far avoided systematic scrutiny. This section evaluates the above narrative together with auxiliary explanations that are often offered for *why* Leicester is different.

Political leadership

In the narrative of the development of Leicester as a multicultural city the role of the Labour Party's political leadership in bringing about radical change is seen as the major factor that facilitated the development of a civic multicultural policy. Multiculturalism as a public policy is counterposed to institutionalised racism, the pursuit of diversity to counteract overt racism aimed at new settlers (Winstone, 1996). The new policy in the late 1970s, it is suggested, marked a radical rupture with civic conventional wisdom by opening up the political market to ethnic recruitment and ensuring that the pursuit of racial and ethnic equality was accompanied by changes in the services delivered by local government. This policy had three key features: the pursuit of equality, the employment of black and ethnic minority staff to ensure that it reflected their proportion within the city's population, and promotional policies to celebrate diversity and combat discrimination within the LCC and civic life. In short, the LCC witnessed a 'municipal revolution' along the lines effected by many radical Labour councils in the early 1980s of which the Greater London Council led by Ken Livingston was the premier example (Ball and Solomos, 1990).

There is much of substance in this narrative, although it overemphasises the *discontinuity* in policy, the importance of the new departure (*Guardian*, 1 January 2002). To be historically accurate, a progressive caucus within the Labour Party had emerged in 1972, at the height of the Ugandan Asian crisis, in opposition to the official leadership which then controlled the LCC (Marett, 1988: 59). This caucus eventually became the basis of the radical left ruling group who ascended to power on the policy of multiculturalism. Hence it consolidated the Labour vote-bank by providing new sources of support and recruitment for the party. Multiculturalism opened up access to inner-city development funds that became the foundations for establishing patron-client relationships between the local authority and ethnic community groups. This enabled new ethnic minority leadership within the city to be co-opted into key structures of power within the local state. Yet apart from the overarching political commitment, the policy generally elided more difficult questions of generating an inter-cultural consensus around which multiculturalism as an ideology could be more firmly rooted in the local soil. In so far as these were addressed, they were confronted primarily in terms of discrimination and the celebration of diversity through religious and cultural festivals such as *Diwali*, *Eid*, and *Vaisaki*. These narrow boundaries have remained the source of both strength and weakness in the multicultural experiment in Leicester.

'Twice migrants' in a buoyant local economy

Political explanations are frequently supplemented by other factors to highlight Leicester's exceptional status. Foremost among these is the assertion that Leicester's diverse and buoyant economy has helped to avoid the kind of structural unemployment common in England's northern industrial towns. Thanks to a thriving, diverse local economy that has traditionally included light engineering, hosiery, boot and shoe and retailing, Leicester, it is claimed, has not experienced the intense competition in the labour markets that has sometimes resulted in dual labour markets—segregated patterns of employment between ethnic and non-ethnic minorities. While this was, to some degree, a characteristic during the early decades of migrant settlement, the changes in the local economy since the manufacturing slump of the 1970s and 1980s have produced more varied patterns of employment with self-employment (Winstone, 1996). Moreover, because East African Asians were 'twice migrants', who arrived with significant entrepreneurial experience, good education and transferable skills, they adapted easily to the local economy by establishing a successful BrAsian business sector (Vertovec, 1994). Today there are over 10,000 registered BrAsian businesses in the city that boast some of the most successful BrAsian businesses in Britain; and many of these have substantial transnational trading links with Europe, South Asia and North America. Ethnic business success in Leicester is symbolised in the Belgrave Road 'Golden Mile' which has become a retail and commercial centre of international renown. Similar centres—Narbrough Road, Evington Road—are emerging in other parts of the city (Martin and Singh, 2002: 7–14).

The generally favourable portrayal of Leicester's local economy normally neglects the significant disparities among and between various ethnic and non-ethnic groups. Thus, for example, in 1991 while self-employment among ethnic groups was above the white average, unemployment among the under-25s of ethnic groups was also significantly higher compared to the white population (Vertovec, 1994: 263). The launch of ethnic minority businesses was probably as much a response to the slump in manufacturing as the outcome of an entrepreneurial drive by the newly arrived East Africans; and the fact that medium- and small-sized ethnic businesses continue primarily to serve ethnic enclaves highlights their relative lack of integration with the wider local economy, notwithstanding their transnational links. Clearly, a much more comprehensive understanding is required of Leicester's ethnic economy and the degree to which it is both a response to local racism and an outgrowth of local conditions that have historically encouraged small businesses.

Competition for public resources

A third factor, which is often unacknowledged, but is certainly implicit in some of the policy and academic research, highlights the fact that the settlement of ethnic minorities in Leicester was, as in other cities, influenced by intense competition for publicly managed resources, in particular housing. In the late 1960s and 1970s the arrival in the city of East African and Ugandan Asians that led to a sharp rise in the ethnic minority population in the city from 5 per cent (1968) to 25 per cent (1975) led to significant pressure on public resources such as education, health and social services. But by and large this pressure did not manifest itself in the demand for public sector housing. While studies elsewhere (Solomos and Singh, 1990) have shown how competition for public sector housing has fuelled racial strife, in Leicester, apart from the Afro-Caribbean community, the demand for public sector housing among ethnic minorities at this juncture remained weak. This was because racial hostility to the allocation of public sector housing to Ugandan Asians, at a time when there were nearly 10,000 people on the city's housing waiting list, put intense pressure on ethnic minorities to settle in areas designated for inner-city redevelopment, where accommodation was affordable and proximate to kith and kin. Fear of physical attacks also deterred many from seeking council accommodation (Marett, 1988: chapter 7). As a consequence Leicester's housing ecology, with its traditional public sector estates in the west and the outskirts of the city, has contributed to a high degree of 'self-segregation' (Phillips, 1981). As inner-city areas designated for redevelopment were vacated by white occupants, ethnic minorities took their place. Belgrave and Highfields remain among those parts of Leicester with the highest concentration of ethnic minorities, even though there is increasing representation in the north and east of the city.

The distribution of public and private sector housing in Leicester in the 1960s and 1970s may well hold the key to the pattern of ethnic minority settlement, but historically it would be unfair to attribute Leicester's relatively good fortune *only* to the availability of cheap private accommodation. If the allocation of public sector housing were institutionally racist, racialised entry barriers in private sector housing also limited the opportunities of more affluent ethnic minorities to settle in Leicester's suburbs (Chessum 2000: 96–119). Whether voluntary or enforced, the pattern of ethnic minority settlement in Leicester remains highly segregated with western and far eastern Leicester predominantly white residential areas and the ethnic minorities confined to the east and the north. Certainly in the 1980s and 1990s there was movement by ethnic minorities to the more affluent suburbs in the east and south, but this has been accompanied by professional 'white flight', which appears to be reinforcing the traditional segregation.

Taken together these three factors are unexceptional: they can be found in other localities in Britain such as West and North London. Indeed, it would appear Leicester's narrative of multicultural 'success' is a reified image of the historical development of the city and the place of ethnic minorities within it. This is perhaps because it was very much a response to the problems of the 1960s and 1970s and served well in promoting the recognition of difference in a highly charged atmosphere of violence and intimidation. Ironically the issues that now confront the political leadership in Leicester are, in some ways, equally if not more challenging than those of the 1970s.

LEICESTER AND DIVERSITY MANAGEMENT IN THE TWENTY-FIRST CENTURY

Leicester today confronts a significant set of issues in ensuring that social and ethnic diversity is effectively managed. As the city heads towards becoming the first 'majority minority' city, three challenges are of special concern to the policy of multiculturalism.

Demographic and social change

Since the 1980s Leicester has witnessed a remarkable demographic and social change that is now a distinctive feature of the city. The ethnic minority population is increasing; while the 2001 Census puts the figure at over 35 per cent of the city's total population, some guesstimates, based on surveys of primary and secondary school pupils, suggest the figure might be even higher. Evidently the age profile of ethnic minorities coupled with higher birth rates among some groups has been the major factor for this growth. Inward migration has contributed too. More recently Leicester has received some 10,000 Somalis, most of who have relocated from the Netherlands; and a sizable number of asylum seekers and Eastern European émigrés have arrived as a result of the war in the Balkans. The city's 'success' as a 'genial' multicultural locality has also attracted ethnic minorities from the northern industrial towns. Most recently, the property boom in London and efficient rail communications have contributed to a new wave of professionals moving into the city, though many of these are located in the suburbs. Of course those who regularly leave, especially ethnic graduates but also the middle-aged and the elderly, need to be offset against the patterns of inward migration. There would appear to be very little detailed information on outward migration, but it is probably not of the magnitude to significantly undermine projected growth. How this demographic change breaks down among the ethnic groups remains to be seen, though the dominance of Indian Gujaratis still prevails despite the increase in the non-Indian ethnic population. Change is most likely to be reflected in the size of the Muslim population which has seen new additions from within Britain, the European Union and from countries like Somalia, Malawi and South Africa (Singh, forthcoming).

Demographic change reflects not only increased diversity in the city's ethnic population, but also increasing social diversity *within* the ethnic groups. Secular changes in patterns of employment, consumption, travel, family and life-styles are also apparent among ethnic minorities as highlighted by such indicators as female employment, divorce rates and family break-ups. For the local policy of multiculturalism these changes raise two specific concerns. First, the emerging white backlash against 'colonisation from below', that is, the spectre of the city's white population becoming a minority in its own locality. This theme has found some resonance in the right-wing national press, among neo-Nazi extremist groups operating in the region, and is probably reflected in the growing political disaffection with the Labour Party in its traditional white strongholds.[3] The backlash is yet to translate into the virulent racism of the 1970s, but its resilience in the context of twenty-three years of official multiculturalism makes it particularly unnerving.

Second, the difficulty of adequately reflecting and representing all constituencies within the city. Arguably the multiculturalism of the 1970s is corporatist, accentuates religious identification and, by accident or design, has encouraged segmentation. Consequently it stands desperately in need of revitalisation such that it becomes more representative, secular and emphasises inter-cultural relations. In the context of emerging hyper-diversity, comparatively multiculturalism as a public policy has embraced new public space and the promotion of rights of 'minorities within minorities' (e.g. women, youth, gays). While LCC policy in the last decade has been to recognise this change, the overall emphasis has been on consolidating the ethnic vote-banks. The failure of 'minorities within minorities' to secure significant representation in structures throughout the local state underscores the domination of traditional community gatekeepers and their close relations with the local structures of power.

Ethnic diversity and social cohesion

Demographic and social change in Leicester also draws attention to the tension between ethnic diversity and social cohesion. Although comparatively Leicester was identified as an example of 'best practice', the LCC's self-assessment on 'community cohesion' is far more sanguine, recognising that the progress made is insufficient to underpin a robust conception of civic multiculturalism.

> Leicester's cultural diversity is an economic and social asset but all our communities do not share equally in its success. Inequality and deprivation mixed with cultural and racial diversity create exceptional complexities. Choice, tolerance and justice are pulled in different directions. Local politicians, health providers, faith leaders and the media wrestle with sensitive contemporary issues such as targeting, deprivation, promoting choice and welcoming integrity. (LCC, 2002: 2)

The 'exceptional complexities' appear to arise from the twin objectives of promoting social and ethnic diversity alongside tackling deprivation, particularly on large council estates with overwhelming white popula-

3 It is difficult to establish a direct causal relationship between the decline in Labour Party's support and the 'white backlash'. However given Labour's decline is most precipitous in its traditional strongholds of white, public sector housing wards, the inference is certainly worthy of further detailed research.

tions. The report notes that thirteen of the city's wards fall into the top 10 per cent of the most deprived wards in Britain (LCC, 2002: 5). Underlying this analysis is an implicit assumption of the dangers of a further polarisation of the city's population along geographical and ethnic lines. There is certainly a perception among the wider local populace that the pursuit of diversity has been privileged at the expense of deprivation. One recent public opinion survey on levels of community satisfaction with LCC service delivery indicated the satisfaction rate among BrAsians was 53 per cent while the comparable figure among whites was 17 per cent (LCC, 2002: 10).

The LCC proposes to tackle these 'exceptional complexities' in four ways. First, by articulating a vision for 'Leicester to be a premier city in Europe with a thriving and diverse society in which everyone is involved' (LCC, 2002: 3). By managing and celebrating diversity the LCC hopes to tap the creative energy within the local community to ensure that 'Leicester remains a model of European best practice, improving integration, sharing innovative ideas and continuing to learn' (LCC, 2002: 3). Second, this vision, it is claimed, is shared by the political leadership of the LCC, its officers and broader organisations within the local state (e.g. Leicester Council of Faiths) that have successfully generated widespread community support to confront potential ethnic tensions within the locality. Third, the LCC proposes to develop a more effective and consistent community engagement through better networking and partnership with local community groups. Revitalisation of neighbourhoods, where development funds are increasingly channelled to targeted areas, is viewed as the key mechanism for eradicating deprivation. Fourth, the LCC intends to continue celebrating diversity by promoting festivals such as *Diwali*, *Vaisaki*, *Eid*, Christmas and the Caribbean carnival, but recognises that the celebration of diversity through ethnic and non-ethnic festivals needs to be embedded in new cultural spaces. To this end the LCC is proposing a new £80 million 'Cultural Quarter' in the city that 'demonstrates both the commitment and willingness to think outside the box [of existing cultural identities] and the ability of staff to work creatively to create new spaces in which communities can come together, learn from each other, and create new forms of intercultural artistic expression' (LCC, 2002: 9).

Political commitment

Political commitment, as the community cohesion self-assessment of the LCC makes clear, is considered the critical variable in shaping a successful multicultural policy. Labour's dominance since 1979 was established primarily through the ethnic vote which eroded Conservative Party presence in the inner-city areas while simultaneously consolidating the Labour vote through new forms of patron-client politics. A measure of this development can be gauged from the observation that in the mid 1980s nearly 10 per cent of the revenue budget of the LCC was allocated to community associations, a large number of which were ethnic minority associations (Willmot, 2002). In some ways this initiative encouraged ethnic participation in local politics, with a quarter of LCC current councillors coming from ethnic minority backgrounds; in others it began to produce large ('wasted') Labour turnouts in wards of ethnic minority councillors, while the Labour vote in predominantly white wards began a secular decline. Interestingly the representation of councillors among ethnic minorities in the city has been confined almost exclusively to the Labour Party. This grave imbalance suggests that multiculturalism as a policy in Leicester has been very much a political project tied to the fortunes of the Labour Party. Being such a project, political integration of ethnic minorities has been delivered almost exclusively through the Labour Party.

The Labour Party's gradual decline in Leicester since the 1990s poses real dilemmas in ensuring political commitment to a form of multiculturalism as a pro-active policy that has been sustained by ethnic constituencies. Whilst it is unlikely that a Liberal Democrat/Conservative combine would deliberately undermine the long-term investment in Leicester as a 'multicultural model', a decision that would have serious repercussions in attracting funding for inner-city programmes, the narrowing of political competition among the three parties increases the potential for out-bidding. In the event of a local regime change what form the new civic vision of multiculturalism will take remains to be seen. Informed observers speculate that a 'thin' commitment to multiculturalism as a public policy might be accompanied by a 'thick' diversion of resources from the inner-city to the outlying areas of majority white settlement. If this were to happen, there is a danger of Leicester reverting to 1970s-styled white political domination based on segmentation and geographical divide. This 'spectre' might be a useful political ploy for the Labour Party to further consolidate the ethnic minority vote. Alternatively critics of the Labour Party's policies in Leicester point to the limitations of the Labour project in fostering political integration across local political parties and civic institutions.

ASSESSING THE LEICESTER MODEL

Leicester as the model of best practice civic multiculturalism in Britain, arguably Europe, is clearly in need of a radical reassessment—an assessment that should be historically based and take into account the peculiarities of the city and the general framework within which race and ethnic relations in Britain have been structured. This brief survey, which is part of such a project (Singh, forthcoming), highlights several issues for the current debate on multiculturalism in Britain and elsewhere.

First, the Leicester model illustrates that political commitment to multiculturalism as a policy is a critical variable in shaping change. Leicester's dramatic transformation from the 'most racist city in Britain' to a model of multiculturalism was accomplished largely by the domination of the Labour Party from 1979 and continuity in leadership. Yet while this domination has succeeded in combating racial discrimination, improving service delivery and celebrating diversity, it has also resulted in the Labour Party being the primary vehicle for political integration among the city's ethnic minorities. The local Labour Party in the last two decades has functioned as an intra-consociational body, aggregating the interests of its segmented sections who have been allowed considerable autonomy in interpreting the theory and practice of multiculturalism. This mode of operation produced an effective coalition for policy delivery but at the expense of evolving a cross-party consensus on multiculturalism as a policy. As support for the Labour Party has declined, both the policy and the interests of Leicester's ethnic minorities seem threatened, though a realignment of ethnic minority councillors with Liberal Democrats and Conservatives cannot be ruled out.

Second, the recent concern of the LCC with community cohesion in an ethnically and socially diverse locality raises the broader issue of what Putnam (2000) has termed shared 'social capital'. Given the high degrees of relative segregation—accommodation, schooling, employment, political, patterns of consumption—of the ethnic and non-ethnic minority population in the city, one might question whether LCC's plans to engineer greater inter-cultural contact will produce the desired outcomes. And even if these outcomes were realised, it is doubtful whether they would articulate a shared vision of a civic future. Whereas historically racism has been a key factor in the city's segregation, it is not unreasonable to suggest that increasingly segregation might well be the outcome of self-selection, of 'parallel lives' by choice rather than fear. If the latter assertion is valid, then the real challenge the Leicester model poses is that a contemporary multicultural city can survive primarily through political or economic integration, however impartial and incomplete this might be. Indeed, a minimal consensual co-existence might recognise the claims to difference without the assumed precondition of social cohesion *à la* community cohesion agenda.

Third, related to the above point, Leicester's exceptionalism probably lies in, if anything, the limited claims the ethnic minorities made on collective goods as they settled in the city, the background of the majority of the migrants and the buoyant local economy. This serendipitous outcome, for all the qualifications introduced above, has gradually produced a virtuous cycle that is now generating problems of 'success'. In so far as these conditions are to be found in other localities—and not in the northern industrial towns of Britain—the lessons for a successful civic multiculturalism are obvious.

Finally, because of the geographical concentration of ethnic minorities in certain localities and their overwhelming support for the Labour Party, the history of the city of Leicester since the 1960s reflects the general patterns of development in Britain. The multicultural model in Leicester was conceived by Labour radicals in opposition to the prevailing conceptions of political integration. Ironically under Tony Blair's 'New Labour' the turn towards community cohesion marks a return to the normative ideals of integration prevalent in the 1960s. If carried to its logical conclusion, the agenda for community cohesion will require a rethinking of the traditional relationship between the Labour Party and its multicultural clients. To what extent this relationship takes the form of a reconstituted, decommunalised, and hyper-diverse multiculturalism, or its subordination to social cohesion, remains to be seen.

In 2003 three related developments that are likely to have profound consequences for the Leicester Model occurred: the release of census data in early 2003, the second Gulf War and the loss of political control by the Labour Party in the May 2003 local elections.

Data for the 2001 Census indicate that anticipated demographic changes are occurring at a lower rate than some of the more alarmist projections suggested. The city's ethnic minority population increased from 28.5 per cent in 1991 to 36.1 per cent in 2001. Within this category there has been a significant increase in the Muslim population. Although no directly comparable figures for 1991 are available, the religious composition of ethnic minorities in the city since 1983 has changed from 13.9 per cent Hindu, 3.8 per cent Sikh and 4.3 per cent Muslim to 14.7 per cent Hindu, 4.2 per cent Sikh and 11.0 per cent Muslim (Vertovec, 1994: 266; National Statistics Online). Consequently the demographic dominance of East African Gujarati Hindus is being challenged by the Muslim community.

The second Gulf War mobilised significant anti-war opposition within Britain. In Leicester this mobilisation was orchestrated by the Leicester Council of Faiths and as in other cities, the Muslim community played a significant part in the protests. This campaign politically mobilised a sizeable section of the local population in the run-up to the May 2003 elections and, as elsewhere in the country (e.g. Birmingham), transnational issues combined with local politics to undermine Labour Party support. Despite the anti-war stance of many sitting local Labour Party councillors, a large section of the Muslim vote went to the Liberal Democrats, who had campaigned on an anti-war platform. This switch of allegiance strategically undermined the Labour Party in its core inner-city wards with the result that Labour was reduced to 20 seats, Liberal Democrat representation increased to 25 and the Conservatives managed to hold on to 9 seats. Overall, ethnic minority representation in the new council declined from 14 seats (all in the Labour Party) to 10, with four Muslims and one Sikh among the new Liberal Democrat councillors.

In the new political configuration, Liberal Democrats have joined with Conservatives to form an alternative administration. This combine has yet to define its policies on civic multiculturalism but will most certainly compromise them in the need to respond to its old and new constituencies alike. Interestingly, all three leading parties have committed themselves to the issue of community cohesion, which is seen as central to urban regeneration. Here the corporatist structures within the local state—Leicester Regeneration Company, national public-sector bodies and voluntary organisations such as the Council of Faiths—have been the key drivers in ensuring this commitment, yet how this translates into policy will be of greater significance.

CAPITAL GAINS

BrASIAN SUBURBAN NORTH-WEST LONDON

Rupa Huq

'The inner-outer suburbs. Always the same.... Just a prison with the cells all in a row. A line of semi-detached torture chambers.' (Orwell, 1937: 13–14)

Ideas of socio-spatial polarisation in the capital have long been propounded in written accounts (Booth, 1893; Orwell, 1939; Pacione, 1997), frequently clustering around a split between the allure of the city and safety of suburbia, or affluent West and dangerous, even odorous, East connoting 'London's tilted social geography' (Rustin, 1996: 2). However, suburban North-West London, a sprawling urban landscape bisected by tube and railway lines and the capital's arterial road network, is more than simply an example of outer London suburban drabness. This chapter explores two particular areas of North-West London: Southall and Wembley. These two locales are now known as areas of Asian-British or BrAsian settlement in London whose reputations spread beyond the capital. Southall is imprinted on the history of British anti-racist struggles for the incidents that took place there in the late 1970s and early 1980s. As will be described, the legacy of some of this era lives on in the area. Wembley has been in the British national consciousness for a number of reasons. Historically it was the home of English football and the twin towers of Wembley Stadium. In the twenty-first century it has also been famed in Britain as home of the Kumars: BBC television's fictitious Punjabi family of the eponymous *Kumars at no. 42*. Southall and Wembley are areas that can only be described as suburban in terms of spatial characteristics but which share richly diverse demographic profiles that are not traditionally associated with the uniformity and whiteness usually implied by the term 'suburbia'.

Common perceptions of ethnic minority peoples in Britain situate them as residing in inner city locations, languishing in multiple deprivation districts; condemned to play out their lives as ghetto-dwellers. For example, Hendry *et al.* (1993: 189) identify the following characteristics of the 'inner city': 'Older housing stock ... in poor state of repair ... high proportion of unemployed people, ethnic minorities, single-parent families.' This is contrasted with their description of 'older suburbs', the defining features of which include 'older population; low rate of unemployment; little penetration by ethnic groups; leisure pursuits largely followed outside [the] area.' However, the contemporary demographic dynamic of areas like Southall and Wembley serve as reminders that received notions of suburbia as resolutely white are now more misplaced than ever and that there is BrAsian life on the margins as well as in what are conceived of as Britian's urban 'centres'. Two small notes of caution must be sounded here. First, data, in large degree, has been shaped by my own eyewitness observations growing up in suburban North-West London in an area equidistantly positioned between Southall and Wembley. Second, the reader may notice that the specificity of London is a key factor in the descriptions that follow; hence the importance of transport links that are stressed throughout.

SOUTHALL

Southall's sizeable Sikh Punjabi population has made it a frequent setting for studies of BrAsians and BrAsian youth in particular (see Alexander, this volume). Examples include Marie Gillespie's studies of television viewing habits (1989, 1995), Gerd Bauman's study on cultural identification (1996), Avtar Brah's earlier work on arranged marriage (1978) and Harwant Bains on the Southall Youth Movement (1988). Southall is an incontestably suburban location on the capital's western edge. It has become a landmark of anti-racist folklore for the struggles around racially motivated disturbances in 1979 and 1981, when young people of Asian origin, provoked by white skinheads and police aggression (Silver, 2001), hit the headlines in a series of what the press were quick to dub 'race riots'. As one of the best-known BrAsian abodes, Southall has had various flashpoint events and names attached to it. In 1979 Blair Peach joined the role-call of Southall martyrs as an Anti-Nazi League activist killed opposing a National Front demonstration, bringing to a close a decade during which Southall was the scene of active resistance to racism that spanned both police brutality and aggression from the extreme right. The source of the 1981 unrest was the Hamborough Tavern, a pub where National Front sympathisers, the band The 4Skins, provocatively decided to stage a concert to an audience of skinheads largely imported from London's East End for the occasion.

Although frequently described as London (e.g. by Gillespie, 1989, 1995), Southall actually lies outside the London postal area in the former county of Middlesex. Indeed, Southall was semi-rural until the turn of the twentieth century. Some traces of its pastoral past can still be seen in places such as the desirable Norwood Green area bounded by Tentelow Lane. Today's Southall is connected to central London by the Paddington rail line (under twenty minutes)—which continues westward to Wales—and by the arterial A4020 Uxbridge Road which eventually finishes up as Oxford Street, W.1. Passing under the Uxbridge Road, at a point in Southall where it is known as The Broadway, The Grand Union Canal was, in the nineteenth and twentieth centuries, an important link in the country's waterways that carried goods across the country, but it is now largely ornamental rather than functional. Over time, the centre of Southall has shifted somewhat. The Broadway is now its main focus. Residential housing off this main drag is largely Edwardian terraced with some pockets of 1930s semis. To the south of the Uxbridge Road beyond the railway station is the original nucleus. Here in what is known as 'old Southall', the housing is predominantly Victorian stock. There are also some concentrations of social housing including the expansive concrete jungle of the Golf Links estate. However, this and others like it, such as the Havelock estate, should not be seen as 'Asian ghettos'. As many commentators point out, Asians generally have a high level of home ownership. Indeed Southall is the highest area of owner-occupier housing in the entire Borough of Ealing. Notable non-residential architecture includes the unusual water tower that resembles a castle opposite the station and the landmark iron bridge at the Uxbridge Road, gateway to Greenford. The area is also home to various examples of light industry including brand names such as Quaker Oats. Other major local employers include Heathrow Airport, across the borough boundary in Hillingdon. Since the early 1990s Southall has also been home to Sunrise Radio, a nationally broadcast Asian station.

Southall is best known for its BrAsian population who began settling in the area from the 1950s onwards. The majority of BrAsian settlement in the area is drawn from respectable Sikh Punjabi-speaking Indians, with Hindu and Pakistani Muslim minorities also present. Indeed it is intra-BrAsian strife that many commentators point to when for example discussing rivalries in youth gangs in Southall. Undoubtedly BrAsian commerce from small businesses has revitalised Southall. While in other parts of London traditional high streets have been in decline, threatened by out-of-town shopping areas, BrAsian clothing stores and Indian restaurants, recommended by London listings magazine *Time Out*, line the main thoroughfares of Southall alongside people selling imitation brand-name watches and counterfeit Asian cassettes and CDs from pitches in the street. Among local controversies in recent years has been the decreasing amount of pavement space available for pedestrians and pushchairs. Long before mainstream British supermarkets began diversifying into 'ethnic ranges', Southall was a magnet for BrAsians from far and wide for its grocery stores and green grocers, to which people would flock for supplies of ghee in catering industry sized tubs, rice by the sack load and various vegetables impossible to obtain elsewhere. Southall Broadway is always crowded on weekends, but on occasions such as *Diwali*, *Eid* or *Vaisaki* it is even more congested than usual.

The affluence of Southall is noticeable from the sort of cars that one sees in the area with its ever-present BMWs and Mercedes. For teenagers and twenty-somethings still residing in the parental home, the use of a car, be it their own or their parents, is often a badge of independence, so it is not uncommon to see BrAsian youths cruising the Broadway with loud Bhangra music booming out of powerful sound systems. Southall has featured in 'ethnic London' guides (e.g. McAuley, 1993) and newspaper articles as an alternative to North London's more fashionable Camden market for buying (implicitly authentic) *objets d'ethno-chic* such as printed fabrics and foodstuffs—*The Observer* food guide (8 June 2003) named Southall as 'best ethnic' area for purchasing pulses and spices. Commerce aside, 1990s research from Ealing Council has shown that many young people were dissatisfied with the range of options on offer regarding entertainment. The Council-owned community venue, Dominion Centre, outside the gates of which our sample was drawn, was seen to follow an irrelevant, municipally regimented programme. Other local attractions on offer that did not tend to figure highly in unprompted responses from BrAsian youth included the Tudor Rose nightclub in King Street—more accustomed to hosting reggae and dancehall jams than Bhangra or other BrAsian events—and a number of Irish pubs which again were not seen as catering for BrAsian tastes. Yellowing posters for Bhangra 'daytimers' and evening concerts are fly-posted all over Southall, and handbills can be picked up in all the Broadway's music shops, but the gatherings they advertise are rarely held in Southall itself. This is despite the town spawning 1980s BrAsian Bhangra acts Alaap and Heera and, prior to this, the (black) reggae outfit Misty in Roots and (white) post-punk band the Ruts. It is more usual for young people from Southall to seek leisure outside the town, for example in Ealing with its superior clubs, cinema and fast food facilities just a three-mile drive or bus ride away.

Politically Southall has always been solidly Labour voting. However, Southall's uneasy positioning in the London Borough of Ealing has been the source of tensions since the dissolution of the old boroughs—of Acton, Ealing and Southall to become the London Borough of Ealing—in 1969 amidst GLC reorganisation and the advent of unitary authorities. There have been constant criticisms that Southall's geography at the borough's western tip has dictated its marginalisation in terms of receiving funds from the centre at the expense of other more marginal (and white) wards, which are seen as more politically advantageous to nurture, a claim which has been the subject of a running debate in the pages of the *Southall Gazette* (Bauman, 1996). Other longstanding grievances include the absence of a Southall tube connection to central London. At various times campaigns have been launched to electrify the tracks on the existing line from Southall to the major London Transport terminus of Ealing Broadway through which the District, Central and Paddington lines run. Such initiatives have always come to nought, again fuelling conspiracy theories. Southall's local representatives include a number of BrAsian councillors. At national level the constituency was represented for years by veteran white left-winger Sydney Bidwell, seen as a unity candidate behind whom all the messy factions of Southall politics could unite, captured in his own unofficial slogan to voters to 'call me Bidwell-Singh'. When Bidwell's tenure ended, ostensibly to 'make way for a younger man', he was replaced at the 1992 election by fellow septuagenarian, Asian Piara Khabra.

While the name of Blair Peach is immortalised in the name of a Southall Primary School, the Hamborough Tavern is no more, having been comprehensively burnt out and firebombed in 1981 (Hamborough Road can still be located in the *London A-Z*). On the spot now stands a Hindu community centre. Other notable sites include the still present Library on South Road and another fine example of Victorian gothic architecture, the obsolete Southall Town Hall on the Uxbridge Road which is now a TEC (Training and Enterprise Council) centre. While the lack of mainstream shops in Southall was once a cause for complaint, over the last ten years an increasing number, such as Pizza Hut and KFC, have appeared on the Broadway and its perpendicular thoroughfare South Road. Other elements have conversely become 'more BrAsian'. The Glassy Junction pub is festooned with Punjabi Sikh symbolism. Clocks on the walls display 'Southall time' and 'Punjab time'. The clientele are predominantly, and sometimes exclusively, male. The soundtrack is Bhangra. In keeping with the Sikh taboo on smoking, a night at the Glassy Junction will be spent in a less smoky atmosphere than a regular pub; which is what the building was a decade earlier. The Liberty cinema on South Road, a listed building, has re-opened, following years of decline, as an Asian picture house named Himalaya Palace Cinema. Its frontage had been used as a shopping centre entrance with largely BrAsian traders, in the way that former cinemas have been converted to bingo halls and churches across Britain. But this re-emergence as a cinema shows a re-reappropriation.

In some ways Southall has served as a model of tolerance and interracial harmony. Waller (1991) may have called it 'this outpost of Asia in West London', yet it is also home to people with roots in Caribbean countries and Ireland who have for years co-existed with little serious difficulty. Furthermore its BrAsian communities are multiple and mixed. The area is home to mosques, Hindu temples and Sikh *gurdwaras*. Despite complaints about Southall receiving a raw deal from the Borough of Ealing, a 1994 exhibition 'The Peopling of Southall', celebrating the area and its ethnic diversity, ran for over a year at the local history museum at the borough's Gunnersbury Park. The events of 1979 and 1981 are significant for demonstrating the militancy of BrAsian youth at a time when they were frequently characterised as being passive, compliant victims of 'Paki-bashing' or 'caught between cultures' (Anwar, 1979). In 1998, when a terror campaign was mounted by the London nail-bomber against targets that seemed to demonstrate the capital's openness and cosmopolitanism, including South London's (predominantly black) Brixton, East London's (largely Bangladeshi) Brick Lane and the 'Admiral Duncan' gay pub in Soho, it was feared that Southall could be next. The area was consequently put on high alert. Such fears ultimately proved to be unfounded as the nail-bomber was nailed before further damage spread. Still many of Southall's residents choose to live there rather than in an ethnic ghetto (as the traditional stereotype would have it) created by those left behind after successive waves of white flight. Consequently the Southall story continues apace with its place in the cartography of the BrAsian nation assured.

WEMBLEY

Long famed for its twin towers and stadium, which staged both legendary football matches and musical concerts, Wembley has also been over the past thirty years home to large numbers of people from Hindu Gujarati backgrounds and other BrAsians. Indeed, the influence of the BrAsian population can be seen in the places of worship. The Christian churches have been in decline for some years; the surviving ones valiantly battle on, protecting their territory against the temples that have sprung up. Among its most famous current residents are the 'Kumars at number 42' (street unspecified). Their extended family includes Ummi, the ageing grandmother with ribald sense of humour, money-mad father Ashwin and mother Madhuri who obsesses about marrying off the programme's star Sanjay, an essentially spoilt kid who hosts his own celebrity chat-show from the family's Wembley in-house studio-cum-sitting room. The programme has not only reinforced Wembley as a BrAsian locale, but has won awards for its deft deployment of humour and generally sensitive portrayal of BrAsians written and performed from an 'insider perspective' by a young BrAsian cast who satirise rather than simply stereotype.

Wembley, like Southall, lies in North-West London, but outside the London postal area. However, it is administratively part of the London borough of Brent; a local authority plagued for many years with associations of 'loony leftism' for its supposedly extreme left policies towards minority groups. Much of the negative publicity was based on exaggerations. Brent is a mixed borough in every sense. In terms of residential tenure it is home to both the notorious Stonebridge Park estate and includes the highest percentage of private rented housing in London. It has longstanding Jewish communities in its outermost fringes to North

Wembley as well as growing numbers of transient people in bed and breakfast accommodation further in. Politically the BrAsian voters have consistently delivered with a turnout proportionately higher than that of the white electorate. Much of the BrAsian vote displays traits of what might normally be seen as natural Conservative tendencies; as in Southall there is an above average level of private home ownership and small business/self employment, yet in terms of political complexion BrAsians have always pretty unswervingly voted Labour. Across the road from Ealing Road Library lies Pavitt Hall—named after the former MP Laurie Pavitt—a converted church and Labour community centre advertising the advice surgeries of Brent South MP Paul Boateng, one of a trio of black MPs elected for the capital in 1987. Wembley's northern part houses Brent Town Hall, the borough's governing headquarters at Forty Lane. North Wembley falls in the Brent North parliamentary seat, which takes in the 1930s suburbia of Kingsbury, Queensbury and Sudbury all with tube-stops. Brent North's long-serving, right-wing Conservative, Sir Rhodes Boyson, repeatedly called for Wembley to be able to secede from the rest of Brent so that it could dissociate itself from the council's 'loony' activities. By 1997 Boyson had been unseated as this once seemingly rock-solid Tory bastion fell to New Labour in a seat transfer that must owe something to the growing number of BrAsians on the electoral roll here. The delivery of the neighbouring seats of Harrow West, Harrow East and Ealing North from Conservative to Labour must also be in part attributable to BrAsian voters who continue to back Labour regardless of personal embourgeoisement.

Unlike Southall, Wembley is well served by London Underground. At Wembley's lower reaches the Piccadilly line stops at Alperton tube station. Further north is Wembley Central on the Bakerloo line and beyond this North Wembley and out at the area's northern-most tip are stations on the Metropolitan line. Alighting at Alperton tube and exiting on to the main Ealing Road, the shops are noticeably 'Asian' in character. The only national chains represented are the Ambala and Royal Indian sweet centres. There are various vegetarian eateries and fresh produce stores in addition to a smattering of discount travel agents. There is also a concentration of sari shops that I remember from my childhood where shopkeepers were susceptible to haggling and the pungent smell of the slow burning incense was always present on the premises. However, the closer one gets towards the centre of Wembley, following Ealing Road northwards, things change. The sari emporiums with the coy expressions of Asian mannequins in the windows looking vacuously on, eventually give way to a preponderance of jewellers—most have heavy security alarms that come into operation on entering and exiting. A slight incline starts before the main High Road begins. My early memories of Wembley include the way the area felt palpably different on match days with visiting supporters in large numbers packing the main pub at the junction of Ealing Road and Wembley High Road, drinking on the benches outside, and perhaps aiming the odd insult at us the BrAsian shoppers. Indeed I suspected that this hostelry was only there for match days as very few BrAsian locals were ever to be seen drinking there. Further on one of the first McDonalds in London is a focal point as a youth hang-out. It would be fair to say that the now rather scruffy-looking High Road looks like it has seen better times. Once this was composed of chain stores with a smaller number of long established independent traders, but soaring rents have seen many leave. Our Price and John Menzies shops, for example, are no more. C&A left long before the entire chain collapsed in Britain. The once futuristic 1960s concrete jungle precinct based around shops in a neo-square situated behind Wembley Central station (served by the Bakerloo line and British Rail into Euston) has also fallen on hard times, with many of its dilapidated units empty and the remainder having become temporary pound stores or charity shops. Out-of-town type shopping such as the Sainsbury's superstore at Hanger Lane with its massive on-site parking facility and in-store low price petrol have left smaller operations unable to compete.

Like the wider borough of Brent to which it belongs, Wembley is an area of rich diversity. Every November annual street decorations are mounted by Brent Council in the Alperton area to commemorate *Diwali* the Hindu festival of lights. These remain up until New Year as *Diwali*'s timing handily runs into the Christmas and twelfth night period. Victorian and Edwardian terraced housing is to be found here. On the approach to the High Road the stock then turns into unremarkable, uniform 1930s semi-detached houses. However, towards the Wembley triangle of the Stadium, Conference Centre and Town Hall houses become larger and more comfortable; encircled with large driveways and set further apart from one another. These streets were once favoured by Jewish families, some of whom are still in the area. The High Road draws in people from outside and is a site where the multiple communities of Wembley rub shoulders: asylum seekers, long established Asian families, increasing numbers of Somalis and suburban net-curtain twitchers are all caught up in the mix.

THE PLACE OF NORTH-WEST LONDON IN BrASIA

Fears of 'suburban neurosis and new town blues' (Clapson, 1998: 121–55; Jackson, 1973), such as Orwell's comment at the top of this chapter, hinting at the dreariness of uniformity in the suburbs, are confounded by the existence of Southall and Wembley. These are vibrant neighbourhoods where inner city and suburb meet. It would be facile to interpret the suburban migration of BrAsians as a sort of 'brown flight'. Instances of this are visible, but continuity and change characterise both Southall and Wembley. As figures of the shrinking populations of British cities attest, general outward drift towards the suburbs is not new. This normally follows a pattern based on familiar roads and public transport routes. A Southall overspill can be seen in parts of neighbouring Greenford, which is increasingly favoured by aspirational-class BrAsian families. Indeed, the three London boroughs of Ealing, Brent and Harrow—between them forming a continuous arc of suburban North-West London—all now have sizeable BrAsian populations. This is evident in both census data and the translation of Council leaflets into various South Asian languages. For many BrAsian residents to live in these areas is a conscious choice, i.e. shaped by 'pull' factors rather than the constraints of 'push' motivations. Others have chosen to stay in the same locations; again this is the case in Southall. There is then no singular North-West London suburban experience.

Comparable 'BrAsian' areas of other British big cities do exist and are dealt with elsewhere in this book. However, the specificity of London in terms of size and diversity are key in understanding the past and present of Southall and Wembley. According to the *Time Out Book of London* (1972: 8): 'London is today less a hundred villages than a modern city, split along American lines—city dwellers and suburban commuters—and along the lines of communication.' Suburbia is all too easily equated with wealth and the inner city with poverty when in reality the two are multi-faceted and complex. As Pacione (1997: 156) puts it: 'The multiplicity of processes that cause poverty are matched by a diversity of poor areas: overspill housing in Havant, Victorian terraces in the outer-city of Harringey, modern estates in Glasgow, picturesque pockets of poverty in Cornwall and holiday resorts throughout the country.' Although *Newsweek* (4 November 1996) trumpeted, 'The food, designers, music, fashion, theatre and journalism make London a great place to live', its description of the capital as 'a hip compromise between the non-stop newness of Los Angeles and the aspic-preserved beauty of Paris sharpened to New York's edge', is not reflected in surveys of inhabitants or 'users', e.g. in the story 'Dirt and beggars loom large in London's image' (*Independent*, 30 March 1994). Crude characterisations of London then are unhelpful. Chambers (1986: 183) very rightly points out 'urban reality is not singular but multiple … inside the city there is always another city.'

Southall and Wembley are ambiguous zones. They are some distance from London's centre and can feel at times very remote. They fall within London's boroughs but not its postcodes. Indeed, it was once alleged that 'postcode prejudice' could operate against job applicants from Southall, although the evidence for this is largely anecdotal so it is difficult to gauge how far this continues in Blair's New Britain. Nonetheless, tube links providing a lifeline to the capital's cultural and economic resources can make areas seem nearer to central London than those without such connections. In dealing with BrAsian North-West London one could have considered other areas. On the branch of the Piccadilly line that travels towards Heathrow Airport, Hounslow is another example of an outer West London suburb with a considerable Asian population who kept Labour in power locally in the 1980s and 1990s. However, there are also obvious differences. The shopping parades of Hounslow and its Treaty Centre are much less obviously 'Asian' than those of Southall or Alperton. Willesden in inner North-West London was the scene of Zadie Smith's celebrated novel *White Teeth* that centred on a Bangladeshi family among its main characters. However, I have chosen not to consider it here; in part because I do not believe that its ethnic make-up is predominantly Asian and also because my logic of inclusion inevitably reflects areas that I myself am familiar with. In conclusion then this has been an admittedly brief tour of suburban Asian North-West London that is far short of comprehensive. However, one hopes that it has provided something of a taster to acquaint the reader with the areas under discussion. For further background information I would inevitably recommend the curious readers to go and see for themselves.

Part III. SIGNATURES

N. Ali, V.S. Kalra and S. Sayyid

The following chapters cover the way in which BrAsians have made their mark on the landscape of these islands, in particular exploring the way in which cultural representations by BrAsians have contributed to the construction of BrAsian identity as almost a distinct civilisation, with its internal divisions, conflicts and fragments but also with its commonalities and unities. The five chapters in this section explore BrAsian signatures in a variety of cultural mediums.

Sanjay Sharma's chapter is ostensibly an account of BrAsian popular music, but on this account he hangs a discussion of two key issues. First, what determines that a particular type of performance is BrAsian: the identity of its producers, its content, its audience? Second, the relationship between postcolonial possibilities and the tension between universalism and particularism. These can be seen in a variety of ways from the 'neo-orientalism' of pop group Monsoon to continuing descriptions of BrAsian music as world music. Asian sounds dis-orient (both in the form of a critique and dismissal of orientalism, and in the sense of producing vertigo) the hegemonic articulation of whiteness and Britishness. These issues of identity and the tension between the universal and particular recur with different degrees of intensity in nearly all the chapters in this section.

Within their 'taster' of South Asian art John Holt and Laura Turney highlight the tension between universal and particular and the way it impacts on the art created by artists of South Asian heritage. The demand for South Asia art to confine itself to being a genre of ethnographic art, painting pictures of 'elephants and tigers', highlights the postcolonial condition of artists who are located in the West but not of the West. However, since BrAsian artists exist in the space between Western (universal) Art and 'Ethnic (i.e. particular) Art', the samplings by Holt and Turney demonstrate the difficulty of containing BrAsian artists within ethnographic notions derived from Western discourses of art.

Comedy clubs, theatre and occasional sitcoms are some of the cultural performances explored in the chapter by Raminder Kaur and Alda Terraciano. In many ways these performing arts are where sustained attempts to elaborate a BrAsian identity have occurred. As the chapter shows, however, BrAsian identities are constantly haunted by the narratives of authentic South Asianness. This tension between an exotica and performances grounded in the actualities of new Britain, where people of colour are part of its urban landscape, is brilliantly exploited by comedians whose redeployment of ethnic stereotypes is not only often very funny but its very incongruity draws attention to the unsettled nature of Brutishness.

Rachel Dwyer provides an account of the development of Hindi popular cinema based and produced in Bombay (Mumbai). There is little doubt that 'Bollywood' is one of the most prolific cinema industries in the world, but Dwyer traces the way in which its globalisation has linked South Asia and the South Asian diasporas not only through patterns of consumption (lower ticket prices) but also through its content which attempts to 'speak' to certain versions of South Asian experiences. The recent wave of valorisation of BrAsianness is often represented through the prism of Bollywood. At the same time Bollywood has been a source of inspiration if not emulation for BrAsian film-makers. Despite its location within the very specific context of the Indian film industry, Bollywood has become a kind of mirror for aspects of BrAsian identity.

The final chapter in this section sets out to examine the impact of the BrAsian presence on the architecture and urban form of Britain. Noha Nasser points out that the meeting of Timurid and Western architecture easily predates the formation of distinct BrAsian communities and suggests that it would also post-date any possible demise of the same communities. Thus transformation of the landscape becomes the resource for any future archaeology. It is not only monumental buildings (mosques and temples) but the very nature of banal, mundane streets being bent and twisted to conform to the needs and ambitions of the BrAsians, which almost literally concretises the signatures of BrAsia. The BrAsian ethnoscape becomes not only an analytical or sociological category but a habitat, a place where actual communities live. Nasser draws attention to the non-virtualisible aspect of the BrAsian experience as a location in border space, but a location that manifests itself in the fabric of Britain's conurbations.

ASIAN SOUNDS

Sanjay Sharma

The 'coolie becoming cool' is a dubious way of capturing the journey of (South) Asian popular music in Britain. Nevertheless, the authorised story of this dance music usually begins by ridiculing early-1970s Bhangra stars as pot-bellied men in garish maroon coloured sequined shirts and obligatory white cricket trousers. In stark contrast, the story climaxes by venerating the latest tabla & bass as *the* multicultural soundtrack of urban Britain in the new millennium. To simply counter-claim that this story has a far more complex multi-layered narrative does little justice to the vicissitudes of BrAsian dance music.

Writing about BrAsian popular music is like charting a map without legitimate borders and boundaries. One is immediately drawn into questions of 'authenticity', location and 'identity': what makes this music Asian? The artists? The lyrics? The sounds? The audience? In attempting to pin down the music's geographical origins, national borders and identifications rapidly become suspect. It is tempting to conclude that BrAsian music is a *diaspora music*, which challenges ethnically proscribed notions of origin, national identity and sense of 'home'. This would be a diaspora of circuitous cultural flows that explode even the more developed accounts of the bi-directional musical movements between only Britain and South Asia. The *Asianness* of BrAsian music exists in the diaspora of global musical multiplicities. We cannot deny the impact of 'Western' musical genres such as soul, funk, hip-hop, reggae, rock and indie upon the development of BrAsian sounds since the 1970s. Moreover it is notable that South Asian pop and Bollywood film music is increasingly being influenced by BrAsian musicians. However, the case is not of these artists simply 'returning home'.[1] Rather, of a transmuted *Britishness* of diasporic Asian music (propelled by the flows of global multicultural capitalism).

It has now become customary to claim that all modern music is syncretic or hybrid. The very nature of music is one of fusion and emer-

1 Hindi film music has been drawing on elements of music from the 'West' for many decades. The recent celebration of fusion and hybridity of Western musical forms often ignores the fact that popular music in the subcontinent has developed in this way. What is notable today is the significant impact of BrAsian artists on contemporary Bollywood sounds.

gence, drawing on different cultural traditions, which constantly evolve. But such a claim ends up saying little about how we come to differentiate between divergent musical styles and genres. The pounding *dhol* of Bally Jagpal's Bhangra and the contrasting esotericism of Talvin Singh's tabla may be lumped together because of a common South Asian instrumentation and geography. Yet it could be argued that these musics occupy genres as different (or similar) as rock and reggae, even though it is not that difficult to trace syncretic musical influences and practices common to both artists. As we shall discover, music has the capacity to disrupt notions of purity and origins. It has the potential to mutate extant identities: both the signifiers 'British' and 'Asian' continue to be transformed by BrAsian music.

This chapter aims to reflect upon the emergence of BrAsian popular music over the last thirty years. The variety of Asian musical styles resists attempts to provide an exhaustive account of their multiple histories. Consequently the intention is to offer an analysis of this music in terms of its relationship to broader cultural transformations in Britain. The chapter is principally organised by identifying three 'moments' in the development of Asian music: invisibility; marginalisation; commodification. These 'moments' appear to follow a time-line from the 1970s onwards, although they do not neatly map on to each of the ensuing decades, and nor are they exclusive. They offer one way of telling a story of BrAsian music—although they cannot capture its 'dis-orienting rhythms'—using an approach that acknowledges that the following account is retrospectively informed by the contemporary political moment: a deeply ambivalent multicultural recognition of a BrAsian presence.

INVISIBILITY: DOING OUR 'OWN' THING

Racism has many faces. From the brutal street violence of neo-fascists to the more subtle forms found in white-collar employment, BrAsians continue to be subjected to these racist practices in Britain. However, there has been a specific kind of racialisation against BrAsians that has rendered them wholly 'other' to the national space. Their so-called foreign ways of life, impenetrable languages, backward religious rituals and obscure exotic habits meant they have not been able to be properly assimilated into the British (white) way of life. It has been a racism of abject exclusion and has lead to an Asian 'invisibility'—outside the national story.

In contrast, Asian music in Britain has offered alternative imaginings of *home* and *belonging*. It has played a significant part in resisting racist exclusions by enabling post-war Asian settlers to forge connections between 'here' and 'there'. The treasured vinyl LPs brought over by migrants in the early 1960s played an essential role in constructing a diasporic popular imaginary of memory, place and identity, and the subsequent technology of the cheaply produced cassette tape sold through local 'Asian' grocery stores, clothes shops and markets was vital in the circulation of Asian music in urban Britain. Replaced now by the compact disc and more specialist shops, the alternative Asian music economy still remains relatively distinct from the 'mainstream' mega-stores. However, during the 1960s and early 1970s it was also the amateur 'playback' singers who recreated a sense of belonging and community during social gatherings. While Bollywood cinema provided an endless supply of love songs, the rhythmic *dhol*-driven Bhangra became the dance music of the many Punjabi migrants in Britain. Originally known as a folk music greeting the New Year (*Vaisaki*), it was adopted by many as the soundtrack for community celebrations, especially weddings.

The politics of wealth and display in Asian weddings leave a lot to be desired, yet they have been integral to the development of popular BrAsian music. Weddings were the spaces that enabled amateur musicians—originally singing religious songs in *gurdwaras* and temples—to form Bhangra bands. By the early 1980s the 'pioneer' Bhangra bands such as Heera and Alaap were in huge demand, and guaranteed that the alcohol-fuelled Punjabi wedding would be a riotous occasion. (It was not uncommon to find ardent Bhangra fans gate-crashing weddings to hear their favourite groups!) While Bhangra embodies a diverse Punjabi cultural specificity, it easily could be reduced to its dominant lyrical content (land, caste and women). Yet the infectious beat of the *dhol* fused with pop electronic instrumentation such as synthesizers, samplers and drum machines made it appeal to a wider Asian audience (Banerji and Baumann, 1990[2]). Furthermore its 'call-and-response' antiphonal quality—*boyliaan*—spirited an energetic affiliation between the performers and the crowd (Kaur and Kalra, 1996). In particular, the female-centred *giddha* enabled women attending Punjabi weddings to express humorous, sexually risqué verses and gender-subversive dance performances.

The fusion of 'traditional' Bhangra sounds with heavier bass-lines was soon to make this music the *contemporary* sound of urban Britain for many young Asians. While bands such as DCS, Premi and Apna Sangeet dominated the wedding circuits it was the (often anonymous) Asian DJs who brought this music to clubland. Up until the early 1980s BrAsian music had been located, or rather confined, to the 'private sphere' of community celebrations and social gatherings. Nevertheless, Bhangra enabled many Asian youth to affirm their identities within a dominant cultural formation that offered either an acculturating process of assimi-

2 Sabita Banerji and Gerd Baumann's (1990) work was one of the first to highlight the development of Bhangra music in Britain. Although, for some of its limitations, see Sharma (1996).

lation into the British nation, or exclusion from it (Sharma, 1996). The question of the invisibility of Asians in the popular-public sphere needs to be understood as a denial of a multi-racist Britain. Alternatively, a radical multicultural musical imaginary, which challenges dominant constructions of a homogeneous Asian enclave defined by fixed ethnic traits, is necessary. Such an understanding is important because it simultaneously acknowledges the socio-cultural exclusions of racism and the dynamic formation of BrAsian identities and their musics.

MARGINALISATION: CROSSING THE TRACKS?

The appearance of the demur seated figure of Sheila Chandra singing her unique chart hit, *Ever So lonely*, on Top of the Pops in the early 1980s neatly captures how Asian music entered into the 'mainstream'. It was likely that the static and exoticised Chandra, miming to a track dominated by a pseudo-Indian classical music sitar riff entrenched neo-orientalist stereotypes of Asians and their music. This process of recognition and exoticisation marks how BrAsian music has entered, yet at the same time been marginalised, in national popular culture. The initial, and deeply Eurocentric, labelling of BrAsian sounds as 'World Music' valorised the ethnic origins of the artists, rather than acknowledged the music's diasporic productions.

However, the marginalisation of Asian dance music did little to arrest its continuing evolution during the 1980s and early 1990s. This period is perhaps best known for the rise of BrAsian record labels, producers, DJs and sound systems. Furthermore developments in digital technologies and the increased availability of Asian dance music on vinyl led to greater experimentation and re-mixing. The Midlands based DJ-producer Bally Sagoo has been the most talented exponent of remixing of not only Bhangra, but Bollywood film music classics and the legendary Qawwali of Nusrat Fateh Ali Khan. Sagoo's albums such as *Star Crazy* (1991) and *Bollywood Flashback* (1994) spawned countless (inferior) re-mix albums. The phenomenon of re-mixing was not surprising given that many Asian youth were fans of black music such as reggae, soul and hip-hop. In particular the largely male phenomenon of playing pounding Asian beats in customised car sound systems was as much about masculine display as it was about claiming an Asian cultural legitimacy and space in the urban public sphere. Furthermore the famous trip-hop collective Massive Attack's remixing of Nusrat's anthemic *Must Must* (1990) did much to promote the credibility of Asian dance music across the music industry. Nevertheless, these fusion re-mixes and Bhangra sounds failed to 'cross over' into the mainstream charts, undoubtedly due to Asian music outlets being excluded from the pop chart compilation practices. Bhangra bands such as Safri Boyz, The Sahotas and

Achanak were in demand on the wedding circuit and club gigs, and were also successfully touring European musical festivals. Yet it appeared that Bhangra music remained 'too ethnic' for the predominantly white British music industry.

However, while Bhangra evaded mainstream pop acceptability, its 'underground' popularity forced it to enter into city club venues during the 1980s, often accompanied with soul and hip-hop music, though initial entry into clubland was vis-à-vis the notorious 'daytimer'. As Banerji and Baumann (1990) note, once discovered by the white press, these events were simplistically depicted as Asian youth (girls) escaping their family's patriarchal restrictions.[3] It is revealing that these reductive accounts failed to stress the everyday racism and exclusionary door policies of many clubs across the major cities in Britain. It was only until the late 1980s that a few clubs, such as *The Wag* and *Limelight* in London, finally opened their doors to Asian youth and their music.

The international success of the Birmingham based artist Apache Indian confounded many critics who considered Asian music as too parochial. Apache Indian originated a 'Bhangramuffin' style fusing reggae with Bhangra, which was expressive of his own hybrid cultural biography. His music articulated a contemporary youthful British multicultural identity, which challenged the narratives of a white only mono-cultural Britain, especially during Thatcher's conservative reign. The music also transgressed fixed notions of ethnic identity amongst both Asians and African-Caribbean groups. In the early 1990s Apache's hit *Movie Over India* remarkably topped both the reggae and Asian music charts.[4] While his music clearly had a pop commercial appeal, it also embodied a political edge. Apache's collaboration with the reggae singer Maxi Priest, in the song *Fe Real*, marked a unique moment of political-musical 'unity' (Back, 1996). It is important to emphasise that the Bhangra music of XLNC, Panjabi Hit Squad or B21 needs to be considered to be as 'hybrid' (or 'traditional') as Apache Indian's music. Terms such as hybridity tend to celebrate musical fusion and *avant-garde* creativity at the expense of actually examining how the music works—both culturally and politically (Sharma *et al.*, 1996; Hutnyk, 2000).

COMMODIFICATION: 'ASIAN KOOL'

If the 1970s and 1980s were about the invisibility and marginalisation of Asian music, then the 1990s heralded the recognition and celebration of

3 The policing of Asian female sexuality and the negotiation/resistance of parental controls have been far more complex than simply escaping family restrictions, see Parmar (1982) and Puwar (2002).

4 To date no other British artist has achieved this kind of cross-chart success. Many listeners initially believed Apache Indian to be an African-Caribbean artist.

this music culture in Britain's major cities. However, this moment cannot be considered outside the increasing commodification of all things Asian (Puwar, 2002). It has never been possible to separate popular music culture from the capitalist marketplace, and the penetration of global capital in the creation of new multicultural markets has led to an acceleration of this process. When the ubiquitous pop star Madonna embraced the exotica of Eastern culture in the 1990s (Kalra and Hutnyk, 1998), South Asian culture ostensibly took centre stage in the Western imagination.

'Asian culture' and 'Asian cool' are certainly not terms that have had a positive association in Britain. To the contrary, the unassimilable 'smelly Paki' has invoked hostile responses of repugnance rather than reverence. Nevertheless, an ambivalent racism in the desire (domination) of otherness has also exoticised elements of Asian culture. The style-media creation of the notion of 'Asian Kool' in the 1990s said much more about the multicultural ideologies and fantasies of influential culture-fashion magazines such as *The Face* and *i-D*, than about the actual productions of Asian dance music. The celebration of *sarees* and trainers, *bindis* and *mehndi* on the dancefloor was represented as a new hybrid metropolitan Asian culture creatively synthesising traditional and modern elements from the East and West respectively. While Bhangra and Bollywood remixes have continued to evolve their own British hybrid musical styles, their ethnicised status meant they were going to be too uncool for the white mainstream. Bally Sagoo's success of having the first Asian language British chart hit, *Dil Cheez* (1996), was short-lived as he was subsequently dropped by Columbia records for poor international album sales. In the mainstream, 'authentic' Asian sounds have increasingly appeared as snatched samples on contemporary R&B and hip-hop hits such as Missy Elliot's *Get Ur Freak On* (2001) and Addictive's *Truth Hurts* (2002).

Asianness and coolness did come together on the release of the album *Anokha* (1997), produced by the talented Talvin Singh. The music defied categorisation as it creatively brought together divergent genres and styles. It mixed evocative Asian lyrics and sounds with contemporary drum & bass beats. The album cover figured a spiky haired Talvin adorned in a retro Mod parka-jacket with a target on the back. Although the contrived image suggested he was trying (to hard?) to reclaim British popular culture from the Asian diasporic perspective, the album was associated with the Anokha nights at the Bluenote club in London's Hoxton Square, which became a fashionable hangout for popstars such as Bjork, and white clubbers wanting to be at the cutting edge of multicultural urban cool. The marketing of Anokha as *The Asian Underground* was always a misnomer, particularly as Asians were never the majority in the crowd (not to mention that those present were mostly aspirational in their middle-classness). Moreover the very idea of the underground played on an Asianness that remained profoundly marginalised in its actual presence (Banerjea, 2000).

The now defunct multicultural style magazine *Second Generation* played a significant role in uncritically celebrating *The Asian Underground* and further accentuating the notion of Asian Kool. It was notable that the magazine's discourse of a new fashionable *hybrid* Asianness was seemingly predicated on a 'rejection' of Bhangra music culture (improperly read as the traditional music of the first generation). While Bhangra never universally appealed to, or defined, Asian youth culture, its own multicultural British working-class roots were being denied by positioning it against the postmodern drum & bass sounds of the Asian underground. In fact it may be contended that Bhangra has remained the 'real' Asian underground music in relation to the white mainstream. This specious splitting of *traditional* and *postmodern* Asian culture did not, however, impede developments in club culture, which embraced the diversity of Asian dance musics. Nation and Outcaste record labels, for instance, have nurtured and supported a range of Asian artists from many different musical genres. Similarly club nights such as *Shaanti* in Birmingham, *Raha* and *Raj & Pablo's Bollywood Nights* in London have continued to celebrate the eclectic Asian dance music scene (Bhangra, Asian beats, Arabic and Latin sounds, reggae, trip-hop, jungle).

The recent 'mainstream' success of artists such as Panjabi Hit Squad, Rishi Rich and Panjabi MC suggests that Bhangra has finally shaken off its so-called traditional-ethnic labelling. The development of the BBC's Asian Network 24/7 internet radio and the success of Panjabi Hit Squad signing with the record label Def Jam UK has meant that Bhangra is no longer confined to an Asian audience. A Bhangra track being piped in the background at Woolworths these days hardly raises an eyebrow from its white customers. Nevertheless, it is interesting to discover that Panjabi MCs anthemic track, *Mundian To Bach Ke* (1993), had appeared four years earlier on his *Legalized* album (which had been hugely successful within the Asian music scene). *Mundian To Bach Ke* gained British chart recognition only when it had been initially re-mixed by USA hip-hop DJs, and then gained airplay via Radio 1 hip-hop DJ Tim Westwood. The re-release of the original track and its phenomenal success throughout clubs in Britain and Europe is an indication that Bhangra music has finally 'come of age'. Nevertheless, this does not mean that the exoticised status of British-diasporic dance music has waned.

DIS-ORIENTING RHYTHMS

It would be a mistake to consider Asian dance music only in relation to its underground subcultures or mainstream success. The 'underground/mainstream' distinction is difficult to sustain in the era of global multicultural capital, which feeds on difference and ethnicity. A productive line of inquiry entails exploring the cultural politics of this music in relation to a highly commodified contemporary popular culture. Moreover when discussing the music's politics, we need to avoid reading it as having an explicitly anti-racist agenda or a determinate political project. Rather this dance music has offered modalities of cultural survival that connect with everyday lived experiences—pleasures, desires, resistances, belonging, racialised subjectivities etc. It has been through the music affirming Asian life and agency in the diaspora, as well as responding to the harsh realities of a multi-racist Britain. For example, Achanak's early 1990s satirical track, *Dhol Tax* (against the Conservative government's infamous 'community charge') urged Asian families to refuse to pay, because it discriminated against large low-income families (Dudrah, 2002a). Instead the mighty beat of the *dhol* offered an alternative musical imaginary for a resistive Asian collectivity. Alternatively Cornershop's remixed chart hit *Brimful of Asha* (1997) was unique for celebrating, for a BrAsian audience, the life of the prolific Indian film playback singer, Asha Bhonsle. Their feel-good song captured her phenomenal impact on the everyday lives of diasporic Asians, and as Nitin Sawhney commented, it was a song dedicated to a woman who was neither oppressed nor exotic.

Examining cultural politics also forces us to acknowledge that being Asian isn't simply commensurate with a progressive political agency. The expressive culture of BrAsian dance music highlights the struggles of a lived diasporic identity. On the one hand the marginalisation of women from the Asian music scene mirrors the wider practices of the British music industry more generally. While on the other hand, patriarchal exclusions specific to Asian cultural production and consumption cannot be denied. However, this has not prevented female performers and DJs such as Amar, Sangeeta, Trickbaby, Hard Kaur, Sista India and DJ Ritu to contest their marginalisation. Furthermore while issues of gender and sexuality have tended to remain peripheral to Asian cultural representation, music has played a crucial role in engendering a diverse range of Asian identifications. The alternative cultural spaces of *Club Kali* and *Shakti* with their lesbian and gay focus have been significant in challenging the heterosexual norm, which permeates much of music culture (Kawale, 2003).

The popular *Raha* 'conscious clubbing' multi-media spectacles (organised by Purple Banana) have regularly attracted a sell-out multi-racial crowd. These 'edu-tainment' events mix live performances and DJs, with poetry, dance, visuals and speeches for raising political awareness and funds for local anti-racist campaigns or international debt relief. Likewise the evocative music of Nitin Sawhney works across conventional boundaries of meaning and pleasure. His albums such as *Beyond*

Skin (1999) and *Prophesy* (2001) poetically celebrate multicultural life, and testify to the dangers of the politicisation of religion or the impending catastrophe of nuclear warfare in South Asia. While Asian dance music should not be reduced to having only an explicit political agenda, groups such as Charged, Blackstar Liner, Badmarsh and Shri, Fun-Da-Mental and Asian Dub Foundation (ADF) have drawn inspiration from roots reggae and African-American consciousness rap. These groups are significant not only for their combative stance against oppression, but for their musical influences and productions that draw upon a range of global musical styles of resistance. The militant rhythms of these groups have played an important role in articulating subjugated knowledges from a standpoint that connects the local (anti-racism) with the global (anti-imperialism).

The stance of punk-dubsters ADF against the unjustly imprisoned Satpal Ram for defending himself against a racist assault exposed the institutional racism of the British justice system. Similarly their EP *Fortress Europe* (2003) highlights the development of a pan-European rise in neo-fascism, border controls and the brutalisation of asylum seekers. ADF have also maintained a close connection with their locality, by supporting the development of community music in the East End of London through their educational wing (ADFED).[5] The merchants of chaos Fun-Da-Mental's biting social critique has targeted transnational capitalist institutions as well as the racist British State. Their sampling of speeches from Malcolm X and Mahatma Gandhi weaved together with Islamic chants and hip-hop beats create a globalising soundscape through which everyday oppressions are connected with a New World (dis-)Order. Fun-Da-Mental's striking musical fusions with Qawwali artists Rizwan and Muazzam (nephews of Nusrat Fateh Ali Khan), highlight how BrAsian music defies national boundaries and cultural authenticities. The disconcerting mixing of Sufi mysticism and invocations with urban break beats and bass-lines pushes beyond simplistic notions of musical syncretism.

MUSICAL FUTURES

To stress that BrAsian dance music cannot be contained by extant categories of identity, place and borders should not lead us to conclude that it is just an ostentatious *masala* mix of eclectic sounds. The musical influences and diversities of artists and bands such as TJ Rehmi, Bally Sagoo, Hard Kaur, Charged, Apache Indian, Trickbaby, LL Cool Singh, Nitin Sawhney, Panjabi Hit Squad, Cornershop, Sista India, Joi and Badmarsh

5 One of ADFEDs aims is to '… promote the growth of community music and music collectivities' (see www.asiandubfoundation.com). By collaborating with the Campaign Against Racism and Fascism (CARF), ADFED has been actively forging links between music and anti-racist politics.

and Shri register the multiple identifications of a contemporary BrAsianness. What is common to this music is not simply the ethnic marker of 'Asian', rather its concomitant articulation of 'roots' (identity, belonging, place) and 'routes' (cultural flows, movements, translations).[6] The global musical adventures of Fun-Da-Mental, Talvin Singh and Nitin Sawhney and their collaborations with other international artists make it difficult to fix the origin of their sounds, especially as it is produced in places such as Mumbai, New York and Johannesburg, as well as in London. Nevertheless, it is argued that their music is uniquely 'made in Britain', even if it is clearly not wholly of it.

The acceleration of global multicultural capitalism in the search for novel markets and exotica may mean the production and circulation of Asian dance music will penetrate the 'white' mainstream. The highly successful West End musical, *Bombay Dreams*, staged by Andrew Lloyd-Webber in collaboration with the now legendary Indian musician A.R. Rehman, is indicative of the further blurring of cultural and national boundaries for BrAsian musical productions. However, the mediocre Lloyd-Webber's dubious motivations for such an exotic venture demonstrate how Asianness has become a commodifiable culture in the global arena. It has increasingly become commonplace for 'exotic' sounds to be included or sampled in mainstream Western pop tunes. The multicultural appetites of cosmopolitan new age urbanites in the West means it is almost obligatory to have 'a bit of the other' in their CD collections; and Asian dance music appears to be at the forefront of the (re)discovery of the East. Nevertheless, this 'diaspora' music has the potential to resist and mutate forces that seek to package and contain its sociality (Sharma, 2003). What remains apparent is that from Bhangra to tabla & bass, Asian sounds continue to make a noise which dis-orientates and transforms British culture.

6 The notion of 'roots' and 'routes' captures the multiple lived experiences of an Asian identity. It acknowledges the locatedness of identity, but at the same time highlights that its formation occurs through diasporic cultural movements and interactions; see Mercer (1994).

RUSHOLME

Nida Kirmani

The 'Curry Mile', which occupies a half-mile stretch of Wilmslow Road, is one of the most popular areas of Manchester among locals and visitors alike. A wander down Wilmslow Road reveals a bustling, polycultural area filled with take-aways, grocers, boutiques and various other shops catering to Asian, Arabic and white clientele amongst others. However, its most striking feature, for which it has earned its nickname, is the massive concentration of 'Indian' restaurants. According to a recent survey commissioned by the City Council, 15,000 diners pass through Rusholme every Friday and Saturday night (http://www.waitrose.com/food_drink/wfi/ingredients/sweettreats/9809078.asp). It is indeed one of Manchester's most renowned features. Despite the area's notoriety, little has yet been written about Rusholme's historical development. Information gleaned in interviews with those who have lived and worked in Rusholme provides an outline of the way in which this street has evolved over the past four decades.

During the 1960s Wilmslow Road was still a 'traditional English street' according to one Rusholme shop owner. At that time there were two or three BrAsian restaurants, but the rest of the road comprised ironmongers, fishmongers, bicycle shops, pubs etc. The BrAsian restaurants basically catered to men newly arrived from Pakistan and India who were working in and around Manchester. However, the majority of the people who lived and owned businesses in Rusholme at that time were Irish. There were also two local cinemas in the area, the Trocadero and the Capital Cinema, which showed English-language films during the week, but also showed Bollywood movies on the weekends. Several respondents hypothesised that it was these movies that first brought BrAsian consumers to Wilmslow Road and one member of the Rusholme business community says the cinemas were the social 'focal point' for the area's Asian community.

In the early 1970s the street started to change, becoming dominated by South Asian-owned businesses. As more and more BrAsians came to Rusholme for the cinema, more businesses catering to BrAsian clientele began to spring up. According to one member of the Rusholme community:

> With the weekend cinema there were record shops, music shops, maga-

zines and … groceries—you know, back home groceries with spices and everything.… Slowly the potential just grew out of one to the other.

Much of the growth in this decade occurred when the men who had been living here started to bring their families over from Pakistan. According to the interviewees, most of Rusholme's customers at this time were local BrAsians.

However, Rusholme's character as the 'Curry Mile' only really took shape during the 1980s and 1990s. One of the major reasons was the increase in the student population and the expansion of the universities. 20–30,000 students living in and around the area guarantee Rusholme businesses, with their geographical location and the appeal of relatively inexpensive curry, a steady stream of customers. The growing popularity of BrAsian food among the white population was also a major contributor to Rusholme's success starting in the 1980s. According to one BrAsian shop owner:

> The thing is … our people … won't go out for a meal two or three times a week because they are cooking the same food at home. The only reason they will go out is on an occasion … and they would sometimes bring their English friends.

With a change in British consumer tastes generally, and with take-aways slowly replacing other kinds of businesses, curry has become a staple of British cuisine, helping to transform Rusholme into the 'Curry Mile'.

Since those days Rusholme has become a mixed community. Despite the stress on its BrAsian character, both by the media and by local people, Rusholme has also seen the growing presence of several non-Asian communities in the area. Of these groups Arabs are the most prominent. Since the late 1990s especially, several Arabic restaurants and take-aways have appeared on Wilmslow Road. Along with these and Arabic grocers, there are two Kurdish restaurants, at least one Afghani take-away and one Persian-influenced take-away. Rusholme is constantly changing. From predominantly Irish, to predominantly Asian, to quite mixed, it is a dynamic space reflecting the changes both in migration patterns and in the market generally.

THE SINGULAR JOURNEY

SOUTH ASIAN VISUAL ART IN BRITAIN

John Holt and Laura Turney

In many ways this chapter aims to provide a snapshot or a taste of 'South Asian' art in Britain that is conceptually at odds with the debate it will introduce; namely, the tension between recognising the contributions and achievements of South Asian artists whilst simultaneously critiquing the marginalisation and exclusion of such artists from what might be called 'the mainstream'. It is a tension between that which is described as 'the particular' being recognised for its 'particularity' whilst suggesting, at the same time, that 'the particular' is no less part of the 'universal' than that which is already considered 'universal'. So in drawing attention to the contributions and work of South Asian artists, are we, at the same time, continuing to mark them as different and separate?

Despite this, it is possible to tell a story of South Asian art in Britain. The story we tell here is necessarily incomplete; a comprehensive review requires more than one chapter in a book. As such, there are omissions, gaps and absences that reflect, of course, the perspectives of the authors. These absences and silences are regrettable but it is hoped this brief overview would encourage the reader to find out more.

This story has a long history and cannot be removed from the context of colonialism and the Empire in the nineteenth century and migration and settlement from South Asia to Britain in the twentieth century. It can not be told simply through an historical framework documenting social, demographic, economic and political changes and inserting peoples, places, movements and works accordingly, but also requires an understanding of how and why peoples, places, movements and works have been documented (or not). The story of South Asian art and artists is one of shifting boundaries, blurred beginnings and uncertain futures. It is also one that has many characters, plots, sub-plots and denouements that are dependent on time and place, and is intersected by questions of ethnicity and gender (among others). Any story we relate here is reliant on a certain set of essentialisms and assumptions that construct a sense of South Asianness regardless of whether the artists and movements included want(ed) or intend(ed) this. Furthermore this story struggles to locate itself both within and without the Eurocentric history of art which has periodically excluded, marginalised, exoticised and denigrated artists and art works of the 'Other' whilst constructing a mythical trajectory that links together the histories and achievements of the so-called 'West' unproblematically.

However, this is not simply a story of South Asian peoples. It is also both a study of the way in which the artistic motifs and symbols of 'South Asia' have been incorporated into the works of 'Western' artists and a consideration of how this incorporation is understood and theorised. Hence, the story of South Asian art and artists does not stand in isolation. Indeed, there is a long and continuing history of exchange and crossover. However, this has not necessarily been on equal terms, as the status and achievements of the 'Western' artist have been elevated in numerous ways above those of artists of South Asian origin; for example, through reference to the 'authentic', the 'spiritual', the 'primitive' and the 'tribal'. Nonetheless, artists have struggled to find voices and spaces from which to work, and it is these voices and spaces that will be considered here.

The issues affecting South Asian art and artists have changed over time as debates have moved on and artists and writers have challenged the Eurocentricity of the art world. Certainly the Britain encountered by artists such as Francis Newton Souza and Avinash Chandra in the 1950s is different to the Britain encountered in the 1980s, 1990s and from 2000 onwards by new generations of artists such as the internationally renowned Anish Kapoor, Chila Kumari Burman, Amrit and Rabindra KD Kaur Singh or Said Adrus.

BEGINNINGS

As mentioned, the story of South Asian art in Britain cannot be disconnected from its colonial roots. The relationship between the concepts of 'art' and 'artists' was transformed (both in Britain and in South Asia) by its encounter with 'the Other'. In Britain the motifs and symbols of the exotic 'East' entered the creative repertoire of artists and designers and in South Asia (post 1850), particularly in India, the British attempted to elevate the status of the artist from that of a humble and traditionally defined position to that of an educated élite. This meant the end of the traditional artists as a class. The Westernisation of India was enthusiastically supported by the literate élite whose command of the English language gave them power over those without it. This linguistic hierarchy was extended to the realms of visual language where it was seen that the aesthetic of traditional India was lacking in the benefits of the European Renaissance. The concepts of chiaroscuro and linear perspective moved the conceptual intentions of the visual arts towards the need to create a facsimile, a likeness of the subject.

In the 1850s the British set up art schools in three major Indian cities, Bombay, Calcutta and Madras. The schools were set up along the lines of the new English art schools, which in turn were modelled on the School of Industrial Arts in London. Thus the schools taught drawing in the Western style exemplified in the aesthetics of South Kensington and by the mid nineteenth century much traditional art began to disappear. In Britain the only major Asian artworks to be seen were in the major museums, particularly the Victoria and Albert and the British Museum. The government acknowledged that Indian artisans had little to learn from their European counterparts in matters of taste, but that the artists needed instruction in scientific drawing. When traditional artisans were made to draw from the antique they couldn't see the point in drawing what they saw as immodest statues of European ladies and gentlemen. The moral of the story is instructive: the students who did benefit from the art schools were not the artisans but those who hailed from English educated groups. The teachers in the new art schools were it seems from South Kensington and they brought with them exemplary drawings by English art students as though to provide evidence of a superior reality (Mitter, 2001). So in the encounter between the arts of Britain and South Asia there was a cross-fertilisation of style, content, technique and subject matter. In South Asia influences from Britain had some impact on the development of the arts either through rejection or incorporation. In Britain of course the same applied. What is of particular interest here is how incorporation, rejection and positioning has been inserted into a discourse of art and artists that has placed South Asia at the periphery.

MOVING FORWARD ... AFTER THE WAR

The story of South Asian art and artists in Britain begins to gain some momentum in the post-war period as artists from India, Pakistan, Sri Lanka and Bangladesh start to settle in Britain. However, the work and developments in South Asian art are not confined to Britain, as there was much movement between Britain and the subcontinent as artists settled in Britain, returned to South Asia and then returned to Britain to settle once more. For example, in 1946 Evan Peries (Sri Lanka) settled in London, returned to Sri Lanka in 1953/4 and subsequently came to live permanently in England. As Araeen points out, this arrival of artists in London from the ex-colonies in the post-war period fits an established pattern of how artists, across countries and history, have travelled from one place to another in search of patronage (Araeen, 1989). See, for example, the concentration of artists in Paris in the late nineteenth and early twentieth centuries. Although many artists struggled when they arrived in Britain (Peries, for example, has been described as lonely, isolated and faced with hostility [Araeen, 1989: 21]), there were some, such as Francis

Newton Souza (India) and Avinash Chandra (India), who became very successful despite initial periods of poverty and unhappiness.[1] These two artists in particular, who had begun to exhibit their work in the 1950s, were phenomenally successful throughout the 1960s. Despite their successes Souza and Chandra were 'othered' or 'particularised' as 'Indian' or 'oriental' painters, their work often described through recourse to the clichéd symbols of the Orient: sensual, erotic, symbolic and spiritual. Although successful in Britain during this period, like many other artists they moved to New York in the 1960s (Chandra in 1965 and Souza in 1967) as British fascination with the 'Other' began to wane. For example, in 1964 the Indian High Commission mounted an exhibition entitled 'Six Indian Painters', which included Khanria. Jenny Lee, Britain's first ever arts minister, attended the opening which nonetheless was ignored by the press, as was an exhibition at the Upper Grosvenor Gallery in 1966 which included leading Indian artists such as Bhuppen Khakkar.

The establishment of artists such as Souza and Chandra was fraught with difficulties. Chandra, when entering a gallery in London to show his work, was asked by the gallery owner if he could paint tigers and elephants and recalled that:

> I was so hurt. There is nothing wrong with painting elephants and tigers, which I perhaps do now or perhaps I should do, to express all that anger which is inside me, but to be asked to do these things because you were an Indian is insulting. (Araeen, 1989: 28, quotes from Araeen, 1988, 'Conversation with Avinash Chandra', *Third Text*, nos 3/4).

This issue, the essentialisation of the 'Indian' artist, continued to be challenged throughout the 1980s and 1990s as South Asian artists struggled to express themselves and their identity without being reducible to cliché, surface and stereotype. These struggles also developed in a country where racism and discrimination against black and minority ethnic peoples increased and extreme right groups became more active. South Asian artists began to work in an increasingly explicitly racialised and racist environment which had found its most vivid encapsulation in Enoch Powell's 'rivers of blood' speech in 1968. In this environment artists have used their work to make statements about gender, ethnicity, racism and spirituality, amongst other things. For example, Chila Kumari Burman, one of the first British South Asian women to study at art school, asserts the right to speak from 'beyond two cultures', challenging the stereotype of the passive, silent Asian female victim by creating self portraits of herself practising Shotokhan (a Japanese martial art) in a sari (see the installation video piece, *Body Weapons: wild woman beyond two cultures*, 1993). Burman says of her work:

1 Souza arrived in Britain in 1949 and attended the Central School of Art and Chandra came to Britain in 1956 after studying painting at the Delhi Polytechnic.

'Stereotypes reinforces mystery', Chila Kumari Burman, 2003.
By kind permission of the artist.

> [It] is about a continual exploration of my dual cultural identity through the manipulation of the photographic image, painting, laser printmaking and scratch video installation works. I'm reclaiming images of us Asian women moving away from the object of the defining gaze towards a position where we become the subject of display clearly under our control. (Burman, 1994: 22)

Other artists, such as Amrit and Rabindra KD Kaur Singh (The Singh Twins), have also worked to find a space in which their creativity can be valued and accepted, although they have found this, at times, a struggle. They have achieved this not, as Burman has done, by subverting the stereotype, but by reasserting what we could describe as 'the traditional' by using miniature forms to express an often subversive and playful perspective on life in contemporary multi-cultural Britain. Their experience of studying art at degree level in Britain elicited the following reflection:

> Self expression was presented to us as the ultimate purpose of Art but was permitted, it seemed, only if it fitted in with contemporary Western ideals of 'acceptable art', namely, an art which tended towards non-figurative, non-decorative representations; an art which was essentially Eurocentric in focus.... (W)e felt it was equally valid to draw upon non-European and ancient artistic traditions for inspiration and to present a modern art within that framework. (Swallow, 1999: 16)

Moving 'back', however, the establishment of a black and/or South Asian art scene continued in Britain from the 1950s. Developments of note include the founding of the New Vision Group by Denis Bowen in

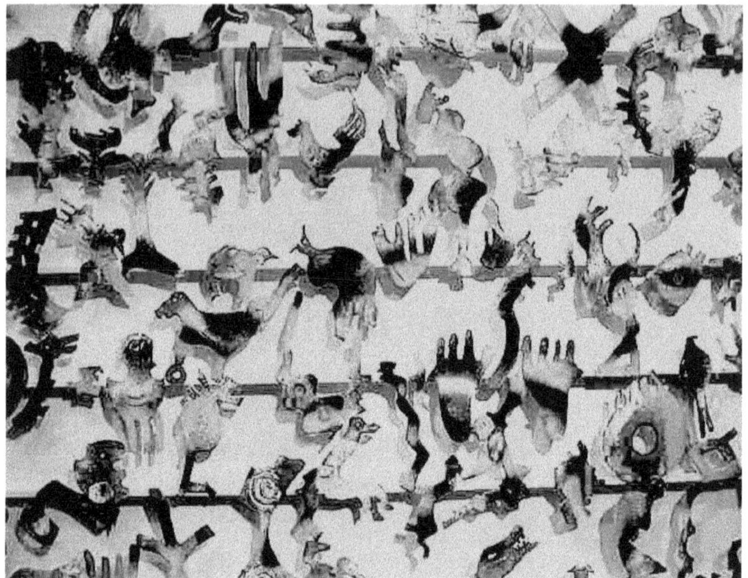

'Nursery Rhymes—for Dimitri', Balraj Khanna, 1997. By kind permission of the artist and Bradford Museums, Galleries and Heritage.

1951 and the opening of the New Vision Centre Gallery in 1956. Bowen was the first person to give Asian artists shows in Britain and provided a venue for young international and unknown abstract artists. Here artists such as Ahmed Parvez (Pakistan), Anwar Jalal Shemza (India) and Balraj Khanna (India) found a space for their work until the gallery's closure in 1966.

Khanna's work, often described through implication as somewhat derivative, is also symbolic of the relationship between centre and periphery in terms of the world of art. His work is compared to Joan Miro or Paul Klee, yet is described as displaying an intrinsic 'Indianness' which Araeen describes as 'a quality invented by Western critics who find it hard to come to terms with Khanna's own modernity' (Araeen, 1989: 43). As such he is positioned as both derivative and 'other' in a way that white, Western, male artists would rarely be. Rothko, Picasso, Hodgkin, Kandinsky and Pollock, to name a few, have all been described as taking inspiration from the 'Other', the 'primitive' and/or the 'Orient'. Positioned in the 'centre', however, they embody the universal rather than the particular.

The opportunities for artists from South Asia were broadened in 1957 when the Imperial Institute (founded in 1887 to mark Queen Victoria's

Golden Jubilee) was renamed the Commonwealth Institute. This and the Africa Centre in Covent Garden were the only galleries in London to have a written policy about showing artists from Africa, Asia and the Caribbean (Araeen, 1989: 130). The two Commonwealth Biennales of Abstract Art held at the Institute proved important in terms of the establishment of South Asian artists in Britain, and in 1965 Rama Rao (Indian) was awarded the £50 prize.

Anwar Shemza's relationship with the British art world is poignantly symbolic of the relationship between a Eurocentric history of art and its 'others'. Having come to Britain in 1956 as a successful writer and artist in Pakistan, his story of what happened whilst at the Slade is indicative of the general discriminatory ethos evident in Britain at that time.

> One evening when I was attending a Slade weekly lecture on the history of art, Professor Gombrich came to the chapter on Islamic art—an art that was—merely functional—from his book 'The Story of Art'. I remember leaving the room for a few minutes before the lecture finished, and sitting on the bench outside. As the students came out, I looked at all their faces; they seemed so contented and self satisfied.... All evening I destroyed paintings, drawings, everything that could be called art.... (Anwar Shemza, quoted in Holt, 1998: 105)

The 'suicide' of his work bears testimony to the crisis of identity he experienced at the time, precipitated by a culturally paranoid British art institution, in which a perceived dissociation was projected on to the 'Other'. The 'Other' in turn internalised and vented anger upon itself. His intention in coming to Britain was to benefit from the environment of Western culture and British art education systems so that he might return to Pakistan as a better painter and, more important, as a teacher. It is ironic that both the education system and the British arts institutions in the main spurned him, and he remained in relative obscurity for most of his life in Britain. Shemza was, as were other Asian artists, not without supporters in Britain. Slade tutor Andrew Forge, and later Denis Bowen, showed faith in the quality of his thinking and work. Shemza was a resistive character and his inner need to make work provided a greater impetus than the doubts foisted upon him by an insensitive and partisan system.

This issue of 'description' and categorisation continues to reverberate today when we think, for example, of descriptive terms such as 'ethnic' or 'primitive'. This has often meant that the art of the non-white artist is positioned behind the West on some abstract chronology of artistic development or evolution. This is forcefully underlined by artist Alnoor Mitha (1997) who argues that the 'history of art' follows an established pattern that observes the achievement of other cultures in the twentieth century on the assumption that they belong to historically receding cultures. This is a history that narrates only the history of the West and excludes those cultures that are seen as external to the *idea* of the West. Araeen writes about the incorporation of objects and art forms from 'beyond' the West:

> It is commonly believed that African peoples themselves were not aware of the aesthetic qualities of what they were producing and that it was the West which 'discovered' these qualities and gave the African 'objects' the status of art. It is true that Africans did not write books on aesthetics, plasticity, or formalism (or whatever relates to art), but to deduce from this that African artists were not aware of what they were doing is to indulge in the kind of stupidity which can only result from a mental blockage or an intellectual dishonesty. (Araeen, 1991: 165)

In this way the West bestows artistic status upon those who, it is believed, have no concept of art to begin with. Furthermore the work of artists such as Anish Kapoor or Permindar Kaur is often evaluated or critiqued from the point of view of a specific cultural heritage. They are denied the aesthetic and artistic universality of the Western artist. And although artists such as Kaur believe the situation (in terms of inclusion) for minority artists and the encouragement of black and Asian children to pursue art has been improved, they are still the victims of tokenism.[2]

THE 1980s AND BEYOND

The interconnections between the social and political milieu and the art world cannot be understated. This context, both in Britain and internationally, provided a focus for a number of artists and thinkers who have sought and continue to seek to challenge racism, discrimination and Eurocentrism in the art world and beyond. For example, in 1984 four anti-racist murals were commissioned by the Greater London Council (GLC) as part of their anti-racism year in Brixton, Notting Hill, Southall and East London. Chila Kumari Burman was among the eight artists to participate. In the same year the Commission for Racial Equality published a report, *The Arts of Ethnic Minorities*, which called for greater attention to and funding for minority ethnic arts whilst the GLC Race Equality Unit organised a conference on 'Black Artists White Institutions' at the Riverside Studios.

In regards to the hegemony of Eurocentrism in the art world (and, of course, beyond), an article by Amrit Wilson (1992) summarised the problems faced by South Asian artists living and working in Britain.

> The Orient of course was a construct of the European colonialist imagination. It grew out of the various colonial relationships, planter and forced labourer, state power and peasantry, imperial power and insurgent nationalist and so on.... But Orientalism is not something we can relegate to history. Its themes still permeate

2 See Permindar Kaur in conversation with Marcelo Spinelli for the British Art Show IV on the web: http://www.illumin.co.uk/britishart/artists/pk/pk_biog.html.

European popular imagery from Thomas Cook brochures to pictures on tea packets ... the experiences of Asians in Britain reflects the same contradictions.... Like Orientalism it seeks to define our culture for us. It tells us that it is about saris and samosas, melas and traditions, and that it is complete and of the past, passive and unchanging, and finally that it is something which needs now only to be recapitulated (Wilson, 1992: 16)

It seems that the damage done by the domination of the Eurocentric view has extended to the Eastern sense of its own spirituality. Indian artist Amal Ghosh, born in India and who later attended the Central School of Art in London, acknowledged the influence on British artists such as Howard Hodgkin and Stephen Cox of Indian spirituality as an inspiration in what Ghosh sees as 'the transition from ignorance to understanding', but Ghosh also observes that what he saw as the materiality of Western thinking had conspired against Indian traditional thought.

In the West 'the spiritual' has remained a problem in our contemporary materialist society. This became increasingly true during the 1950s and 1960s, when the majority of first generation South Asians and South Asian artists were arriving in Britain. There are now at least three generations of artists of South Asian origins practicing in Britain and Europe, each having a different relationship with the cultures of South Asia, but with minimal references to the spiritual content of their cultural tradition. (Ghosh, 2001: 79)

Artists such as Gurminder Sikand and Balrak Khaima have retained the spiritual ethos of their work it seems without recourse to the exotic. But the problem of not being trapped in an expectation derived from political polemic is one that is yet another trap to conspire against British South Asian identity being constructed in its own terms.

Another key event in the development of a 'South Asian' arts scene occurred in 1987 when the Indian Artists in the UK (IAUK) association opened the Horizon Gallery in London in order to provide a platform for artists from the Asian subcontinent working in Britain. It exhibited works by Sutapa Biswas, Avinash Chandra and Amal Ghosh. Further to this, in 1988 Rasheed Araeen organised 'The Essential Black Art' at the Chisenhale Gallery, London, which subsequently went on tour and in 1989 Anish Kapoor was selected to represent Britain at the Venice Biennale.

Kapoor is described as one of the most internationally influential sculptors of his generation. He was born in Bombay but has lived and worked in London since the early 1970s where he was educated at Chelsea School of Art. His work has been exhibited all over the world and is held in a number of public and private collections. Kapoor's creativity is concerned with an engagement with deep-rooted metaphysical polarities. These polarities are manifest in his work, for example, absence/presence—to be/not to be—the intangible/the tangible.

Kapoor's sculptures reveal a fascination with light and darkness as he confronts us with notions of space/not space. For example, Kapoor's work exhibited in 1989 at the Lisson Gallery—the exhibition, *Void Fields*—contained some of Kapoor's most famous pieces in which apparently solid sandstone forms with interiors that were filled with ultramarine blue pigment were testament to silence and contemplation. Pier Luigi Tazzi writes that Kapoor achieves this effect (a manifestation of 'the void') through:

> ... his knowledgeable use of materials—the pigments and their dispersability, stone and its hardness, surfaces that are reflective and others opaque, chasms and protrusions—with the 'spiritual' import of his own research and the illusions of sight and the mind. Kapoor's work is always metonymic, never metaphorical, even when it draws from the vast repertoire of universal symbolism. (Bhabha and Tazzi, 1998: 104)

Without doubt Kapoor stands as one of the world's most important contemporary artists. In 1991 Kapoor's often astonishingly overwhelming work was recognised again when he won the Turner Prize. He is an enormously inventive and versatile artist whose works not only take over the physical space of the gallery but psychological space as well, as his work is transformed by the physical, psychological (and for some spiritual) experiences of the viewer. His 2002 installation at the Tate Modern in London was staggeringly grand in concept, design and experience. Drawing on Greek mythology, *Marsyas*, which was composed of three steel rings joined by a single span of red PVC membrane, occupied the whole length of the Tate Modern's Turbine Hall.

In 1989 the Hayward Gallery in London held a major exhibition titled *The Other Story: Afro Asian Artists in Post-War Britain.* This exhibition was certainly a landmark in terms of the recognition of the work of both black and South Asian artists. Other important developments in the 1990s included the creation of the Institute of International Visual Arts (inIVA), which was established in 1993 as an independent non-profit making organisation with support from the Arts Council and London Arts Board. InIVA's remit has been to encourage knowledge and understanding of contemporary visual art in Britain and abroad by giving priority to visual art practice and scholarship that has not been adequately represented or disseminated. As the hegemony of the art and artists of the West has been steadily challenged by both organisations and individuals alike, so too has the public profile of South Asian art in Britain been steadily rising throughout the 1990s and into the new millennium. For example, in 1995 Cartwright Hall hosted an exhibition—*Intelligent Rebellion: Women Artists of Pakistan*—curated by Salima Hashmi and Nima Poovaya-Smith. This exhibition gave space and a voice to those who had never before been heard in Britain. The exhibition was described by its curators as:

> … overturning a number of stereotypes that the West may have, about contemporary art practised in a Muslim country. Belying their usual image of seclusion and subjugation, women have actually dominated the arts in Pakistan. (Poovaya-Smith and Hashmi, 1995)

Much of the most innovative work in raising the profile of South Asian art has occurred in the North West. For example, in addition to the work of Cartwright Hall (where, incidentally, you can find Britain's only permanent collection of contemporary South Asian art) in 1995/6, *Tampered Surface: Six Artists from Pakistan* (curated by Alnoor Mitha and Richard Hilton) was held at Huddersfield and Oldham art galleries. Recently the work in the North West has been consolidated by the establishment of *Shisha* in 2001. In 1997, to mark the fiftieth anniversary of the independence of India and Pakistan, there were several major exhibitions that took place across the country, many of which were held in the north of England. Building on the work of Alnoor Mitha and others in the North, it was identified that there was need for an organisation to facilitate and centralise this work and in 2001 *Shisha* was finally formed as an independent 'diversifying agency' to promote work of South Asian origin, acting as a link between artists, galleries and theorists in Britain and South Asia. *Shisha* promises to be a significant initiative for both Britain and South Asia fostering awareness amongst people in Britain generally as well as amongst the British South Asian peoples who can take pride in the contemporary visual arts of South Asia. Indeed, in July 2002 *Shisha* initiated the project ArtSouthAsia, the first international programme of visual culture from Bangladesh, India, Pakistan and Sri Lanka. As a result the North West cities of Oldham, Preston, Liverpool and Manchester saw significant events and exhibitions curated by individuals from each of the contributing countries.

All these developments have a significance and importance in that they mark the continuing development of South Asian artists in Britain and across the diaspora as they assert the right to tell their own stories and to create in their own ways without being constrained by the expectations of the mainstream. The story, of course, continues and now, at least, South Asians in Britain (and elsewhere) are no longer expected to paint elephants and tigers.

UPRISINGS

Paul Bagguley and Yasmin Hussain

Britain has witnessed sequences of uprisings (or in more comman parlance'riots') involving racial factors since the late 1950s, when whites and African-Caribbeans fought in Nottingham and in Notting Hill, London. The 'riots' of 1981 and 1985 have been seen by subsequent commentators as community insurrections against the police. The antecedents on those occasions involved heavy policing of predominantly African-Caribbean communities. Of particular relevance here though was the 'riot' that took place in Manningham, Bradford on 10–12 June 1995, mainly involving BrAsians. This was again popularly blamed on heavy policing, although the official reports simply blamed it on 'anti-social' individuals (The Bradford Commission Report, 1996: 11). The 'riots' of 2001 are more complex: whilst there are characteristics similar to those of before, where policing is involved, other factors have also emerged. In 2001 Britain saw another summer of rioting in its cities, in Oldham on May 26, Leeds on June 5, Burnley on June 23 and Bradford on July 7. Although comparable to those of 1981 and 1985, these 'riots' were, in significant ways, quite different from earlier years, and mark a departure in Britain's racial politics. Ethnic minority communities in all the areas where violence erupted have had their lives affected by ongoing, mundane and persistent racism. The spread of unrest was linked to an increase in racial violence, the long-standing mistrust and disillusionment with the police, the overt and taunting presence of the British National Party (BNP) and other far-right groups and the entrenched poverty and unemployment that existed within the cities. The towns concerned have variable proportions of people of South Asian origin and large numbers reporting themselves as Muslims. For instance, in Burnley over 6 per cent, in Oldham over 11 per cent and in Bradford over 16 per cent of people reported themselves as Muslims in the 2001 Census.

The uprisings/'riots' of 1981 and 1985 should be seen as part of the 'wave' of action starting in the late 1970s, and as often arising in response to neo-fascist mobilisations. The parallels with 2001 are striking in this respect. In 1981 a new anti-immigrant 'Nationality Act' was being debated in parliament (compare to asylum seekers), and (usually National Front [NF]) marches were banned for periods of up to a month in Leicester, Wolverhampton,

Leeds, Barnsley, Doncaster, Rotherham, London, Sheffield and Oxford. On 23 May 1981 in Coventry 10,000 white and BrAsian people marching for protection against racist attacks were met by a counter-demonstration of neo-fascists from the NF and the British Movement, and on 1 July 1981 disturbances around a neo-fascist skinheads' concert in Southall led to disturbances between the local BrAsian community and the police (Cowell *et al.*, 1982). However, there is a tendency to focus on the social base of the 'rioters' as being 'African-Caribbean' young men. This ignores the role of BrAsians and whites in some 'riots', as well as the involvement of women, children and older people in some instances. In this respect there is a sharp contrast with 2001.

The 'riots' of 2001 have generated the now to be expected raft of official reports (Burnley Task Force, 2001; Cantle, 2001; Ritchie, 2001). These are poor relatives of the official investigations into earlier waves of 'rioting' such as that produced by Lord Scarman in 1981. They say little about the 'riots' themselves and tend to focus on broader issues around the management of public services. Most strikingly they have promulgated an ideology of 'community cohesion' organised around crude functionalist ideas of social integration where all should come to share a common social identity. This has led to a re-evaluation of earlier accounts of 'riots', especially those of the 1980s. First, those accounts have ignored the role of neo-fascist mobilisations in provoking some of those 'riots', resulting in a partially misleading focus on the role of the police, because those 'riots' that were most closely analysed—St Paul's in Bristol and Brixton—were indeed responses to police action, while others were not. Second, all analyses of the 1980s riots (with the notable exception of Keith, 1993) have over-emphasised the role of young African-Caribbean men, and consequently misrepresented both the ethnic and class unity of those events.

The 2001 'riots' themselves differ in substance from those of the 1980s, and how they are approached theoretically and politically is also quite different. In substance the 'riots' were more ethnically homogenous. In Bradford on 7 July 2001 what started as multi-ethnic became an event involving almost entirely BrAsians of Pakistani descent. What the riots are expressing are new modes of 'racialistion' (Miles, 1989) on the one hand and new ethnic identities on the other. The old racialisation of Britain's ethnic minorities, crudely put, saw African-Caribbeans as 'having problems', whilst BrAsians 'have culture'. This also shaped academic research. The new racialisation is rapidly pathologising the

Muslim communities of northern England. Discourses of gang-culture, forced marriages, drug abuse, inter-generational conflict, resistance to integrating and speaking English and being Muslim are all routinely mobilised to explain away racism and justify dubious policies. Thus the uprisings of 2001 can be seen as part of the process by which BrAsians and Muslims are dis-articulated in a process accelerated by a sequence of events which included the post 9/11 'war on terror', British involvement in the war in Iraq and the subsequent attacks on London's transport network on 7 July 2005. Increasingly Muslims came to signify the potential enemy within, distinct from the 'integrated' BrAsians.

SOUTH ASIAN / BRASIAN PERFORMING ARTS

Raminder Kaur and Alda Terracciano

To appreciate fully the depth and diversity of South Asian performance in Britain, we need to begin long before the oft-cited post war migration period, with the era when maritime technology had transformed journeys to and from the East into a routine affair and ships carried to Britain a diverse cross-section of people from the Indian subcontinent—*ayahs* (nannies), *lascars* (seamen), students, doctors, revolutionaries, traders, princes and performers. By the nineteenth century South Asian street musicians had become a regular component of metropolitan life in the heart of the empire, religious ceremonies/performances had become a part of the 'exotica' entering the everyday life of white British neighbourhoods, and visiting Indian dance companies were widely applauded by the aristocracy sitting in the 'king seat' of main theatre houses in London.

South Asian performing traditions have been modified by the travels of migrants to Africa, the Caribbean and elsewhere from a subcontinent as vast and diverse as the cultures of Europe. Such patterns of migration have been reflected in a variety of artistic productions within the communities settled in Britain. Throughout their journeys South Asian performing arts have, in the main, refused the reductive logic of compartmentalisation operated by Eurocentric media and cultural institutions. The frisson produced by their interplay with mainstream or other dominant forms of culture over the years reveals complex processes of cultural negotiation variously enacted by the communities in their everyday life. In responding to questions of exile and cultural hybridism, the performing arts produced within BrAsian communities reflect something akin to what Jacques Derrida (1976) has described as 'difference': an irreducible distance both from the 'homeland' and the acquisitive land.[1] This conflux of two or more trajectories in languages, histories and cultures has opened a creative space that here will be specifically explored in the areas of dance, theatre and comedy. However, such distinctions in the performing arts should not be perceived as inherent in the artistic

1 For a detailed analysis of Derrida's concept of 'difference' within the linguistic arena set up in Tara Arts theatre productions see Terracciano, 1997.

traditions imported from the subcontinent, as performances may well thrive on a blend of dance, theatre and comedy as well as ritualistic elements around the time of religious festivals. Rather, these separations reflect an inclination to compartmentalisation and professionalism operating within the European artistic context from which the South Asian performing arts could not remain unaffected.

Moreover the long presence of South Asians in Britain makes the reference to first and second generation Asians irrelevant from a historical point of view—the distinction only refers to post-war migration. Thus throughout this exploration, a flexible understanding of categories of identity is also required. On the one hand the term 'British Asian' only reflects the condition experienced by migrants in the latter part of the twentieth century, when nation-states were carved out of what were previously colonial and colonised territories, subsumed under the nomenclature of the British Raj. On the other anti-racist campaigning and alliances with British-based African-Caribbean communities in post-war Britain provided for another arena of identity politics where Asian, however momentarily, became aligned to the category of 'Black British' (CCCS, 1982; Hall, 1996a; Gilroy, 1993b). Furthermore there is the fragmentation of Asian identities to consider in terms of Indian, Pakistani, Bangladeshi, Sri Lankan, Trinidadian Indian etc. and their regional constituencies. Our identity referents need, therefore, to be understood differentially in the varying spatial and temporal contexts explored here.

DANCE

Ever since South Asians set foot in Britain they have been the object of a gaze which exoticised them as different—in the process, conjuring up a mixed bag of metaphors: mysterious, sensual, sly, untrustworthy, odd, odorous, even regally connected. It was a gaze that easily transferred itself from the people to their associated musical and performative activities. In the late eighteenth century many South Asian street musicians were brought over to Britain as servants by army officers and traders, but after the death of their 'owners', the servants were often left to fend for themselves. Unable to obtain work, some of them resorted to playing in the streets. Others came as seamen and jumped ships to earn their living in the 'taprooms' of England and Scotland. In addition, there were conjurers and other 'novelty' performers. To name just a few of those recalled by Rosina Visram, there was an 'East Indian Gentoo' who in 1790 enthralled passers-by with his card tricks and thought-reading, a snake charmer who lured the curious in Limehouse, and in 1886 five Punjabis who arrived in London with a performing bear to entertain the public. The latter stayed only a few months, returning to the subcontinent with their furry friend (Visram, 1986: 58–61).

It would appear that in a time when theatres and music halls were, in the main, out of bounds for these 'exotic-looking' performers, the streets enabled a ready-made stage, much as they would in India.[2] South Asians in Britain did not need to try hard in order to become a 'spectacle' for the native English. They apparently became sights of interest by their presence alone. This observation applied very much to Indian royalty who presented themselves at courts, state balls and dances, naval and military reviews and other public spectacles. Their wealth and splendour bedazzled onlookers and many of the princes became indispensable as exotica in Edwardian England (Visram, 1986: 173). The Diamond Jubilee celebrations of Queen Victoria in 1897 were a case in point. Indian princes, *maharajahs*, *nawabs* and aristocracy gave the occasion 'a tinge of the romantic and the exotic in the eyes of the popular press. India's rich variety of native royalty, coupled with their wealth and flamboyance, meant that their doings were always newsworthy' (Vadgama, 1984: 32).

The romanticised aspects of orientalism also played their part in perceptions of working class mortals from the subcontinent.[3] When two Parsis, for instance, came to London to learn shipbuilding, they ended up 'playing up' to the curiosity of the crowds that used to constantly gather around them whilst they worked (Visram, 1986: 181). Whether they were performers or not, South Asians in Britain were subjects of an unflinching gaze—either of curiosity or wonder, or its obverse, suspicion and hatred.

After the Second World War a large-scale and more permanent settlement of South Asians in Britain began. Beginning with performances in front rooms and hired halls at special events, the performing arts eventually branched out into a series of distinct outfits with stages and audiences. Dance was an integral part of many of these performances. As the subcontinent thrived in a rich variety of classical dance repertoires, it was these that were first re-created as performances for diasporic audiences.

> In the early years, the role of the dancer was comparatively simple. More often than not, in the UK on a short stay with a husband whose posting had brought him to the West, she would replicate her classical training by passing it on to a number of selected pupils. There were very few outlets for performance, and the audiences were rather small. Consequently the importance of the private concert, set up by a *rasika* at their home, for a few knowledgeable invited guests. (Khan *et al.*, 2000: 1).

2 The streets continue to be an important arena for South Asian performances in Britain, particularly in the form of festivals (*mela*) and processions as for *Jagganathan* and *Vaisaki* from the 1970s. However, these outdoor performances operate nowadays in a much more regulated fashion as a consequence of local council initiatives and planning.

3 For an in-depth analysis on the concept of orientalism see Edward Said's *Orientalism* (1985) and Ronald Inden's *Imagining India* (1990).

Some performers continued Indian styles, trying to retain the 'authentic' music and rhythms of Indian dances, such as Bharatiya Natyam and Kathak. Nahid Siddiqui, for instance, was trained in Kathak in the 1970s in Pakistan. She came to Britain, first to teach dance from 1984, then setting up her own company in 1991. Whilst seeing herself as a traditional Kathak dancer, she explored its forms through ideas such as Sufism, nature and the *fakirs* (mendicants) of Punjab.

It is dance along with singing and playing musical instruments that was taught in classes to children whose parents were eager for them to keep in touch with their Indian heritage. This retrenchment did indeed bolster Eurocentric expectations of South Asian arts as the Other, the exotic. Initially BrAsians gathered to learn and teach music and dance in their houses. By the 1970s community-specific, culture-focused institutions had been established to provide cultural activities. In 1972 the first overseas branch of the Bharatiya Vidhya Bhavan (Institute of Indian Culture) was set up in London to promote Indian arts and culture, to be followed by a number of others in the rest of the country.[4] Consisting of a bookshop, a small library and two or three classrooms, six years later the Institute moved to a disused church in its present site in West London to hold classes and staged performances. Teachers were invited over from India in order to instruct in singing, musical instruments and physical exercises such as yoga. By the 1980s several companies and productions had emerged as a response to encouragement from the funding bodies of the art establishment. In general dancers and other cultural practitioners were adopted 'with a vision to take "heritage" arts beyond the immediate community and make artistic space for Indian dance in the mainstream' (Khan *et al.*, 2000: 2). Similarly, but in a less traditionalist mode to the Bharatiya Vidhya Bhavan classes and performances, the Akademi (formerly the Academy of Indian Dance) was founded in 1979 with the aim to place South Asian dance as a force to be reckoned with in British art, society and education. Other prominent dance organisations that have provided a focal point for the BrAsian dance landscape include SAMPAD, a development organisation for the arts of the subcontinent based in the Midlands, AdiTi, a London-based national organisation for South Asian dance in Britain (established in 1989), and Kadam, a Bedford-based development agency for South Asian dance (established in 1990).

However, as pointed out by Nadir Tharani:

> [T]his marginalisation together with the protectionist penchant for tradition perpetuates the historical judgements on South Asian arts and confirms its representation as strange and exotic, its location as the Other. It reinforces the opposition between tradition and contemporaneity bestowed by Modernism. This allows

4 The Bharatiya Vidhya Bhavan was founded by K.M. Munshi in 1937 in India, having been inspired by the philosophy and politics of Mahatma Gandhi.

the dominant culture to continue to appropriate and install these forms within its own divergent terrain, subjecting them to the wand of Reason after activating them with the motor of Progress. (Tharani, 1988: 43).

Thus a fair number of BrAsian dancers emerged from the early 1980s onwards who sought to innovate within classical Indian dance in order to incorporate and merge with contemporary trends. An exemplary figure here is Shobana Jeyasingh who founded her company in 1988 to pursue experimental forms of dance, combining Bharatiya Natyam with other dance repertoires to make for a dynamic, invigorating hybrid between various cultural references. She has gone on to forge a dance language responsive to the times and explorative of her BrAsian identity. However, Jeyasingh prefers not to see herself or her work as a 'fusion' of two discrete entities—the East and the West, the traditional and the modern. In an interview she stated: 'I'm very allergic to the word fusion because it suggests carpentry rather than dance!'[5] Rather, as her company policy asserts, she prefers a more fluid and heterogeneous identity of 'urban', and 'seeks to create work which is Asian in technique, British in context and personal and contemporary in vision'.[6] Her choreography for the company includes national tours of *Configurations* (1988), *Defile* (1989), *Correspondence* (1990), *Romance...with footnotes* (1991), *Raid* (1995), *Palimpsest* (1996), *Intimacies of a Third Order* (1998) and *Fine Frenzy* (1999). Many of these works involve experimental collaborations with artistes from a variety of backgrounds. In 1993, for instance, she commissioned the choreographer, Richard Alston, to develop a piece for her company. He called it *Delicious Arbor* and set the dance to a score by the seventeenth-century composer Henry Purcell. Jeyasingh took issue with critics who described it as 'exotic' to see her dancers moving to Purcell's 'white' music. She insisted that she combined East and West as messily and thoroughly as they are in her own life. Jeyasingh asserted, 'Purcell, like Shelley, like David Bowie, is not "the Other", it is part of my heritage. And in dance terms, Rumani Devi and Merce Cunningham are also part of my heritage.' Thus her creations are not a process of bringing together two discrete entities, the Eastern and the Western, but something much more heterogeneous, a dynamic and fluid response to her experiences. She is 'part of a process of cultural interpenetration that's both careful and haphazard'—as a result, her work defies simplistic traditional/modern dichotomies.[7] The success of such shows has meant a shift from their marginal positions to the core of mainstream performance arts, where Indian dance-based performances are made available in mainstream concert halls, theatres, festivals, film and on video.

5 26 February 2003, www.londondance.com.

6 http://www.britishcouncil.org/arts/theatredance/companies/dance1_009.html.

7 http://www.artandculture.com/arts/artist?artistId=1222.

By the 1990s another important trend had begun to emerge, in which funded Dance-in-Education and Community Dance projects (community not in a specifically Indian sense) worked within schools, communities and amongst minority groups. Often these activities accompanied tours in performing venues. This decade also saw the intensification of the debate about whether diasporic South Asian performances should be evaluated in terms of their ethnic associations and reference points or judged according to their generalised competence as an art form.[8] Diasporic artists increasingly began to voice their disagreements to being seen as tokens of the ethnic arts, and asked for the liberty to express their artistic visions any which way they chose (Araeen, 1987). These are questions that have raised as many responses and answers as there are performers in the various genres.

THEATRE

As with dance, so with theatre: the development of a BrAsian theatre aesthetic and production has also been influenced by a complex web of cultural, political and economic relations between Britain and the subcontinent, referred to above in terms of 'orientalism'. This phenomenon has been particularly visible in the critical response to the imports of South Asian dance/drama performances at the turn of the nineteenth century. Whilst acknowledging the artistic value of classical traditions and techniques, theatre critics and reviewers of South Asian dance/theatre performances generally reinforced the conceptual remoteness of Indian theatre from the British context. South Asian theatre was often trapped in a mythical past, which not only denied the existence of new and experimental theatre undertaken in the subcontinent, but also work practised in Britain. Disregarded by most West End impresarios, these forms pointed towards a cultural landscape that embraced hybridity as the necessary outcome of colonisation.[9] At the same time casting policies operated by

8 This is a debate that has been paralleled for other creative endeavours of diasporic people in Britain. Stuart Hall (1996a) comments on two 'cultural or political dominants' in post-war black experience in Britain. The first moment describes when the term 'black' was coined to refer to common experiences of racism and marginalisation in Britain. Along with this came challenges to dominant regimes of representation through music, style and later literary, visual and cinematic forms. The question of black artists' access to rights of representation was also raised. The second moment describes another kind of politics where black cultural workers have to struggle on two fronts—as people marked by colour and as artists. The shift is about a movement from a struggle over the relations of representation to a politics of representation itself—that is, it is a move to get away from notions of the innocent, essentialist black subject and judge artworks on a non-racialised platform.

9 See Homi Bhabha's (1994) critique of any essentialisation of cultural entities, such as the English, the Indian etc., and of the 'hybrid' as the coming together of two 'authentic' and distinctive entities. East-West fusions may well be seen to simultaneously energise the 'Eastern' and regenerate the 'Western' in a dynamic crucible. However, whatever preceded

a number of impresarios often stifled the talent of Asian actors by engaging them in predictably stereotypical roles. Interestingly, diasporic South Asian art practitioners reacted against the racism experienced within the entertainment industry by enacting strategies of resistance both on a personal and collective level.

At a time when hybridity was already evident in the theatre halls of the Indian subcontinent, a number of theatre groups emerged in Britain at the beginning of the last century to explore similarities and connections between theatre traditions practised in India and Europe.[10] The orientalising gaze was thus resisted in various ways, as they began to engage in performances that were either openly indebted to the Western traditions of expressive arts, or were developed to become a direct challenge to them. On 4 November 1915, for instance, the Union of East and West and the Indian Art and Dramatic Society presented a *Grand Performance in Aid of the Wounded Indian Troops* at the Town Hall in Chiswick. The programme included extracts from the religious epic the *Mahabharata* and K.N. Das Gupta's adaptations from Tagore and the *Arabian Nights Story*, accompanied by the music of Sullivan, Mascagni Clutsam and Indian songs by Ali Khan.[11] Some years later in the programme of their production of Niranjan Pal's *The Goddess* the Indian Players made a specific note that the play would be performed with an all-Indian cast of players 'speaking in accentual English'.[12] Early ama-

the 'hybrids' cannot be assumed to be versions of regional purity, as the process of colonisation had long affected 'original' cultures.

10 The remit of the present work does not allow delving too extensively into the effects of the assimilation of European theatrical forms in Indian theatre. However, it is worth reminding that in the subcontinent the assimilation of alien devices like the proscenium arch, which was introduced in Hindi theatre in the mid nineteenth century by Pārasī (or Parsee) amateur companies, had far reaching consequences in the shaping of new theatre formulas. In this case it represented a major change in the way theatre was experienced by the audiences, formally located on the three sides of the stage. More generally, the introduction of technological devices like microphones and electric lights would either make obsolete previous theatre practices or change their meaning within classical and popular dramatic structures. For instance, in Kathakali performances, originally played in the rural villages of Kerala, the musical compositions and rhythms played before the start of the performances with highly resonant instruments like the clarinet originally served to attract people's attention and gather them around the performing area. Similarly, the use of torches to light the stage may have influenced the richness of costumes and use of make up, as they were employed to focus the attention of the audience to the face and the hands of the performers. Taking such performances into closed theatres has inevitably bestowed a new meaning to the above practices. (See Narayana Birendra, 1981; Awasthi Suresh, 1983; and Ottai Antonella, 1986).

11 The Society was set up 'to establish a common meeting place for East and West in the field of art, literature, music and the drama'. See programme of the play, *Grand Performance in Aid of the Wounded Indian Troops*, Town Hall, Chiswick, 4 November 1915, Theatre Museum Archive.

12 Programme of the show, *The Goddess*, by Niranjan Pal, Duke of York's Theatre, London, 6 June 1922, Theatre Museum Archive.

teur theatre groups, such as the India Office Dramatic Society and the Indian Students' Union Play-Reading Circle, also revealed an interest in drawing both from Indian and European theatre traditions. Their work, mostly unrecognised by theatre critics and entrepreneurs, anticipated the research of later groups from the 1970s as they looked at submerged connections between continents as a tool to defy essentialist views of cultural and artistic activities.

The soil that allowed these seeds to grow was provided by the political activities that, in the years after the Second World War, were spurred in Britain by colonial independence. Self-help and support organisations, often set up in conjunction with white liberals and radical activists, provided a space for social activities and various forms of entertainment. By 1945—the year in which Asians, Africans and West Indians living in Britain united in a Subject People's Conference and in the later Fifth Pan-African Congress in Manchester—nearly all associations in Britain were leaning towards a common front for the colonial independence of their countries of origin in tandem with international black struggles. The many Indian leagues and workers' associations, which after Indian independence started to concentrate their efforts for the improvement of their living conditions in Britain, were pivotal in bonding their people's struggles to those of other African and Caribbean groups. Within such organisations, different forms of entertainment also started to thrive: in the case of the India League it was the newly emerging Indian film industry. Conceived initially 'as the spearhead of the Indian independence lobby', after 1947 it focused its activity on easing the relationship between Indian and British people by the distribution of films imported from the subcontinent.[13] As the Asian population grew, so did the amount of imports and the number of cinema halls built in the country—an interest, which after the onslaught of video technology in the 1980s, transferred itself into mainstream cinemas to meet the demand for Indian commercial films.

Interestingly, by the mid 1940s white leftist theatre companies had started to show an increasing interest to include African, Caribbean and Asian plays in their repertoire. In 1943 Unity Theatre, a radical, left-wing company founded in 1936 with a distinctive communist and anti-imperialist agenda produced the documentary drama *India Speaks*, by Mulk Raj Anand. The cast was composed entirely of BrAsian people living in Britain. This was a particularly remarkable case considering the casting policies operating within many theatre houses of the times. Some years later Zia Mohyeddin, a Pakistani actor who became famous for his interpretation of Doctor Aziz in E.M. Forster's *A Passage to India*, remarked:

13 See Dilip Hiro, 1991: 124.

> It was somehow assumed that black and Asian actors weren't good enough.... This is why some people who were not Asian, not even remotely Asian, constantly played Asian parts. And because they had specialised in playing these parts, the directors felt more comfortable using them. I don't know whether the directors felt comfortable because they knew these people, or because they couldn't cope with the real thing.[14]

While the mainstream sector continued for many years to offer a limited range of roles to Asian actors, in the early 1960s an increasing number of community theatre groups started to perform in original languages, such as Hindi, Urdu, Bengali and Gujarati, establishing what was later called the Language Theatre Movement. Among them were the Maharashtrian Theatre Group and the Asian Artists Association in London, The East-West Community Theatre Group in Birmingham and a number of other small groups especially active in the East Midlands. Away from the glamorous spotlights of the London West End, these groups performed plays directly imported from the subcontinent in community halls, front rooms and other alternative spaces, which were also used for dance performances and other social/religious gatherings.

The genres performed were mostly drawing-room comedies, melodramas and thrillers, with dialogues often interwoven with songs, dances and plots that tended to reinforce values and customs imported from India. As reflected in Naseem Khan's seminal report on 'Ethnic Arts' in Britain (Khan, 1976), it seems that public funding assessors at the time tended to perceive these productions as less worthy of institutional support than the work produced by groups performing in English and focusing on the social realities of Asian people in Britain. This attitude clearly disregarded the fact that these plays offered an important *trait d'union* with the subcontinent both on a cultural and linguistic level. By resisting the homogenising trends imparted by mainstream institutions and funding bodies, they offered a unique opportunity to express linguistic, religious and cultural differences otherwise disregarded at work, in education and other sectors of society. Besides, the opportunity for young people to establish a creative contact with a linguistic universe only spoken at home was going to be crucial for later artistic currents, as shown in the development of poetry and lyrics. As in the case of Raas and Garba folk dances, especially popular within the Gujarati community and later popularised through open-air festivals and *mela*, poetry has also entered the wider domain of cultural production when funded as a live art event rather than an obscure community activity. A good case in point is offered by the *mushaira* (Urdu poetry readings very popular

14 Zia Mohyeddin in Pines, 1992: 73. Interestingly Mohyeddin came to international fame in 1960 with his interpretation of the Indian doctor in this memorable adaptation by Santha Rama Rau for the Oxford Playhouse, later transferred to Broadway.

within Pakistani communities), which, with their increasing use of music and the performative attitude of the readers, have started to be enjoyed by wider and varied audiences all over the country.[15]

A trend that directly addressed contemporary socio-political issues in Britain started to take roots in London and other major cities in the early 1970s. Pivotal to its development was the contribution of theatre professionals and aspirant artists coming from the former East African colonies whose take on questions of racism, exile and diaspora within the British urban context reflected previous experiences of cultural and geographical displacement. As these young artists started to perform in fringe venues, community spaces, temples and private houses, the intent to bring a new dimension to the creative exploration of Asian multiple identities became immediately evident. A good case in point is offered by the Tara Arts group, founded in 1976 in response to the racist murder of an Asian teenager in Southall.[16] A radical, political stance became its hallmark for some years, with plays focusing on colonial paradigms, the tensions between communities and the changing roles assumed by Asian women within the new cultural environment. Historical connections between the subcontinent and Europe were also elaborated through a distinctive theatrical vocabulary. In particular the process of cultural negotiation, which Asian communities would experience in their everyday life, was effectively enacted on stage by the actors who could draw from their double, or sometimes multiple sensitivity and creatively engage with several cultural traditions. This unique position enabled the group to devise a specific formula of 'theatre for all', aiming at communicating with Asian, African, Caribbean and the indigenous white communities. Questions of identity, cultural hybridisation and race relations were at the heart of plays like *Sacrifice*, by Rabindranath Tagore, staged in 1977 at the Battersea Arts Centre, *Relationships*, a poetry recital, produced in 1977 and *Fuse*, the first original production presented in 1978 at the London Drama and Tape Centre in Holborn.

By the mid 1980s Tara's political perspective had started to be filtered through a theatrical language increasingly concerned with stylistic experimentation. Between 1983 and 1989 the company focused on

15 Performance poetry in the public sphere came to fruition in the 1990s, particularly with the activities of younger generations of Asians who drew from *mushaira* and other South Asian traditions and merged them with other forms such as West African/New York griot traditions of story-telling and rap-based MC-ing to make for a peculiarly British and urban blend of performance commentary. Key figures here include the Manchester-based Samshad and the London-based Joyoti Grech, Sujhdev Sandhu, Parm Kaur and Raman Mundair.

16 Tara Arts was the first Asian theatre company to be revenue funded by the Arts Council of England (then Arts Council of Great Britain). For an in-depth analysis of Tara Arts history see Alda Terracciano (1996). Archival material and historical information on Tara Arts can be viewed on http//www.salidaa.org.uk.

a distinctive aesthetic research based on the study of Indian and other non-European theatre techniques, alongside Sanskrit drama and mostly anti-realist trends in theatre and cinema, for which Bombay movies provided an important source of inspiration. Much of this work entailed the rewriting of Western theatrical classics to evolve a sophisticated counter-practice to racist assumptions, while imparting new viewpoints on received stories and histories. The phase reached its maturity with the production of *The Government Inspector* in 1989 under the direction of the visiting theatre director from New Delhi, Anuradha Kapur. Unsuspected similarities and cross-fertilisation between Eastern and Western theatre traditions emerged, leading the company to a provocative fusion of different styles, as they resonated throughout the streets of Birmingham, Leicester, London and Britain's other multicultural metropolises.[17]

During the 1980s a number of other theatre companies also progressed, their ways uncovering cultural, historical, economic and artistic connections between Europe and its former colonies which history had so often overlooked. These included the Hounslow Arts Co-operative, the Asian Co-operative, Madhav Sharma's Actors Unlimited and the British Asian Theatre Company. The groups variously pushed forward the boundaries of social theatre by exploring the linguistic and cultural universes of the South Asian diaspora both for their communities and their mostly white, young audiences (Kaur, 2000). Some of them told their stories in a variety of languages where myths intermingled with scenes of real life, bringing to the stage a new generation of young people born or brought up in Britain and therefore claiming their fair share of the 'cool Britannia'.[18] In this respect drama became an exceptional medium to convey the changing modalities of BrAsian identities well before the film industry would take an interest in this area of British urban life. The work of playwrights such as Farrukh Dhondy and later Meera Syal, Rukhsana Ahmad, Parv Bancil and Tanika Gupta seemed to contribute to challenging Eurocentric views on BrAsian life by freeing their characters from the stereotypical roles of shopkeepers, restaura-

17 It is worth noting that a unique eclecticism permeated most of Verma's work during these years, as evident in his production of *Danton's Death* (1989), *Tartuffe* (1990), *Oedipus the King* (1991), *Troilus and Cressida* (1993) and *The Bourgeois Gentilhomme* (1994). These productions are emblematic of Tara's attempt to create a 'theatre of connections' both on the level of text and of *mise en scène*, which, with all the due differences, can be aligned with the theatre research of other European contemporaries such as Eugenio Barba, Peter Brook and Ariane Mnouchkine.

18 As arts policy has, of late, shifted from the concept of multiculturalism to that of cultural diversity, artists started to take a critical stance with regards to a proper acknowledgement of diasporic contributions to modern Britain. To put it in the words of playwright and director Parv Bancil, when discussing his play *Made in England* (1998): 'I was particularly interested with the "cool Britannia" aspect of the Labour propaganda machine. I wanted to know if I—a British Asian—was included in this "celebration".' (Bancil, 2000: 90).

teurs or post office employees. Finally, with companies like Tamasha, Kali, Chandica Theatre, Moti Roti and venues like the Watermans Arts Centre in London, The Haymarket Studio in Leicester, the Drum and the Birmingham Rep in Birmingham, a nurturing space has been provided for newer generations of playwrights, directors and actors to engage in the exciting dialogue between times, cultures and theatre traditions that South Asian theatre artists had been pioneering in Britain for the last two centuries.

COMEDY

One more important area to consider in our exploration of the performance arts is comedy. As is its promiscuous wont, comedy is a component of virtually all dramas, dances and other types of performances whether it be spoken or through mime. Many of the films produced by the Asian diaspora also rely strongly on comedy interspersed amongst the high drama and novel scenarios, for example *Bhaji on the Beach* (dir. Gurinder Chadha, 1994), *East is East* (dir. Damien O'Donnell, 1999), *Bend it Like Beckham* (dir. Gurinder Chadha, 2002) and *Anita and Me* (dir. Metin Huseyin, 2002). As with the professionalisation of dance and theatre, comic stand-ups began to take on a prominent role as a force to be reckoned with on their own grounds around the 1990s.

Cornerstones of contemporary Asian diasporic comedy include a dialogue with colonial narratives premised upon essentialisms and stereotypes, where age-old assumptions are turned on their head. As the art critic, Manick Govinda, summarised for the 1980s, these include(d): 'Asian woodentops in *Eastenders*, exotica in *The Far Pavilions*, Asians as barbarians and savages in *Indiana Jones and the Temple of Doom*, Asians as silly 'Pakis' in *Mind Your Language* etc.' (*Bazaar*, spring 1988). Once BrAsians began to fine-tune their comedic acts, the exotic, the barbaric, the effeminate and the holy or sacred were ripped apart with abandon. It is not incidental that the title of one of the more successful comedy television programmes, *Goodness Gracious Me!* invoked reappropriating British comedian/actor Peter Sellers' trademark quip on the Indian accent. Subject matter also strongly revolves around astute commentaries on the parent generation, as well as observations on the contemporary British socio-political milieu.

The uses and effects of this type of comedy are multiple. First, as we have already mentioned, comedy's uses as a socio-political weapon inverts age-old truisms and clichés based on South Asian culture, ethnicity and associated concepts. Second, it serves as an indirect means of deflecting potentially aggressive or uncomfortable situations in the diaspora context, which then can be translated for the staged performance. Third, it provides a lateral narrative of diasporic consciousness, rewriting the assumed and taken-for-granted by jettisoning it into the orbit of the ludicrous. A set piece by the stand-up, Sody Funjabi, invokes these themes with characteristic panache:

> You know the British, they look after their minorities: for example, the British have a service that takes the minorities off the streets and puts a roof over their heads. This service is called the Police Force. Bloody brilliant service!
>
> But the only problem of living in England is that it costs too much to telephone India. So I tell you what to do: you get drunk, you get arrested and when the police give you your one telephone call—you call your family back in Bombay. The old bill pay your phone bill! Bloody brilliant service! (Sody Funjabi, 2000, from the performance *This is your life Mr Funjabi*)

Clearly comedy has the potential of transgressing normative categories of thought. It highlights the phenomenon of a 'surplus of meaning' and the crucial catalyst of excess, which disrupts totalising analytical schemas with moments of madness and 'ludism'—a trait symptomatic of the comic enterprise. Using techniques of inversion, subversion, irony, exaggeration and exposure of taboo subjects amongst others, comedy encapsulates the dynamic nuances, contradictions and contestations of BrAsian life, which defy straightforward sociological or anthropological parameters of analysis.

One Nation Under a Groove...Innit was a regular event at the Middlesex-based Watermans Arts Centre and became a banner for several BrAsian performers in this trade. The unit became a production house for comedy dramas, such as *Arrange that Marriage, Don't Look at my Sister...Innit!*, and *Papa was a Bus Conductor*, which all explored the history and cultural mores of BrAsian life in 1990s Britain in a parodic fashion. Several of the comedians also had parallel careers as straight actors—Nina Wadia and Sanjeev Bhaskar to name but two. Even musicians such as Nitin Sawhney had a part to play in the comedy group Secret Asians along with Sanjeev Bhaskar. With an alliance between Bhaskar and actress Meera Syal, already known for her Asian input into the multi-racial television comedy show *The Real McCoy*, the seeds of the award-winning *Goodness Gracious Me* (produced by Anil Gupta) phenomenon were firmly planted. The show was first transmitted on Radio Four catering to a largely white middle-class audience before it was broadcast on television in 1998, viewed by a broader constituency of people in Britain, and then overseas via BBC World.[19] Rather than being seen as subjects to be treated with caution, BrAsians have been compared to the Jewish diaspora in America for their irreverent sense of humour. In 1996 when the BBC producer Anil Gupta first broached the

19 It is noteworthy that radio has also been an important media for much of the Asian diaspora, particularly when franchises became available to target minority audiences from the 1980s.

subject of an Asian sitcom, the reaction was, 'What! Asians have a sense of humour!?' A few years later BrAsian points of reference have entered firmly into the national narratives of viewing audiences.

As with dance, theatre and poetry, BrAsian comedy also grew directly from the drawing room or 'parlour'. A good example of this process started with the social club for young adults called the Young Putoharis where young BrAsians got together to 'have a laugh' and eventually led to the formation of the comedy group the Funjabis in 1996 under the inspiration of Sody Kahlon. Other comedians had more mundane backgrounds—people realising that they had a flair for comedy and leaving their trade altogether to do the club circuit: a case in hand being the ex-structural engineer Jeff Mirza. Many of the comedy acts touch upon subjects familiar to Asian diasporas but also (bar the occasional Indian phrases) accessible to mainstream audiences. Some have chosen to amplify controversial subjects—Shazia Mirza is a Muslim comedienne who, clad top-to-toe in burqa, lampoons orthodoxy in a dead-pan style. Television has injected oxygen into live performances, and one-off shows such as *Asian Mega Mela Malai: The Cream of Comedy* (2003) have showcased a wide variety of multiracial performers. Along with other performances/media offerings, BrAsian comedy has contributed a lot towards bringing together several arms of the South Asian diaspora. Some of it has looped back to the subcontinent where comedy programmes and films have met with enthusiastic reception.

Dance, theatre and comedy have been the key focus of our enquiry here. Having said this, we have seen how easily these art forms would link with other expressive arenas articulating the many facets of BrAsian identities long before mainstream media began to take an interest in their self-crafted stories. Moreover, while their critiques and subversions of dominant stereotypes of diasporic Asians have come more to the fore towards the latter part of the twentieth century, it is to earlier precedents that one must turn to find the seeds of their counteracting strategies.

Throughout we have noted how it is not only the performative arts that have defied reification as distinct activities but also the identities associated with them. We have tried to still the constant waters of change to highlight some exemplary moments in the history of South Asian performing arts in Britain. The description of 'South Asian performance' itself needs to be put under erasure: are the arts described in this chapter South Asian or even BrAsian by virtue of their motifs and/or their practitioners? Indeed, should these performances be indexed or evaluated in terms of any ethnic associations at all, or should they be judged according to the level of 'excellence' reached by the artists in their chosen art form?[20] Of course, such an idea of 'artistic excellence' panders to a dominant and rather romantic and often self-serving view of an artist as a heroically gifted individual standing outside society. By the 1980s diasporic artists increasingly had begun to voice their disagreement of being hemmed in by the expectations and assumptions laid down by racial/ethnic associations. They appealed for the liberty to express their artistic visions however they wished, as 'cultures of origins' can be shackles just as well as they can be resources. Indeed, it seems that while cultural associations offered themselves as creative pools to draw from, problems arose when they became categories to fall in to according to funding criteria set up in a context severely tipped towards mainstream white culture. However, the difficulty for BrAsian (as well as other ethnically marked) performers goes beyond mere questions of the funding policy of various governmental agencies. Rather, it goes to the way the (liberal) discourse of performance interacts with the racialised context in which BrAsians find themselves. Thus BrAsian performers often find themselves fêted as a representative voice of the BrAsian condition, while the 'BrAsian condition' continues to be treated as being particular and parochial. As Toni Morrison is supposed to have ruefully commented, her novel *Beloved* is a novel about enslaved African Americans, while James Joyce's *Ulysses* is not a novel about a summer day in Dublin, it's a story about Everyman. For the most part BrAsian performing arts continue to be located within an ethnographic and exoticised context.

20 See footnote 8.

VASCO DA GAMA

AbdoolKarim Vakil

'The history of this expansion of England', Sir John Seely stated in his popular and enduringly influential lectures on *The Expansion of England*, 'must necessarily begin with the two ever memorable journeys of Columbus and Vasco da Gama' (Seely, 1883: 123). The reason being, as Edgar Prestage, the Camões Professor of Portuguese at the University of London's King's College, spelt out on the occasion of the fourth centenary in 1925 of the death of da Gama, that 'Our Indian Empire grew out of Bombay ceded by the Portuguese as part of the dowry of Catherine of Braganza when she married Charles II, but it derives indirectly from the Voyage of Vasco da Gama, and the Union Jack now waves over many lands which his countrymen were the first Europeans to find and govern, especially India and Ceylon. It is therefore fitting that Britishers should honour the man who opened the way of Empire for them' (Prestage, 1925: 2–3). Da Gama, as H. Reade had somewhat more succinctly put it at the special session of the Royal Asiatic Society of Great Britain and Ireland held to commemorate the fourth centenary of his landing at Calicut, 'was the man who gave India to Europe and to England' (Reade, 1898: 589–90).

Little is known about Vasco da Gama, nor, in truth, does it much matter here. Even Seely, whose book and whose vision of history and empire shaped generations of British statesmen no less than pupils, has no more interest in da Gama or even in his voyage than the bearing of its 'pregnant' possibilities under and for the English. For the point about da Gama, even for this imperial historiography, is rather the event it names, for all intents and purposes exchangeable with the date 1498, or the discovery of the sea route to India.

For Hume, Adam Smith and William Robertson, from a seventeenth-century Enlightenment perspective, da Gama's voyage, together with Columbus', made up the 'greatest and most important events recorded in the history of mankind' (Smith, [1776] 1976: II, 141). Alexander von Humboldt writing in the nineteenth century dates the global impact of the West and the crucial period during which the balance of power tipped in its favour to the six years between Columbus' and da Gama's voyages (Humboldt, 1837: 20–1). For Serge Latouche, towards the close of the twentieth century, echoing Paul Valéry's reflections from the abyss of the 1930s, 'the time of the finite world began with Vasco da Gama and Magellan' (Latouche, 1996: 8). To paraphrase an aside of Samir Amin's on the occasion of the 1998 quincentenary of da Gama's voyage: 1492 or 1498, Portuguese and Spaniards are welcome to argue it out; we can split the difference, the point is the consequent formation of a polarised mercantile capitalism (Amin, 1998: 43). Each of these, and many others besides, encode different readings of da Gama's voyage (see Vakil, 1998a, 1998b), but what they share is its privileging in the historiographical narrative constitutive of the discourse of the West and the Rest.

In the same year of 1925 that Englishmen were invited to honour da Gama's memory for opening Britain's route to India and empire, and British immigration officers were busy abusing the newly passed Special Restriction (Coloured Alien Seamen) Order to keep Indians from making the reverse journey into England (Visram, 2002: 205–16), K.M. Panikkar visited the beach of Belem 'from which Vasco da Gama set out on his fateful voyage'. There, as he later recalled, as he 'marvelled at the momentous changes unleashed on the world by that trivial event' (Panikkar, 1977: 242), the idea came to him for the study that would eventually result in his *Asia and Western Dominance*. The book and its presiding architecture, however, owed less to that day in Belem than to his involvement in the protracted process towards Indian independence, or, symbolically more pertinent still, his witnessing the departure of the European warships from Asia following the evacuation of their bases on mainland China and the declaration of the People's Republic in 1949. For it is this closure of the cycle, rather than its 1498 origins, that more significantly structures his *Survey of the Vasco da Gama Epoch of Asian History, 1498–1945*, as its subtitle describes it. And for all that the opening line of Panikkar's first chapter does describe 'Vasco da Gama's arrival at the port of Calicut on the southwest coast of India on May 27, 1498' as 'mark[ing] a turning-point in the history of India and Europe' (Panikkar, 1953: 23), and despite his insistence on the unity of the Vasco da Gama epoch, it is only from the nineteenth century, in the wake of the Industrial and French Revolutions, that he sees Europe as indeed coming to challenge the basis of Asian societies. Contemporary historiography reinforces this view. The world economy of the fifteenth century, when da Gama arrives in the Indian Ocean, was a polycentric regional system dominated by Asia, which Europe entered on Asian terms. As the, likely apocryphal, story has it, when asked upon his return what commodities were to be found there and what they wanted from us, and told by da Gama that pepper, cinnamon, ginger, amber and musk was what was to be had and gold, silver, velvet and scarlet cloth was what was to be paid for it, the Count of Vimioso quipped: 'it seems to me then that it is they rather who had discovered us!' (cited in Fonseca, 1998: 122).

The economic and political hegemony of the West can only be dated from the Industrial Revolution. The story the West tells itself though, from the chronicles of the voyages of discovery and the enterprises of conquest, through the formation of the discourses of history, geography and the social sciences, is the narrative of the rise and triumph of the West predicated on the exceptionality of Europe.

It is the discursive triumph in instituting a representation of the relation between Asia and the West dominated by the West that BrAsian genealogy disrupts. BrAsians unstitch the national narrative of Britishness. BrAsian history gets back to basics: it brings the Empire back in. BrAsian, too, is a genealogical construct, but one which undoes the immigrant genealogy of descent with its focus on the 'second' and 'third generations', and on a 'contemporary South Asian presence' traced to its point of origin at the moment and place of arrival on British soil. Like Enoch Powell's 'citizens of the Commonwealth who', in his infamous pronouncement of 1972, 'have no more connection or affinity with the United Kingdom than with China or Peru' (cited by Marshall in Gardiner, 1990: 82), 'Asians' come into British social history much as their fathers and grandfathers came into Britain in the 1950s: as immigrants; aliens, in perception, if not (yet then) in law. The immigrant genealogical perspective reproduces and enshrines the amnesiac amazement of the (white) British faced with the arrival of 'these poor, benighted people' who, in Stuart Hall's bitingly witty depiction of 1978, 'for reasons which the British sometimes find it hard to bring to mind, picked themselves up out of their villages ... and, quite uninvited made this long, strange and apparently unpredictable journey to the doors of British industry—which, as you know, out of the goodness of their hearts gave them jobs' (Hall, 1978: 24).

The critique of this immigrant genealogy begins, as Bhikhu Parekh did in his follow up talk in the same 1978 BBC TV series on Multi-Racial Britain, by firmly placing any discussion of 'the relations between the Asian immigrants and native Britons' squarely against 'the background of their colonial encounter and the unequal economic and political power relationship generated by it' (Parekh, 1978: 37). Though confronting the collective colonial amnesia head on, Parekh's remains, as it then perhaps could not but remain, an immigrant critique of the immigrant genealogy. Extending the relation back in time and on to the Empire, it leaves Britain to the 'native Britons' repatriating the Asian through his immigrant genealogy back and beyond the geography of the nation-state into the realm of a (still white) British history made elsewhere.

A BrAsian approach shares with this critique of immigrant genealogy its preoccupation with the constitutive role of the colonial in the analysis of the postcolonial. But it takes Parekh's riposte to the resentful racist, that he 'cannot accept the benefits accruing from Britain's occupation of other lands, and deny their inhabitants a right to benefit from Britain' (Parekh, 1978: 51), and reinscribes it with Fanon's reminder that 'the entire Third World went into the making of Europe' (cited in Said, 2000: 480). The BrAsian critique is postcolonial in its conception of the colonial and its constitutiveness. It is concerned not merely to reinscribe colonialism and its legacies in the postcolonial, but to critique the very distinctness of the categories of home and empire, metropolitan centre and colonial periphery which projected the imperial into the confines of the Empire, and structured the imperial narrative through the discourse of discovery and expansion.

PLANET BOLLYWOOD

Rachel Dwyer

In 2002 the hotly contested term 'Bollywood' became a buzzword in Britain as London's 'Bollywood summer' saw a whole range of events connected with Indian popular cinema, from museum exhibitions to film festivals, department store themed promotions and exposure in several publications. Given these events were not engineered to coincide, their occasion rather shows how an awareness of this cinema, hitherto known only as vague exotica, had penetrated public awareness in the early 2000s. This cinema is known in Britain as 'Bollywood', a term which, despite its being contested in India, especially in the film industry, has entered the *Oxford English Dictionary* (2001) and is now here to stay.

This chapter focuses on the dominant form of Indian cinema, the Hindi cinema produced in Bombay. Hindi cinema is unique in the world as a national, popular, independent cinema, free from much state control, which has enormous domestic audiences, its popularity threatened only occasionally by Hollywood's global reach. Hindi cinema has been part of the life of BrAsians for several decades and it is no coincidence that the events of 2002 took place at a time of increased visibility of BrAsians in all walks of life. This chapter looks at Hindi cinema in Britain, tracing the complex dynamic between the Indian producers and BrAsians in the wider context of British culture.

HISTORICAL BACKGROUND

From its beginnings Indian cinema was international. Developing from nineteenth-century Indian public culture, itself a product of the imperial encounter, cinema's hybrid nature combined Western technologies and modes such as melodrama with indigenous visual and performative traditions. In the early period of silent cinema, American cinema was the most widely screened cinema in India, thanks to good distribution and its relatively low cost due to the economy of scale. Furthermore from the early days many foreigners have worked in the Indian cinema industry, often as technicians although also as directors. Notable figures include the American Ellis Duncan who, despite not knowing the language, worked in Tamil cinema for seventeen years, introducing the actor MGR; several Germans, who worked in Bombay Talkies (including

Joseph Wirschung, who was later the cameraman for *Pakeezah/The Pure One*, 1971, and Franz Osten—who had earlier directed several silent films including *Light of Asia/Prem Sanyas*, 1925—who directed several of their most famous films including *Acchut Kanya/The Untouchable Girl*, 1936); and the Australian 'Fearless Nadia', who was India's first stunt queen. However, the first entirely Indian film was made as early as 1913, immediately establishing some of the distinctive characteristics that are a part of Indian cinema.

Indian cinema soon devolved into many cinemas, separated by language and style as well as production, distribution and audience. During the silent era language was not a divisive issue. Although the films had title cards, usually in two or three languages, they were of little significance since, given low levels of literacy, the films also had presenters to explain the action (or rather to embellish it, given that the narratives were often already familiar to the audience) in local languages to musical accompaniments. Lip reading reveals that sometimes the actors were even speaking English. However, with the coming of sound in the 1930s, language became an important issue as the producers aimed to reach as large an audience as possible rather than confining the films to local language areas. The obvious choice was 'Hindustani', a *lingua franca* which comprised many dialects understood over much of north India. It can be loosely identified as the colloquial form both of Hindi, which became the national language of India after independence, and of Urdu, later the national language of Pakistan. However, during this period many films were made in two versions, one in the local language of the studio and one in Hindi. India's major film centres in the 1930s were Bombay (Mumbai), Calcutta (Kolkata), Poona (Pune) and Lahore, with Bombay, despite lying outside the Hindi belt, becoming the centre of the Hindi film industry. After independence and partition in 1947 other popular national cinemas evolved, notably in Pakistan, based in Lahore ('Lollywood'), and important local cinemas, notably in south India. Hindi cinema remains dominant in South Asia, finding major audiences across the region, even where there have been attempts to prevent screenings, such as in Pakistan where pirate copies of Hindi films are widely available.

In addition to the various popular cinemas made in a variety of languages, other cinemas emerged in India in the 1950s (see Nandy, 1995, 1998; Rajadhyaksha, 1996a and b; Prasad, 1998; Dwyer, 2000a: chapter 3; Dwyer and Patel, 2002: chapter 2). The first of these was an 'art' cinema, typified by the films of Satyajit Ray, one of the world's most acclaimed directors. Art cinema has limited distribution in India but is seen worldwide, including in Britain, though largely within the arthouse and festival circuit. South Asian art films are mostly in Bengali, with Calcutta remaining the centre for much art cinema, although strong traditions exist in other regions, notably Kerala. Cinemas other than the popular are also produced in Hindi, including the 1970s *avant garde* cinema of Mani Kaul and Kumar Shahani and the 'middle cinema' (new cinema, parallel cinema) typified by that of Shyam Benegal. Since the 1990s a new younger generation of film makers, such as Kaizad Gustad and Dev Benegal, has been experimenting with films in Hindi and in English (often called 'Hinglish') intended also for an international audience. These cinemas have production and distribution circuits different from the (popular) Hindi cinema and are seen in the West but only by selective audiences.

BOLLYWOOD AND THE SOUTH ASIAN DIASPORA

Hindi cinema is also a global cinema, though different in scale from that of Hollywood (see Dwyer, 2000b). It is hugely popular outside Western Europe and North America, often more so than local and Hollywood cinemas. Some films have proved to be massive international hits, such as *Awaara/The Vagabond* (1951), which was remade in several languages worldwide. One of the reasons for the appeal of Hindi cinema in many countries is its cheaper ticket prices, the result of being cheaper to screen than Hollywood cinema. But it is also celebrated as a non-Western form, upholding other traditions and values, suitable for family viewing and concerned with issues such as Westernisation, nationalism and so on.

Although Hindi cinema was screened occasionally in Europe and North America in the 1930s to the 1950s, it never found large audiences or international recognition, even after the vastly popular *Mother India* (1957) received an 'Oscar' nomination. Only one mainstream Hindi film has been shown at the London Film Festival, V. Shantaram's *Do Aanken Barah Haath/Two Eyes, Twelve Hands*, in 1957. Thus Hindi films came to be screened in the West only for the diasporic Asian markets and, despite their popularity with people of South Asian origin, have yet to reach the mainstream audiences in Europe and America.

It was several years after the first substantial groups of South Asians settled in Britain in the 1950s that Indian films began to be shown in Britain for Asian audiences. (Sardar, 1998, gives a vivid account of his childhood recollections of watching Indian cinema in Britain.) This was mostly on Sunday mornings and other 'off-peak' times at cinemas that screened mainly English-language films. Occasionally stars coming over from India appeared in specially organised events, but although these attracted large BrAsian audiences they were few and far between. Hindi films, then, provided one of the few arenas for entertainment which was not in English, in which the first generation of early migrants had varying levels of competence. However, the 1960s saw the presence of BrAsians increase with major migrations, this time from East Africa. These 'twice migrants' arrived having already acquired the skills necessary to develop infrastructures for maintaining their culture in alien environments—religious organisations, education, community organisations, media, theatre and, of course, cinema, which they had screened in East Africa, and which had also found an African audience.

At this time the British media made no provision for ethnicised minorities. Although the Indian media were set up along the lines of its British counterparts—notably radio and the print media—and the BBC World Service radio had been broadcasting in South Asian languages for several decades, these were not intended for British audiences and no provision for such programming was made. With the increasing South Asian presence in Britain, the BBC began making a few Asian programmes for radio and television in its (tellingly named) 'Immigrants' Unit', founded in 1965. This later became the Asian Unit, hosting entertainment and debates in Hindi-Urdu as well as focusing on English language learning. In the late 1980s the programming switched to English with the establishment in 1987 of Network East, now renamed the Asian Network. Importing some Asian dramas and screening the occasional Hindi film (with subtitles), quiz shows, news reviews and so on brought it closer to the mainstream BBC. Meanwhile the first new television channel for almost two decades, Channel 4, went on air in the 1980s with a brief to give more coverage to minority programming, which included seasons of Indian films, although usually shown after midnight. Film Four later began producing films made by Indian directors and BrAsians until its demise in 2002. (See Dudrah, this volume.)

The lack of programmes in South Asian languages in mainstream media was compensated for by the rise of independent media, notably Asian radio. The most popular of these was Sunrise Radio, which began in 1989. It was 24-hour, available locally in several areas of Britain with large Asian populations, then across Britain and Europe by satellite. Sunrise offered a unique combination of community programmes, such as phone-ins and 'family introductions' (aiming at marriage), alongside a mix of news, music and other features.

THE VIDEO REVOLUTION

The advent of the VCR in the 1980s had a massive impact on the South Asian community's consumption of media. Video shops mushroomed in the high streets, and films and religious programmes as well as other items such as video news magazines became available. This was the first time that BrAsian audiences had access to such a wide choice of both the ever-popular Hindi movies and films in their mother-tongues (mostly Gujarati and Punjabi), which quickly found audiences. Coupled with a general fall in cinema audiences in Britain during this time, Indian films were no longer shown in cinema halls.

Another drastic change in media for BrAsians took place in the 1990s with the arrival of cable and satellite Asian programmes, simultaneous with their arrival in South Asia. Various channels have come and gone in Britain, with the main channels at present being Zee TV (launching as TV Asia in 1992, changing its name in 1995), Sony TV, Star TV and B4U. Much of their programming is composite, consisting of programmes made for several South Asian countries by private and government channels, mostly in Hindi-Urdu with some English and other languages, alongside programmes made locally for the British Asian market. Although soap operas are gaining more airtime alongside news, lifestyle and other programmes, as with television in South Asia, film and film-related shows form a significant part of the programming. While most film material concerns the Hindi cinema, Pakistani serials, which were heroine-oriented and quite naturalistic, were widely regarded as more interesting than their Indian counterparts, although the slicker more glamorous Indian serials of the last few years (notably *Kyun ki saas kabhi bahu thi*) have become hugely popular with BrAsians as well as in India and Pakistan.[1]

Surprisingly, this new television, rather than reducing cinema audiences, began to act as a major marketing tool for films, just as it did in India. The practice of 'video holdback' was begun in India in 1994 by Sooraj Barjatya for the release of his film *Hum Aapke Hain Koun...!/ What am I to You?*, which broke all box-office records. It is hard to say how much the return to cinema of the BrAsian audience was due to this 'video holdback' and how much part of the general trend in the West at the time, partly due to new technologies. Old cinemas reopened with new names, screening only Indian films, although the video shop, also selling the new cheap audio cassettes and film magazines, continued to prosper until the advent of the DVD (usually pirated) at the end of the decade. Perhaps the most surprising aspect of this return to cinema though was the change in audience composition. Often supposed to be comprised of bored housewives and the elderly, who watched Hindi films to while away the time and because their English was not good enough for them to enjoy British television, audiences now included a new group of Hindi film goers emerging from the British South Asian diaspora.

THE BrASIAN MARKET

BrAsians are mainly Punjabi- or Gujarati-speaking, with a significant number of Sylheti speakers from Bangladesh (see Peach, this volume). There are very few mother-tongue Hindi speakers in this diaspora, although many people of Pakistani origin learn Urdu. The audience, how-

1 Thanks to Fahimeh Fifi Haroon for this detail.

ever, is drawn from all sections of the BrAsian community and many young BrAsians are encouraged by their families to watch Hindi films in order to learn the language, which they might otherwise not do.

BrAsians who have mainly been socialised in Britain (through schooling, through work and living in large metropolitan areas) have grown up with Hollywood and British cinema and British television and other British media. For many of them the mainstream public sphere is mostly white with, hence, only a limited BrAsian presence. The BrAsian public presence is marked out mostly in religious places, shopping streets and cinema halls. Their private sphere consists of a dynamic mixture of South Asian and British elements, creating a wide spectrum of interaction with different cultural possibilities. It is possible that a specifically BrAsian civil society, which is neither the mainstream public sphere nor a private one, may be emerging around the sites of the new BrAsian public culture of fashion, music, clubs and so on. The signs of this are not clear nor is the future certain, but this certainly seems a likely development.

The overseas market has long been of vital importance to the commercial Hindi film industry, which recognises it as a territory for the purposes of film distribution and exhibition with equal, or even superior, status to any of the distributional territories of India. The recent expansion in the overseas market has led to its subdivision into new territories, namely Britain, the largest market, North America and the Gulf, with the rest of the world labelled the general overseas territory. In some cases success overseas can make the difference between a film's financial viability and disaster. For some top-ranking Bombay producers the British territory alone is reckoned to yield as much as, if not more than, a top Indian territory. For example, Yash Raj Films reckon to earn more from Britain than from the Bombay territory while the North American market is somewhat smaller. Even though the audience is smaller in these areas the ticket prices are higher—sometimes ten times the top Indian ticket price. The producers are also keen on hard currency, making it easier for them to take their units overseas in future productions. The Bombay underworld has been quick to notice this, and it is said they usually demand the money from the overseas territory as protection money.

Some films seem to cater particularly for the diaspora by showing that members of the diaspora understand 'Indian values' and that however 'foreign' they are—by birth, language and so on—their hearts are still Indian. These films place wealthy Indians, whether diasporic or Indian residents, on an equal footing. Even when a film is set in Europe or the United States, interactions with white people are limited, and racism is rarely encountered, perhaps providing a fantasy of how the West should be for young BrAsians. These films may appeal to Indian audiences for different reasons—perhaps because of their display of consumerist possibilities, travel to foreign locations, expensive fashions and glamorous houses. Indeed, the diasporic audience does not favour Indian action movies, or gritty urban dramas, preferring the big-budget romances, typified by the cinema of Yash Chopra, which has inspired younger film-makers such as Aditya Chopra and Karan Johar (Dwyer, 2002).

Nevertheless, although many film makers are thought to tailor their films towards the diasporic audience, there is little evidence to support this. The presence of a BrAsian may be thought to interest the British audience, but while the Indian audience's reaction to this character may be different, it is not necessarily more or less successful as a marketing ploy. The BrAsian in the Hindi film speaks English with an Indian accent, lives in a house that looks like an upmarket Indian metropolitan house (or just a film set), and lives a lifestyle that would not be recognisably BrAsian to an audience in Britain, but may be to audiences elsewhere. The Indian film makers visit London regularly where they watch Hollywood and other cinemas, but they do not carry out market research on this audience or indeed on their Indian audience. However, they do find the tourist boards very helpful in finding locations and arranging permissions, and some producers claim it is cheaper for them to shoot overseas as they have the stars' undivided attention while out of India.

With the increased importance of the diasporic market, the Bombay producers' big ambition is now to reach beyond the Asian market, which is large enough to get films into the top ten but not to earn serious amounts of money. The largest-grossing Hindi film to date, *Kabhi Khushi Kabhie Gham/Sometimes Happiness, Sometimes Sorrow* (dir. Karan Johar, 2001) made £2.5m., while Gurinder Chadha's *Bend it like Beckham* took £7m. in the first weekend. This is still small compared to a Hollywood blockbuster. In response to this potential, the producers are becoming distributors and making efforts to get films shown in mainstream cinemas, screening subtitled prints. However, at present Asian audiences for Hindi cinema are said to be falling as the DVD, often pirated, is a cheaper and more attractive option with the flexibility of the video but greater quality, boosted by the rising popularity of home cinema systems.

So although Indian films are often very popular in the rest of the non-Euro-American world (Nigeria, the Gulf states, Turkey and so on), they are still not attracting non-Asian audiences in Britain. The glamorous stars, fashion and music have great appeal but the stories and acting are often regarded as unintentionally comic, an attitude often promoted by BrAsians, for whom the problems are tempered with nostalgia and for whom the films provide sufficient attractions to override these misgivings. Even today, although 'Bollywood' is a familiar word in Britain, when Hindi films are shown on British terrestrial television they have a unique status in that they are always shown in the early hours of the morning and listings do not review them as they do all other films, whatever their language. Even an 'Oscar' nomination for *Lagaan/Once Upon a Time in India* (2001) did not help to open up the mainstream markets. There is no little irony in that within India in recent years Hollywood has become increasingly popular while Hindi films have mostly done badly at the box office. As budgets and production values increase, the cost of failure becomes more serious. Yet when Hindi films are hits in India they return ever increasing amounts of money from the box office. Furthermore, 'Bollywood' has become a recognised brand of film-making. This is undoubtedly because of the cultural significance it has to so many BrAsians, who are now taking major roles in the British media, as they are in many other walks of life.

BRASIAN FILMS

One of the first BrAsian films was *My Beautiful Laundrette* (dir. Stephen Frears, 1985), with a screenplay by Hanif Kureishi. It seemed to appear as a rebuttal to the 'Raj Revival' films (*Heat and Dust*, Merchant-Ivory, 1983; A *Passage to India*, David Lean, 1985) and the television epic serial of Paul Scott's *Raj Quartet*, *The Jewel in the Crown*, 1984, (discussed in Rushdie, 1991). *Laundrette*, featuring a gay relationship between a BrAsian and a white skinhead, presented a new subjectivity and image of the BrAsian, away from the exotica and romance of colonialism. Although Kureishi's subsequent film scripts were less successful in their depiction of BrAsian gritty realism, his novel adapted for television, *The Buddha of Suburbia*, was an excellent BrAsian view of London and suburbia in the 1970s, taking a serious and subversive look at postcolonial themes of the diaspora, exotica and interracial sexuality with a new stylish glamour.

Among key figures in British cinema is the BrAsian director Gurinder Chadha whose *Bhaji on the Beach* (1994), a day's visit to the seaside by a group of BrAsian women, raised many serious social issues affecting the communities, offset by comic moments and a warm sympathy, while her international hit, *Bend it like Beckham* (2002), showed the life choices of a young Sikh girl in Southall: 'Who wants to make *aloo gobi* when you can bend it like Beckham?' The film did well in the United States—although no one knew of the British footballer, David Beckham—and in Indian metros, while the Hindi-dubbed version, *Football-shootball, hay Raba!* found its own audience. Chadha's latest film, *Bride and Prejudice* (2004), is an adaptation of *Pride and Prejudice* with Bollywood's Aishwarya Rai as an Indian in a relationship with a white Englishman. Another great success was *East is East* (dir. Damien O'Donnell, 1999), scripted by Ayub Khan Din, the story of a family whose father tries to teach his reluctant children about Pakistani culture, resisted and supported by his English-Irish wife. Meera Syal, best known for her television comedy (*Goodness Gracious Me!* and *The Kumars at No. 42*) and for scripting Lloyd-Weber's *Bombay Dreams*, also scripted a film, *Anita and Me* (dir. Metin Huseyin, 2002), adapted from her novel about a BrAsian growing up in a white community. In 2002 Asif Kapadia's *The Warrior*, made with Indian actors, and with its minimal dialogue in Hindi, was put forward by Britain as a British film for the Academy Awards ('Oscars'), but was disallowed on the grounds that it was made in Hindi, although films made in the 'older' minority languages (Welsh, Gaelic) are allowed, thus raising serious questions about how British are BrAsians.

These film-makers are mostly great fans of Bollywood films, notably Gurinder Chadha who regularly views Hindi films, but their cinema draws on a more British style of film making with occasional tributes to Hindi film, often in their soundtracks which may use Hindi film songs alongside BrAsian music. They are less 'Indian' than films made by NRIs (non-resident Indians) such as Deepa Mehta and Mira Nair, whose films are akin to the Indian 'new' or middle-brow cinema and use Indian film and theatre actors. Kapadia's film is unlike any of these, a more international 'art' film, emphasising the visual component with its striking images and shots and its defamiliarisation of landscape, time and place.

While few in number, these films form a major part of British cinema in the 2000s and BrAsian actors (Archie Punjabi, Parminder Nagra, Saeed Jaffrey) are becoming more visible, while Indian actors (Om Puri, Ayesha Dharker, Anupam Kher) are becoming increasingly familiar to British audiences.

Clearly, BrAsians are very much located in a South Asian 'mediascape', the transnational media flow between South Asia and the diasporic communities (Appadurai, 1997). Indian film producers are increasingly aware of their importance as consumers of cinema towards whom they market their products. BrAsians consume Indian films and other media as part of their new culture, for which markets are now being found among the non-Asian community. BrAsian films have yet to find the wide audiences in South Asia that BrAsian music has, but this is perhaps because the issues that these films depict are not regarded as part of the pleasure of film viewing to many of the Indian audiences. Nearly all BrAsian films refer to racism, whether overt or insidious; the negotiation of new BrAsian identities—by young and old—of gender, sexuality and so on; the way in which the hero/heroine persuades family and other community members to accept these new identities; and the criticism of forced marriages, domestic violence and other 'private matters'. None of these issues is discussed in Hindi cinema, although similar themes are found in the 'non-commercial' cinemas. Nevertheless, these films are making significant inroads into the audiences in the large metropolitan cities, notably those who consume the new youth films made in India.

WRITINGS

Yasmin Hussain

BrAsian women's imaginative writings were initially published alongside other 'black' women writers in particular during the 1970s and most of the 1980s. The anthologisation and taxonomy of 'black' British cultural production is telling in this context. Publishing houses were reluctant to publish literature from minority women. Collections of stories and poems in anthologies were typical of the way in which black British discourse has been gathered in the post-war period. It was symptomatic of a publishing industry that is reluctant to commit itself financially to minority authors. Anthologies such as *Charting the Journey: Writings by Black and Third World Women* (1988) edited by S. Grewal *et al.* and *Watchers and Seekers: Creative Writing by Black Women in Britain* (1987) edited by R. Cobham and M. Collins became appropriate outlets for the women to publish their work. These anthologies recognised the diverse diasporic conditions under which black British cultural production took place, whether African, Caribbean or BrAsian, yet they all signal the hyphenated, the cross-cultural and the postcolonial. The issues of migration, race and gender are fundamental to the minority experiences, as it is specific to diasporic communities. BrAsian women's subjectivity as a migratory phenomenon exists in multiple locations, and by adopting such a stance the manner in which their presence traverses geographical and national boundaries becomes apparent. Therefore BrAsian women's writing should be read as a series of boundary crossings and not as a fixed ethnically-bound category of writing, thus redefining identities away from the exclusion and marginality which exists within mainstream British literary production.

Creative writing by BrAsian women as a collective is intricately connected with the development of British black feminism. BrAsian female authors articulated a perspective within their texts which mirrored their socially experienced grievances. Bringing together these disparate voices in a common forum was to some extent a polemical act. Many writers explored the workings of a 'black' identity which was, at the same time, imposed and embracing. Leena Dhingra's essay, 'Breaking Out of the Labels' provides a brief narration of what she terms 'the label-fitting-fighting game' (Dhingra, 1987: 105) as she describes the labels of identity imposed on her and the subsequent racism she encounters: 'a girl from India, an Indian girl, a coloured, a paki, a black, a wog, an Asian, and recently graduated to becoming a member of an ethnic minority' (Dhingra, 1987: 103). Dhingra's experiences of being denigrated and the problems of asserting her own identity are echoed in many other BrAsian women's texts, as in those of African-Caribbean women. Dhingra reminds the reader that access to Indian culture has been strengthened and given direction by the writers' understanding of themselves as part of a wider black community (Cobham, 1987). She describes the black identity embracing herself and others as a: 'fellowship ... seeing reflections in each other and sharing a whole new world of common experience and history' and calls this a 'shared reality' (Dhingra, 1987: 107).

Within the body of writings by BrAsian women, it is possible to focus and modulate the critical approach these women bring to their work by looking at several of the shared thematic concerns and characteristics of black literature. These are not only thematic for the literature but also central concerns within black writing. BrAsian women's literature is strongly marked by the encounter of two or more contrasting cultures and their interaction within the diasporic communities. These literary texts explore the intersections of race, gender, class, ethnicity and generation in different discourses, practices and political contexts which become defining features of experience. The women mirrored their social and personal grievances, within their literary work, and discussed their experiences of living in Britain. In the mid 1980s BrAsian women began to publish under the label of Asian, instead of 'black', for instance Debjani Chatterjee, *I was that Woman* (1989). They also began to publish as a collective under this category, for example *Flaming Spirit: stories from the Asian women writers collective* (1994), edited by Rukhsana Ahmad and Rahila Gupta. Conflict between individualism and communalism is at the heart of BrAsian women's literature, written as the women struggle for independence and self-reliance while clinging to traditional requirements of the minority culture. The women focused upon within the texts are 'new women' because they recognise themselves as individuals, and choose a strategy, no matter what the outcome, to overcome the pressure to conform to the role or category others want to see them enact.

The strategy used by the 'new woman' within the texts involves a journey into herself within both a psychological and a geographical context, questioning conventional and traditional assumptions. This process forces her to display characteristics that show an obvious shift from the ideal traditional woman that is desired to the one which is criticised and rejected. Journey had previously strongly structured the literature written by immigrants as the writers recounted the transformation of migration, its effects and problems. Journey continues to be central to BrAsian women's writing, it gives structure and pattern to the narrative, but changes occur in its use. The journey of immigration has been closely followed by the journey into settlement and now the journey into self. Writers treat journey as a means of self-knowledge, not only through re-entry into a collective historical experience but also through an exploration or rediscovery of personal experience.

Farhana Sheikh's *The Red Box* (1991) and Ravinder Randhawa's *A Wicked Old Woman* (1987) begin with their main protagonists embarking on a journey, thus establishing immediately each novel's preoccupation with place and displacement. But BrAsian women writers, like black African-Caribbean women within the diasporas, use journey largely for a specific critical approach, generating a growth of consciousness where voyages over geographical space become a metaphor for the journey into the self. The journeys, whether real or in the imagination, may enact the retrieval of the collective past but are essentially about exploration and discovery of the self. The novels succeed in documenting this process and trace the self-discovery of their main protagonists; in essence, the emphasis is on story as a means of fixing identity. Movement in and out of time frames is also used. This movement in time and space, in the conscious and the unconscious, offers a means for conceptualising this process of dislocation and displacement. This displacement is not purely physical—the movement of bodies in space and time—it also has a representational component, suggesting the process in which the narratives of belonging have to be re-thought and re-told. The experience of displacement has been central to the formation of contemporary South Asia and its diasporas (Sayyid, 2003). The journeying of BrAsian women writers can be seen as a metaphor of the experience of displacement of past and present, of South Asia and Britain, of self and society.

METROPOLITAN BORDERLANDS

THE FORMATION OF BRASIAN LANDSCAPES

Noha Nasser

Borderlands refer to spaces of cohabitation and exchange between the 'British' urban tradition and the 'South Asian' settlement paradigm resulting in hybrid cosmopolitan neighbourhoods. South Asian settlers transferred their own particular conceptualisations of space, built forms and functional requirements to the new context, modifying British urban forms to their own designs. How they have adapted, utilised and given new meanings to the built forms of an established British urban tradition is the subject of this chapter. Borderlands also draw attention to the political context of postcolonial British hegemony and the negotiations between identity and locality that have given rise to 'BrAsian' urban landscapes. This chapter examines the distinct way in which BrAsian presence has marked itself architecturally and in the urban form.

FIRST ENCOUNTERS

The first modest architectural exchanges between Britain and South Asia date back to the colonialist period when the meeting of Timurid (Mughal) and Western influences created new nuanced hybrid architectural styles of striking originality. On the subcontinent, vernacular forms and decorative motifs were fused with neo-classical and neo-gothic styles to produce such stunning examples of syncretic architecture as the Government House in Calcutta, the Victoria Terminus in Bombay and the Albert Hall in Jaipur. These buildings signified an assertion of British dominance over the local vernacular as testimony to its *imperium*.

At the heart of empire, however, the motives for importing non-indigenous architectural styles were of a different nature. The increasing infatuation with the mystique of the Orient brought 'exoticised' fads to the architecture of imperial cities (King, 1990). Some of these buildings were monuments to the triumphs of imperialism, but many were constructed to indulge the imperialist fantasy. For example, the Brighton Pavilion (1823) portrays an exuberant theme-park reconstruction of a Maharaja's palace as an object of exotic consumption. Here the architect John Nash uses the playful forms of Timurid architecture—domes, filigree screens and archways—to echo the most elaborate stonework found in the colonies. Similarly the construction of the Shah Jehan Mosque (1889) in Woking, Britain's first purpose-built mosque, is a simple geometric form styled in Indo-Saracenic fashion. The central arched portal and two flanking doorways on the façade reflect an overall richness of detail; embellished with colour, surface textures and elements of decoration, such as four green *chhatri* (cupolas on white columned turrets) representing miniature minarets, as well as a parapet lined with distinct motifs. A large green central dome spans the prayer hall. To a large extent the selection of this particular stylistic vocabulary owes its origins to European orientalism which reduced the regional diversity of architectural traditions found in the subcontinent to the simplistic imagery of the dome, minaret and arch. This form of imagery was considered mysterious and irrational in contrast to the rational European rectilinear identity, creating a fictive polarised view of the Orient (Dodds, 2002).

POSTCOLONIALISM IN BRITISH CITIES

Space and its politics of identity and power have always been considered a fundamental part of colonialist, and more recently, postcolonialist discourse (Said, 1989, 1993; Vidler, 1992; Jacobs, 1996). The city as the main spatial arena of encounters between the Self and the Other is therefore the most obvious site of appropriation, contestation and resistance. It is the place where legacies of imperialist ideologies and practices can still be seen through processes of segregation, re-territorialisation, marginalisation and displacement of migrant communities—described by Jacobs (1996: 87) as 'managed "multicultural" cohabitation'. The nature and outcome of this spatial politics relies in great measure on the arrangement of power under which various coalitions express their sense of self and their desire for the spaces that constitute their 'home'. The varying results arise from a protracted struggle in which the Other might be ordered or harnessed, or in some cases domesticated, through 'self-conscious gestures of reconciliation' (Jacobs, 1996).

The evocation of identity in cities is largely the result of inter-ethnic encounters in which ethnic boundaries are demarcated as 'contested realms of identity' (Vidler, 1992). The mélange of BrAsian communities in Britain, of diverse ethnic, national and religious origins, creates a complex geography of identities which are activated within particular conditions and circumstances and for particular purposes (AlSayyad, 2001). The various origins of identity, whether the nation, ethnic origin, faith, sect or even the religious movement, have manifested themselves in the establishment of places of worship in Britain and the adoption of distinct symbolism and imagery as a display of assertiveness towards the community at large, amongst competing BrAsian communities, or amongst competing intra and inter-faith communities. However, these boundaries are not given, but constructed, manipulated, subject to change and situational (Colombijn and Erdentug, 2002). Spatially these sites of encounter and cohabitation have been described metaphorically as 'borderlands' denoting a condition between two extremes—a place of mutual transformation and exchange between British cultural dominance and the South Asian paradigm. According to AlSayyad (2001) borderlands are sites of resistance in which differences are emphasised, temporary boundaries are drawn, and social networks are formalised, but they are also sites of cultural production (Rosaldo, 1989). If encounters between the Self and Other shape the migrant experience and redefine identity, then where do these encounters take place and how can they be defined? Metcalf (1996) has argued that borderlands are most likely to be found in built or altered environments infused with new meanings in the new setting which may be distinguished by markers of symbolic expression. The visibility of this expression, however, has an inverse relationship with the nature of inter-ethnic relations (Colombijn and Erdentug, 2002). Therefore, in places where relations are good, ethnic symbols are 'over-communicated' and can be associated with functional, visual or spatial markers which help delineate the ethnic boundary (Nasser, 2005). In British towns and cities BrAsian borderlands are found in heterogeneous neighbourhoods where changes to the homes, shops, buildings and streetscapes are a result of the on-going relationship between expressions of identity and existing built forms, but also where there is an emergence of new forms (Nasser, 2003).

THE FORMATION OF BRASIAN BORDERLANDS

At the time of settlement of large numbers of BrAsians in Greater London and in the industrial cities of the Midlands, West Yorkshire and Lancashire, an out-movement of the British middle class from the industrial inner and middle-ring neighbourhoods to the outer suburbs was already underway (Whitehand and Carr, 2001). This movement left a significant percentage of the industrial built heritage largely redundant and open to adaptation, conversion and transformation by the new settlers. Simultaneously the increasing secularisation of British society left many of the picturesque churches available for appropriation. Thus it was largely the industrial urban heritage that the BrAsian communities inherited.

The highly regular and well-differentiated layout of the industrial urban landscape of the late Victorian and Edwardian (1875–1918) period offered a morphological frame governing future urban change. These neighbourhoods also offered a number of advantages for the early settlers. The High Street, a major thoroughfare of commercial ribbon development connecting the neighbourhoods to the city centre, made these areas readily accessible to the central business, commercial and industrial districts. The major neighbourhood thoroughfares were also traditionally a social space where shops, public buildings, chapels, churches and schools, as well as local government buildings, created the main visual features which were later appropriated by the incoming settlers (Chadwick, 1978). The commercial area contrasted with the residential neighbourhoods characterised by regular streets, long street blocks, standardised plot sizes and repetitive two storey terraces (Kostof, 1991). Occasionally the monotony of the long blocks was interrupted by a corner shop serving the daily needs of the residents. The terrace houses had a basic plan: two floors, with two rooms each. For variation and enlargement there was the cellar and the attic, and a back extension, or 'lean-to', for the kitchen-cum-scullery (Muthesius, 1982). Out-migration by the British middle classes had left many of the terraces vacant and ready for occupation by incoming settlers, and as a result the housing stock was both cheap and non-competitive (Dahya, 1974; Slater, 1996). This housing type also had the advantage of being capable of absorbing large numbers of male workers. With the arrival of families came greater diversification along the residential streets in owner-occupied terrace housing in close proximity to the commercial thoroughfares. Since the 1960s the urban character of these industrial neighbourhoods and streets has gradually changed, suggesting that these communities have responded and adapted to local conditions.

The urban segregation of these communities has received considerable attention in which racial politics, discriminatory practices and policies governing housing and settlement are believed to have created ethnic 'ghettos' (Rex and Moore, 1967; Peach, 1975; Smith, 1989; Boal, 2000). Although this has been demonstrated, Peach (2000) has argued the term 'ghetto' is not necessarily negative, but that in many cases ethnic communities segregate voluntarily as a means of maintaining social cohesion, cultural values and social networks. In Glasgow, for example, Bowes *et al.* (2000) have shown that one of the major deciding factors for Pakistani families has been their preference to live in areas in close proximity to Asian shops, the mosque, good schools and transport. The preference to be well-connected to areas of BrAsian services places increasing importance on transport networks acting as 'corridors' of ethnic expansion. In the case of North-West Greater London, BrAsian settlements have been established in Southall, Alperton, Wembley, Kingsbury and Golders Green along a 'corridor' following the no. 83 bus route connecting the major BrAsian High Streets of Southall and Ealing Road.

The ability of BrAsian communities to adapt to the local urban tradition and its associated building types in order to attain their social, cultural, economic and physical aspirations suggests a degree of integration. However, such integration is distinct from state directed projects of assimilation which, to consume the settler, transforms their identities in such a way that they become indistinguishable from the 'host' community. Such assimilationist policies are belied by the logic of racism which continues to mark the host/immigrant distinction as another variant of the West and the Rest dyad. In other words, the racism that establishes and institutionalises the host-immigrant hierarchy, making it possible to think in terms of assimilation, is also what prevents erosion of the host-immigrant hierarchy and prevents assimilation being realised (Sayyid, 2004). Adaptation also determines hybridity or the mutual transformation that takes place between the new context and BrAsian aspirations and lifestyles. The degree of hybridisation is ultimately conditioned by shifting positions of power (AlSayyad, 2001), which in the case of Britain has been influenced by (i) the growth and organisation of BrAsian communities from small nationalist groupings to more established diverse sectarian communities with a stronger economic and social position; (ii) the weakening of both Western supremacist discourses and Britain's place within the world. This postcolonial condition makes it more difficult to articulate an unquestioning cultural hierarchy in which white British society is considered to be superior to BrAsian settlers; and (iii) the development of British antiracist and multicultural discourses which have influenced the ability of BrAsian communities to express themselves in different forms. In the built environment these changes have shifted from the appropriation and adaptation of dwellings, to the transformation of more diverse and dispersed building types within BrAsian settled neighbourhoods, to the creation and (re)production of architectural idiom and symbolism in new cultural forms. In the following sections these ongoing processes in the metamorphosis of parts of the British urban landscape into distinct BrAsian borderlands are discussed with particular focus on the homes, shops and religio-cultural buildings. The discussion sets these processes in the context of the challenges, both spatial and temporal, that BrAsian communities have faced in creating a 'home' for themselves.

FILLING OUT THE BORDERLANDS

The settlement of families in the mid 1960s created a major impetus for urban transformation. Earlier attempts by mainly male congregations to consecrate space for ritual were relatively few and widely dispersed. In many cases these spaces were informal and temporary making it difficult to trace their origins. Nevertheless, the first mosques are known to have been founded in Liverpool (1887), Woking (1889) and London (1924); the earliest officially-listed Sikh *gurdwara*s were located in Liverpool and Newcastle (1958); and the first two Hindu *mandir*s believed to have opened were in Birmingham and Coventry (1967) (Naylor and Ryan, 2003).

However, large-scale conversion of space for religious and cultural use accompanied the settlement of women and children and the sudden increase in size of congregations. The need to establish places in which cultural values and religious practice could be perpetuated became the primary concern. The difficulty in securing financial support from local authorities and Community Relations Councils (CRCs) placed the onus on the communities themselves to raise sufficient funds to purchase property for their use. As a result the relatively affordable terrace house offered the most readily appropriated vernacular building type. As a space the building was capable of internal modification and integration of religious and educational functions. Modifications included the demolition of internal walls and additions to the rear. Barton's (1986) description of the first Bengali mosque in Bradford (1969) highlights processes of adaptation and functional differentiation of a residential building type, and the constraints that this carried in response to the spatial requirements for Muslim ritual and cultural elaboration. Bradford's first Bengali mosque comprised two adjacent terrace houses on Howard Street. The dividing wall between the properties was retained although the internal partitions between the front and back rooms were removed in order to create two large rooms for children's classes and prayers. The orientation to Mecca for prayer, the *qibla*, was located in the corner of the inner room imposing awkward and oblique prayer lines to the walls. The other necessary functions, such as a place for ablution, were accommodated in the cellar along with the kitchen. The toilet was located outside in the back-yard. The attics, comprised of two bed-sits, were used to accommodate the leader in prayer, the *imam.* Although the terrace house was relatively adaptable, spatial constraints were most acute during celebrations, and in many cases communities would hire public halls in which to hold their functions. The sharp rise in the number of worshippers during these occasions also created strong opposition by neighbours and local authorities to convert dwellings into religious sites. This resulted in the widespread issuance of enforcement notices on the grounds that these changes constituted 'material change of use' as accorded in Town and Country Planning legislation (Gale and Naylor, 2002), and presented a 'loss of amenity' to neighbours (Barton, 1986). Nonetheless, communities remained adamant and appealed against the planning authorities to the Department of the Environment (Barton, 1986; Gale and Naylor, 2002).

In the late 1960s expanding congregations were outgrowing the existing residential spaces that they had appropriated. In the built environment this created an impetus for claiming more territory and visibly shaping a BrAsian presence in the city. There were a number of initial conceptions to construct purpose-built places of worship, such as the Central Mosque in Birmingham or the Hindu Shikharbaddha Mandir in North-West London, but varying obstacles of land acquisition, construction costs and planning permission slowed down their realisation. Communities turned to the acquisition of the more commodious buildings of the industrial heritage which had fallen into disuse. In particular churches, warehouses, schools, community halls, even cinemas and clubs were building types that were converted to cultural use. The most convenient to adapt were those buildings that had a previous religious use resulting in the widespread conversion of churches, synagogues and other building types of religious affiliation by these communities. Any other building type required engagement with the formal processes of planning application. The antagonistic nature of inter-ethnic relations at this time had a direct influence on the outward expression of all appropriated buildings, residential or otherwise. Modifications were restrained to interiors with no extravagant indication of the use of the building nor the application of religious symbols or motifs except the odd banner or sign aimed primarily at signifying a place of worship to the faith community. The objective was to ensure the building was 'under-communicating' its function and blending in with its surroundings. The most significant aspect of the process of diversification was the emergence of the temple-cum-community centre which was specifically intended to provide additional religious, educational and social functions such as a conference hall, library, kitchen and welfare services. For the most part the rehabilitation of redundant buildings was an important means of tackling the functional and physical obsolescence of the industrial built heritage, imbuing these buildings with new cultural and functional meaning.

The rehabilitation of structures once attributed to British culture and society has been contentious, particularly amongst conservationists seeking to preserve the heritage of a distinctly 'British nation'. The politicisation of heritage as a means of constructing and redefining 'Britishness' and national identity has evoked wide-spread dissent over the re-use of listed buildings by the Other (Eade, 1996; Jacobs, 1996). In Spitalfields, East London, the declaration of an urban conservation area based on its Georgian heritage in 1969 and the listing of most of the Georgian buildings in 1976, led to a 'managed' displacement of the Bengali-based garment manufacturing industry based on a nostalgic return to its historic, white, English roots (Jacobs, 1996). The revival of nationalist sentiment by conservationist opposition was particularly strong at the time the Bengali community needed to construct an additional floor to the Brick Lane Mosque, an appropriated eighteenth-century listed Georgian building. The changes were internal modifications which did not require planning permission, but 'for many non-Muslims the mosque building was a physical expression of both a local English heritage and a gentrified, Georgian present' (Eade, 1996: 220). To overcome the threat to Georgian Spitalfields by the Bengali community, the opposition directed its efforts

Fig. 1. Transformation of Ladypool Road, Birmingham, 1952.

towards spatially regulating and controlling their presence through a discrete and 'genteel gentrification' of the area (Jacobs, 1996).

A reverse movement of 'ethnic gentrification' was taking place on the High Streets bisecting BrAsian settlements. This process was marked by a significant increase in the number of Asian-owned businesses. In Bradford, for example, Dahya (1974) records a total of five BrAsian-owned grocers/butchers and cafés in 1959, 133 enterprises in 1966 and 260 in 1970. Economic expansion was attributed to businesses run by family and kinship networks and specialising in the service industry and manufacturing of goods catering for a BrAsian clientele. Initially the corner shop, grocer/butcher and the café were established as venues for social interaction and exchange. However, over time services diversified catering for all aspects of everyday life. The services that emerged were of three types: local enterprises catering for South Asian traditions; businesses that served the wider BrAsian population; and those businesses that helped BrAsians interact with formal institutions of British state. The introduction and proliferation of a distinctive service industry established a familiar environment to its BrAsian clientele, gradually transforming the character of the streets (Figure 1). The High Streets have since become vibrant commercial areas, teeming with people buying and selling their goods in elaborate window displays and on the pavements. Signs and notices on the fascias of shops in Urdu, Hindi and Gujarati indicate their specialisation, whether it is a book store, jeweller, butcher selling *halal* meat, restaurant, or Muslim bank. Colourful displays of saris and fabric shops, jewellers and '*bhajia* houses' jostle with grocers selling tropical vegetables, exotic spices, bakeries and shops selling Asian sweets piled high in the shop windows. Interspersed amongst the accountants, income tax consultancies, importers and exporters, immigration and advisory bureaus, driving schools, insurance firms, real estate and travel agencies are BrAsian community organisations that act as community mediators. For the most part the buildings still proclaim their Victorian and Edwardian origins, but the ambience of the street is distinctly different from its non-Asian counterpart, both visually and audibly. This suggests that the changing character of these commercial areas is the result of spatial and functional, rather than morphological transformations. The active use of the pavement as an extension to the shop space for the arrangement of displayed goods and produce reflects a different conceptualisation of public space by the incoming community originating from the traditional market economy in which trade takes place in all parts of the city. The commercial revival of many of these areas has had a positive effect on dealing with economic obsolescence. By establishing a secondary economic base in the city, BrAsians have successfully converted run-down buildings into marketable property and revived the shop-house concept contributing to the overall urban regeneration of these areas.

This phase in the development of BrAsian borderlands is the South Asian response to the hegemonic imperialist legacies that have been manifested through processes of segregation, gentrification and the politicisation of heritage. It reflects an ambivalent stance towards anti-racism and multiculturalism in the 1960s and 1970s by the state and local authorities during which co-existence with the Other was both ordered and harnessed. Within these spatial constraints BrAsian communities re-territorialised the industrial neighbourhoods by claiming space for their specific needs and lifestyles. The most significant developments are the growth in importance of religious-cum-community centres and the High Street as venues for community life. These developments demonstrate an adaptation to the new context through processes of appropriation, conversion, dispersal and diversification. Nevertheless, the nature of inter-ethnic relations influenced the outward representation of these communities in which symbols and motifs were both discrete and 'under-communicated'. But more positive, adaptation also demonstrates how the incoming community has economically and physically revitalised substantial parts of the industrial urban landscape.

UN/SETTLED BORDERLANDS

As Britain's ethnically marked minorities began to make in-roads into the political arenas of large conurbations, local authorities began to shift in the 1980s to a more pluralistic model of welfare provision which recognised that life opportunities of ethnicised minorities were adversely affected by notions of 'racial disadvantage'. The assertiveness of ethnicised minorities also led to the conclusion that policies of assimilation in which ethnically marked communities were to erase their identities and histories as a price of admission into the white host society were no longer tenable in a world in which notions of white superiority were increasingly difficult to sustain. The effect of municipal multiculturalism was the provision of financial assistance for ethnically marked communities to engage in cultural activities deriving from their ethnicity. The planning profession also underwent a multicultural conversion, a change marked by the publication of the *Planning for a Multi-Racial Britain* report (RTPI/CRE, 1983) which emphasised that local and structural plans should be sensitive to the development needs of different groups. But the absence of national guidelines has meant there have been wide-ranging regional variations in the report's adoption (Gale and Naylor, 2002). The ability of some BrAsian communities to succeed in their struggle for place is attributed to them becoming sufficiently established and well-organised to negotiate with public bodies on their own terms (Vertovec, 1996; Gale and Naylor, 2002).

With respect to the built environment, an assertiveness of BrAsian communities has led to the emergence of distinctive forms of architectural expression and co-opting by some local authorities and national development agencies in matters of finance, land acquisition and the granting of planning permission for new cultural forms. Gale and Naylor (2002), for example, have noted that since the late 1970s Leicester City Council have actively demonstrated their 'positive action initiative' by co-opting the construction of sites of worship such as the Conduit Street Mosque through the sale of land to the Leicester Islamic Centre for a quarter of the market value, and by making available local and national grants to the Jain Samaj for the establishment of the Jain Centre. Similarly in Birmingham the city council made available grants for the refurbishment and conversion of Green Lane Mosque (1980), a listed Victorian public library and swimming baths, to serve as a community centre with a library, offices, prayer hall, school and car park. National development agencies had also by the 1990s come to accept that the establishment of ethnic community projects were desirable forms of urban development, such as the financing of the Gujarat Hindu Society Temple in Preston by English Partnerships and the Millennium Commission (Gale and Naylor, 2002).

The late 1970s and early 1980s also saw planning authorities permitting the conversion of dwellings into religious use. The house mosques/temples were being established by smaller groupings of residents of a particular religious sect or movement who required localised places of worship and a community centre serving their immediate neighbourhood. These sites tended to be on corner lots allowing them to be extended to the rear and sides. At the same time these groups felt compelled to create a visual feature by virtue of the building's prominent location in the neighbourhood, but, more important, by the remodelling of the elevation as a form of religious representation. Rectangular fenestrations, such as windows and doorways, were framed by arches, religious motifs lined the parapets, and vestigial domes and minarets adorned the corners of the building, signifying the building's use and its users. More recently, many local communities have raised sufficient funds to construct purpose built premises on adjacent sites in accordance with architectural styles expressive of a specific religious identity.

The conscious act of remodelling elevations with ornamental features and decorative motifs has been a major development in the metamorphosis of the British urban landscape as a means of redefining the presence of the Other. Not only were localised community centres in the heart of residential neighbourhoods undergoing this form of transformation, but more prominent sites as well. In Birmingham, for example, the Soho Road Guru Nanak Nishkam Sewark Jatha, located on a major thoroughfare that winds its way through a Sikh-settled area, was converted from a Polish ex-servicemen's club to a *gurdwara* in 1978. Over the ensuing ten years residential property adjacent to the club was acquired along with land to the rear, allowing the construction of considerable extensions accommodating educational and social functions. In the early 1990s the *gurdwara* committee made a planning application for the remodelling of the exterior to add a grand entrance surmounted by a dome and other ornamental features. According to Gale (2004), there was little objection by the city council on aspects of style which he argues reflects the council's growing acceptance of such projects as potential landmarks. Today the Soho Road *gurdwara* is an imposing landmark on the urban landscape. It occupies almost an entire street block and is three storeys high. Many of its features have been inspired from the model of the Golden Temple of Amritsar. The extensive use of three different types of coloured marble on the elevation has been used for embellishment and for delineating prominent features such as the grand entrance, fenestrations and the parapet. The main building is set back from the street accentuating the impressive three storey *deorhi*, or grand entrance to the sanctum sanctorum. At the third level of the *deorhi* a central projecting window is framed by arches and crowned by a shallow elliptical cornice. Above the three-storey entrance a large ribbed central dome creates a strong visual feature, topped by an inverted lotus symbol and a golden *kal*. At the base of the central dome are four smaller cupolas, or *chhatris*, on turrets, one on either corner. The roofline is defined by a heavily decorated parapet of repeated smaller *chhatris* and turrets. The overall effect

Fig. 2. Sikh Mandir, Handsworth, Birmingham.

Fig. 3. Birmingham Central Mosque, Highgate, Birmingham.

is rather elaborate and by no means discrete, on the contrary, it employs a stylistic vocabulary that is inspired from the Indian subcontinent and intended to 'over-communicate' a Sikh identity in the area.

The introduction of a repertoire of exotic forms such as the dome, *chhatris*, *shikhara* (bee-hive shaped dome), arch and minaret has created a new cultural urban landscape in Britain (Figures 2 and 3). The traditionally rectilinear identity of the British skyline dominated by the pointed church spire towering over the highly regular swathe of low rise brick buildings and pitched roofs are today vying with the new addition of distinctly sinuous forms. But to what extent have these forms been accepted as being part of a new British urban landscape? In Preston, for example, Gale and Naylor (2002) have demonstrated how the planning process has been the lens by which the creative stylistic expressions of BrAsian communities have been 'domesticated' in order to preserve the 'Britishness' of the urban landscape. They describe how a proposal for constructing the Gujarat Hindu Society Temple in a residential neighbourhood received strong opposition from locals on the grounds that the building was 'alien' to the area and that it would generate large volumes of traffic. Planning permission was granted, but under the condition that the building had to comply with the character of the area in terms of scale, materials and style of the surrounding terrace houses. Faced with the challenge, the Gujarat Hindu Society was able to creatively combine local forms with elements from Hindu temple architecture as a 'self-conscious gesture of reconciliation'. In the process a stylistic hybridity between the two traditions created an innovative fusion of brickwork and slate roofing with a *shikhara* and marble entrance supported on four ornately decorated pillars. Examples of architectural hybridity in new cultural forms can be found across many British cities—the result of negotiations between locality and identity that have been part of the struggle of BrAsian communities in expressing their sense of belonging in an urban context. A particularly stunning example is that of the Edinburgh Central Mosque, which represents a meeting of two rather different traditions: Highland castle architecture inscribed with an 'Islamic' sensibility (Figure 4). The massing of the building suggests its strong Scottish architectural language articulated by the location of four stone-clad octagonal towers at either corner of the building. The towers are imposing features contributing to the overall fortified look of the building; clad in a stone finish encircled by large Arabic script inlaid in red brick, small slot windows and lead-covered pinnacles. One tower has been used as a base for the minaret, an octagonal stone-clad shaft and abstracted balcony capped with a lead-clad semi-dome. A central *iwan*-like portal frames the entrance, pierced by a series of recessed pointed arches marking a recognisable feature of the 'Islamic' tradition. The *iwan* is also clad in stone, adding to the overall heaviness of the building, separated from the

Fig. 4. Edinburgh Central Mosque represents a meeting of two rather different traditions: Highland castle architecture inscribed with an 'Islamic' sensibility.

two flanking towers by a narrow strip of glazing. The pointed pinnacles of the towers create a disharmony with the curved forms of the domes, creating a language of confusion, an ambivalent aesthetic.

The ambivalence associated with the interpretation of these new cultural forms opens up the debate between 'tradition' and 'modernity' in architectural expression. On the one hand the indiscriminate use of historic or extant design features and models by BrAsian communities in their cultural buildings reflects an emotional tie with the past and the meanings and value that these architectural conventions ascribe. On the other hand a more *avant garde* approach attempts to reinterpret various aesthetic themes through exploration based on the setting, form, function and use of technology to create a new semblance of architectural identity that does not violate cultural principles. The Shri Swaminarayan Mandir in Neasden is a stunning example of the former approach, a reproduction of a traditional Hindu temple, literally imported from India and designed according to ancient Hindu *Shilpashastras* (texts on architecture). The *mandir* and adjoining cultural complex occupy a 3.85 acre site at the heart of a London residential suburb, but according to Naylor and Ryan (2003: 179) the proposal to construct the *mandir* was marked with con-

Fig. 5. Shri Swaminarayan Mandir in Neasden, London.

flict and controversy as local residents 'developed new senses of territoriality' to what they considered a visual intrusion and invasion of a predominantly white British space. Planning permission was granted as the construction of the temple commenced in India. It was carved out of limestone and marble by 1,500 sculptors then shipped in massive pieces for assembling. Visually it is a stunning example of the grandeur of North Indian religious architecture characterised by a spectacular assemblage of seven *shikharas* made up of layer upon layer of architectural elements such as *kapotas* and *gavaksas* and fluted domes, three over the *gopurams* (entrance) and one over the sanctum sanctorum (Figure 5). The temple is raised on a high platform to add to its grandeur. The use of traditional building techniques, like the post and beam and corbelled vaulting, pilasters and brackets, are heavily embellished and intricately ornamented with interlaced forms and carvings of deities. The adjacent cultural centre stands in stylistic contrast using the more domestic *haveli* aesthetic. An intricately carved two-storey timber gallery defines the entrance. It is decorated using elaborate traditional wooden craftsmanship. A series of timber posts, beams and ornate brackets support an arched gallery above. The ground floor of the cultural complex is finished in white marble in contrast to the brick-red coloured plaster finish of the top floor. Here a series of bays are defined by exposed timber posts, beams and brackets supporting a timber overhanging canopy. Observed within the urban landscape, the idiosyncratic treatment and usage of architectural features, forms, materials and ornamentation in the Shri Swaminarayan Mandir in Neasden bears no relationship to either time or context, but evokes a strong visual image to the users and to non-Hindus alike.

A more modernist, *avant garde* approach, on the other hand, has been adopted in the Glasgow Mosque. In this building, first opened in 1984, the architects have made an attempt to move away from a strictly traditional approach by exploring the use of modern technology, materials and abstraction as a means of reinterpreting various aesthetic themes associated with religious architecture in the Muslim world. The steel frame structure of the building allows the external fabric to be articulated freely between brick-clad solids and glazed voids. Light penetrates the interior through a glazed dome and a series of brick-clad buttresses that lean outwards from the building, freeing the sides. The buttresses function to control the intimacy of the building's internal functions whilst still allowing light in. The dome is an outstanding feature of the building, created through the fusion of a traditional architectural element with modern materials. It is raised on a metal drum, angular and onion-shaped in form, with tinted glass panels. The main entrance, however, is a protruding light-frame brick *iwan*-like portal framed by a pointed arch that tapers out as it meets the ground. From the ceiling of the portal hang large symbolic *muqarnas* or stalactite structures that can be seen from the outside. A single-storey arcade of pointed archways adjoins the main building from which springs a minaret. The form of the minaret is both simple and abstract, functioning as a spatial landmark. The Glasgow Mosque still communicates its function through the use of abstract reinterpretations of 'Muslim' imagery and symbolism but at the same time employs local materials and modern technology to arrive at an innovative expression.

The numerous examples of hybrid postcolonial architecture that have arisen in Britain over the past twenty years is a reversal of the exchanges during the colonialist period when British hegemony was expressed through the fusion of neo-classical and neo-gothic styles with the local vernacular. The reproduction of this language in the heart of the ex-empire is a way of redefining and reasserting a South Asian paradigm over the local British vernacular. Most significant is the revival and reanimation of the imagery associated with orientalism which is both recognisable and understood in Britain as representing a specific identity. Hence, the utilisation of motifs, symbols and elements are in effect a subverting force playing on an essentialised and 'commodified' cultural image, giving BrAsians an outward expression and meaning to their presence and a way of redefining their identity in Britain in no uncertain terms.

The recent construction of a 'disneyfied' BrAsian identity has become a major determinant in the place-making of BrAsian borderlands by local authorities. The growing importance of tourism as a generator of income has been a significant factor in this trend as essentialised, romantic notions of South Asian culture has increasingly become a commodity for consumption. Both Leicester and Birmingham City Councils, for example, actively sought to co-opt landmark projects in the 1980s and 1990s, particularly places of worship along major urban thoroughfares, with the

Fig. 6. The 'theming' of Ladypool Road, Birmingham, has involved the design of street furniture with a distinctly 'South Asian' flavour.

dual intention of attracting tourism and ensuring that they are being seen as co-opting a 'multicultural city' (Gale and Naylor, 2002). To a large extent BrAsian communities have actively encouraged and promoted such consumable notions of culture. For example, in the case of the development of Brick Lane as a 'Banglatown', Jacobs (1996: 100) notes that local businessmen 'traded on an essentialised notion of their culture as a component part of a broader plan to control redevelopment in their favour: acquire land, ensure social amenity and establish opportunities for Bengali youths to enter the "City" workforce'. Similarly the invention of the 'Balti Triangle' in Birmingham or the 'Curry Mile' in Manchester have been examples of tourism-led redevelopment projects by city councils. In Birmingham's Ladypool Road, the heart of the 'Balti Triangle' in Balsall Heath, substantial funding was allocated to the enhancement and theme-ing of the streetscape to promote the area's BrAsian image. On the city council's tourist website, the 'Balti Triangle' boasts fifty 'Balti houses' offering a distinct Pakistani and Kashmiri cuisine as well as shops selling everything 'exotic' from colourful saris to Balti cooking pots. It is no surprise that the city council are keen to promote the area since the restaurant turnover is estimated at generating in excess of £7 million. Part of the council's place-making strategy was to commission PRASADA (Practice, Research and Advancement in South Asian Art and Architecture) at De Montfort University, Leicester to design the street furniture—street lamps, benches, rubbish bins and bollards—according to a BrAsian aesthetic (Figure 6). The result has been a project based on the 'repackaging of difference', structured by commercial interest and the need to present an attractive South Asian ambience. In the process of representing these areas as 'exotic landscapes' of attraction, the area has shifted from a place of production (serving the needs of the BrAsian community) to a place of consumption (by the larger society) (Loukaitou-Sideris, 2002; Hester, 2002).

Behind the visible face of a consumable South Asianness are the less conspicuous residential neighbourhoods which have seen gradual, incremental and small-scale transformation. The nature of these transformations has been the result of a number of factors such as the growth in affluence of households and the above-average size of extended families. Morphological changes, such as additions to the front, side and rear, as well as the conversion of the attic and basement for additional living space, suggest considerable modifications to the density of built-up area within the plot as well as the volumetric expansion of the building's fabric. Smaller and less formal alterations to window frames from timber to double glazing, the installation of a distinctly floral-pattern glass panelling and doors are most probably the combined effect of increased affluence, the adoption of technical innovations and the tendency for imitation amongst neighbours. The general robustness of the terrace house to adapt to the changing needs and family-size of its occupants is one reason why there has not been a trend of out-movement from the late-Victorian and Edwardian neighbourhoods. Not that there is not a substantial presence of BrAsian communities and buildings in the suburbs (Naylor and Ryan, 2002), but by maximising and extending the terrace house, sufficient space has been created to fulfil their cultural requirements.

Civilisations sign their names in monuments and in bricks and mortar. Such writing leaves its traces even when the civilisation that gave it birth has disappeared from memory or even history. If tomorrow BrAsians were to disappear from these islands, the signs of a BrAsian civilisation would be discernible. The betwixt and between nature of built form which contains BrAsian settlers of these islands should not stop us from recognising the emergence of a distinct way of life and how it is etched in bricks and mortar. This tension between relative fixity and apparent permanence of the built environment, and fluidity and mobility of the form that combines traditions of South Asia and Britain, is itself testimony to the postcolonial context of BrAsian borderlands. The postcolonial points to the intermediate, a recognition of the passing of one way of life and the not-completed establishment of another way of life. Thus BrAsian built environments can be seen as mirroring this transition, and perhaps the BrAsian civilisation is itself a transitory way of life.

ZEE TV

Rajinder Dudrah

Zee TV-Europe is the most popular non-terrestrial channel in the European South Asian diaspora. Zee TV-Europe broadcasts from its studios in Northolt, Middlesex in West London and is distinct from the specific workings of Zee TV in South Asia. Its emergence in 1992 and its development since it took over from the TV Asia channel in 1995 (Dudrah, 2002: 166–8) can be seen as responding to the historical marginalisation and misrepresentation of European South Asian audiences in the mainstream audio and visual spheres. It can also be viewed as providing an outlet for diasporic South Asian audiences to engage with their local and global senses of selfhood.

The mainstream media of the European Community member states have been shown to disseminate and construct problematic images of black minorities, thereby fuelling 'Euro-whiteness' (see for instance Ross, 1996 and Malik, 2002 on the representation of black people in the mainstream media in Britain). Also television programmes aimed specifically at non-white groups tend to be constructed as 'minority' programming (see Cohen and Gardner, 1983; Gilroy, 1983; Ross, 1996: chapter 5; Cottle, 1998; Malik, 2002). The way in which mainstream television in Britain responded to the supposed needs of black communities must be understood in the specific historical context in which they originated, i.e. a policy atmosphere which was dominated by the race-relations issue in which 'race' not racism was seen as the problem, and black communities were thought to be in need of assimilation into the white British way of life. Issues of poor representation and lack of access to the means of media production were at the forefront of demands from black communities and campaigning organisations who argued for change, and, as Karen Ross puts it, '[p]ublic service broadcasting, so called, became the target for dissatisfaction and viewed as part of the same oppressive structure which operated against black autonomy in the real world' (Ross, 1996: 120). In Britain at the time of writing (February 2004) a number of such 'minority' programmes are shown: in magazine formats, documentary series and as film and drama imports from South Asia which are shown intermittently as part of a season or series of programmes throughout the year. The current composition of regular minority television in Britain includes BBC2's

Black Britain, *Network East* and *East*, and Central Television's *Eastern Mix*. These programmes are presented as being by and for 'minorities'—'others' and not part of the mainstream of British broadcasting scheduling and its concomitant identities.

Other programmes such as the BBC's comedy sketch show *Goodness Gracious Me* (2000), the BBC's comedy chat show format of *The Kumars at No. 42* (2001) and Channel 4's television adaptation of Zadie Smith's novel *White Teeth* (2002) have been interesting achievements in British television that have articulated a more complex sense of British cultural identity through television address. However, such programmes have only been possible as a result of the ongoing struggles by black media professionals for access to the means of production for more elaborate black representation (cf. Cottle, 1998; Malik, 2002: chapter 1). With these latter programmes being few and far between, there still appears to be little space available in the British broadcasting schedule for programmes that offer black-*British* identities—hybrid or diasporic ways of thinking about identity that can encompass both the British culture in which these audiences are living and the original homelands to which they wish to retain a sense of connectedness. It is in such a context that Zee TV-Europe appears.

Zee TV's schedule in Europe combines South Asian and Western programme formats. In addition to feature films from Bollywood (see Dwyer, this volume), its programming includes popular South Asian films from Bangladesh, Pakistan, Sri Lanka and other parts of India. These, together with a range of other news, current affairs and business programmes, religious, comedy, film review and health shows, drama serials from India and Pakistan and South Asian sports, form the basis of the Zee TV schedule. The schedule, which is uniform right across Europe and can, therefore, be seen to offer possibilities of an audio-visual pan-South Asian European identity, is available on Zee Text (accessible on television sets throughout Europe with teletext service provided by the non-terrestrial channels), in the British South Asian popular press in Britain and some European national and local mainstream newspapers.

Zee TV in Europe is now in its tenth year of operation. Since its initial European broadcast the Zee network has diversified into four main channels: Zee TV, Zee Music, Zee Cinema and Zee Alpha Punjabi. The first three in particular continue to broadcast predominantly Hindi language programming. The Zee Alpha Punjabi channel, which, as one would expect, broadcasts its programmes primarily in Punjabi, is part of the umbrella group of Zee's Alpha regional channels from South Asia that also include Alpha Gujarati, Alpha Marathi and Alpha Bangla. The Zee network is obviously keen to capitalise on the variety of linguistic and cultural traditions within South Asia and its diasporas.

Alongside the broadcasting of Zee TV in Europe and more globally, a number of other channels have come and gone over the past few years as part of other media networks. Those broadcasting in 2004 included Sony TV (Sony TV Asia), the Bollywood 4 U network (B4U Movies and B4U Music), the Star TV channels (Star TV and Star Plus), ARY Digital, Ekushey TV, PTV Prime, Asian Television Network, Vectone TV (Vectone India, Vectone Urdu, Vectone Tamil), SAB TV and the South For You channel. Channels such as Channel East and the Reminiscent television network (RTV), having being on-air for a year or two, had to withdraw their services due to the lack of sustainable viewer subscriptions and competition from other channels.

Also of interest here are the kinds of adverts aired on these channels. Increasingly, cultural and social services (e.g. black British immigration and criminal law services) and diasporic South Asian products (e.g. subcontinental foods and stores, and retailers such as jewellers) are being advertised. In part this is due to the rates offered by the non-terrestrial channels, which are much more competitive than their mainstream counterparts, but primarily because these channels are viewed as an appropriate vehicle to relay messages to South Asian audiences.

Clearly this is a fast-changing mediascape in which Zee TV and other channels are in intense competition for similar South Asian audiences and advertising revenues made available by the increasing liberalisation and deregulation of the international audio-visual spheres.

BIBLIOGRAPHY

Adams, C., 1987, *Across Seven Seas and Thirteen Rivers: life stories of pioneer Sylhetti settlers in Britain*, London: THAP Books.

ADP (Asian Drug Project), 1995, *Substance Use: an assessment of the young Asian community in Tower Hamlets and a summary of the development work of the Asian Drug Project*, London: Asian Drug Project.

Agamben, G., 2005, *State of Exception*, University of Chicago Press.

Ahmad, F., 2001, 'Modern Traditions? British Muslim women and academic achievement', *Gender and Education*, 13, 2, pp. 137–52.

——, 2003, '"Still in progress?": methodological dilemmas, tensions and contradictions in theorizing South Asian Muslim women' in N. Puwar and P. Ranghuram (eds), *South Asian Women in the Diaspora*, Oxford: Berg.

——, T. Modood and S. Lissenburgh, 2003, *South Asian Women and Employment in Britain: the interaction of gender and ethnicity*, London: Policy Studies Institute.

Ahmad, R. and R. Gupta (eds), 1994, *Flaming Spirit: stories from the Asian women writers' collective*, London: Virago.

Ahmad, W.I.U., 1989, 'Policies, Pills and Political Will: a critique of policies to improve the health status of ethnic minorities', *Lancet*, 1, 8630, pp. 148–50.

——, 1993, *Race and Health in Contemporary Britain*, Buckingham: Open University Press.

——, 1996, 'Family Obligations and Social Change among Asian Communities' in W.I.U. Ahmad and K. Atkin (eds), *Race and Community Care*, Buckingham: Open University Press.

——, 2000, 'Introduction' in W.I.U. Ahmad (ed.), *Ethnicity, Disability and Chronic Illness*, Buckingham: Open University Press.

——, K. Atkin and R. Chamba, 2000, 'Causing Havoc among Their Children: parental and professional perspectives on consanguinity and childhood disability' in W.I.U. Ahmad (ed.), *Ethnicity, Disability and Chronic Illness*, Buckingham: Open University Press.

W.I.U. Ahmad, K. Atkin and L. Jones, 2002, 'Young Asian Deaf People and Their Families: negotiating relationships and identities', *Social Science and Medicine*, 55, 10, pp. 1757–69.

Al Ahmad, J., 1997, *Gharbzadegi: Weststruckness*, Costa Mesa, CA: Mazda Publishers.

Alam, M.Y., 1998, *Annie Potts is Dead*, Glasshoughton (British Midlands): Springboard Fiction.

——, 2002, *Kilo*, Glasshoughton (British Midlands): Route.

Aldrich, H.E., J. Cater, T.P. Jones and D. McEvoy, 1981, 'Business Development and Self-segregation: Asian enterprise in three British cities' in C. Peach, V. Robinson and S. Smith (eds), *Ethnic Segregation in Cities*, London: Croom Helm, pp. 170–90.

Aldrich, H.E. and R. Waldinger, 1990, 'Ethnicity and Entrepreneurship', *Annual Review of Sociology*, 16, pp. 111–35.

Alexander, C., 1996, *The Art of Being Black: the creation of black British youth identities*, Oxford University Press.

——, 2000, *The Asian Gang: ethnicity, identity, masculinity*, Oxford: Berg.

——, 2002, 'Beyond Black: rethinking the colour/culture divide', *Ethnic and Racial Studies*, 25, 4, pp. 552–71.

Ali, N., 2002, 'Kashmiri Nationalism Beyond the Nation-State', *South Asia Research*, 22, 2, pp. 145–60.

Ali, Y., 1991, 'Echoes of Empire: towards a politics of representation' in J. Cromer and S. Harvey (eds), *Enterprise and Heritage: cross currents of national culture*, London: Routledge.

Allen, S., 1971, *New Minorities, Old Conflicts*, New York: Random House.

Alliez, Eric, 1996, *Capital Times: tales from the conquest of time*, trans. Georges van den Abbeele, Minneapolis: Minnesota University Press.

Almond, Ian, 2004, 'Borges the Post-Orientalist: images of Islam from the edge of the West', *Modern Fiction Studies*, 50, 2 (summer), pp. 435–59.

AlSayyad, N., 2001, 'Prologue: hybrid culture/hybrid urbanism: Pandora's Box of the "third place"' in N. AlSayyad (ed.), *Hybrid Urbanism: on the identity discourse and the built environment*, Westport, CT: Praeger.

Amin, A., 2002, *Ethnicity and the Multicultural City: living with diversity*, Report for Department of Transport, Local Government and the Regions.

Amin, K. and R. Richardson, 1992, *Politics for All: equality, culture and the General Election 1992*, London: Runnymede Trust.

Amin, Samir, 1998, 'A Mundialização actual e o futuro' in *Essas outras histórias qua há para contar. Colóquio Internacional em tempos de Expo*, Lisbon: Salamandra.

Anderson, D., 2005, *Histories of the Hanged: the dirty war in Kenya and the end of empire*, New York: W.W. Norton.

Ang, Ien, Sharon Chalmers, Lisa Law and Mandy Thomas (eds), 2000, *Alter/Asians: Asian-Australian identities in art, media and popular culture*, London: Pluto Press.

Anionwu, E. and K. Atkin, 2001, *The Politics of Sickle Cell and Thalassaemia*, Buckingham: Open University Press.

Anthias, F. and N. Yuval-Davis, 1992, *Racialised Boundaries*, London: Routledge.

Anwar, M., 1973, 'Pakistani Participation in the 1972 Rochdale By-election', *New Community*, 2, 4, pp. 418–23.

——, 1975, 'Asian Participation in the 1974 Autumn Election', *New Community*, 4, 3, pp. 376–83.

——, 1979, *The Myth of Return: Pakistanis in Britain*, London: Heinemann.

——, 1980, *Votes and Policies*, London: Commission for Racial Equality.

——, 1984, *Ethnic Minorities and the 1983 General Election*, London: Commission for Racial Equality.

——, 1986, *Race and Politics*, London: Tavistock.

——, 1994, *Race and Elections*, Coventry: Centre for Research in Ethnic Relations.

——, 1998a, *Between Cultures: continuity and change in the lives of young Asians*, London: Routledge.

——, 1998b, *Ethnic Minorities and the British Electoral System*, London and Coventry: Operation Black Vote and Centre for Research in Ethnic Relations.

—— and D. Kohler, 1975, *Participation of Ethnic Minorities in the General Election, October 1974*, London: Community Relations Commission.

Appadurai, Arjun, 1997, *Modernity at Large: cultural dimensions of globalization*, New Delhi: Oxford University Press.

Appaiah, A., 2003, *Hindutva: ideology and politics*, New Delhi: Deep and Deep.

Araeen, R., 1987, 'From Primitivism to Ethnic Arts', *Third Text*, 1.

——, 1989, *The Other Story: Afro-Asian artists in post-War Britain*, London: South Bank Centre.

——, 1991, 'From Primitivism to Ethnic Arts' in S. Hiller (ed.), *The Myth of Primitivism: perspectives on art*, London: Routledge.

Asad, T., 1993a, *Genealogies of Religion: discipline and reasons of power in Christianity and Islam*, Baltimore, MD: Johns Hopkins University Press.

——, 1993b, 'Multiculturalism and British Identity in the Wake of the Rushdie Affair' in Talal Asad, 1993, *Genealogies of Religion: discipline and reasons of power in Christianity and Islam*, Baltimore, MD: Johns Hopkins University Press, pp. 239–68.

——, 2003, *Formations of the Secular: Christianity, Islam and modernity*, Stanford University Press.

Atkin, K., 1996, 'Race and Social Policy' in N. Lunt and D. Coyle (eds), *Welfare and Policy*, Basingstoke: Taylor and Francis.

——, 2003, 'Primary Health Care and South Asian Populations: institutional racism, policy and practice' in S. Ali and K. Atkin (eds), *South Asian Populations and Primary Health Care: meeting the challenges*, Oxford: Radcliffe.

—— and J. Rollings, 1996, 'Looking After Their Own? Family care giving in Asian and Afro-Caribbean communities' in W.I.U. Ahmad and K. Atkin (eds), *Race and Community Care*, Buckingham: Open University Press.

Atkin, K., W.I.U. Ahmad and E. Anionwu, 1998, 'Screening and Counselling for Sickle Cell Disorders and Thalassaemia: the experience of parents and health professionals', *Social Science and Medicine*, 47, 11, pp. 1639–51.

Atkin, K., W.I.U. Ahmad and L. Jones, 2002, 'Being Deaf and Being Other Things: young Asian deaf people negotiating identities', *Sociology of Health and Illness*, 24, 1, pp. 21–45.

Awasthi, S., 1983, *Drama: the gift of gods, culture, performance and communication in India*, Tokyo: Institute for the Study of Languages and Cultures of Asia and Africa, Nihon Eishin.

Back, L., 1993, 'Race, Identity and Nation within an Adolescent Community in South London', *New Community*, 19, pp. 217–33.

——, 1996, *New Ethnicities and Urban Culture: racisms and multi-culture in young lives*, London: UCL Press.

Bagchi, A.K., 1973, 'Foreign Capital and Economic Development in India' in K. Gough and H. Sharma (eds), *Imperialism and Revolution in South Asia*, London: Monthly Review Press.

Baig, M.R.A., 1967, *In Different Saddles*, Bombay: Asia Publishing House.

Bailey, Frederick, 1969, *Stratagems and Spoils: a social anthropology of politics*, London: Routledge.

Bains, H., 1988, 'Southall Youth: an old-fashioned story' in P. Cohen and H. Bains (eds), *Multi-Racist Britain*, London: Macmillan.

Balagangadhara, S.N., 1994, *The Heathen in His Blindness: Asia, the West and the dynamic of religion*, Leiden: Brill.

Bald, S.R., 1995, 'Negotiating Identity on the Metropolis' in R. King, J. Connell and P. White (eds), *Writing Across Worlds, Literature and Migration*, London: Routledge.

Bale, J. and F. Gibb, 2002, 'Girl forced to marry at 16 wins annulment', *The Times Online*, 14 April 2002, http://www.thetimes.co.uk/article/0%2C%2C2-277377%2C00.html.

Ball, Wendy and John Solomos (eds), 1990, *Race and Local Politics*, London: Macmillan.

Ballard, C., 1978, 'Arranged Marriages in the British Context', *New Community*, VI, 3, pp. 181–96.

——, 1979, 'Conflict, Continuity and Change: second generation South Asians' in V. Saifullah Khan (ed.), *Minority Families in Britain: support and stress*, London: Macmillan.

Ballard, R., 1982, 'South Asian Families' in R. Rapoport, M. Fogarty and R. Rapoport (eds), *Families in Britain*, London: Routledge & Kegan Paul. Also online: http://www/art.man.ac.uk/CASAS/pdfpapers/families/pdf.

——, 1987, 'The Political Economy of Migration: Pakistan, Britain and the Middle East' in J. Eades (ed.), *Migrants, Workers and the Social Order*, London: Tavistock.

——, 1989, 'Social Work and Black People: what's the difference?' in C. Rojeck, G. Peacock and S. Collins (eds), *The Haunt of Misery: critical essays in social work and helping*, London: Routledge.

——, 1990, 'Migration and Kinship: the differential effect of marriage rules of the process of Punjabi migration to Britian' in C. Clarke, C. Peach and S. Vertovec (eds), *South Asians Overseas: migration and ethnicity*, Cambridge University Press.

——, 1994a, 'Introduction: the emergence of Desh Pardesh' in R. Ballard (ed.), *Desh Pardesh: the South Asian presence in Britain*, London: Hurst & Company.

—— (ed.), 1994b, *Desh Pardesh: the South Asian presence in Britain*, London: Hurst.

—— and C. Ballard, 1977, 'The Sikhs' in J. Waton (ed.), *Between Two Cultures*, Oxford: Blackwell.

Bancil, P., 2000, 'Made in England' in *Black and Asian Plays Anthology*, London: Aurora Metro Press.

Banerjea, K., 2000, 'Sounds of Whose Underground?: the fine tuning of diaspora in an age of mechanical reproduction', *Theory, Culture and Society*, 17, 3, pp. 64–79.

Banerji, S. and G. Baumann, 1990, 'Bhangra 1984–8: fusion and professionalisation in a genre of South Asian dance music' in P. Oliver (ed.), *Black Music in Britain: essays on the Afro-Asian contribution to popular music*, Milton Keynes: Open University Press.

Banton, M., 1955, *The Coloured Quarter*, London: Jonathan Cape.

——, 1987, 'The Battle of the Name', *New Community*, 14, pp. 170–5.

Barrett, A.G., T.P. Jones and D. McEvoy, 1996, 'Ethnic Minority Business: theoretical discourse in Britain and North America', *Urban Studies*, 33, 4–5, pp. 783–809.

Barton, S.W, 1986, *The Bengali Muslims of Bradford*, Leeds: Monograph Series, Community Religions Project, Department of Theology and Religious Studies, University of Leeds.

Basit, T.N., 1996, '"Obviously I'll have an arranged marriage": Muslim marriage in the British context', *Muslim Education Quarterly*, 13, pp. 4–19.

——, 1997, *Eastern Values; Western Milieu: identities and aspirations of adolescent British Muslim girls*, Aldershot: Ashgate.

Basu, A. and A. Goswami, 1999, 'Br-Asian Entrepreneurship in Great Britain: factors influencing growth', *International Journal of Entrepreneurial Behaviour & Research*, 5, 5, pp. 251–75.

Bauman, G., 1996, *Contesting Culture: discourses of identity in multi-ethnic London*, Cambridge University Press.

Bauman, Z., 1989, *Modernity and the Holocaust*, Ithaca, NY: Cornell University Press.

——, 1992, *Intimations of Post Modernity*, London: Routledge.

bbc.co.uk/asiannetwork

Beetham, D., 1970, *Transport and Turbans: a comparative study in local politics*, London: Oxford University Press for the Institute of Race Relations.

Bennet, L., 1957, *Anancy Stories and Dialect Verse*, Kingston, Jamaica: Pioneer.

Benson, S., 1996, 'Asians have Culture, West Indians have Problems: discourses of race and ethnicity in and out of anthropology' in T. Ranger, Y. Samad and O. Stuart (eds), *Culture, Identity and Politics*, Aldershot: Avebury, pp. 47–56.

Bernal, Martin, 1987, *Black Athena: the Afroasiatic roots of Western civilization*, London: Vintage Books.

Berthoud, R., 2000, 'Ethnic Employment Penalties in Britain', *Journal of Ethnic and Migration Studies*, 26, July, pp. 389–416.

Beynon, John and John Solomos (eds), 1987, *The Roots of Urban Unrest*, Oxford: Pergamon Press.

Bhabha, H., 1994, *The Location of Culture*, London: Routledge.

—— and P.L. Tazzi, 1998, *Anish Kapoor*, Los Angeles: University of California Press and London: Hayward Gallery.

Bhachu, P., 1985, *Twice Migrants: East African Sikh settlers in Britain*, London: Tavistock.

——, 1988, 'Apni Marzi Kardi' in S. Westwood and P. Bhachu (eds), *Enterprising Women: ethnicity, economy and gender relations*, London: Routledge.

——, 1991, 'Ethnicity Constructed and Reconstructed: the role of Sikh women in cultural elaboration and educational decision-making in Britain', *Gender and Education*, 3, 1, pp. 45–60.

——, 1996, 'The Multiple Landscapes of Trans-national Asian Women in the Diaspora' in V. Amit-Talai and C. Knowles (eds), *Re-Situating Identities: the politics of race, ethnicity and culture*, Peterborough, ON: Broadview Press.

——, 2004, *Dangerous Designs: Asian women fashion the diaspora economies*, London: Routledge.

Bhakta, P., S. Katbamna and G. Parker, 2000, 'South Asian Carers: experiences of primary health care teams' in W.I.U. Ahmad (ed.), *Ethnicity, Disability and Chronic Illness*, Buckingham: Open University Press.

Bhatt, C., 1997, *Liberation and Purity: race, new religious movements and the ethics of postmodernity*, London: UCL Press.

——, 2001, *Hindu Nationalism: origins, ideologies and modern myths*, Oxford: Berg.

Bhattacharyya, G., 1998, *Tales of Dark-Skinned Women*, London: UCL Press.

Bhopal, K., 1997, *Gender, 'Race' and Patriarchy: a study of South Asian women*, Aldershot: Ashgate.

——, 1998, 'How Gender and Ethnicity Intersect: the significance of education, employment and marital status', *Sociological Research Online*, 3, 3, pp. 1–16.

——, 1999, 'South Asian Women and Arranged Marriages in East London' in R. Barot, H. Bradley and S. Fenton (eds), *Ethnicity, Gender and Social Change*, Basingstoke: Macmillan.

——, 2000, 'South Asian Women in East London: the impact of education', *European Journal of Women's Studies*, 7, pp. 35–52.

Boal, F. (ed.), 2000, *Ethnicity and Housing: accommodating differences*, Aldershot: Ashgate.

Bonnet, A., 2003, 'From White to Western: "racial decline" and the idea of the West in Britain 1890–1930', *Journal of Historical Sociology*, 16, 3.

Booth, C., 1893, *Life and Labour of the People of London* (16 vols), London: Williams and Worgate.

Borges, Jorge Luis, 2000, *Selected Non Fictions*, Harmondsworth: Penguin.

Boulton, M.L. and P. Smith, 1992, 'Ethnic Preferences and Perceptions Among Asian and White British Middle School Children', *Social Development*, 1, pp. 55–6.

Bourdieu, P., 1992, *The Logic of Practice*, Cambridge: Polity Press.

—— and Passeron, J., 1977, *Reproduction in Education and Society*, London: Sage.

Bowes, A., N. Dar and D. Sim, 2000, 'Housing Preferences and Strategies: an exploration of Pakistani preferences in Glasgow' in F. Boal (ed.), *Ethnicity and Housing: accommodating differences*, Aldershot: Ashgate.

Bowling, B. and P. Phillips, 2002, *Racism, Crime and Justice*, Essex: Longman.

Bradby, H., 1999, 'Negotiating Marriage: young Punjabi women's assessment of their individual and family interests' in R. Barot, H. Bradley and S. Fenton (eds), *Ethnicity, Gender and Social Change*, Basingstoke: Macmillan.

Bradford Commission, 1996, *The Bradford Commission Report*, London: The Stationery Office.

Bradford Heritage Recording Unit (BHRU), 1987, *Destination Bradford: a century of immigration*, Bradford: Bradford Libraries and Information Service.

Bradford Population Forecasts Information Bulletin, February 2000, Bradford: Bradford Metropolitan District Council, Policy and Research Unit, 2000.

Brah, A., 1978, 'South Asian Teenagers in Southall: their perceptions of marriage, family and ethnic identity', *New Community*, VI, 3, pp. 197–206.

——, 1979, 'Inter-generational and Inter-ethnic Perceptions: a comparative study of South Asian and English adolescents and their parents in Southall, West London', PhD thesis, University of Bristol.

——, 1993, '"Race" and "Culture" in the Gendering of Labour Markets: South Asian young Muslim women and the labour market', *New Community*, 29, pp. 441–58.

——, 1996, *Cartographies of Diaspora*, London: Routledge.

——, 2002, 'Global Mobilities, Local Predicaments: globalization and the critical imagination', *Feminist Review*, 70.

——, 2004, 'Gendered Embodiment, Scattered Belongings: Sikh women in the diaspora', *International Journal of Punjab Studies*, 11, 1.

—— and S. Shaw, 1992, *Working Choices: South Asian women and the labour market*, Department of Employment Research Paper 91, London: HMSO.

Brah, H., 1998, *Bourgeois Nationalism or Proletarian Internationalism*, London: Harpal Brah.

Brennan, T., 1999, 'Poetry and Polemic', *Race and Class*, 41, 1/2, pp. 23–34.

'Britain to rebrand ethnic minorities', *The Times*, 8 August 2005.

Brown, C., 1984, *Black and White Britain*, Third PSI survey, London: Policy Studies Institute.

—— and P. Gay, 1985, *Racial Discrimination: 17 years after the act*, London: Policy Studies Institute.

Brown, J., 1994, *Modern India: the origins of an Asian democracy*, Oxford University Press.

Brown, S.M., 2000, 'Religion and Economic Activity in the Br-Asian Population', *Ethnic and Racial Studies*, 23, 6, pp. 1035–61.

Building Cohesive Communities: a Report of the Ministerial Group on Public Order and Community Cohesion, London: Home Office (UK), 2001.

Bulmer, M. and J. Solomos, 1999, *Ethnic and Racial Studies Today*, London: Routledge.

Burlet, S. and H. Reid, 1998, 'A Gendered Uprising: political representation and minority ethnic communities', *Ethnic and Racial Studies*, 21, 2, pp. 270–87.

Burman, Chila Kumari, 1994, *With Your Own Face On It* (exhibition catalogue), London: Watermans Art Centre.

Burnley Task Force, 2001, *Report of the Burnley Task Force*.

Butt, J. and K. Mirza, 1996, *Social Care and Black Communities*, London: HMSO.

Callaghan, John, 1993, *Rajani Palme Dutt: a study in British Stalinism*, London: Lawrence and Wishart.

Cameron, E., F. Badger, H. Evers and K. Atkin, 1989, 'Black Old Women and Health Carers' in M. Jefferys (ed.), *Growing Old in the Twentieth Century*, London: Routledge.

Campaign against Racism and Fascism/Southall Rights, 1981, *Southall: birth of a black community*, London: Institute of Race Relations and Southall Rights.

Carey, S.F., 2000, '*Looking for the Buzz: heroin—the drug of choice. Drug use amongst Bangladeshi youths on the Ocean estate*, final report, London: Community Partnership, London Borough of Tower Hamlets.

Carmichael, F. and R. Woods, 2000, 'Ethnic Penalties in Unemployment and Occupational Attainment', *International Review of Applied Economics*, 14, 1, pp. 71–98.

Carmichael, Stokely and Charles V. Hamilton, 1967, *Black Power: the politics of liberation in America*, Harmondsworth: Penguin Books.

Carrington, A., n.d., *An Action Study Report on Drug Misuse and the African-Caribbean Community*, Bradford: Bradford Drugs Prevention Team / Bradford West Indian Community Centre Association (also reported in Gilman, 1993).

Cashmore, E. and B. Troyna, 1990, *Introduction to Race Relations*, Brighton: Falmer Press.

Castles, S. and M. Miller, 1993, *The Age of Migration: international population movements in the modern world*, Basingstoke: Macmillian.

Cavanagh, T.E., 1984, *The Impact of Black Electorate*, Washington, DC: Joint Centre for Political Studies.

CCCS, 1982, *The Empire Strikes Back: race and racism in 70s Britain*, London: Hutchinson.

Centre For Research Into Ethnic Relations, 1990, 'Research Programme 1989–1993', *Occasional Paper in Ethnic Relations*, 6.

Cesaire, A., 1955, *Discourse on Colonialism*, New York University Press.

Chadwick, G.F., 1978, 'The Face of the Industrial City: two looks at Manchester' in H.J. Dyos and M. Wolff (eds), *The Victorian City: images and realities*, London: Routledge & Kegan Paul.

Chamba, R., M. Hirst, D. Lawton, W.I.U. Ahmad and B. Beresford, 1999, *On the Edge: a national survey of minority ethnic parents caring for a severely disabled child*, Bristol: Policy Press.

Chambers, I., 1986, *Popular culture: the metropolitan experience*, London: Routledge.

Chatterjee, D., 1989, *I was that Woman*, Frome: Hippopotamus Press.

Chattoo, S. and W.I.U. Ahmad, 2003, 'The Meaning of Cancer: illness, biography and social identity' in D. Kelleher and G. Cahill (eds), *Identity and Health*, London: Routledge.

Chaudhuri, K.N., 1991, *Asia before Europe: economy and civilisation of the Indian Ocean from the rise of Islam to 1750*, Cambridge University Press.

Chessum, Lorna, 2000, *From Immigrants to Ethnic Minority: making black community in Britain*, Aldershot: Ashgate.

Choudhury, Y., 1993, *The Roots and Tales of the Bangladeshi Settlers*, Birmingham: Sylheti Social History Group.

Clapson, M., 1998, *Invincible Green Suburbs, Brave New Towns*, Manchester University Press.

Clark, D., 1975, 'Recollections of Resistance: Udham Singh and the IWA', *Race and Class*, 17, 1, pp. 75–7.

Cobham, R. and M. Collins (eds), 1987, *Watchers and Seekers: creative writing by black women in Britain*, London: Women's Press.

Cohen, A. (ed.), 1974, *Urban Ethnicity*, London: Tavistock.

Cohen, P., 1988, 'The Perversions of Inheritance: studies in the making of multi-racist Britain' in P. Cohen and H.S. Bains (eds), *Multi-Racist Britain*, London: Macmillan.

—— and C. Gardner, 1983, *It Ain't Half Racist, Mum*, London: Comedia.

Cohn, Bernard S., 1996, *Colonialism and its Forms of Knowledge: the British in India*, Princeton University Press.

Colombijn, F. and A. Erdentug, 2002, 'Introduction: urban space and ethnicity' in F. Colombijn and A. Erdentug (eds), *Urban Ethnic Encounters: the spatial consequences*, London: Routledge.

Commission For Racial Equality, 1988, 'Ethnic Classification System Recommended by CRE', press statement, 7 December 1988.

Commission on the Future of Multi-Ethnic Britain, London: Profile Books, 2000.

Community Cohesion: a report of the Independent Review Team chaired by Ted Cantle, London: Home Office, 2001.

'Community Pride not Prejudice: making diversity work in Bradford', online at http://www.bradford2020.com/pride/, 2001.

Connelly, N., 1988, *Care in the Multi-racial Community*, London: Policy Studies Institute.

Constantine, S., 1980, *Unemployment in Britain Between the Wars*, London: Longman.

Cottle, S., 1998, 'Making Ethnic Minority Programmes Inside the BBC: professional pragmatics and cultural containment', *Media, Culture, Society*, 20, 2, pp. 295–317.

Cowell, D. *et al.* (eds), 1982, *Policing the Riots*, London: Junction Books.

CRE (Commission for Racial Equality), 1995, Census data, London: CRE.

Dahya, B., 1974, 'The Nature of Pakistani Ethnicity in Industrial Cities in Britain' in A. Cohen (ed.), *Urban Ethnicity*, London: Tavistock, pp. 77–118.

Dale, A., N. Shaheen, E. Fieldhouse and V. Kalra, 2002a, 'Labour Market Prospects for Pakistani and Bangladeshi Women', *Work, Employment and Society*, 16, 1, pp. 5–26.

——, 2002b, 'Routes into Education and Employment for Young Pakistani and Bangladeshi Women in the UK', *Ethnic and Racial Studies*, 25, 6, pp. 942–68.

Dalmia, Vasudha, 1996, *The Nationalisation of Hindu Traditions*, New Delhi: Oxford University Press.

Dalrymple, W., 2002, *White Mughals*, London: HarperCollins.

Daniel, W.W., 1968, *Racial Discrimination in England*, Harmondsworth: Penguin.

Darr, A., 1997, 'Consanguineous Marriage and Genetics: a model for genetic health service delivery' in A. Clarke and E. Parsons (eds), *Culture, Kinship and Genes*, London: Macmillan.

Datta, V.N., 1978, *Madan Lal Dhingra and the Revolutionary Movement*, New Delhi: Vikas Publishing House.

Davidson, Alan , 1999, *The Oxford Companion to Food*, Oxford University Press.

Davies, Norman, 2000, *The Isles: a history*, London: Pimlico.

Deakin, N. (ed.), 1965, *Colour and the British Electorate*, London: Pall Mall Press.

Denham, L., 2001, *Building Cohesive Communities: a report of the Ministerial Group on Public Order and Community Cohesion*, London: Home Office.

Department of Education Science, 1965, *Circular 7/65*, London: HMSO.

Department of Health, 1989, *Caring for People: community care in the next decade and beyond* (Cm 849), London: HMSO.

Derrida, J., 1976, *Of Grammatology*, Baltimore, MD: Johns Hopkins University Press.

——, 1998, *Religion*, London: Polity Press.

Desai, R., 1963, *Indian Immigrants in Britain*, Oxford University Press.

de Souza, A. and M. Shaheen (eds), 1992, *Crossing Black Waters*, London: Working Press.

Dhingra, L., 1987, 'Breaking Out of Labels' in R. Cobham and M. Collins (eds), *Watchers and Seekers: creative writing by black women in Britain*, London: Women's Press, p. 30.

——, 1988, *Amritvela*, London: Women's Press.

Dhondy, F., 1987, 'Speaking in Whose Name?', *New Statesman*, 24 April 1987.

Dodds, J., 2002, *New York Masjid: the mosques of New York City*, New York: Powerhouse Books.

Donald, J. and A. Rattansi (eds), 1992, *'Race', Culture and Difference*, London: Sage.

Drury, B., 1990, 'Blackness: a situational identity', paper given at *New Issues in Black Politics* conference, University of Warwick, 14–16 May 1990.

——, 1991, 'Sikh Girls and the Maintenance of an Ethnic Culture', *New Community*, 17, 3, pp. 387–99.

——, 1996, 'The Impact of Religion, Culture, Racism and Politics on the Multiple Identities of Sikh Girls' in T. Ranger, Y. Samad and O. Stuart (eds), *Culture, Identity and Politics*, Aldershot: Avebury.

Du Bois, W.E.B., 1947, *The World and Africa: an inquiry into the part which Africa has played in world history*, New York: Viking Press.

Dudrah, R.K., 2002a, 'Drum N Dhol: British Bhangra music and diasporic South Asian identity formation', *European Journal of Cultural Studies*, 5, 3, pp. 363–83.

——, 2002b, 'Zee TV in Europe: non-terrestrial television and the construction of a pan-South Asian European identity', *Contemporary South Asia*, 11, 1, pp. 163–81.

Dutt, R., 1901, *The Economic History of India*, London: Routledge & Kegan Paul.

Dwyer, C., 1999, 'Veiled Meanings: British Muslim women and the negotiation of differences', *Gender, Place and Culture*, 6, 1, pp. 5–26.

Dwyer, Rachel, 2000a, *All You Want is Money, All You Need is Love: sex and romance in modern India*, London: Cassell.

——, 2000b, '"Indian Values" and the Diaspora: Yash Chopra's films of the 1990s', *West Coast Line*, autumn 2000 and in Parthiv Shah (ed.), *Figures, Facts, Feelings: a direct diasporic dialogue*, catalogue to accompany a British Council exhibition, November 2000: pp. 74–82.

——, 2002, *Yash Chopra*, London: British Film Institute/Berkeley, CA: University of California Press.

——, 2005, *100 Bollywood Films*, London: British Film Institute.

—— and Divia Patel, 2002, *Cinema India: the visual culture of the Hindi film*, London: Reaktion/New Brunswick, NJ: Rutgers University Press/New Delhi: Oxford University Press.

Eade, J., 1996, 'Nationalism, Community and the Islamization of Space in London' in B.D. Metcalf, *Making Muslim Space in North America and Europe*, Berkeley, CA: University of California Press.

——, T. Vamplew and C. Peach, 1996, 'The Bangladeshis: the encapsulated community' in *Ethnicity in the 1991 Census*, volume 2: *the ethnic minority populations of Great Britain*, London: Office for National Statistics.

Ealing International Friendship Council, 1968, *A Report of the Education Committee*, unpublished.

Eisenstadt, S., 1971, *From Generation to Generation*, New York: Monthly Review Press.

Electoral Commission, 2001, *Election 2001: The Official Results*, London: Electoral Commission.

——, 2002, *Voter Engagement Among Black and Minority Ethnic Communities*, London: Electoral Commission.

Elkins, M. and J. Olagundoye, 2001, *The Prison Population in 2000: a statistical review*, London: Home Office.

English Indices of Deprivation 2004, Neighbourhood Renewal Unit, Office of the Deputy Prime Minister.

Fawcett, J.T. and F. Arnold, 1987, 'Explaining Diversity: Asian and Pacific immigration systems' in J.T. Fawcett and B. Carino (eds), *Pacific Bridges*, New York: Centre for Migration Study.

Fenton, S., 2003, *Ethnicity*, Cambridge: Polity Press.

Fisher, M.H., 1996, *The First Indian Author in English: Dean Mahomed (1759–1851) in India, Ireland and England*, Oxford University Press.

Fonseca, Luís Adão da, 1998, 'Vasco da Gama e a Expansão Portuguesa' in *Da Ocidental Praia Lusitana—Vasco da Gama e o Seu Tempo*, Lisbon: CNCDP.

Forward, M., 1995, 'Syed Ameer Ali: a bridge-builder?', *Islam and Christian Muslim Relations*, 6, 1, pp. 50–1.

Foucault, M., 1970, *The Order of Things: an archaeology of the human sciences*, London: Tavistock.

——, 1974, *The Archaeology of Knowledge*, London: Tavistock.

Foyster *et al.*, 1990, 'I landed twice as many jobs as my two friends—but then they are black', *Today*, 11 September 1990.

Frankenberg, R., 1993, *White Women, Race Matters: the social construction of whiteness*, London: Routledge.

Frean, A., 2002, 'Arranged Marriages Total 1,000 a Year', *The Times Online*, 24 April 2002. Also at http://www.thetimes.co.uk/article/0,,2-277379,00.html.

Fredrickson, G., 2001, *Racism: a short historical introduction*, Princeton University Press.

Fryer, P., 1984, *Staying Power: the history of black people in Britain*, London: Pluto Press.

Furedi, F., 1998, *The Silent War: imperialism and the changing perception of race*, London: Pluto Press.

Gale, R., 2004, 'Urban Planning and the Geography of Religion: South Asian faith groups and the planning process in Birmingham', PhD thesis, Oxford University.

—— and S. Naylor, 2002, 'Religion, Planning and the City: the spatial politics of ethnic minority expression in British cities and towns', *Ethnicities*, 2, 3, pp. 387–409.

Garcia, José Manuel (ed.), 1999, *A Viagem de Vasco da Gama à Índia 1497–1499*, Lisbon: Academia de Marinha.

Gardiner, Juliet, 1990, *The History Debate*, London: Collins & Brown.

Gardner, K. and A. Shakur, 1994, 'I'm Bengali, I'm Asian and I'm Living Here' in R. Ballard (ed.), *Desh Pardesh: the South Asian presence in Britain*, London: Hurst.

German soldier's letter published in *Frankfurter Zeitung*, and quoted in P. Mason, 1986, *A Matter of Honour*, London: Macmillan, p. 413.

Ghai, D.P. and Y.P. Ghai, 1970, *Portrait of a Minority*, Oxford University Press.

Ghosh, A., 2001, 'The Transcending Vision: another vision' in A. Ghosh and J. Lamba (eds), *Beyond Frontiers: contemporary British art by artists of South Asian descent*, London: Saffron.

Gillespie, M., 1989, 'Technology and Tradition: audiovisual culture among South Asian families in West London', *Cultural Studies*, 3, 3, pp. 226–39.

——, 1995, *Television, Ethnicity and Cultural Change*, London: Routledge.

Gilman, M., 1993, *An Overview of the Main Findings and Implications of Seven Action Studies into the Nature of Drug Use in Bradford*, Bradford: Home Office Drugs Prevention Team (also reported in Carrington, n.d.)

Gilroy, P., 1983, 'Channel 4: bridgehead or bantustan', *Screen*, 24, pp. 130–6.

——, 1987, *There Ain't No Black in the Union Jack*, London: Routledge.

——, 1992, 'The End of Antiracism' in J. Donald and A. Rattansi (eds), *'Race', Culture and Difference*, London: Sage, pp. 49–61.

——, 1993a, *Small Acts: thoughts on the politics of black cultures*, London: Serpent's Tail.

——, 1993b, *The Black Atlantic: modernity and double consciousness*, London: Verso.

Giroux, H., 1996, *Fugitive Cultures*, London and New York: Routledge.

Glasgow, D., 1980, *The Black Underclass*, London: Jossey Bass.

Goldberg, D.T., 2002, *The Racial State*, Oxford: Blackwell.

Gooden, T., 1999, *Carers and Parents of African Caribbean and Asian Substance Users in Nottingham: a needs analysis*, draft final report, Nottingham: ORCHID (Organisational Change Innovation Development) / NBI (Nottingham Black Initiative).

Gopal, R., 1963, *British Rule in India*, London and New Delhi: Asia Publishing House.

Green, J. and F.E. Murton, 1996, 'Diagnosis of Duchenne Muscular Dystrophy: parents' experiences and satisfaction', *Child Care, Health and Development*, 22, 2, pp. 113–28.

Green, J. and H. Statham, 1996, 'Psychological Aspects of Prenatal Screening and Diagnosis' in T. Marteau and M. Richards (eds), *The Troubled Helix: social and psychological implications of the new human genetics*, Cambridge University Press.

Gregory, Derek, 2004, *The Colonial Present: Afghanistan, Palestine, Iraq*, Oxford: Blackwell.

Greenberger, A.J., 1969, *The British Images of India: a study in the literature of imperialism 1880–1960*, Oxford University Press.

Grewal, Shabnum, Jackie Kay, Lilianne Landor, Gail Lewis and Praktibhan Parmar (eds), 1988, *Charting the Journey: writings by black and Third World women*, London: Sheba Feminist Publishers.

Grove, Peter and Colleen Grove, 2000, *Curry, Spice and All Things Nice: the what, where, when*, Surbiton: Grove Publications.

Halbfass, Wilhelm, 1988, *India and Europe: an essay in philosophical understanding*, New Delhi: Motilal Banarsidas.

Hall, K., 2002, *Lives in Translation: Sikh youth as British Citizens*, Philadelphia: University of Pennsylvania Press.

Hall, S., 1978, 'Racism and Reaction' in *Five Views of Multi-Racial Britain*, London: CRE.

——, 1987, 'Urban Unrest in Britain' in J. Benyon and J. Solomos (eds), *The Roots of Urban Unrest*, Oxford: Pergamon Press.

——, 1990, 'Cultural Identity and Diaspora' in J. Rutherford (ed.), *Identity: culture, community and difference*, London: Lawrence and Wishart.

——, 1992a, 'New Ethnicities' in J. Donald and A. Rattansi (eds), *'Race', Culture and Difference*, London: Sage, pp. 252–9.

——, 1992b, 'Power and Discourse' in S. Hall and B. Gieben, *The Formation of Modernity*, Cambridge: Polity Press.

——, 1996a, 'New Ethnicities' in D. Morley and K.H. Chen (eds), *Stuart Hall: critical dialogues in cultural studies*, London: Routledge.

——, 1996b, 'When was "the Post-Colonial"? Thinking at the limit' in I. Chambers and L. Curti, *The Postcolonial Question: common skies, divided horizons*, London: Routledge.

——, 2000a, 'Conclusion: the multicultural question' in B. Hesse (ed.), *Un/settled Mutliculturalisms, Diasporas, Entanglements, Transruptions*, London: Zed Books.

——, 2000b, 'Old and New Identities, Old and New Ethnicities' in J. Solomos and L. Black (eds), *Theories of Race and Racism*, London: Routledge.

——, 2001, *Different*, London: Phaidon Press.

——, C. Critcher, T. Jefferson, J. Clarke and B. Roberts, 1978, *Policing the Crises: mugging, the state and law and order*, London: Palgrave Macmillan.

Halstead, M., 1988, *Education, Justice and Cultural Diversity*, London: Falmer Press.

Harding, S., 2003, 'Mortality of Migrants from the Indian Subcontinent to England and Wales: effect of duration of residence', *Epidemiology*, 14, 3, pp. 287–92.

Hardt, M. and A. Negri, 2001, *Empire*, Cambridge, MA: Harvard University Press.

Hart, William D., 2000, *Edward Said and the Religious Effects of Culture*, Cambridge University Press.

Hartman, P. and C. Husband, 1974, *Racism and the Mass Media*, London: Davis-Poynter.

Hasan, R., 2000, 'Riots and Urban Unrest in Britain in the 1980s and 1990s: a critique of dominant explanations' in M. Lavalette and G. Mooney (eds), *Class Struggle and Social Welfare*, London: Routledge.

Hazareesingh, S., 1986, 'Racism and Cultural Identity: an Indian perspective', *Dragon's Teeth*, 24, pp. 4–10.

Hegel, G.W.F., 1987, *Lectures on the Philosophy of Religion*, ed. Peter C. Hodgson, Berkeley: University of California Press.

Hendry, L., J. Shucksmith, J. Love and A. Glendinning, 1993, *Young People's Leisure and Lifestyles*, London: Routledge.

Hennink M., I. Diamond and P. Cooper, 1999, 'Young Asian Women and Relationships: traditional or transitional?', *Ethnic and Racial Studies*, 22, 5, pp. 867–91.

Hesse, B., 1999, 'Reviewing the Western Spectacle: reflexive globalization through the black diaspora' in Avtar Brah *et al.*, *Globalization, Migration, Environment*, London: Macmillan.

——, 2000 'Introduction: Un/settled Multiculturalisms' in B. Hesse (ed.), *Un/settled Multiculturalisms: diasporas, entanglements, transruptions*, London: Zed Books.

——, 2004a, 'Im/Plausible Deniability: racism's conceptual bind', *Social Identities*, 10, 1.

——, 2004b, 'Discourse on Institutional Racism: the genealogy of a concept' in Ian Law, Deborah Phillips and Laura Turney (eds), *Institutional Racism in Higher Education*, London: Trentham Books.

——, 2005 (forthcoming), 'Racialized Modernity: "Europe"/"Non-Europe"' in David Goldberg, Kim Furumoto and Dragan Kujundzic (eds), *tRACES: race, critical theory and deconstruction*, Durham, NC: Duke University Press.

Hester, J.F., 2002, 'Repackaging Difference: the Korean "theming" of a shopping street in Osaka, Japan' in F. Colombijn and A. Erdentug (eds), *Urban Ethnic Encounters: the spatial consequences*, London: Routledge.

Hiro, D., 1991 [1971], *Black British White British*, London: HarperCollins.

Holt, John, 1998, 'Anwar Jalal Shemza: a search for the "significant"', *Third Text*, 42, spring, pp. 104–8.

Home Office, 1998, *Statistics on Race and Criminal Justice System*, a Home Office publication under Section 95 of the Criminal Justice Act 1991, London: HMSO.

——, 2000, *Statistics on Race and the Criminal Justice System 2000*, A Home Office publication under Section 95 of the Criminal Justice Act 1991, London: Home Office.

——, 2001, *United Kingdom Anti-drugs Co-ordinator's Annual Report 2000/01*, a report on progress since 2000 of the Government's ten-year anti-drugs strategy, London: Home Office, Department for Education and Skills, HM Customs and Excise, Department of Health, Foreign and Commonwealth Office.

Housee, S. and S. Sharma, 1999, '"Too Black, Too Strong?": anti-racism and the making of South Asian political identities in Britain' in T. Jordan and A. Lent (eds), *Storming the Millennium*, London: Lawrence and Wishart.

Hughes, R.M., 1855, *The Laws Relating to Lascars and Asiatic Seamen Employed in the British Merchant Service*, London: Smith, Elder.

Humboldt, Alexandre de, 1837, *Examen Critique de lá Géographie du Nouveau Continent et des progrès de l'astronomie nautique aux 15 et 16 siècles*, vol. 4, Paris: Librarie Gide.

Husband, C. (ed.), 1975, *White Media and Black Britain*, London: Arrow Books.

——, 1996, 'Defining and Containing Diversity: community, ethnicity and citizenship' in W.I.U. Ahmad and K. Atkin (eds), *Race and Community Care*, Buckingham: Open University Press.

Hussain, Y., K. Atkin and W.I.U. Ahmad, 2002, *South Asian Disabled People and their Families*, Bristol: Policy Press.

Hutchins, F.G., 1967, *The Illusion of Permanence: British imperialism in India*, Princeton University Press.

Hutnyk J., 1996, 'Media, Research, Politics, Culture', *Critique of Anthropology*, 16, 4, pp. 417–28.

——, 2000, *Critique of Exotica: music, politics and the culture industry*, London: Pluto Press.

Inden, R., 1986, 'Orientalist Constructions of India', *Modern Asian Studies*, 20, 3, pp. 401–46.

——, 2000, *Imagining India*, London: Hurst (repr. of 1990 edn).

Jack, C.M., L. Penny and W. Nazar, 2001, 'Effective Palliative Care for Minority Ethnic Groups: the role of a liaison worker', *International Journal of Palliative Nursing*, 7, 4, pp. 375–80.

Jackson, A., 1973, *Semi-Detached London*, London: Geo. Allen and Unwin.

Jacobs, J.M., 1996, *Edge of Empire: postcolonialism and the city*, London and New York: Routledge.

Jacobson, J., 1997, 'Religion and Ethnicity: dual and alternative sources of identity among young British Pakistanis', *Ethnic and Racial Studies*, 20, 2, pp. 238–56.

——, 1998, *Islam in Transition: religion and identity among British Pakistani youth*, London: Routledge.

Jaffrelot, Christophe, 1996, *The Hindu Nationalist Movement and Indian Politics*, London: Hurst.

Jeffers, S., 1991, 'Black Sections in the Labour Party: the end of ethnicity and "godfather" politics' in P. Werbner and M. Anwar (eds), *Black and Ethnic Leaderships*, London: Routledge.

Jeffrey, P., 1976, *Migrants and Refugees: Muslim and Christian families in Bristol*, Cambridge University Press.

Jenkins, R., 1966, address given on 23 May 1966 to a meeting of the Voluntary Liaison Committees, London: National Council for Civil Liberties.

Jenks, L.H., 1963, *The Migration of British Capital to 1875*, London: Nelson.

Jeyasingham, M., 1992, 'Acting for Health: ethnic minorities and the community health movement' in W.I.U. Ahmad (ed.), *The Politics of Race and Health*, Bradford Race Relations Research Unit, Bradford University Press.

Jhutti, J., 1998, 'Dowry Among Sikhs in Britain' in W. Menski (ed.), *South Asians and the Dowry Problem*, GEMS no. 6, Stoke-on-Trent: Trentham Books.

John, D.W., 1969, *Indian Workers' Association in Britain*, Oxford University Press.

Jones, T., 1993, *Britain's Ethnic Minorities*, London: Policy Studies Institute.

——, D. McEvoy and G. Barrett, 1994, 'Success or Just Survival?', *New Economy*, 1, pp. 51–6.

Josephides, S., 1991, 'Organisational Splits and Political Ideology in the Indian Workers Associations' in Pnina Werbner and Mohammed Anwar (eds), *Black and Ethnic Leaderships*, London: Routledge.

Jowell, R. *et al.*, 1986, *British Social Attitudes: The 1986 Report*, Social and Community Planning Research, London: Gower.

Kalra, V., 2000a, *From Textile Mills to Taxi Ranks: experiences of migration, labour and social change*, Aldershot: Ashgate.

——, 2000b, '*Vilayeti* Rhythms: beyond bhangra's emblematic status to a translation of lyrical texts', *Theory, Culture and Society*, 17, 3, pp. 80–102.

—— and J. Hutnyk, 1998, 'Brimful of Agitation, Authenticity and Appropriation: Madonna's Asian Kool', *Postcolonial Studies*, 1, 3, pp. 339–56.

—— and S. Sharma, 1996, 'Re-Sounding (Anti)Racism, or Concordant Politics? Revolutionary Antecedents' in S. Sharma, J. Hutnyk and A. Sharma (eds), *Dis-Orienting Rhythms: the politics of the new Asian dance music*, London: Zed Books.

Kaur, R., 2000, 'Dramas of Diaspora', *International Journal of Punjab Studies*, 17, 2 (July-Dec), pp. 343–63.

—— and V. Kalra, 1996, 'New Paths for South Asian Identity and Musical Creativity' in S. Sharma, J. Hutnyk and A. Sharma (eds), *Dis-Orienting Rhythms: the politics of the new Asian dance music*, London: Zed Books.

Kawale, R., 2003, 'A Kiss is Just a Kiss…or is it? South Asian lesbian and bisexual women and the construction of space' in N. Puwar and P. Raghuram (eds), *South Asian Women in the Diaspora*, Oxford: Berg.

Keith, M., 1993, *Race, Riots and Policing: lore and disorder in a multi-racist society*, London: UCL Press.

Kelleher, D. and S. Hillier, 1996, *Researching Cultural Differences in Health*, London: Routledge.

Khan, N., 1976, *The Arts Britain Ignores*, London: Commission for Racial Equality.

——, S. Chitra, W. Ginnie and R. Piali, 2000, 'Moving Margins: South Asian dance in the UK', paper presented at Natya Kala Conference, www.narthaki.com/info/articles/article13.html.

Khanum, S., 1995, 'Education and the Muslim Girl' in M. Blair, J. Holland and S. Sheldon (eds), *Identity and Diversity: gender and the experience of education*, Clevedon: Multilingual Matters.

Kiernan, V.G., 1969, *The Lords of Human Kind*, London: Weidenfeld & Nicolson.

Kincaid, D., 1973, *British Social Life in India 1608–1937*, London: Routledge & Kegan Paul.

King, A.D., 1990, *Urbanism, Colonialism and the World-Economy*, London and New York: Routledge.

King, Christopher, 1994, *One Language, Two Scripts: the Hindi movement in nineteenth-century North India*, New Delhi: Oxford University Press.

King, Richard, 1999, *Orientalism and Religion: postcolonial theory, India and the mystic East*, London and New York: Routledge.

Knott, Kim, 1986, *Religion and Identity, and the Study of Ethnic Minority Religions in Britain*, Community Religions Project Research Papers no. 3, Department of Theology and Religious Studies, University of Leeds.

——, 1992, *The Role of Religious Studies in Understanding the Ethnic Experience*, Community Religions Project Research Papers no. 7, Department of Theology and Religious Studies, University of Leeds.

Kogbara, D., 1988, 'When is a Black not a Black?', *Independent*, 30 November 1988.

Kostof, S., 1991, *The City Shaped: urban patterns and meaning through history*, London: Thames and Hudson.

Kramer, J., 1991, 'Letter from Europe', *New Yorker*, 14 January 1991, pp. 60–75.

Kundnani, A., 2001a, 'From Oldham to Bradford: the violence of the violated', *Race and Class*, 43, 2, pp. 105–10.

——, 2001b, 'The Summer of Rebellion: special report', *CARF*, 1 August 2001.

Kureishi, H., 1986, 'Bradford' in *In Trouble Again: a special issue of travel writing*, Granta 20, London: Penguin, pp. 149–70.

——, 2005, 'The Carnival of Culture', *The Guardian*, 4 August 2005.

Laclau, E., 1990, *New Reflections on the Revolutions of Our Time*, London: Verso.

Latouche, Serge, 1996, *The Westernization of the World*, Oxford: Polity Press.

Law, I., 1996, *Racism, Ethnicity and Social Policy*, Brighton: Harvester Wheatsheaf.

Layard, Austin H., 1853, *Discoveries in the Ruins of Nineveh and Babylon: with travels in Armenia, Kurdistan and the desert: being the result of a second expedition undertaken for the Trustees of the British Museum*, London: John Murray.

Layton-Henry, Z., 1980, 'Immigration' in Z. Layton–Henry (ed.), *Conservative Party Politics*, London: Macmillan.

Lazreg, M., 1988, 'Feminism and Difference: the perils of writing as a woman on women in Algeria', *Feminist Studies*, 14, spring, pp. 81–107.

Le Lohe, M.J., 1975, 'Participation in Elections by Asians in Bradford' in I. Crewe (ed), *The Politics of Race*, London: Croom Helm.

——, 1984, *Ethnic Minority Participation in Local Elections*, Bradford University Press.

Leicester City Council, 2002, *Community Cohesion: Beacon Council Scheme*, pp. 1–13.

Leitner, M., J. Shapland and P. Wiles, 1993, *Drugs Usage and Drug Prevention: the views and habits of the general public*, London: HMSO.

Levick, P., 1992, 'The Janus Face Nature of Community Care Legislation: an opportunity for radical possibilities', *Critical Social Policy*, 12, 1, pp. 75–92.

Lewis, P., 1994/2002, *Islamic Britain*, London: I.B. Tauris.

——, 1997, 'Arenas of Ethnic Negotiation: cooperation and conflict in Bradford' in T. Modood and P. Werbner (eds), *The Politics of Multiculturalism in the New Europe: racism, identity and community*, London: Zed Books, pp. 126–46.

Light, I. and P. Bhachu (eds), 1993, *Immigration and Entrepreneurship: culture, capital and ethnic networks*, New Brunswick, NJ: Transaction Books.

Light, I. and S. Karageorgis, 1994, 'The Ethnic Economy' in N. Smelser and R. Swedberg (eds), *Handbook of Economic Sociology*, Princeton University Press and New York: Russell Sage Foundation.

Lijphart, A., 2001, 'Turnout' in R. Rose (ed), *International Encyclopaedia of Elections*, London: Macmillan.

Local Government Association, 2002, *Draft Guidelines on Community Cohesion*, London: LGA.

London City Mission Magazine, 1 August 1857, p. 217.

London Skills Forecasting Unit, 1999, *Strength Through·Diversity: ethnic minorities in London's economy*, London: LSFU.

Loukaitou-Sideris, A., 2002, 'Regeneration of Urban Commercial Strips: ethnicity and space in three Los Angeles neighborhoods', *Journal of Architectural and Planning Research*, 19, 4, pp. 334–50.

Lowe, Lisa, 1996, *Immigrant Acts: on Asian Americans and cultural politics*, Durham, NC: Duke University Press.

Maan, B., 1992, *The New Scots: the story of Asians in Scotland*, Edinburgh: John Donald.

Macey, M., 1999, 'Class, Gender and Religious Influences on Changing Patterns of Pakistani Muslim Male Violence in Bradford', *Ethnic and Racial Studies*, 22, 5, pp. 845–66.

——, 2002, 'Interpreting Islam: young Muslim men's involvement in criminal activities in Bradford' in B. Spalek (ed.), *Islam, Crime and Criminal Justice*, Cullompton, Devon: Willan Publishing.

Macpherson, W., 1999, *The Stephen Lawrence Inquiry: report of an inquiry by Sir William Macpherson of Cluny* (Cm 4262-I), London: HMSO.

Mahony, G.V., 2001, 'Race Relations in Bradford', a paper submitted to the Bradford Race Review, available online at http://www.bradford2020.com/pride/docs/Section7.doc.

Malik, S., 2002, *Representing Black Britain: Black and Asian images on television*, London and New Delhi: Sage.

Mamdani, M., 1976, *Politics and Class Formation in Uganda*, London: Monthly Review Press.

Mandair, Arvind-pal S., forthcoming, *Religion and the Politics of Translation*, Manchester University Press.

Manneheim, K., 1952, 'The Problem of Generations' in P. Kecskemeti (ed.), *Essays on the Sociology of Knowledge*, London: Routledge & Kegan Paul.

Marett, Valerie, 1988, *Immigrants Settling in the City*, University of Leicester Press.

Marquese, Mike, 1994, *Anyone but England: cricket and the national malaise*, London: Verso.

Marsh, P., 1967, *The Anatomy of a Strike*, London: Institute of Race Relations.

Martin, John and Gurharpal Singh, 2002, *Asian Leicester*, Stroud: Sutton Publishers.

Marx, K., 1867 (1967), *Capital: a critique of political economy*, vol. I: *the process of capitalist production*, New York: International Publishers.

Mason, D., 1986, 'Controversies and Continuities in Race and Ethnic Relations Theory' in J. Rex and D. Mason (eds), *Theories of Race and Ethnic Relations*, Cambridge University Press.

——, 2000, *Race and Ethnicity in Modern Britain*, Oxford University Press.

Mayhew, H., 1861, *London Labour and the London Poor*, London: Griffin, Bohn & Co.

Mazower, M., 1999, *Dark Continent: Europe's twentieth century*, Harmondsworth: Penguin.

McAuley, I., 1993, *Guide to Ethnic London*, London: Immel Publishing.

McLoughlin, S., 2005, 'Migration, Diaspora and Transnationalism: transformations of religion and culture in a globalising age' in John R. Hinnells (ed.), *The Routledge Companion to the Study of Religions*, London: Routledge.

Mehmood, T., 1983, *Hand on the Sun*, London: Penguin.

Menski, W. (ed.), 1998, *South Asians and the Dowry Problem*, GEMS no. 6, Stoke-on-Trent: Trentham Books.

Mercer, K., 1994, *Welcome to the Jungle: new positions in black cultural studies*, London: Routledge.

Metcalf, B.D., 1996, 'Introduction: sacred words, sanctioned practice, new communities' in B.D. Metcalf (ed.), *Making Muslim Space in North America and Europe*, Berkeley: University of California Press.

Metcalf, H., T. Modood and S. Virdee, 1996, *Asian Self-Employment: the interaction of culture and economics in England*, London: Policy Studies Institute.

Miles, R., 1989, *Racism*, London: Routledge.

Milloy, J. and R. O'Rourke, 1991, *The Woman Reader*, London: Routledge.

Mir, G. and A. Nocon, 2002, 'Partnership, Advocacy and Independence: service principles and the empowerment of minority ethnic people', *Journal of Learning Disabilities*, 6, 2, pp. 153–62.

Mir, G. and P. Tovey, 2003, 'Asian Carers Experience of Medical and Social Care: the case of cerebral palsy', *British Journal of Social Work*, 33, pp. 465–79.

Mitchell, Timothy, 2000, *Rule of Experts: Egypt, techno-politics, modernity*, Berkeley: University of California Press.

Mitha, A., 1997, 'Artscene', *Yorkshire and Humberside Arts*, June, 3.

Mitropoulos, A., 2001, 'Movements Against the Enclosures: virtual is preamble', online at http://www.antimedia.net/xborder/.

Mitter, P., 2001, 'Indian Artists and the Raj: Westernisation and nationalism 1850–1947' in A. Ghosh and J. Lamba (eds), *Beyond Frontiers: contemporary British art by artists of South Asian descent*, London: Saffron.

Modell, B. and A. Darr, 2002, 'Genetic Counselling and Customary Consanguineous Marriage, *Nature Reviews Genetics*, 3, pp. 225–9.

Modood, T., 1988a, '"Black", Racial Equality and Asian Identity', *New Community*, 14, pp. 397–404.

——, 1988b, 'Who is Defining Who?', *New Society*, 4 March 1988, pp. 4–5.

——, 1990a, 'Catching Up with Jesse Jackson: being oppressed and being somebody', *New Community*, 17, 1, pp. 87–98.

——, 1990b, 'British Asian Muslims and the Rushdie Affair', *Political Quarterly*, 61, 2, pp. 143–60.

——, 1992a, 'British Muslims and the Rushdie Affair' in J. Donald and A. Rattansi (eds), *'Race', Culture and Difference*, London: Sage, pp. 260–77.

——, 1992b, *Not Easy Being British: colour, culture and citizenship*, London: Runnymede Trust and Stoke-on-Trent: Trentham Books.

——, 2005, *Multicultural Politics: racism, ethnicity and Muslims in Britain*, University of Edinburgh Press.

——, S. Beishon and S. Virdee, 1994, *Changing Ethnic Identities*, London: Policy Studies Institute.

Modood, T., R. Berthoud, J. Lakey, J. Nazroo, P. Smith, S. Virdee and S. Beishon (eds), 1997, *Ethnic Minorities in Britain: diversity and disadvantage*, London: Policy Studies Institute.

Mohanty, C.T., 1988, 'Under Western Eyes: feminist scholarship and colonial discourse', *Feminist Review*, 30, autumn, pp. 65–88.

Moore, R., 1975, *Racism and Black Resistance in Britain*, London: Pluto Press.

Morris, M.D. *et al.*, 1969, *Indian Economy in the Nineteenth Century: a symposium*, New Delhi: School of Economics Press.

Morrison, T., 1992, *Playing in the Dark: whiteness and the literary imagination*, Cambridge, MA: Harvard University Press.

Mukherjee, M., 1944, *W.C. Bonnerjee: snapshots from his life and his London letters*, Calcutta: Deshbandhu Book Depot.

Mukherjee, R., 1974, *The Rise and Fall of The East India Company*, New York: Monthly Review Press.

Murji, 1994, 'White Lines: culture, "race" and drugs' in R. Coomber (ed.), 1994, *Drugs and Drug Use in Society*, Dartford, Kent: Greenwich University Press.

Murphy, D., 1987, *Tales from Two Cities: travels of another sort*, London: Penguin.

Muthesius, S., 1982, *The English Terrace House*, New Haven, CT: Yale University Press.

Nandy, Ashis, 1995, 'An Intelligent Critic's Guide to the Indian Cinema' in *The Savage Freud and Other Essays on Possible and Retrievable Selves*, New Delhi: Oxford University Press, pp. 196–236.

—— (ed.), 1998, *The Secret Politics of Our Desires: innocence, culpability and popular cinema*, London: Zed Books.

Nanton, P., 1989, 'The New Orthodoxy: racial categories and equal opportunity policy', *New Community*, 15, pp. 549–64.

Narayana, B., 1981, *Hindi Drama and Stage*, New Delhi: Bansal & Co.

Nasser, N., 2003, 'The Challenge of Ethnoscapes', *Urban Morphology*, 7, 1, pp. 45–8.

——, 2005, 'South Asian Muslims in Britain: expressions of identity in architecture and urbanism', *Journal of Islam and Christian-Muslim Relations*, 16, 1, pp. 61–78.

National Council for Civil Liberties (NCCL), 1980, *The Death of Blair Peach: the supplementary report of the unofficial committee of enquiry*, London: NCCL.

NatWest, 2000, *Ethnic Minority Businesses*, London: National Westminster Bank.

Naylor, S. and J. Ryan, 2002, 'Mosques in the Suburbs: negotiating religion and ethnicity in South London', *Social and Cultural Geography*, 3, 1, pp. 39–59.

——, 2003, 'Mosques, Temples and Gurdwaras: new sites of religion in twentieth-century Britain' in D. Gilbert, D. Matless and J. Short (eds), *Historical Geographies of Twentieth-Century Britain*, Oxford: Blackwell, pp. 163–83.

Nazir, P., 1981, 'Transformation of Property Relations in the Punjab', *Economic and Political Weekly*, XVI, 8, Bombay.

Nazroo, J., 1997, *The Health of Britain's Ethnic Minorities*, London: Policy Studies Institute.

Nead, L., 1995, *Chila Kumari Burman: beyond two cultures*, London: Kala Press.

Newham Annual Residents Survey 2004/05, a report by Taylor Nelson Sofres plc for the London Borough of Newham.

Niranjana, Tejaswini, 1992, *Siting Translation: history, post-structuralism and the colonial context*, Berkeley and Los Angeles: University of California Press.

Nugent, N. and R. King, 1979, 'Ethnic Minorities, Scapegoating and the Extreme Right' in R. Miles and A. Phizacklea (eds), *Racism and Political Action in Britain*, London: Routledge & Kegan Paul.

Oberoi, Harjot, 1994, *The Construction of Religious Boundaries*, New Delhi: Oxford University Press.

O'Brien, Patrick K., 1990, 'The Imperial Component in the Decline of the British Economy before 1914' in Michael Mann (ed.), *The Rise and Decline of the Nation State*, Oxford: Blackwell.

Office for National Statistics, *Census 1991*, Local Based Statistics Table 6.

——, *Census 2001*, Key Statistics Table 6.

Office of Population Censuses and Surveys (OPCS), 1993, *1991 Census: Ethnic Group and Country of Birth (Great Britain)*, London: HMSO.

Ohri, S., 1988, 'The Politics of Racism, Statistics and Equal Opportunity: towards a black perspective' in A. Bhat, R. Carr-Hill and S. Ohri (eds), *Britain's Black Population: a new perspective*, Aldershot: Gower.

Oldham Independent Review Panel, *The Oldham Independent Review*.

Ommer, R. and G. Panting (eds), 1980, *Working Men Who Got Wet*, St John's, NF: Maritime History Group, Memorial University of Newfoundland.

Orwell, G., 1937, *Coming up for Air*, London: Penguin.

——, 1939, *The Road to Wigan Pier*, Harmondsworth: Penguin.

Ottai, A. (ed.), 1986, *Teatro Oriente/Occidente*, Rome: Università degli Studi di Roma, La Sapienza, Bulzoni.

Ouseley, H., 2001, *Community Pride not Prejudice: making diversity work in Bradford*, Bradford 2020 Vision.

Owens A. and G. Randhawa, 2004, '"It's Different from My Culture; They're Very Different": providing community-based "culturally competent" palliative care for South Asians in the UK', *Health and Social Care in the Community*, 12, 5, pp. 414–21.

Pacione, M., 1997, *Urban Restructuring and the Reproduction of Inequalities in Britain's Cities*, London: Routledge.

Pagden, A., 1995, *Lords of all the World: ideologies of empire in Spain, Britain and France, c.1500 – c.1800*, New Haven, CT: Yale University Press.

Palme Dutt, R., 1940, *India To-day*, London: Victor Gollancz.

Pandey, Gyan, 1989, *The Construction of Communalism in Colonial North India*, New Delhi: Oxford University Press.

Panikkar, K.M., 1953, *Asia and Western Dominance*, London: George Allen & Unwin.

——, 1977, *An Autobiography*, Madras: Oxford University Press.

Panjabi, Camellia, 2000, *50 Great Curries of India*, London: Kyle Cathie.

Papastergiadis, N., 1997, 'Tracing Hybridity in Theory' in P. Werbner and T. Modood, 1997, *Debating Cultural Hybridity: multi-cultural identities and the politics of anti-racism*, London: Zed Books.

Parekh, Bhikhu, 1978, 'Asians in Britain: problem or opportunity' in *Five Views of Multi-Racial Britain*, London: CRE.

——, 2000, *Rethinking Multi-culturalism: cultural diversity and political theory*, Basingstoke and New York: Palgrave.

Parker, H., F. Measham and J. Aldridge, 1995, *Drug Futures: changing patterns of drug use amongst English youth*, Institute for the Study of Drug Dependence (ISDD), Research Monograph 7, London: ISDD.

Parkes, Graham (ed.), 1987, *Heidegger and Asian Thought*, Honolulu: University of Hawaii Press.

—— (ed.), 1991, *Nietzsche and Asian Thought*, Honolulu: University of Hawaii Press.

Parmar, P., 1982, 'Gender, Race and Class: Asian women and resistance' in CCCS, *The Empire Strikes Back: race and racism in 70s Britain*, London: Hutchinson.

——, 1990, 'Black Feminism: the politics of articulation' in J. Rutherford (ed.), 1990, *Identity*, London: Lawrence and Wishart.

Patel, K., 1993, 'Minority Ethnic Access to Services' in Harrison (ed.), 1993, *Race, Culture and Substance Problems*, University of Hull, pp. 33–46.

——, 1997, 'A Preliminary Enquiry into the Nature, Extent and Responses to Drug Problems (if any) within the Asian Population of Bradford', *Social Work Education*, 8, 1, pp. 39–41.

——, K. Sherlock, M. Chaudry and J. Buffin, 1998, *Drug Use Amongst Asian Communities in Cheetham Hill*, Manchester: Lifeline / Preston: University of Central Lancashire.

Patel, K., I. Wardle, J. Bashford and M. Winters, 2001, *The Evaluation of Nafas: a Bangladeshi drug service*, Preston: Ethnicity and Health Unit, Faculty of Health, University of Central Lancashire.

Patel K. and C. Wibberley, 2002, 'Young Asians and Drug Use', *Journal of Child Health Care*, 6, 1, pp. 51–9.

Patel, P., 1997, 'Third Wave Feminism and Black Women's Activism' in H.S. Mirza (ed.), *Black British Feminism*, London: Routledge.

Patnaik, P., 1975, 'Imperialism and the Growth of the Indian Capitalism' in R. Blackburn (ed.), *Explosion in a Subcontinent*, Harmondsworth: Penguin.

Peach, C. (ed.), 1975, *Urban Social Segregation*, London: Longman.

——, 1990, 'Estimating the Growth of the Bangladeshi Population of Great Britain', *New Community*, 16, 4, pp. 481–91.

——, 1994, 'Three Phases of South Asian Emigration' in J.M. Brow and R. Foot, *Migration: the Asian presence*, Basingstoke: Macmillian.

——, 1996, 'Introduction' in C. Peach (ed.), *Ethnicity in the 1991 Census volume 2: the ethnic minority populations of Great Britain*, London: Office for National Statistics.

——, 1998, 'London and New York: contrasts in British and American models of segregation', *International Journal of Population Geography*, 5, 4, pp. 319–54.

——, 2000, 'The Consequences of Segregation' in F.W. Boal (ed.), *Ethnicity and Housing: accommodating differences*, Aldershot: Ashgate.

Pearson, M., 1986, 'The Politics of Ethnic Minority Health Studies' in T. Rathwell and D. Phillips (eds), *Health, Race and Ethnicity*, London: Croom Helm.

Performance and Innovation Unit, 2002, *Ethnic Minorities and the Labour market: interim analytical report*, London: Cabinet Office.

Perkins, Anne, 2000, *Nation and Word: religious and metaphysical language in European national consciousness*, Aldershot: Ashgate.

Phillips, D., 1981, 'The Social and Spatial Segregation of Asians in Leicester' in P. Jackson and S.J. Smith (eds), *Social Interaction and Ethnic Segregation*, London: Academic Press, pp. 101–21.

——, 2003, 'Experiences and Interpretations of Segregation, Community and Neighbourhood' in *Housing and Black and Minority Ethnic Communities*, London: Office of the Deputy Prime Minister, pp. 36–49.

Phoenix, A., 1997, 'Theories of Gender and Black Families' in H.S. Mirza (ed.), *Black British Feminism: a reader*, London: Routledge.

Pines, J. (ed.), 1992, *Black and White in Colour*, London: BFI Publishing.

Poovaya-Smith, N. and S. Hashmi, 1995, *An Intelligent Rebellion: women artists of Pakistan* (exhibition catalogue), Bradford: City of Bradford Metropolitan Council, Arts, Museums and Libraries Division.

Poovaya-Smith, N. and C. Hopper (eds), 1997, *Cartwright Hall Art Gallery and its Collections*, Bradford: City of Bradford Metropolitan Council, Arts, Museums and Libraries Division.

Portes, A. (ed.), 1995, *The Economic Sociology of Immigration: essays on networks, ethnicity and entrepreneurship*, New York: Russell Sage Foundation.

Prasad, Madhava, 1998, *Ideology of the Hindi Film: a historical construction*, New Delhi: Oxford University Press.

Prestage, Edgar, 1925, 'The Fourth Centenary of the Death of Vasco da Gama', *Geographical Journal*, LXV, 1, pp. 1–4.

Procter, J., 2000, *Writing Black Britain 1948–1998*, Manchester University Press.

Putnam, R.D., 2000, *Bowling Alone: the collapse and revival of American community*, New York: Simon and Schuster.

Puwar, N., 2002, 'Multi-cultural Fashion: stirrings of another sense of aesthetics and memory', *Feminist Review*, 71, pp. 63–87.

——, 2003, 'Melodramatic Postures and Constructions' in N. Puwar and P. Ranghuram (eds), *South Asian Women in the Diaspora*, Oxford: Berg.

—— and P. Raghuram (eds), 2003, *South Asian Women in the Diaspora*, Oxford: Berg.

Quijano, A., 1972, *Nationalism and Capitalism in Peru: a study in neo-imperialism*, London: Monthly Review Press.

Rabasa, J., 1993, *Inventing America: Spanish historiography and the formation of Eurocentrism*, Normoan: University of Oklahoma Press.

'Race Row MP Vows to Speak Out', *Evening Standard*, 13 July 2001.

Rafique, M., 1992, 'Ethnicity and Enterprise: a comparison of Muslim and non-Muslim owned Asian businesses in Britain', *New Community*, 19, 1, pp. 43–60.

Rajadhyaksha, Ashish, 1996a, 'Indian Cinema: origins to independence' in G. Nowell-Smith (ed.), *The Oxford History of World Cinema*, Oxford University Press, pp. 398–409.

——, 1996b, 'India: filming the nation' in G. Nowell-Smith (ed.), *The Oxford History of World Cinema*, Oxford University Press, pp. 678–89.

Ralph, O., 1997, *Naoroji: the first Asian MP*, London: Hansib.

Ramji, H., 2003, 'Engendering Diasporic Identities' in N. Puwar and P. Ranghuram (eds), *South Asian Women in the Diaspora*, Oxford: Berg.

Ramsey, M. and J. Spiller, 1997, *Drug Misuse Declared: results of the 1996 British Crime Survey*, London: Home Office.

Randhawa, G. and A. Owens, 2004, 'The Meanings of Cancer and Perceptions of Cancer Services among South Asians in Luton, UK', *British Journal of Cancer*, 91, 1, pp. 62–8.

Randhawa, R., 1987, *A Wicked Old Woman*, London: Women's Press.

Ravenstien, E.G., 1885, 'The Laws of Migration', *Journal of the Statistical Society*, 48.

Ray, M. and E. Jacka, 1996, 'Indian Television: an emerging regional force' in John Sinclair *et al.*, *New Patterns in Global Television: peripheral vision*, New York: Oxford University Press.

Reade, H., 1898, 'Vasco da Gama', *Journal of the Royal Asiatic Society*, pp. 589–604.

Reus-Smit, C., 2004, *American Power and World Power*, Cambridge: Polity.

Rex, J., 1991, *Ethnic Identity and Ethnic Mobilisation in Britain*, Monograph in Ethnic Relations, 5, Centre for Research in Ethnic Relations, University of Warwick.

—— and R. Moore, 1967, *Race, Community and Conflict: a study of Sparkbrook*, London: Oxford University Press.

Rex, J. and S. Tomlinson, 1979, *Colonial Immigrants in a British City: a class analysis*, London: Routledge & Kegan Paul.

Ritchie, D., 2001, *Oldham Independent Review Panel Report*.

Robinson, M., 2001, *Communication and Health in a Multi-ethnic Society*, Bristol: Policy Press.

Robinson, V., 1986, *Transients, Settlers and Refugees: Asians in Britain*, Oxford: Clarendon Press.

——, 1996, 'The Indians: onwards and upwards' in C. Peach (ed.), *Ethnicity in the 1991 Census volume 2: the ethnic minority populations of Great Britain*, London: Office for National Statistics.

Rocherson, Y., 1988, 'The Asian Mother and Baby Campaign: the construction of ethnic minority health needs', *Critical Social Policy*, 22, pp. 4–23.

Rorty, Richard, 1989, *Contingency, Irony and Solidarity*, Cambridge University Press.

Rosaldo, R., 1989, *Culture and Truth: the remaking of social analysis*, Boston, MA: Beacon Press.

Rose, E. *et al.*, 1969, *Colour and Citizenship: a report on British race relations*, London: Oxford University Press.

Ross, K., 1996, *Black and White Media: black images in popular film and television*, Cambridge: Polity Press.

Roy, A., 1988, 'Asians Protest: we are not black', *Sunday Times*, 26 June 1988.

Roys, P., 1988, 'Social Services' in A. Bhat, R. Carr-Hill and S. Ohri (eds), *Britain's Black Population: a new perspective*, Aldershot: Gower.

RTPI/CRE, 1983, *Planning for a Multi-Racial Britain*, London: CRE.

Rushdie, Salman, 1991, 'Outside the Whale' in *Imaginary Homelands*, London: Granta, pp. 87–101.

Rustin, M., 1996, 'Perspectives on East London' in T. Butler and M. Rustin (eds), *Rising in the East: the regeneration of East London*, London: Lawrence and Wishart.

Ruthven, M., 1991, *A Satanic Affair: Salman Rushdie and the wrath of Islam*, London: Hogarth Press.

Saggar, S., 2000, *Race and Representation: electoral politics and ethnic pluralism in Britain*, Manchester University Press.

Saghal, G. and N. Yuval-Davis (eds), 1992, *Refusing Holy Orders*, London: Virago.

Said, E., 1978 (1985), *Orientalism*, London: Routledge & Kegan Paul (1985 edn, London: Penguin).

——, 1989, 'Representing the Colonized: anthropology's interlocuturs', *Critical Inquiry*, 15, pp. 205–25.

——, 1993, *Culture and Imperialism*, London: Chatto and Windus/Vintage.

——, 2000, *Reflections on Exile*, London: Granta.

Saifullah Khan, V., 1977, 'The Pakistanis: Mirpuri villagers at home and in Bradford' in J.L. Watson (ed.), *Between Two Cultures: migrants and minorities in Britain*, Oxford: Blackwell, pp. 57–89.

Sakai, Naoki, 1997, *Translation and Subjectivity: on 'Japan' and cultural nationalism*, Minneapolis: Minnesota University Press.

Salter, J., 1873, *The Asiatic In England: sketches of sixteen years' work among Orientals*, London: Seeley, Jackson and Halliday.

Samad, Y., 1992, 'Book Burning and Race Relations: political mobilization of Bradford Muslims', *New Community*, 18, 4, pp. 507–19.

——, 1997, 'The Plural Guises of Multiculturalism: conceptualising a fragmented paradigm' in T. Modood and P. Werbner (eds), *The Politics of Multiculturalism in the New Europe: racism, identity and community*, London: Zed Books, pp. 240–60.

—— and J. Eade, 2002, *Community Perceptions of Forced Marriage*, London: Foreign and Commonwealth Office, Community Liaison Unit.

Sardar, Ziauddin, 1998, 'Dilip Kumar Made Me Do It' in A. Nandy (ed.), *The Secret Politics of Our Desires: innocence, culpability and popular cinema*, London: Zed Books, pp. 19–91.

Sayyid, S., 1997 (2003a), *A Fundamental Fear: Eurocentrism and the emergence of Islamism*, London: Zed Books (2003a, 2nd edn).

——, 2003, 'Displacing South Asia', *Contemporary South Asia*, 12 (December), 4, pp. 465–9.

——, 2004, 'Slippery People: the immigrant imaginary and the grammar of colour' in I. Law, D. Philips and L. Turney (eds), *Institutional Racism in Higher Education*, London: Trentham Books.

Scammell, G.V., 1990, *First Imperial Age: European overseas expansion 1400–1715*, London: Routledge.

Scarman, Lord, 1981, *The Scarman Report*, London: Home Office.

Schmitt, C., 1996, *The Concept of the Political*, University of Chicago Press.

Seely, J., 1883, *The Expansion of England*, Macmillan

SEU (Social Exclusion Unit), 1998, *Bringing Britain Together: a national strategy for neighbourhood renewal*, London: Stationery Office.

Shah-Kazemi, S.N., 2001, *Untying The Knot: Muslim women, divorce and the Shariah*, London: published with the support of the Nuffield Foundation.

Sharma, Krishna, 1986, *Bhakti and the Bhakti Movement: a new perspective*, New Delhi: Munshiram Manoharlal.

Sharma, S., 1996, 'Noisy Asians or Asian noise?' in S. Sharma, J. Hutnyk and A. Sharma (eds), *Dis-Orienting Rhythms: the politics of the new Asian dance music*, London: Zed Books.

——, 2003, 'The Sounds of Alterity' in M. Bull and L. Back (eds), *The Auditory Culture Reader*, Oxford: Berg.

——, J. Hutnyk and A. Sharma (eds), 1996, *Dis-Orienting Rhythms: the politics of the new Asian dance music*, London: Zed Books.

Shaw, A., 1988, *A Pakistani Community in Britain*, Oxford: Blackwell.

——, 1994, 'The Pakistani Community in Oxford' in R. Ballard (ed.), *Desh Pardesh: the South Asian presence in Britain*, London: Hurst.

——, 2000, *Kinship and Continuity: Pakistani families in Britain*, Amsterdam: Harwood Academic Publishers.

Shaw, M., 2000, *Theory of the Global State: globality as an unfinished revolution*, Cambridge University Press.

Sheikh, F., 1991, *The Red Box*, London: Women's Press.

Sheikh, N., J. Fountain, J. Bashford and K. Patel, 2001, *A Review of Current Drug Service Provision for Black and Minority Ethnic Communities in Bedfordshire*, final report to Bedfordshire Drug Action Team, August 2001, Preston: Ethnicity and Health Unit, Faculty of Health, University of Central Lancashire.

Sheikh, N., J. Fountain, J. Jhurana, A. Syed and K. Patel, 2002, *Planning Drug and Alcohol Services for Adults from Black and Minority Ethnic Communities in Waltham Forest and Redbridge*, Preston: Centre for Ethnicity and Health, University of Central Lancashire.

Shephard, J.E., n.d., *A.J. Mahomet: from street Arab to Evangelist*, Ventnor, Isle of Wight: W.B. Tomkins.

Shukra, K., 1990, 'Black Sections in the Labour Party' in H. Goulbourne (ed), *Black Politics in Britain*, Aldershot: Avebury.

Siddique, M., 1993, *Moral Spotlight on Bradford*, Bradford: M.S. Press.

Silver, S., 2001, 'Echoes of the Past', online at http://www.searchlightmagazine.com/stories/EchosOfPast.htm.

Singh, A.K., 1963, *Indian Students in Britain: a survey of their adjustment and attitudes*, London: Asia Publishing House.

Singh, Gurharpal, 2000, *Ethnic Conflict in India*, London: Macmillan.

——, forthcoming (2006), *Leicester: the making of a multicultural city*.

Singh, R., 1994, 'Introduction' in *Here to Stay: Bradford's South Asian communities*, Bradford: City of Bradford Metropolitan Council, Arts, Museums and Libraries, pp. 9–21.

——, 2002, *The Struggle for Racial Justice: from community relations to community cohesion*, Bradford: Print Plus UK.

Sivanandan, A., 1976, *Race, Class and the State: the black experience in Britain*, London: Institute of Race Relations.

——, 1982, *A Different Hunger: writings on black resistance*, London: Pluto Press.

——, 1985, 'RAT and the Degradation of the Black Struggle', *Race and Class*, XXVI, 4.

——, 1986, *From Resistance to Rebellion: Asian and Afro-Caribbean struggles in Britain*, London: Institute of Race Relations.

——, 2000, *Where the Dance Is*, London: Arcadia Books.

——, 2002, 'A Radical Black Political Culture' in K. Owusu (ed.), *Black British Culture and Society*, London: Routledge.

Slater, T.R., 1996, 'Birmingham's Black and South-Asian Population' in A.J. Gerrard and T.R. Slater (eds), *Managing a Conurbation: Birmingham and its region*, Studley: Brewin Books.

Slatter, D., 2004, *Geopolitics and the Post-Colonial: rethinking North-South relations*, Oxford: Blackwell.

Smith, Adam, 1976, *An Inquiry into the Nature and Causes of the Wealth of Nations*, ed. by Edwin Cannan, University of Chicago Press.

Smith, L.K., J.L. Botha, A. Benghiat and W.P. Steward, 2003, 'Latest Trends in Cancer Incidence among UK South Asians in Leicester, *British Journal of Cancer*, 89, pp. 70–3.

Smith, S., 1993, *Electoral Registration in 1991*, London: OPCS.

Smith, S.J., 1989, *The Politics of Race and Residence*, Cambridge: Polity Press.

Social Exclusion Unit, 2000, *Report of the Policy Action Team*, 12: *young people*, London: HMSO.

Solomos, J., 1989, *Race and Racism in Contemporary Britain*, London: Macmillan.

——, 1992, 'The Politics of Immigration Since 1945' in P. Braham, A. Rattansi and R. Skellington (eds), *Racism and Anti-racism: inequalities, opportunities and policies*, London: Sage.

——, 1993, *Race and Racism in Britain*, Basingstoke: Macmillan.

—— and Gurharpal Singh, 1990, 'Race Equality, Housing and the Local State' in Wendy Ball and John Solomos (eds), *Race and Local Politics*, London: Macmillan, pp. 95–114.

Southall Black Sisters, 1990, *Against the Grain: a celebration of survival and struggle*, London: Southall Black Sisters.

Southall Rights, 1980, *23 April 1979*, London: Crest.

Spivak, G.C., 1988, 'Reading The World: literary studies in the eighties' in *In Other Worlds: essays in cultural politics*, New York: Routledge, p. 102.

——, 1990, *The Post-Colonial Critic*, New York: Routledge.

——, 1993, *Outside in the Teaching Machine*, London: Routledge.

——, 1999, *A Critique of Postcolonial Reason: toward a history of the vanishing present*, Cambridge, MA: Harvard University Press.

Starrs, C., L. Robertson and C. Holme, 2002, 'Forced Marriage "a Huge Mistake"', *Herald*, 24 April 2002. Also at http://www.theherald.co.uk/news/archive/24-4-19102-1-10-44.html.

State Research, 1981, *State Research Bulletin*, 4, 25, London: State Research.

Stopes-Roe, M. and R. Cochrane, 1990, *Citizens of this Country: the Asian British*, Clevedon: Multilingual Matters.

Stuart, O., 1996, 'Yes, We Mean Black Disabled People Too: thoughts on community care and disabled people from black and minority ethnic communities' in W.I.U. Ahmad and K. Atkin (eds), *Race and Community Care*, Buckingham: Open University Press.

Swales, J.D., 1996, 'Frederick Akbar Mahomed (1849–1884): pioneer of clinical research', *Journal of Human Hypertension*, 10, pp. 139–40.

Swallow, Deborah, 1999, '...To a Modern Revival' in A.K. Singh and A.K. Singh, *Twin Perspectives: paintings by Amrit and Rabindra KD Kaur Singh*, Birmingham: Twin Studios, pp. 14–19.

Taagepera, R., 1978, 'Size and Duration of Empires: systematics of size', *Social Science Research*, 7, pp. 180–96.

Talbani, A. and P. Hasanali, 2000, 'Adolescent Females between Tradition and Modernity: gender role socialization in South Asian immigrant culture', *Journal of Adolescence*, 23, 5 (October), pp. 615–27(13).

Tatla, Darshan Singh, 1999, *The Sikh Diaspora: the search for statehood*, London: UCL Press.

Taylor, C., 1993, *Multiculturalism and 'The Politics of Recognition'*, with commentary by Amy Gutmann (ed.), Steven C. Rockefeller, Michael Walzer and Susan Wolf, Princeton University Press.

Taylor, S., 1979, 'The National Front: anatomy of a political movement' in R. Miles and A. Phizacklea (eds), *Racism and Political Action in Britain*, London: Routledge & Kegan Paul.

Terracciano, A., 1996, 'Il Teatro Black in Gran Bretagna. Oriente e Occidente in Cinque Messe in Scena del Tara Arts Group', BA dissertation, Istituto Universitario Orientale, Naples.

——, 1997, 'Il Teatro Black', *Drammaturgia*, vol. IV, Rome: Salerno Editori.

——, 2002, 'Crossing Lines: an analysis of integration and separatism within black theatre in Britain', PhD dissertation in History of Theatre, Istituto Universitario Orientale, Naples.

Tharani, N., 1988, 'Heads under the Sands: Western appropriation of South Asian arts' in O. Kwesi (ed.), *Storms of the Heart: an anthology of black arts and culture*, London: Camden Press.

Time Out Book of London, 1972, London: Time Out Publications.

Times Higher Education Supplement, 'CIA outrages UK academics by planting spies in classroom', 3 June 2005.

Tinker, H., 1977, *The Banyan Tree: overseas emigrants from India, Pakistan and Bangladesh*, London: Oxford University Press.

Todd, J. and B. Butcher, 1982, *Electoral Registration in 1981*, London: OPCS.

Todorov, T., 1984, *The Conquest of America*, New York: Harper and Row.

Troyna, B., 1982, 'Reporting the National Front: British values observed' in C. Husband (ed.), *'Race' in Britain: Continuity and Change*, London: Hutchinson.

Turning Point: a review of race relations in Bradford, Bradford Metropolitan District Council, 1981.

Uppal, I.S., 1988, '"Black": the word making Asians angry', *Daily Mail* (London), 28 June 1988.

Vadgama, K., 1984, *India in Britain: the Indian contribution to the British way of life*, London: Robert Royce.

Vakil, AbdoolKarim, 1998a, 'Vários Vascos da Gama' in Diogo Ramada Curto (ed.), *O Tempo de Vasco da Gama*, Lisbon: Difel-Expo98-CNCDP.

——, 1998b, 'O descobrimento do caminho marítimo para a Índia na memória histórica britânica' in Jorge Flores (ed.), *O Centenário da Índia [1898] e a Memória da Viagem de Vasco da Gama*, Lisbon: CNCDP.

Van der Veer, Peter, 1994, *Religious Nationalism: Hindus and Muslims in India*, New Delhi: Oxford University Press.

Venn, Couze, 2000, *Occidentalism: modernity and subjectivity*, London: Sage.

——, 2005, *The Postcolonial Challenge: towards alternative worlds*, London: Sage.

Vertovec, S., 1994, 'Multiculturalism, Multi-Asian, Multi-Muslim Leicester: dimensions of social complexity, ethnic organisation and local interface', *Innovations*, 7, 3, pp. 259–76.

——, 1996, 'Multiculturalism, Culturalism and Public Incorporation', *Ethnic and Racial Studies*, 19, 1, pp. 49–69.

Vidler, A., 1992, *The Architectural Uncanny: essays in the modern unhomely*, Cambridge, MA: MIT Press.

Visram, R., 1986, *Ayahs, Lascars and Princes: the story of Indians in Britain 1700–1947*, London: Pluto Press.

——, 1989, 'The First World War and the Indian soldiers', *Indo-British Review*, XVI, 2, p. 21.

——, 2002, *Asians in Britain: 400 years of history*, London: Pluto Press.

Wade, B. and P. Souter, 1992, *Continuing to Think: the British Asian girl*, Clevedon, Somerset: Multilingual Matters.

Wadsworth, M., 1998, *Comrade Sak: Shapurji Saklatvala MP, a political biography*, Leeds: Peepal Tree Press.

Waldinger, R., 1995, 'The Other Side of Embeddedness: a case study of the interplay of economy and ethnicity', *Ethnic and Racial Studies*, 18, 3, pp. 555–80.

—— *et al.* (eds), 1990, *Ethnic Entrepreneurs: immigrant business in industrial society*, London: Sage.

Walker, R. and W.I.U. Ahmad, 1994, 'Windows of Opportunity in Rotting Frames: care providers' perspectives on community care', *Critical Social Policy*, 40, pp. 46–9.

Wall, C., 1990, *Changing Our Own Words: essays on criticism, theory and writing by black women*, London: Routledge.

Waller, R., 1991, *British Almanac of Politics*, London: Routledge.

Wanvari, A., 1996, 'Outward Bound Chandra Takes Zee TV Global', *Cable and Satellite Asia*, September/October, pp. 11–17.

Warwick, R., 1994, 'Introduction' in *Writers of the Asian Diaspora*, London: Commonwealth Institute.

Watson, J.L. (ed.), 1977, *Between Two Cultures: migrants and minorities in Britain*, Oxford: Blackwell.

Werbner, P., 1988, 'Taking and Giving: working women and female bonds in a Pakistani immigrant neighbourhood' in S. Westwood and P. Bhachu (eds), *Enterprising Women: ethnicity, economy and gender relations*, London: Routledge.

——, 1990a, *The Migration Process: capital, gifts and offerings among British Pakistanis*, Oxford: Berg.

——, 1990b, 'Renewing an Industrial Past: British Pakistani entrepreneurship in Manchester', *Migration*, 8, pp. 17–41.

——, 2002, *Imagined Diasporas among Manchester Muslims*, London: James Currey and Santa Fé, NM: School of American Research Press.

——, 2003, *Pilgrims of Love: the anthropology of a global Sufi cult*, London: Hurst.

—— and M. Anwar (eds), 1991, *Black and Ethnic Leaderships*, London: Routledge.

Westwood, S., 1991, 'Red Star over Leicester: racism, the politics of identity and black youth in Britain' in P. Werbner and M. Anwar (eds), *Black and Ethnic Leaderships in Britain*, London: Routledge.

Whitehand, J.W.R and C. Carr, 2001, *Twentieth Century Suburbs: a morphological approach*, London: Routledge.

Wickramasinghe, Priya *et al.*, 2002, *The Food of India*, London: Murdoch Books.

Willmot, Ross, 2002, 'Migration, Voting Patterns and Ethnic Minority Councillors', presentation given at the conference 'Leicester Past and Present: migration and the making of the modern city', University of Leicester, 12 October 2002.

Wilson, A., 1978, *Finding a Voice: Asian women in Britain*, London: Virago.

——, 1992, 'Beyond an Assertion of Identity' in A. de Souza and S. Merali (eds), *Crossing Black Waters*, London: Working Press.

Wink, A., 1997, *Al-Hind, The Making of the Indo-Islamic World*, volume 2: *The Slave Kings and the Islamic Conquest 11–13th Centuries*, Leiden: Brill.

Winstone, Paul, 1996, 'Managing a Multi-ethnic and Multicultural City in Europe: Leicester', *ISSJ*, 147, pp. 32–41.

Wolf, E.R., 1982, *Europe and the People without History*, Berkeley: University of California Press.

Wood, D., 1960, 'The Immigrant in the Towns' in J.A.G. Griffith, J. Henderson, M. Usborne and D. Wood, *Coloured Immigrants in Britain*, Oxford University Press.

Young, K., 1992, 'Class, Race and Opportunity' in R. Jowell *et al.*, *British Social Attitudes*, the 9th Report, Aldershot: SCPR.

Young, R., 1990, *White Mythologies: writing history and the West*, London: Routledge.

Zubaida, S. (ed.), 1970, *Race and Racism*, London: Tavistock.

INDEX

Achanak, 321, 324
Ali, Syed Ameer, 148
All India Muslim League, 148
Altab Ali, 52
Apache Indian, 269, 321, 325
architecture, 374–91
art, 157, 329–39
Asian Dub Foundation, 85, 270, 325
Asian Youth Movements (AYM), 119–20, 123–4, 138, *see also* Southall Youth Movement

Bangladesh: 117, 393; migration, 115, 163, 168–9
Bangladeshis: 59, 116, 117, 138, 230–3, 310, 314; and art, 331; and cinema and TV, 366; and drugs, 91; and education, 171–2; and employment, 170—2, 212–23; geographical distribution of, 175–7; and health care, 250, 252; and housing, 175, 232; and marriage, 274; migration, 168–9; and policing, 236; and politics, 192, 194, 197; population, 112, 168–70, 173–4; and segregation, 177–81; youths, 265, 267; *see also* Bengal and Bengalis, Sylhet and Sylhettis
Bengal and Bengalis: 83, 84, 109, 132, 159; and architecture, 379, 380–1, 390; and cinema and TV, 363; and drugs, 91; migration, 132, 160, 163; youths, 265, 270; *see also* Sylhet and Sylhettis
Bhangra, 77, 183, 270, 308, 309, 317–23, 326
Bharatiya Vidhya Bhavan (Institute of Indian Culture), 346
Bhaskar, Sanjeev, 355
Bhownagree, Mancherjee, 147, 201
Bhutto, Benazir, 200
Birmingham: 26, 60, 84, 108, 119, 155, 179, 234, 321, 323, 351, 353; architecture, 354, 378, 379, 383, 384, 389, 390; politics, 188, 192, 197, 198, 204, 205, 206, 207
Blackburn: 59–60, 132, 234; politics, 189, 208
Blair, Tony, 60, 87, 200, 303, 313
Blunkett, David, 276
Bollywood, 77, 183, 317, 319, 320, 322, 327, 353, 362–70, 393
Bowen, Denis, 333–4, 335
Bradford: 26, 33, 55, 81, 85, 110–40, 155, 184, 240, 257, 258, 263, 266, 267; architecture, 379, 381; politics, 193, 195, 197, 202, 205, 206
Bradford 12, the, 57–8, 120, 125, 263, 340, 341
Bradford Blacks, 55, 263
Bradford Council for Mosques (BCM), 128, 130–4
Bristol: 153, 341; politics, 196
British Empire, 6, 15–16, 30, 40, 77, 143, 144, 148–9, 159–60, 163–5, 329, 344, 358–61, 374
British National Party (BNP), 82, 119, 208, 241, 340
Burman, Chila Kumari, 330, 332–3, 336
Burnley: 112, 142, 239–41, 340; politics, 208

Cambellpore: migration, 115, 169–70
Cartwright Hall, 338–9
Chadha, Gurinder, 109, 354, 369, 370
Chaggar, Gurdip Singh, 51, 263
Chandra, Avinash, 330, 332, 337
cinema, 77, 183, 270, 309, 327, 350, 353, 354, 362–70, *see also* Bollywood
colonialism/coloniality, 2–10, 14–21, 28–31, 36, 44, 62, 77, 84, 94–105, 114, 148–9, 159–60, 164–5, 182–3, 185, 187, 273, 282, 329–31, 336–7, 358–61, 369, 374, 389
comedy, 310, 354–6, 369, 393
Commission for Racial Equality (CRE), 40, 56, 64, 70, 111, 124, 207, 259, 336
communism, 80, 83–7, 90
Communist Party of Great Britain (CPGB), 77, 83, 84, 87, 201
Community Relations Commission (CRC), 40, 192, 259
Conservative Party, 83, 117, 134, 147, 158, 191, 196–9, 201–9, 300–2, 304, 311, 321
Cornershop, 324, 325
Coventry: 60, 108, 155, 341; architecture,

378; politics, 201
Cryer, Ann, 276
cuisine, 14, 62–3, 72–3, 327–8
culture and cultural identity: 7, 9, 14, 15, 17–19, 35, 38–43, 45–6, 49–51, 56, 58, 60–1, 67–71, 76–7, 79, 103–7, 113–14, 116, 121, 131, 135–40, 218, 225; and architecture, 379, 380, 383, 387, 389–90; and art, 333–7; and cinema and TV, 367, 369, 370, 393; clash, 52–5, 259–62, 264, 273; and health care, 246–53, 256–7; and literature, 371–2; and marriage, 273–5, 278–88; and music, 319–21, 324, 326; and performing arts, 343, 350, 352, 354, 357; youths, 258–62, 264–71

da Gama, Vasco, 13–14, 358–9
dance, 344–8
Dhingra, Madan Lal, 149
Dholakia, Lord, 200
drugs and drug use, 91–2, 238, 258, 266, 342
Duncan-Smith, Iain, 199

East Africa and East African Asians: 138, 303; and cinema and TV, 364–5; geographical distribution of, 177; migration, 43–8, 160, 165, 166–7, 168–9, 170, 293, 296; and performing arts, 352; youths, 265
East India Company, 158–9, 170
education, 8, 16, 25, 26, 36–7, 39, 41, 46, 48–9, 52, 59, 69, 112, 117, 127–8, 144, 153, 171–2, 212, 219–20, 232, 240, 266, 286
Edward VII, King of England, 148
employment and labour, 8, 15, 21, 26, 36, 39, 41–4, 48, 51, 66–7, 69, 77–8, 82, 86–7, 91, 115, 118, 144, 146–7, 149–50, 151–5, 170–3, 211–29, 231–2, 266, 277, 295–6
ethnicity and ethnic identity: 3–9, 19, 21–4, 27, 53, 64–71, 75–6, 77–9, 86, 88, 89, 111, 112, 113–19, 134–40, 165, 168–9, 173, 183, 186, 212, 218, 225–6, 290, 341–2; and architecture, 375–6, 383; and art, 329; and health care, 245, 251–4, 256–7; and music, 321, 324, 326; and performing arts, 354, 357; youths, 261–2, 264–5, 268–71

First World War, 15, 84, 143, 148–52, 165–6
Foucault, Michel, 1, 2, 10
Fun-Da-Mental, 325, 326

Gandhi, M.K., 77, 83–4, 99, 325
gay and gays, 51, 289–90, 324, 369
George IV, King of England, 147
Ghosh, Amal, 337
Glasgow: 146, 149, 272, 274, 283; architecture, 377, 389; politics, 201, 202
Gujarat and Gujaratis: 61, 116, 132, 293, 298, 303, 310; and architecture, 383, 386; and cinema and TV, 366, 394; migration, 45, 46, 160, 163, 169; and performing arts, 351

Hague, William, 199
health care, 26, 221, 244–55, 256–7
Hegel, G.W.F., 93, 97, 98, 100–6
Hindus and Hinduism: 45, 59, 61, 94, 95, 97, 98, 99, 102, 103, 106, 135, 138, 148, 154, 165, 307, 309, 310, 312; and architecture, 378, 379, 383, 386–8; and employment, 218, 220–1; and health care, 252; and housing, 175; and marriage, 275, 283, 286–8; and policing, 237; population, 112, 168, 303; youths, 265–6
Honeyford, Ray, 126–8, 130, 132, 133, 138
housing: 33, 36, 39, 41–2, 48, 60, 69, 114, 115–16, 152, 175, 223, 232, 240; and architecture, 377, 391; *see also* Leicester, Southall, Wembley
Howard, Michael, 199

identity: 5–10, 16, 20, 24, 26, 35, 52–6, 108, 154–6, 181, 315, 341; and architecture, 374–6, 377–8, 386, 389; and art, 332; and cinema and TV, 367, 393; and health care, 246, 251–3; and literature, 371–3; and marriage, 284; and music, 317–18, 325; and performing arts, 344, 347, 352, 353, 356–7; youths, 258–9, 263, 269; *see also* culture and cultural identity, ethnicity and ethnic identity, politics and political identity, religion and religious identity, sexuality and sexual identity
India: 2–3, 4, 14–15, 32, 43, 45, 53, 59, 94–5, 97–9, 101, 102, 116, 123, 125, 158–60, 163, 164, 166, 330–1, 339, 358–60, 362–4, 366, 367, 369, 388,

393; migration, 44, 144, 147–8, 158–60, 168–9, 343
Indian Workers Association (IWA), 42, 77, 78, 79, 81, 85, 86, 122n, 153
Indians: 3, 5, 13–15, 28, 45, 94, 95, 108, 138, 230–1, 298, 307, 327; and art, 331, 332; and education, 172; and employment, 170–3, 213–23; geographical distribution of, 175–7; and health care, 252; and housing, 175, 232; migration, 168–9, 294; and policing, 236; and politics, 192, 194, 197; population, 112, 168–70, 173–4; and segregation, 177–81; youths, 265; *see also* Gujarat and Gujaratis, Punjab and Punjabis
Indology, 2–3, 9, 95, 98–104, 186
Institute of International Visual Arts (inIVA), 338

Jenkins, Roy, 39
Jeyasingh, Shobana, 347
Jinnah, M.A., 154
July 7 attacks on London, *see* terrorism and terrorists

Kapadia, Asif, 370
Kapoor, Anish, 157, 330, 336, 337–8
Kashmir and Kashmiris: 113, 117, 134, 138, 139, 184, 200, 390; migration, 32, 80n, 113, 117, 160, 163, 165–7, 169, 170; *see also* Mirpur and Mirpuris
Khalon, Sody 'Funjabi', 355, 356
Khan, Nusrat Fateh Ali, 320, 325
Khanna, Balraj, 334
Khomeini, Ayatollah, 58, 133, 182, 184
Krishnawarma, 149
Kureishi, Hanif, 120, 125–6, 186, 369

Labour Party, 65, 77, 83, 85, 86, 87, 139, 158, 184, 195–8, 200, 201–7, 209, 232, 291, 294–5, 299, 300–4, 308–9, 311, 314
Language Theatre Movement, 351
Leeds: 80, 112, 155, 266, 340–1; politics, 198
Leicester: 177, 256, 263, 291–304, 340, 353, 354; architecture, 383, 389, 390–1; housing, 296–7; politics, 189, 198, 201, 205, 294–5, 300–4
Liberal Party, Liberal Democrats and Liberal/SDP Alliance, 50, 191, 195–8, 200–5, 207, 301–4
literature, 61, 120–4, 139–40, 371–3
Liverpool: 26, 143, 149, 153, 160, 339; architecture, 378
London: 10, 13, 26, 109, 119, 122, 143, 146, 149, 177, 213, 217, 224, 234, 270, 274, 297, 298, 321, 322, 323, 325, 326, 331, 336, 340, 342, 343, 346, 351, 352, 353, 354, 362; architecture, 376, 377, 378, 380, 387–8, 392; politics, 192, 205; *see also* Newham, Southall, Tower Hamlets, Wembley
Luton: 257; politics, 205

Mahomed, Frederick Akbar, 147
Mahomed, Sake Dean, 147
Mahomet, Albert J, 147
Manchester: 91, 112, 119, 217, 263, 327–8, 339, 350; architecture, 390; politics, 206; *see also* Rusholme
marriage, 50–1, 119, 129, 258, 260, 272–88, 342, 370
Mehmood, Tariq, 85, 111, 120–4, 139–40
Menon, Krishna, 77, 87, 154, 201
migration, 15–16, 20–3, 36–55, 62, 77–8, 82, 143–7, 151–2, 155–6, 158–67, 245, 266, 329, 331, 343–4, 360, 371, 373, *see also* Bangladesh, Bangladeshis, Bengal and Bengalis, Campbellpore, East Africa and East African Asians, Gujarat and Gujaratis, India, Indians, Kashmir and Kashmiris, Mirpur and Mirpuris, Pakistan, Pakistanis, Punjab and Punjabis, Sylhet and Sylhettis
Mirpur and Mirpuris: 113–15, 116, 117–19, 126, 127, 129, 132; migration, 32, 80n, 113–15, 117, 132, 163, 165–7, 170
Mirza, Shazia, 356
Mitha, Alnoor, 335, 339
Mohyeddin, Zia, 350–1
Mulk Raj Anand, 154, 350
multiculturalism: 16, 17, 19, 62, 93–4, 97, 98, 103–4, 105–7, 111, 124–9, 132–3, 138, 186; and architecture, 378, 382, 383, 390; and health care, 245–7; and Leicester, 291–5, 298–304; and music, 317–18, 320, 321–6
Munshi Abdul Karim, 145
Murphy, Dervla, 125–9
music, 269–70, 308, 317–26, 370
Muslim Council of Britain, 133n
Muslims and Islam: 9, 26–7, 45, 58–9, 60, 76, 89, 94, 95, 97, 106, 143, 145, 148, 149, 151, 154, 155, 165, 166, 182–7, 231, 298, 304, 307, 340, 342; and art,

339; and architecture, 379, 380, 383, 386–7, 388; in Bradford, 111, 116, 127–9, 130–9; and employment, 220–1; and health care, 250–1, 252; and marriage, 275, 279, 283, 285–8; and performing arts, 356; and policing, 235, 237, 238–9, 240, 241–3; and politics, 69, 182–7, 198, 200, 202, 206, 209; population, 112, 168, 303; youths, 264, 265–8

Naoroji, Dadabhai, 148, 160, 201
Nasira Begum, 51, 58
National Front, 56, 57, 82, 119, 120, 123, 128, 208, 294, 306, 340–1
National Health Service (NHS), 25, 248, 249
Newham, 230–3, 263
Nottingham: 37, 340; politics, 202, 206

Oldham, 81, 83, 84, 112, 142, 179, 218, 239–41, 266, 339, 340
Orientalism: 2, 60, 89, 97, 186, 282; and architecture, 374–5, 389; and art, 332, 336–7; and music, 320; and performing arts, 345, 348–9

Pakistan: 15, 45, 117, 122, 127–8, 163, 164, 166, 200, 338–9, 363, 366, 393; migration, 32, 168–9
Pakistani Workers Association, 77, 78
Pakistanis: 13, 108, 231–3, 307, 327–8, 341; and architecture, 377, 390; and art, 331; in Bradford, 113–19, 126–8, 130, 134, 135, 137–40; and cinema and TV, 366, 369; and drugs, 91; and education, 171–2; and employment, 170–3, 212–23; geographical distribution of, 175–7; and health care, 249–50, 252; and housing, 175, 232; and marriage, 272, 274, 275; migration, 32–4, 160, 168–9, 294; and performing arts, 350, 352; and policing, 236, 237; and politics, 192, 194, 195, 197, 200, 202, 205; population, 112, 168–70, 173–4; and segregation, 177–81; youths, 260, 265, 267; *see also* Campbellpore, Kashmir and Kashmiris, Mirpur and Mirpuris
Palme Dutt, Rajani, 77, 80, 84, 87
Panjabi Hit Squad, 323, 325
Panjabi MC, 323
Peach, Blair, 56, 306, 309
performing arts, 343–4, 356–7, *see also* comedy, dance, poetry, theatre
Peries, Evan, 331
poetry, 61, 324, 351–2
police and policing, 9–10, 16, 25, 26, 27, 51, 56–8, 65, 68, 92, 123, 234–43, 263, 290, 306, 340–1
politics and political identity: 15, 16–17, 18–31, 35, 38, 41–2, 50, 52, 55–9, 61, 65–6, 67–71, 74–90, 117, 120–4, 133–40, 147–9, 151, 182–7,188–210, 232, 294–5, 300–4, 308–9, 310–1; and art, 337; European parliament, 205; General elections, 193–8, 201–5, 208; local elections, 205–6, 208, 209; and music, 324–5; and performing arts, 350, 352, 354; youths, 262–4, 267
Portugal and Portuguese, 13, 14
postcolonialism/postcoloniality, 2–10, 11–12, 16–21, 23–7, 30–1, 59, 76, 89, 93–4, 97, 98, 100, 102, 104–6, 120, 160, 163–7, 185, 284, 361, 369, 371, 374–6, 378, 389, 391
Powell, Enoch, 41, 49, 85, 332, 360
Preston: 339; architecture, 383, 386
Punjab and Punjabis: 60, 108, 115, 116, 306, 307, 309; and cinema and TV, 366, 393; and marriage, 274; migration, 45, 46, 115, 149, 152, 160, 163, 165–7, 169, 170; and music, 319; and performing arts, 344; youths, 260

Qawwali, 320, 325

racism and anti-racism: 8, 16, 17, 18, 20, 24–31, 39–41, 47, 49–52, 55–8, 60, 65–70, 76, 114, 126–9, 138, 145–6, 150–1, 152–3, 159, 160, 164–5, 184, 186, 233, 289–90, 293–4, 299, 302, 306, 340–2; and architecture, 378, 382; and art, 332, 336; and cinema and TV, 367, 370; and education, 239; and employment, 43, 48, 82, 153, 212, 219, 223, 224, 296; and health care, 244–51, 253–5, 256; and housing, 239, 297, 377; and literature, 371–2; and marriage, 278, 282; and music, 318, 320, 321–2, 324–5; and performing arts, 344, 349, 352–3; and policing, 234–8, 240–3, 262–3; and politics, 82, 85, 87, 119–20, 153, 206–8; and sport, 108–9; and youths, 261–3, 264, 266, 268, 270, 271
religion and religious identity: 45, 49, 52, 59–61, 93–107, 117, 119, 130–40, 145, 168, 182–7, 295; and architecture, 375,

379–80, 383–6; and employment, 218, 220–1; and health care, 251–3, 256; and marriage, 275, 287–8; youths, 264, 265, 267–8
riots/uprisings: 25, 56–7, 59–60, 65, 124, 131, 134, 138, 139, 212, 258, 262–3, 266, 267, 291–2, 306, 340–2; and policing, 234–5, 238–41, 242–3
Rochdale: 33; politics, 193, 195–6
Rushdie, Salman, 26, 58, 69, 71, 94, 110, 111, 128, 130–3, 138, 139, 182, 186, 209
Rusholme, 327–8

Sagoo, Bally, 320, 322, 325
Saklatvala, Shapurji, 77, 80, 83–4, 86, 87, 201
Salisbury, Lord, 148
Sawhney, Nitin, 269, 324, 325, 326, 355
Scarman, Lord: and the Scarman report, 85, 239, 242, 341
Scottish National Party, 200
Second World War, 16, 35, 123, 152, 154–5, 158, 161, 164, 166, 345, 350
September 11 attacks on United States, *see* terrorism and terrorists
sexuality and sexual identity, 289–90, 324, 370, *see also* gay and gays
Sheffield, 119, 149, 153, 179, 341
Shemza, Anwar Jalal, 334, 335
Siddiqui, Nahid, 346
Sikhs and Sikhism: 38, 45, 59, 80, 81, 85, 94, 95, 97, 98, 106, 109, 116, 118, 123, 135, 138, 145, 154, 155, 165, 166, 304, 306, 307, 309; and architecture, 378, 384–6; and cinema and TV, 369; and employment, 218, 220–1; and health care, 252; and housing, 175; and marriage, 274–5, 277, 283, 284, 286–8; and policing, 237; and politics, 69; population, 112, 168, 303; youths, 260, 265–6
Singh, Sophia Duleep, 201
Singh, Talvin, 269, 318, 322, 326
Singh Twins, The, 330, 333
Singh, Udham (Mohamad Singh Azad), 84–5, 123
Sivanandan, Ambalavaner, 74–5, 80, 85–6, 88–9
Smith, Zadie, 314, 393
South Asia and South Asians: anthropology of, 75–82, 85–90, 113–19, 130–2, 273–4, 276–80, 283–5, 288; classification of, 2–10, 14, 64, 75–7, 79, 94–5, 101–7, 251, 325, 329, 337, 343–4, 356–7, 360, 370, 371; *see also* Bangladesh, Bangladeshis, India, Indians, Pakistan, Pakistanis, Sri Lanka, Sri Lankans
Southall: 25, 37, 42, 55, 56–7, 79, 80, 122, 124, 263, 292, 305–10, 312–14, 336, 341, 352, 369; architecture, 377; housing, 307; politics, 188, 202, 308–9
Southall Black Sisters, 55, 263
Southall Youth Movement (SYM), 263, 306
Souza, Francis Newton, 330, 331–2
sport, 108–9
Sri Lanka, 86, 163, 393
Sri Lankans: 74; and art, 331
Steele, David, 50
Sunrise Radio, 307, 365
Syal, Meera, 353, 355, 369
Sylhet and Sylhettis: 366; migration, 160, 163, 169–70

Tara Arts, 352–3
television, 3, 365–6, 368, 392–4
terrorism and terrorists: 9, 59, 76, 139, 184, 243, 310; July 7 attacks on London, 10, 185, 186, 342; September 11 attacks on United States, 58, 59, 89, 111, 131, 136, 243, 267, 268, 291, 342; war on terror, 9, 16, 76, 184, 185, 187, 342
Thatcher, Margaret, 49, 128, 321
theatre, 348–54
Tower Hamlets: 91, 170, 177; politics, 207

UK Action Committee on Islamic Affairs (UKACIA), 133
uprisings, *see* riots

Vara, Shailesh, 199
Vaz, Keith, 201–2, 209
Victoria, Queen of England, 145, 159, 345

Wadia, Nina, 355
war on terror, *see* terrorism and terrorists
Wembley: 305–6, 310–14; architecture, 377; housing, 310, 312; politics, 310–11
Woking: 145, 160; architecture, 375, 378
Women: 38, 41, 48, 50–1, 55–6, 60, 118, 170, 171–2; and art, 332–3, 338–9; and employment, 213, 215, 217; and health care, 253; and literature, 371–3; and marriage, 274, 276–86, 288; and music, 319, 321, 324; and performing arts,

352; and policing, 236; and politics, 201, 205; youths, 260–1, 268

youth and youths: 52–8, 111, 121–4, 134, 234, 258–71, 306, 309–10; and employment, 220; and music, 321; and policing, 238–43; and politics, 262–3, 267

Zee TV, 3, 366, 392–4

Lightning Source UK Ltd.
Milton Keynes UK
UKHW010643080223
416669UK00005B/699